GLOBAL STUDIES

JAPAN AND THE PACIFIC RIM

STAFF

Ian A. Nielsen	Publisher
Brenda S. Filley	Production Manager
Lisa M. Clyde	Developmental Editor
Charles Vitelli	Designer
Cheryl Nicholas	Permissions Coordinator
Lisa Holmes-Doebrick	Administrative Coordinator
Shawn Callahan	Map Rendering and Graphics
Meredith Scheld	Graphics
Libra Ann Cusack	Typesetting Coordinator
Juliana Arbo	Typesetter
Diane Barker	Editorial Assistant

GLOBAL  STUDIES

JAPAN AND THE PACIFIC RIM

Dr. Dean Collinwood
Weber State University

The Dushkin Publishing Group, Inc., Sluice Dock, Guilford, Connecticut 06437

Japan and the Pacific Rim

OTHER BOOKS IN THE GLOBAL STUDIES SERIES

- Africa
- China
- Latin America
- The Soviet Union and Eastern Europe
- The Middle East
- Western Europe
  India and South Asia

- Available Now

©1991 by The Dushkin Publishing Group, Inc., Guilford, Connecticut 06437. All rights reserved. No part of this book may be reproduced, stored, or transmitted by any means mechanical, electronic, or otherwise—without written permission from the publisher.

First Edition

Manufactured by The Banta Company, Harrisonburg, Virginia 22801

Library of Congress Catalog Number: 91-71258

ISBN: 0-87967-863-1

Japan and the Pacific Rim

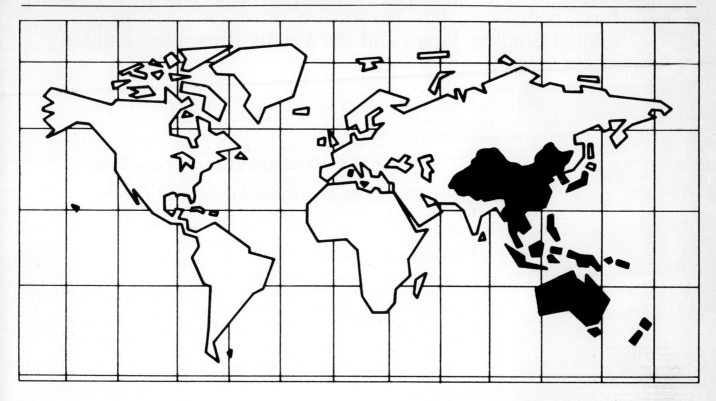

AUTHOR/EDITOR

Dr. Dean Collinwood

The author/editor of *Global Studies: Japan and the Pacific Rim* is an associate professor of sociology and anthropology at Weber State University in Utah. His Ph.D. is from the University of Chicago; his M.Sc. in international relations is from the University of London, and his B.A., in political science with a minor in Japanese, is from Brigham Young University. He has been a Fulbright Scholar at the University of Tokyo and Tsuda College in Japan and has conducted fieldwork throughout Asia and Southeast Asia. Dr. Collinwood resided in Asia in 1968–1971 and again in 1985–1987, completing his most recent fieldwork there in 1990. Under the auspices of the National Endowment for the Humanities and others, he has lectured throughout the United States on the nature of the Japanese mind. Dr. Collinwood also has an interest in the cultures of the Caribbean and has written two books on the Bahamas. He is currently combining his interest in the Caribbean and in Asia by conducting a study of the growth of the Rastafarian movement in Japan.

SERIES CONSULTANT

H. Thomas Collins
PROJECT LINKS
George Washington University

Contents

Global Studies: Japan and the Pacific Rim, First Edition

Pacific Rim   Page 5

Pacific Islands   Page 11

Japan   Page 20

Introduction

THE GLOBAL AGE

As we approach the end of the twentieth century, it is clear that the future we face will be considerably more international in nature than was ever believed possible in the past. Each day, print and broadcast journalists make us aware that our world is becoming increasingly smaller and substantially more interdependent.

The energy crisis, world food shortages, nuclear weaponry, and regional conflicts that threaten to involve us all—all make it clear that the distinctions between domestic and foreign problems are all too often artificial, that many seemingly domestic problems no longer stop at national boundaries. As Rene Dubos, the 1969 Pulitzer Prize recipient, stated: ". . . [I]t becomes obvious that each [of us] has two countries, [our] own and planet earth." As global interdependence has become a reality, it has become vital for the citizens of this world to develop literacy in global matters.

THE GLOBAL STUDIES SERIES

It is the aim of this Global Studies series to help readers acquire a basic knowledge and understanding of the regions and countries in the world. Each volume provides a foundation of information—geographic, cultural, economic, political, historical, artistic, and religious—which will allow readers better to understand better the current and future problems within these countries and regions and to comprehend how events there might affect their own well-being. In short, these volumes attempt to provide the background information necessary to respond to the realities of our global age.

Author/Editor

Each of the volumes in the Global Studies series is crafted under the careful direction of an author/editor—an expert in the area under study. The author/editors teach and conduct research and have traveled extensively through the regions about which they are writing.

In this *Japan and the Pacific Rim* volume, the author/editor has written introductory essays on the Pacific Rim, Japan, and the Pacific islands, and country reports for each of the countries included. In addition he has been instrumental in the selection of the world press articles that appear in this volume.

Contents and Features

The Global Studies volumes are organized to provide concise information and current world press articles on the regions and countries within those areas under study.

Regional Essays

For *Global Studies: Japan and the Pacific Rim,* the author/editor has written narrative essays focusing on the religious,

(United Nations/Yutaka Nagata)

The Global Age is making all countries and all peoples more interdependent.

cultural, sociopolitical, and economic differences and similarities of the countries and peoples in the region. The purpose of the regional essays is to provide readers with an effective sense of the diversity of the area as well as an understanding of its common cultural and historical backgrounds. Accompanying the essays are maps showing the boundaries of the countries within the region.

Country Reports

Concise reports are written for each of the countries within the region under study. These reports are the heart of each Global Studies volume. *Global Studies: Japan and the Pacific Rim* contains 20 country reports, including Japan.

The country reports are composed of five standard elements. Each report contains a small, semidetailed map visually positioning the country amongst its neighboring states; a detailed summary of statistical information; a current essay providing important historical, geographical, political, cultural, and economic information; a historical timeline, offering a convenient visual survey of a few key historical events; and four graphic indicators, with summary statements about the country in terms of development, freedom, health/welfare, and achievements, at the end of each report.

A Note on the Statistical Summaries

The statistical information provided for each country has been drawn from a wide range of sources. The 10 most frequently referenced are listed on page 240. Every effort has been made to provide the most current and accurate information available. However, occasionally the information cited by these sources differs to some extent; and, all too often, the most current information available for some countries is dated. Aside from these discrepancies, the statistical summary of each country is generally quite complete and reasonably up to date. Care should be taken, however, in using these statistics (or, for that matter, any published statistics) in making hard comparisons among countries. We have also provided comparable statistics on the United States, which follow on the next two pages.

World Press Articles

Within each Global Studies volume are reprinted a number of articles carefully selected by our editorial staff and the author/editor from a broad range of international periodicals and newspapers. The articles have been chosen for currency, interest, and their differing perspectives on the subject countries. There are a total of 42 articles in *Global Studies: Japan and the Pacific Rim.*

The articles section is preceded by an annotated table of contents as well as a topic guide. The annotated table of contents offers a brief summary of each article, while the topic guide indicates the main theme(s) of each article. Thus, readers desiring to focus on articles dealing with a particular theme, say, religion, may refer to the topic guide to find those articles.

Glossary, Bibliography, Index

At the back of each Global Studies volume, readers will find a glossary of terms and abbreviations, which provides a quick reference to the specialized vocabulary of the area under study and to the standard abbreviations (NIC, ASEAN, etc.) used throughout the volume.

Following the glossary is a bibliography, which lists general works, national histories, literature in translation, current events publications, and periodicals that provide regular coverage on Japan and the Pacific Rim.

The index at the end of the volume is an accurate reference to the contents of the volume. Readers seeking specific information and citations should consult this standard index.

Currency and Usefulness

This first edition of *Global Studies: Japan and the Pacific Rim,* like other Global Studies volumes, is intended to provide the most current and useful information available necessary to understand the events that are shaping the cultures of the region today.

We plan to revise this volume on a regular basis. The statistics will be updated, essays rewritten, country reports revised, and articles completely replaced as new information becomes available. In order to accomplish this task we will turn to our author/editor, our advisory boards, and—hopefully—to you, the users of this volume. Your comments are more than welcome. If you have an idea that you think will make the volume more useful, an article or bit of information that will make it more current, or a general comment on its organization, content, or features that you would like to share with us, please send it in for serious consideration for the next edition.

(UN photo/John Isaac)

Understanding the problems and lifestyles of other countries will help make us literate in global matters.

United States of America

Comparing statistics on the various countries in this volume should not be done without recognizing that the figures are within the timeframe of our publishing date and may not accurately reflect today's conditions. Nevertheless, comparisons can and will be made, so to enable you to put the statistics of different countries into perspective, we have included comparable statistics on the United States. These statistics are drawn from the same sources that were consulted for developing the statistical information in each country report.

The United States is unique. It has some of the most fertile land in the world, which, coupled with a high level of technology, allows the production of an abundance of food products—an abundance that makes possible the export of enormous quantities of basic foodstuffs to many other parts of the world. The use of this technology also permits the manufacture of goods and services that exceed what is possible in a majority of the rest of the world. In the United States are some of the most important urban centers in the world focusing on trade, investment, and commerce as well as art, music, and theater.

GEOGRAPHY

Area in Square Kilometers (Miles):
9,372,614 (3,540,939)
Capital (Population): Washington, DC
(638,432)
Climate: temperate

PEOPLE

Population
Total: 255,000,000
Annual Growth Rate: 0.7%
Rural/Urban Population Ratio: 21/79
Ethnic Makeup of Population: 80%
white; 11% black; 6.2% Spanish
origin; 1.6% Asian and Pacific
Islander; 0.7% American Indian,
Eskimo, and Aleut

Health
Life Expectancy at Birth: 71.5 years
(male); 78.5 years (female)
Infant Mortality Rate (Ratio):
8.9/1,000
Average Caloric Intake: 138% of FAO
minimum
Physicians Available (Ratio): 1/520

Religion(s)
55% Protestant; 36% Roman
Catholic; 4% Jewish; 5% others

Education
Adult Literacy Rate: 99.5% (official;
estimates vary widely)

COMMUNICATION

Telephones: 182,558,000
Newspapers: 1,676 dailies;
approximately 63,000,000 circulation

TRANSPORTATION

Highways—Kilometers (Miles):
6,208,552 (3,866,296); 5,466,612
(3,398,810) paved
Railroads—Kilometers (Miles):
270,312 (167,974)
Usable Airfields: 15,422

GOVERNMENT

Type: federal republic
Independence Date: July 4, 1776
Head of State: President George Bush
Political Parties: Democratic Party;
Republican Party; others of minor
political significance
Suffrage: universal at 18

MILITARY

Number of Armed Forces: 2,116,800
*Military Expenditures (% of Central
Government Expenditures):* 29.1%
Current Hostilities: currently none

ECONOMY

Per Capita Income: $16,444
Gross National Product (GNP): $4.2
trillion
Inflation Rate: 5%
Natural Resources: metallic and
nonmetallic minerals; petroleum;
arable land
Agriculture: food grains; feed crops;
oilbearing crops; cattle; dairy
products
Industry: diversified in both capital-
and consumer-goods industries

FOREIGN TRADE

Exports: $250.4 billion
Imports: $424.0 billion

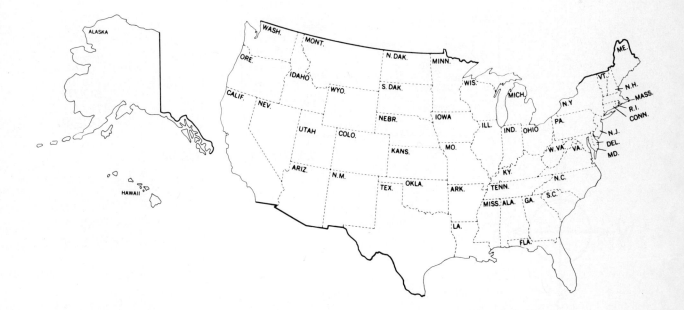

GLOBAL 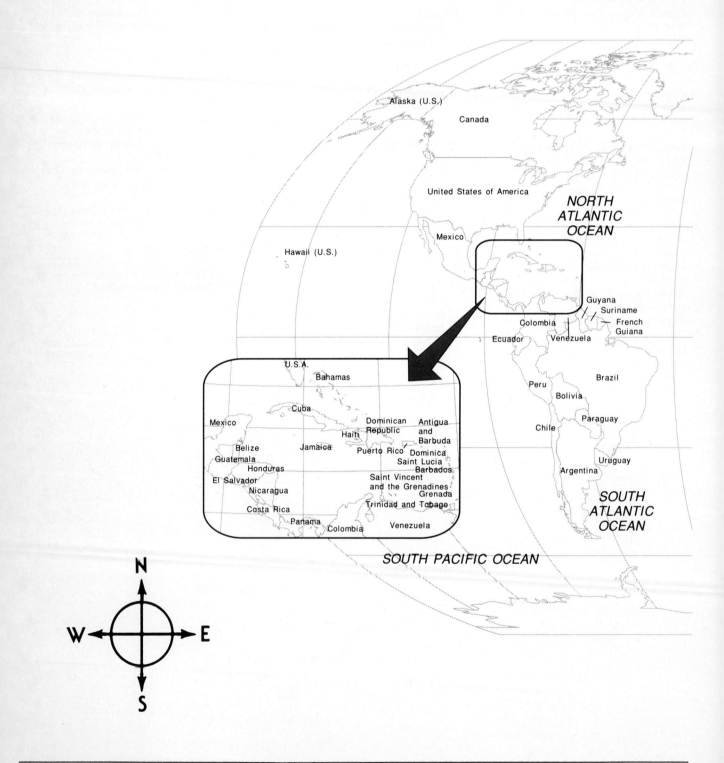 STUDIES

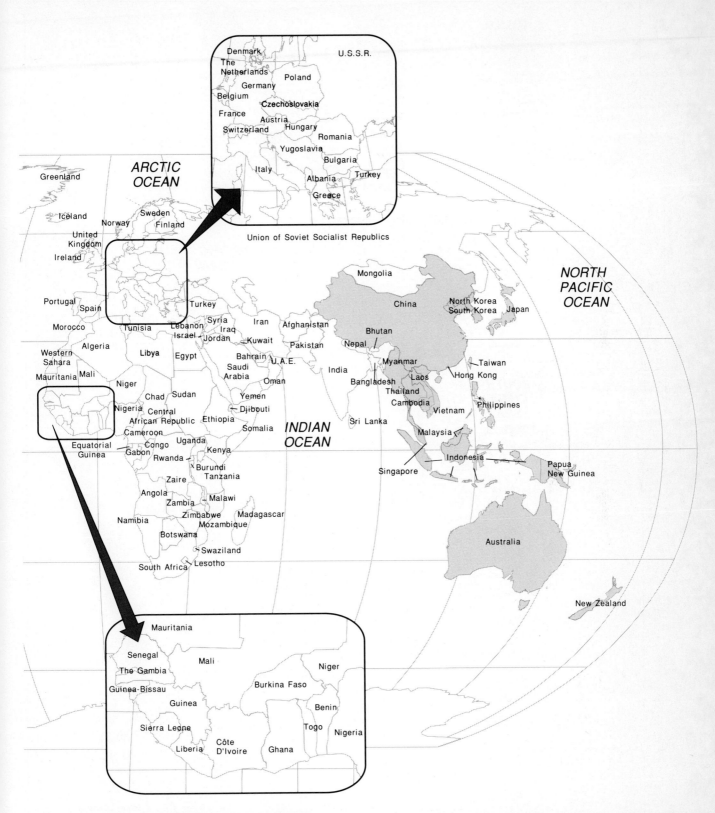

This map has been developed to give you a graphic picture of where the countries of the world are located, the relationship they have with their region and neighbors, and their positions relative to the superpowers and power blocs. We have focused on certain areas to more clearly illustrate these crowded regions.

Pacific Rim Map

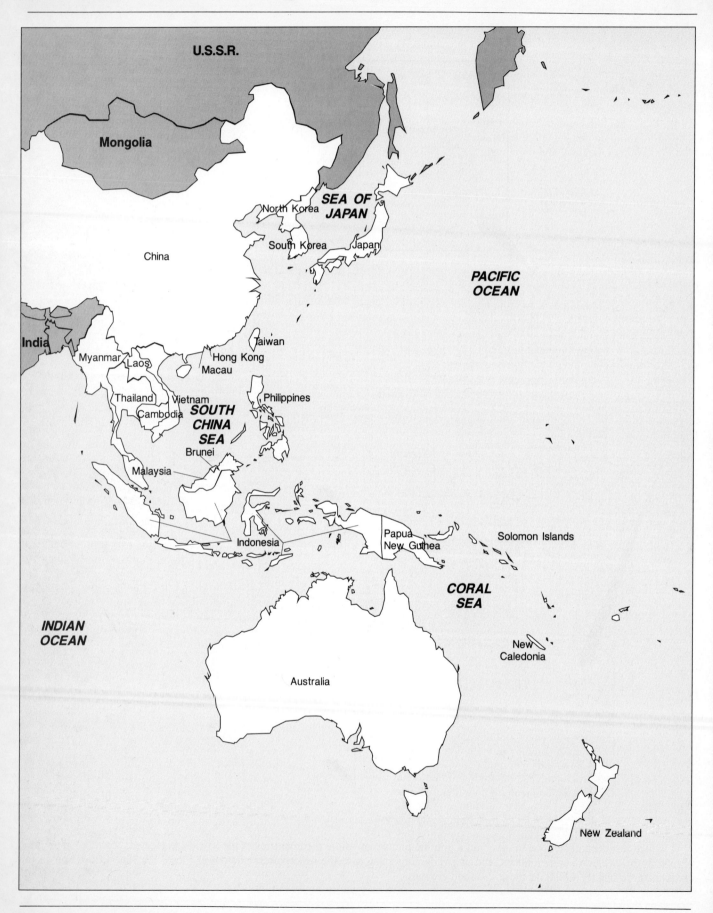

U.S.S.R.

Mongolia

China

North Korea

SEA OF JAPAN

South Korea

Japan

PACIFIC OCEAN

India

Taiwan

Myanmar

Laos

Hong Kong

Macau

Thailand

Vietnam

Philippines

Cambodia

SOUTH CHINA SEA

Brunei

Malaysia

Indonesia

Papua New Guinea

Solomon Islands

CORAL SEA

INDIAN OCEAN

New Caledonia

Australia

New Zealand

The Pacific Rim: Diversity and Interconnection

WHAT IS THE PACIFIC RIM?

The term "Pacific Rim," as used in this book, refers to 20 countries or administrative units along the western side of the Pacific Ocean, plus the numerous islands of the South Pacific. It is not a simple matter to decide which countries to include in a definition of the Pacific Rim. If we were thinking geographically, for instance, we might have included Mexico, Chile, Canada, the United States, the Soviet Union, and numerous other countries that border the Pacific Ocean, while eliminating Burma and Laos, since they are not technically on the rim of the Pacific. But our definition stems from recent changes in economic and geopolitical power that have affected the countries of Asia, Southeast Asia, and the South Pacific, such that they are increasingly referred to as a single bloc by international corporate and political leaders.

Most people living in the region we have defined do not think of themselves as "Pacific Rimmers." In addition, many social scientists, particularly anthropologists and comparative sociologists, would prefer not to apply a single term to such a culturally, politically, and sociologically diverse region. Yet there is something arising from the region itself that points to the validity of a single, all-encompassing term. This powerful force is the yen—the Japanese currency—flowing throughout the Pacific Rim in the form of aid or investment, facilitating development and helping other regional countries to create their own engines of economic growth.

In the 1960s, when the Japanese economy had completely recovered from the devastation of World War II, the Japanese looked to North America and Europe for markets for their increasingly high-quality products. Japanese business continues to seek out markets and resources globally; but in the 1980s, in response to the movement toward a truly common European economic community as well as in response to free-trade agreements among North American countries, Japan began to invest more heavily in countries nearer its own borders. The Japanese hoped to guarantee themselves market and resource access should they find their products frozen out of the emerging European and North American economic blocs. The unintended consequences of this policy were the revitalization of many nearby economies and the solidification of lines of communication between governments and private citizens within the region. Recognizing this interconnection has prompted many people to refer to the countries we treat in this book as a single unit, the Pacific Rim.

TROUBLES IN THE RIM

The current preponderance of media images of billionaire Japanese businesspeople and chauffeur-driven Hong Kong Chinese has overshadowed the hard realities of life for most people in the Rim. For the most part, Pacific Rim countries

(UN photo by J. M. Micaud)

In areas of the Pacific Rim such as Vietnam, Laos, and Cambodia, conditions are so grim that thousands of people elect to leave their homelands and become homeless "boat people," trusting that they will find a better place to live. These people are living at the Hawkings refugee camp in Singapore in conditions that are barely survivable.

WARFARE IN SELECTED PACIFIC RIM COUNTRIES						
	Civil Only	*Civil/ International*	*International Only*	*Religious/ Ethnic*	*UN Involved*	*Superpower Involved*	*Estimated Total Deaths*
Myanmar (Burma)	•						6,000 since 1985
Cambodia		•			•	•	2.2 million since 1970
China-Tibet	•						1.2 million since 1956
Indonesia-East Timor		•		•		•	100,000 since 1975
Philippines	•			•		•	35,000 since 1972

Adapted from *The Nation* (January 9, 1989), p. 47.

have not met the needs of their peoples. Whether it is the desire of affluent Japanese for larger homes and two-car garages, or of rice farmers in Myanmar (Burma) for the right to sell their grain for personal profit, or of Chinese students to speak their minds in public without repression—in these and many other ways, the Pacific Rim has failed its peoples. In Vietnam, Laos, and Cambodia, for example, life is so difficult that thousands of families have risked their lives to leave their homelands. Some have swum across the wide Mekong River on moonless nights to avoid detection by guards, while others have sailed into the South China Sea on creaky and overcrowded boats, hoping that people of good-will rather than marauding pirates will find and transport them to a land of safety. As you read this, some 120,000 Vietnamese are waiting in refugee camps in Hong Kong, the Philippines, Malaysia, Thailand, Singapore, and Japan—waiting to start a new life away from the troubles of the Pacific Rim.

Warfare

Of all the Rim's troubles, warfare has been the most devastating. Not only have there been wars in which foreign powers like the United States and the Soviet Union have been involved, but there have been numerous battles between tribes and races and religions. (The chart above provides a sample of how many people have been killed in recent years in selected countries in the Pacific Rim.)

Overpopulation

Another serious problem is overpopulation. There are well over 2 billion people living in the Pacific Rim. Of those, 1.1 billion are Chinese, and even though China's government has implemented the strictest family-planning policies in world history, the country's annual growth rate is such that more than 1 million more inhabitants are added *every month*. This means that more new Chinese are born each year than make up the entire population of Australia. Couples in some countries, including Japan, Taiwan, and South Korea, have been voluntarily limiting family size. Other states, such as

China and Singapore, have promoted family planning though government incentives and punishments. The effort is paying off; the United Nations (UN) now estimates that the proportion of the global population living in Asia will remain relatively unchanged between now and the year 2025, and China's share will decline to approximately 19 percent by then.

But already, so many children have been born that Pacific Rim governments simply cannot meet their needs. For these newcomers, schools must be built, health facilities provided, houses constructed, and jobs created. This is not an easy challenge for many Rim countries. Moreover, as the population density increases, the quality of life decreases. In crowded New York City, for example, the population is 1,100 per square mile, and many people, thinking that is too high, have left the city for the suburbs. Yet in Tokyo, the density is 2,400 per square mile, and in Manila it is 51,000! Demographers predict that by the year 2000 many of the world's largest cities will be in the Pacific Rim: Shanghai, China is projected to have 12 million people; Jakarta, Indonesia will have well over 13 million; Manila in the Philippines will be home to 11 million; and Bangkok, Thailand will have nearly 11 million. Migration to the cities will continue despite miserable conditions for many: in some Asian cities, 50 percent of the population live in slum housing. One incredibly rapid-growth country is the Philippines; home to only about 7 million in 1898, when it was acquired by the United States, it will have 130 million people in the year 2020.

Absolute numbers alone do not tell the whole story. In many Rim countries, 40 percent or more of the population are under age 15. Governments must provide schooling and medical care as well as plan for future jobs and housing for all these children. Moreover, as these young people age, they will require increased medical and social care. Some scholars have pointed out that between 1985 and 2025, the numbers of old people will double in Japan, triple in China, and quadruple in Korea. In Japan, where replacement-level fertility was achieved in the 1960s, government officials are already concerned about the ability of the nation to care for the growing number of retirement-age people while paying the higher wages that the increasingly scarce number of younger workers are demanding.

(UN photo by Shaw McCutcheon)

By the year 2025 the numbers of elderly people in China will triple. Even with the strict enforcement of limiting each family to only one child, China will be faced with the increasing need of caring for retirement-age citizens. This group of elderly men in a village near Chengdu is just the tip of this enormous problem.

Political Instability

One consequence of the overwhelming problems of population growth, urbanization, and continual military conflict is disillusionment with government. Many Japanese are disappointed with the money scandals that have plagued their Liberal Democratic Party in recent years, the Australians nearly threw out the ruling Labor Party in the 1990 elections, and the Liberals and Nationals in New Zealand have been voted in and out of office numerous times.

But these examples constitute the normal workings of government and do not represent the kind of disillusionment we are talking about. Rather, we mean that in many countries of the Pacific Rim, people are challenging the very right of the government to rule or are demanding a complete change in the political philosophy that undergirds governments. For instance, at least three groups oppose the government of Cambodia because it was installed by the military of Vietnam. In some Rim countries, opposition groups armed with sophisticated weapons donated by foreign nations roam the countryside, capturing towns and military installations.

The government of the Philippines has barely survived six coup attempts in half a decade; elite military dissidents want to impose the old Marcos-style patronage government, while armed rural insurgents want to install a communist government. Thousands of students have been injured or killed protesting the authoritarian governments of South Korea, China, and Myanmar, and half a million residents of Hong Kong have taken to the streets to oppose Great Britain's decision to turn over the territory to China in 1997. Military takeovers, political assassinations, and repressive policies have been the norm in most of the countries in the region. Millions of people have spent their entire lives under governments they have never agreed with, and unrest is bound to continue because those now alive are showing less and less patience with imposed government.

Part of the reason is that the region is so fractured, between countries and, especially, within countries. In some states, dozens of different languages are spoken, people practice very different religions, families trace their roots back to many different racial and ethnic origins, and wealth is distributed so unfairly that some people become well

TYPES OF GOVERNMENTS IN SELECTED PACIFIC RIM COUNTRIES

PARLIAMENTARY DEMOCRACIES
Australia
Fiji
New Zealand
Papua New Guinea

CONSTITUTIONAL MONARCHIES
Brunei
Japan
Malaysia
Thailand

REPUBLICS
Indonesia
Philippines
Singapore
South Korea
Taiwan

SOCIALIST REPUBLICS
China
Laos
Myanmar
North Korea
Vietnam

OVERSEAS TERRITORIES/COLONIES
Hong Kong
French Polynesia
Macau
New Caledonia

ECONOMIC DEVELOPMENT IN SELECTED PACIFIC RIM COUNTRIES

Economists have divided the Rim into five zones, based on the level of development, as follows:

DEVELOPED NATIONS
Australia
Japan
New Zealand

NEWLY INDUSTRIALIZING COUNTRIES (NICs)
Hong Kong
Singapore
South Korea
Taiwan

RESOURCE-RICH DEVELOPING ECONOMIES
Brunei
Indonesia
Malaysia
Philippines
Thailand

COMMAND ECONOMIES
Cambodia
China
Laos
Myanmar
North Korea
Vietnam

LESS DEVELOPED ECONOMIES
Papua New Guinea
South Pacific Islands

educated and well fed while others nearby remain illiterate and malnourished. Under these conditions, it has been difficult for the peoples of the Rim to agree upon the kinds of government that will best serve them; all are afraid that their particular language, religion, ethnic group, and/or social class will be negatively affected by any leader not of their own background.

Identity Confusion

A related problem is that of confusion about personal and national identity. Many nation-states in the Pacific Rim were created in response to Western pressure. Before Western influences came to be felt, many Asians, particularly Southeast Asians, did not identify themselves with a nation but, rather, with a tribe or an ethnic group.

Uneven Economic Development

While the Japanese are wrestling with questions of meaning and purpose, Laotians and others are worrying about where their next meal will come from. Such disparity brings us to the next major problem afflicting the Pacific Rim, namely, uneven economic development.

Other Asians, especially those in the northern states of Japan, Korea, and China, are struggling with their identities

because rapid economic change seems to render the traditions of the past meaningless. For instance, almost all Japanese will state that Japan is a Buddhist country, yet only 15 percent today claim any actual religious affiliation. Moreover, economic success has produced a growing interest in the meaning of life in a Japanese world in which one's physical needs are always fully met.

The *developed nations* are characterized by political stability and long-term industrial success. Their per capita income is comparable to those of Canada, Northern Europe, and the United States, and they have achieved a level of economic sustainability. These countries are closely linked to North America. Japan, for instance, exports one-third of its products to the United States.

The *newly industrializing countries* (NICs) are currently capturing world attention because of their rapid growth. Hong Kong, for example, exports more manufactured products than do the Soviet Union and Eastern Europe combined. Taiwan, famous for cameras and calculators, has had the highest gross national product (GNP) growth in the world for the past 20 years. South Korea is tops in shipbuilding and steel manufacturing and is the tenth-largest trading nation in the world.

The *resource-rich developing nations* have tremendous natural resources but have been held back economically by

(UN photo by John Isaac)

Some of the Pacific Rim nations are resource-rich, but development has been curtailed by the innate political instability and a strong inbred culture. This worker is farming as his ancestors did with techniques that have not changed for hundreds of years.

extreme political instability and religious/cultural factionalism. Indonesia illustrates this problem. People think of it as a Muslim country, as overall it is 88 percent Muslim, but in regions like North Sumatra, 30 percent are Protestant; in Bali, 94 percent are Hindu; and in East Timor, 49 percent are Catholic and 51 percent are animist. Coups and counter-coups rather than peaceful political transitions seem to be the norm, because the people have not yet developed a sense of unified nationalism. The Philippines is another example. Although it is not a member of the Association of Southeast Asian Nations (ASEAN), its conditions are similar to those of ASEAN states. With 88 different languages spoken, its people spread out over 12 large islands, a population explosion (the average age is 16), and huge debts left by the Marcos regime, the Philippines is a classic case of fragmentation. Moreover, it cannot decide whether it should love or hate its former colonial overseer, the United States. Indecision on this point is providing fodder for the anticolonial New People's (Communist) Army, which in turn is opposed by vigilante groups who will fight anyone who opposes the government. Such conditions do not contribute to sustained economic progress.

Command economies lag far behind the rest, not only because of the endemic inefficiency of the system but because military dictatorships and continual warfare have sapped the strength of the people. Significant changes in these countries may be in the offing, now that the superpowers, which promoted and financed warfare because of their ideological commitment to either the promotion or containment of communism, are now reevaluating their positions in light of the end of the Cold War. Moreover, as the superpowers withdraw somewhat from Asia, the door is being opened for more active involvement in the region by Japan. Historically having directed its trade to North America and Europe, Japan is now finding its Asian/Pacific neighbors to be convenient recipients of its powerful economic and cultural influence.

Many of the *less developed economies* are the small micro-states of the South Pacific with limited resources and tiny internal markets. Others, like Papua New Guinea, have only recently achieved political independence and are searching for a proper role in the world economy.

THE NEW OPTIMISM

Warfare, overpopulation, political instability, identity confusion, and uneven development would seem to be an unresolvable set of problems for the Pacific Rim, but as the 1990s began there was reason for optimism about some of these issues. Reunification talks between North and South Korea seemed to take on a new urgency, giving hope that the military tension between the two states would begin to ease. Similarly, the superpowers seemed more anxious than ever before to encourage a resolution of the continuing Cambodian civil war. There were signs of some movement away from military dictatorship in Myanmar, and China was trying to reestablish relationships with the West which had been severed in the aftermath of the Tiananmen Square massacre.

But most heartening of all was the flood of reports on the growing economic strength of many Pacific Rim countries. Typical was the World Bank's *World Development Report 1988,* which favorably compared Pacific Rim countries' 1986 investment and savings percentages with those of 20 years earlier; in almost every case, there had been a tremendous improvement in the economic capacity of these countries.

The rate of economic growth in the Pacific Rim has been astonishing. In 1987, for example, the growth rate of real gross domestic product (GDP) in the United States was only 3.5 percent over the previous year. By contrast, in Hong Kong, the rate was 13.5 percent; in Taiwan, 12.4 percent; in Thailand, 10.4 percent; and in South Korea, 11.1 percent. The significance of these data is that historically the economies of North America have been regarded as the engine behind Pacific Rim growth, and yet today growth in the United States and Canada trails far behind those of the Rim economies. This anomaly can be explained, in part, by the hard work and saving ethic of Pacific Rim peoples and by their external-market-oriented development strategies. But hard work and clever strategies without venture capital and foreign aid would not have produced the economic dynamo that the world is now witnessing. This is why Japan's financial contributions to the region, coming in chunks much larger than those of the United States, are so crucial. This is also why we consider that Japan and Japanese investment and aid are central to our definition of the Pacific Rim as an identifiable region.

Japan has been investing in the Asia/Pacific region for several decades. However, growing protectionism in its traditional markets as well as changes in the value of the yen and the need to find cheaper sources of labor (labor costs are 75 percent less in Singapore and 95 percent less in Indonesia) have now raised Japan's level of involvement so high as to give its actions the upper hand in determining the course of development and political stability for the entire region. This heightened level of investment started to gain momentum in the mid-1980s. Between 1984 and 1989 Japan's overseas development assistance to the ASEAN countries amounted to $6.1 billion. In some cases, this assistance translated to more than 4 percent of the annual national budget and nearly 1 percent of GDP. Private Japanese investment in ASEAN countries, plus Hong Kong, Taiwan, and South Korea, was $8.9 billion between 1987 and 1988. In recent years the Japanese government or Japanese business has invested $582 million in an auto-assembly plant in Taiwan, $5 billion in an iron and steel complex in China, and $2.3 billion in a bullet-train plan for Malaysia.

Japan also is importing more from Rim countries. In 1988–1989 Japan's imports from Korea, Taiwan, Hong Kong, and ASEAN countries increased 24 percent over the previous year. Clearly, Pacific Rim countries are becoming more dependent on Japan as a market for their products.

JAPANESE INFLUENCE, PAST AND PRESENT

This is certainly not the first time in modern history that Japanese influence has swept over Asia and the Pacific. A major thrust began in 1895, when Japan, like the European powers, started to acquire bits and pieces of the region. By 1942 the Japanese were in control of Taiwan, Korea, Manchuria and most of the populated parts of China, and Hong Kong; what are now Vietnam, Laos, and Cambodia; Thailand; Burma (now Myanmar); Malaysia; Indonesia; the Philippines; part of New Guinea; and dozens of South Pacific islands. In effect, by the 1940s the Japanese were the dominant force in precisely the area they influence in the 1990s and which we are calling the Pacific Rim. The similarities do not end there, for while most Asians of the 1940s were apprehensive about or openly resistant to Japanese rule, many people welcome the Japanese invaders and even helped them to take over their countries. This was because they believed that Western influence was out of place in Asia and that Asia should be for Asians. They hoped that the Japanese military would rid them of Western rule,

and it did: after the war, very few Western powers were able to regain control of their Asian and Pacific colonies.

Similarly in the 1990s, many Asians and Pacific islanders are apprehensive about excessive Japanese financial and industrial influence in their countries, but they welcome Japanese investment anyway, because they believe that it is the best and cheapest way they can rid their countries of poverty and underdevelopment. So far they are right, for by copying the Japanese model of economic development, and thanks to Japanese trade, foreign aid, and investment, the entire region—some countries excepted—is gaining such a reputation for economic strength that many people believe the next 100 years will be called the "Pacific Century," just as the previous 100 years were called the "American Century." It would not be far-fetched to call it the "Japanese Century" and to rename the Pacific Rim the "Pacific Community" or the "Yen Bloc," as some observers are already doing. (It is important to note, however, that many Rim countries are beginning to challenge Japan's economic dominance.)

Why have the Japanese re-created in the 1990s a modern version of the old Greater East Asian Co-Prosperity Sphere of the imperialistic 1940s? We cannot find the answer in the propaganda of wartime Japan: fierce devotion to emperor and nation and belief in the superiority of Asians over all other races are no longer the propellants in the Japanese economic engine. Rather, Japan courts Asia and the Pacific today for the very same reason it conquered them militarily 50 years ago: to acquire resources to sustain its civilization. Japan is about the size of California, but it has five times as many people and not nearly as much arable land. Much of Japan is mountainous; many other parts are off limits because of active volcanoes (one-tenth of all the active volcanoes in the world are in Japan), and after 2,000-plus years of intensive and uninterrupted habitation, the natural forests are long since consumed, as are most of the other natural resources—all of which were scarce to begin with.

In short, Japan continues to extract resources from the rest of Asia and the Pacific because it is the same Japan as before—environmentally speaking, that is. Take oil, for example. In the early 1940s Japan needed oil to keep its industries (as well as its military machines) operating, but the United States wanted to punish Japan for its military expansion in Asia, so it shut off all shipments to Japan of any kind, including oil. That may have seemed politically right to the policymakers of the day, but it did not change Japan's resource environment; Japan still did not have its own oil, and it still needed as much oil as before. So Japan decided to capture a nearby nation that did have natural reserves of oil; in 1941 it attacked Indonesia and obtained by force the oil it had been denied by trade.

Japan has no more domestic resources now than it did 50 years ago, and yet its needs—for food, minerals, lumber, paper—are even greater. You name it, Japan does not have it. A realistic comparison is to imagine trying to feed half the

(UN photo by Nichiro Gyogyo)

Japan is surrounded with resources that must be utilized for its population to survive. This factory ship is a floating cannery that processes the salmon harvested from the Pacific.

population of the United States from the natural output of the state of Montana. As it happens, however, Japan sits astride the continent of Asia, which is rich in almost all the materials it needs. For lumber there are the forests of Malaysia, for food there are the farms and ranches of New Zealand and Australia, and for oil there are Indonesia and Brunei, the latter of which sells 50 percent of its exports to Japan. A quest for resources is why Japan is flooding its neighbors with Japanese yen, and that, in turn, is creating the interconnected trading bloc of the Pacific Rim.

Catalyst for Development

In addition to the need for resources, Japan has turned to the Pacific Rim in an attempt to offset the anti-Japanese import or protectionist policies of its historic trading partners. Because so many import tariffs are imposed on products sold directly from Japan, Japanese companies find they can avoid or minimize tariffs if they cooperate on joint ventures in Rim countries and have products shipped from there. The result is that both Japan and its host countries are prospering as never before. Sony Corporation, for example, assembles parts made in both Japan and Singapore to construct videocassette

recorders at its Malaysian factory, for export to North America, Europe, and other Rim countries. Toyota Corporation intends to build its automobile transmissions in the Philippines and its steering-wheel gears in Malaysia, and to build the final product in whichever country intends to buy its cars. In 1989 alone, Japan gave Indonesia $1.8 billion in loans for infrastructural improvements and invested or loaned another $2.6 billion throughout the rest of the region.

So helpful has Japanese investment (as well as North American and European investment) been in spawning indigenous economic powerhouses that many other Rim countries are now reinvesting in the region. In particular, Hong Kong, Singapore, Taiwan, and South Korea are now in a position to seek cheaper labor markets in Indonesia, Malaysia, the Philippines, and Thailand. In 1989 they invested $4 billion in the resource- and labor-rich economies of Southeast Asia.

Eyed as a big consumer as well as a bottomless source of cheap labor is the People's Republic of China. Many Rim countries such as South Korea, Taiwan, Hong Kong, and Japan are working hard to increase their trade with China (Taiwan exchanged $2.6 billion of goods with China in 1989, despite an official policy prohibiting trade due to the formal state of war that exists between the two countries). Japan was especially eager to resume economic aid to China in 1990. For its part, China is establishing free-enterprise zones which will enable it to participate more fully in the regional economy.

Japan and a handful of other economic powerhouses of the Rim are not the only big players in Rim economic development. The United States and Canada remain major investors in the Pacific Rim (in computers and automobiles, for example), and Europe maintains its historical linkages with the region (such as in oil). But there is no question that Japan is the main catalyst for development in the region. For instance, U.S. companies invested $4 billion in the Rim in 1989, but Japan invested nearly $13 billion. Moreover, this level of investment is likely to continue for at least the next decade, because Japan is awash in investment monies seeking a home. Almost all the top 20 banks in the world are Japanese, and the volume of the Japanese stock market is the biggest in the world, even though the value of its stocks declined 37 percent in 1990. Many of the world's wealthiest business executives are Japanese, and they are eager to find places to invest their capital.

Not everyone is pleased with the way Japan is giving aid or making loans. Particularly in the Pacific Rim, money invested by the Japan International Development Organization (JIDO) is usually connected very closely to the commercial interests of Japanese companies. For instance, commercial-loan agreements often require that the recipient of low-interest loans purchase Japanese products.

Nevertheless, it is clear that many countries would be a lot worse off without Japanese aid. JIDO aid around the world in 1988 was $10 billion. Japan is the dominant supplier of foreign aid to the Philippines and a major investor; in Thailand, where U.S. aid recently amounted to $20 million,

Japanese aid was close to $100 million. Moreover, some of this aid gets recycled from one country to another within the Rim—Thailand, for example, receives more aid from Japan than any other country, but it supplies major amounts of aid to other nearby countries. Thus we can see the growing interconnectivity of the region.

In the militaristic 1940s Japanese dominance in the region produced antagonism and resistance, but it also gave subjugated countries new highways, railways, and other infrastructural improvements. Today host countries continue to benefit from infrastructural advances, but they also get quality manufactured products. Once again Asian, Southeast Asian, and South Pacific peoples have begun to talk about Japanese domination. The difference is that this time no one seems upset about it; people no longer believe that Japan has military aspirations against them, and they regard Japanese investment as a first step toward becoming economically strong themselves. Many people are eager to learn the Japanese language, and in some cities, such as Seoul, Japanese has displaced English as the most valuable business language. Nevertheless, to deter negative criticism arising from its prominent position in the Rim, Japan has increased its gift-giving, such that in 1989 it surpassed the United States as the world's most generous donor of foreign aid.

POLITICAL AND CULTURAL CHANGES

Although economic issues are important to an understanding of the Pacific Rim, political and cultural changes are also crucial. For instance, the new, noncombative relationship between the United States and the Soviet Union means that special-interest groups and governments in the Rim will be less able to rely on the strength and power of those superpowers to help advance or uphold their positions. Communist North Korea, for instance, which has long relied on the Soviet bloc for not only trade but also ideological support, may no longer be able to count on the Soviet Union as an ideological ally. That is, it is no longer possible for North Korea to pattern itself after a communist model that itself no longer models communism. North Korea may begin to look for new ideological neighbors or, more significantly, to consider major modifications in its own approach to organizing society.

Similarly, ideological changes are afoot in Myanmar (Burma), where the populace is tiring of life under a military dictatorship. The military may no longer be able to look for support to the crumbling non-Western world. For a long while, too, it looked as though the Western world was content to let the Cambodians engage in internecine warfare as long as it did not spill over into other regions. Objecting to the Vietnam-installed Cambodian government as a puppet of Hanoi, the United States seemed to show little flexibility when the prospect of including the current government in a final peace solution was proposed. Now, however, the United States is moving toward compromise on this issue, and talks on a ceasefire and a coalition government are finally making

headway. In the case of Hong Kong, the British government shied away from extreme political issues and agreed to the peaceful annexation in 1997 of a capitalist bastion by a communist nation, China. It is highly unlikely that such a decision would have been made had the issue of Hong Kong's political status arisen during the anticommunist years of the Cold War.

One must not get the impression, however, that suddenly peace has arrived in the Pacific Rim. A very hot war is still in progress in Cambodia, communist insurgents in the Philippines are waging a continuing battle to overthrow the elected government, and border disputes among countries in Southeast Asia and between Japan and the Soviet Union and Taiwan, the reunification of Korea, and many other issues remain stumbling blocks to the creation of a region at peace with itself and its neighbors. But outside support for extreme ideological positions seems to be giving way to a pragmatic search for peaceful solutions. This should have a salutary effect throughout the region.

The growing pragmatism in the political sphere is yielding changes in the cultural sphere. Whereas communist Chinese formerly looked upon Western dress and music as decadent, many Chinese now openly seek out these cultural commodities and are finding ways to merge these things with the command economy in which they live. It is also increasingly clear to most leaders in the Pacific Rim that international mercantilism has allowed at least one regional country, Japan, to rise to the highest ranks of world society, first economically and now culturally and educationally. The fact that one Asian nation has accomplished this is living proof that others can as well.

Rim leaders also see, however, that Japan achieved its position of prominence only because it was willing to change traditional mores and customs and accept outside modes of thinking and acting. Religion, family life, gender relations, recreation, and many other facets of Japanese life have altered during Japan's rapid rise to the top. Many other Pacific Rim nations—including Thailand, Singapore, and South Korea—seem determined to follow Japan's lead in this regard. Therefore we are witnessing in certain high-growth economies in the Rim significant cultural changes: a reduction in family size, a secularization of religious impulses, a desire for more leisure time and better education, and a move toward acquisition rather than being as a determinant of one's worth. That is, more and more people are likely to judge others' value by what they own rather than what they believe or do. Buddhist values of self-denial, Shinto values of respect for nature, and Confucian values of family loyalty are giving way slowly to Western-style individualism and the drive for personal comfort and monetary success. Formerly close-knit communities, such as those in American Samoa, are finding themselves struggling with drug abuse and gang-related violence just as in the metropolitan countries. These changes in political and cultural values are at least as important as economic growth in projecting the future of the Pacific Rim.

The Pacific Islands: Opportunities and Limits

PLENTY OF SPACE, BUT NO ROOM

There are about 30,000 islands in the Pacific Ocean. Most of them are found in the South Pacific and are divided into three mammoth regions: Micronesia, consisting of some 2,000 islands with such names as Palau, Nauru, and Guam; Melanesia, where 200 different languages are spoken on such islands as Fiji and the Solomon Islands; and Polynesia, consisting of such islands as Hawaii, Samoa, and Tahiti.

Straddling both sides of the equator, these territories are characterized as much by what is *not* there as by what *is*— that is, between every tiny island lie hundreds and often thousands of miles of open ocean. A case in point is the Cook Islands. Associated with New Zealand, this island group contains only 88 square miles of land but is spread over 850,000 square miles of open sea. So expansive is the space between islands that early explorers from Europe and the Spanish lands of South America often bypassed dozens of islands which lay just beyond view in the vastness of the world's largest ocean.

However, once the Europeans found and set foot on the islands, they inaugurated a process that irreversibly changed the history of island life. A case in point was the discovery of the Marquesas Islands by the Peruvian Spaniard Alvaro de Mendana. Mendana landed there in 1595 with some women and children and, significantly, 378 soldiers. Within weeks he had planted three Christian crosses, declared the islands to be the possession of the king of Spain, and killed 200 islanders. Writes historian Ernest S. Dodge:

> . . .The Spaniards opened fire on the surrounding canoes for no reason at all. To prove himself a good marksman one soldier killed both a Marquesan and the child in his arms with one shot as the man desperately swam for safety. . . . The persistent Marquesans again attempted to be friendly by bringing fruit and water, but again they were shot down when they attempted to take four Spanish water jars. Magnanimously the Spaniards allowed the Marquesans to stand around and watch while mass was celebrated. . . . When [the islanders]

(UN photo by Nagata Jr.)

In the South Pacific area of Micronesia there are some 2,000 islands spread over an ocean area of 3 million square miles. There remain many relics of the diverse cultures found on these islands; these boys are walking between the highly prized stone discs that were used as money on the islands of the Yap District.

THE CASE OF THE DISAPPEARING ISLAND

It wasn't much to begin with, but the way things are going, it won't be anything by the year 2000. Nauru, a tiny 8^1/$_2$-square-mile dot of phosphate dirt in the South Pacific, is being gobbled up by the Nauru Phosphate Corporation. Made of bird droppings mixed with marine sediment, Nauru's high-quality phosphate has a ready market in Australia, New Zealand, Japan, and other Pacific Rim countries, where it is used in industry, medicine, and agriculture (as fertilizer).

Many South Pacific islanders with few natural resources to sell to the outside world envy the 4,500 Nauruans. The Nauruans pay no taxes, yet the government, thanks to phosphate sales, is able to provide them with free health and dental care, bus transportation, newspapers, and schooling (including higher education if they are willing to leave home temporarily for Australia, with the trip paid for by the government). Rent for government-built homes, supplied with telephones and electricity, costs about $5 a month. Nor do Nauruans have to work particularly hard for a living, since most laborers in the phosphate pits are imported from other islands; most managers and other professionals come from Australia, New Zealand, or England.

Phosphate is Nauru's only export, and yet the country makes so much money from it that, technically speaking, Nauru is the richest country per capita in the world. Unable to spend all the export earnings (even though it owns and operates five Boeing 737s, several hotels on other islands, and the tallest skyscraper in Melbourne, Australia), the government puts lots of the money away in trust accounts for a rainy day.

It all sounds nice, but the rub is that the island is being mined away. Already there is only just a little fringe of green left along the shore where everyone lives, and the government is starting to think about the year 2000 (or sooner: some estimates put the end of the island as early as 1992), when even the ground under people's homes will be mined and shipped away. Some think that topsoil should be brought in to see if the moonlike surface of the excavated areas can be revitalized. Others think that moving out makes sense—with all its money, the government could just buy another island somewhere and move everyone (an idea that Australia suggested years ago, even before Nauru's independence in 1968). Of course, since the government owns the phosphate company, it could just put a halt to any more mining. But if it does, what would Nauru be to anybody? On the other hand, if it doesn't, will Nauru *be* at all?

---

attempted to take two canoe loads of . . . coconuts to the ships half the unarmed natives were killed and three of the bodies hung in the rigging in grim warning. The Spaniards were not only killing under orders, they were killing for target practice. . . .

—From *Islands and Empires; Western Impact on the Pacific and East Asia* (Minneapolis: University of Minnesota Press, 1976), p. 18.

As it turned out, there were plenty of Pacific islands for the Europeans to discover, since the islanders were skilled navigators and boat builders and, by the time of Europe's Age of Exploration, had built settlements on almost every inhabitable island. "Pacifying" the people on these islands was, in general, accomplished by violence and represents a gruesome chapter of human history. The European explorers insisted that the islanders learn European languages, wear European clothing, convert to Christianity and pay homage to European monarchs. This Eurocentric approach to other cultures constituted arrogance, since the islanders already had their own languages, clothing, religions, and kings. They could not understand how the islands they owned could, by verbal pronouncement, become the property of someone else. Nor could they understand why people said they were "discovered" when they had always known where they were.

COMING OF AGE

The Pacific islands today, despite the ravages of colonization and disease (measles, influenza, and slave labor decimated the populations of many islands), are perhaps more interconnected than ever before. For one thing, the population, now about 2.2 million, excluding whites, is increasing, and many islanders are moving to islands with bigger towns, more jobs, and more excitement. Hawaii, for example, is peopled now with Japanese, Samoans, Filipinos, Koreans, whites, and many others; pure Hawaiians are a minority, and despite efforts to preserve the Hawaiian language, it is dying out. Similarly, Fiji is now populated by more immigrants from India than by native Fijians. New Caledonians are outnumbered by Indonesians, Vietnamese, French, and Polynesians. And, of course, whites have long outnumbered the Maoris on New Zealand.

Island trade involving vast distances brought otherwise disparate people together in the past; it continues to do so today. The relatively dry, flat, coral islands export phosphate, while the volcanic islands, well endowed with water, flora, and fauna, export foodstuffs. It is still meaningful to speak of the Pacific Islands as divided into three racial/cultural groups (the Micronesians with ties to Asia; the Melanesians with probable ties to Africa; and the Polynesians, who some speculate may have ancient ties with South America). But the islanders' common history of colonization (by Spain, Great Britain, France, Germany, and, briefly, Japan), and the common conditions of everyday life—everyone, for example, knows how to raise bananas, coconuts, and yams, and how to roast pigs and fish—draw them continually toward one common culture.

Politically, however, the region is a hodgepodge. Some islands, like Western Samoa and Nauru, have been independent for decades, but most remain in some kind of loose association with the United States, Britain, France, New Zealand, or Australia. Some of these relationships are continuations of colonial-era influences, while others are the result of the termination of such influences after the two world wars. For example, after World War I, Germany lost its colonies in the region (e.g., German Samoa). After the defeat of Japan in World War II, the Marshall Islands, the Marianas, and the Carolines were assigned by the United Nations to the United States as a trust territory. The French Polynesian islands have chosen to remain overseas territories of France, although in recent years there has been a growing desire for autonomy, which France has attempted to meet in various ways while still retaining control. The United Nations' decolonization policy has made it possible for numerous islands to achieve complete or partial independence, although many are so small that true economic independence will never be possible and many have chosen to remain in some type of limited voluntary association with their former colonial overseers.

Although some exotic exports like copra (dried coconut meat) and mother-of-pearl find their way to Japanese and Western consumers, the controlling powers today seem to prefer to consume not the products but the islands themselves. Britain, France, and the United States have all used coral atolls to test hydrogen bombs, and the United States is now proposing to dispose of its entire European stockpile of nerve gas on one of the atolls. Phosphate mining on some of the raised coral islands is also depleting living space and destroying the natural environment.

THE PACIFIC COMMUNITY

Particularly since the end of World War II, the various islands, often at the urging of Australia or New Zealand, have banded together in numerous regional and economic associations, including the South Pacific commission, the South pacific Islands Fisheries Development Agency, the South Pacific Regional Trade and Economic Agreement, and the South Pacific Forum, to name a few. These organizations have produced a variety of duty-free agreements among countries and made joint decisions about regional transportation and cultural exchanges. Regional art festivals and sports competitions are now a regular feature of island life. A regional university in New Zealand attracts several thousand island students a year, as do universities in Hawaii. Most significant, however, is the development of a stronger sense of regional identity—despite sharp rivalries among some island states—which is allowing the scattered islands to speak with a more unified voice on such matters as nuclear testing and environmental destruction.

No amount of cooperation, however, can overcome the obvious and limiting conditions of economic life in the islands. Exports are primarily of agricultural products rather than of more profitable manufactured items, and small size combined with vast distances between markets make it unlikely that the region will ever be able to affect the world economy substantially. Japan is the largest single purchaser of Pacific Island products. Islanders import consumer items mostly from Australia, France, and the United States; they export primarily to Japan, the United States, Europe, Australia, and New Zealand.

Negative effects of modernization are seen in growing crime rates and other signs of social dissolution on some islands. Young Samoans, for example, are currently afflicted with many of the same problems—gangs, drugs, and so on—as are their U.S. inner-city counterparts. Samoan authorities now report increases in incidences of rape, robbery, and other socially dysfunctional behaviors.

Japan Map

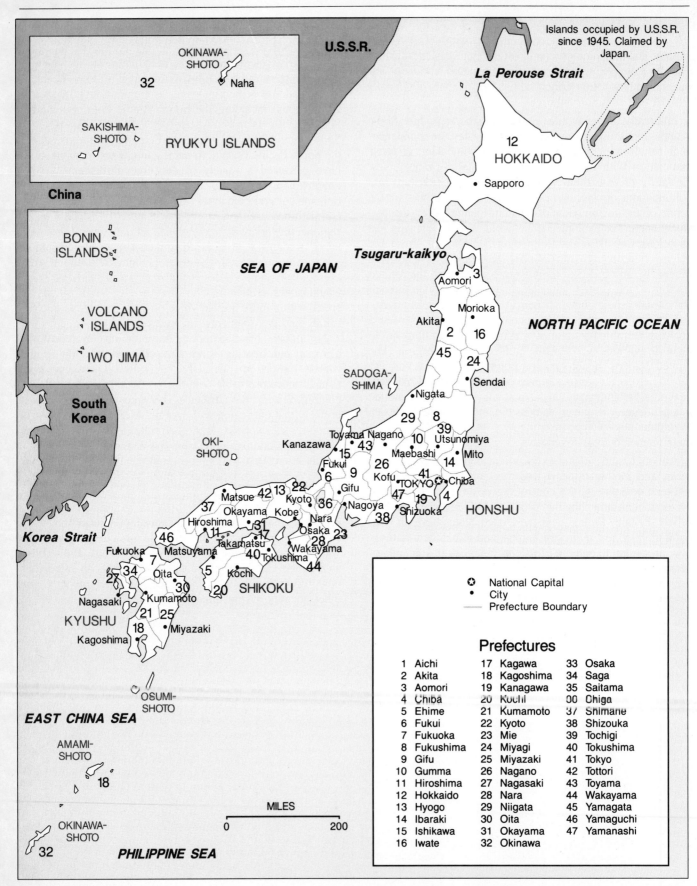

OKINAWA-SHOTO
32
Naha

SAKISHIMA-SHOTO
RYUKYU ISLANDS

China

BONIN ISLANDS

VOLCANO ISLANDS

IWO JIMA

South Korea

SEA OF JAPAN

U.S.S.R.

Islands occupied by U.S.S.R. since 1945. Claimed by Japan.

La Perouse Strait

12
HOKKAIDO
Sapporo

Tsugaru-kaikyo

Aomori
3

Morioka
Akita
2
16
45
24
Sendai

NORTH PACIFIC OCEAN

SADOGA-SHIMA

Niigata

29
8
Toyama Nagano
39
Kanazawa
43
10
Utsunomiya
15
Maebashi
Mito
Fukui
26
14
6
9
Kofu
41
Gifu
47
TOKYO
Chiba
OKI-SHOTO
22
36
19
4
Matsue
42
13
Kyoto
Nagoya
38
Shizuoka
37
Okayama
Kobe
Nara
HONSHU
Hiroshima
31
Osaka
23
46
11
17
28
Takamatsu
Wakayama
Fukuoka
7
Matsuyama
40
Tokushima
44
34
Oita
5
Kochi
27
30
20
SHIKOKU
Nagasaki
Kumamoto
KYUSHU
21
25
18
Miyazaki
Kagoshima

OSUMI-SHOTO

EAST CHINA SEA

AMAMI-SHOTO
18

Korea Strait

MILES
0   200

OKINAWA-SHOTO
32

PHILIPPINE SEA

Legend

⊛ National Capital
• City
— Prefecture Boundary

Prefectures

1 Aichi	17 Kagawa	33 Osaka
2 Akita	18 Kagoshima	34 Saga
3 Aomori	19 Kanagawa	35 Saitama
4 Chiba	20 Kochi	36 Shiga
5 Ehime	21 Kumamoto	37 Shimane
6 Fukui	22 Kyoto	38 Shizuoka
7 Fukuoka	23 Mie	39 Tochigi
8 Fukushima	24 Miyagi	40 Tokushima
9 Gifu	25 Miyazaki	41 Tokyo
10 Gumma	26 Nagano	42 Tottori
11 Hiroshima	27 Nagasaki	43 Toyama
12 Hokkaido	28 Nara	44 Wakayama
13 Hyogo	29 Niigata	45 Yamagata
14 Ibaraki	30 Oita	46 Yamaguchi
15 Ishikawa	31 Okayama	47 Yamanashi
16 Iwate	32 Okinawa	

Japan

GEOGRAPHY

Area in Square Kilometers (Miles):
377,835 (145,882) (slightly smaller
than California)
Capital (Population): Tokyo
(8,300,000)
Climate: tropical in south to cool in
north

PEOPLE

Population
Total: 123,642,000
Annual Growth Rate: 0.4%
Rural/Urban Population Ratio: 23/77
Ethnic Makeup of Population: 99.4%
Japanese; 0.6% others (mostly
Korean)
Language: Japanese

Health
Life Expectancy at Birth: 76 years
(male); 82 years (female)
Infant Mortality Rate (Ratio): 5/1,000
Average Caloric Intake: 124% of FAO
minimum
Physicians Available (Ratio): 1/646

Religion(s)
83% Shinto and Buddhist; 16%
others; 1% Christian

JAPANESE INCOME

After working an average work week of 46.8 hours, the average male
worker in Japan earned $33,100 in 1989, an increase of about 3 percent
from the previous year. Even after inflation, his earnings were 3 percent
more than in the previous year. (If his wife worked, she probably earned
only half his salary.) Like almost everyone (90 percent), this male
worker had to pay income tax, which on average was about $1,700.
Twice during the year his company paid him large bonuses, with which
he likely purchased a car or major household items. The amounts of
these bonuses were a matter of serious negotiation between his labor
union and management. Typically, he would have saved 15 to 25 percent
of his income.

Education
Adult Literacy Rate: 99.9%

COMMUNICATION

Telephones: 64,000,000
Newspapers: 124

TRANSPORTATION

Highways—Kilometers (Miles):
1,098,900 (681,318)

Railroads—Kilometers (Miles): 27,327
(16,943)
Usable Airfields: 156

GOVERNMENT

Type: constitutional monarchy
Independence Date: May 3, 1947
(constitutional monarchy established)
Head of State: Emperor Akihito;
Prime Minister Toshiki Kaifu
Political Parties: Liberal Democratic
Party; Japan Socialist Party;
Democratic Socialist Party; Japan
Communist Party; Komeito Party
Suffrage: universal at 20

MILITARY

Number of Armed Forces: 246,000
*Military Expenditures (% of Central
Government Expenditures):* 1 % of
GNP
Current Hostilities: none

ECONOMY

Currency ($ U.S. Equivalent): 145
yen = $1
Per Capita Income/GNP:
$15,600/$1,914.1 billion
Inflation Rate: 2.1%
Natural Resources: negligible oil and
minerals
Agriculture: rice; sugar beets;
vegetables; fruit; animal products
include pork, poultry, dairy and eggs,
fish
Industry: metallurgy; engineering;
electrical and electronics; textiles;
chemicals; automobiles; fishing

FOREIGN TRADE

Exports: $270 billion
Imports: $210 billion

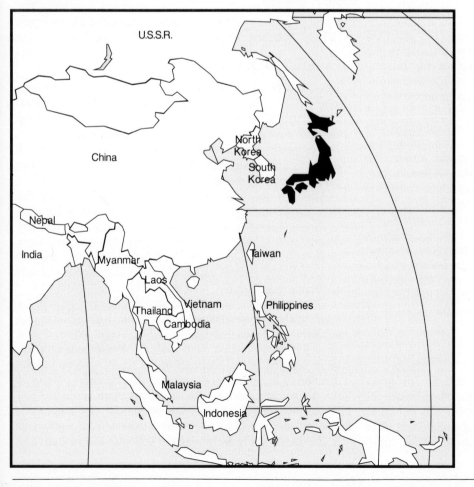

Japan: Driving Force in the Pacific Rim

HISTORICAL BACKGROUND

The Japanese nation is thought to have begun about 250 B.C., when ancestors of today's Japanese people began cultivating rice, casting objects in bronze, and putting together the rudiments of the Shinto religion. However, humans are thought to have inhabited the Japanese islands as early as 20,000 B.C. Remnants of these early peoples are, perhaps, the non-Oriental Ainu people who still occupy parts of the northern island of Hokkaido. Asiatic migrants from China and Korea and islanders from the South Pacific occupied the islands between 250 B.C. and A.D. 400, contributing to the population base of modern Japan.

Between A.D. 300 and 710 military aristocrats, claiming divine approval, established their rule over individual clans, of which the Yamato clan became the most powerful. Under Yamato rule, the Japanese began to import ideas and technology from nearby China, including the Buddhist religion and the Chinese method of writing—which the elite somewhat awkwardly adapted to spoken Japanese, an entirely unrelated language. The Chinese bureaucratic style of government and architecture was also introduced; Japan's first permanent capital was constructed at the city of Nara between 710 and 794.

As Chinese influence waned in the period 794–1185, the capital was relocated to Kyoto, with the Fujiwara family wielding real power under the largely symbolic figurehead of the emperor. A warrior class controlled by *shoguns,* or generals, held power at Kamakura between 1185 and 1333 and successfully defended the country from invasion by the Mongols. Buddhism became the religion of the masses, although Shintoism was often embraced simultaneously. Between 1333 and 1568 a very rigid class structure developed along with a feudalistic economy controlled by feudal lords (*daimyos*) who reigned over their own mini-kingdoms.

In 1543 Portuguese sailors landed in Japan, followed 6 years later by the Jesuit missionary Francis Xavier. An active trade with Portugal began, and many Japanese (perhaps half a million), including some feudal lords, converted to Christianity. The Portuguese introduced firearms to the Japanese and perhaps taught them Western-style techniques of building castles with moats and stone walls. Wealthier feudal lords were able to utilize these innovations to defeat weaker rivals, and by 1600 the country was unified under a military bureaucracy, although feudal lords still retained substantial sovereignty over their fiefs. During this time the general Hideyoshi attempted an unsuccessful invasion of nearby Korea.

The Tokugawa Era

In the period between 1600 and 1868, called the Tokugawa Era, the social, political, and economic foundations of modern Japan were put in place. The capital was moved to Tokyo, cities began to grow in size, and a merchant class arose which was powerful enough to challenge the hege- mony of the centuries-old warrior class. Strict rules of dress and behavior for each of the four social classes (samurai, farmer, craftsman, and merchant) were imposed, and the Japanese people learned to discipline themselves to these codes. Western ideas came to be seen as a threat to the established ruling class. The military elite expelled foreigners and put the nation into two centuries of extreme isolation from the rest of the world. Christianity was banned, as was most trade with the West. Even Japanese living abroad were forbidden from returning, for fear that they were contaminated with foreign ideas. During the Tokugawa Era indigenous culture expanded rapidly. Puppet plays and a new form of drama called *kabuki* became popular, as did *haiku* poetry and Japanese pottery and painting. The samurai code, called *bushido,* along with the concept of *giri,* or obligation to one's superiors, suffused Japanese society. Also during this period, literacy among males rose to about 40 percent, higher than most European countries of the day. Samurai busied themselves with the education of the young, using teaching methods that included strict discipline, hard work, and self-abnegation.

During the decades of isolation Japan grew culturally strong but militarily weak. In 1853 a U.S. naval squadron appeared in Tokyo Bay to insist that Japan open up its ports to foreign vessels needing supplies and desiring to trade. Similar requests had been denied in the past, but the sophistication of the U.S. ships and their advanced weaponry convinced the Japanese military rulers that they no longer could keep Japan isolated from the outside.

The Era of Modernization

Treaties with the United States and other Western nations followed, and the dislocations associated with the opening of the country to the world soon brought discredit to the ruling shoguns. Provincial samurai took control of the government. The emperor, long a figurehead away from the center of power in Kyoto, was moved to Tokyo in 1868, beginning the period known as the Meiji Restoration.

Although the Meiji leaders came to power with the intention of ousting all the foreigners and returning Japan to its former state of domestic tranquillity, they quickly realized that the nations of the West were determined to defend their newly won access to the ports of Japan. To defeat the foreigners, they reasoned, Japan must first acquire their knowledge and technology.

Thus, beginning in 1868, the Japanese leaders launched a major campaign to modernize the nation. Ambassadors and scholars were sent abroad to learn about Western-style government, education, and warfare. Implementing these ideas resulted in the abolition of the feudal system and the division of Japan into prefectures under the direct control of the Tokyo government. Social classes were abolished and Western-style dress, music, and education were embraced. The old samurai class turned its attention from warfare to leadership in the government, in schools, and in business.

(Photo credit Reuters/Bettmann)

The Japanese emperor has long been a figurehead in Japan. In 1926 Hirohito, pictured above, became emperor and ushered in the era named Showa. He died on January 7, 1989, having seen Japan through World War II and witnessed its rise to the economic world power it is today. He was succeeded by his son, Akihito, whose reign has been named Heisei by the Japanese government.

Factories and railroads were constructed, and public education was expanded. By 1900 Japan's literacy rate was 90 percent, the highest in Asia. Parliamentary rule was established along the lines of the government in Prussia, agricultural techniques were imported from the United States, and banking methods were adopted from Britain.

Japan's rapid modernization soon convinced its leaders that the nation was strong enough to begin doing what other advanced nations were doing: acquiring empires. Japan went to war with China, acquiring the Chinese island of Taiwan in 1895. In 1904 Japan attacked Russia and successfully acquired Korea and access to Manchuria (both areas having been in the sphere of influence of Russia). Siding against Germany in World War I, Japan was able to acquire Germany's Pacific empire—the Marshall, Caroline, and Mariana Islands. Western nations were surprised at Japan's rapid empire-building but did little to stop it.

The Great Depression of the 1930s caused serious hardships in Japan because, being resource-poor yet heavily populated, the country had come to rely on trade to supply its basic needs. Many Japanese advocated the forced annexation of Manchuria as a way of providing needed resources. This was accomplished easily in 1931. With militarism on the rise, the Japanese nation began moving away from democracy and toward a military dictatorship. Political parties were eventually banned, and opposition leaders were jailed and tortured.

WORLD WAR II AND THE JAPANESE EMPIRE

The battles of World War II in Europe, initially won by Germany, promised to realign substantially the colonial empires of France and other European powers in Asia. The military elite of Japan declared its intention of creating a Greater East Asia Co-Prosperity Sphere—in effect, a Japanese empire created out of the ashes of the European empires that were now dissolving. In 1941, under the guidance of General Hideki Tojo and with the tacit approval of the emperor, Japan captured the former French colony of Indochina (Vietnam, Laos, and Cambodia), bombed Pearl Harbor in Hawaii, and captured oil-rich Indonesia. These victories were followed by others: Japan captured all of Southeast Asia, including Burma, Thailand, and Malaya, the Philippines, and parts of New Guinea; and expanded its hold in China and in the islands of the South Pacific. Many of these conquered peoples, lured by the Japanese slogan of "Asia for the Asians," were initially supportive of the Japanese, believing that Japan would rid their countries of European colonial rule. It soon became apparent, however, that Japan had no intention of relinquishing control of these territories and would go to brutal lengths to subjugate the local peoples. Japan soon dominated a vast empire, the constituents of which were virtually the same as those making up what we call the Pacific Rim today.

In 1941 the United States launched a counter offensive against the powerful Japanese military. (American history books refer to this offensive as the Pacific Theater of World War II, but the Japanese call it the Pacific War. We use the term World War II in this text, for reasons of clarity and consistency.) By 1944 U.S. troops had ousted the Japanese from most of their conquered lands and were beginning to attack the home islands themselves. Massive firebombing of Tokyo and other cities, combined with the dropping of two atomic bombs on Hiroshima and Nagasaki, convinced the Japanese military rulers that they had no choice but to surrender.

This was the first time in Japanese history that Japan had been conquered, and the Japanese were shocked to hear their emperor Hirohito—whose voice had never been heard on radio—announce on August 14, 1945 that Japan was defeated. The emperor cited the suffering of the people—almost 2 million Japanese had been killed—devastation of the cities brought about by the use of a "new and most cruel bomb," and the possibility that without surrender, Japan as a nation might be completely "obliterated." Emperor Hirohito then encouraged his people to look to the future, to keep pace with progress, and to help build world peace by accepting the

(Photo credit U.S. Navy)

On December 7, 1941, the Japanese entered World War II by bombing Pearl Harbor. This photograph, taken by an attacking Japanese plane, shows Pearl Harbor and a line of American battleships about to be attacked.

surrender ("enduring the unendurable and suffering what is insufferable").

This attitude smoothed the way for the American Occupation, led by U.S. General Douglas MacArthur. Defeat seemed to inspire the Japanese people to adopt the ways of their more powerful conquerors and to eschew militarism. Under the Occupation forces, the Japanese Constitution was rewritten in a form that mimicked that of the United States. Industry was restructured, labor unions encouraged, land reform accomplished, and the nation as a whole was demilitarized. Economic aid from the United States as well as the prosperity in Japan that was occasioned by the Korean War in 1953 allowed Japanese industry to begin to recover from the devastation of war. The United States returned the governance of Japan back to the Japanese people by treaty in 1951 (although some 60,000 troops still remain in Japan as part of an agreement to defend Japan from foreign attack). By the late 1960s the Japanese economy was more than self-sustaining, and the United States was Japan's primary trading partner. Trade with Japan's former empire was minimal because of the resentment against Japanese wartime brutalities. Even as recently as the late 1970s anti-Japanese riots and demonstrations occurred upon the visit of Japanese officials to Southeast Asian nations.

Between the 1960s and 1980s Japan experienced an era of unprecedented economic prosperity. Annual economic growth was three times as much as in other industrialized nations. Japanese couples voluntarily limited their family size so that each child born could enjoy the best of medical care and social and educational opportunities. The fascination with the West continued, but eventually, rather than "modernization" or "Americanization," the Japanese began to speak of "internationalization," a term that reflects both their capacity for and their actual membership in the world community politically, culturally, and economically.

In the mid-1980s the Japanese government as well as private industry began to accelerate the drive for diversified markets and resources. This was partly in response to protectionist trends in countries in North America and Europe with whom Japan had accumulated huge trade surpluses, but it was partly due to changes in Japan's own internal social and economic conditions. Japan's recent resurgence of interest in its neighboring countries and the origin of the bloc of nations we are calling the Pacific Rim can be explained by both external protectionism and internal changes. This time, however, Japanese influence—no longer linked with militarism—is being welcomed by virtually all nations in the region.

DOMESTIC CHANGE

What internal conditions are causing Japan's renewed interest in Asia and the Pacific? One change involves wage structure. For several decades Japanese exports were less expensive than competitors' because Japanese workers were not paid as well as workers in North America and Europe. Today, however, the situation is reversed: average manufacturing wages in Japan are now higher than those paid to workers in the United States. School teachers, college professors, and many other white-collar workers are also better off in Japan. These wage differentials are the result of successful union activity and demographic changes.

Whereas prewar Japanese families—especially those in the rural areas—were large, today's modern household typically consists of a couple and only one or two children. As this low birth rate began to affect the supply of labor, companies were forced to entice workers with higher wages. An example is McDonald's, increasingly popular in Japan as a fast-food outlet. Whereas young people working at McDonald's outlets in the United States are paid at or slightly above the legal minimum wage of $4.25 an hour, McDonald's employees in Japan are paid as much as $7.10

an hour because there are simply fewer youths available (many schools prohibit students from working during the school year). In 1989 the average household income in Japan was about $7,500 more per year than in the United States.

Given conditions like these, Japanese companies find they cannot be competitive in world markets unless they move their operations to countries like the Philippines or Singapore, where an abundance of laborers keeps wage costs 75 to 95 percent lower than in Japan. Abundant, cheap labor (as well as a desire to avoid import tariffs) is also the reason so many Japanese companies are being constructed in the economically depressed areas of the U.S. Midwest and South.

Another internal condition that is spurring Japanese interest in the Pacific Rim is a growing public concern for the home environment. Beginning in the 1970s the Japanese courts handed down several landmark decisions in which Japanese companies were held liable for damages to people caused by chemical and other industrial wastes. Japanese industry, realizing that it no longer had a carte blanche to make profits at the expense of the environment, began moving some of its smokestack industries to new locations in

(Photo credit United Motor Manufacturing)

As the economy of Japan began to develop, manufacturing wages rose to a point that made their products no longer competitive in world markets. In response, Japanese industry began to build manufacturing facilities in partnership with foreign companies. These American workers are busy in a Toyota-General Motors plant in the midwestern United States.

Third World countries, just as other industrialized nations had already done. This has turned out to be a wise move for many companies because it has put their operations closer to their raw materials, which, in combination with cheaper labor costs, has allowed them to remain globally competitive. It also has been a tremendous benefit to the host countries, although environmental groups in many Rim countries are also now becoming active, and industry in the future may be forced to effect actual improvements in their operations rather than move polluting technologies to "safe" areas.

Attitudes toward work are also changing in Japan. Although the average Japanese worker still works about 6 hours more per week than does the typical North American worker, the new generation of workers—those born and raised since World War II—are not so eager to sacrifice as much for their companies as were their parents. Recent policies have eliminated weekend work in many industries, and sports and other recreational activities are becoming increasingly popular. Given these conditions, Japanese corporate leaders are finding it more cost-effective to move operations abroad to countries like South Korea, where labor legislation is weaker and long work hours remain the norm.

MYTH AND REALITY OF THE ECONOMIC MIRACLE

The Japanese economy, like any other economy, must respond to market as well as social and political changes to stay vibrant. It just so happens that, this time, Japan's attempt to keep its economic boom alive has created the conditions that, in turn, are furthering the economies of all the countries in the Asia/Pacific region. If a regional "yen bloc" (so called because of the dominance of the Japanese currency, the yen) is created in the process, it will simply be the result of Japan doing what it calculates it has to do to remain competitive in the world market.

Outsiders today are often of the impression that whatever Japan does—whether targeting a certain market or reorienting its economy toward regional trade—turns to gold, as if the Japanese possess some secret of success that others do not. But there is no such secret that other nations could not understand or employ themselves. Japanese success in business, education, and other fields is the result of hard work, advance planning, persistence, and outside help.

However, even with those ingredients in place Japanese enterprises often fall short. In many industries, for example, Japanese workers are less efficient than are workers in other countries. Japan's national railway system was once found to have 277,000 more employees on its payroll than it needed. The system was so poorly managed for so many years that an investigation revealed the system had by 1988 accumulated a total public debt of $257 billion. Multimillion-dollar train stations had been built in out-of-the-way towns, for no other reason than that a member of the Diet (Congress) happened to live there and had pork-barreled the project. Both government and industry have been plagued by bribery and corrup-

tion, as in the Recruit Scandal of the late 1980s that caused many implicated government leaders, including the prime minister, to resign.

THE 10 COMMANDMENTS OF ECONOMIC SUCCESS

Still, the success of modern Japan has been phenomenal, and it would be helpful to review in detail some of the bases of that success. We might call these the 10 commandments of Japan's economic success.

1. Some of Japan's entrenched business conglomerates (called *zaibatsu*) were broken up by order of the U.S. Occupation commander after World War II; this allowed competing businesses to get a start. Similarly, the physical infrastructure—roads, factories—were destroyed during the war. This was a blessing in disguise, for it paved the way for newer equipment and technologies to be put in place quickly.

2. The United States, seeing the need for an economically strong Japan in order to offset the growing attraction of communist ideology in Asia, provided substantial reconstruction aid. For instance, Sony Corporation got started with help from the Agency for International Development (AID)—an organization to which the United States is a major contributor. Mazda Motors got its start by making Jeeps for U.S. forces during the Korean War. Other Rim countries that are now doing well can also thank U.S. generosity: Taiwan

(Photo credit Sony Corporation of America)

A contributing factor in the economic development of Japan was investment from the Agency for International Development (AID). The Sony Corporation is an example of just how successful this assistance could be. These women are assembling products that will be sold all over the world.

received $5.6 billion and South Korea received $13 billion in aid during the period 1945–1978.

3. Japanese industry looked upon government as a facilitator and received useful economic advice as well as political and financial assistance from government planners. (In this regard, it is important to note that many of Japan's civil servants are the best graduates of Japan's colleges and universities.) Also, the advice and help coming from the government were fairly consistent over time, because the same political party, the Liberal Democratic Party, remained (and still remains) in power for almost the entire postwar period.

4. Japanese businesses selected an export-oriented strategy that stressed building market share over immediate profit.

5. Except in certain professions such as teaching, labor unions in Japan were not as powerful as in Europe and the United States. This is not to suggest that unions have not been effective in gaining benefits for workers, but the structure of the union movement—individual company unions rather than industry-wide unions—moderated the demands for improved wages and benefits.

6. Company managers stressed employee teamwork and group spirit and implemented policies such as "lifetime employment" and quality-control circles, which contributed to group morale. In this they were aided by the Japanese tendency to grant to the company some of the same level of loyalty traditionally reserved for families. In certain ways, the gap between workers and management was minimized.

7. Companies benefited from the Japanese ethic of working hard and saving much. For most of Japan's postwar history, workers have worked 6 days a week, arriving early and leaving late. The paychecks were carefully managed to include a substantial savings component—generally between 15 and 25 percent. This guaranteed that there were always enough cash reserves for banks to offer company expansion loans at low interest.

8. The government spent relatively little of its tax revenues on social-welfare programs or military defense, preferring instead to invest public funds in private industry.

9. A relatively stable family structure (i.e., few divorces and substantial family support for young people until marriage) produced employees who were reliable and psychologically stable.

10. The government as well as private individuals invested enormous amounts of money and energy into education, on the assumption that in a resource-poor country, the mental energies of the people would need to be exploited to their fullest.

Some of these conditions for success are now part of immutable history, but some, such as the emphasis on education, are open to change as the conditions of Japanese life change. A relevant example is the practice of lifetime employment. Useful as a management tool when companies were small and *skilled* laborers were difficult to find, it is now giving way to a freer labor market system. In some

industries, as many as 30 percent of new hires quit after 2 years on the job. In other words, the aforementioned conditions for success were relevant to at least one particular era of Japanese and world history and may not be relevant to other countries or other times. Selecting the right strategy for the right era has perhaps been the single most important condition for Japanese economic success.

COMMON CHARACTERISTICS

All of these conditions notwithstanding, Japan would never have achieved economic success without its people possessing certain social and psychological characteristics, many of which can be traced to the various religious/ethical philosophies that have suffused Japan's 2,000-year history. Shintoism, Buddhism, Confucianism, Christianity, and other philosophies of living have shaped the modern Japanese mind. This is not to suggest that Japanese are tradition-bound; nothing could be further from the truth, even though many Westerners think "tradition" when they think Japan.

It is more accurate to think of Japanese people as imitative, preventive, pragmatic, obligative, and inquisitive, rather than traditional. These characteristics are discussed in this section.

Imitative

The capacity to imitate one's superiors is a strength of the Japanese people; rather than representing an inability to think creatively, it constitutes one reason for Japan's legendary success. It makes sense to the Japanese to copy a success, whether it is their bosses, or a company in the United States, or an educational curriculum in Europe. It is true that imitation can produce conformity, but in Japan's case, it is often conformity based on respect for the superior qualities of someone or something rather than simple, blind mimickry.

Once Japanese people have mastered the skills of their superiors, they then believe they have the moral right to a style of their own. Misunderstandings on this point arise often when East meets West. An American school teacher, for example, was recently sent to Japan to teach Western art to elementary-school children. Considering her an expert, the children did their best to copy her work to the smallest detail. Misunderstanding that this was at once a compliment and the first step toward creativity, the teacher removed all of her art samples from the classroom in order to force the students to paint something from their own imaginations. Because the students found this to be a violation of their approach to creativity, they did not perform well, and the teacher left Japan believing that Japanese education teaches conformity and compliance rather than creativity and spontaneity.

There is a lesson to learn from this episode as far as predicting the future role of Japan vis-à-vis the West. After decades of imitating the West, Japanese people are now beginning to feel that they have the skills and the moral right to create styles of their own. We can expect to see, therefore, an explosion of Japanese creativity in the near future. Some observers have recently noted, for example, that the international fashion industry seems to be gaining more inspiration from designers in Tokyo than from those in Milan, Paris, or New York. And as of the mid-1980s the Japanese have annually registered more new patents with the U.S. Patent Office than have Americans.

Preventive

Japanese individuals, families, companies, and the government prefer long-range over short-range planning, and they greatly prefer foreknowledge over postmortem analysis. Assembly-line workers test and retest every product to prevent customers from receiving defective products. Store clerks plug in and check electronic devices in front of a customer to prevent bad merchandise from sullying the good reputation of the store. Insurance companies do a brisk business in Japan, and even though Japanese citizens are covered by the government's national health plan, many people buy additional coverage—e.g., cancer insurance—just to be safe.

This concern with prevention trickles down to the smallest details. At train stations, as many as five recorded warnings are given of an approaching train to commuters standing on the platform. Parent-teacher associations send teams of mothers around the neighborhood to determine which streets are the safest for the children. They then post signs designating certain roads as "school passage roads" and instruct children to take those routes even if it takes longer to walk to school. The Japanese reason that it is better to avoid an accident than to have an emergency team ready when a child is hurt. Whereas Americans say, "If it ain't broke, don't fix it," the Japanese say, "Why wait 'til it breaks to fix it?"

Pragmatic

Rather than pursue a plan because it ideologically fits some preordained philosophy, the Japanese try to be pragmatic on most points. Take drugs, for example. Many nations say that drug abuse is an insurmountable problem that will, at best, be contained but probably never eradicated, because to do so would violate civil liberties. But, as a headline in *The Asahi Evening News* proclaimed not long ago, "Japan Doesn't Have a Drug Problem and Means to Keep It That Way." Reliable statistics support this claim, but that is not the whole story, because in 1954 Japan had a serious drug problem, with 53,000 drug arrests in one year. At the time, the authorities concluded that they had a serious problem on their hands and must do whatever was required to solve the problem. The government passed a series of tough laws restricting the production, use, exchange, and possession of all manner of drugs, and it gave the police the power to arrest all violators. Users were arrested as well as dealers because, it was reasoned, if the addicts were not left to buy the drugs,

(Photo credit Dean Collinwood)

Social problems such as drugs and homelessness are minimal in Japan. Neither the state nor the culture condones the plight of poverty, and there are few places in Japan that could be called a ghetto. Homeless people are a rare sight in Japan.

the dealers would be out of business. Their goal at the time was to arrest all addicts even if it meant that certain liberties were briefly circumscribed. The plan, based on a do-what-it-takes pragmatic approach, worked, and today Japan is one of the only industrialized countries without a widespread drug problem. In this case, to pragmatism was added the Japanese tendency to work for the common rather than the individual good.

This approach to life is so much a part of the Japanese mindset that many Japanese cannot understand why the United States and other industrialized nations have so many unresolved social and economic problems. For instance, when it comes to the trade imbalance, it is clear that one of the West's most serious problems is a low savings rate (making money scarce and interest high); another is inferior-quality products. Knowing that these are problems, the Japanese wonder why North Americans and Europeans do not just start saving more and working more carefully. They say to themselves, "We did it; why can't you?"

Obligative

The Japanese have a great sense of duty toward those around them. There are thousands of Japanese workers who work late without pay to improve their job skills so that they will not let their fellow workers down. Good deeds done by one generation are remembered and repaid by the next, and lifetime friendships are kept by exchanging appropriate gifts and letters. North Americans and Europeans are often considered untrustworthy friends, because they do not keep up the level of close, personal communications that the Japanese expect of their own friends; nor do these Westerners have as strong a sense of place, station, or position.

Duty to the group is closely linked to respect for superior authority. Every group—indeed, every relationship—is seen as a mixture of people with inferior and superior resources. These differences must be acknowledged, and no one is disparaged for bringing less to the group than someone else. However, equality is assumed when it comes to basic commitment to or effort expended for a task. Slackers are not welcome. Obligation to the group along with respect for superiors motivated Japanese pilots to fly suicide missions during World War II, and it now causes workers to go the extra mile for the good of the company.

Changes in the intensity of commitment, however, are increasingly apparent among modern Japanese. More Japanese than ever before are beginning to feel that their own personal goals are more important than those of their companies or extended families. This is no doubt a result of the Westernization of the culture since the Meiji Restoration in the late 1800s and especially of the experiences of the growing number of Japanese—approximately half a million in a given year—who live abroad and then take their newly acquired values back to Japan. (About half of these away Japanese live in North America and Western Europe.)

Inquisitive

The image of dozens of Japanese businesspeople struggling to read a book or newspaper while standing inside a packed commuter train is one not easily forgotten, symbolizing as it does the intense desire amongst the Japanese for knowledge, especially knowledge of foreign cultures. Nearly 6 million Japanese traveled abroad in 1986 (many to pursue higher education), and for those who did not, the government and private radio and television stations provided a continuous stream of programming about everything from Caribbean cuisine to French ballet. The Japanese have a yen for foreign styles of dress, foreign cooking, and foreign languages. The Japanese study languages with great intensity: every student is required to study English, and many others study Chinese, Greek, Latin, Russian, and others, with French being the most popular after English.

Observers inside and outside of Japan are beginning to comment that the Japanese are recklessly discarding Japanese culture in favor of foreign ideas and habits, even when they make no sense in the Japanese context. A tremendous intellectual debate (called *Nihonjin-ron*) is now taking place in Japan over the meaning of being Japanese and the Japanese role in the world. There is certainly value in these concerns, but, as was noted previously, the secret about Japanese

(Photo credit Dean Collinwood)

The Japanese are by nature a very inquisitive people. Foreign food, foreign dress, foreign languages, and foreign travel are of great interest to the average Japanese. The sign above these travel posters reads "Advance Your Summer Plans."

traditions is that they are not traditional. That is, the Japanese seem to know that in order to succeed they must learn what they need to know for the era in which they live, even if it means modifying or eliminating the past. This is probably the reason why the Japanese nation has endured for more than 2,000 years, whereas many other empires have long since fallen. In this sense, the Japanese are very forward-looking people and, in their thirst for new modes of thinking and acting, they are, perhaps, revealing their most basic and useful national personality characteristic. Given this attitude toward learning, it should come as no surprise that formal schooling in Japan is a very serious business to the government and to families. It is to that topic that we now turn.

SCHOOLING IN JAPAN

Probably most things we have heard about Japanese schools are distortions or outright falsehoods. We hear that Japanese children are highly disciplined, for example, yet in reality, Japanese schools at the elementary and junior-high levels are rather noisy, unstructured places, with children racing around the halls during breaks and getting into fights with classmates on the way home. Many readers may be surprised to learn that Japan has a far lower percentage of its college-age population enrolled in higher education than is the case in the United States—35 percent as compared to 50 percent. Moreover, the Japanese government does not require young people to attend high school (they must attend only until age 15), but 94 percent do anyway. Given these and other

(Photo credit Reuters/Bettmann)

Doing well in school is seen by students as fulfilling their obligation to their families. Education is held in high regard and is seen as an important element in achieving a better life; it is supported very strongly by parents.

realities of school life in Japan, how can we explain the consistently high scores of Japanese on international tests and the general agreement that Japanese high school graduates know almost as much as college graduates in the United States?

Structurally, schools in Japan are similar to those in many other countries: there are kindergartens, elementary, junior high, and high schools. Passage into elementary and junior high is automatic, regardless of student performance level. But admission to high school and college is based on test scores from entrance examinations. Preparing for these examinations occupies the full attention of students in their final year of junior high and high school, respectively. Both parents and school authorities insist that studying for the tests be the primary focus of a student's life at those times. For instance, members of a junior-high-school soccer team may only be allowed to play on the team for their first 2 years; during their last year they are expected to be studying for their high school entrance examinations. School policy reminds students that they are in school to learn and to graduate to the next level, not to play sports. Many students even attend after-hours "cram schools" (*juku*) several nights a week to prepare for the exams.

Time for recreational and other nonschool activities is restricted, because Japanese students attend school 240 days out of the year (as compared to about 180 in U.S. schools), including Saturday mornings. Summer vacation is only 6 weeks long, instead of 3 months. Japanese youth are expected to treat schooling as their top priority—over part-time jobs (usually prohibited by school policy during the school year), sports, dating, and even family time. A student who does well in school is generally thought to be fulfilling his or her obligations to the family. The reason for this focus on education is that Japanese parents realize that only through education can Japanese youths find their place in society. Joining the army is generally not an option for Japanese youth, opportunities for farming are limited because of land scarcity, and most major companies will not hire a new employee who has not graduated from college or a respectable high school. Thus, the Japanese find it important to focus on education—to do one thing and do it well.

Japanese teachers are held in high regard, partly because when mass education was introduced, many of the high-status samurai class took up teaching to replace their martial activities. In addition, in modern times the Japan Teacher's Union has been active in agitating for higher pay for teachers. As a group, teachers are the highest-paid civil servants in Japan. Public school teachers visit the home of each student each year to merge the authority of the home with that of the school, and they insist that parents (usually mothers) play active supporting roles in the school.

Some Japanese youth dislike their system, and discussions are currently underway among Japanese educators on how to improve the quality of life for students. Occasionally the pressure of taking examinations (called "exam hell") causes some students to commit suicide, but these are infrequent occurrences (the overall suicide rate in Japan is much lower than in the United States). Most Japanese youth enjoy school and value the time they have to be with their friends, whether in class, walking home, or attending cram school. Some of those who fail their college entrance exams continue to study privately (some for many years) and re-take the exam each year until they pass. Others will travel abroad and enroll in foreign universities that do not have such rigid entrance requirements. Still others will enroll in vocational training schools. But everyone in Japan realizes that education, not money, name, or luck, is the key to success.

Parents whose children are admitted to the prestigious national universities—such as Tokyo, Kyoto, Waseda, and Keio Universities—consider that they have much to brag about. Other parents are willing to pay as much as $35,000 on average for 4 years of college at the private (but not so prestigious) universities. Once admitted, students find that life slows down a bit. For one thing, parents pay more than 65 percent of the costs, and about 3 percent is covered by scholarships. This leaves only 30 percent to be earned by the students; this usually comes from tutoring high-school students who are studying for the entrance exams. Contemporary parents are also willing to pay the cost of a son or daughter traveling to North America or Europe either before college begins or during summer break—a practice that is becoming de rigueur for Japanese students.

College students may take 15 or 16 courses at a time, but classes usually only meet once or twice a week, and sporadic attendance is the norm. Straight lecturing rather than class discussion is the typical learning format, and there is very little homework beyond studying for the final exam. Students generally do not challenge the professor's statements in class, but some students develop rather close avuncular-type relationships with their professors outside of class. Hobbies, sports, and club activities (things the students did not have time to do while in public school) occupy the center of life for many college students. Equally important is the cementing of friendships which will last throughout a lifetime and be useful in one's career and private life.

THE JAPANESE BUSINESS WORLD

Successful college graduates begin their careers in April, when most companies do their hiring. They may have to take an examination to determine how much they know about electronics or stocks and bonds, and they may have to complete a detailed personality profile. Finally, they will have to submit to a very serious interview with company management. During interviews, the managers will watch their every move, and the applicants will be careful to avoid saying anything that will give them "minus points."

Once hired, individuals are put in training sessions in which they learn the company song and company policy on numerous matters. They may be housed in company apartments (or may continue to live at home), permitted to use a company car or van, and advised to shop at company grocery stores. Almost never are employees married at this time, and so they are expected to live a rather spartan life for the next few years.

Employees are expected to show considerable deference to their section bosses, even though, on the surface, bosses do not appear to be very different from other employees. Bosses' desks are out in the open, near the employees, they wear the same uniform, they socialize with the employees after work, and, even in a factory, they are often on the shop floor rather than sequestered away in private offices. Long-term employees often come to see the section leader as an uncle-figure (bosses are usually male) who will give them advice about life, be the best man at their weddings, and provide informal marital and family counseling as needed.

Japanese company life can be described as somewhat like a large family rather than a military squad; employees (sometimes called associates) often obey their superiors out of genuine respect rather than forced compliance. Moreover, competition between workers is reduced, because everyone hired at the same time receives more or less the same pay and most workers receive promotions at about the same time. Only later in one's career are individualistic promotions given.

Employees are expected to work hard, for not only are Japanese companies in competition with foreign businesses, but they also must survive the fiercely competitive business climate at home. Indeed, it is probably the case that the Japanese skill in international business was developed at home. There are, for example, some 580 electronics companies and 7,000 textile enterprises competing for customers in Japan. And whereas the United States has only four automobile-manufacturing companies, Japan has nine. All of these companies entice customers with deep price cuts or unusual services, hoping to edge out unprepared or weak competitors. Many companies fail. There were once, for instance, almost 40 companies in Japan that manufactured calculators, but today only 6 remain, the rest victims of tough internal Japanese competition.

At about age 28, after 6 years of working and saving money for an apartment, a car, and a honeymoon, the typical Japanese male worker marries. The average bride, about age 25, will have taken private lessons in flower arranging, the tea ceremony, sewing, cooking, and perhaps a musical instrument like the *koto,* the Japanese harp. She probably has not graduated from college, although she may have attended a specialty college for a while. If she is working, she likely is paid much less than her husband, even if she has an identical position (despite equal-pay laws enacted in the late 1980s). She may spend her time in the company preparing and

(Photo credit Reuters/Bettmann)

In the Japanese business world, employment is taken very seriously and is seen as a lifelong commitment. These workers are going to jobs that, in many ways, are more a part of their lives than their families.

serving tea for clients and employees, dusting the office, running errands, and answering telephones. When she has a baby she will be expected to quit (although more women are choosing to remain on the job).

Because the wife is expected to serve as the primary caregiver for the children (rarely more than two, and often just one), the husband is expected to always make his time available for the company. He may be asked to work weekends, to stay out late most of the week (about 4 out of 7 nights), or even to be transferred to another branch in Japan or abroad without his family. This loyalty is rewarded in numerous ways: unless the company goes bankrupt or the employee is unusually inept, he will be permitted to work for the company until he retires, usually at about age 55 or 60, even if the company no longer really needs his services; he and his wife will be taken on company sightseeing trips; the company will pay most of his health-insurance costs (the government pays the rest); and he will have the peace of mind that comes from being surrounded by lifetime friends and workmates. His association with company employees will be his main social outlet, even after retirement; upon his death, it will be his former workmates who organize and direct his Buddhist funeral services.

THE FAMILY

The loyalty once given to the traditional Japanese extended family, called the *ie,* has now been transferred to the modern company. This is logical historically, since the modern company once began as a family business and was gradually expanded to include more workers, or "siblings." Thus, whereas the family is seen as the backbone of most societies, it might be more accurate to argue that the *kaisha,* or company, is the basis of modern Japanese society. As one Japanese commentator explained, "In the West, the home is the cornerstone of people's lives. In Tokyo, home is just a place to sleep at night. . . . Each family member—husband, wife, and children—has his own community centered outside the home."

Thus, the common image that Westerners hold of the centrality of the family to Japanese culture may be inaccurate. For instance, father absence is epidemic in Japan. It is an unusual father who eats more than one meal a day with his family. He may go shopping or to a park with his family when he has free time from work, but he is more likely to go golfing with a workmate. The children's schooling occupies the bulk of their time, even on weekends. And with fewer children than in earlier generations and with appliance-equipped apartments, many Japanese women rejoin the workforce after their children are self-maintaining.

Japan's divorce rate, while rising, is still considerably lower than in other industrialized nations, a fact that may seem incongruent with the conditions described above. Yet, as explained by one Japanese sociologist, Japanese couples "do not expect much emotional closeness; there is less pressure on us to meet each other's emotional needs. If we become close, that is a nice dividend, but if we do not, it is not a problem because we did not expect it in the first place."

Despite these modifications in our image of the Japanese family, Japanese families do have significant roles to play in society. Support for education is one of the most important. Families, especially mothers, support the schools by being actively involved in the parent-teacher association; by insisting that children be given plenty of homework, and by saving for college so that the money for tuition is available without the college student having to work.

Another important function of the family is mate selection. About half of current Japanese marriages are arranged by the family. Families will ask a go-between (an uncle, boss, or other trusted person) to compile a list of marriageable candidates. Criteria such as social class, blood type, and occupation are considered. Photos of prospective candidates are presented to the unmarried son or daughter, who has the option to veto any of them or to date those he or she finds acceptable. Young people, however, increasingly select their mates with little or no input from parents.

Finally, families in Japan, even, those in which the children are married and living away from home, continue to gather for the purpose of honoring the memory of deceased family members or to enjoy one another's company for New Year's Day, Children's Day, and other celebrations.

WOMEN IN JAPAN

Ancient Confucian values held that women were legally and socially inferior to men. This produced a culture in feudal Japan in which the woman was expected to walk several steps behind her husband when in public, to eat meals only after the husband had eaten, to forgo formal education, and to serve the husband and male members of the family whenever possible. A good woman was said to be one who would endure these conditions without complaint. This pronounced gender difference can be seen today in myriad ways, including in the preponderance of males in positions of leadership in business and politics, in the smaller percentage of women college graduates, and in the pay differential between women and men.

Given the Confucian values noted above, one would expect that all top leaders would be males. However, women's roles are also subject to the complexity of both ancient and modern cultures. Between A.D. 592 and 770, for instance, of the 12 reigning emperors, half were women. In rural areas today, women take an active decision-making role

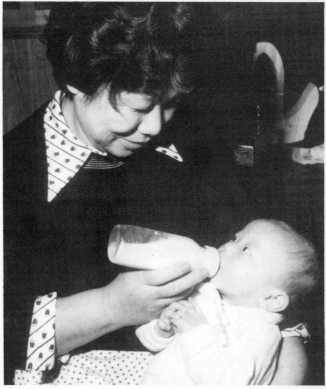

(Photo credit UN photo by Jan Corash)

In Japan, not unlike many other parts of the world, economic well-being requires two incomes. Still, there is strong social pressure on women to stop working once they have a baby. All generations of family members take part in childrearing.

in farm associations. In the urban workplace, some women occupy typically pink-collar positions (nurses, clerks and so on), but many women are also doctors and business executives.

Thus, it is clear that within the general framework of gender inequality imposed by Confucian values, Japanese culture, especially at certain times, has been rather lenient in its application of those values. There is still considerable social pressure on women to stop working once they marry, and particularly after they have a baby, but it is clear that many women are resisting that pressure: one out of every three employees in Japan is female, and nearly 60 percent of the female workforce consists of married women. In 1989 an equal-pay law was enacted which makes it illegal to pay women less for doing comparable work (although it may take years for companies to comply fully). And the Ministry of Education has mandated that home-economics and shop classes now be required for both boys and girls; that is, both girls and boys will learn to cook and sew as well as construct things out of wood and metal.

In certain respects, Japanese women seem more assertive than women in the West. For example, in the most recent national elections, a wife challenged her husband for his seat in the House of Representatives (something that has not been done in the United States, where male candidates usually expect their wives to stump for them). Significantly, too, the head of the leading opposition party, the Japan Socialist Party, and the person who would become prime minister should the Liberal Democrats lose, is an unmarried woman, Takako Doi. Women have been elected to the powerful Tokyo Metropolitan Council and awarded professorships at prestigious universities such as Tokyo University. And while women continue to be used as sexual objects in pornography and prostitution, certain kinds of demeaning behavior, such as rape and serial killing, are less frequent in Japan than in Western societies. Indeed, western women visiting Japan often report that they felt free to walk outside alone at night for the first time in their lives. Nevertheless, much of the traditional subservience expected of women remains apparent throughout Japanese culture, and modern Japanese women are learning to blend this expectation with the modern realities of the workplace and home.

RELIGION/ETHICS

There are many holidays in Japan, most of which have a religious origin. This fact, as well as the existence of numerous shrines and temples, may leave the impression that Japan is a rather religious country. This is not true, however.

Only about 15 percent of the Japanese people claim any active religious affiliation, although many will stop by a shrine occasionally to ask for divine help in passing an exam, finding a mate, or recovering from an illness.

Nevertheless, modern Japanese culture sprang from a rich religious heritage. The first influence on Japanese culture came from the animistic Shinto religion, from whence modern Japanese acquired their respect of the beauty of nature. Confucianism brought a respect for hierarchy and education. Taoism stressed introspection, and Buddhism taught the need for good behavior now in order to acquire a better life in the future.

Shinto was selected in the 1930s as the state religion and was used as a divine justification for Japan's military exploits of that era, but most Japanese today will say that Japan is, culturally, a Buddhist nation. Some new Buddhist denominations have attracted thousands of followers. The rudiments of Christianity are also a part of the modern Japanese consciousness, but few Japanese have actually joined Christian churches.

Most Japanese regard morality as springing from within the group rather than pronounced from above. That is, a Japanese person may refrain from stealing so as not to offend the owner of an object or bring shame upon the family, rather

(Photo credit The Bettmann Archive)

Religion in Japan, while not having a large active affiliation, is still an intricate part of the texture and history of the culture. This temple in Kyoto was founded in the twelfth century.

than because of a divine prohibition against stealing. Thus we find in Japan a relatively small rate of violent—that is, public—crimes, and a much larger rate of white-collar crimes such as embezzlement, in which offenders believe that they can get away with something without creating a public scandal for their families.

THE GOVERNMENT

The Constitution of postwar Japan became effective in 1947 and firmly established the Japanese people as the ultimate source of sovereignty, with the emperor as the symbol of the nation. The national Parliament, or Diet, is empowered to pass legislation. The Diet is divided into two houses: the House of Representatives, with 511 members elected for 4-year terms; and the House of Councillors, with 252 members elected for 6-year terms from each of the 47 prefectures of Japan as well as nationally. The prime minister, assisted by a Cabinet, is also the leader of the party with the most seats in the Diet. Prefectures are governed by an elected governor and an assembly, and cities and towns are governed by elected mayors and town councils. The Supreme Court, consisting of a chief judge and 14 other judges, is independent of the legislative branch of government.

Japan's Constitution forbids Japan from engaging in war or from having military capability that would allow it to attack another country. Japan does maintain a small self-defense force, but it relies on a security treaty with the United States in case of serious aggression against it. In recent years the United States has been encouraging Japan to assume more of the burden of the military security of the Asian region, and Japan has increased its expenditures in absolute terms. But until the Constitution is amended, Japan is not likely to initiate any major upgrading of its military capability. This is in line with the general wishes of the Japanese people, who, since the devastation of Hiroshima and Nagasaki, have become firmly committed to a pacifist foreign policy. Moreover, Japanese leaders fear that any significant increase in military capability would re-ignite dormant fears about Japanese intentions within the increasingly vital Pacific Rim area.

This tendency toward not wanting to get involved militarily is reflected in Japan's most recent performance on the world stage. They were slow to play any significant part in supporting military expenditures for the war in the Middle East, even when the outcome had a direct potential effect on their economy. When Iraqi President Saddam Hussein invaded Kuwait in August 1990 and subsequently brought on the wrath of a coalition of countries led by the United States in January 1991, it generated an initial commitment from Japan of only $2 billion (later increased to $9 billion, still a small fraction of the cost) and no personnel of any kind. This meager support was criticized by some foreign observers who pointed out the fact that Japan relies heavily on gulf oil.

The Japanese people support a broad spectrum of political parties, including the Japan Communist Party, the Demo-cratic Socialist Party, the Clean Government Party (affiliated with a Buddhist denomination), and the Japan Socialist Party, which is the largest opposition party. However, since 1955, the majority of the population has supported the conservative Liberal Democratic Party (LDP). Relying on big business for financial support and on the rural farming community for votes, the LDP has steered Japan through 4 decades of phenomenal economic growth and rapid social change. Despite revelations of sexual improprieties, bribery, and other scandals, the leaders of the LDP continue to receive the support of the Japanese people because their policies have permitted Japan to succeed economically—it is now the second-largest economic power in the world.

In the most recent elections, in early 1990, the LDP won 275 seats, while the runner-up challenger, the Japan Socialist Party, captured 136. The current prime minister, Toshiki Kaifu, was somewhat reluctantly selected by his party after scandals forced the resignations of the previous two prime ministers. The LDP won despite its support of a very unpopular 3-percent sales-tax plan.

Party politics in Japan is a mixture of Western-style democracy and feudalistic personal relationships. The LDP, for example, is actually many parties rolled into one. The party is divided into 9 or 10 factions, each with a group of loyal younger members headed by a powerful member of the Diet. The senior member has a duty to pave the way for the younger members politically, but they, in turn, are obligated to support the senior member in votes and in other ways. The faction leader's role in gathering financial support for faction members is particularly important, because Diet members are expected by the electorate to be patrons of numerous causes, from charity drives to the opening of a constituent's fast-food business. Because parliamentary salaries are inadequate to the task, outside funds, and thus the faction, are crucial. The size and power of the various factions are often the critical elements in deciding who will assume the office of prime minister and who will occupy which Cabinet seats. The role of these intraparty factions is so central to Japanese politics that attempts to ban them have never been successful.

The factional nature of Japanese party politics means that Cabinet and other political positions are frequently rotated. This would yield considerable instability in governance were it not for the stabilizing influence of the Japanese bureaucracy. Large and powerful, the career bureaucracy is responsible for drafting more than 80 percent of the bills submitted to the Diet. Many of the bureaucrats are graduates from the finest universities in Japan, particularly Tokyo University, which provides some 80 percent of the senior officials in the nearly two dozen national ministries. Many of them consider their role in long-range forecasting, drafting legislation, and implementing policies to be superior to that of the elected officials under whom they work. They reason that whereas the politicians are bound to the whims of the people they represent, bureaucrats are committed to the nation of Japan—to, as it were, the *idea* of Japan. Thus, government

Prepottery, paleolithic culture 20,000 B.C.–4,500 B.C.	Jomon culture with distinctive pottery 4,500 B.C.–250 B.C.	Yayoi culture with rice agriculture, Shinto religion, and Japanese language 250 B.C.–A.D. 300	The Yamato period; warrior clans import Chinese culture A.D. 300–700	The Nara period; Chinese-style bureaucratic government at the capital at Nara 710–794	The Heian period; the capital is at Kyoto 794–1185	The Kamakura period; feudalism and shoguns; Buddhism is popularized 1185–1333	The Muromachi period; Western missionaries and traders arrive; feudal lords control their own domains 1333–1568	The Momoyama period; feudal lords become subject to one central leader; attempted invasion of Korea 1568–1600

service is considered a higher calling than careers in private business, law, or other fields.

In addition to the bureaucracy, Japanese politicians have leaned heavily on big business to support their policies of postwar reconstruction, economic growth, and social reform. Business has accepted heavy taxation so that social-welfare programs such as the national health plan are feasible, and they have supported political candidates through substantial financial help. In turn, the government has seen its role as that of facilitating the growth of private industry (some critics claim that the relationship between government and business is so close that Japan is best described not as a nation but as "Japan, Inc."). Consider, for example, the powerful Ministry of International Trade and Industry (MITI). Over the years it has worked closely with business, particularly the Federation of Economic Organizations (Keidanren) to forecast potential market shifts, develop strategies for market control, and generally pave the way for Japanese businesses to succeed in the international marketplace. The close working relationship between big business and the national government is an established fact of life in Japan, and despite criticism from countries with a more laissez-faire approach to business, it will undoubtedly continue into the future, because it has served Japan well.

WHITHER JAPAN?

During the past 4½ decades of political stability, the Japanese have accomplished more than anyone, including themselves, thought possible. Japan's literacy rate is 99.9 percent, 100 percent of Japanese households have telephones, 99 percent have color televisions, and 75 percent own automobiles. Nationalized health care covers every Japanese citizen, and the Japanese have the highest life expectancy in the world. With only half the population of the United States, a land area about the size of Great Britain, and extremely limited natural resources (it has to import 99.6 percent of its oil, 99.8 percent of its iron, and 86.7 percent of its coal), Japan has nevertheless created the second-largest economy in the world. Where does it go from here?

When the Spanish were establishing hegemony over large parts of the globe, they were driven in part by the desire to bring Christianity to the "heathen." The British, for their part, believed that they were taking "civilization" to the savages of the world. China and the Soviet Union have been strongly committed to the ideals of communism, while the United States has felt its mission to be that of expanding democracy and capitalism.

(Photo credit Dean Collinwood)

Foreign firms do a large business in Japan; the United States alone has 170 companies. This shelf in a Japanese supermarket has many brands familiar to Americans.

What about Japan? For what reason do Japanese businesses buy up hotels in New Zealand and skyscrapers in New York? What role does Japan have to play in the world in addition to spawning economic development? What values will guide and perhaps temper Japan's drive for economic dominance?

These are questions that the Japanese people themselves are attempting to answer; but finding no ready answers, they are beginning to encounter more and more difficulties with the world around them and within their own society. Animosity over the persistent trade imbalance in Japan's favor continues to grow in Europe and North America as well as in some countries of the Pacific Rim. To deflect these criticisms, Japan has substantially increased its gift-giving to foreign governments, including allocating money for the stabilization or growth of democracy in Nicaragua and Eastern Europe and for easing the foreign-debt burden of Mexico and other countries.

What Japan has been loathe to do, however, is remove the "structural impediments" that make it difficult for foreign companies to do business in Japan. For instance, 50 percent of the automobiles sold in Iceland are Japanese, which means

| The Tokugawa Era; self-imposed isolation from the West 1600–1868 | The Meiji Restoration; modernization; Taiwan and Korea are under Japanese control 1868–1912 | The Taisho and Showa periods; militarization leads to war and Japan's defeat 1912–1945 | Japan surrenders; U.S. Occupation imposes major changes in organization of Japanese society 1945 | Sovereignty is returned to the Japanese people by treaty 1951 | The newly merged Liberal-Democratic Party wins control of the government 1955 | Japan passes the threshold of economic self-sustainability 1960s | Student activism; the Nuclear Security Treaty with the United States is challenged late 1960s | 1980s–1990s |

| The ruling party is hit by scandals but retains control of the government | Japan reacts to protectionism in major markets by turning attention to the Pacific Rim | Hirohito dies; Emperor Akihito succeeds Toshiki Kaifu becomes prime minister, but the LDP loses some seats to the Socialist Party |

less profit for the American and European manufacturers who used to dominate car sales there. Yet, because of high tariffs and other regulations, very few American and European cars have been sold in Japan. Beginning in the mid-1980s Japan began to dismantle many of these trade barriers, and it has been so successful that it now has a lower overall average tariff on nonagricultural products than the United States—its severest critic in this arena.

But Japanese people worry that further opening of their markets may destroy some fundamentals of Japanese life. Rice, for instance, costs much more in Japan than it should, because the Japanese government protects rice farmers with subsidies and forbids most rice imports from abroad. The Japanese would prefer to pay less for rice at the supermarket, but they also argue that foreign competition would prove the undoing of many small rice farmers, whose land would then be sold to housing developers. This, in turn, would destroy more of Japan's scarce arable land and weaken the already shaky traditions of the Japanese countryside—the heart of Japan.

Now more than 300 foreign firms do business in Japan, and some of them, like Polaroid and Schick, control the Japanese market in their products. Since 1980 foreign investment in Japan has grown about 16 percent annually. In the case of the United States, the profit made by American firms doing business in Japan (there are 170 of them) in 1 year is just about equal to the amount of the trade imbalance between Japan and the United States. Japanese supermarkets are filled with foreign foodstuffs, and the radio and television airwaves are filled with the sounds and sights of Western music and dress. Japanese youth are as likely to eat at McDonald's or Kentucky Fried Chicken outlets as at tradi-

tional Japanese restaurants, and many Japanese have never worn a kimono nor learned to play a Japanese musical instrument. It is clear to many observers that, culturally, Japan already imports much more from the West than the West does from Japan.

Given this overwhelming Westernization of Japan as well as Japan's current capacity to continue imbibing Western culture, even the change-oriented Japanese are beginning to ask where they, as a nation, are going. Will national wealth, as it slowly trickles down to individuals, produce a generation of hedonistic youth who do not appreciate the sacrifices of those before them? Will wealthy Japanese people be satisfied with the small homes and tiny yards that their forebears had to accept? Will there ever be a time when, strapped for resources, the Japanese will once again seek hegemony over other nations? What future role should Japan assume in the international arena, apart from economic development? If these questions remain to be answered, circumstances of international trade have at least provided an answer to the question of Japan's role in the Pacific Rim countries: it is clear that for the next several decades Japan will continue to shape the pace and nature of economic development, and thus the political environment, of the entire Pacific Rim.

DEVELOPMENT

Japan is now entering a postsmokestack era in which primary industries are being moved abroad, producing a hollowing effect inside Japan and increasing the likelihood of rising unemployment. Nevertheless, prospects for continued growth are excellent.

FREEDOM

Japanese citizens enjoy full civil liberties, opposition parties and ideologies are seen as natural and useful components of democracy. Certain people, however, such as those of Korean ancestry, have been subject to both social and official discrimination—an issue that is gaining the attention of the Japanese.

HEALTH/WELFARE

The Japanese live longer on average than any other people on earth. Every citizen is provided with inexpensive medical care under a national health system, but many people still prefer to save substantial portions of their income for health emergencies and old age.

ACHIEVEMENTS

Japan has achieved virtually 100% literacy, and although there are poor areas, there are no slums inhabited by a permanent underclass. The gaps between the social classes appear to be less pronounced than in many other societies. The country seems to be entering an era of remarkable educational and technological achievement.

Australia (Commonwealth of Australia)

GEOGRAPHY

Area in Square Kilometers (Miles):
7,686,850 (2,867,896)
Capital (Population): Canberra
(289,000)
Climate: generally arid to semi-arid;
temperate in the south and east;
tropical in the north

PEOPLE

Population

Total: 16,923,000
Annual Growth Rate: 1.3%
Rural/Urban Population (Ratio):
15/85
Languages: official: English; others
spoken: native languages
Ethnic Makeup of Population: 95%
white; 4% Asian; 1% Aboriginal and
others

Health

Life Expectancy at Birth: 73 years
(male); 80 years (female)
Infant Mortality Rate (Ratio): 8/1,000
Average Caloric Intake: 118% of FAO
minimum
Physicians Available (Ratio): 1/615

Religion(s)

26% Anglican; 26% Roman Catholic;
24% other Christian; 24% other or
no affiliation

Education

Adult Literacy Rate: 98%

COMMUNICATION

Telephones: 8,700,000
Newspapers: 15

A LAND OF HEAT AND HARD WORK

Some people emigrate to Australia with the hope that the relatively inexpensive land and strong economy will easily provide them with a high standard of living. But in character, many parts of Australia are like the American Wild West of the 1870s: sweaty and persistent hard work (and luck) are the only keys to success. For example, cattle ranches in parts of Australia can have as many as 70,000 head of cattle to be cared for over a 5-million-acre spread. Just providing water in the arid climate is a formidable task; dozens of wells must be dug to reach the water table lying far below the earth's surface. Ranchers must also contend with daily temperatures over 100° Fahrenheit and bush fires that destroy hundreds of acres of grassland and roast sheep and cattle alive. The extensive comforts of city life in Sydney, Canberra, Melbourne, and other coastal cities depend on the back-breaking work of thousands of ranchers and farmers in the hot but valuable interior.

TRANSPORTATION

Highways—Kilometers (Miles):
837,872 (51,948)
Railroads—Kilometers (Miles): 40,478
(25,096)
Usable Airfields: 524

GOVERNMENT

Type: federal parliamentary state
Independence Date: January 1, 1901
Head of Government: Prime Minister
Robert Hawke; chief of state: Queen
Elizabeth II, represented by Governor
General William George Hayden
Political Parties: Australian Labor
Party; Liberal Party; National Party;
Australian Democratic Party
Suffrage: universal and compulsory at
age 18

MILITARY

Number of Armed Forces: 69,600
*Military Expenditures (% of Central
Government Expenditures):* n/a
Current Hostilities: none

ECONOMY

Currency ($ U.S. Equivalent): 1.27
Australian dollars = $1
Per Capita Income/GNP:
$14,300/$240.8 billion
Inflation Rate: 8%
Natural Resources: bauxite;
diamonds; coal; copper; iron; oil;
gas; other minerals
Agriculture: beef; wool; mutton;
wheat; barley; sugarcane; fruit
Industry: mining; industrial and
transportation equipment; food
processing; chemicals; steel; motor
vehicles

FOREIGN TRADE

Exports: $43.2 billion
Imports: $48.6 billion

ARAFURA SEA

INDIAN OCEAN

Darwin

GULF OF CARPENTARIA

CORAL SEA

Wyndham

Cooktown

Derby

Cairns

Northern Territory

Townsville

Alice Springs

Queensland

Western Australia

Rockhampton

Charlesville

Southern Australia

Brisbane

Bourke

Geraldton

Coolgardie

Port Augusta

New South Wales

Perth

Newcastle
Sydney
CANBERRA

Albany

INDIAN OCEAN

Adelaide

Victoria

Melbourne

★ National Capital
• City
- - - State/Provence Boundry

Tasmania
Hobart

MILES
0   500

THE LAND NO ONE WANTED

Despite its out-of-the-way location, far south of the main trading routes between Europe and Asia, explorers from Portugal, Spain, and the Netherlands began investigating parts of the continent of Australia in the seventeenth century. The French later made some forays along the coast, but it was the British who first found something to do with a land that others had disparaged as useless: they decided to send their prisoners there. The British had long believed that the easiest solution to prison overcrowding was expulsion. For many years convicts had been sent to the American colonies, but after American independence was declared in 1776, Britain decided to begin sending prisoners to Australia.

Australia seemed like the ideal spot for a penal colony: it was isolated from the centers of civilization; it had some good harbors; and although much of the continent was a flat, dry, riverless desert with only sparse vegetation, the coastal fringes were well suited to human habitation. Indeed, although the British did not know

it in the 1700s, they had discovered a huge continent which was endowed with abundant natural resources. Along the northern coast (just south of Indonesia and New Guinea) was a tropical zone with heavy rainfall and tropical forests. The eastern coast was wooded with valuable pine trees, while the western coast was dotted with eucalyptus and acacia trees. Minerals, especially coal, gold, nickel, petroleum, iron, and bauxite, were plentiful, as were the many species of unique animals: kangaroos, platypus, and koalas, to name a few.

The British chose to build their first penal colony in what is now Sydney. By the 1850s, when the practice of transporting convicts stopped, more than 150,000 prisoners, including hundreds of women, had been sent there and to other colonies. Most of them were illiterate English and Irish from the lower classes. Upon completing their sentences they were set free to settle on the continent. These individuals, their guards, and gold prospectors constituted the beginning of modern Australian society.

RACE RELATIONS

They certainly did not constitute the beginning of human habitation on the continent, however. Tens of thousands of Aborigines (literally, "first inhabitants") inhabited Australia and the nearby island of Tasmania when Europeans first made contact. Living in scattered tribes and speaking hundreds of entirely unrelated languages, the Aborigines, whose origin is unknown (some scholars see connections to Africa, the Indian subcontinent, and the Melanesian islands), survived by fishing and nomadic hunting. Succumbing to European diseases, violence, forced removal from their lands, and finally neglect, thousands of Aborigines died during the first centuries of contact. Indeed, the entire Tasmanian race (originally 5,000 people) is now extinct.

Most Aborigines eventually adopted European ways, including Christianity. Today they live in the cities or work for cattle and sheep ranchers. Others reside on reserves (tribal reservations) in the central and northern parts of Australia. There they continue to live as they have

(Australian Information Service photo)

When Europeans first discovered Australia they found the continent inhabited by Aborigines who had survived for millennia by fishing and nomadic hunting. With the Europeans came disease, violence, and neglect. Most Aborigines eventually adapted to these newcomers' customs, but some continued to live in their traditional ways on tribal reservations.

European exploration of the Australian coastline begins 1600s	British explorers first land in Australia 1688	The first shipment of English convicts arrives 1788	The gold rush lures thousands of immigrants 1851	Australia becomes independent within the British Commonwealth 1901

always done, organizing their religion around plant or animal sacred symbols, or totems, and initiating youth into adulthood through lengthy and sometimes painful rituals.

Of the six British colonies established in Australia, none felt a compelling need to unite into a single nation until the 1880s, when other European powers began taking an interest in settling the continent. A unified and largely independent Australia thus came into existence as recently as 1901. Populated almost entirely by whites from Great Britain or Europe (whites still constitute about 95 percent of Australia's population), Australia has maintained close cultural and diplomatic links with Britain and the West, at the expense of ties with the geographically closer nations of Asia.

Reaction against Polynesians, Chinese, and other Asian immigrants in the late 1800s produced an official "White Australia" policy, which remained intact until the 1960s and effectively excluded non-whites from settling in Australia. Also in the 1960s the government made an effort to restore land and some measure of self-determination to Aborigines. Evidence of continued racism can be found, however, in such graffiti painted on walls of high-rise buildings as: "Go home Japs!" (in this case, the term "Jap," or, alternatively, "wog," refers to any Asian, regardless of nationality).

ECONOMIC PRESSURES

Despite the prevalence of this sort of attitude, events since World War II have forced Australia to reconsider its position, at least economically, vis-à-vis Asia and Southeast Asia. The impressive industrial strength of Japan now allows its people to enjoy higher per capita income than that of Australians, and Singapore is not far behind. Moreover, since Australia's economy is based on the export of primary goods (for example, minerals, wheat, beef, and wool) rather than the much more lucrative consumer products manufactured from raw resources, it is likely that Australia will continue to lose ground to the more economically aggressive and heavily populated Asian economies.

This will be a new experience for Australians, whose standard of living has been the highest in the Pacific Rim for decades. Building on a foundation of sheep (imported in the 1830s and now supplying more than a quarter of the world's supply of wool), mining (gold was discovered in 1851), and agriculture (Australia is nearly self-sufficient in food), Australia has now developed its manufacturing sector such that Australians are able to enjoy a standard of living equal in most respects to that of North Americans.

But as they look toward the year 2000, Australians fear that the growing tendency to create mammoth trading blocs (e.g., the United States and Canada—and maybe Mexico; the European Community, including parts of Eastern Europe; and the Pacific Rim, headed by Japan) might exclude Australian products from preferential trade treatment or eliminate them from certain markets altogether. Beginning in 1983, therefore, the Labor government of Prime Minister Robert ("Bob") Hawke began to establish collaborative trade agreements with Asian countries, a plan that seems to have the support of the electorate, even though it will mean reorienting Australia's foreign policy away from its traditional posture Westward. In 1990 voters returned the Labor Party to a fourth successive term in power, albeit narrowly.

Despite such trade initiatives, the economic threat to Australia remains. Even in the islands of the Pacific, an area that Australia and New Zealand generally have considered their own domain for economic investment and foreign aid, new investments by Asian countries are beginning to winnow Australia's sphere of influence.

THE AMERICAN CONNECTION

Australia has never been conquered by a foreign power, not even by Japan during World War II. Political power is shared back and forth between the Australian Labor Party and the Liberal-National Country Party coalition, and its Constitution is based on both British parliamentary democracy (Australia is an independent member of the British Commonwealth) and the U.S. model. The country is seen by the world community as both internally stable and culturally aligned with the West. Thus, the United States has come to depend on Australia as an ally in its military objectives in the South Pacific and Southeast Asia. A military mutual-assistance agreement, ANZUS (for Australia, New Zealand, and the United States) was concluded after World War II (New Zealand withdrew in 1986). And just as it had sent troops to fight Germany during World Wars I and II, Australia sent troops to fight in the Korean War in 1950 and the Vietnam War in the 1960s—although anti-Vietnam War sentiment in Australia strained relations somewhat with the United States at that time. Australia also joined the United States and other countries in 1954 in establishing the Southeast Asia Treaty Organization (SEATO), an Asian counterpart to the North Atlantic Treaty Organization (NATO) and designed to contain the spread of communism.

Given the constant political tension over the U.S. military bases in the Philippines there has been talk of moving U.S. operations to the Cockburn Sound naval base in Australia—a move that the current Australian government appears to welcome. U.S. military aircraft already land in Australia, and submarines and other naval craft call at Australian ports. The Americans also use Australian territory for surveillance facilities. There is historical precedence for this level of close cooperation: before the U.S. invasion of the Japanese-controlled Philippines in the 1940s, the United States based its Pacific theater military headquarters in Australia; moreover, Britain's inability to lead the fight against Japan had forced Australia to look to the United States.

A few Australians resent the violation of sovereignty represented by the U.S. bases, but most regard the United States as a solid ally. Indeed, many Australians regard their country as the Southern Hemisphere's version of the United States: both countries have space and vast resources, both were founded as disparate colonies that eventually united and obtained independence from Great Britain, and both share a language and Western cultural heritage. Unlike New Zealand, which has distanced itself from the United States by refusing to allow nuclear-armed ships to enter its ports and has withdrawn from ANZUS, Australia has joined with the United States in attempting to dissuade

Australia is threatened by Japan during World War II
1940s

Australia proposes the South Pacific Commission
1947

Australia joins New Zealand and the United States in the ANZUS military security agreement
1951

Australia joins SEATO
1954

Relations with the United States are strained over the Vietnam War
1960s

The Australian Labor Party wins for the first time in 23 years; Gough Whitlam is prime minister
1972

After a constitutional crisis, Whitlam is replaced by opposition leader J. M. Fraser
1975

1980s–1990s

South Pacific states from declaring the region a nuclear-free zone. Yet it has also maintained good ties with the small and vulnerable societies of the Pacific through its leadership in such regional associations as the South Pacific Commission and the South Pacific Forum. It has also condemned nuclear-bomb testing programs in French-controlled territories.

AUSTRALIA AND THE PACIFIC

Australia was not always possessed of good intentions toward the islands around it. For one thing, white Australians thought of themselves as superior to the brown-skinned islanders; and for another, Australia preferred to use the islands' resources for its own economic gain, with little regard for the islanders themselves. At the end of World War I, for example, the phosphate-rich island of Nauru, formerly under German control, was assigned to Australia as a trust territory. Until phosphate mining was turned over to the islanders in 1967, Australian farmers consumed large quantities of phosphate but paid only half the market price. Worse, only a tiny fraction of the proceeds went to the Naurun people. Similarly, in Papua New Guinea, Australia controlled the island without taking significant steps toward its domestic development until the 1960s, when, under the guidance of the United Nations, it did an about-face and facilitated changes that advanced the successful achievement of independence in 1975.

In addition to access to cheap resources, Australia was reluctant to relinquish control of these islands in that it saw them as a shield against possible military attack. It learned this lesson well in World War II. In 1941 Japan, taking advantage of the Western powers' preoccupation with Hitler, moved quickly to expand its imperial designs in Asia and the Pacific. The Japanese first disabled the U.S. Navy by attacking its warships docked in Pearl Harbor, Hawaii. They then moved on to oust the British in Hong Kong and the Gilbert Islands, and the Americans in Guam and Wake Island. Within 5 months the Japanese had taken control of Burma, Malaya, Borneo, the Philippines, Singapore, and hundreds of tiny Pacific islands, which they used to create an immense defensive perimeter around the home islands of Japan. They also had captured part of New Guinea and were keeping a large force there, which greatly concerned the Australians. Yet fighting was kept away from Australia proper when the Japanese were successfully engaged by Australian and American troops in New Guinea. Other Pacific islands were regained from the Japanese at a tremendous cost in lives and military hardware. Japan's defeat came only when islands close enough to Japan to be attacked by U.S. bomber aircraft were finally captured. Japan surrendered in 1945, but the colonial powers learned that possession of small islands could have strategic importance. This experience is part of the reason for

Australia strengthens its economic ties with Asian countries

Depletion of the ozone layer is believed to be responsible for a rapidly rising incidence of skin cancer among Australians

The Labor Party is reelected to a fourth term, with Bob Hawke as prime minister

their reluctance to grant independence to the vast array of islands over which they have exercised control.

There is no doubt that such stressful historical episodes have drawn the English-speaking countries of the South Pacific closer together, and closer to the United States. But recent realignments in the world economic system are creating strains. When the United States insists that Japan take steps to ease the billowing U.S.–Japan trade imbalance, Australia sometimes comes out the loser. For instance, both Australia and the United States are producers of coal, and given the nearly equal distance between those two countries and Japan, it would be logical to expect that Japan would buy coal at about the same price from both countries. In fact, however, Japan pays $7 a ton more for American coal than for Australian coal, a discrepancy directly attributable to Japan's attempt to reduce the trade imbalance with the United States. Resentment against the United States over such matters is likely to grow, and managing such international tensions will no doubt challenge the skills of the leadership of Australia well into the next century.

DEVELOPMENT

Mining of nickel, iron ore, and other metals continues to supply a substantial part of Australia's gross domestic product. In recent years Japan rather than Great Britain has become Australia's primary trading partner. Seven out of 10 of Australia's largest export markets are Asian countries.

FREEDOM

Australia is a parliamentary democracy adhering to the ideals incorporated in English common law. Constitutional guarantees of human rights apply to all of Australia's nearly 17 million citizens. However, social discrimination continues, and despite improvements since the 1960s, the Aborigines remain a neglected part of Australian society.

HEALTH/WELFARE

Like New Zealand, Australia has developed a complex system of social welfare, including government-funded hospital and medical care, maternity payments, and aid to those unemployed, widowed, or aged. Education is the province of the several states. Public education is compulsory. Australia boasts several world-renowned universities.

ACHIEVEMENTS

The vastness and challenge of Australia's interior lands, called "the outback," have inspired a number of Australian writers to create outstanding poetry and fictional novels. In 1973 Patrick White became the first Australian to win a Nobel Prize in Literature. Jill Ker Conway and Colleen McCullough are other well-known Australian authors.

Brunei (Negara Brunei Darussalam)

GEOGRAPHY

Area in Square Kilometers (Miles):
5,770 (2,228) (slightly larger than
Delaware)
Capital (Population): Bandar Seri
Begawan (51,000)
Climate: tropical

PEOPLE

Population
Total: 372,000
Annual Growth Rate: 7.1%
Rural/Urban Population (Ratio): n/a
Ethnic Makeup of Population: 64%
Malay; 20% Chinese; 16% others
Languages: official: Bahasa Melayu;
others spoken: English, Chinese,
Iban, and native dialects

Health
Life Expectancy at Birth: 74 years
(male); 77 years (female)
Infant Mortality Rate (Ratio):
10/1,000
Average Caloric Intake: n/a
Physicians Available (Ratio): 1/2,176

Religion(s)
60% Muslim; 32% Buddhist and
indigenous beliefs; 8% Christian

A LITTLE-KNOWN HAVEN

Brunei's capital and main center of population is Bandar Seri Begawan,
previously known as Brunei Town. Located approximately 10 miles
from the mouth of the Brunei River, the town boasts pleasant sightseeing
opportunities for travelers, including nearby beaches, the Hassanal
Bolkiah Aquarium, and the Sultan Omar Ali Saifuddin Mosque, considered one of the most impressive examples of modern Islamic architecture in Southeast Asia. Visitors to the country are treated warmly, even
when passing through immigration and customs; yet, due to its healthy
reserves of foreign exchange earned from oil and gas revenues, the
government has not actively pursued tourism.

Education
Adult Literacy Rate: 45%

COMMUNICATION

Telephones: 44,620
Newspapers: n/a

TRANSPORTATION

Highways—Kilometers (Miles): 1,090
(676)
Railroads—Kilometers (Miles): 13 (8)
Usable Airfields: 2

GOVERNMENT

Type: Constitutional sultanate
Independence Date: January 1, 1984
Head of State: Sultan and Prime
Minister Sir Muda Hassanal Bolkiah
Mu'izzaddin Waddaulah
Political Parties: Brunei National
United Party (inactive); Brunei
National Democratic Party (the first
legal party now banned)
Suffrage: None

MILITARY

Number of Armed Forces: 4,500
*Military Expenditures (% of Central
Government Expenditures):* $197.6
million (17%)
Current Hostilities: None

ECONOMY

Currency ($ U.S. Equivalent): 1.88
Bruneian dollars (B$) = $1
Per Capita Income/GNP:
$16,000/$3.3 billion
Inflation Rate: 2.5%
Natural Resources: oil; gas; forest
products
Agriculture: rice; vegetables; arable
crops; fruits
Industry: oil (prime industry
employing 7% of entire population);
rubber; pepper; sawn lumber; gravel;
animal hides

FOREIGN TRADE

Exports: $2.07 billion
Imports: $800 million

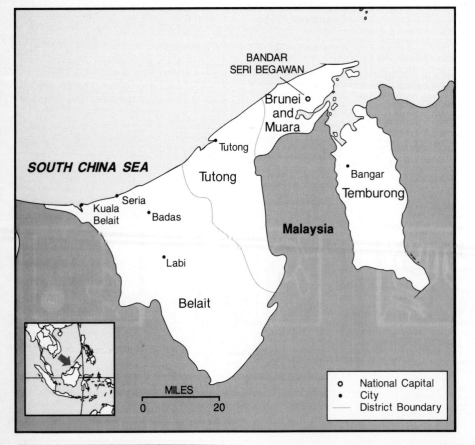

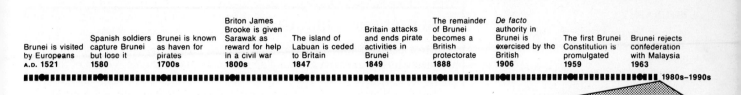

			Briton James Brooke is given			Britain attacks	The remainder	*De facto*		

Brunei is visited by Europeans A.D. 1521 | Spanish soldiers capture Brunei but lose it 1580 | Brunei is known as haven for pirates 1700s | Sarawak as reward for help in a civil war 1800s | The island of Labuan is ceded to Britain 1847 | Britain attacks and ends pirate activities in Brunei 1849 | of Brunei becomes a British protectorate 1888 | authority in Brunei is exercised by the British 1906 | The first Brunei Constitution is promulgated 1959 | Brunei rejects confederation with Malaysia 1963

1980s–1990s

Brunei gains independence from Britain

The Sultan of Brunei, Hassanal Bolkiah, is said to be the richest person in the world, with assets of $25 billion

A WEALTHY COUNTRY

Hardly bigger than the state of Delaware and home to only 372,000 inhabitants, Brunei rarely captures the headlines. But perhaps it should, for despite its tiny size, Brunei boasts the highest per capita income ($16,000) of any country in Southeast Asia and one of the highest in the world. The secret? Oil. First discovered in Brunei in the late 1920s, oil and natural gas today almost entirely support the sultanate's economy, which boasts an economic-growth rate of nearly 7 percent per year. Currently Brunei is in the middle of a 5-yer plan designed to diversify its economy and lessen its dependence on oil revenues, but some 98 percent of the nation's revenues continues to depend on the sale of oil and natural gas.

HISTORY

A sultan ruled over the entire island of Borneo and other nearby islands during the sixteenth century. Advantageously located on the northwest coast of the island of Borneo, along the sea lanes of the South China Sea, Brunei was a popular resting spot for traders; and, during the 1700s, it became known as a haven for pirates. In the 1800s the sultan then in power agreed to the kingdom becoming a protectorate of Great Britain; his country, however, had already been whittled away to its current size.

In the 1960s it was expected that Brueni, which is surrounded on three sides by Malaysia, would join the newly proposed Federation of Malaysia; but it refused to do so, preferring to remain under British control. The decision to remain a colony of Britain was made by Sultan Sir Omar Ali Saifuddin. Educated in British Malaya, the sultan retained a strong affection for British culture and frequently visited the British Isles. (Brunei's 1959 Constitution, promulgated during Sir Omar's reign, reflected this attachment: it declared Brunei a self-governing state, with its foreign affairs and defense remaining the responsibility of Britain.)

In 1967 Sir Omar abdicated in favor of his son, who became the 29th ruler in succession. Sultan (and Prime Minister) Sir Muda Hassanal Bolkiah Mu'izzaddin Waddaulah oversaw Brunei's gaining of independence, in 1984. He now is approaching his silver anniversary as head of state; thanks to Brunei's oil wealth, it is believed that the sultan is the richest person in the world.

A DIVERSE POPULATION

Brunei's largest ethnic group is Malays, who account for 64 percent of the population; Chinese, Ibans, and other indigenous peoples are also well represented. Europeans make up only a small portion of Brunei's populace.

Brunei is an Islamic nation with Hindu roots; Islam is the official state religion. Modern Brunei is a constitutional monarchy, headed by the sultan, a chief minister, and a Council. All major decisions are in the hands of the sultan, and the Constitution provides him with supreme executive authority in the state.

An issue of some magnitude in recent years is the chronic labor shortage. The government and Brunei Shell (a consortium owned jointly by the Brunei government and Shell Oil) are the largest employers. To operate the vigorous oil and gas industry, they must compete with non-oil private-sector enterprises of the work force. (Naturally, these large employers have the advantage, since they have the resources to provide more generous fringe benefits and pay levels.) To compensate for the labor deficit, foreign workers must be recruited—indeed, one-third of all workers in Brunei are foreigners. This figure is of some concern to the government, which is apprehensive of the sort of social tensions that have become evident in other countries with large foreign-worker populations.

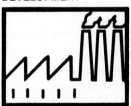

DEVELOPMENT

Brunei's economy is a mixture of the modern and the ancient: foreign and domestic entrepreneurship, government regulation and welfare statism, and village tradition. Chronic labor shortages are managed by the importation of thousands of foreign workers.

FREEDOM

Although Islam is the official state religion, the government practices religious tolerance. Matters related to Islam are dealt with by Islamic courts; in most respects, however, the legal system in Brunei is derived from the British system. The Constitution provides the sultan with supreme executive authority.

HEALTH/WELFARE

The country's massive oil and natural-gas revenues support wide-ranging benefits to the population, e.g., subsidized food, fuel, and housing, and free medical care and education. This distribution of wealth is reflected in Brunei's generally favorable quality-of-life indicators.

ACHIEVEMENTS

Most of Brunei's college students attend university abroad, but an important project has been the construction of a modern campus that will accommodate 1,500 to 2,000 students. Since independence, the government has tried to strengthen and improve the economic, social, and cultural life of its people.

Cambodia (People's Republic of Kampuchea)

GEOGRAPHY

Area in Square Kilometers (Miles):
181,040 (69,881) (slightly smaller than Oklahoma)
Capital (Population): Phnom Penh (500,000 est.)
Climate: tropical

PEOPLE
Population

Total: 6,991,000
Annual Growth Rate: 2.2%
Rural/Urban Population (Ratio): 90/10
Ethnic Makeup of Population: 90% Khmer (Cambodian); 5% Chinese; 5% others
Languages: official: Khmer; others spoken: French

Health

Life Expectancy at Birth: 47 years (male); 50 years (female)
Infant Mortality Rate (Ratio): 131/1,000
Average Caloric Intake: 85% of FAO minimum
Physicians Available (Ratio): n/a

Religion(s)

95% Buddhist; 5% others

Education

Adult Literacy Rate: 48%

COMMUNICATION

Telephones: 7,315
Newspapers: 16

TRANSPORTATION

Highways—Kilometers (Miles): 13,351 (8,277)
Railroads—Kilometers (Miles): 612 (379)
Usable Airfields: 9

GOVERNMENT

Type: people's republic
Independence Date: November 9, 1953
Head of State: President Prince Norodom Sihanouk; Prime Minister Son Sann; Head of State Hunsen
Political Parties: Democratic Kampuchea (DK also known as Khmer Rouge); Khmer People's National Liberation Front; National United Front for an Independent, Neutral, Peaceful, and Cooperative Cambodia
Suffrage: universal at 18

MILITARY

Number of Armed Forces: 45,200
Military Expenditures (% of Central Government Expenditures): n/a
Current Hostilities: border disputes with Vietnam and civil war

ECONOMY

Currency ($ U.S. Equivalent): 218 riels — $1
Per Capita Income/GNP: $960/$10.4 billion
Inflation Rate: n/a
Natural Resources: timber; gemstones; iron ore; manganese; phosphates; hydropower potential
Agriculture: rice; rubber; maize; beans; soybeans
Industry: rice processing; fishing; wood and wood products; rubber; cement; gem mining

FOREIGN TRADE

Exports: $32 million
Imports: $147 million

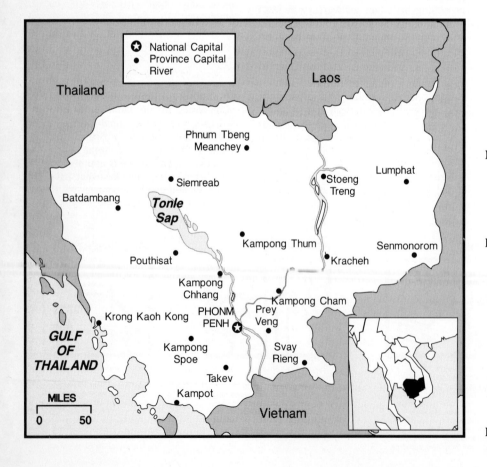

A LAND OF TRAGEDY

In Khmer (Cambodian) the word *Kampuchea,* which for a time during the 1980s was the official name of Cambodia, means "country where gold lies at the foothill." But there is no gold in Cambodia today and hardly any food. Nor is there safety, stability, or sanity, for Cambodia is one of the poorest countries in the world and a haven for military madmen who would kill a man for wearing glasses or a woman for simply being in the way.

Cambodia was not always a place to be pitied. In fact, at times it was the dominant power of Southeast Asia. Around the fourth century A.D. India, with its pacifist Hindu ideology, began to influence in earnest the original Chinese base of Cambodian civilization. The Indian script came to be used, the name of its capital city was an Indian word, its kings had Indian titles, and many of its Khmer people believed in the Hindu religion. The mile-square Hindu temple Angkor Wat, built in the twelfth century, still stands as a symbolic reminder of Indian influence, Khmer ingenuity, and the Khmer Empire's glory.

But the Khmer Empire, which at its height included parts of present-day Burma, Thailand, Laos, and Vietnam, was gradually reduced both in size and power until, in the 1800s, it was paying tribute to both Thailand and Vietnam. Continuing threats from these two countries, as well as wars and domestic unrest at home, led the king of Cambodia to appeal to France for help. France, eager to offset British power in the region, was all too willing to help. A protectorate was established in 1863, and French power grew apace until, in 1887, Cambodia became a part of French Indo-China, a conglomerate consisting of the countries of Laos, Vietnam, and Cambodia.

The Japanese temporarily evicted the French in 1945 and, while under Japanese control, Cambodia declared its "independence" from France. Heading the country was the young King Norodom Sihanouk. Controlling rival ideological factions, some of which were pro-West while others were procommunist, was difficult for Sihanouk, but he built unity around the idea of permanently expelling the French, who finally left in 1955. King Sihanouk then abdicated his throne in favor of his father so that he could, as premier, personally enmesh himself in political governance. He took the title Prince Sihanouk, by which he is known to most people today.

From the beginning Sihanouk's government was bedeviled by border disputes with Thailand and Vietnam and by the incursion of communist Vietnamese soldiers into Cambodia. Sihanouk's ideological allegiances were (and remain) confusing at best; but to his credit, he was able to keep Cambodia officially out of the Vietnam War, which raged for years (1950–1975) on its border. In 1962 Sihanouk announced that his country would remain neutral in the Cold War struggle between the West and the communist powers.

Neutrality, however, was not seen as a virtue by the United States, whose people were becoming more and more eager either to win or to quit the war with North Vietnam. A particularly galling point for the U.S. military was the existence of the so-called Ho Chi Minh Trail, a supply route through the tropical mountain forests of Cambodia. For years North Vietnam had been using the route to supply its military operations in South Vietnam, and Cambodia's neutrality prevented the United States, at least legally, from military action against the supply line.

All this changed in 1970 when Sihanouk, out of the country at the time, was evicted from office by his prime minister, General Lon Nol, who was supported by the United States and South Vietnam. Shortly thereafter the United States, now at its peak of involvement in the Vietnam War, began extensive military action in Cambodia, and the years of official neutrality came to a bloody end.

THE KILLING FIELDS

Most of these international political intrigues were lost on the bulk of the Cambodian population, only half of whom could read and write, and almost all of whom survived, as their forebears had before them, by cultivating rice along the Mekong River valley. The country had almost always been poor, so villagers had long since learned that, even in the face of war, they could survive by hard work and reliance on extended-family networks. Most farmers probably thought that the war next door would not seriously alter their lives. But they were profoundly wrong, for just as the United States had an interest in having a pro-U.S. government in Cambodia, the North Vietnamese desperately wanted Cambodia to be procommunist.

North Vietnam's choice to control the Cambodian government was the Khmer Rouge, a communist guerrilla army led by Pol Pot, one of a group of students influenced by the left-wing ideology taught in Paris universities during the 1950s. Winning control in 1975, the Khmer Rouge launched a hellish 3½-year extermination policy, resulting in the deaths of between 1 million and 3 million fellow Cambodians—that is, between one-fifth and one-third of the entire Cambodian population.

The official goal was to eliminate anyone who had been "polluted" by prerevolutionary thinking, but what actually happened was random violence, torture, and murder.

It is difficult to describe the mayhem and despair that engulfed Cambodia during those years. Cities were emptied of people. Teachers and doctors were killed or sent as slaves to work in the rice paddies. In Cambodia, where Buddhism is as culturally central as Catholicism is to Rome, thousands of Buddhist monks were killed or died of starvation as the Khmer Rouge carried out its program of eliminating all religions. Many people were shot for no other reason than to terrorize the remainder into submission. Explains Leo Kuper:

> Those who were dissatisfied with the new regime were . . . 'eradicated,' along with their families, by disembowelment, by beating to death with hoes, by hammering nails into the backs of their heads and by other cruel means of economizing on bullets.
>
> Persons associated with the previous regime were special targets for liquidation. In many cases, the executions included wives and children. There were summary executions too of intellectuals, such as doctors, engineers, professors, teachers and students, leaving the country denuded of professional skills.

Leo Kuper, *International Action Against Genocide* (London: Minority Rights Group, Report No. 53, 1984), p. 8.

The Khmer Rouge wanted to alter the society completely. Children were removed from their families, private ownership of property was eliminated. Money was outlawed. Even the calendar was started over, at year zero. One observer explained just how totalitarian the rulers were:

> [In 1979] there was no small piece of soap or handkerchief anywhere. Any person who had tried to use a toothbrush was considered bourgeois and punished. Any person wearing glasses was considered an intellectual who must be punished.

Vietnamese military leader Bui Tin, quoted by Diane Cole in "Cambodians Cope with Khmer Rouge," *The Salt Lake Tribune,* January 26, 1990, p. 16.

A kind of bitter relief came in late 1978, when Vietnamese troops, traditionally Cambodia's enemy, invaded Cambodia, drove the Khmer Rouge to the borders of Thailand, and installed a puppet government. This entity still exists and is cur-

| France gains control of Cambodia A.D. 1863 | Japanese invasion; King Norodom Sihanouk is installed 1940s | Sihanouk wins Cambodia's independence from France 1953 | General Lon Nol takes power in a U.S.–supported coup 1970 | The Khmer Rouge, under Pol Pot, overthrow the government and begin a reign of terror 1975 | Vietnam invades Cambodia and installs a puppet government 1978 | 1980s–1990s |

| Sihanouk resigns as head of the coalition government | All factions, plus Vietnam, meet in Indonesia to discuss peace | Vietnam withdraws most of its troops from Cambodia; the Khmer Rouge gains strength |

rently headed by Hun Sen, a former Khmer Rouge soldier who defected and fled to Vietnam in the 1970s. Although almost everyone was relieved to see the Khmer Rouge pushed out of power, the Vietnamese intervention was almost universally condemned by other nations. This was because the Vietnamese were taking advantage of the chaos in Cambodia to further their aim of creating a federated state of Vietnam, Laos, and Cambodia. Vietnam had the strongest military in the region, thanks to years of training and hardware buildup by the Soviet Union and the United States during the Vietnam War. Its virtual annexation of Cambodia eliminated Cambodia as a buffer state between Vietnam and Thailand, further destabilizing the international relations of the region.

COALITION GOVERNANCE

The United States and others refused to recognize the Vietnam-installed regime, instead granting recognition to the Coalition Government of Democratic Kampuchea. This entity consists of three groups: the communist Khmer Rouge, led by Khieu Samphan and Pol Pot and backed by China; the anticommunist Khmer People's National Liberation Front, led by former Prime Minister Son Sann; and the Armee Nationale Sihanoukiste, led by Prince Sihanouk. It is obvious that these three groups, all former enemies, cannot constitute a workable government for Cambodia. Moreover, the Khmer Rouge still has the strongest army of the three and would likely dominate the other two should the coalition regain control

of the capital city, Phnom Penh. Nevertheless, the United Nations has granted its Cambodia seat to this coalition, and the United States has refused to help the Vietnamese-installed government of Hun Sen.

Vietnam had hoped that its capture of Cambodia would be easy and painless. Instead, the Khmer Rouge and others resisted so much that Vietnam had to send in 200,000 troops, of which 25,000 died. Moreover, other countries, including the United States and Japan, strengthened their resolve to isolate Vietnam in terms of international trade and development financing. After 10 years the costs to Vietnam in remaining in Cambodia were so great that Vietnam announced it would pull out its troops. By 1989 most of the Vietnamese troops were gone, but the war between the government they installed and the coalition continued and even intensified.

Soon it became apparent that the Khmer Rouge faction of the coalition was once again gaining control of important parts of the countryside. In 1990 U.S. President George Bush announced that the United States was withdrawing its recognition of the coalition, due to the likelihood that the murderous Khmer Rouge would once again come to power. The United States is now holding talks with Vietnam, but success appears to be years away, since all the principal players in Cambodia's tragedy remain locked in antagonism. Moreover, numerous diplomatic attempts by France and others to solve the stalemate have been disappointing.

No single group seems acceptable or

capable of leadership. Sihanouk's loyalties are unclear, Hun Sen is seen as a puppet of Vietnam, Khieu Samphan heads the hated Khmer Rouge, and Son Sann's army is thought to be too weak to withstand anyone. Part of the reason for the absence of good leaders is that under the Khmer Rouge government, the best-educated people were annihilated. It is estimated that before the Khmer Rouge came to power in 1975, for example, Cambodia had 1,200 engineers, 21,000 teachers, and 500 doctors. After the purges, the country was left with only 20 engineers, 3,000 teachers and 54 doctors.

Poverty and malnutrition are rampant, but efforts at international relief from such groups as the Red Cross and Oxfam have been frustrated by the fact that the soldiers who control the borders consume the food and supplies before they reach the interior. Moreover, the renewed military activity since the pullout of the Vietnamese troops has prevented farmers from planting or harvesting rice. So many Cambodians have been killed in battle or have died of disease and starvation that one U.S. filmmaker entitled his film on the tragedy of Cambodia "The Killing Fields," and such it is likely to remain for many years to come.

DEVELOPMENT	FREEDOM	HEALTH/WELFARE	ACHIEVEMENTS
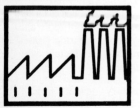			
In the past, China, the United States, and others built roads and industries in Cambodia, but the country remains an impoverished state whose economy rests on fishing and farming. Continual warfare for nearly 2 decades has prevented industrial development.	Few Cambodians can remember political stability, much less political freedom. Every form of human-rights violations has been practiced in Cambodia since before the arrival of the barbaric Khmer Rouge. Today's Cambodians wish more for food than for freedoms.	Almost all doctors were killed or died during the Khmer Rouge regime, and warfare has disrupted normal agriculture. Thus, disease is rampant, as is malnutrition. The few trained international relief workers in Cambodia find it impossible to make a dent in the country's enormous problems.	During most of the Vietnam War, the Cambodian government was able to steer a neutral course, despite pressure from the superpowers to choose sides. It thereby prevented—for a while—the bloodshed that was transpiring in neighboring Vietnam.

China (People's Republic of China)

GEOGRAPHY

Area in Square Kilometers (Miles):
9,572,900 (3,696,100) (slightly larger
than the contiguous United States)
Capital (Population): Beijing
(8,500,000)
Climate: varied

PEOPLE

Population
Total: 1,130,065,000
Annual Growth Rate: 1.1%
Rural/Urban Population Ratio: 54/46
Ethnic Makeup of Population: 94%
Han Chinese; 6% minority groups
(the largest being Chuang, Hui,
Uighur, Yi, and Miao)

Health
Life Expectancy at Birth: 68 years
(male); 70 years (female)
Infant Mortality Rate (Ratio):
33/1,000
Average Caloric Intake: 104% of FAO
minimum
Physicians Available (Ratio): 1/668

Religion(s)
officially atheist; but Taoism,
Buddhism, Islam, Christianity,
ancestor worship, and animism do
exist

Education
Adult Literacy Rate: 70%

THE TEACHINGS OF CONFUCIUS

Confucius (550–478 B.C.) was a Chinese intellectual and minor political figure. He was not a religious leader, nor did he ever claim divinity for himself or divine inspiration for his ideas. As the feudalism of his era began to collapse, he proposed that society could best be governed by paternalistic kings who set good examples. Especially important to a stable society, he taught, were respect and reverence for one's elders. Within the five key relationships of society (ruler and subject, husband and wife, father and son, elder brother and younger brother, and friend and friend), people should always behave with integrity, propriety, and goodness.

The writings of Confucius—or, rather, the works written about him by his followers and called the *Analects*—eventually became required knowledge for anyone in China claiming to be an educated person. However, rival ideas such as Legalism (a philosophy advocating authoritarian government) were at times more popular with the elite; and at one point, 460 scholars were buried alive for teaching Confucianism. Nevertheless, much of the hierarchical nature of Asian culture today can be traced to Confucian ideas.

COMMUNICATION
Telephones: 8,000,000
Newspapers: more than 1,500

TRANSPORTATION
Highways—Kilometers (Miles):
962,800 (596,936)
Railroads—Kilometers (Miles): 52,500
(32,550)
Usable Airfields: 330

GOVERNMENT
Type: one-party Communist state
Independence Date: October 1, 1949
Head of State: President Yang
Shangkun
Political Parties: Chinese Communist
Party; several small and politically
insignificant non-Communist parties
Suffrage: universal over 18

MILITARY
Number of Armed Forces: 3,030,000
on active duty; 8,580,300 in People's
Militia
*Military Expenditures (% of Central
Government Expenditures):* 14.6%
Current Hostilities: border tensions
with Soviet Union on northern
boundary and to west (Afghanistan);
skirmishes on Vietnam border

ECONOMY
Currency ($ U.S. Equivalent): 4.72
yuan = $1 (March 1988)
Per Capita Income/GNP: $258/$350
billion
Inflation Rate: 7%
Natural Resources: coal; oil; hydroelectric sites; natural gas; iron ores;
tin; tungsten
Agriculture: food grains; cotton; oil
seeds; pigs; tea
Industry: iron and steel; coal;
machinery; light industry; armaments

FOREIGN TRADE
Exports: $51.6 billion
Imports: $58.2 billion

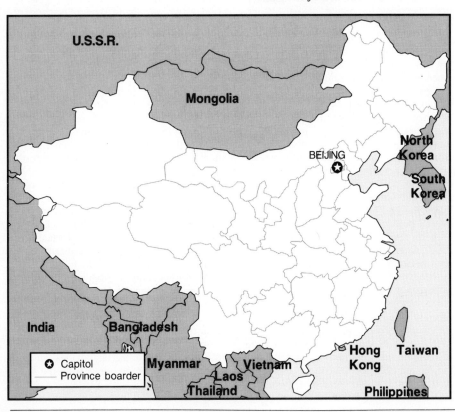

U.S.S.R.

Mongolia

BEIJING

North Korea

South Korea

India   Bangladesh

Myanmar   Vietnam

Laos

Thailand

Hong Kong   Taiwan

Philippines

⊙ Capitol
----- Province boarder

CHINA

Shakespeare, Columbus, Charlemagne, Julius Caesar, Plato, and Aristotle are names that bespeak historicity to students of Western civilization. But they are all relative newcomers when compared to the great figures of Chinese history. Indeed, China was a thriving culture at least 1,500 years before Plato was born. Therefore, an important characteristic of China is that it is very old—in fact, it may be the oldest surviving civilization. There is evidence of human civilization in China as early as 20,000 years ago, at the end of the last Ice Age; a distinctly Chinese culture is distinguishable as early as 2000 B.C. The first documented Chinese dynasty, the Shang, began about 1523 B.C., although legends suggest that an imperial government was in existence much earlier than that. Over the centuries of documented history the Chinese people were ruled by a dozen imperial dynasties, enjoyed hundreds of years of stability and amazing cultural progress; and they endured more hundreds of years of chaos, military mayhem, and hunger. Yet China and the Chinese people remain intact—a strong testament to the tenacity of human culture.

A second characteristic is that the People's Republic of China (P.R.C.) is big. It is the third-largest country in the world, accounting for 6.5 percent of the world's landmass. Much of China—about 40 percent—is mountainous; but large, fertile plains have been created by China's numerous rivers, most of which flow toward the Pacific Ocean. China is blessed with substantial reserves of oil, minerals, and many other natural resources. Its large size and geopolitical location—it is bordered by the Soviet Union, Pakistan, India, Nepal, Bhutan, Myanmar, Laos, Vietnam, North Korea, and Mongolia—have caused the Chinese people over the centuries to think of their land as the Middle Kingdom: that is, the center of world civilization.

However, its unwieldy size has been the undoing of numerous emperors who found it impossible to maintain its borders in the face of outside "barbarians" determined to possess the riches of Chinese civilization. During the Ch'in Dynasty (221–207 B.C.) a 1,500-mile-long, 25-foot-high wall, the so-called Great Wall, was erected along the northern border of China, in the futile hope that invasions from the north could be stopped. Although the P.R.C.'s national boundaries are now recognized by international law, recent Chinese governments have found it necessary to "pacify" border areas by settling as many Han Chinese there as possible, to prevent se-cession by China's numerous ethnic minorities.

A third important characteristic of modern China is its large population. With 1.13 billion people, China is home to about 20 percent of all human beings alive today. About 94 percent of China's people are Han, or ethnic, Chinese; the remaining 6 percent are divided into 56 separate minority groups, numbering some 60 million people. Many of these ethnic groups speak mutually unintelligible languages, and although they often appear to be Chinese, they derive from entirely different cultural roots; some are Muslims, some are Buddhists, some are animists. As one moves away from the center of Chinese civilization in the eastern provinces, the influence of the minorities increases. The Chinese government has accepted the reality of ethnic influence and has granted a degree of limited autonomy to some provinces with heavy populations of minorities.

China has so many people that it often seems, in historical retrospection, to have treated its people as expendable objects. For instance, in the Taiping Rebellion of 1851–1865, it is believed that 20 million people died. In the conflict between Communist and Nationalist armies in the 1920s and 1930s, it is estimated that 11 million people lost their lives in just one war-torn province. Over the centuries, millions more have died of hunger and malnutrition, because for much of its history, China has not been able to feed its people.

In the 1950s Premier Mao Zedong encouraged couples to have many children, but this policy was reversed in the 1970s, when a formal birth-control program was inaugurated. Urban couples today are permitted to have only one child and are penalized if they have more. Penalties include expulsion from the Chinese Communist Party (CCP), dismissal from work, or a 10-percent reduction in pay for up to 14 years after the birth of the second child. The policy is strictly enforced in the cities, but Chinese demographers admit that it has had only a marginal impact on overall population growth, because some 85 percent of China's people live in rural areas, where they are allowed more children in order to help with the farmwork. In the city of Shanghai, which is expected to have a population of 13.3 million people by the year 2000, authorities have recently removed second-child privileges for farmers living near the city and for such former exceptional cases as children of revolutionary martyrs and workers in the oil industry. Despite these and other restrictions, it is estimated that 15 million to 17 million new Chinese will be born each year until the end of the century.

Over the centuries millions of people have found it necessary or prudent to leave China in search of food, political stability, or economic opportunity. Those who emigrated a thousand or more years ago are now fully assimilated into the cultures of Southeast Asia and elsewhere and identify themselves accordingly. More recent émigrés (in the past 200 years or so), however, constitute visible, often wealthy, minorities in their new host countries, where they have become the backbone of the business community. Ethnic Chinese constitute the majority of the population in Singapore and a sizable minority in Malaysia. Important world figures such as Corazon Aquino, the president of the Philippines, and Goh Chok Tong, the prime minister of Singapore, are part or full Chinese. The Chinese constituted the first big wave of the 6.5 million Asian-Americans to call the United States home. Thus the influence of China continues to spread far beyond its borders.

A fourth crucial characteristic of China is its history of imperial and totalitarian rule. Except for a few years in the early part of this century, China has been controlled by imperial decree, military order, and patriarchal privilege. Confucius taught that a person must be as loyal to the government, as a son should be to his father. Following Confucius by a generation or two was Shang Yang, of a school of governmental philosophy, called Legalism, that advocated unbending force and punishment against wayward subjects. Compassion and pity were not considered qualities of good government.

Mao Zedong, building on this heritage as well as that of the Soviet Union's Joseph Stalin and Vladimir Lenin, exercised strict control over both the public and private lives of the Chinese people. Dissidents were summarily executed (generally people were considered guilty once they were arrested), the press was strictly controlled, and recalcitrants were forced to undergo "reeducation" to correct their thinking. Religion of any kind was suppressed, and churches were turned into warehouses. It is estimated that during the first 3 years of CCP rule more than 1 million opponents of Mao's regime were executed. During the Cultural Revolution (1966–1976) Mao, who apparently thought that a new mini-revolution in China might restore his eroding stature in the Chinese Communist Party, encouraged young people to report to the authorities anyone suspected of owning books from the West or having contact with Westerners. Even party functionaries were purged if it was believed that their thinking had been corrupted by Western influences.

Historically, authoritarian rule in China has been occasioned, in part, by China's mammoth size, its unwieldy, mostly illiterate population, and by the ideology of some of its intellectuals. The modern Chinese state has arisen from these same pressures as well as some new ones. It is to these that we now turn.

ORIGINS OF THE MODERN STATE

The Chinese had traded with such non-Asian peoples as the Arabs and Persians for hundreds of years before European contact. But in the 1700s and 1800s the British and others extracted something new from China in exchange for merchandise from the West: the permission of foreign citizens to live in parts of China without being subject to Chinese authority. Though this process of granting extra-territoriality to foreign powers, China slowly began to lose control of its sovereignty. The age of European expansion was not, of course, the first time in China's long history that its ability to rule itself was challenged; the armies of Kublai Khan successfully captured the Chinese throne in the 1200s, as did the Manchurians in the 1600s. But these outsiders, especially the Manchurians, were willing to rule China on-site and to imbibe as much Chinese culture as they could; eventually they became indistinguishable from the Chinese.

The European powers, on the other hand, preferred to rule China (or, rather, parts of it) from afar as a vassal state, with the proceeds of conquest being drained away from China to enrich the coffers of the European monarchs. Beginning in 1834, when the British forced the Chinese to cede Hong Kong island, the Western powers began to nibble away at China's sovereignty. Britain, France, and the United States all extracted unequal treaties from the Chinese that gave them privileged access to trade and ports along the eastern coast. By the late 1800s Russia was in control of much of Manchuria, and Germany and France also had wrested special economic privileges from the ever-weakening Chinese government. Further affecting the Chinese economy was the loss of many of its former tributary states in Southeast Asia. China lost Vietnam to France, Burma to Britain, and Korea to Japan. During the violent Boxer Rebellion of 1900 the Chinese people showed how frustrated they were with the declining fortunes of their country.

Thus weakened internally and embarrassed internationally, the Manchu rulers of China began to initiate reforms that would strengthen their ability to compete with the Western and Japanese powers. A constitutional monarchy was proposed by the Manchu authorities but was preempted by the republican revolutionary movement of Western-trained Sun Yat-sen. Sun and his armies wanted an end to imperial rule; their dreams were realized in 1912, when Sun's Kuomintang, or Nationalist Party, took control of the new Republic of China.

Sun's Western approach to government was received with skepticism by many Chinese who distrusted the European model and preferred the thinking of Karl Marx and the approach of the Soviet Union. In 1921 Mao Zedong and others organized the Soviet-style Chinese Communist Party, which grew quickly and began to be seen as an alternative to the Kuomintang. After Sun's death in 1925 Chiang Kai-shek assumed control of the Kuomintang and waged a campaign to rid the country of Communist influence. Although Mao and Chiang cooperated when necessary—for example, to resist Japanese incursion into Manchuria—they eventually came to be such bitter enemies that they brought a ruinous civil war to all of China.

Mao derived his support from the rural areas of China, while Chiang depended on the cities. In 1949, facing defeat, Chiang Kai-shek's Nationalists retreated to the island of Taiwan, where, under the name Republic of China (R.O.C.), they contin-

(UN/photo by A. Holcombe)

During Mao Zedong's Great Leap Forward huge agricultural communes were established and farmers were denied the right to grow crops privately. The government's strict control of these communes met with chaotic results; there were dramatic drops in agricultural output.

The Shang Dynasty is the first documented Chinese dynasty 1523-1027 B.C.	The Chou Dynasty and the era of Confucius, Laotze, and Mencius 1027-256	The Ch'in Dynasty, from which the word China is derived 211-207	The Han Dynasty 202 B.C.-A.D. 220	The Three Kingdoms period; the Tsin and Sui Dynasties A.D. 220-618	The T'ang Dynasty, during which Confucianism flourished 618-906	The Five Dynasties and Sung Dynasty periods 906-1279	The Yuan Dynasty is founded by Kublai Khan 1260-1368	The Ming Dynasty 1368-1644	The first European settlement is established by the Portuguese in Macau 1557

ued to insist on their right to rule all of China. The Communists, however, controlled the mainland (and have done so for more than 4 decades) and insisted that Taiwan was just a province of the People's Republic of China. These two antagonists are officially (but not in actuality) still at war. In the 1950s the United States had to intervene to prevent an attack on Taiwan from the mainland.

Initially world opinion sided with Taiwan, and it was granted diplomatic recognition by many nations and given the China seat in the United Nations (UN). In the 1970s, however, many nations, including the United States, came to believe that it was dysfunctional to withhold recognition and standing from such a large and powerful nation as the P.R.C. Because both sides insisted that there could not be two Chinas, nor one China and one Taiwan, the UN proceeded to give the China seat to mainland China, and dozens of countries broke off formal diplomatic relations with Taiwan in order to establish a relationship with China.

PROBLEMS OF GOVERNANCE

The China that Mao came to control was a nation with serious economic and social problems. Decades of civil war had disrupted families and wreaked havoc on the economy. Mao believed that the solution to China's ills was to whole-heartedly embrace socialism. Businesses were nationalized and state planning replaced private initiative. Slowly the economy improved. In 1958, however, Mao decided to enforce the tenets of socialism more vigorously, so that China would be able to take an economic "Great Leap Forward." Workers were assigned to huge agricultural communes and were denied the right to grow crops privately. All enterprises came under the strict control of the central government. The result was economic chaos and a dramatic drop in both industrial and agricultural output.

Exacerbating China's problems was the growing rift between the P.R.C. and the Soviet Union. China insisted that its brand of communism was more true to the principles of Marx and Lenin and criticized the Soviets for selling out to the West. As relations with (and financial support from) the Soviet Union withered, China

found itself increasingly isolated from the world community, a circumstance worsened by serious conflicts with India, Indonesia, and other nations. To gain friends, the P.R.C. provided substantial aid to communist insurgencies in Vietnam and Laos, thus contributing to the eventual severity of the Vietnam War.

In 1966, Mao found that his power was waning in the face of Communist Party leaders who favored a more moderate approach to internal problems and external relations. To regain lost ground, Mao urged young students, called Red Guards, to fight against anyone who might have liberal, capitalist, or intellectual leanings. He called it the Great Proletarian Cultural Revolution, but it was an *anti*cultural purge; books were burned, and educated people were arrested and persecuted. In fact, the whole country remained in a state of domestic chaos for more than a decade.

Soon after Mao died, in 1976, Deng Ziaoping, who had been in and out of Communist Party power several times before, came to occupy the senior position in the CCP. A pragmatist, he was willing to modify or forgo strict socialist ideology if he believed that some other approach would work better. Often pressed by hardliners to tighten governmental control, he nevertheless was successful in liberalizing the economy and permitting exchanges of scholars with the West. In 1979 he accepted formalization of relations with the United States—an act seen as a signal of China's opening up to the world.

Deng's liberal image was severely tarnished, however, in 1989, when thousands of students and workers were brutally attacked by government forces during prodemocracy demonstrations in Beijing's Tiananmen Square. Sensing a shift in the wind under Deng's leadership, students, some of whom had studied abroad, pressed the government to crack down on corruption in the Chinese Communist Party and to permit greater freedom of speech and other civil liberties. The protest received wide international media coverage and became an embarrassment to the Chinese leadership, especially after students constructed a large statue in the square similar in appearance to the Statue of Liberty in New York harbor. After

weeks of continual demonstrations, some party leaders seemed inclined at least to talk with the students, but hardliners apparently insisted that the prodemocracy movement must be crushed if the CCP was to remain in firm control of the government. Thousands were injured or killed in the crackdown in Tiananmen Square, and hundreds more were systematically hunted down and brought to trial for sedition and for spreading counter-revolutionary propaganda.

In the wake of the crackdown many nations reassessed their relationships with the People's Republic of China. The United States, Japan, and other nations halted or canceled foreign-assistance and exchange programs with China. The people of Hong Kong, who are scheduled to come under P.R.C. control in 1997, staged massive demonstrations against the Chinese government's brutality. Foreign tourism all but ceased, and foreign investment declined.

The withdrawal of financial support and investment has been particularly troublesome to the Chinese leadership. The Chinese have accepted their need to modernize (although not necessarily to Westernize) the economy. They realize that they are far behind other nations in many ways. For instance, the Taiwanese, with whom mainlanders share a common heritage but who inhabit an island just a fraction the size of the P.R.C. and without its abundant resources, have long since eclipsed the mainland in terms of economic prosperity. Economic experts in China have recently suggested using Taiwan as a model for future Chinese development.

Already China has established several capitalist enclaves, called Special Economic Zones (SEZs), throughout China to catalyze the economy. Still, the withdrawal of warm economic support from the West and Japan remains a problem that the Chinese leadership is actively trying to solve. Japan's support in particular is valued, because Japan is China's main creditor. Like every other trading nation, Japan is eager to penetrate China's massive consumer market, but after the 1989 massacre Japan temporarily halted its loan-assistance program. China responded to the international pressure by

| The Manchu or Ch'ing Dynasty 1644-1912 | Trading rights and Hong Kong island are granted to Britain 1834 | The Sino-Japanese War 1894-1895 | Sun Yat-sen's republican revolution ends centuries of imperial rule; the Republic of China is established 1912 | The Chinese Communist Party is organized 1921 | Chiang Kai-shek begins a long civil war with the Communists 1926 | Mao Zedong's Communist Army defeats Chiang Kai-shek 1949 | A disastrous economic reform, the Great Leap Forward, is launched by Mao 1958 | The Cultural Revolution; Mao dies 1966-1976 | The United States and China establish diplomatic relations 1979 |

1980s–1990s

Economic and political liberalization begins under Deng Ziaoping; the P.R.C. and Britain agree to return Hong Kong to Chinese

China increases its relationship with Taiwan; the Tiananmen Square massacre provokes international outrage

Crackdowns on dissidents and criminals result in hundreds of arrests and executions

releasing the well-known dissidents Fang Lizhi and Li Shuxian, but many investors remain wary of China's reliability as a trading partner and investment-venture location.

THE SOCIAL ATMOSPHERE

It is difficult to predict the future, but many believe that when the aging Communist Party leadership is replaced by younger leaders, the P.R.C. might once again broach the question of democratization and liberalization. In the meantime, it is evident that the Communist Party has effected a major change in Chinese society. Historically, the loyalty of the masses of the people was placed in their extended families and in the feudal warlords, who, at times of weakened imperial rule, were nearly sovereign in their own provinces. Communist policy has been to encourage the masses to give their loyalty to the centrally controlled Communist Party, at the expense of both family and prominant or formerly wealthy individuals in the local community. The size of families has been reduced to the extent that "family" as such has come to play a less important role in the lives of ordinary Chinese. At times the government has encouraged family members to spy on their own siblings or parents and to report any deviations from communist orthodoxy to the authorities.

Furthermore, historical China was a place of great social and economic inequality between the classes. The wealthy feudal lords and their families and those connected with the imperial court and bureaucracy had access to the finest in educational and cultural opportunities, while around them lived illiterate peasants who often could not feed themselves, let alone pay the often heavy taxes imposed on them by feudal and imperial elites. The masses often found life to be bitter, but they found solace in the teachings of the three main religions of China (often adhered to simultaneously): Confucianism, Taoism, and Buddhism. Islam, animism, and Christianity have also been significant to many people in China.

The Chinese Communist Party, by legal decree and by indoctrination, has attempted to suppress people's reliance on religious values to cope with their problems; since the late 1970s religious activity has once again been permitted, but atheism is still preferred. The CCP also has attempted to reverse the ranking of the classes; the values of hard work and simplicity of the peasants have been elevated, while the refinement and education of former elites have been denigrated. Rural life has been valued over urban life. Homes of formerly wealthy capitalists have been taken over by the government and turned into museums, where the opulent life of the capitalist owners is disparaged. During the Cultural Revolution high-school students who wanted to attend college had first to spend 2 years in manual labor in factories and on farms to help them learn to relate to the peasants and working class. So much did revolutionary ideology and fervor take precedence over education that schools and colleges were shut down for several years and the length of compulsory education was reduced (although during the liberalizations that occurred in the early 1980s, the educational enterprise regained some of its lost ground).

Changes of this sort have struck at the very heart of the Chinese heritage. Confucianism had extolled the virtues of scholarly learning and cultural refinement as well as respect and loyalty to one's family. Buddhism, with its stress on spiritual merit and the doctrine of re-birth, and Taoism, with its emphasis on the contemplative life, had added a pronounced "other-worldiness" to Chinese thinking. The ideology of Maoist communism has thus radically altered Chinese society and created a major break with Chinese history. Where these changes will lead is impossible to say, but it is clear that China will never be the same. If it moves toward greater democratization and societal liberalization in the future, the process will likely be slow and halting, given China's long history of authoritarian rule.

DEVELOPMENT

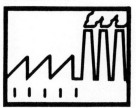

In the early years of communist control authorities stressed the value of establishing heavy industry and collectivizing agriculture. More recently the P.R.C. has attempted to reduce its isolation from the world economy by establishing trading relationships with the United States, Japan, and others and by constructing free-enterprise zones.

FREEDOM

Until the late 1970s the Chinese people were controlled by Chinese Communist Party cadres who monitored both public and private behavior. Some economic and social liberalization occurred in the 1980s. However, the 1989 Tiananmen Square massacre reminded Chinese and the world that, despite some reforms, the People's Republic of China is still very much a dictatorship.

HEALTH/WELFARE

The communist government has overseen dramatic improvements in the provision of social services for the masses. Life expectancy has increased from 45 years in 1949 to 65 years (overall) today. Health care is available at low cost to the patient. The government has attempted to eradicate such diseases as malaria and tuberculosis.

ACHIEVEMENTS

Chinese culture has, for thousands of years, provided the world with classics in literature, art, pottery, ballet, and other arts. Under communism, the arts have been marshaled in the service of communist ideology and have lost some of their dynamism. Since 1949 literacy has increased dramatically and now stands at about 70%—the highest in Chinese history.

Hong Kong

GEOGRAPHY

Area in Square Kilometers (Miles):
1,062 (658) (about 1¹/₃ the size of
New York City)
Capital: Victoria
Climate: subtropical

PEOPLE

Population
Total: 5,656,000
Annual Growth Rate: 2.1%
Rural/Urban Population Ratio: 9/91
Ethnic Makeup of Population: 98%
Chinese (mostly Cantonese); 2%
European and Vietnamese
Languages: official: English and
Cantonese Chinese; other spoken:
other Chinese dialects

Health
Life Expectancy at Birth: 76 years
Infant Mortality Rate (Ratio):
10/1,000
Average Caloric Intake: n/a
Physicians Available (Ratio): 1/1,000

Religion(s)
90% a combination of Buddhism and
Taoism; 10% Christian

Education
Adult Literacy Rate: 78%

COMMUNICATION
Telephones: 2,900,000
Newspapers: 63

TRANSPORTATION
Highways—Kilometers (Miles): 1,160
(719)
Railroads—Kilometers (Miles): 34
(21)
Usable Airfields: 2

GOVERNMENT
Type: colonial (British Crown colony)
Independence Date: Chinese
sovereignty to be reestablished on
July 1, 1997

Head of State: Queen Elizabeth II;
head of government Governor Sir
David Wilson (appointed by the
United Kingdom)
Political Parties: insignificant
Suffrage: universal for those over 21
years and residents of Hong Kong for
7 years

MILITARY
Number of Armed Forces: foreign
relations and defense the
responsibility of British Armed
Forces, 12,000 of whom are stationed
in Hong Kong; also a Royal Hong
Kong Police Force and an auxiliary
police force
*Military Expenditures (% of Central
Government Expenditures):* 4.3%
Current Hostilities: none

ECONOMY
Currency ($ U.S. Equivalent): 7.80
Hong Kong dollars = $1
Per Capita Income/GNP:
$9,642/$41.8 billion
Inflation Rate: 5.5%
Natural Resources: none
Agriculture: vegetables; livestock
(cattle, pigs, poultry); fish
Industry: light—textiles and clothing;
electronics; clocks and watches; toys;
plastic products; metalware; footwear;
heavy—shipbuilding and ship
repairing; aircraft engineering

FOREIGN TRADE
Exports: $47.6 billion
Imports: $47.4 billion

HONG KONG'S RESTLESS PEOPLE

As recently as 1989 Chinese student protesters fleeing the authorities in
the People's Republic of China (P.R.C.) made their way to Hong Kong,
where they were smuggled across the border to safety. Ironically, while
these exiles were finding refuge in Hong Kong, thousands of other
people were planning to leave the British colony. Among them were
several hundred Vietnamese boat people who, induced by a United
Nations repatriation program, were voluntarily returning to Vietnam
after enduring many years in Hong Kong's crowded detention camps.
Another group of departees is made up of Hong Kong's well-educated
middle class. Hong Kong government officials predict that 60,000
people a year—about 1,150 people a week—will leave Hong Kong in 1991
and 1992, and that the figure will increase substantially after that. Some
people are leaving because they fear life under the Chinese Communists
(Hong Kong is scheduled to revert to P.R.C. control in 1997). Others are
worried about China's new, problem-plagued nuclear plant, which is
scheduled to start up in 1992 and which is located at Daya Bay, just 30
miles from Hong Kong. Still others are taking advantage of Britain's
offer to allow up to 225,000 Hong Kong residents to settle in England.

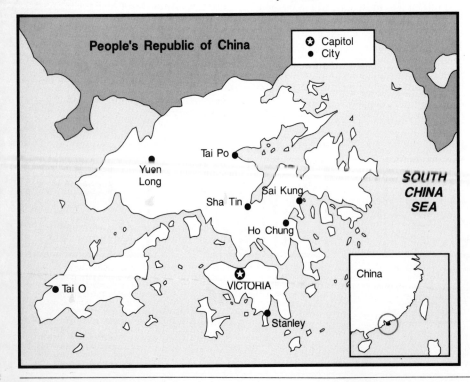

People's Republic of China

⊛ Capitol
● City

Tai Po

Yuen Long

Sai Kung

Sha Tin

Ho Chung

SOUTH CHINA SEA

Tai O

VICTORIA

Stanley

China

HISTORICAL BACKGROUND

Opium started it all for Hong Kong. The addictive drug from which such narcotics as morphine, heroin, and codeine are made, opium had become a major source of income for British merchants in the early 1800s. When the Chinese government declared the opium trade illegal and confiscated more than 20,000 large chests of opium, which had been on their way for sale to the increasingly addicted residents of Canton, the merchants persuaded the British military to intervene and restore their trading privileges. The British Navy attacked and occupied part of Canton. Three days later the British Navy forced the Chinese to agree to their trading demands, including a demand that they be ceded the tiny island of Hong Kong (meaning "Fragrant Harbor"), where they could pursue their trading and military business without the scrutiny of the Chinese authorities.

Initially the British government was not pleased with the acquisition of Hong Kong; on it existed only a small fishing village, and the island had been annexed without the foreknowledge of the authorities in London. Shortly, however, the government found the island's harbor a useful place to resupply ships and to anchor military vessels in the event of further hostilities with the Chinese. The harbor turned out to be one of the finest natural harbors along the coast of China. On August 29, 1842, China reluctantly signed the Treaty of Nanking, which ended the first Opium War and gave Britain ownership of Hong Kong island "in perpetuity."

Twenty years later a second Opium War caused China to lose more of its territory; Britain acquired permanent lease rights over Kowloon, a tiny part of the mainland facing Hong Kong Island. By 1898 Britain realized that its miniscule Hong Kong naval base would be too small to defend itself against sustained attack by French or other European navies seeking privileged access to China's markets. The British were concerned in particular about the scarcity of agricultural land on Hong Kong and Kowloon. In 1898 they persuaded the Chinese to lease them more than 350 square miles of land adjacent to Kowloon. Thus, the colony of Hong Kong consists of Hong Kong Island (as well as numerous small, uninhabited islands nearby), the Kowloon Peninsula, and the agricultural lands which came to be called the New Territories.

POPULATION PROBLEMS

From its inauspicious beginnings Hong Kong has grown into a dynamic, modern society, wealthier and more densely populated than its promoters would have ever dreamed in their wildest imaginations. Hong Kong is now home to 5.7 million people, or some 13,902 people per square mile. Furthermore, most of the New Territories are mountainous or are needed for agriculture, so the bulk of the population is packed into about one-tenth of the land space. This gives Hong Kong the dubious honor of being one of the most densely populated human spaces ever created. Millions of people live stacked on top of one another in 30-story-high public tenement buildings. The rent for some apartments in Hong Kong exceeds that of apartments in Tokyo, costing their tenants thousands of dollars each month. Even Hong Kong's excellent harbor has not escaped the population crunch; approximately 10 square miles of former harbor have been filled in and now constitute some of the most expensive real estate on earth.

Why are there so many people in Hong Kong? One reason is that, after occupation by the British, many Chinese merchants moved their businesses to Hong Kong, under the correct assumption that trade would be given a freer hand there than on the mainland. Eventually Hong Kong became the home of mammoth trading conglomerates. The laborers in these highly profitable enterprises came to Hong Kong, for the most part, as political refugees from mainland China in the early 1900s. Another wave of immigrants arrived in the 1930s upon the invasion of Manchuria by the Japanese, and yet another influx came after the Communists took over China in 1949. Thus, like Taiwan, Hong Kong has become a place of refuge for those in economic or political trouble on the mainland. This fact was underscored in 1989, when many students who had demonstrated against the Chinese government in Beijing escaped to Hong Kong.

Extreme overcrowding plus a favorable climate for doing business have produced a society rife with social and economic inequalities. Some of the richest people on earth live in Hong Kong, as do some of the most wretchedly poor, notable among whom are the recent refugees from China and Southeast Asia, some of whom have joined the traditionally poor boat peoples living in Aberdeen Harbor. Although surrounded by poverty, many of Hong Kong's economic elites have not found it inappropriate to indulge in ostentatious displays of wealth. The children of the poor, on the other hand, must resign themselves to playing on the teeming streets of Central, Causeway Bay, or Tsimshatsui.

Workers are on the job 6 days a week, morning and night, yet the average pay for a worker in industry is only about $4,800 per year. With husband, wife, and older children all working (school is free and compulsory through junior-high school), families can survive; some even make it into the ranks of the fabulously wealthy. Indeed, the desire to make money was the primary reason why Hong Kong was settled in the first place. That fact is not lost on anyone who lives there today. Noise and air pollution, traffic congestion, and dirty and smelly streets do not deter migrants from abandoning the countryside in favor of the consumptive lifestyle of the city.

CULTURAL LIFE

Materialism has not wholly effaced the cultural arts and social rituals that are essential to a cohesive society. Indeed, with 98 percent of Hong Kong's residents hailing originally from mainland China, the superstitions and cultural heritage of China's long history abound. Some residents hang small eight-sided mirrors outside windows to frighten away malicious spirits, while others choose for the names of their companies or products Chinese characters which they hope will bring them luck. Even modern skyscrapers are designed, following ancient Chinese customs, so that their main entrances are in balance with the elements of nature.

Buddhist and Taoist beliefs remain central to the lives of many residents. In the back rooms of many shops, for example, are erected small religious shrines; joss sticks burning in front of these shrines are thought to bring good fortune to the proprietors. Elaborate festivals, such as those at New Year's, bring the costumes, art, and dance of thousands of years of Chinese history to the crowded streets of Hong Kong. And, of course, the British legacy may be found in the cricket matches, ballet troupes, philharmonic orchestras, English-language radio and television broadcasts, and the legal system under which capitalism has flourished.

THE END OF AN ERA

Britain has been in control of this tiny speck of Asia for some 150 years. Except during World War II, when the Japanese occupied Hong Kong for about 4 years, the territory has been governed as a Crown Colony of Great Britain, with a governor appointed by the British sovereign. However, Britain's rule will soon come to an end. In 1984 British Prime Minister Margaret Thatcher and Chinese leader Deng Xiaoping concluded 2 years of acrimonious negotiations over the fate of Hong Kong upon the expiration of the New Territories' lease in 1997. Britain claimed the right to control Hong Kong

| The British begin to occupy and use Hong Kong Island; the first Opium War A.D. 1839–1842 | The Treaty of Nanking cedes Hong Kong to Britain 1842 | The Chinese cede Kowloon and Stonecutter Island to Britain 1856 | England gains a 99-year lease on the New Territories 1898 | The Boxer Rebellion 1898–1900 | Sun Yat-sen overthrows the emperor of China to establish the Republic of China 1911 | The Sino-Japanese War 1931–1945 | Chinese Communists declare war on Japan 1932 | The Japanese attack Pearl Harbor and take Hong Kong 1941 | Communist victory in China produces massive immigration into Hong Kong 1949 |

1980s–1990s

Britain and China begin negotiations over Hong Kong's future; and agree to the return of Hong Kong to China

Mass demonstrations in Hong Kong against the Tiananmen Square massacre

Hong Kong is scheduled to become a Special Administrative District of the People's Republic of China

Island and Kowloon forever—a claim disputed by China, which argued that the treaties granting these lands to Britain had been imposed on them by military force. Hong Kong Island and Kowloon, however, constitute only about 10 percent of the colony; the other 90 percent was to return automatically to China at the expiration of the lease. The various parts of the colony having become fully integrated, it seemed desirable to all parties to keep the colony together as one administrative unit. Moreover, it was felt that Hong Kong Island and Kowloon could not survive alone.

The British government had hoped that the People's Republic of China (P.R.C.) would agree to the status quo, or that it would at least permit the British to maintain administrative control over the colony should it be returned to China. Many Hong Kong Chinese felt the same way, since they had, after all, fled to Hong Kong to escape the Communist regime in China. For its part, the P.R.C. insisted that the entire colony be returned to its control by 1997. After difficult negotiations, Britain agreed to return the entire colony to China as long as China would grant important concessions. Foremost among these were that the capitalist economy and lifestyle, including private-property ownership and basic human rights, would not be changed for 50 years. The P.R.C. agreed to govern Hong Kong as a Special Administrative Region (SAR) within China and to permit British and local Chinese to serve in the administrative apparatus of the territory.

The Joint Declaration of 1984 was drafted by top governmental leaders, with very little input from the people of Hong Kong. This fact plus fears about what P.R.C. control will mean to the free wheeling lifestyle of Hong Kong's ardent capitalists have caused many residents to pack their bags. Thousands of residents, carrying $10 billion in assets, have resettled in Canada, Bermuda, Australia, the United States, and Britain. It has been reported in the Hong Kong press that as many as one-third of the population of Hong Kong would like to emigrate before the mainland Chinese take control in 1997.

Many residents believe the Chinese Communist Party authorities will not honor the provisions of the Joint Declaration. This belief was given momentum in 1989 when the Chinese military brutally suppressed the student prodemocracy movement in Beijing. In Hong Kong, some 1.5 million people—the largest assemblage ever in the colony's history—took to the streets to protest the massacre.

This kind of response might lead outsiders to conclude that everyone in Hong Kong is unequivocally opposed to the departure of the British. However, although there are large British and American communities in Hong Kong, and although English is the language of government, many residents have little or no contact with the Western aspects of Hong Kong life and feel very little, if any, loyalty to the British Crown. They assert that they are, first and foremost, Chinese, and that as such they can govern themselves without the involvement of any Western power. This, of course, does not amount to a popular endorsement of the People's Republic of China's claim to govern Hong Kong, but it does imply that the residents of Hong Kong, if they have to be governed by others, would rather they be Chinese. Moreover, some believe that the Chinese government may actually help rid Hong Kong of financial corruption and allocate more resources to the poor.

The natural links with the P.R.C. have been expanding steadily for years. In addition to a shared language and culture, there are in Hong Kong thousands of new immigrants with strong family ties to the People's Republic. And there are increasingly important commercial ties. Hong Kong has always served as south China's entrepôt to the rest of the world for both commodity and financial exchanges. For instance, for years Taiwan has circumvented its regulations against direct trade with China by transshipping its exports through Hong Kong. Commercial trucks plying the highways between Hong Kong and the P.R.C. form a bumper-to-bumper wall of commerce between the two regions. Thus it is recognized that China needs Hong Kong to remain more or less as it is, and that, therefore, the transition to Chinese rule may be less jarring to local residents than is expected. Most observers believe that even after the transition to Chinese rule, Hong Kong will remain, along with Tokyo, one of the financial and trading centers of Asia and of the world.

DEVELOPMENT

Hong Kong is one of the financial and trading dynamos of the world. Between 1981 and 1988 it averaged an annual economic growth rate of 9.6%. Hong Kong annually exports billions of dollars worth of products. Hong Kong's political future may be uncertain after 1997, but its fine harbor is sure to continue to bolster its economy.

FREEDOM

Hong Kong has been an appendage to one of the world's foremost democracies for some 150 years. Its residents have enjoyed the civil liberties guaranteed by British law. After 1997 a new Basic Law—currently being implemented with the consent of the Chinese government—will take full effect.

HEALTH/WELFARE

Schooling is free and compulsory in Hong Kong through junior-high school. The government has devoted large sums for low-cost housing, aid for refugees, and social services such as adoption. Housing, however, is cramped and inadequate for the population.

ACHIEVEMENTS

Hong Kong has the capacity to hold together a society where the gap between rich and poor is enormous. The boat people have been subjected to discrimination, but most other groups have found social acceptance and opportunities for economic advancement.

Indonesia (Republic of Indonesia)

GEOGRAPHY

Area in Square Kilometers (Miles):
1,919,440 (740,903) (nearly 3 times
the size of Texas)
Capital (Population): Jakarta
(7,800,000)
Climate: tropical; hot, humid; more
moderate in highlands

PEOPLE

Population
Total: 190,136,000
Annual Growth Rate: 1.8%
Rural/Urban Population Ratio: 75/25
Languages: official: Bahasa
Indonesia; others spoken: English,
Dutch, Javanese, others
Ethnic Makeup of Population: 45%
Javanese; 14% Sudanese; 7.5%
Madarese, 7.5% coastal Malays, 26%
others

Health
Life Expectancy at Birth: 58 years
(male); 63 years (female)
Infant Mortality Rate (Ratio):
75/1,000
Average Caloric Intake: 105% of FAO
minimum
Physicians Available (Ratio): 1/8,234

Religion(s)
88% Muslim; 9% Christian; 2%
Hindu; 1% others

Education
Adult Literacy Rate: 72%

COMMUNICATION
Telephones: 999,320
Newspapers: 252

EXPLOSIVE ISLANDS

Located in an area that geologists call "the belt of fire," Indonesia has
more volcanoes per square mile than any other country in the world. Out
of 500 volcanoes, 128 are active and 65 more are considered dangerous.
An eruption of Krakatau in 1883 killed 35,000 people. In 1990 Mount
Kelud, 390 miles east of Jakarta, erupted, spewing lava on nearby towns
and dumping ash on towns 30 miles away. Kelud has erupted 8 times
since 1811, claiming the lives of nearly 6,000 people. Its most recent
explosion killed 15, injured 48, and required the evacuation of 4,000
villagers.

TRANSPORTATION

Highways—Kilometers (Miles):
119,500 (74,000)
Railroads—Kilometers (Miles): 6,964
(4,318)
Usable Airfields: 435

GOVERNMENT

Type: republic
Independence Date: August 17, 1945
Head of State: President Suharto
Political Parties: GOLKAB (quasi-
official); Indonesia Democracy Party;
Development Unity Party
Suffrage: universal at age 17 and
married persons regardless of age

MILITARY

Number of Armed Forces: 282,000
*Military Expenditures (% of Central
Government Expenditures):* 2.1%
Current Hostilities: none

ECONOMY

Currency ($ U.S. Equivalent): 1,805
Indonesian Rupiahs (Rp) = $1
Per Capita Income/GNP: $338/$80
billion
Inflation Rate: 8%
Natural Resources: oil; minerals;
forest products
Agriculture: subsistence food
production; rice; cassava; peanuts;
rubber; cocoa; coffee; copra; other
tropical products
Industry: petroleum; textiles, mining;
cement; chemical fertilizer; timber;
food; rubber

FOREIGN TRADE

Exports: $21.0 billion
Imports: $13.2 billion

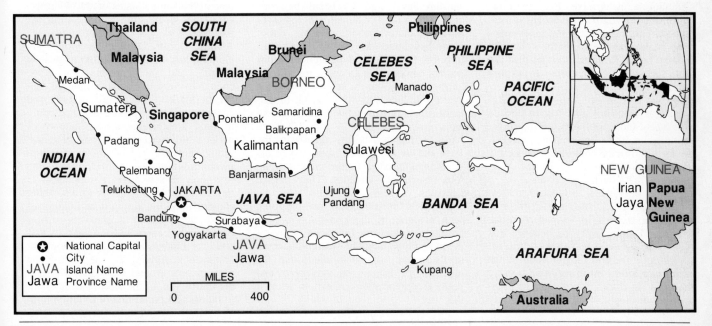

A KALEIDOSCOPIC CULTURE

Present-day Indonesia is a kaleidoscope of some 300 languages and more than 100 ethnic groups. Beginning about 5000 B.C. people of Mongoloid stock settled the islands in successive waves of migration from what are now China, Thailand, and Vietnam. Animism—the nature-worship religion of these peoples—was altered substantially (but never completely lost) about A.D. 200, when Hindus from India began to settle in the area and wield the dominant cultural influence. Five hundred years later Buddhist missionaries and settlers began converting Indonesians in a proselytizing effort that produced strong political and religious antagonisms. In the thirteenth century Muslim traders began the Islamization of the Indonesian people; today 88 percent of the population claim the Muslim faith. Commingling with all these influences were cultural inputs from the islands of Polynesia.

The real roots of the Indonesian people undoubtedly go back much further than any of these historic cultures. In 1891 the fossilized bones of a man who used stone tools, camped around a fire, and probably had a well-developed language were found on the island of Java. Named *Pithecanthropus erectus,* or erect ape-man, these important early human fossils, popularly called Java Man, have been dated at about three-quarters of a million years ago. Fossils similar to Java Man have been found in Europe, Africa, and Asia.

Modern Indonesia was sculpted by the influence of many outside cultures. In the 1500s Portuguese Catholics, eager for Indonesian spices, made contact with Indonesia and left 20,000 converts to Catholicism, many mixed Portuguese-Indonesian communities, and dozens of Portuguese "loan words" in the Indonesian-style Malay language. In the following century Dutch Protestants established the Dutch East India Company, to exploit Indonesia's riches. Eventually the Netherlands was able to gain complete political control; it reluctantly gave it up in the face of insistent Indonesian nationalism, as recently as in 1950. Before that, however, the British briefly controlled one of the islands, and the Japanese ruled the country for 3 years during the 1940s.

Initially Indonesians, including then President Sukarno, welcomed the Japanese as helpers in their fight for independence from the Dutch. Everyone believed that the Japanese would leave soon. Instead, they forced farmers to give food to the Japanese soldiers, made everyone worship the Japanese emperor, neglected local industrial development in favor of military

projects, and took 270,000 young men away from Indonesia to work elsewhere as forced laborers; fewer than 70,000 survived to return home. Military leaders who attempted to revolt against Japanese rule were executed. Finally, in August 1945, the Japanese abandoned their control of Indonesia according to the terms of surrender with the Allied powers.

Consider what all these influences mean for the culture of modern Indonesia. After all, some of the most powerful ideologies ever espoused by humankind—supernaturalism, Islam, Hinduism, Buddhism, Christianity, mercantilism, colonialism, and nationalism—have had an impact on Indonesia. Take music, for example. Unlike Western music, which most people just listen to, Indonesian music, played on drums and gongs reminiscent of Africa and the Polynesian islands, is intended as a somewhat sacred ritual in which all members of a community are expected to participate. Even the instruments themselves are considered sacred. Dances are often the main element in a religious service whose goal might be a good rice harvest, spirit possession, or exorcism. This may seem decidedly foreign and exotic to Westerners, but familiar musical styles can be heard here and there around the country. In the eastern part of Indonesia, for instance, the Nga'dha peoples, converted to Christianity in the early 1900s, sing Christian hymns to the accompaniment of bronze pot gongs and drums. On the island of Sumatra, Minang Kabau peoples, converted to Islam in the 1500s, use local instruments to accompany Islamic poetry singing. Communal feasts in Hindu Bali, circumcision ceremonies in Muslim Java, and Christian baptisms among the Bataks of Sumatra all represent borrowed cultural traditions. Thus, out of many has come one magically rich culture. But the faithful of different religions are not always able to work together in harmony. For instance, in the 1960s, when average Indonesians were trying to distance themselves from the radical communists, many decided to join Christian faiths. Threatened by this tilt toward the West and by the secular approach of the government, many fundamentalist Muslims resorted to violence. They burned Christian churches, threatened Catholic and Baptist missionaries, and opposed such projects as the construction of a hospital by Baptists. Indonesia is one of the most predominately Muslim countries in the world, and it is clear that the hundreds of Islamic socioreligious and political organizations intend to keep it that way.

A LARGE LAND, LARGE DEBTS

Unfortunately, the economy is not so richly endowed. About 75 percent of the population live in rural areas; more than half of the people engage in fishing and small-plot rice and vegetable farming. Forty percent of the gross national product comes from agriculture. The average income per person is only $338 a year, and inflation consumes about 8 percent of that annually.

Even more worrisome is the level of government debt. Indonesia, the fourteenth-largest country in the world, is blessed with large oil reserves (Pertamina is the state-owned oil company) and minerals and timber of every sort (also state-owned), but to extract these natural resources has required massive infusions of capital, most of it borrowed. In fact, Indonesia has borrowed more money than any other country in Asia ($53 billion owed in 1989) and must allocate 40 percent of its national budget just to pay the interest on the loans. Low oil prices in the 1980s made it difficult for the country to keep up with its debt burden.

To cope with these problems, Indonesia has relaxed government control over foreign investment and banking and seems to be on a path toward privatization of other parts of the economy. Still, the gap between the modernized cities and the traditional countryside continues to plague the government.

Indonesia's financial troubles seem puzzling, because in land, natural resources, and population, the country appears quite well-off. With 741,101 acres of land, Indonesia is the second-largest country in Asia (after China). Were it superimposed on a map of the United States, its 13,677 tropical islands would stretch from California, past New York, and out to Bermuda in the Atlantic Ocean. Oil and hardwoods are plentiful (the forests are similar to those in Brazil), and the population is large enough to constitute a viable internal consumer market. But transportation and communication are problematic and costly in such archipelagic states. Indonesia's national airline, Garuda Indonesia, is currently launching a $3.6 billion development program which will bring into operation 50 new aircraft stopping at 13 new airports. New seaports are also under construction. But the cost of linking together the thousands of islands is a major drain on the economy. Moreover, exploitation of Indonesia's amazing panoply of resources is drawing the ire of more and more people around the world who fear the destruction of the world's ecosystem. Indonesia's population of about 190 mil-

Java Man lived here **1.7 million years** B.C.	Buddhism gains the upper hand A.D. **600**	Muslim traders bring Islam to Indonesia A.D. **1200**	The Portuguese begin to trade and settle in Indonesia **1509**	Dutch traders begin to influence Indonesian life **1596**	The Japanese defeat the Dutch **1942**	Indonesian independence from the Netherlands; President Sukarno retreats from democracy and the West **1949–1950**	General Suharto takes control of the government from Sukarno and establishes his New Order pro-Western government **1965**	Anti-Japanese riots take place in Jakarta **1974**	Indonesia invades East Timor **1975**

■■■■■■■■■■■■■■■■■■■■■●■■■■■■■■■■■■■■■■■■■●■■■■■■■■■■■■■■■■■■■●■■■■■■■■■■■■■■■■■●■■■■■■■■■■■■■■●■■■■■■■■■■■●■■■■■■■■■■■■■■■●■■■■■■■■■■■■■■■■■●■■■■■■■■■■■■■■■■■●■■■ **1980s–1990s**

Economic reforms aim to increase foreign investment	Oil revenues slump; the rupiah is devalued	China restores diplomatic relations after 22 years

lion is one of the largest in the world, but 28 percent of the people cannot read or write. Only about 600 people per 100,000 attend college, as compared to 3,580 in nearby Philippines. Moreover, since almost 70 percent of the population reside on or near the island of Java, on which the capital city, Jakarta, is located, educational and development efforts have concentrated there, at the expense of the communities on outlying islands. Many children in the out islands never complete the required 6 years of elementary school; and some ethnic groups, for example, on the islands of Irian Jaya (New Guinea) and Kalimantan (Borneo), continue to live isolated in small tribes, much as they did thousands of years ago. By contrast, the modern city of Jakarta, with its classical European-style buildings, is predicted to have a population of more than 13 million by the year 2000.

The current government is aware that with 3 million new Indonesians entering the labor force every year and 42 percent of the total population under age 15, serious efforts must be made to increase employment opportunities. For the 1990s the government has earmarked millions of dollars to promote the tourism industry, a labor-intensive industry that could bring as many as 2 million visitors to Indonesia per year and provide jobs for many. New-hotel construction alone is budgeted at $1.5 billion for 1990–1992. Nevertheless, the most pressing problem is to finish the many projects for which World Bank and Asian Development Bank loans have already been received.

POLITICAL PROBLEMS

Just as the Dutch East India Company (VOC) had difficulty colonizing the highly diverse and fragmented Spice Islands (which are now part of Indonesia), establishing the current political and geographic boundaries of the Republic of Indonesia has been a bloody and protracted task. So fractured is the culture that many people doubt whether there really is a single country that one can call Indonesia. During the first 15 years of independence (1950–1965) there were revolts by Muslims and pro-Dutch groups, indecisive elections, several military coups, battles against U.S.-supported rebels, and serious territorial disputes with Malaysia and the Netherlands. In 1966 nationalistic President Sukarno, who had been a founder of Indonesian independence, lost power to Army General Suharto. (Many Southeast Asians had no family names until influenced by Westerners; Sukarno and Suharto each used only one name.) Anticommunist feeling grew during the 1960s, and thousands of suspected members of the Indonesian Communist Party (PKI) and other communists were killed before the PKI was banned in 1966. President Suharto's so-called New Order government continues to rule with an iron hand, suppressing student and Muslim dissent and controlling the press and the economy.

FOREIGN RELATIONS

In 1974, upon the visit of the prime minister of Japan, antigovernment and anti-Japanese riots broke out in Jakarta. Many believed that Suharto and the Japanese were in collusion to exploit the Indonesian economy. (Today Japanese yen continue to flow into Indonesia, as elsewhere in the Pacific Rim. Many tourist-industry projects are financed by the Japanese. In 1988 Japanese investments totaled $256 billion. Other nations, including Taiwan, South Korea, West Germany, and the United States, are also heavy investors.) In 1975, ignoring the disapproval of the United Nations, Suharto ordered the invasion and annexation of East Timor, a Portuguese colony. Thus, with its earlier harassment of the new Federation of Malaysia, its military invasions of Dutch-controlled Irian and Portuguese-held East Timor, and its violent treatment of Chinese nationals within its own borders, Indonesia has not established itself as a good political neighbor. Moreover, the glaring inequalities between the social classes, between the urban and rural areas, and between the dozens of distinct ethnic and religious groups presage many years of instability ahead.

DEVELOPMENT

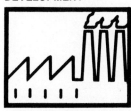

Indonesia continues to be hamstrung by its heavy reliance on foreign loans, a burden inherited from the Sukarno years. Current Indonesian leaders speak of "stabilization" and "economic dynamism." When there are oil stoppages in the Middle East, Indonesia's economy improves. Fifty-five percent of Indonesians are farmers and fishermen.

FREEDOM

Sukarno's Guided Democracy style of government resulted in the suppression of many civil rights and the crushing of left-wing groups, including the Communist Party. Demands for Western-style human rights are frequently heard, but only the army has the power to impose order on the numerous and competing political groups, many imbued with religious fervor.

HEALTH/WELFARE

Indonesia has one of the highest birth rates in the Pacific Rim; 42% of the population are under age 15. Many of these children will grow up in poverty, never learning even to read or write their national language, Bahasa Indonesian. Currently, 26% of the population are illiterate.

ACHIEVEMENTS

The largely Hindu island of Bali continues to attract tourists from around the world who are fascinated by the beauty of Balinese music and dancing. The dancers' glittering gold costumes and unique choreography epitomize the "Asian-ness" of Indonesia. Despite its heavy debt, Indonesia continues to pay its bills on schedule.

Laos (Lao People's Democratic Republic)

GEOGRAPHY

Area in Square Kilometers (Miles):
236,800 (91,400)
Capital (Population): Vientiane
Climate: tropical monsoon

PEOPLE

Population

Total: 4,024,000
Annual Growth Rate: 2.2%
Rural/Urban Population (Ratio):
85/15
Ethnic Makeup of Population: 50%
Lao; 20% tribal Thai; 15%
Phoutheung (Kha); 15% Meo,
Hmong, Yao, and others
Languages: official: Lao; others
spoken: French, English

Health

Life Expectancy at Birth: 48 years
(male); 51 years (female)
Infant Mortality Rate (Ratio):
126/1,000
Average Caloric Intake: 94% of FAO
minimum
Physicians Available (Ratio): 1/6,495

Religion(s)

85% Buddhist; 15% traditional
indigenous and others

WHAT'S FOR DINNER?

When the first entity that could be called the nation of Laos was formed in the fourteenth century A.D. the country's name was Lang Xang, meaning "Land of a Million Elephants." One of the founders of Laos was said in legend to have been sent by God and to have arrived on earth riding on an elephant. Elephants are still used as beasts of burden in Laos, but other animals, such as water buffalo, oxen, horses, chickens, and ducks, are more important to Laotian daily life. Animals are often tied up underneath Laotian houses, which are built up on stilts. Quail, snakes, deer, wild chickens, and fish add protein to the rice-based Laotian diet.

Recently North American cultural sensitivities were offended: city dwellers complained that Laotian Hmong immigrants (a mountain people who were severely persecuted by the communists and who subsequently emigrated *en masse*) were catching rats in city parks and cooking them for dinner.

Education

Adult Literacy Rate: 85%

COMMUNICATION

Telephones: 8,136
Newspapers: n/a

TRANSPORTATION

Highways—Kilometers (Miles):
27,527 (17,066)
Railroads—Kilometers (Miles): none
Usable Airfields: 50

GOVERNMENT

Type: communist state
Independence Date: July 19, 1949
Head of State: Acting President
Phoumi Vongvichit; Prime Minister
Kaysone Phomvihan
Political Parties: Lao People's
Revolutionary Party
Suffrage: universal at 18

MILITARY

Number of Armed Forces: 55,150
*Military Expenditures (% of Central
Government Expenditures):* 3.8%
Current Hostilities: boundary dispute
with Thailand

ECONOMY

Currency ($ U.S. Equivalent): 700
new kips = $1
Per Capita Income/GNP: $500/$500
million
Inflation Rate: 35%
Natural Resources: timber;
hydropower; gypsum; tin; gold;
gemstones
Agriculture: rice; potatoes;
vegetables; coffee; sugarcane; cotton
Industry: tin mining; timber; electric
power; agricultural processing

FOREIGN TRADE

Exports: $57 million
Imports: $219 million

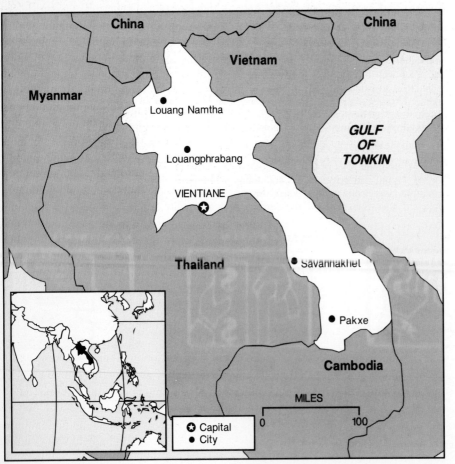

THE REALITY OF LAOTIAN LIFE

Laos seems a sleepy place. Almost everyone lives in small villages where the only distraction might be the Buddhist temple gong announcing the day. Water buffalo plow quietly through centuries-old rice paddies, while young Buddhist monks in saffron robes make their silent rounds for rice donations. Villagers build their houses on stilts for safety from annual river flooding and top them with thatch or tin. Barefoot children play under the palm trees or wander to the village Buddhist temple for school in the outdoor courtyard. Mothers stay home to weave brightly colored cloth for the family and to prepare meals—on charcoal or wood stoves—of rice, bamboo shoots, pork, duck, and snakes seasoned with hot peppers and ginger.

Below the surface, however, Laos is a nation divided against itself. Although the national name Laos is taken from the dominant ethnic group of the same name, there are actually about 70 ethnic groups in the country. Over the centuries they have battled one another for supremacy, for land, and for tribute money. The constant feuding has weakened the nation and served as an invitation for neighboring countries to annex portions of Laos forcibly, or to align themselves with one or another of the Laotian royal families or generals for material gain. China, Burma, Vietnam, and especially Thailand—with which Laotian people share many cultural and ethnic similarities—have all been involved militarily in Laos. France, the United States, and the Soviet Union have also contributed to the tragic military history of the country.

Historically, the cause of unrest was often palace jealousies which led one member of the royal family to fight against a kinsman for dominance. More recently Laos has been seen as a pawn in the battle of the Western powers for access to the rich natural resources of Southeast Asia or as a "domino" that some did and others did not want to fall to communism.

ECONOMIC DEVASTATION

The results of these struggles have been devastating. Laos is now one of the poorest countries in the world, with the average Laotian earning only $45 a year. There are few industries in the country, so most people survive by subsistence farming—that is, farming just what they need to eat rather than growing food to sell. In fact, some hill peoples in the long mountain range that separates Laos from Vietnam continue to use the most ancient farming technique known, slash-and-burn farming, an unstable method of land use

that only allows 3 or 4 years of good crops before the soil is depleted and the farmers must move to new ground.

Even if all Laotian farmers used the most modern techniques and geared their production to cash crops, it would still be difficult to export food (or, for that matter, anything else), because of Laos's woefully inadequate transportation network. There are no railroads, and muddy, unpaved roads make many mountain villages completely inaccessible by car or truck. Moreover, Laos is landlocked. In a region of the world where wealth flows toward those countries with the best ports (Singapore and Hong Kong, for example), having no access to the sea is a serious impediment to economic growth. And finally, the controlled economy has not been open to lucrative Western trade and investment. Until recently the country was closed to tourists; despite the official promotion of tourism since 1989, the government still allows visits only to a few cities.

Nonetheless, some economic progress has been made in the past decade. Laos is

once again self-sufficient in its staple crop, rice, and electricity generated from dams along the Mekong River is sold to Thailand to earn foreign exchange. Laos imports various commodity items from Thailand, Singapore, Japan, and other countries, and it has received foreign aid from the Soviet Union and Eastern European nations as well as from the Asian Development Bank. Exports to Thailand, China, and the United States include teakwood and various minerals.

LAOTIAN HISTORY

The Laotian people, originally migrating from south China through Thailand, settled Laos in the thirteenth century A.D., when the area was controlled by the Khmer (Cambodian) Empire. Early Laotian leaders expanded the borders of Laos through warfare with Cambodia, Thailand, Burma, and Vietnam. Internal warfare, however, led to a loss of autonomy in 1833, when Thailand forcefully annexed the country (against the wishes of Vietnam, which also had designs on Laos). In

(UPI/Bettmann)

Laos is one of the poorest countries in the world. With few industries in the country most people survive by subsistence farming. These fishermen spend their day catching tiny fish, measuring 2 to 5 inches, that must suffice to feed their families.

| The first Laotian nation is established **1300s** A.D. | Vietnam annexes most of Laos **1833** | Laos comes under French control **1885** | The Japanese conquer Southeast Asia **1940s** | France grants independence to Laos **1949** | South Vietnamese troops, with U.S. support, invade Laos **1971** | Pathet Lao Communists gain control of the government **1975** | Laos signs military and economic agreements with Vietnam **1977** | **1980s–1990s** |

Border dispute with Thailand strains relations

The government liberalizes some aspects of the economy

Prince Souphanouvang retires from government leadership

the 1890s France, determined to have a part of the lucrative Asian trade and to hold its own against growing British strength in Southeast Asia, forced Thailand to give up its hold on Laos. Laos, Vietnam, and Cambodia were combined into a new political entity, which the French called Indochina. Between these French possessions and the British possessions of Burma and Malaysia lay Thailand; thus, France, the United Kingdom, and Thailand effectively controlled mainland Southeast Asia for several decades.

There were several small uprisings against French power, but these were easily suppressed until the Japanese conquest of Indochina in the 1940s. The Japanese, with their "Asia for Asians" philosophy, convinced the Laotians that European domination was not a given. In 1949 Laos was granted independence, although full French withdrawal did not take place until 1954.

Prior to independence Prince Souphanouvong had organized a communist guerrilla army, with help from Ho Chi Minh and the Vietnamese communist Viet Minh. This army called itself the Pathet Lao (meaning "Lao Country"). In 1954 it challenged the authority of the government in Vientiane. Civil war ensued, and by 1961, when a ceasefire was arranged, the Pathet Lao had captured about half of Laos. The Soviet Union supported the Pathet Lao, whose strength was in the northern half of Laos, while the United States supported a succession of pro-Western but fragile governments in the south. A coalition government consisting of Pathet Lao, pro-Western, and neutralist leaders was installed in 1962, but it collapsed in 1965, when warfare once again broke out.

During the Vietnam War, U.S. and South Vietnamese forces bombed and invaded Laos in an attempt to disrupt the North Vietnamese supply line known as the Ho Chi Minh Trail. Communist battlefield victories in Vietnam encouraged and aided the Pathet Lao army, which became the dominant voice in a new coalition government established in 1974. The Pathet Lao controlled the government exclusively by 1975. In the same year the government proclaimed a new People's Democratic Republic of Laos. It also abolished the 622-year-old monarchy and sent the king and the royal family to a detention center in order to learn Marxist ideology. Vietnamese Army support and flight by many of those opposed to the communist regime have permitted the Pathet Lao to maintain control of the government.

The Pathet Lao government was sustained militarily and economically by the Soviet Union and other Eastern Bloc nations for more than 15 years. However, with the recent upheaval in Eastern Europe and the end of the Cold War, Laos has begun to look elsewhere, including to noncommunist countries, for possible linkages. It is likely that the next decade will bring significant changes to Laos's international commitments.

DO BUDDHISM AND COMMUNISM MIX?

Trying to teach communism to a very Buddhist country has not been easy. Popular resistance has caused the government to retract many of the regulations it has tried to impose on the Buddhist church (technically, the *Sangha*, or order of the monks—the Buddhist equivalent of a clerical hierarchy). Repealed after mass protest were laws forbidding the wearing of the traditional saffron robe by monks and the prohibition against the ancient act of monks begging for rice. As long as the Buddhist hierarchy limits its activities to helping the poor, it seems to be able to avoid running afoul of the communist leadership.

Intellectuals, especially those known to have been functionaries of the French administration, have fled the country, leaving a leadership vacuum. As many as 300,000 people—more than the entire population of the capital city, Vientiane—are thought to have left the country for refugee camps in Thailand and elsewhere. Many have taken up permanent residence in foreign countries. With a total population of only 4 million people, the Laotian exodus has imposed a significant drain on Laos's intellectual resources.

DEVELOPMENT

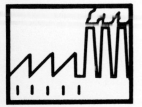

Communist rule after 1975 isolated Laos from world trade and foreign investment. The planned economy has not been able to gain momentum on its own. In 1986 the government loosened restrictions so that government companies could keep a portion of their profits. A goal is to integrate Laos economically with Vietnam and Cambodia.

FREEDOM

Laos is ruled by the political arm of the Pathet Lao Army. Opposition parties and groups as well as opposition newspapers and other media are outlawed. Lack of civil liberties as well as poverty have caused many thousands to flee the country.

HEALTH/WELFARE

Laos is typical of the least developed countries in the world. The birth rate is high, but so is infant mortality. Most Laotians eat less than an adequate diet. Life expectancy is low, and many Laotians die from illnesses for which medicines are available in other countries. Many doctors fled the country when the communists came to power.

ACHIEVEMENTS

The original inhabitants of Laos, the Kha, have been looked down upon by the Lao, Tai, and other peoples for centuries. But under the communist regime, the status of the Kha has been upgraded and discrimination formally proscribed.

Macau

GEOGRAPHY

Area in Square Kilometers (Miles): 16 (6) (about one-tenth the size of Washington, DC)
Capital (Population): Macau (402,000)
Climate: subtropical

PEOPLE

Population
Total: 442,000
Annual Growth Rate: 1.1%
Rural/Urban Population Ratio: 100% urban
Ethnic Makeup of Population: 95% Chinese; 3% Portuguese; 2% others
Languages: official: Portuguese; other spoken: Cantonese

Health
Life Expectancy at Birth: 75 years (male); 79 years (female)
Infant Mortality Rate (Ratio): 7/1,000
Average Caloric Intake: n/a
Physicians Available (Ratio): 1/2,470

Religion(s)
predominantly Buddhist

Education
Adult Literacy Rate: 100%

COMMUNICATION

Telephones: 55,643
Newspapers: 8

THE LEGEND OF A-MA

Every May the people of Macau celebrate the Feast of A-Ma, a Chinese goddess after whom the Portuguese named Macau. During the festival, the entire fishing fleet comes to port to honor this patroness of fishermen and seamen at the temple that bears her name, located at the entrance of the Inner Harbor.

According to legend, A-Ma was a poor girl looking for a passage to Canton. She was refused by the wealthy junk owners, but a lowly fisherman took her aboard. Soon a storm wrecked all the boats but the one carrying A-Ma. When it landed in Macau, she disappeared, only to reappear later as a goddess at the spot where the fisherman built her temple.

TRANSPORTATION

Highways—Kilometers (Miles): 90 (56)
Railroads—Kilometers (Miles): none
Usable Airfields: none

GOVERNMENT

Type: overseas territory of Portugal; scheduled to revert to China in 1999
Independence Date: —
Head of State: President Mário Alberto Soares; Governor Carlos Melancia
Political Parties: Association to Defend the Interests of Macau; Macau Democratic Center; Group to Study the Development of Macau; Macau Independent Group
Suffrage: universal at 18

MILITARY

Number of Armed Forces: defense is the responsibility of Portugal
Military Expenditures (% of Central Government Expenditures): n/a
Current Hostilities: none

ECONOMY

Currency ($ U.S. Equivalent): 8.03 patacas = $1
Per Capita Income/GNP: n/a
Inflation Rate: 9.5%
Natural Resources: fish
Agriculture: rice; vegetables
Industry: clothing; textiles; toys; plastic products; furniture; tourism

FOREIGN TRADE

Exports: $1.7 billion
Imports: $1.6 billion

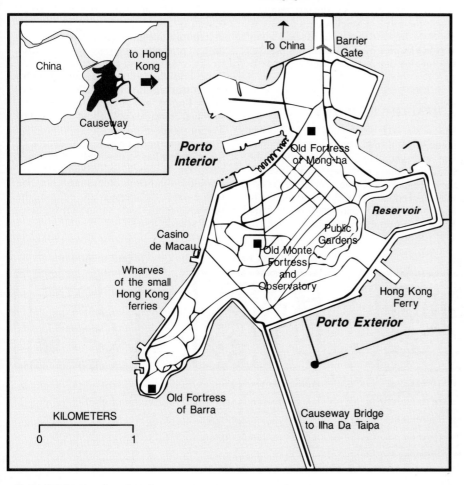

| A Portuguese trading colony is established at Macau A.D. 1557 | Portugal declares sovereignty over Macau 1849 | China signs a treaty recognizing Portuguese sovereignty over Macau 1887 | Immigrants from China flood the colony 1949 | Procommunist riots in Macau 1967 | Portugal begins to loosen direct administrative control over Macau 1970s | Macau becomes a Chinese territory wholly administered by Portugal 1976 | 1980s–1990s |

China and Portugal sign an agreement scheduling the return of Macau to Chinese control in 1999

50,000 illegal Chinese immigrants seek permanent residency status in Macau

MACAU

Just 17 miles across the Pearl River estuary from British Hong Kong is another speck of foreignness on Chinese soil: the Portuguese territory of Macau (sometimes spelled Macao). The oldest permanent outpost of European culture in the Far East, Macau has the highest population density of any political entity in the world: although it consists of only about 6 square miles in area, it is home to nearly half a million people. Some 95 percent of these are Chinese. This percentage has varied throughout Macau's history, depending on conditions within China itself; during the World War II Japanese occupation of China, for instance, Macau's Chinese population is believed to have doubled.

Macau was frequented by Portuguese traders as early as 1516, but it was not until 1557 that the Chinese agreed to Portuguese settlement of the land; it did not, however, acknowledge Portuguese sovereignty. Indeed, the Chinese government did not recognize the Portuguese right of "perpetual occupation" until 1887.

In 1987, after 9 months of negotiation, Chinese and Portuguese officials, meeting in Beijing, signed an agreement that will end European control of the first and last colonial outpost in China. For close to 450 years the Portuguese will have administered the tiny colony of Macau; the transfer to Chinese control is scheduled for December 20, 1999.

The agreement is similar to that signed by Britain over the fate of Hong Kong.

China agrees to allow Macau to maintain its capitalist way of life for 50 years, to elect local leaders, and to permit its residents to travel freely without Chinese intervention. Yet unlike in Hong Kong, where residents have either staged massive demonstrations against future Chinese rule or have emigrated from the colony, Macau residents have not seemed bothered by the new arrangements.

"CITY OF THE NAME OF GOD"

Since it was established in the sixteenth century as a trading colony (with interests in oranges, tea, tobacco, and lacquer), Macau has been heavily influenced by Roman Catholic priests of the Dominican and Jesuit orders; and so Christian churches, interspersed with Buddhist temples, abound. The name of Macau itself reflects its deep and enduring religious roots; the city's official name is "City of the Name of God in China, Macau, There is None More Loyal." Macau has perhaps the highest density of churches and temples per square mile in the world.

A HEALTHY ECONOMY

Macau's modern economy is a vigorous blend of light industry, fishing, and tourism and gambling. Revenues from the latter two sources are impressive; indeed, they account for 25 percent of gross domestic product (GDP). Today there are five major casinos and many other gambling opportunities in Macau, which,

along with the considerable charms of the city itself, attract more than 4 million foreign visitors a year, most of them Hong Kong Chinese with plenty of money to burn. Macau's gambling industry is run by a syndicate of Chinese businesspeople operating under the name Macau Travel & Amusement Company, which won monopoly rights on all licensed gambling in Macau in 1962.

Export earnings derived from light-industry products (such as textiles, fireworks, plastics, and electronics) are also critical to the colony. Macau's leading export markets are the United States, Germany, France, and Hong Kong; ironically, Portugal consumes only about 3 percent of Macau's exports.

As might be expected, the success of the economy has its downside. In Macau's case, the hallmarks of modernization—crowded apartment blocks and bustling traffic—are threatening to eclipse the remnants of the old, serene Portuguese-style seaside town.

DEVELOPMENT

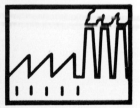

The development of industries related to gambling and tourism (tourists are primarily from Hong Kong) has been very successful. Most of Macau's foods, energy, and fresh water are imported from China; Japan and Hong Kong are the main suppliers of raw materials.

FREEDOM

Portugal and China have long had an interest in settling the Macau question, but only in 1987 was an agreement signed between those countries, which will lead in 1999 to the return of Macau to Chinese authority. Currently the governor of Macau is nominated by the president of Portugal.

HEALTH/WELFARE

Macau has very impressive quality-of-life statistics. It has a low infant mortality rate and very high life expectancy for both males and females. Literacy is universal. In recent years the unemployment rate has been a low 2%.

ACHIEVEMENTS

Considering its unfavorable geographical characteristics, such as negligible natural resources and a port so shallow and heavily silted that ocean-going ships must lie offshore, Macau has had stunning economic success. Its annual economic growth rate is approximately 5%.

Malaysia

GEOGRAPHY

Area in Square Kilometers (Miles):
329,750 (121,348) (slightly larger than New Mexico)
Capital (Population): Kuala Lumpur (977,000)
Climate: tropical

PEOPLE
Population
Total: 17,511,000
Annual Growth Rate: 2.3%
Rural/Urban Population Ratio: 62/38
Ethnic Makeup of Population: 59% Malay and other indigenous; 32% Chinese; 9% Indian and Pakistani
Languages: Peninsular Malaysia—Malay (official); English, Chinese dialects, Tamil; Sabah—English, Malay, numerous tribal dialects, Mandarin and Hakka dialects; Sarawak—English, Malay, Mandrin, and numerous tribal dialects

Health
Life Expectancy at Birth: 65 years (male); 71 years (female)
Infant Mortality Rate (Ratio): 30/1,000
Average Caloric Intake: 117% of FAO minimum
Physicians Available (Ratio): 1/2,853

Religion(s)
Peninsular Malaysia Malays nearly all Muslim, Chinese predominantly Buddhists, Indians predominantly Hindu; Saba—33% Muslim, 17% Chrisitan, 45% other; Sarawak—35% tribal religion; 24% Buddhist and Confucianist, 20% Muslim, 16% Christian, 5% other

Education
Adult Literacy Rate: 65% overall

COMMUNICATION
Telephones: 994,860
Newspapers: n/a

THE PROTON SAGA

Malaysians, once fearful of Japan and its military might, are now welcoming the Japanese into their industries and businesses. With Japanese money (more than $2 billion in 1989) and Malaysian labor, Malaysia's attempt to industrialize is starting to bear fruit. A recent successful example is the $320 million joint venture between the Malaysian government-owned Heavy Industries Corporation and Mitsubishi Motor Corporation of Japan. The new venture has produced a Malaysian car called the Proton Saga, which is being exported to New Zealand, England, Jamaica, and several countries in Asia. The company is planning to sell the car in the United States beginning in 1993.

The Proton Saga, which Malaysians are proud to call their "national car," captured 47 percent of Malaysia's market in its first year. At full capacity, the company will produce 100,000 cars a year.

TRANSPORTATION
Highways—Kilometers (Miles): 29,026 (17,996)
Railroads—Kilometers (Miles): 1,801 (1,116)
Usable Airfields: 121

GOVERNMENT
Type: constitutional monarchy
Independence Date: August 31, 1957
Head of State: Prime Minister Dr. Mahathir bin Mohamad; Paramount Ruler (King) Azlan Muhibbuddin Shah ibni Sultan Yusof Izzudin
Political Parties: Peninsular Malaysia: National Front Confederation and others; Sabah: Berjaya Party and others; Sarawak: coalition Sarawak National Front and others
Suffrage: universal at 21

MILITARY
Number of Armed Forces: 695,000
Military Expenditures (% of Central Government Expenditures): 3.8%

Current Hostilities: dispute over the Spratly Islands with China, the Philippines, Taiwan, and Vietnam; Sabah is claimed by the Philippines

ECONOMY
Currency ($ U.S. Equivalent): 2.72 ringgit = $1
Per Capita Income/GNP: $1,870/$34.3 billion
Inflation Rate: 3.6%
Natural Resources: oil; natural gas; bauxite; iron ore; copper; tin; timber; fish
Agriculture: rubber; palm oil; rice; coconut; pepper; timber
Industry: rubber and palm-oil manufacturing and processing; light manufacturing; electronics; tin mining and smelting; logging and processing timber; petroleum production and refining; food processing

FOREIGN TRADE
Exports: $18 billion
Imports: $12.1 billion

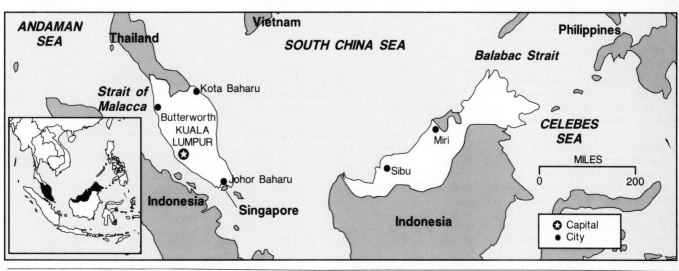

A FRACTURED NATION

About the size of Japan and famous for its production of natural rubber and tin, Malaysia sounds like a true political, economic, and social entity. But do not be deceived, for Malaysia, although it has all the trappings of a modern nation-state, is one of the most fragmented nations on earth.

Consider its land, for example. West Malaysia, wherein reside 86 percent of the population, is located on the Malay Peninsula between Singapore and Thailand; but East Malaysia, with 60 percent of the land, is located on the island of North Borneo, some 400 miles of ocean away.

Similarly, Malaysia's people are divided along racial, religious, and linguistic lines. Fifty-nine percent of the population of 17 $1/2$ million are Malays and other indigenous peoples, many of whom adhere to the Islamic faith or animist beliefs; 32 percent are Chinese, most of whom are Buddhist, Confucian, or Taoist; and 9 percent are Indians and Pakistanis, some of whom follow the Hindu faith. Bahasa Malaysia is the official language, but English, Arabic, two forms of Chinese, Tamil (from India), and other languages are also spoken. Thus, although the country is called Malaysia (a name applied only 30 years ago), the odds are that the typical people living in Kuala Lumpur, the capital, or in the many villages in the countryside, would not think of themselves first and foremost as Malaysians.

Malaysia culture is also fragmented because each ethnic group tends to adhere to the architecture, social rituals, and norms of etiquette peculiar to itself. Thus, one finds Moorish (Islamic) architecture alongside concrete and steel highrises, and store-front signs in Chinese characters hang next to signs in Malay, English, or Hindi. The Chinese, originally imported in the 1800s from south China by the British, in order to work the rubber plantations and tin mines, have become so economically powerful that their cultural influence extends far beyond their actual numbers.

Malaysia's history is equally fragmented. Originally controlled by numerous sultans who gave allegiance to no one or only reluctantly to various more powerful states in surrounding regions, Malaysia first came to Western attention in 1511, when the prosperous city of Malacca, founded on the west coast of the Malaya Peninsula about A.D. 1400, was conquered by the Portuguese. The Dutch took Malacca away from the Portuguese in 1641. The British seized it from the Dutch in 1824 (the British had already acquired an island off the coast and had established the port of Singapore). By 1888 the British were in control of most of the area that is now called Malaysia.

However, British hegemony did not mean total control, for each of the many sultanates—the bases for the 13 states that constitute Malaysia today—continued to act more or less independently of the British, engaging in wars with one another and maintaining an administrative apparatus apart from the British. And some groups, such as the Dayaks, an indigenous people living in the jungles of Borneo, remained more or less aloof from the various intrigues of modern state-making and developed little or no identity of themselves as citizens of any modern nation.

MODERN POLITICS

It is hardly surprising, then, that Malaysia has had a difficult time emerging as a modern nation. Nor is it likely that there would be an independent Malaysia had it not been for the Japanese, who defeated the British in Southeast Asia during World War II and preached their doctrine of "Asia for Asians"

After the war Malaysian demands for independence from European domination grew more persuasive; Britain attempted in 1946 to meet these demands by proposing a partly autonomous Malay Union. However, ethnic rivalries and power-sensitive sultans created such enormous tension that the plan was scrapped. In an uncharacteristic display of cooperation, some 41 different Malay groups organized the United Malay National Organization (UMNO) to oppose the British plan. In 1948 a new Federation of Malaya was attempted, which granted considerable freedom within a framework of British supervision, allowed sultans to retain power over their own regions, and placed certain restrictions on the power of the Chinese living in the country.

Opposing any agreement short of full independence, a group of Chinese communists began a guerrilla war, which came to be known as The Emergency, against the government and against capitalist ideology. Lasting for more than a decade, The Emergency, at its peak, involved some 250,000 government troops.

The three main ethnic groups—Malayans, represented by UMNO; Chinese represented by the Malayan Chinese Association, or MCA; and Indians, represented by the Malayan Indian Congress, or MIC—were able to cooperate long enough in 1953 to form a single political party under the leadership of Abdul Rahman. This party demanded and received complete independence for the Federation in 1957, although some areas, such as the oil-rich sultanate of Brunei on the island of Borneo, refused to join the new Federation. Upon independence the new Federation of Malaya (not yet called Malaysia), excluding Singapore and the territories on the island of Borneo, became a member of the British Commonwealth of Nations and was admitted to the United Nations.

In 1963 a new Federation was proposed which included Singapore and the lands on Borneo. Brunei, an Islamic sultanate and British dependency, again refused to join the new Federation. Singapore joined but withdrew in 1965. Thus, what is known as the Federation of Malaysia acquired its current form in 1966 and is known today as a rapidly developing Third World nation that is attempting to govern itself according to democratic principles.

Malaysia's political troubles, however, based on the severe ethnic divisions in the country, remain a constant feature of life. Hundreds of people have been killed in ethnic clashes in Kuala Lumpur, and every election is a test of the ability of the government to maintain the fragile political status quo. This has been particularly difficult in an era of growing Islamic fundamentalism. In control of the government at the moment is a multiracial coalition of some 11 different parties, called the National Front, each threatening to withdraw at any moment over some pressing domestic issue. In addition, Malaysia has had boundary disputes with neighboring nations, particularly the Philippines and Indonesia, both of which have claimed ownership of parts of North Borneo. Between 1963 and 1965 Indonesia conducted raids across the border, and British troops were called in to defend Malaysian claims.

ECONOMIC DEVELOPMENT

Malaysia continues to be known for its abundance of raw materials, especially rubber, tin, petroleum, and timber. Rice, coconut oil, and pepper are also major exports. Malaysia has had to endure the cyclical fluctuations of market demand for its products. In general, however, the economy has prospered since independence was achieved in 1957, thanks particularly to Japan and the United States, which have been eager to acquire Malaysian products. In fact, since 1985 the economy has grown at an average annual rate of nearly 5 percent, faster than both Japan and the United States.

Until 1989 Japan was Malaysia's primary investor, investing millions of dollars each year. Although Taiwan now invests more in Malaysia, and although Japan is perceived as being somewhat selfish with its technology, the Malaysians

| The city of Malacca is established; it becomes a center of trade and Islamic conversion A.D. 1403 | The Portuguese capture Malacca 1511 | The Dutch capture Malacca 1641 | The British obtain Malacca from the Dutch 1824 | Japan captures the Malay Peninsula 1941 | The British establish the Federation of Malaya; communist guerrilla war begins, lasting for a decade 1948 | The Federation of Malaya achieves independence under Prime Minister Tengku Abdul Rahman 1957 | The Federation of Malaysia, including Singapore but not Brunei, is formed 1963 | Singapore leaves the Federation of Malaysia 1965 | Demonstrations for economic and ethnic equality engulf the nation; the New Economic Policy is instituted 1970s |

1980s–1990s

| Malaysia attempts to build an industrial base | Mahathir Mohamad is reelected to the office of prime minister | The New Economic Policy, proclaimed a success, comes to an official end |

value Japanese know-how in doing business. In 1988, for example, Japanese were brought in to manage Malaysia's automobile-manufacturing plant (a joint venture with Mitsubishi Corporation); shortly thereafter the company made a profit for the first time.

Despite its recent successes, however, Malaysia's economy has had serious problems. These stem not from insufficient revenues (until 1990 Malaysia was blessed with an annual budget surplus) but from inequitable distribution. the Malay portion of the population in particular continues to feel economically deprived as compared to the wealthier Chinese and Indian segments. At one time these upper-class households received, on average, 16 times the income of the poorest Malay families. Furthermore, most Malaysians are farmers, and poverty in some of the rural areas has been acute.

Riots in the 1960s and 1970s, involving thousands of college students, were headlined in the Western press as having their basis in ethnicity. This was partly true, but economic equality was the core issue. The government's New Economic Policy (NEP), promulgated in the 1970s, was, like Affirmative Action programs in the United States, an attempt to change the structural barriers that prevented Malays from fully enjoying the benefits of the economic boom. Under Prime Minister Mahathir Mohamad, it was determined that Malays should be assisted until they held a 30-percent interest in Malaysian businesses. In 1990 the government announced that the figure had reached an impressive 20 percent. Unfortunately, many Malays have insufficient capital to maintain ownership in businesses, so the government has been called upon to acquire substantial amounts of Malaysian businesses in order to prevent their being purchased by non-Malays.

In addition, the system of special privileges and opportunities for Malays has had the effect of creating a Malay elite, who now compete with the Chinese and Indian elites economically and thus promote continued ethnic tension. Nonetheless, the goals of the NEP have been attained to a greater extent than most observers thought possible. Educational opportunities for the poor have been increased, farmland development has proceeded on schedule, and the poverty rate has dropped to 17 percent. Perhaps most impressive is that economic targets set for the mid-1990s, such as yearly increases in manufacturing output and the proportion of the gross domestic product derived from manufacturing versus agriculture, had been achieved by 1988.

MALAYSIA'S CURRENT LEADERSHIP

In a polity so fractured as Malaysia's, one would expect rapid turnover among political elites. But Prime Minister Mahathir Mohamad, a Malay, has continued to receive the support of the electorate for more than a decade. His most recent challenge came from the main opposition party, the Chinese Democratic Action Party (DAP) in the 1986 elections, but Mahathir remained firmly in office. The policies that have sustained his reputation as a credible leader include the NEP, with its goals of economic diversification, privatization, and wealth equalization, and his nationalist—but moderate—foreign policy. Malaysia has been an active member of ASEAN and has worked hard to maintain good diplomatic relations with the Western nations, while simultaneously courting Japan and other Pacific Rim nations for foreign investment and export markets (Mahathir's Look East policy).

Success has not been achieved, however, without some questionable practices. The government seems unwilling to regulate economic growth, even though strong voices have been raised against industrialization's deleterious effects on the teak forests and other aspects of the environment. Moreover, the blue-collar workers who are the muscle behind Malaysia's success are prohibited from forming labor unions, and outspoken critics have been silenced. Charges of government corruption are becoming more frequent and more strident. Future Malaysian governments will no doubt have to address these complaints if they wish to maintain the support of the people in this divisive land.

DEVELOPMENT

Malaysia continues to struggle to move its economy away from agriculture. Attempts at industrialization have been successful: Malaysia is now the third-largest producer of semiconductors in the world, and manufacturing now accounts for 24% of the gross domestic product. Still, the average per capita income of Malaysians is much lower than those of Japan and Singapore.

FREEDOM

Malaysia is attempting to govern according to democratic principles. The Parliament consists of a Senate and a House of Representatives, with the government headed by a prime minister and Cabinet. Ethnic rivalries, however, severely hamper the smooth conduct of government and limit individual liberties.

HEALTH/WELFARE

City dwellers have ready access to educational, medical, and social opportunities, but the quality of life declines dramatically in the countryside, where reside 62% of the population. A third of the inhabitants of Malaysia cannot read or write—one of the highest illiteracy rates in the Pacific Rim.

ACHIEVEMENTS

Malaysia has made some impressive economic improvements. The government's New Economic Policy has been effective in achieving a measure of redistribution of wealth, and since 1985 the economy's growth rate has been a stunning 5% per year.

Myanmar (Union of Myanmar)

GEOGRAPHY

Area in Square Kilometers (Miles):
678,500 (261,901) (slightly smaller than Texas)
Capital (Population): Rangoon (2,459,000)
Climate: tropical monsoon and equatorial

PEOPLE

Population
Total: 41,277,000
Annual Growth Rate: 2.0%
Rural/Urban Population Ratio: 76/24
Ethnic Makeup of Population: 68% Burman; 9% Shan; 7% Karen; 4% Rakline; 3% Chinese; 8% Mon, Indian, and others
Languages: 60% Burmese

Health
Life Expectancy at Birth: 53 years (male); 56 years (female)
Infant Mortality Rate (Ratio): 97/1,000
Average Caloric Intake: 106% of FAO minimum
Physicians Available (Ratio): 1/5,120

Religion(s)
85% Buddhist; 15% animist, Muslim, Christian, or others

Education
Adult Literacy Rate: 78%

BUDDHISM

Siddhartha Gautama was born about 563 B.C. in what is today Nepal. He was raised in luxury and was expected to follow in his father's footsteps as a ruler and warrior. At about age 35 Gautama had a sudden insight that so impressed him that people started calling him the Buddha, meaning "the awakened" or "enlightened one." What did the Buddha realize? That life is characterized by pain and separation from the true Way, because people have selfish cravings; and pain and separation can be eliminated by renouncing selfish desires. By following a lifestyle that includes right views, thoughts, speech, action, livelihood, effort, awareness, and concentration a person achieves a state of eternal enlightenment and freedom from cravings and pain, called Nirvana.

Over the centuries Buddha's teachings have been formalized under the aegis of an extensive hierarchy of priests. In Myanmar, where most of the people are Buddhist, these religious authorities, called the Sangha, exercise considerable power, both spiritually and politically.

COMMUNICATION

Telephones: 53,000
Newspapers: 2

TRANSPORTATION

Highways—Kilometers (Miles): 27,000 (16,740)
Railroads—Kilometers (Miles): 3,991 (2,474)
Usable Airfields: 81

GOVERNMENT

Type: military government
Independence Date: January 4, 1948
Head of State: General Saw Maung
Political Parties: National League for Democracy; League for Democracy and Peace; National Unity Party; more than 100 others
Suffrage: universal at 18

MILITARY

Number of Armed Forces: 200,000 plus 73,000 paramilitary personnel
Military Expenditures (% of Central Government Expenditures): 21%
Current Hostilities: none

ECONOMY

Currency ($ U.S. Equivalent): 6.51 kyats = $1
Per Capita Income/GNP: $200/n/a
Inflation Rate: 23%
Natural Resources: crude oil; timber; tin; antimony; zinc; copper; tungsten; lead; coal; marble; limestone; precious stones; natural gas

Agriculture: teak; rice; corn; oilseed; sugarcane; pulses
Industry: agricultural processing; textiles; footwear; wood and wood products; petroleum refining; copper, tin, tungsten, and iron mining; construction materials; pharmaceuticals; fertilizer

FOREIGN TRADE

Exports: $311 million
Imports: $536 million

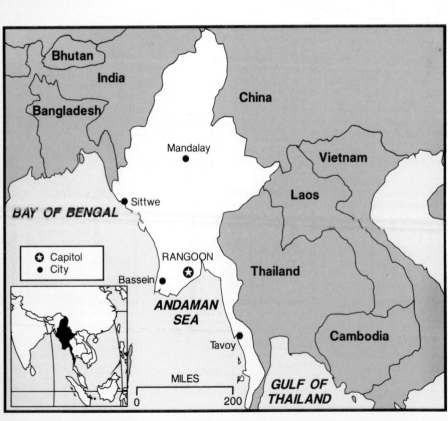

THE CONTROLLED SOCIETY

Myanmar (as Burma was renamed in 1989) is a totalitarian society in which every telephone is owned by the military government, as well as every radio station, every railroad, and all major companies. Tourists are allowed to stay only 2 weeks (for many years the limit was 24 hours), must register with the government, and may stay only at government-approved hotels. The citizens of Myanmar may not leave their country by car or train to visit any of the surrounding countries, because all the roads are closed off by government decree and the railroads terminate at the border. Until a minor liberalization of the economy in 1989, all foreign exports—every grain of rice, every peanut, every piece of lumber—had to be exported by the government rather than by the people who produced them.

Observers attribute this state of affairs to military commanders who overthrew the legitimate government in 1962, but the roots of Myanmar's political and economic dilemma actually go back to 1885, when the British overthrew the Burmese government and declared Burma a colony of Britain. In the 1930s European-educated Burmese college students organized strikes and demonstrations against the British. Seeing that the Japanese Army had successfully toppled other European colonial governments in Asia, the students determined to assist the Japanese during their invasion of the country (in 1941). Once the British had been expelled, however, the students organized the Anti-Fascist People's Freedom League (AFPFL) to oppose Japanese rule.

When the British tried to resume control of Burma after World War II, they found that the Burmese people had given their allegiance to U Aung San, one of the original student leaders. U Aung San and the AFPFL insisted that the British grant full independence to Burma, which they reluctantly did in 1948. So determined were the Burmese to remain free of foreign domination that, unlike most former British colonies, they refused to join the British Commonwealth of Nations, an economic association of former British colonies. This was the first of many decisions that would have the effect of isolating Burma from the global economy.

THE ISOLATIONIST IMPULSE

Unlike Japan, with its nearly homogeneous population and single, national language, Myanmar is a multiethnic state; in fact, only about 60 percent of the people speak Burmese. For hundreds of years ethnic factions have warred against one another for dominance. Upon the withdrawal of the British in 1948 some ethnic groups, particularly the Kachins, the Karens, and the Shans, embraced the communist ideology of change through violent revolution. Their rebellion against the government in the capital city of Rangoon had the effect of removing from government control large portions of the country. Headed by U Nu (U Aung San and several of the original government leaders having been assassinated shortly before independence), the government considered its precarious position and determined that to align itself with the communist forces then ascendent in the People's Republic of China and other parts of Asia would strengthen the hand of the ethnic separatists, whereas to form alliances with the capitalist world would invite a repetition of decades of Western domination. U Nu thus attempted to steer a decidedly neutral course during the Cold War era and to be as tolerant as possible of separatist groups within Burma. Burma refused U.S. economic aid, had very little to do with the warfare afflicting Vietnam and the other Southeast Asian countries, and was not eager to join the Southeast Asian Treaty Organization (SEATO) or the Asian Development Bank.

Some factions of Burmese society were not pleased with U Nu's relatively benign treatment of separatist groups. In 1958 a political impasse allowed Ne Win, a military general, to assume temporary control of the country. National elections were held in 1962, and a democratically elected government was installed in power. Shortly thereafter, however, Ne Win staged a military coup. The military has controlled Burma ever since.

Under Ne Win, competing political parties were banned, the economy was nationalized, and the country's international isolation became even more pronounced. Ne Win even withdrew from the Conference of Nonaligned Nations, although Burma had earlier been one of its leading proponents.

ECONOMIC STAGNATION

Years of ethnic conflict, inflexible socialism, and self-imposed isolation have severely damaged economic growth in Myanmar. Despite an abundance of valuable teak and rubber trees in its forests, sizable supplies of minerals in the mountains to the north, onshore oil, rich farmland in the Irrawaddy Delta, and a reasonably well-educated population (78 percent can read and write), in 1987 the United Nations (UN) declared Burma one of the Least Developed Countries (LDCs) in the world. Debt incurred in the 1970s exacerbated the problem, as did Burma's fear of foreign investment. Thus, by 1988, Burma's per capita income was only $200 a year.

Today Myanmar's industrial base is still very small; some 70 percent of the population of 41 million make their living by farming (rice is a major export) and by fishing. Only 10 percent of Myanmar's gross domestic product (GNP) comes from the manufacturing sector (as compared to, for example, 45 percent in Taiwan). In the absence of a strong economy, black marketeering has increased, as have other forms of illegal economic transactions. For instance, it is estimated that 80 percent of the heroin smuggled into New York City comes from the jungles of Myanmar and northern Thailand, where it is grown and processed by an estimated 10,00 young men calling themselves the Shan United Army.

Over the years the Burmese have been advised by economists to open up their country to foreign investment and to develop the private sector of the economy. They have resisted the former idea, because of their deep-seated fear of foreign domination; and they have similar suspicion of the private sector, because it was formerly controlled almost completely by ethnic minorities (the Chinese and Indians). The government has relied on the public sector to counterbalance the power of the ethnic minorities.

Beginning in 1987, however, the government began to admit publicly that the economy was in serious trouble. To counter massive unrest in the country, the military authorities agreed to permit foreign investment from countries such as Malaysia, South Korea, Singapore, and Thailand and to allow trade with China and Thailand. In 1989 the government signed oil exploration agreements with South Korea, the United States, the Netherlands, Australia, and Japan.

POLITICAL STALEMATE

Despite these reforms, the country remains in a state of turmoil. In 1988 thousands of students participated in 6 months of demonstrations to protest the lack of democracy in Burma and to demand multiparty elections. General Saw Maung brutally suppressed the demonstrators, imprisoning many students and killing some 3,000 of them. He then took control of the government and reluctantly agreed to multiparty elections. Some 170 political parties registered for the elections, which were scheduled for 1990—the first elec-

| Burman people enter the Irrawaddy Valley from China and Tibet 800 B.C. | The city of Pagan (Bagan) becomes the center of Burmese life A.D. 100 | The Portuguese are impressed with Burmese wealth 1500s | The First Anglo-Burmese War 1824-1826 | The Second Anglo-Burmese War 1852 | The Third Anglo-Burmese War results in the loss of Burmese sovereignty 1885 | The Japanese invade Burma 1941 | Burma gains independence from Britain 1948 | General Ne Win takes control of the government in a coup 1962 | The official name of the country is changed to Socialist Republic of the Union of Burma 1974 |

1980s–1990s

| Economic crisis; the prodemocracy movement is crushed | General Saw Maung takes control of the government; Burma's name is changed to Myanmar | The first multi-party elections in 30 years; pro-democracy parties win a big victory; Buddhist monks protest |

tions in 30 years. Among these were the National Unity Party (a new name for the former Burma Socialist Program Party, the only legal party since 1974) and the National League for Democracy, a new party headed by Aung San Suu Kyi, daughter of slain national hero U Aung San.

The campaign was characterized by the same level of military control that had existed in all other aspects of life since the 1960s. Martial law, imposed in 1988, remained in effect; all schools and universities were closed; opposition-party workers were intimidated; and, most significantly, the three most popular opposition leaders were placed under house arrest and barred from campaigning. The United Nations began an investigation of civil-rights abuses during the election, but once again students were at the forefront in opposing these measures. Several students even hijacked a Burmese airliner to demand the release of Aung San Suu Kyi.

As the votes were tallied, it became apparent that the Burmese people were eager to end military rule; the National League for Democracy won 80 percent of the seats in the National Assembly. But the military junta refused to step down, and as of this writing, it remains in control of the government. Hundreds of students who fled the cities during the 1988 crackdown on student demonstrations have now joined rural guerrilla organizations, such as the Burma Communist Party and the Karen National Union, to continue the fight against the military dictatorship. Among those most vigorously opposed to military rule are Buddhist monks. Five months after the elections, monks in the capital city of Rangoon boycotted the government by refusing to conduct religious rituals for soldiers. Tens of thousands of people joined in the boycott. The government responded by threatening to shut down monasteries in the cities of Rangoon and Mandalay.

THE CULTURE OF BUDDHA

For a brief period in the 1960s Buddhism was the official state religion of Burma. Although this status was repealed by the government in order to weaken the power of the Buddhist leadership, or Sangha, vis-à-vis the polity, Buddhism, representing the belief system of 85 percent of the population, remains the single most important cultural force in the country. Even the Burmese alphabet is based, in part, on Pali, the sacred language of Buddhism. Buddhist monks joined with college students after World War II to pressure the British government to withdraw from Burma, and they have brought continual pressure to bear on the current military junta.

Historically, so powerful has been the Buddhist Sangha in Burma that four major dynasties have fallen because of it. This has not been the result of ideological antagonism between church and state (indeed, Burmese rulers have usually been quite supportive of Buddhism) but, rather, because Buddhism soaks up resources that might otherwise go to the government or to economic development. Believers are willing to give money, land, and other resources to the religion, because they believe that such donations will bring them spiritual merit; the more merit one acquires, the better one's life will be the next time one is born. Thus, all over Myanmar, but especially in older cities such as Pagan (Bagan), one can find large, elaborate Buddhist temples, monuments, or monasteries, some of them built by kings and other royals on huge, untaxed parcels of land. These monuments drained resources from the government but brought to the donor unusual amounts of spiritual merit. As Burmese scholar Michael Aung-Thwin explains it, "One built the largest temple because one was spiritually superior, and one was spiritually superior because one built the largest temple."

DEVELOPMENT

Primarily an agricultural nation, Myanmar has a poorly developed industrial sector. Until recently the government forbade foreign investment and severely restricted tourism. In 1989, recognizing that the economy was on the brink of collapse, the government permitted foreign investment and signed contracts with Japan and others for oil exploration.

FREEDOM

Myanmar is a military dictatorship. Until 1989 only the Burma Socialist Program Party was permitted. Other parties, while now legal, are intimidated by the military junta. The democratically elected National League for Democracy has not been permitted to assume office. The government has also restricted the activities of the Buddhist Church.

HEALTH/WELFARE

The Myanmar government provides free health care and government pensions to citizens, but the quality and availability are erratic. Malnourishment and preventable diseases are common, and infant mortality is high. Overpopulation is not a problem; Myanmar is one of the most sparsely populated nations in Asia.

ACHIEVEMENTS

Myanmar is known for the beauty of its Buddhist architecture. Pagodas and other Buddhist monuments and temples dot many of Myanmar's cities, especially Pagan, one of Myanmar's earliest cities. Politically, it is notable that the country was able to remain free of the warfare that engulfed much of Indochina during the 1960s and 1970s.

New Zealand

GEOGRAPHY
Area in Square Kilometers (Miles): 268,680 (98,874) (about the size of Colorado)
Capital (Population): Wellington (328,000)
Climate: temperate; sharp regional contrasts

PEOPLE
Population
Total: 3,296,000
Annual Growth Rate: 0.4%
Rural/Urban Population (Ratio): 16/84
Ethnic Makeup of Population: 88% white; 9% Maori; 3% Pacific Islander
Languages: official: English; others spoken:

Health
Life Expectancy at Birth: 72 years (male); 78 years (female)
Infant Mortality Rate (Ratio): 10/1,000
Average Caloric Intake: 132% of FAO minimum
Physicians Available (Ratio): 1/522

Religion(s)
81% Christian; 18% unaffiliated; 1% others

Education
Adult Literacy Rate: 99%

COMMUNICATION
Telephones: 2,110,000
Newspapers: 34 dailies

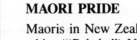

MAORI PRIDE

Maoris in New Zealand have, for the most part, been assimilated into white ("Pakeha") New Zealand culture: they speak English, some use the birth-control pill for family planning, and a few have become millionaires by buying and selling real estate. Some are married to whites, others to Japanese, and others to Indians. Yet pride in being Maori is coming back. Not only are white schools teaching more about Maori culture, but Maoris themselves are setting up language "nests" or preschools, open to both Maoris and whites, where only Maori is spoken. Maori-inspired clothing designs have become fashionable, as has the Maori custom of facial tattooing.

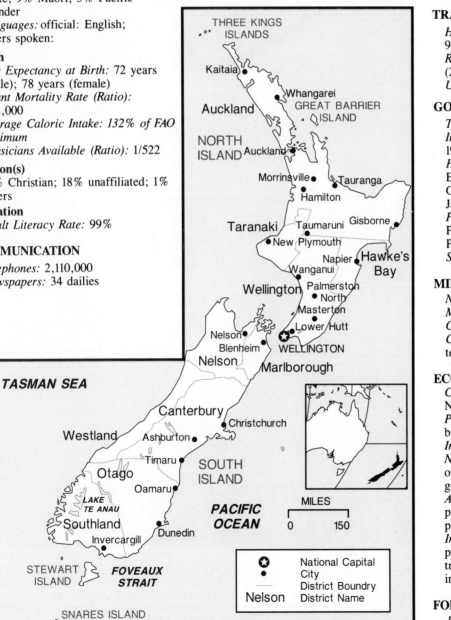

TRANSPORTATION
Highways—Kilometers (Miles): 92,648 (57,441)
Railroads—Kilometers (Miles): 4,716 (2,923)
Usable Airfields: 157

GOVERNMENT
Type: parliamentary democracy
Independence Date: September 26, 1970
Head of State: Chief of State Queen Elizabeth II, represented by Governor General Paul Reeves; Prime Minister James Bolger
Political Parties: New Zealand Labor Party; National Party; Democratic Party; Socialist Unity Party
Suffrage: universal at 18

MILITARY
Number of Armed Forces: 12,548
Military Expenditures (% of Central Government Expenditures): 2.1%
Current Hostilities: none; disputed territorial claim in Antarctica

ECONOMY
Currency ($ U.S. Equivalent): 1.65 New Zealand dollars = $1
Per Capita Income/GNP: $11,126/$37 billion
Inflation Rate: 10%
Natural Resources: natural gas; iron ore; sand; coal; timber; hydropower; gold; limestone
Agriculture: wool; meat; dairy products; wheat; barley; potatoes; pulses; fruits; vegetables; fishing
Industry: food processing; wood and paper products; textiles; machinery; transportation equipment; banking; insurance; tourism; mining

FOREIGN TRADE
Exports: $8.9 billion
Imports: $7.5 billion

ITS PLACE IN THE WORLD

New Zealand, like Australia, is decidedly an anomaly among Pacific Rim countries. More than 90 percent of the population are of British descent, English is the official language, and most people, even many of the original Maori inhabitants, are Christians. Great Britain claimed the beautiful, mountainous islands officially in 1840, after agreeing to respect the property rights of Maoris, most of whom lived on the North Island.

New Zealand, although largely self-governing since 1907 and fully independent as of 1947, has always maintained very close ties with the United Kingdom. It has, in fact, attempted to re-create British culture—customs, architecture, even vegetation—in the South Pacific. So close were the links with England in the 1940s, for example, that England purchased fully 88 percent of New Zealand's exports (mostly agricultural and dairy products), while 60 percent of New Zealand's imports came from England. And believing itself to be very much a part of the British Empire, New Zealand always sided with the Western nations on matters of military defense.

These efforts to maintain close contact with Great Britain have not derived entirely from the cultural roots of the inhabitants. They have also been encouraged by the extreme geographical isolation of the country from the mainstream of European, North American, and Asian activity. Until the 1940s New Zealand had always wanted the British to increase their involvement in Asia and the South Pacific (by acquiring more islands or building up naval bases), so as to improve the chance that the United Kingdom would be in a position to come to the aid of New Zealand in a time of crisis. New Zealand had involved itself somewhat in the affairs of nearby islands in the late 1800s and early 1900s. But the purpose was not to assist weaker islands but, rather, to extend the power of the British Empire and put New Zealand in the middle of a mini-empire of its own. New Zealand annexed the Cook Islands in 1901 and took over German Samoa in 1914. In 1925 it assumed formal control over the atoll group known as the Tokelau Islands.

REGIONAL RELIANCE DEVELOPS

During World War II (or, as the Japanese call it, the Pacific War), Japan's rapid conquest of the Malay Archipelago, its seizure of many South Pacific islands, and its plans to attack Australia demonstrated

to New Zealanders the futility of relying on the British to guarantee their security. After the war, and for the first time in its history, New Zealand began to pay serious attention to the real needs and ambitions of the peoples nearby rather than to focus on Great Britain. In 1944 and again in 1947 New Zealand joined with Australia

and other colonial nations to create regional associations on behalf of the South Pacific Islands. One of the organizations, the South Pacific Commission, has itself spawned many regional subassociations dealing with trade, education, migration, and cultural and economic development. Generally neglecting the islands it had

(The Peabody Museum of Salem photo)

Maoris occupied New Zealand before the European settlers moved there. It did not take the Maoris long to see that the newcomers were intent on depriving them of their land, but it wasn't until the 1920s that the government finally took control of these unscrupulous land-grabbing practices. Today the Maoris have created a lifestyle that preserves key parts of their traditional culture while incorporating the skills necessary for survival in a white world.

| Maoris, probably from Tahiti, settle the islands **1300s** A.D. | New Zealand is discovered by Dutch navigator A. J. Tasman **1642** | Captain James Cook explores the islands **1769** | Great Britain declares sovereignty **1840** | A gold rush attracts new immigrants **1865** | New Zealand becomes an almost independent dominion of Great Britain **1907** |

controlled during its imperial phase in the early 1900s, New Zealand cooperated with the United Nations in their decolonization during the 1960s (although Tokelau, by choice, remains under the control of New Zealand) while at the same time increasing development assistance. New Zealand's first alliance with Asian nations came in 1954, when it joined the Southeast Asian Treaty Organization (SEATO).

New Zealand's new international focus certainly did not mean the end of cooperation with its traditional allies, however. In fact, the common threat of the Japanese during World War II had strengthened cooperation between Australia and the United States to the extent that, in 1951, New Zealand joined a three-way, regional security agreement known as ANZUS (for Australia, New Zealand, and the United States). Moreover, because the United States was, at war's end, a Pacific/Asian power, any agreement with the United States was likely to bring New Zealand into more, rather than less, contact with Asia and the Pacific. Indeed, New Zealand sent troops to assist in all of the United States' military involvements in Asia: the occupation of Japan in 1945, the Korean War in 1950, and the Vietnam War in the 1960s. And, as a member of the British Commonwealth, it sent troops in the 1950s and 1960s to fight Malaysian communists and Indonesian insurgents.

NEW ZEALAND'S NEW INTERNATIONALISM

Beginning in the 1970s, especially when the Labor Party of Prime Minister Norman Kirk was in power, New Zealand shifted decidedly away from its British Empire orientation and toward a more regional alignment. Under Labor, New Zealand defined its sphere of interest and responsibility as the South Pacific, where it hoped to be seen as a protector and benefactor of smaller states. Of immediate concern to many island nations was the issue of nuclear testing in the Pacific. Both the United States and France had undertaken tests by exploding nuclear devices on tiny Pacific atolls. In the 1960s

the United States had ceased these tests, but France continued. New Zealand argued on this issue on behalf of the smaller islands before the United Nations, but France did not stop the testing. Eventually, the desire to end testing congealed into the more comprehensive position that the entire Pacific should be declared a nuclear-free zone. Not only testing but also the transport of nuclear weapons through the area would be prohibited under the plan.

New Zealand's Labor government issued a ban on the docking of ships with nuclear weapons in New Zealand, despite the fact that such ships were a part of the ANZUS security agreement. When the National Party regained control of the government in the late 1970s, the nuclear ban was revoked, and the foreign policy of New Zealand tipped again toward its traditional allies. The National government argued that, as a signatory to ANZUS, New Zealand was obligated to open its docks to U.S. nuclear ships. However, under the subsequent Labor government of Prime Minister David Lange, New Zealand once again began to flex its muscles over the nuclear issue. Lange, like his Labor predecessors, was determined to create a foreign policy based on moral rather than legal rationales. In 1985 a U.S. destroyer was denied permission to call at a New Zealand port, even though its presence there was due to joint ANZUS military exercises. Because the United States refused to say whether or not its ship carried nuclear weapons, New Zealand insisted that the ship could not dock. Diplomatic efforts to resolve the stand-off were unsuccessful, and in 1986 New Zealand, claiming it was not fearful of foreign attack, formally withdrew from ANZUS.

The issue of superpower use of the Pacific for nuclear-weapons testing is still of major concern to the New Zealand government. The nuclear-test-ban treaty signed by the United States in 1963 has limited its involvement in that regard, but France has continued to test atmospheric weapons, and both the United States and Japan have proposed using uninhabited Pacific atolls to dispose of nuclear waste.

In the 1990s a new issue has come to the fore: nerve-gas disposal. As tensions have eased between the superpowers, the U.S. military has proposed disposing of most of its European stockpile of nerve gas on an atoll in the Pacific. The atoll is located within the trust territory granted to the United States at the conclusion of World War II. The plan is to burn the gas safely away from areas of human habitation, but those islanders living closest (albeit hundreds of miles away) worry that residues from the process could contaminate the air and damage humans, plants, and animals. The religious leaders of Melanesia, Micronesia, and Polynesia have condemned the plan not only on environmental grounds, but also on the ground that outside powers should not be permitted to use the Pacific region without the consent of the inhabitants there—a position with which the Labor government of New Zealand strongly concurs.

ECONOMIC CHALLENGES

The New Zealand government's new foreign-policy orientation has caught the attention of observers around the world, but more urgent to New Zealanders themselves is the state of their own economy. Until the 1970s New Zealand had been able to count on a nearly guaranteed export market in the United Kingdom for its dairy and agricultural products. Moreover, cheap local energy supplies as well as inexpensive oil from the Middle East had produced several decades of steady improvement in the standard of living. Whenever the economy showed signs of being sluggish, the government would artificially protect certain industries to ensure full employment.

All of this came to a halt beginning in 1973, when Britain joined the European Community (EC) and when the Organization of Petroleum Exporting Countries (OPEC) sent the world into its first oil shock. New Zealand actually has the potential of near self-sufficiency in oil, but the easy availability of Middle East oil over the years prevented the full development of local oil and gas reserves. As for exports, New Zealand had to find new

Socialized
medicine is
implemented
1941

New Zealand
becomes fully
independent

New Zealand
backs creation
of the South
Pacific
Commission
1947

Restructuring of
export markets
1950s

New Zealand
forges foreign
policy more
independent of
traditional allies
1970s

1980s–1990s

The Labor Party
comes to power

New Zealand
abrogates the
ANZUS treaty

outlets for its agricultural products, which it did by contracting with various countries throughout the Pacific Rim. Currently a third of New Zealand's trade is within the Pacific Rim. In the transition to these new markets, farmers complained that the manufacturing sector—intentionally protected by the government as a way of diversifying New Zealand's reliance on agriculture—was getting unfair favorable treatment. Subsequent changes in government policy toward industry resulted in a new phenomenon for New Zealand: unemployment. Moreover, New Zealand had constructed a rather elaborate social-welfare system since World War II, so regardless of whether economic growth was high or low, social-welfare checks still had to be sent. In the 1970s New Zealanders, for the first time, began to notice a decline in their standard of living, and 2 decades later the economy remains stagnant. New Zealand's economic growth rate is the lowest of all Pacific Rim countries (only 1.1 percent per year, as compared to more than 9 percent in Thailand and Singapore); inflation, at about 10 percent per year, is higher than in any other country in the region; and its per capita income is lower than in Hong Kong, Australia, and Japan.

New Zealanders are well aware of Japan's economic strength and the potential it has for benefiting their own economy through joint ventures, loans, and trade.

Yet they also worry that Japanese wealth may constitute a symbol of New Zealand's declining strength as a culture. For instance, in the 1980s as Japanese tourists began traveling *en masse* to New Zealand, complaints were raised about the quality of New Zealand's hotels. Unable to find the funds for a massive upgrading of the hotel industry, New Zealand agreed to allow Japan to build its own hotels; they reasoned that the local construction industry could use an economic boost and that the better hotels would encourage well-heeled Japanese to spend even more tourist dollars in the country. However, they also believed that with the Japanese owning the hotels, New Zealanders might be relegated to low-level jobs.

Concern about their status vis-à-vis nonwhites had never been much of an issue to Anglo-Saxon New Zealanders; they always assumed that nonwhites were inferior. Many settlers of the 1800s believed in the Social Darwinistic philosophy that the Maori and other brown- and black-skinned cultures would gradually succumb to their European betters. It did not take long for the Maoris to realize that, land guarantees notwithstanding, the whites intended to deprive them of their land and culture. Violent resistance to these intentions occurred in the 1800s, but Maori land holdings continued to be gobbled up, usually deceptively, by white farmers and sheep herders. Government

control of these unscrupulous practices was lax until the 1920s. Since that time many Maoris (whose population has increased to about 300,000) have intentionally sought to create a lifestyle that preserves key parts of traditional culture while incorporating the skills necessary for survival in a white world.

Now, however, Maoris and whites alike feel the social leveling that is the consequence of years of economic stagnation. Moreover, both worry that the superior financial strength of the Japanese and newly industrializing Asian and Southeast Asian peoples may diminish in some way the standing of their own cultures. The Maoris, complaining recently about Japanese net fishing and its damage to their own fishing industry, have a history of accommodation and adjustment to those who would rule over them; but for the whites, submissiveness, even if it is imposed from afar and is largely financial in nature, will be a new and challenging experience.

DEVELOPMENT

Government protection of manufacturing has allowed this sector to grow at the expense of agriculture. Nevertheless, New Zealand continues to export large quantities of dairy products, wool, meat, fruits, and wheat. Full development of the Maui oil and gas deposits could alleviate New Zealand's unnecessary dependency on foreign oil.

FREEDOM

New Zealand partakes of the democratic heritage of English common law and subscribes to all the human-rights protections that other Western nations have endorsed. Maoris, originally deprived of much of their land, are now guaranteed the same legal rights as whites. Social discrimination against Maoris is much milder than with many other colonized peoples.

HEALTH/WELFARE

New Zealand established old-age pensions as early as 1898. Child-welfare programs were started in 1907, followed by the Social Security Act of 1938, which augmented the earlier benefits and added a minimum-wage requirement and a 40-hour work week. A national health program was begun in 1941.

ACHIEVEMENTS

New Zealand is notable for its efforts on behalf of the smaller islands of the Pacific. In addition to advocating a nuclear-free Pacific, New Zealand has promoted interisland trade and has established free trade agreements with Western Samoa, the Cook Islands, and Niue. It provides educational and employment opportunities to islanders who reside within its borders.

North Korea (Democratic People's Republic of Korea)

GEOGRAPHY

Area in Square Kilometers (Miles):
120,540 (44,358) (slightly smaller than Mississippi)
Capital (Population): P'yongyang (2,639,000)
Climate: temperate

PEOPLE

Population
Total: 21,293,000
Annual Growth Rate: 1.7%
Rural/Urban Population (Ratio): 38/62
Ethnic Makeup of Population: Korean
Language: Korean

Health
Life Expectancy at Birth: 69 years (male); 75 years (female)
Infant Mortality Rate (Ratio): 27/1,000
Average Caloric Intake: n/a
Physicians Available (Ratio): 1/370

Religion(s)
Buddhism and Confucianism

Education
Adult Literacy Rate: 95% est.

COMMUNICATION

Telephones: 30,000
Newspapers: 11

FROM WHENCE THE KOREAN NATION?

According to Korean myth, in 2333 B.C. the god Hanul took human form and descended from heaven to Paektusan Mountain, in what is now North Korea. He was a god with three qualities: as a teacher, a king, and a creator. He found tribes of people living on the Korean Peninsula and remained with them for 93 years, teaching them and creating the laws and customs of the Korean people. Eventually he returned to heaven, but his influence was so powerful that until recent times, Korean dates and calendars were reckoned from the year of his arrival. At one time the worship of Hanul was the primary religion of Korea, but today that faith has been replaced by numerous other religions.

TRANSPORTATION

Highways—Kilometers (Miles): 20,280 (12,573)
Railroads—Kilometers (Miles): 4,535 (2,811)
Usable Airfields: 50

GOVERNMENT

Type: communist state
Independence Date: September 9, 1948
Head of State: President Kim Il-sŏng; Premier Yon Hyong-muk
Political Parties: Korean Workers' Party (only legal party)
Suffrage: universal at 17

MILITARY

Number of Armed Forces:
Military Expenditures (% of Central Government Expenditures): 22%
Current Hostilities: continuing border conflicts with South Korea

ECONOMY

Currency ($ U.S. Equivalent): 0.97 won = $1
Per Capita Income/GNP: $1,180/$20 billion
Inflation Rate: n/a
Natural Resources: hydroelectric power; oil; iron ore; copper; lead; zinc; coal; uranium; manganese; gold; salt
Agriculture: rice; corn; potatoes; soybeans; pulses; livestock and livestock products; fish
Industry: machinery; military products; electric power; chemicals; mining; metallurgy; textiles; food processing

FOREIGN TRADE

Exports: $2.4 billion
Imports: $3.1 billion

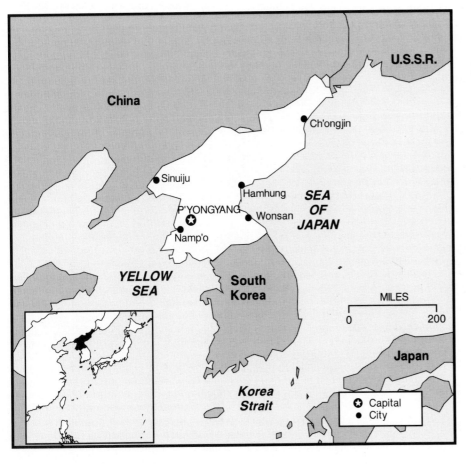

A COUNTRY APART

The area we now call North Korea has, at different times in Korea's long history, been separated from the South. In the fifth century A.D. the Koguryo Kingdom in the North was distinct from the Shilla, Paekche, and Kaya Kingdoms of the South. Later the Parhae Kingdom in the North remained separate from the expanded Shilla Kingdom in the South. Thus, the division of Korea in 1945 into two unequal parts was not without precedent. Yet this time, the very different paths of development that the North and South have taken render the division more poignant and, to those separated without hope of reunion, more emotionally painful.

With the strong backing of the Soviet Union, North Korea, under the leadership of Kim Il Sung, pursued in the mid-1940s a hardline communist policy for both political and economic development. At the end of the war with Japan, taking advantage of the temporary division of the nation to establish a communist buffer state between itself and the capitalist West, the Soviet Union, which had entered the war against Japan just eight opportunistic days before the Japanese surrender, quickly moved troops into position above the 38th Parallel, the line dividing areas of temporary occupation by U.S. and Soviet forces. Headquarters were established in the northern city of P'yongyang, and when United Nations representatives arrived in Korea in 1948 to oversee elections and ease the transition to an independent Korea, the Soviet military refused to allow them access to areas above the 38th Parallel. The 38th Parallel came to represent not only the division of Korea but also the boundary of the free world from the communists. Elections proceeded in the South, and the beginning of two separate political systems was under way.

THE KOREAN WAR (1950–1953)

Although not pleased with the idea of division, the South, without a strong army, resigned itself to the reality of the moment. In the North, a well-trained military, with Soviet and Chinese help, began preparations for a full-scale invasion of the South. The North attacked in June 1950, shortly after U.S. troops had vacated the South, and quickly overran most of the Korean Peninsula. The South Korean government requested the aid of the United Nations, which dispatched personnel from 19 nations, under the command of U.S. General Douglas MacArthur. (A U.S. intervention was ordered on June 27 by President Harry Truman.)

MacArthur's troops advanced against the North's armies and by October were in control of most of the peninsula. However, with massive Chinese help, the North once again moved south. In response, UN troops decided to inflict heavy destruction on the North through the use of jet fighter/bomber planes. Whereas South Korea was primarily agricultural, North Korea was the industrialized sector of the peninsula. Bombing of the North's industrial targets severely damaged the economy, forcing several million North Koreans to flee south to escape both the war and the communist dictatorship under which they found themselves.

Eventually the UN troops recaptured South Korea's capital, Seoul. Realizing that further fighting would lead to an expanded Asian war, the two sides agreed to ceasefire talks. They signed a truce in 1953 which established a 2.5-mile-wide demilitarized zone (DMZ) for 155 miles across the peninsula and more or less along the former 38th Parallel division. The Korean War took the lives of more than 54,000 American soldiers, 58,000

(UPI/Bettmann photo by Norman Williams)

The Korean War evolved with the communist-backed North Koreans attacking the South after U.S. troops pulled out in 1949. The North Koreans overwhelmed the South and, in response, the United Nations, under U.S. General Douglas MacArthur, dispatched armed personnel. The war ground on for 3 years and resulted in a ceasefire but no declared peace; officially, the two Koreas are still in a state of war. Pictured above are U.S. Marines, with captured North Koreans.

South Koreans, and 500,000 North Koreans—but when it was over, both sides occupied about the same territory as they had at the beginning. Yet because neither side has ever declared peace, the two countries remain officially in a state of war. The borders of the two Koreas, like the borders of wartorn Cambodia, are some of the most volatile areas in Asia.

Four decades after the Korean War, scholars are still debating whether it should be called the United States' first losing war and whether or not the bloodshed was really necessary. To understand the Korean War, one must remember that in the eyes of the world it was more than a civil war amongst different kinds of Koreans. The United Nations, and particularly the United States, saw North Korea's aggression against the South as the first step in the eventual communization of the whole of Asia. Just a few months before North Korea attacked, China had fallen to the communist forces of Mao Zedong, and communist guerrilla activity was being reported throughout Southeast Asia. The "Red Scare" frightened many Americans, and witchhunting for suspected communist sympathizers—a college professor who might have taught about Karl Marx in class or a news reporter who might have praised the educational reforms of a communist country—became the everyday preoccupation of such groups as the John Birch Society and the supporters of U.S. Senator Joseph McCarthy.

In this highly charged atmosphere it was relatively easy for the U.S. military to promote a war whose aim it was to contain communism. Containment rather than defeat of the enemy was the policy of choice, because the West was weary after battling Germany and Japan in World War II. The containment policy also underlay the United States' approach to Vietnam. Practical though it may have been, this policy denied Americans the opportunity of feeling satisfied in victory, since there was to be no victory, just a stalemate. Thus, the roots of the United States' dissatisfaction with the conduct of the Vietnam War actually began in the policies shaping the response to North Korea's offensive in 1950. North Korea was indeed contained, but the communizing impulse of the North remains unabated.

TENSIONS PERSIST

South Korea claims to have discovered four secret tunnels which were excavated underneath the DMZ by North Korea to facilitate spying activities or an armed invasion. Sporadic violence along the border has left patrolling soldiers dead and tensions high. The assassination of former South Korean President Park Chung Hee and attempts on the lives of other members of the South Korean government have been attributed to North Korea, as was the bombing of Korean Airlines Flight 858 in 1987. So wary of the North are South Korean authorities that advocacy of any cause favored by the North can result in arrest. A number of South Koreans have been arrested for spying for the North, and the well-known dissident and head of the Unification Church, Reverend Moon Sun Myung, has been arrested for illegally traveling to North Korea for the purpose of hastening reunification.

The North, seeing in the growing demand for free speech in the South a chance to further its aim of communizing the peninsula, has been angered at the brutal suppression of dissidents by the South Korean authorities. Although the North's argument is bitterly ironic, given its own brutal suppression of human rights, it is nonetheless accurate in its view that the government in the South has been blatantly dictatorial. To suppress opponents, the South Korean government has, among other things, abducted its own students from Europe, abducted opposition leader Kim Dae Jung from Japan, tortured dissidents, and violently silenced demonstrators. All of this is said to be necessary because of the need for unity in the face of the threat from the North, although, as pointed out by scholar Gavan McCormack, the South seems to use the North's threat as an excuse for maintaining a rigid dictatorial system.

In this atmosphere, it is not surprising that the formal reunification talks begun in 1971 have produced little. The North insists, among many other things, that the talks cannot proceed until South Korea stops participating in joint military exercises with the United States and repeals its anticommunist laws. Some progress was made in 1985, when North Korea and South Korea agreed to brief exchange visits of 100 residents who had been separated by the war. This was the first time that the border had been opened in 40 years. And in 1990 North Korea returned to the United States the remains of five American soldiers killed during the Korean War—an act that may signal North Korea's willingness to engage in meaningful dialogue with the West.

Some nearby countries seem to prefer to maintain the status quo. For instance, some Japanese argue that it is in Japan's national interest to keep the two Koreas divided, so as to retard the growth of South Korea's already competitive economy. Still, most people welcome any movement toward North-South dialogue.

THE CHANGING INTERNATIONAL LANDSCAPE

North Korea has good reason to promote better relations with the West. In 1989 South Korea initiated trading relationships with the Soviet Bloc countries of Eastern Europe and even established diplomatic relations with some of them. At the same time the Soviet Union indicated its desire to reduce its military expenditures worldwide. These events may mean that unless North Korea comes out of its isolation from the West, it may find itself more and more alone in world politics, and certainly in world trade.

Nevertheless, it is not likely that North Koreans will quickly retreat from the communist model of development they have espoused for so long. For one thing, the North Korean economy is tightly linked with those of the two leading communist nations, China and the Soviet Union. Foreign aid from these two benefactors helped North Korea to rebuild its roads, power plants, and industries, while labor shortages caused by the massive southward migration during the war were overcome in part by new residents from China and ethnic Koreans from Manchuria.

What is more, many North Koreans are strongly committed to the Marxist-Leninist ideology of the Soviet Union and the Maoist ideology of communist China. Particularly strong is the belief in *juche*, or self-reliance, a term that implies the complete absence of influence from outside cultures, especially "imperialistic" ones. Nurturing this belief from the beginning has been North Korean leader Kim Il-sŏng, whom many North Koreans call Great Leader. In power since 1945, Kim is the longest-governing ruler in the communist world. Kim had been a communist guerrilla fighting against the Japanese and in the 1940s had spent 4 years in exile in the Soviet Union. During his tenure he has promoted the development of heavy industries, the collectivization of agriculture, and the linkage of North Korea militarily with China and the Soviet Union. Governing with an iron hand, he has seen to it that his people eschew in their personal attire and private lives any tendency to behave like people in the "decadent" West. He has also kept international tensions high by continuing to assert North Korea's intention of communizing the South. Unlike communist

Kim Il-sŏng comes to power **1945**	The People's Democratic Republic of Korea is created **1948**	The Korean War begins **1950**	A truce is arranged between North Korea and UN troops **1953**	A U.S. spy boat, the *Pueblo*, is seized by North Korea **1968**	A U.S. spy plane is shot down over North Korea **1969**	Reunification talks begin **1971**	**1980s–1990s**

The border is opened temporarily for brief exchange visits by separated relatives

North Korea hosts a world conference of leftist activists

Kim Il-sŏng, at age 78, is reelected

leaders in Eastern Europe, Kim still commands the respect of those around him. In 1990, at age 78 and despite rumors that his son Kim Chong-il might take the reins of power, he was reinstated for another term.

With Kim still in charge, it is not likely that bold policy changes will be forthcoming. Still, North Korean officials know that the recent diplomatic initiatives of the South require a response. Responding to Seoul's overwhelmingly successful hosting of the 1988 Summer Olympics, P'yongyang sponsored the World Youth and Student Festival, a political gathering of left-leaning activists from around the world. Approximately 15,000 people attended, including some 90 Americans. Never before has North Korea allowed so many foreigners, including journalists, into its country. Similarly, in 1990 North Korea announced that it would open a small stretch of the heavily guarded border with the South on August 15 (the day in 1945 when the Japanese left Korea after 35 years of colonial control). South Korea proposed the same thing, but neither side actually followed through.

Clearly, the North Korean government is hoping that these actions will bring it some badly needed international goodwill. But more than good public relations will be needed if North Korea is to prosper in the new, post–Cold War climate in which it can no longer rely on the generosity or moral support of the Soviet Union and its allies in Eastern Europe. When communism was introduced in North Korea in 1945, the government nationalized

major companies and steered economic development toward heavy industry. In contrast, the South concentrated on heavy industry to balance its agricultural sector until the late 1970s but then geared the economy toward meeting consumer demand. Thus, the standard of living in the North for the average resident remains far behind that of the South, and unless a broader trading front is opened up, the North will continue to lag behind.

RECENT TRENDS

There is evidence that some liberalization is taking place within North Korea. In 1988 the government drafted a law that would allow foreign companies to establish joint ventures inside North Korea. Tourism is also being promoted as a way of earning foreign currency, and recently the government permitted two small Christian churches to be established. Nevertheless, years of a totally controlled economy in the North and shifting international alliances indicate many difficult years ahead for North Korea. Moreover, the bad blood between North and South would suggest only the slowest possible reconciliation of the world's most troubled peninsula.

Although political reunification seems to be years away, social changes are becoming evident everywhere as a new generation, unfamiliar with war, comes to adulthood. Young women are spending more time at the hair stylist and are challenging tradition by wearing brightly colored Western-style clothing. Young couples who only a few

years ago would have submitted to their parents' wishes about whom to marry now prefer to select their own mates. Outward signs of affection which were traditionally discouraged—such as holding hands in public or going on dates after work—are now becoming an accepted part of North Korean life.

Part of the reason for these changes is that North Koreans are being exposed to outside sources of news and ideas. In the past North Korean-made radios were not equipped to tune in anything but local stations. Now many North Koreans own radios that receive signals from other countries. South Korean stations are now heard in the North, as are news programs from the Voice of America. Modern North Korean history, however, is one of repression and control, first by the Japanese and then by the Kim government, who used the same police surveillance apparatus as did the Japanese during their 35-year occupation of the peninsula. It is not likely, therefore, that a massive push for democracy will be forthcoming soon from a people long accustomed to dictatorship. North Korea in the foreseeable future will remain a country apart.

DEVELOPMENT

Already more industrialized than South Korea at the time of the Korean War, North Korea built on this foundation with massive assistance from China and the Soviet Union. Heavy industry was emphasized, however, to the detriment of consumer goods. Economic isolation presages difficult times ahead.

FREEDOM

Kim Il-sŏng's mainline communist approach has meant that the human rights commonplace in the West have never been experienced by North Koreans. Suppression of dissidents, a controlled press, and restrictions on travel have kept North Koreans isolated from the world.

HEALTH/WELFARE

Under the Kim government, illiteracy has been greatly reduced, and North Koreans have access to free medical care, schooling, and old-age pensions. Government housing is available at low cost, but shoppers are often confronted with empty shelves and low-quality goods.

ACHIEVEMENTS

North Korea has developed its resources of aluminum, cement, and iron into solid industries for the production of tools and machinery while developing military superiority over South Korea, despite a population numbering less than half that of South Korea.

Papua New Guinea (Independent State of Papua New Guinea)

GEOGRAPHY

Area in Square Kilometers (Miles):
461,690 (178,612) (slightly larger than California)
Capital (Population): Port Moresby (152,000)
Climate: tropical

PEOPLE

Population
Total: 3,823,000
Annual Growth Rate: 3.5%
Rural/Urban Population Ratio: 86/14
Languages: 715 indigenous languages; English; pidgin English; Motu
Ethnic Makeup of Population: predominantly Melanesian and Papuan; some Negrito, Micronesian, and Polynesian

Health
Life Expectancy at Birth: 54 years (male); 56 years (female)
Infant Mortality Rate (Ratio): 68/1,000
Average Caloric Intake: 85% of FAO minimum
Physicians Available (Ratio): 1/14,040

Religion(s)
nominal Christians; indigenous beliefs

Education
Adult Literacy Rate: 32%

UNREST IN BOUGAINVILLE

In 1988 residents of the Papua New Guinea island of Bougainville, where many World War II battles were fought, revolted against a large Australian-owned, open-pit copper mine. The mine was closed, and the rebels, many of whom were armed with bow and arrows, declared Bougainville an independent nation.

Prime Minister Rabbie Namaliu's government in Port Moresby responded by imposing an economic blockade and cutting off electricity service to the island. Later battles with government troops ended in death for many people. New Zealand sponsored peace talks between the rebels and the government, and an agreement was reached in August 1990; the government lifted the blockade and restored electricity. In early 1991, however, violence again erupted, and dozens of people were killed. Amnesty International has claimed that both sides have acted with undue violence. The issue remains unresolved.

COMMUNICATION

Telephones: 51,700
Newspapers: 1

TRANSPORTATION

Highways—Kilometers (Miles): 19,200 (11,904)
Railroads—Kilometers (Miles): ——
Usable Airfields: 455

GOVERNMENT

Type: parliamentary democracy
Independence Date: September 16, 1975
Head of State: Prime Minister Rabbie Namaliu
Political Parties: Pangu Party; People's Progress Party; United Party; Papua Besena; National Party; Melanesian Alliance
Suffrage: universal at 18

MILITARY

Number of Armed Forces: 3,200
Military Expenditures (% of Central Government Expenditures): 1.3%
Current Hostilities: none

ECONOMY

Currency ($ U.S. Equivalent): 1.15 kina = $1
Per Capita Income/GNP: $770/$2.5 billion
Inflation Rate: 5%
Natural Resources: gold; copper; silver; natural gas; timber; oil potential
Agriculture: coffee; cocoa; coconuts; palm kernels; tea; rubber; sweet potatoes; fruit; vegetables; poultry; pork
Industry: copra crushing; palm-oil processing; wood processing and production; mining; construction; tourism

FOREIGN TRADE

Exports: $1.4 billion
Imports: $1.2 billion

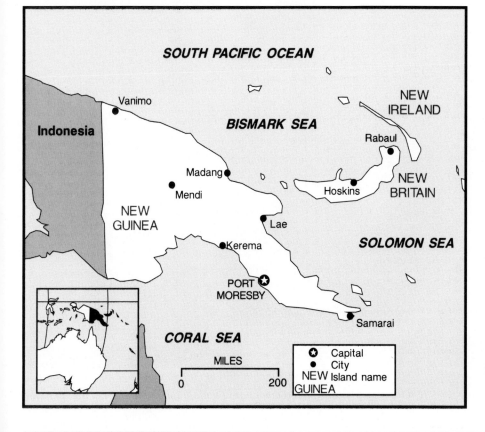

SOUTH PACIFIC OCEAN
Vanimo
Indonesia
BISMARK SEA
NEW IRELAND
Rabaul
Madang
Mendi
Hoskins
NEW BRITAIN
NEW GUINEA
Lae
Kerema
SOLOMON SEA
PORT MORESBY
Samarai
CORAL SEA
MILES
0   200
⊕ Capital
● City
NEW GUINEA Island name

TERRA INCOGNITA

Papua New Guinea is today an independent nation and a member of the British Commonwealth. Occupying the eastern half of New Guinea, the second-largest island in the world, Papua New Guinea is probably the most overlooked of all the nations in the Pacific Rim.

It was not always overlooked, however. Spain claimed the vast land in the mid-sixteenth century, followed by Britain's East India Company in 1793. The Netherlands laid claim to part of the island in the 1800s and eventually came to control the western half (now known as Irian Jaya, a province of the Republic of Indonesia). In the 1880s German settlers occupied the northeast part of the island; and in 1884 Britain signed a treaty with Germany, which gave it about half of what is now Papua New Guinea. In 1906 Britain gave its part of the island to Australia. Australia invaded and quickly captured the German area in 1914. Eventually the League

(UN photo)

Despite contact with the civilized world, through exploitation of their mineral and forest resources, many of the natives of Papua New Guinea have retained their culture since the Stone Age.

| The main island is sighted by Portuguese explorers A.D. 1511 | The Dutch annex the west half of the island 1828 | A British protectorate over part of the eastern half of the island; the Germans control the northeast 1884 | Gold is discovered in Papua New Guinea 1890 | Australia assumes control of the British part of the island 1906 | Australia invades and captures the German-held areas 1914 | Australia is given the former German areas as a trust territory 1920 | Japan captures the northern part of the island; Australia resumes control in 1945 1940s | Australia grants independence to Papua New Guinea 1975 | Several successful elections for prime minister and other national officials are held 1970s–1980s |

1980s–1990s

| A revolt against the government begins on the island of Bougainville | 600 army soldiers storm Parliament, demanding higher pay | An economic blockade of Bougainville is lifted, but violence continues |

of Nations and, later, the United Nations gave the captured area to Australia to administer as a trust territory.

During World War II the northern part of New Guinea was the scene of bitter fighting between a large Japanese force and Australian and U.S. troops. The Japanese had apparently intended to use New Guinea as a base for the military conquest of Australia. Australia resumed control of the eastern half of the island after Japan's defeat, and it continued to administer Papua New Guinea's affairs until 1975, when it granted independence. The capital is Port Moresby, where, in addition to English, the Motu language and a hybrid language known as New Guinea Pidgin are spoken.

STONE AGE PEOPLES MEET THE TWENTIETH CENTURY

Why did the area attract so much attention? The coastline and some of the interior are swampy, mosquito- and tick-infested; the high, snow-capped mountainous regions are densely forested and difficult to traverse; and until the 1890s few minerals were known to exist. But perhaps most daunting to early would-be settlers and traders were the local inhabitants. Consisting of hundreds of sometimes warring tribes, with totally different languages and customs, the New Guinea populace was determined to prevent outsiders from settling the island. Many adventurers were killed, their heads displayed in tribal villages as victory trophies. The origins of these peoples are

unknown, but some tribes share common practices with Melanesian islanders. Others appear to be Negritos, and some may be related to the Australian Aborigines.

Australians and other Europeans found it beneficial to engage in trade with coastal tribes who supplied them with unique tropical lumbers, such as sandalwood and bamboo, and foodstuffs such as sugarcane, coconut, and nutmeg. Rubber and tobacco are also indigenous. Tea, which grows well in the highland regions, is an important cash crop. But the resource that was most important for the economic development of Papua New Guinea was gold. It was discovered there in 1890; two major gold rushes occurred in 1896 and 1926. Prospectors came mostly from Australia and were hated by the local tribes; some prospectors were killed and cannibalized. A large number of airstrips in the otherwise undeveloped interior eventually were built by miners who needed a safe and efficient way of receiving supplies. Today copper is more important than gold—copper is, in fact, the largest single earner of export income for Papua New Guinea.

The tropical climate that predominates in all areas except the highest mountain peaks produces an impressive variety of plant and animal life. Botanists and other naturalists for years have been attracted to the island for scientific study. Despite extensive contacts with these and other whites over the past 100 years, including experience with schools and universities

established by the Australian government, some inland mountain tribes continue to live much as they must have done in the Stone Age. Thus the country lures not only mining concerns and naturalists but also anthropologists looking for clues to humankind's early lifestyles.

Most of the nearly 4 million Papuans live by subsistence farming. Agriculture for commercial trade is limited by the absence of a good transportation network: most roads are unpaved, and there is no railway system. Air travel on tiny aircraft and helicopters is common, however; New Guinea boasts more than 450 airstrips, most of them unpaved and dangerously situated in mountain valleys. The harsh conditions of New Guinea life have produced some unique ironies. For instance, Papuans who have never ridden in a car or truck may have flown in a plane dozens of times. Given the discrepancies in socialization of the Papuan peoples and the difficult conditions of life on their island, it will likely be many decades before Papua New Guinea is able to participate fully in the Pacific Rim community.

DEVELOPMENT

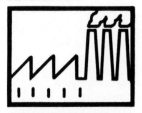

Agriculture (especially coffee and copra) is the mainstay of Papua New Guinea's economy. Copper, gold, and silver mining are also important, but large-scale development of other industries is inhibited by rough terrain, illiteracy, and a bewildering array of spoken languages—some 700. There are substantial reserves of untapped oil.

FREEDOM

Papua New Guinea is a member of the British Commonwealth and officially follows the English heritage of law. However, in the country's numerous, isolated small villages, effective control is wielded by village elites with personal charisma; tribal customs take precedence over national law—of which many inhabitants are virtually unaware.

HEALTH/WELFARE

Three-quarters of Papua New Guinea's population have no formal education. Daily nutritional intake falls far short of recommended minimums, and tuberculosis and malaria are common diseases. At its current birth rate (35 per 1,000, as compared to 29 per 1,000 globally), Papua New Guinea's population (now 3.8 million) will double by the year 2005.

ACHIEVEMENTS

Papua New Guinea is world-famous for its varied and beautiful flora and fauna, including orchids, birds of paradise, butterflies, and parrots. Dense forests cover 70 percent of the country, and some parts receive as much as 350 inches of rain a year.

Philippines (Republic of the Philippines)

GEOGRAPHY

Area in Square Kilometers (Miles):
300,000 (110,400) (slightly larger than Arizona)
Capital (Population): Manila (6,000,000)
Climate: tropical marine

PEOPLE

Population
Total: 66,117,000
Annual Growth Rate: 2.5%
Rural/Urban Population Ratio: 59/41
Ethnic Makeup of Population: 95.5% Malay; 1.5% Chinese; 3% others
Languages: official: Pilipino (based on Tagalog) and English

Health
Life Expectancy at Birth: 63 years (male); 69 years (female)
Infant Mortality Rate (Ratio): 48/1,000
Average Caloric Intake: 92% of FAO minimum
Physicians Available (Ratio): 1/1,090

Religion(s)
83% Roman Catholic; 9% Protestant; 5% Muslim; 3% Buddhist and others

Education
Adult Literacy Rate: 87%

COMMUNICATION

Telephones: 872,900
Newspapers: 472, of which about 20 are dailies

TRANSPORTATION

Highways—Kilometers (Miles): 156,000 (96,720)
Railroads—Kilometers (Miles): 378 (234)
Usable Airfields: 237

GOVERNMENT

Type: republic
Independence Date: July 4, 1946
Head of State: President Corazon C. Aquino; Vice President Salvador H. Laurel
Political Parties: PDP-Laban; Struggle of Philippine Democrats; Nationalista Party; Liberal Party; the Philippine Communist Party has quasi-legal status
Suffrage: universal at 15

MILITARY

Number of Armed Forces: 112,000
Military Expenditures (% of Central Government Expenditures): 2.1%
Current Hostilities: dispute over the Spratly Islands with China, Malaysia, Taiwan, and Vietnam; claims Malaysian state of Sabah

ECONOMY

Currency ($ U.S. Equivalent): 22.46 Philippine pesos = $1
Per Capita Income/GNP: $625/$40.5 billion
Inflation Rate: 10.6%
Natural Resources: timber; crude oil; nickel; cobalt; silver; gold; salt; copper
Agriculture: rice; coconut; corn; sugarcane; bananas; pineapple; mango; animal products; fish
Industry: food processing; chemicals; textiles; pharmaceuticals; wood products; electronics assembly; petroleum refining; fishing

FOREIGN TRADE

Exports: $8.1 billion
Imports: $10.5 billion

THE RICH GET RICHER; THE POOR GET CHILDREN

Visitors to the Philippines' capital of Manila are often stunned by the stark contrast between the rich and the poor. The rich drive to their air-conditioned, high-rise offices in luxury cars, while alongside the highways are thousands of the poor, who live in tin shacks with no plumbing, few jobs, and inadequate food. Because the shantytowns are not conducive to the upscale image that Manila would like to show the world, white picket fences have been built alongside major thoroughfares to hide the squalor from the view of visiting dignitaries.

One-quarter of the 6 million Manila residents are squatters who cannot sustain themselves, let alone their children. Yet the Philippines continues to have one of the highest birth rates in Asia, and nearly 60 percent of the population are under age 20.

SOUTH CHINA SEA

Laoag

LUZON

MANILA

Lucena

Catarman

SAMAR

PHILIPPINE SEA

PALAWAN

SULU SEA

Butuan

MINDANAO

MALAYSIA

MINDANAO SEA

MILES
0   150

⭐ Capital
● City
SAMAR Island name

THIS IS ASIA?

The Philippines is a land with close historic ties to the West. Eighty-three percent of Filipinos, as the people of the Philippines are known, are Roman Catholics, and most—even rice-paddy farmers in isolated mountain regions—speak at least some English. Many use English daily in business and government. In fact, English is the language of instruction at school. Moreover, when they discuss their history as a nation, Filipinos will mention Spain, Mexico, the Spanish-American War, the United States, and cooperative Filipino-American attempts to defeat the Japanese in World War II. The country was even named after a European, King Philip II of Spain. If this does not sound like a typical Asian nation, it is because Philippine nationhood essentially began with the arrival of Westerners. That influence continues to dominate the political and cultural life of the country.

Yet the history of the region certainly did not begin with European contact; indeed, there is evidence of human habitation in the area as early as 25,000 B.C. Beginning about 2,000 B.C. Austronesians, Negritos, Malays, and other tribal peoples settled many of the 7,107 islands that constitute the modern Philippines. Although engaged to varying degrees in trade with China and Southeast Asia, each of these ethnic groups (nearly 60 distinct groups still exist) lived in relative isolation from one another, speaking different languages, adhering to different religions, and, for good or ill, knowing nothing of the concept of national identity.

Although some 5 million ethnic peoples remain marginated from the modern mainstream, for most islanders the world changed in the mid-1500s, when soldiers and Roman Catholic priests from Spain began conquering and converting the population. Eventually the disparate ethnic groups came to see themselves as one entity, Filipinos, a people whose lives were controlled indirectly by Spain from Mexico—a fact that, unique among Asian countries, linked the Philippines with the Americas. Thus, the process of national-

identity formation for Filipinos began in Europe.

Some ethnic groups assimilated rather quickly, marrying Spanish soldiers and administrators and acquiring the language and cultural outlook of the West. The descendants of these mestizos (mixed peoples, including local/Chinese mixes) have become the cultural, economic, and political elite of the country. Others, particularly among the Islamic communities on the Philippine island of Mindanao, resisted assimilation right from the start and continue to challenge the authority of Manila. Indeed, the communist insurgency, reported so often in the news and the focus of attention of both former President Ferdinand Marcos and his successor Corazon Aquino, is in part an attempt by marginated ethnics and others to regain the cultural independence that their peoples lost some 400 years ago.

As in other Asian countries, the Chinese community has played an important but controversial role in Philippine life. Dominating trade for centuries, the Phil-

(United Nations photo by J. M. Micaud)

The Philippines has suffered from the misuse of funds entrusted to the government over the past several decades. The result has been a polarity of wealth, with many citizens living in severe poverty. Slums such as Tondo in Manila, pictured above, are a common sight in many of the urban areas of the Philippines.

Negritos and others begin settling the islands 25,000 B.C.	Malays arrive in the islands 2,000 B.C.	Chinese, Arabs, and Indians control parts of the economy and land A.D. 400–1400	The islands are named for the Spanish King Philip II 1542	Local resistance to Spanish rule 1890s

ippine Chinese have acquired clout (and enemies) that far exceeds their numbers (fewer than 1 million). President Aquino is of part-Chinese ancestry; some of the resistance to her presidency stems from her lineage.

FOREIGN INTEREST

Filipinos occupy a resource-rich, beautiful land. Monsoon clouds dump as much as 200 inches of rain on the fertile, volcanic soil. Rice and corn grow well, as do hemp, coconut, sugarcane, and tobacco. Tuna, sponges, shrimp, and hundreds of other kinds of marine life flourish in the ocean. Part of the country is covered with dense tropical forests yielding bamboo and lumber and serving as habitat to thousands of species of plant and animal life. The northern part of Luzon island is known for its terraced rice paddies.

Given this abundance, it is not surprising that several foreign powers have taken a serious interest in the archipelago. The Dutch held military bases in the country in the 1600s, the british briefly controlled Manila in the 1800s, and the Japanese overran the entire country in the 1940s. But it was Spain, in control of most of the country for more than 300 years (1565–1898), that established the cultural base for the modern Philippines. Spain's interest in the islands—its only colony in Asia—was primarily material and secondarily spiritual. It wanted to take part in the lucrative spice trade and fill its galleon ships each year with products from Asia for the benefit of the Spanish Crown. It also wanted (or, at least, Rome wanted) to convert the so-called heathens (nonbelievers) to Christianity. The Catholic friars were particularly successful in winning converts to Roman Catholicism because, despite some local resistance, there were no competing Christian denominations in the Philippines and because the Church quickly gained control of the resources of the island, which it used to entice converts. Resisting conversion were the Muslims of the island of Mindanao, a group that continues to remain on the fringe of Philippine society. Eventually a Church-dominated society was established that mirrored in structure—social-class divisions as well as religious and social values—the mother cultures of Spain and Mexico.

THE U.S. ERA

Spanish rule in the Philippines came to an inglorious end in 1898 at the end of the Spanish-American War. Spain granted independence to Cuba and ceded the Philippines, Guam, and Puerto Rico to the United States. Filipinos hoping for independence were disappointed to learn that yet another foreign power had assumed control of their lives. Resistance to American rule cost several thousand lives in the early years, but soon Filipinos realized that the U.S. presence was fundamentally different from that of Spain. Of course, the United States was interested in trade and it certainly could see the advantage of having a military presence in Asia, but it viewed its primary role as one of tutelage. American officials believed that the Philippines should be granted independence, but only when the nation was sufficiently schooled in the process of democracy. Unlike Spain, the United States encouraged political parties and attempted to place Filipinos in positions of governmental authority.

Preparations were underway for independence when the Pacific War with Japan broke out. The war and the occupation of the country by the Japanese undermined the economy, devastated the capital city of Manila, caused divisions among the political elite, and delayed independence. After Japan's defeat the country was, at last, granted independence, on July 4, 1946. Manuel Roxas, a well-known politician, was elected president. Despite armed opposition from communist groups, the country, after several elections, seemed to be maintaining a grasp on democracy.

MARCOS AND HIS AFTERMATH

Then, in 1965, Ferdinand E. Marcos, a senator and former guerrilla fighter with the United States armed forces, was elected president. He was reelected in 1969. Rather than addressing the serious problems of agrarian reform and trade, Marcos maintained people's loyalty through an elaborate system of patronage, whereby his friends profited from the misuse of government power and money. Opposition to his rule manifested itself in violent demonstrations and in growing communist insurgency. In 1972 Marcos declared martial law, arrested some 30,000 oppo-

nents, and shut down newspapers as well as the National Congress. Marcos continued to rule the country by personal proclamation until 1981. He remained in power thereafter, and he and his wife, Imelda, and their extended family and friends were increasingly criticized for corruption. Finally, in 1986, after nearly a quarter-century of Marcos rule, an uprising of thousands of dissatisfied Filipinos overthrew Marcos, who fled to Hawaii, where he died in 1990.

Taking on the formidable job of president was Corazon Aquino, the wife of murdered opposition leader Benigno Aquino. Aquino's People Power revolution had a heady beginning. Many observers believed that at last Filipinos had found a democratic leader around whom they could unite and who would end corruption and put the persistent communist insurgency to rest. Aquino, however, was immediately beset by overwhelming economic, social, and political problems.

Opportunists and factions of the Filipino military and political elite still loyal to Marcos have attempted numerous coups d'etat in the years of Aquino's administration. Much of the unrest comes from within the military, which became accustomed to direct involvement in government during Marcos' martial-law era. Some communist separatists have turned in their arms at Aquino's request, but many continue to plot violence against the government. Thus, the sense of security and stability that Filipinos need in order to attract more substantial foreign investment and to reestablish the habits of democracy continues to elude them.

Nevertheless, the economy is showing signs of improvement. Some countries, particularly Japan and the United States and, more recently, Hong Kong, have invested heavily in the Philippines, as have half a dozen international organizations. In fact, some groups now complain that further investment is unwarranted, because already allocated funds have not yet been fully utilized. Moreover, misuse of funds entrusted to the government—a serious problem during the Marcos era—continues, despite Aquino's promise to eradicate corruption. In 1990 there were suggestions that Aquino would run again for the presidency, despite the 1987 constitution (enacted after she came to power)

| A treaty ends the Spanish-American War 1898 | The Japanese attack the Philippines 1941 | General Douglas MacArthur makes a triumphant return to Manila 1944 | The United States grants complete independence to the Philippines 1946 | Military-base agreements are signed with the United States 1947 | Ferdinand Marcos is elected president 1965 | Marcos declares martial law 1972 | 1980s–1990s |

| Martial law is lifted | Corazon Aquino and her People Power movement drive Marcos into exile | Marcos dies in exile in Hawaii; the military-base lease reaches its deadline |

forbidding a president to hold office for more than one term.

SOCIAL PROBLEMS

One problem in the Philippines seems never to go away: extreme social inequality. As in Malaysia, where ethnic Malays have constituted a seemingly permanent class of poor peasants, Philippine society is fractured by distinct classes. Chinese and mestizos constitute the top of the hierarchy, while Muslims and most country dwellers form the bottom. About half the Filipino population of 66 million make their living in agriculture and fishing; but even in Manila, where the economy is stronger than anywhere else, thousands of residents live in abject poverty as urban squatters. Disparities of wealth are striking: some modern hotels in Manila, for example, charge for a single night's stay as much as the average Filipino makes in an entire year ($625). Worker discontent is such that the Philippines lost more work days to strikes between 1983 and 1987 than any other Asian country.

Also occupying the government's attention is the problem of the six U.S. military bases, the largest of which are Subic Bay Naval Base and Clark Air Base. The United States pays the Philippine government $385 million each year to lease the land on which the bases are built, plus $128 million in base-connected direct aid. The leasing agreements began in 1947; the current lease expires in 1991. Communists and other anti-U.S. groups in the Philippines regard the bases as an obstacle to their political aims and as a symbol of

colonialism and imperialism. Indeed, occupying many acres of valuable land and port space and bringing as many as 40,000 Americans at one time into the Philippines, the bases are a visible symbol of American influence in the Pacific.

As the 1991 lease deadline neared, anti-base groups expanded their tactics beyond protest demonstrations, to the random killing of U.S. military personnel. The U.S. government responded by declaring the area a danger zone for Americans and offering to pay the passage home of military dependents. Peace Corps workers were also told to gather at U.S. military bases for safety, although one was taken hostage before the order was given. Japanese nationals have also been captured as hostages.

The Philippine government holds that the bases provide a sense of security in an otherwise volatile world. (Indeed, U.S. war planes helped President Aquino to survive one of the most dangerous coup attempts against her government.) On the other hand, the Philippine government recognizes that it must make some kind of concession to the growing sense of nationalism in the country. For its part, the U.S. military, although happy to have received an invitation from Singapore to move its installations there, has nevertheless invested billions of dollars in the Philippines; it would rather stay put, for both economic and strategic reasons. And many Filipinos agree that keeping the bases is a good idea—esepcially for the economy. Hundreds of thousands of Filipinos make their entire livelihood either directly or

indirectly because of the bases—an infusion of money that amounts to 3 percent of the entire Philippine economy.

CULTURE

Philippine culture is a rich amalgam of Asian and European customs. Family life is valued, and few people have to spend their old age in nursing homes. Divorce is frowned upon. Women have traditionally involved themselves in the worlds of politics and business to a greater degree than do women in other Asian countries. Educational opportunities for women are about the same as that for men; literacy in the Philippines is estimated at 88 percent. Unfortunately, many college-educated men and women are unable to find employment befitting their skills. Discontent among these young workers continues to grow, as it does among the many rural and urban poor.

Nevertheless, many Filipinos take a rather relaxed attitude toward work and daily life. They enjoy hours of sports and folk dancing or spend their free time in conversation with neighbors and friends, with whom they construct patron/client relationships. In recent years the growing nationalism has been expressed in the gradual replacement of the English language with Filipino, a version of the Malay-based Tagalog language.

DEVELOPMENT

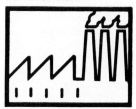

In 1989 the Philippines owed $27.9 billion in foreign debt. Payback from development projects has been so slow that about 51 percent of the earnings from all exports has to be spent just to service the debt. The Philippines sells most of its products to the United States, Japan, Hong Kong, Britain, and the Netherlands.

FREEDOM

Marcos' one-man rule meant that both the substance and structure of democracy was ignored. The Philippine Constitution is similar in many ways to that of the United States, and thus far the Aquino administration has adhered to its principles more closely than any of its predecessors.

HEALTH/WELFARE

Quality of life varies considerably between the city and the countryside. Except for the numerous urban squatters, city residents generally have better access to health care and education. Most people still do not have access to safe drinking water. The gap between the upper-class elite and the poor is pronounced and growing.

ACHIEVEMENTS

Under President Corazon Aquino, inflation has abated and foreign investment ($3.5 billion in loans and grants in 1989) has increased.

Singapore (Republic of Singapore)

GEOGRAPHY

Area in Square Kilometers (Miles):
633 (244) (slightly less than 3½
times the size of Washington, DC)
Capital (Population): Singapore
(2,334,400)
Climate: tropical

PEOPLE

Population
Total: 2,721,000
Annual Growth Rate: 1.3%
Rural/Urban Population (Ratio):
almost entirely urban
Ethnic Makeup of Population: 76%
Chinese; 15% Malay; 6% Indian, 3%
others
Languages: official: Malay, Mandarin
Chinese, Tamil, and English

Health
Life Expectancy at Birth: 72 years
(male); 77 years (female)
Infant Mortality Rate (Ratio): 8/1,000
Average Caloric Intake: 134% of FAO
minimum
Physicians Available (Ratio): 1/10,494

THE PERANAKANS

Most ancestors of the 2.7 million contemporary Singaporeans moved to
the island from various parts of China only about 150 years ago. A few
Singaporeans, however, including Prime Minister Lee Kuan Yew, can
trace their origins back to the fifteenth century, when Chinese traders
moved to the Malacca Straits, married local Malay women, and stayed
to create a uniquely blended culture of Chinese and Malay traditions.
Useful to their various European overlords as interpreters, these people,
called Peranakans ("locally born"), became the backbone of Singapore's upper class.

Religion(s)
42% Buddhist and Taoist; 18%
Christian; 16% Muslim; 5% Hindu;
others

Education
Adult Literacy Rate: 87%

COMMUNICATION

Telephones: 1,110,000
Newspapers: 7 dailies

TRANSPORTATION

Highways—Kilometers (Miles): 2,597
(1,610)
Railroads—Kilometers (Miles): 38
(23)
Airports: 6

GOVERNMENT

Type: republic within the British
Commonwealth
Independence Date: August 9, 1965
Head of State: President Wee Kim
Wee; Prime Minister Goh Chok Tong
Political Parties: People's Action
Party; Workers' Party; Singapore
Democratic Party; National Solidarity
Party; United People's Front; Barisan
Sosialis; communist party illegal
Suffrage: universal and compulsory at
20

MILITARY

Number of Armed Forces: 55,600
*Military Expenditures (% of Central
Government Expenditures):* 5%
Current Hostilities: none

ECONOMY

Currency ($ U.S. Equivalent): 1.88
Singapore dollar = $1
Per Capita Income/GNP:
$8,782/$49.6 billion
Inflation Rate: 3.5%
Natural Resources: fish; deepwater
ports
Agriculture: rubber; copra; fruit;
vegetables
Industry: petroleum refining;
electronics; oil-drilling equipment;
rubber processing and rubber
products; processed food and
beverages; ship repair, financial
services; biotechnology

FOREIGN TRADE

Exports: $46 billion
Imports: $53 billion

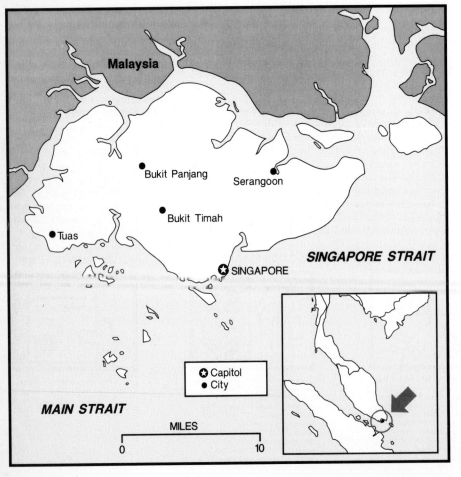

THE ECONOMIC ANOMALY

North Americans are well-off, it is often said, because they inhabit a huge continent that overflows with natural resources. This explanation for prosperity does not fit even remotely the case of Singapore. The inhabitants of this tiny, flat, humid island, located near the equator off the tip of the Malay Peninsula, must import even their drinking water from another country. With only 244 square miles of land (including 54 mostly uninhabited islets), Singapore is only half the size of Hong Kong; however, it has one of the highest per capita incomes ($8,782) in Asia. With more than 11,000 people per square mile, one of the highest population densities in Asia, Singapore might be expected to have the same problem of slums that characterize parts of other crowded areas. But unemployment in Singapore is only 2.8 percent, inflation is low, and most of its 2.7 million people own their own homes. Eighty percent of the residences are government-built apartments, but they are spacious by Asian standards and are well-equipped with labor-saving appliances. Seventy-six percent of the inhabitants are Chinese, yet the language of government and commerce is English (which is one of the four official languages of the country). Many Singaporeans speak English as their mother tongue.

What accounts for such anomalies? Imperialism, geography, and racism are the primary factors. For most of its recorded history, beginning in the thirteenth century, Singapore was controlled variously by the rulers of Thailand, Java, Indonesia, and even India. In the early 1800s the British were determined to wrest control of parts of Southeast Asia from the Dutch and expand their growing empire. Facilitating their imperialistic aims was Sir Stamford Raffles, a Malay-speaking British administrator who not only helped defeat the Dutch in Java but also diminished the power of local elites in order to fortify his position as lieutenant-governor.

Arriving in Singapore in 1919, Raffles found it to be a small, neglected settlement with an economy based on fishing. But he believed that the island's geographic location—at the tip of the Malay Peninsula and astride the busy sea lane

between the Far East and London—endowed it with great potential as a trans-shipment port. He established policies that facilitated its development just in time to benefit from the British exports of tin, rubber, and timber leaving Malaya. Perhaps most important was his declaration of Singapore as a free port. Skilled Chinese merchants and traders, escaping racist discrimination against them by Malays on the Malay Peninsula, flocked to Singapore, where they prospered in the free-trade atmosphere.

In 1924 the British began construction of a naval base on the island, the largest in Southeast Asia, which was nonetheless overcome by the Japanese in 1942. Returning in 1945, the British continued to build Singapore into a major maritime center. Today oil supertankers from Saudi Arabia must exit the Indian Ocean through the Strait of Malacca and skirt Singapore to enter the South China Sea for deliveries to Japan and other Asian nations. Thus,

Singapore has found itself in the enviable position of helping to refine and transship millions of barrels of Middle Eastern oil.

Singapore is now the second-busiest port in the world (Rotterdam in the Netherlands is number one). It has become the largest shipbuilding and -repair port in the region and a major shipping-related financial center. Singapore's economy has been growing at rates between 6 and 12 percent for the past decade, making it one of the fastest-growing economies in the world. In recent years the government has aggressively sought out investment from nonshipping-related industries in order to diversify the economy.

A UNIQUE CULTURE

Britain maintained an active interest in Singapore throughout its empire period. At its peak there were some 100,000 British military men and their dependents stationed there, many of whom remained until 1971. Thus, British culture, from the

(Reuters/Bettmann photo by Dominic Wong)

Singapore, one of the most affluent nations in Asia, still has a startlingly large section of its population mired in poverty. This woman, huddled with her life possessions, is one of many who eke out a bare existence in the thriving island state.

79

The British return to Singapore **1945**	Full elections and self-government; Lee Kuan Yew comes to power **1959**	Singapore, now unofficially independent of Britain, briefly joins the Malaysia Federation **1963**	Singapore becomes an independent republic **1965**	Singapore joins the newly created Association of Southeast Asian Nations (ASEAN) **1967**	The last British troops leave Singapore **1971**

1980s–1990s

Singapore becomes the second busiest port in the world

Singapore achieves one of the highest per capita incomes in the Pacific Rim

Prime Minister Lee steps down and Goh Chok Tong is appointed

architecture of the buildings, to the leisure of a cricket match, to the prevalence of the English language, is everywhere present in Singapore. Yet because of the heterogeneity of the population (76 percent are Chinese, 15 percent are Malay, and 6 percent are Indian), Singapore accommodates many philosophies and belief systems, including Confucianism, Buddhism, Islam, Hinduism, and Christianity. In recent years the government has attempted to promote the Confucian ethic of hard work and respect for law, as well as the Mandarin Chinese language, in order to develop a greater Asian consciousness among the people. But most Singaporeans seem content to avoid extreme ideology, in favor of pragmatism; they prefer to believe in whatever approach works—that is, whatever allows them to make money and have a high standard of living. Like the Japanese (whom many Singaporeans admire because of their high-quality products and self-discipline), Singapore residents save as much as 30 percent of their income. Out of every 100,000 inhabitants, 1,713 attend college, as compared to only 680 in neighboring Malaysia. Eighty-seven percent can read and write.

Yet this success has come with a price. The government keeps a firm hand on the people. Citizens, for example, can be fined as much as $250 for dropping a candy wrapper on the street or driving without a seat belt. Political dissidents are arrested, and the press cannot publish whatever it wishes without often generating the government's ire. Government leaders argue that order and hard work are

necessities, since being a tiny island, Singapore could easily be overtaken by the envious and more politically unstable countries nearby; with few natural resources, Singapore must instead develop its people into disciplined, educated workers. Few deny that Singapore is an amazingly clean and efficient city-state, yet in recent years younger residents have begun to wish for a greater voice in government.

The law-and-order tone is largely because, since its separation from Malaysia in 1965, Singapore had been controlled by one man, Prime Minister Lee Kuan Yew, and his Political Action Party (PAP). On November 26, 1990 Lee resigned his office, and on November 28 he was replaced by his chosen successor Goh Chok Tong. Goh had been the deputy prime minister and was the designated successor-in-waiting since 1984. The transition has been smooth and the PAP's hold on the government remains intact.

Originally the PAP came into prominence in 1959, when the issue of the day was whether or not Singapore should join the proposed Federation of Malaysia. Singapore joined Malaysia in 1963, but serious differences persuaded Singaporeans to become an independent nation 2 years later. Lee, a Cambridge-educated, ardent anticommunist with old roots in Singapore, gained such strong support as prime minister that not a single opposition-party member has been elected since 1968. The two main goals of the administration have been to utilize fully Singapore's primary resource—its deepwater port—and to develop a strong Singaporean identity. The

first goal has been achieved in a way that few would have thought possible; the question of national identity, however, continues to be problematic.

Creating a Singaporean identity has been difficult because of the heterogeneity of the population, which is likely to increase as foreign workers are imported to fill gaps in the labor supply and because of Singapore's history as a lackey of several larger nations. First Singapore was a colony of Britain, then it became an outpost of the Japanese Empire, followed by a return to Britain. Next Malaysia drew Singapore into its fold, and finally, in 1965, Singapore became independent. All these changes transpired within the lifetime of many contemporary Singaporeans, so their confusion regarding identity is understandable. Many still have a sense that their existence as a nation is tenuous, and they look for direction.

Younger Singaporeans believe that more grass-roots involvement in government and more self-determination in personal matters will add meaning to their lives. To date such opportunities have been denied them, and it will be a measure of the new prime minister's statesmanship as to how willing he will be to loosen the longstanding grip the PAP has had on the reins of government.

DEVELOPMENT

Development of the deepwater Port of Singapore has been so successful that at any single time, 400 ships are in port. Singapore has also become a base for fleets engaged in offshore oil exploration and a major financial center, "the Switzerland of Southeast Asia."

FREEDOM

Under Prime Minister Lee, Singaporeans have had to adjust to a strict regiment of behavior involving both political and personal freedoms. Citizens want more freedoms but realize that law and order have helped produce their high quality of life. Opposition voices have been silenced since 1968, when the Political Action Party captured all the seats in the government.

HEALTH/WELFARE

Eighty percent of Singaporeans live in government-built dwellings. A government-created pension fund, the Central Provident Fund, takes up to one-quarter of workers' paychecks; some of this goes into a compulsory savings account which can be used to finance the purchase of a residence. Other forms of welfare are not condoned.

ACHIEVEMENTS

Housing remains a serious problem for many Asian countries, but virtually every Singaporean has access to adequate housing. Replacing swamplands with industrial parks has helped to lessen Singapore's reliance on its deepwater port. Singapore successfully overcame a communist challenge in the 1950s to become a solid home for free enterprise in the region.

South Korea (Republic of Korea)

GEOGRAPHY

Area in Square Kilometers (Miles): 98,480 (38,013) (slightly larger than Indiana)
Capital (Population): Seoul (9,646,000)
Climate: temperate

PEOPLE

Population
Total: 43,045,000
Annual Growth Rate: 0.8%
Rural/Urban Population (Ratio): 25/75
Ethnic Makeup of Population: homogeneous Korean
Language: Korean

Health
Life Expectancy at Birth: 66 years (male); 73 years (female)
Infant Mortality Rate (Ratio): 23/1,000
Average Caloric Intake: 119% of FAO minimum
Physicians Available (Ratio): 1/1,132

Religion(s)
Buddhism; Shamanism; Confucianism; Christianity

Education
Adult Literacy Rate: more than 90%

WOMEN IN MODERN KOREA

According to the traditions of Confucianism, a woman had three people whom she was to obey throughout her lifetime: her father until she married; her husband after marriage; and her son after her husband's death. The subservience mandated by this ancient custom can still be seen throughout South Korean society at the interpersonal level, but times are changing in the public arena. Women may vote in Korea (more than 80 percent did so in the last presidential election), and half a dozen women have been appointed to the Cabinet at various times since 1948. Fifty-four women have served in the legislature, and there are women judges, lawyers, and newspaper editors and reporters. Women account for about 35 percent of the South Korean workforce. About 21 percent of all civil servants are women, but there has never yet been a woman president.

COMMUNICATION

Telephones: 4,800,000
Newspapers: 68 dailies

TRANSPORTATION

Highways—Kilometers (Miles): 62,936 (39,020)
Railroads—Kilometers (Miles): 3,106 (1,926)
Usable Airfields: 105

GOVERNMENT

Type: republic
Independence Date: August 15, 1948
Head of State: President Roh Tae-woo; Prime Minister Kang Young Houn
Political Parties: Democratic Justice Party; Peace and Democracy Party; Korea Reunification Democratic Party; New Democratic Republican Party; others
Suffrage: universal at 20

MILITARY

Number of Armed Forces: 650,000
Military Expenditures (% of Central Government Expenditures): 5%
Current Hostilities: disputed Demarcation Line with North Korea; disputed Liancourt Rocks, claimed by Japan

ECONOMY

Currency ($ U.S. Equivalent): 1,140 won = $1
Per Capita Income/GNP: $4,600/$200 billion
Inflation Rate: 5%
Natural Resources: coal; tungsten; graphite; molybdenum; lead; hydropower
Agriculture: rice; root crops; barley; vegetables; fruit; livestock and livestock products; fish
Industry: textiles; clothing; footwear; food processing; chemicals; steel; electronics; automobile production; shipbuilding

FOREIGN TRADE

Exports: $62.3 billion
Imports: $61.3 billion

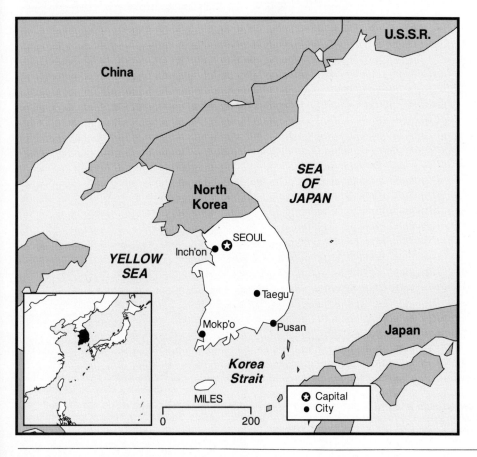

EARLY HISTORY

Korea has been inhabited by hominid groups for at least half a million years. (Descendants from these early peoples may be the Ainus of northern Japan, the inhabitants of Sakhalin Island, and the Siberian Eskimos.) Distinct from these groups, the early Koreans migrated to the Korean Peninsula from Central Asia and, benefiting from close contact with the civilization of China, established prosperous kingdoms as early as 1000 B.C.

Another era, that of King Sejong, who ruled Korea from 1418–1450, is notable for its many scientific and humanistic accomplishments. Ruling his subjects according to Neo-Confucian thought, Sejong taught improved agricultural methods; published books on astronomy, history, religion, and medicine (the Koreans were the first to invent movable metal type); and was instrumental in the invention of sundials, rain gauges, and various musical instruments. Of singular importance was his

invention of *han-qul*, a simplified writing system that even uneducated peasants could easily learn. Before *han-qul*, Koreans used the more complicated Chinese characters to represent sounds in the Korean language.

REGIONAL RELATIONS

For most of its history Korea remained at least nominally independent of foreign powers. China, however, always wielded tremendous cultural influence and at times politically dominated the Korean Peninsula. Similarly, Japan often cast longing eyes toward Korea but was never able to control affairs successfully there until the beginning of the twentieth century.

Korean influence on Japanese culture was pronounced in the 1400s and 1500s, when, through peaceful trade as well as forced labor, Korean artisans and technicians taught advanced skills in ceramics, textiles, painting, and other arts to the Japanese. (Historically, the Japanese had

received most of their cultural influence from China via Korea.)

In this century the direction of influence was reversed—to the current Japan-to-Korea flow—with the result that the two cultures share numerous qualities. Ironically, cultural closeness has not eradicated emotional distance: modern Japanese continue to discriminate against Koreans who live in Japan, and Japanese brutality during the years of occupation (1905–1945) remains a frequent topic of Korean conversation.

Japan finally achieved its desire to rule Korea in 1905, when Russia's military, along with its imperialistic designs on Korea, was soundly defeated by the Japanese in the Russo-Japanese War; Korea was granted to Japan as part of the peace settlement. Unlike other expansionist nations, Japan was not content to rule Korea as a colony but, rather, attempted the complete cultural and political annexation of the peninsula. Koreans had to adopt

(Reuters/Bettmann photo by Tony Chung)

When Korea was divided, the South Koreans received large amounts of economic and military aid from the United States which allowed them to follow the Japanese model of development. As their industrial base grew and they focused on specific markets, South Korea became an economic powerhouse. These workers in the Hyundai shipyards typify the industrious South Koreans.

Japanese names, serve in the Japanese Army, and pay homage to the Japanese emperor. Some 1.3 million Koreans were forcibly sent to Japan to work in coal mines or to serve in the military. The Korean language was not taught in school, and more than 200,000 books on Korean history and culture were burned.

Many Koreans joined clandestine resistance organizations. In 1919 a Declaration of Korean Independence was announced in Seoul by resistance leaders, but the brutally efficient Japanese police and military crushed the movement. They killed thousands of demonstrators, tortured and executed the leaders, and set fire to the homes of those suspected of cooperating with the movement. Despite suppression of this kind throughout the 35 years of Japanese colonial rule, a provisional government was established by the resistance in 1919, with branches in Korea, China, and Russia. However, a very large police force—1 Japanese for every 40 Koreans—kept such efforts in check.

One resistance leader, Syngman Rhee, vigorously promoted the cause of Korean independence to government leaders in the United States and Europe. Rhee, supported by the United States, became the president of South Korea after the defeat of the Japanese in 1945.

Upon the surrender of Japan, the victorious Allied nations decided to divide Korea into two zones of temporary occupation for the purposes of overseeing the orderly dismantling of Japanese rule and establishing a new Korean government. The United States was to occupy all of Korea south of the 38th Parallel of latitude (a demarcation running east and west across the peninsula, about 150 miles north of the capital city of Seoul), while the Soviet Union was to occupy Korea north of that line. The United States was uneasy about permitting the Soviets to move troops into Korea, as the Soviet Union had entered the war against Japan just 8 days before Japan surrendered, and its commitment to the democratic intentions of the Allies was questionable. Nevertheless, it was granted occupation rights.

In 1948 the United Nations attempted to enter the zone occupied by the Soviet Union in order to oversee democratic elections for all of Korea. Denied entry, UN advisors proceeded with elections in the South, which brought Syngman Rhee to the presidency. The North created its own government, with Kim Il-sŏng at the head. Tensions between the two governments resulted in the elimination of trade and other contacts across the new border. This was difficult for each side, because the Japanese had developed industries in the North, while the South remained primarily agricultural. Each side needed the other's resources; in their absence, considerable civil unrest occurred. Rhee's government responded by suppressing dissent, rigging elections, and using strong-arm tactics on critics. Autocratic rule, not unlike that of the colonial Japanese, has been the norm in South Korea ever since, and citizens, particularly university students, have been quick to take to the streets in protest of human-rights violations by the various South Korean governments. Equally stern measures were instituted by the communist government in the North, so that despite nearly a half-century of Korean rule, the repressive legacy of the Japanese police state remains for all Korean people.

AN ECONOMIC POWERHOUSE

Upon the establishment of two separate political entities in Korea, the North chose a communist model of economic restructuring. South Korea, bolstered by massive infusions of economic and military aid from the United States, pursued a decidedly capitalist strategy. The results of this choice have been dramatic. South Korea today is often said to be the fastest-growing economy in the world; by the year 2010 it is expected that per capita income for Koreans will equal that of European economies. About 75 percent of South Korean people live in urban centers, where they have access to good education and jobs. Manufacturing accounts for 30 percent of the gross domestic product, a fact that North Americans can attest to by the number of Hyundai automobiles and Samsung television sets they buy. Economic success and recent improvements in the political climate seem to be slowing the rate of outward migration. Some Koreans have even returned home in recent years.

Following the Japanese model, Korean businesspeople work hard to capture market share rather than to gain immediate profit—that is, they are willing to sell their products at or below cost for several years in order to gain the confidence of consumers, even if they make no profit. Once a sizable proportion of consumers buy their product and trust its reliability, they begin to raise prices to a profitable level. (In contrast, many investors in American companies want to see a profit right away.)

Many South Korean businesses are now investing in other countries, and South Korea is now a creditor rather than a debtor member of the Asian Development Bank—it is now in a position to loan money to other newly industrializing countries (NICs) rather than to borrow from nations wealthier than itself. Given this kind of economic strength, it is now claimed by some that Japan's towering economic powerhouse could be challenged by a unified Korea and that, therefore, Japan (which is separated from Korea by only 150 miles) is not interested in promoting reunification. The situation is not unlike European countries' concern about the economic strength of a unified Germany.

SOCIAL PROBLEMS

Economically, South Korea is an impressive showcase for the fruits of capitalism. Politically, however, the country has been wracked with problems. Under Presidents Syngman Rhee (1948–1960), Park Chung Hee (1964–1979), and Chun Doo Hwan (1981–1987), South Korean government was so centralized as to constitute a virtual dictatorship. Human-rights violations, suppression of workers, and other acts incompatible with the tenets of democracies were frequent occurrences. Student uprisings, military revolutions, and political assassinations became more influential than the ballot box in forcing a change of government. The current president, Roh Tae-woo, came to power in 1987 in the wake of a mass protest against the excesses of the previous government.

A primary focus of the South Korean government's attention at the moment is the several U.S. military bases in South Korea, currently home to 43,500 U.S. troops. The government (and apparently most of the 42 million South Korean people), though not always happy with the military presence, believes that the U.S. troops are useful in deterring possible aggression from North Korea. Many university students, however, are offended at the presence of these troops. They claim that the Americans have suppressed the growth of democracy by propping up authoritarian regimes—a claim readily admitted by the United States, which believed during the Cold War era that the containment of communism was a higher priority. Strong feelings against U.S. involvement in South Korean affairs have precipitated hundreds of violent demonstrations, sometimes involving as many as 100,000 protesters. The United States' refusal to withdraw its forces from South Korea has left an impression with many Koreans that Americans are hard-line, Cold War ideologues who are unwilling to bend in the face of changing international alignments. By contrast, Soviet leader Mikhail Gorbachev's foreign-policy initiatives have earned him considerable respect among South Korean college students.

The Yi dynasty begins a 518-year reign over Korea A.D. 935	Korea pays tribute to Mongol rulers in China 1637	Korea opens its ports to outside trade 1876	Japan formally annexes Korea at the end of the Russo-Japanese War 1910	Korea is divided into North and South 1945	North Korea invades South Korea: the Korean War begins 1950	Ceasefire agreement; the DMZ is established 1953	President Park Chung Hee is assassinated 1979

1980s–1990s

Democratization movement | The 1988 Summer Olympic Games are held in Seoul | President Roh Tae-woo meets with Soviet President Mikhail Gorbachev to discuss reunification

In 1990 U.S. Secretary of Defense Richard Cheney announced that, in an effort to reduce U.S. military costs in the post--Cold War era, the United States would pull out several thousand of its troops from South Korea and close three of its five air bases by about 1993. The United States also declared that it expects South Korea to pay more of the cost of the U.S. military presence, in part as a way to reduce the unfavorable trade balance between the two countries. The South Korean government has agreed to build a new U.S. military base about 50 miles south of the capital city of Seoul, where current operations would be relocated. South Korea would pay all construction costs—estimated at about $1 billion—and the U.S. would be able to reduce its presence within the Seoul metropolitan area, where many of the anti-U.S. demonstrations take place.

However, protesters demand that U.S. troops be withdrawn, not just relocated. Although surveys show that about 90 percent of South Koreans want the United States military to remain in the country as a defense against North Korea and the possible remilitarization of Japan, it is easy to see why some people detest the American presence. In the Philippines, for example, 6,000 registered prostitutes reside in villages near Subic Bay Naval Base, and when the fleets come in the number of prostitutes working the area swells to 16,000. In South Korea, the U.S. military's main role often has seemed to be the propping up of authoritarian, right-wing governments.

POPULAR DISSATISFACTION

Such situations are particularly offensive to the numerous Christian clergy and their congregations in South Korea. The country has more Christians than any other Asian nation except the Philippines. With their close ties to their European and American mother-churches, Korean Christians have been a strong voice for democracy and human rights in the country.

Another increasingly vocal group is South Korean youth. In addition to the bases question, student protesters are angry at the South Korean government's willingness to open more Korean markets to U.S. products. The students want the United States to apologize for its alleged assistance to the South Korean government in violently suppressing an antigovernment demonstration in 1981 in Kwangju, a southern city that is a frequent locus of antigovernment as well as labor-related demonstrations and strikes. Protesters were particularly angered by President Roh Tae-woo's silencing of part of the opposition by convincing two opposition parties to merge with his own to form a large Democratic Liberal Party (DLP), not unlike that of the Liberal Democratic Party (LDP) which has ruled Japan almost continuously since World War II.

Ironically, demands for Roh's resignation have increased at precisely the moment he has been instituting changes designed to strengthen both the economy and the freedoms of South Korea. Under Roh's administration, trade and diplomatic initiatives have been launched with Eastern European nations and with China and the Soviet Union. Similarly, relaxation of the tight controls on labor-union activity has given workers more leverage in negotiating with management. Unfortunately, union activity, exploding after decades of suppression, has produced crippling industrial strikes—as many as 2,400 a year, and once again the police have been called out to restore order. In fact, since 1980, riot police have fired an average of more than 500 tear-gas shells a day at a cost to the South Korean government of $51 million.

Frequent strikes and walk-outs, along with the never-ending stream of student protesters and the potential military threat from North Korea, have produced a society in which there is a constant feeling of unease. Some South Koreans have emigrated to build new lives elsewhere in Asia and in North and South America. However, the emerging democratization and continued economic strength of South Korea may entice many Koreans to return home.

DEVELOPMENT

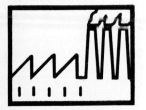

The South Korean economy is booming. Recent attempts to increase trade with socialist countries will further strengthen it. Construction of new homes and businesses is everywhere evident. Industrial workers have had to bear the brunt of the negative aspects of industrialization: low wages and long hours.

FREEDOM

Suppression of political dissent, manipulation of the electoral process, and restrictions on labor-union activity have been features of every South Korean government since 1948. Martial law has been frequently invoked, and governments have been overthrown by mass uprisings of the people. The current president, Roh Tae-woo, has promised reforms.

HEALTH/WELFARE

Korean men usually marry at about age 27, women at about 24. In 1960 Korean women, on average, gave birth to 6 children; in 1990 the expected births per woman were 1.6. The average South Korean baby born today can expect to live to be about 70 years old, as compared to 75 for U.S. newborns.

ACHIEVEMENTS

South Korea achieved self-sufficiency in agricultural fertilizers during the 1970s, which has increased production of all food commodities. The country has shown steady growth in the production of cereal grains and vegetables. The formerly weak industrial sector is now balancing out agriculture in its contribution to the gross national product.

Taiwan (Republic of China)

GEOGRAPHY

Area in Square Kilometers (Miles):
36,002 (22,320) (about the size of
West Virginia)
Capital (Population): Taipei
(2,637,000)
Climate: subtropical

PEOPLE
Population
Total: 20,454,000
Annual Growth Rate: 1.1%
Rural/Urban Population Ratio: 28/72
Ethnic Makeup of Population: 84%
Taiwanese; 14% Mainlander Chinese;
2% aborigine

Health
Life Expectancy at Birth: 70 years
(male); 76 years (female)
Infant Mortality Rate (Ratio):
6.3/1,000
Average Caloric Intake: n/a
Physicians Available (Ratio): 1/1,010

Religion(s)
93% mixture of Buddhism,
Confucianism, and Taoism; 4.5%
Christian; 2.5% others

TAIWAN BAMBOO, A SYMBOL OF ASIA

In central Taiwan, near the city of Taichung, is a 6,000-acre forest
research station, located approximately 4,000 feet above sea level. This
forest is unique because its trees are mostly bamboo. Bamboo, of which
there are some 200 species, is a member of the grass family, but some
varieties grow to be more than 150 feet high and 1 foot in diameter. Some
species have been known to grow nearly 2 feet a day.

With more than a dozen varieties of bamboo, the Hsitou Bamboo
Forest preserves a plant that is now being slowly displaced by plastic and
steel but which remains the single most useful building material throughout Asia and Southeast Asia. In Korea and elsewhere, bamboo is used as
scaffolding on most construction jobs; in China, the small tips of new
bamboo shoots are used as food in many dishes; in Japan, bamboo is
fashioned into fans, flowerpots, water pipes, and a flute-like musical
instrument called a *shakuhachi.* Chopsticks, baskets, and even paper
have been made from bamboo.

Education
Adult Literacy Rate: 92%

COMMUNICATION
Telephones: 7,159,210
Newspapers: 168

TRANSPORTATION
Highways—Kilometers (Miles): 19,981
(12,349)
Railroads—Kilometers (Miles): 2,526
(1,556)
Usable Airfields: 37

GOVERNMENT
Type: one-party presidential regime
Head of State: President Lee Teng-hui
Political Parties: Nationalist Party
(Kuomintang); Democratic People's
Party; other minor parties
Suffrage: universal over 20 years

MILITARY
Number of Armed Forces: 369,000
*Military Expenditures (% of Central
Government Expenditures):* 39.4%
Current Hostilities: officially (but not
actually) in a state of war with the
People's Republic of China

ECONOMY
Currency ($ U.S. Equivalent): 27.02
New Taiwan dollars = $1
Per Capita Income/GNP:
$6,200/$119.1 billion
Inflation Rate: % 5%
Natural Resources: coal; gold;
copper; sulphur; oil; natural gas
Agriculture: rice; tea; bananas;
pineapples; sugarcane; sweet
potatoes; wheat; soybeans; peanuts
Industry: steel; pig iron; aluminum;
shipbuilding; cement; fertilizer;
paper; cotton; fabrics

FOREIGN TRADE
Exports: $66.1 billion
Imports: $52.5 billion

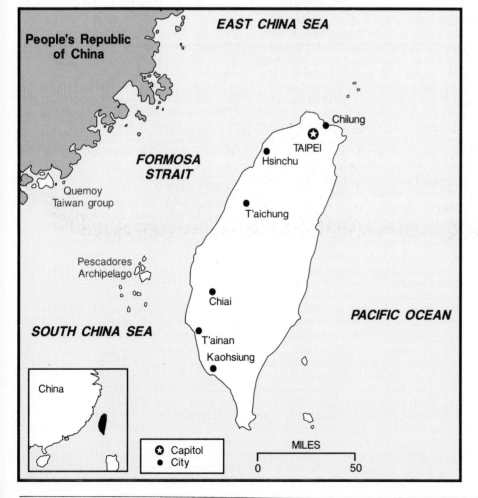

A LAND OF REFUGE

It has been called "beautiful island," "treasure island," and "terraced bay island," but to the people who have settled there, Taiwan (formerly called Formosa) has come to mean "refuge island."

Typical of the earliest refugees of the island were the Hakka peoples of China, who, tired of persecution on the mainland, fled to Taiwan (and to Borneo) before A.D. 1000. In the seventeenth century tens of thousands of Ming Chinese soldiers, defeated at the hands of the expanding Manchu army, sought sanctuary in Taiwan. In 1949 a third major wave of immigration to Taiwan brought thousands of Chinese Nationalists, retreating in the face of the victorious Red Chinese armies. Hosting all these newcomers were the original inhabitants of the islands, various Malay-Polynesian-speaking tribes whose descendants live today in mountain villages throughout the island.

Other outsiders have shown interest in Taiwan, too: Portugal, Spain, the Netherlands, Great Britain, and France have all either settled colonies or engaged in trade along the coasts. But the non-Chinese power that has had the most influence is Japan. Japan treated parts of Taiwan as its own for 400 years before it officially acquired the entire island in 1895, at the end of the Sino-Japanese War. From then until 1945 the Japanese ruled Taiwan with the intent of fully integrating it into Japanese culture. The Japanese language was taught in schools, college students were sent to Japan for their education, and the Japanese style of government was implemented. Many Taiwanese resented the harsh discipline that the Japanese imposed, but they also recognized that the Japanese were building a modern, productive society. Indeed, the basic infrastructure of contemporary Taiwan—roads, railways, schools, and so on—was constructed during the Japanese colonial era (1895–1945). Japan still lays claim to the Senkaku Islands, a chain of uninhabited islands, which the Taiwanese say belong to Taiwan. In 1990 maritime authorities in Japan blocked access to the islands by Taiwanese fishing vessels, an act that provoked a condemnation from Taipei.

After Japan's defeat in World War II Taiwan became the island of refuge of the anti-Communist leader Chiang Kai-shek and his 3 million Kuomintang (KMT, or Nationalist Party) followers, many of whom had been prosperous and well-educated businesspeople and intellectuals in China. These Mandarin-speaking mainland Chinese, called Mainlanders, now constitute about 14 percent of Taiwan's population of 20 million.

During the 1950s the leader of the People's Republic of China (P.R.C.), Mao Zedong, planned an invasion of Taiwan. However, Taiwan's leaders succeeded in obtaining military support from the United States to prevent the attack. They also convinced the United States to provide substantial amounts of foreign aid (which the United States willingly gave, perceiving it as an attempt to contain communism) to Taiwan as well as to grant it diplomatic recognition as the only legitimate government for all of China.

Over the past 4 decades both mainland China and Taiwan have threatened to invade each other's territory, but neither has done so, even though they officially remain in a state of war. Both also claim to be the only legitimate China.

Because neither side has been willing to accept the sovereignty of the other, for over 20 years mainland China was denied membership in the United Nations; Taiwan held the "China seat." In the early 1970s world opinion on the "two Chinas" issue began to change. Many countries believed that a nation as large and powerful as the People's Republic of China should not be kept out of the United Nations nor out of the mainstream of world trade in favor of the much smaller Taiwan. In 1971 the United Nations withdrew its China seat from Taiwan and gave it to China. The United States and many other countries wished to establish diplomatic relations with China but were denied that opportunity as long as they granted recognition to Taiwan. In 1979 the United States, preceded by many other nations, switched diplomatic recognition from Taiwan to China. Foreign-trade offices in Taiwan remained unchanged, but embassies were renamed "institutes"; and as far as official diplomacy was concerned, Taiwan became a non-nation.

AN ECONOMIC POWERHOUSE

Diplomatic maneuvering has not affected Taiwan's stunning postwar economic growth. Like Japan, Taiwan has been described as an economic miracle. In the past 20 years Taiwan has enjoyed more years of double-digit economic growth than any other nation on earth. With electronics leading the pack of exports, about 45 percent of Taiwan's gross domestic product (GDP) comes from manufacturing, a higher percentage than for any other country in Asia. Taiwan has been open to foreign investment and, of course, to foreign trade. Of interest is that, despite Taiwan's official policy of no contact and no communication with the People's Republic of China, annual trade with the mainland—processed mostly through Hong Kong—exceeds $3 billion and is expected to increase in the future. In fact,

China is now Taiwan's seventh-largest trading partner. In 1988 Taiwan passed legislation to permit direct trading with China, including postal and cultural exchanges.

As one of the Newly Industrializing Countries (NICs) of Asia, Taiwan certainly no longer fits the label "underdeveloped." Taiwan holds large stocks of foreign reserves and currently carries a trade surplus with the United States (in Taiwan's favor) 4 times greater than Japan's, when counted on a per capita basis. Per capita income is $6,200. The Taipei stock market has been so successful—outperforming both Japan and the United States in 1989, for example—that some workers were reportedly quitting their jobs to play the market, thereby exacerbating Taiwan's already serious labor shortage.

Successful Taiwanese companies have begun to invest heavily in other countries where land and labor are plentiful and less expensive. Thailand and the Philippines have been targeted for Taiwanese investment, as have Australia, the United States, and other countries. Between 1986 and 1989 some 200 Taiwanese companies invested $1.3 billion in Malaysia alone (Taiwan has now supplanted Japan as the largest outside investor in Malaysia). Even the socialist countries of Myanmar (Burma), Cambodia, Laos, and Vietnam are being considered for Taiwanese investment, a move encouraged by Taiwan's recent lifting of its ban on trade with socialist nations. Investment in mainland China is also increasing; a 1990 survey found that out of 1,400 Taiwanese companies, 38 percent had already invested in China or were planning to do so.

WHAT HAPPENED TO CONFUCIUS?

Taiwan's economic success is attributable in part to its educated population, many of whom constituted the cultural and economic elite of China before the communist revolution. Despite resentment of the mainland immigrants by native-born Taiwanese, everyone, including the lower classes of Taiwan, has benefited from this infusion of talent and capital. Yet the Taiwanese people are beginning to pay a price for their sudden affluence. It is said that Taipei, the capital city of Taiwan, is awash in money, but it is also now awash in air pollution and traffic congestion. Traffic congestion in Taipei is rated near the worst in the world; 10.5 million vehicles—more than 1 for every 2 people—cram Taiwan's highways, while concrete highrises have displaced the lush greenery of the mountains. Many residents spend their earnings on luxury foreign cars and on cigarettes and alcohol, whose con-

| Portuguese sailors are the first Europeans to visit Taiwan A.D. **1590** | Taiwan becomes part of the Chinese Empire **1700s** | The Sino-Japanese War ends; China cedes Taiwan to Japan **1895** | Taiwan achieves independence from Japan **1945** | Nationalists, under Chiang Kai-shek, retreat to Taiwan **1947-49** | A de facto separation of Taiwan from China; Chinese aggression is deterred with U.S. assistance **1950s** | China replaces Taiwan in the United Nations **1971** | U.S. President Richard Nixon visits China to open relations **1972** | Chiang Kai-shek dies and is succeeded by his son, Chiang Ching-Kuo **1975** | The United States breaks off diplomatic recognition of Taiwan, in favor of China **1979** |

■■I●I■■■■■■■■■■I●I■■■■■■■■■■I●I■■■■■■■■■■■■■■■I●I■■■■■■■■■■I●I■■■■■■■■■I●I■■■■■■■■■■I●I■■■■■■■■■■■■■■■■■■I●I■■■■■■■■■I●I■■■ **1980s-1990s**

The first two-party elections in Taiwan's history are held; 38 years of martial law end

Chiang Ching-Kuo dies; Lee Teng-hui is the first native-born Taiwanese to be elected president

Relations with China improve

sumption rate has been increasing by about 10 percent a year. Many Chinese traditions—for instance, the roadside restaurant serving noodle soup—are giving way to 7-Elevens selling Coca-Cola and ice cream.

Some Taiwanese despair of ever turning back from the growing materialism; they wish for the revival of traditional Chinese (that is, Confucian) ethics, but they doubt that it will happen. Still, the government, which has been dominated since 1949 by the conservative Mandarin migrants from the mainland, sees to it that Confucian ethics are vigorously taught in school. And there remains in Taiwan more of traditional China than in China itself, because, unlike the Chinese communists, the Taiwanese authorities have had no reason to attempt an eradication of the values of Buddhism, Taoism, or Confucianism. Nor has grinding poverty—often the most serious threat to the cultural arts—negatively affected literature and the fine arts, as it has in China. Parents, with incense sticks burning before small religious altars, still emphasize respect for authority, the benefits of harmonious cooperative effort, and the inestimable value of education. Traditional festivals dot each year's calendar, and temples are filled with worshippers praying for health and good luck.

But the Taiwanese will need more than luck if they are to escape the consequences of their intensely rapid drive for material comfort. Some people contend that the island of refuge is being destroyed by success. Violent crime, for instance, once hardly known in Taiwan, is now commonplace. Six thousand violent crimes, including rapes, robberies, kidnappings, and murder, were reported in 1989—a 22-percent increase over 1988. Extortion against wealthy companies and abductions of the children of successful families are causing a wave of fear among the rich.

Furthermore, there are signs that the economy is heading for a slowdown. In the early 1990s labor shortages are forcing some companies to operate at 60 percent of capacity; low-interest loans are hard to get, because the government fears that too many people will simply invest in get-rich stocks instead of in new businesses; and inflation is taking a bigger bite out of profits.

POLITICAL LIBERALIZATION

These disturbing trends notwithstanding, in recent years the Taiwanese people have had much to be grateful for in the political sphere. Until 1986 the government, dominated by the influence of the Chiangs, had permitted only one political party, the KMT, and had kept Taiwan under martial law for nearly 4 decades. A marked political liberalization began near the time of Chiang Ching-Kuo's death, in 1987. The first opposition party, the Democratic Progressive Party, was formed, martial law (officially, the "Emergency Decree") was lifted, and the first two-party elections were held in 1986. Significantly, in 1988, for the first time a native-born Taiwanese, Cornell-educated Lee Teng-hui, was elected to the presidency, and further Taiwanization of the government is anticipated.

Nevertheless, the Taiwanese people, like their counterparts in Singapore, have over the years accustomed themselves to limited civil liberties, because violators have often been silenced by force. It is still against the law for any group to advocate publicly the independence of Taiwan—that is, to advocate international acceptance of Taiwan as a sovereign state, separate and apart from China. It would appear, however, that most Taiwanese would prefer a legally recognized separation from the People's Republic of China. As opposition parties proliferate, the independence issue could become a more urgent topic of political debate. In the meantime, contacts with the P.R.C. increase daily; Taiwanese students are now being admitted to China's universities, and Taiwanese residents may now visit relatives in the P.R.C. President Lee has publicly promoted better relations with the People's Republic (the first president to do so), but China has vowed to invade Taiwan if it should ever declare independence. Under these circumstances, many—probably most—Taiwanese will likely remain content to let the rhetoric of reunification continue while enjoying the reality of de facto independence.

DEVELOPMENT

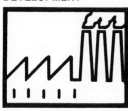

Taiwan has vigorously promoted export-oriented production, particularly of electronic equipment. In the 1980s manufacturing became the leading sector of the economy, employing more than one-third of the workforce. Ninety-nine percent of Taiwanese households own color televisions, and other signs of affluence are abundant.

FREEDOM

For nearly 4 decades Taiwan was under martial law. Opposition parties were not tolerated, and individual liberties were limited. A liberalization of this pattern began in 1986. Taiwan now seems to be on a path toward greater democratization. In 1991, 5,574 prisoners, including many political prisoners, were released in a general amnesty.

HEALTH/WELFARE

Taiwan has one of the highest population densities in the world. About 92 percent of the population can read and write. Education is compulsory to age 15, and the country boasts more than 100 institutions of higher learning. Social programs, however, are less developed than those in Singapore, Japan, and some other Pacific Rim countries.

ACHIEVEMENTS

From a largely agrarian economic base, Taiwan has been able to transform its economy into an export-based dynamo with international influence. Today only 20 percent of the population work in agriculture.

Thailand (Kingdom of Thailand)

GEOGRAPHY

Area in Square Kilometers (Miles):
514,000 (198,404) (slightly more than
twice the size of Wyoming)
Capital (Population): Bangkok
(4,700,000)
Climate: tropical

PEOPLE

Population
Total: 55,116,000
Annual Growth Rate: 2.18%
Rural/Urban Population Ratio: 80/20
Ethnic Makeup of Population: 75%
Thai; 14% Chinese; 4% Malay; 7%
others
Languages: Thai; English; dialects;
others

Health
Life Expectancy at Birth: 64 years
(male); 70 years (female)
Infant Mortality Rate (Ratio):
34/1,000
Average Caloric Intake: 105% of FAO
minimum
Physicians Available (Ratio): 1/8,150

Religion(s)
95% Buddhist; 4% Muslim; 1%
others

Education
Adult Literacy Rate: 89%

MONKS BEFORE MARRIAGE

In some parts of Thailand, a young man who has never served as a
Buddhist monk is not considered prime marriage material. Young
women may think of him as an "unripe person." To overcome this
stigma, many young Thai men shave their heads and accept a temporary
ordination into the Buddhist priesthood.

This important rite of passage into adulthood is usually undertaken
during the monsoon season, when daily rain prevents extensive labor in
the rice paddies. The process is not particularly difficult, and boys spend
much of the time chatting and resting. However, recruits are expected to
don a saffron robe and go from door to door each morning to beg for
rice from the faithful; both the giver and the receiver are said to gain
spiritual merit for this deed, and the family of the young monk receive
even more spiritual merit for having enrolled their son as a monk. After
a few weeks or months most young men return to their normal lives,
with spiritual merit to their names and a heightened chance of marriage.

COMMUNICATION

Telephones: 739,500
Newspapers: 23 dailies in Bangkok

TRANSPORTATION

Highways—Kilometers (Miles):
44,534 (27, 611)
Railroads—Kilometers (Miles): 3,940
(2,442)
Usable Airfields: 103

GOVERNMENT

Type: constitutional monarchy
Independence Date: traditional
founding date: 1238
Head of State: King Bhumibol
Adulyadej; Acting Prime Minister
(General) Sunthorn Kongsompong
Political Parties: Democratic Party;
Social Action Party; Thai Nation
Party; People's Party (2); Thai
Citizens Party; United Democracy
Party; others
Suffrage: universal at 21

MILITARY

Number of Armed Forces: 283,000
*Military Expenditures (% of Central
Government Expenditures):* 2.9%
Current Hostilities: boundary dispute
with Laos

ECONOMY

Currency ($ U.S. Equivalent): 25.72
baht = $1
Per Capita Income/GNP:
$1,160/$64.5 billion
Inflation Rate: 5.4%
Natural Resources: tin; rubber;
natural gas; tungsten; tantalum;
timber; lead; fish; gypsum; lignite;
fluorite
Agriculture: rice; cassava; rubber;
corn; sugarcane; coconuts; soybeans
Industry: tourism; textiles and
garments; agricultural processing;
beverages; tobacco; cement; electric
appliances and components;
electronics; furniture; plastics

FOREIGN TRADE

Exports: $19.9 billion
Imports: $25.1 billion

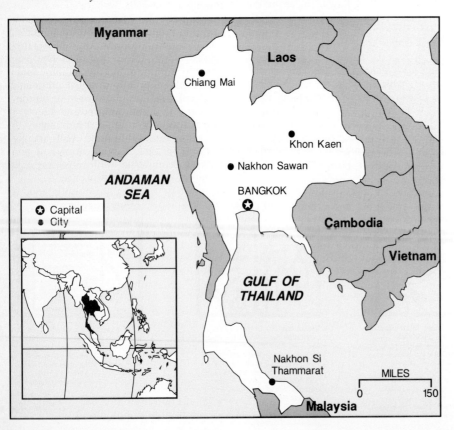

THAILAND'S ANCIENT HERITAGE

The roots of Thai culture extend into the distant past. People were living in Thailand at least as early as the Bronze Age; and by the time Thai people from China (some scholars think from as far away as Mongolia) had established the first Thai dynasty in the Chao Phya Valley in A.D. 1238, some communities, invariably with a Buddhist temple or monastery at their center, had been thriving in the area for 600 years. Early Thai culture was greatly influenced by Buddhist monks and traders from India and Sri Lanka (Ceylon).

By the seventeenth century Thailand's ancient capital, Ayutthaya, boasted a larger population than did London of the same period. Ayutthaya was known around the world for its wealth and for the beauty of its architecture, particularly its religious edifices. Attempts by European nations to obtain a share of the wealth were so inordinate that in 1688 the king expelled all foreigners from the country. Later, warfare with Cambodia, Laos, and Malaya yielded tremendous gains in power and territory for Thailand, but it was periodically afflicted by Burma which briefly conquered Thailand in the 1760s (as it had done in the 1560s). The Burmese were finally defeated in 1780, but the destruction of the capital required the construction of a new city near what is today Bangkok.

Generally speaking, the Thai people have been blessed over the centuries with benevolent kings, many of whom were open to new ideas from Europe and North America. Gathering around them advisors from many nations, they improved transportation systems, education, and farming while maintaining the central place of Buddhism in Thai society. Occasionally, royal support for religion overtook other societal needs, at the expense of the power of the government.

The gravest threat to Thailand came during the era of European colonial expansion. However, although both France and Britain forced Thailand to yield its holdings in Southeast Asia, Thailand—which means "Free Land"—was never completely conquered by European powers.

MODERN POLITICS

Since 1932, when a constitutional monarchy replaced the absolute monarchy, Thailand (formerly called Siam) has weathered 17 attempted or successful military or political coup d'états (most recently in 1991). The Constitution has been revoked and replaced numerous times; governments have fallen under votes of no-confidence; students have mounted violent demonstrations against the government; and the military has, at various times, imposed martial law or otherwise curtailed civil liberties.

Clearly, Thai politics are far from stable. Nevertheless, there *is* a sense of stability in Thailand. Miraculously, its people were spared the direct ravages of the Vietnam War, which raged nearby for 20 years. And despite all the political upheavals, the same royal family has been in control of the Thai throne for 9 generations, although its power has been severely delimited for some 60 years. Furthermore, before the first Constitution was enacted, in 1932, the country had been ruled continuously, for more than 700 years, by often brilliant and progressive kings. At the height of Western imperialism, when France, Britain, Holland, and Portugal were in control of every country on or near its borders, Thailand remained free of Western domination, although it was forced, sometimes at gunpoint, to relinquish sizable chunks of its holdings in Cambodia and Laos to France, and holdings in Malaya to Britain. The reasons for this singular state of independence were the diplomatic skill of Thai leaders, Thai willingness to Westernize the government, and the desire of Britain and France to let Thailand remain interposed as a neutral buffer zone between their respective armies in Burma (today known as Myanmar) and Indochina.

The current king, Bhumibol Adulyadej, born in the United States and educated in Switzerland, is highly respected as head of state. The king is also the nominal head of the armed forces, and his support is critical to any Thai government. Despite Thailand's structures of democratic government, any administration that has not also received the approval of the military elites, many of whom hold seats in the Senate, has not prevailed for long. The military has been a rightist force in Thai politics, resisting reforms from the left that might have produced a stronger labor-union movement, more freedom of expression (many television and radio stations in Thailand are controlled directly by the military), and less economic distance between the social classes. Military involvement in government increased substantially during the 1960s and 1970s, when a communist insurgency threatened the government from within and the Vietnam War destabilized the external environment.

Until the February 1991 coup, there had been signs that the military was slowly withdrawing from direct meddling in the government. This may be because the necessity for a strong military appeared to have lessened since the end of the Cold War. In late 1989, for example, the Thai government signed a peace agreement with the Communist Party of Malaya, which had been harassing villagers along the Thai border for more than 40 years.

Unlike some democratic governments which have one dominant political party and one or two smaller opposition parties, party politics in Thailand are characterized by diversity. Indeed, so many parties compete for power that no single party is able to govern without forming coalitions with others. Parties are often founded on the strength of a single charismatic leader rather than on a distinct political philosophy, a circumstance that makes the entire political setting rather volatile. The Communist Party remains banned.

FOREIGN RELATIONS

Thailand is a member of the United Nations (UN) and of the Association of Southeast Asian Nations (ASEAN). Throughout most of its modern history it has maintained a pro-Western political position. During World War I Thailand joined with the Allies, and during the Vietnam War it allowed the United States to stage air attacks on North Vietnam from within its borders; it also served as a major rest and relaxation center for American soldiers. During World War II, Thailand briefly allied itself with Japan but made decided efforts after the war to reestablish its former Western ties.

Thailand's international positions have seemingly been motivated more by practical need than by ideology. During the colonial era Thailand linked itself with Britain because it needed to offset the influence of France; during World War II it joined with Japan in an apparent effort to prevent its country from being devastated by Japanese troops; during the Vietnam War it supported the United States because the United States seemed to offer Thailand its only hope of not being directly engaged in military conflict in the region.

Currently Thailand seems to be tilting somewhat away from its close ties with the United States and toward a closer relationship with Japan. Disputes with the United States in the late 1980s, over import tariffs and international copyright matters, cooled the prior warm relationship. Moreover, Thailand found in Japan a more ready, willing, and cooperative economic partner than the United States. Japan and Taiwan are now the leading foreign investors in Thailand.

During the Cold War and especially during the Vietnam War era the Thai military strenuously resisted the growth of communist ideology inside Thailand, and the Thai government refused to engage in normal diplomatic relations with the communist regimes on its borders. Because of military pressure, elected officials refrained from advocating improved relations with the communist governments. However, in 1988 Prime Minister Prem Tinslanond, a former general in the army who had been in control of the government for 8 years, stepped down from office, and opposition to normalization of relations seemed to mellow. The subsequent prime minister, Chatichai Choonhavan, who was ousted in the 1991 military coup, invited Cambodian leader Hun Sen to visit Thailand, and he also made overtures to Vietnam and Laos. Chatichai's goal was to open the way for trade in the region by helping to settle the agonizing Cambodian conflict. He also hoped to bring stability to the region so that the huge refugee camps in Thailand, the largest in the world, could be dismantled and the refugees repatriated. The intentions of the new Thai government in these regards are as yet unclear.

THE RICE CULTURE
Part of the thrust behind Thailand's diplomatic initiatives is the changing needs of its economy. For decades Thailand saw itself as an agricultural country; indeed, nearly 70 percent of the workforce remain in agriculture today, with rice as the primary commodity. Rice is Thailand's single most important export and a major source of government revenue. Every morning Thai families sit down on the floor of their homes around a large bowl of rice; holidays and festivals are scheduled to coincide with the various stages of planting and harvesting rice; and in rural areas, school is dismissed at harvest time so that all members of a family can help in the fields. So central is rice to the diet and the economy of the country that the verb "to eat," translated literally, means "to eat rice." Thailand is the fifth-largest exporter of rice in the world.

(UN/photo by Saw Lwin)

Rice is Thailand's single most important export and utilizes for a majority of the agricultural workforce. Today the government is attempting to diversify this reliance on rice, encouraging farmers to grow a wider variety of crops that are not so dependent on world markets and the weather.

King Rama I
ascends the
throne, begin-
ning a nine-
generation
dynasty
1782

King Mongkut
builds the first
road in Thailand
1868

Coup;
constitutional
monarchy
1932

The country's
name is
changed from
Siam to
Thailand
1939

Thailand joins
Japan and
declares war on
the United
States and
Britain
1942

Thailand
resumes its
historical pro-
Western stance
1946

Communist
insurgency
threatens
Thailand's
stability
1960s-1970s

Student protests
usher in
democratic
reforms
1973

1980s-1990s

A military coup
attempt is
thwarted

Chatichai
Choonhavan
replaces a
former army
general as
prime minister

Chatichai is
deposed in a
military coup

Unfortunately, Thailand's dependence on rice subjects its economy to the cyclical fluctuations of weather (sometimes the monsoons bring too little moisture) and market demand. Thus, in recent years the government has invested millions of dollars in economic diversification. Not only have farmers been encouraged to grow a wider variety of crops, but tin, lumber, and offshore oil and gas production have also been promoted. Foreign investment in export-oriented manufacturing has been warmly welcomed. Japan in particular benefits from trading with Thailand in food and other commodities, and sees Thailand as one of the more promising places to relocate smokestack industries. For its part, Thailand seems to prefer Japanese investment over that from the United States, because the Japanese seem more willing to engage in joint ventures and to show patience while enterprises become profitable.

Thailand's shift to an export-oriented economy is paying off. The growth rate of the gross domestic product in 1988 was an amazing 11 percent which places it as high or higher than all the newly industrializing countries (NICs) of Asia (Hong Kong, South Korea, Singapore, Taiwan, and China). Furthermore, unlike the Philippines or Indonesia, Thailand has been able to achieve this incredible growth without high inflation. The current military leadership, however, may alter these trends. It cited widespread corruption in the economy as a major reason for staging its takeover of the government in 1991.

SOCIAL PROBLEMS

Industrialization in Thailand, as everywhere, draws people to the cities. It is estimated that, by the year 2000, Bangkok will have a population of 10.7 million, making it one of the largest cities in the world. Numerous problems, particularly traffic congestion and overcrowding, already complicate life for Bangkok residents, and solving them may alter important elements of Thai life. Yet a majority of Thai people still make their living on farms, where they grow rice, rubber, and corn, or tend chickens and cattle, including the ever-present water buffalo. Thus, it is in the countryside (or "upcountry," as everywhere but Bangkok is called in Thailand) that the real culture of Thailand may be found. There, for example, one still finds villages of typically fewer than 1,000 inhabitants, with houses built on wooden stilts alongside a canal or around a Buddhist monastery. One also finds, however, unsanitary conditions, higher rates of illiteracy, and lack of access to potable water. The provision of social services does not meet demand even in the cities, but rural residents are particularly deprived.

THE CULTURAL MILIEU

Culturally, Thai people are known for their willingness to tolerate (although not necessarily to assimilate) diverse lifestyles and opinions. Buddhist monks, who shave their heads and vow celibacy, do not find it incongruous to beg for rice in

districts of Bangkok known for prostitution and wild night life. And worshipers seldom object when a noisy, congested highway is built alongside the serenity of an ancient Buddhist temple.

This relative openness has mitigated ethnic conflict among Thailand's numerous minority groups. The Chinese, for instance, who are often disliked in other Asian countries because of their dominance of the business sectors, are able to live with little or no discrimination in Thailand; indeed they constitute the backbone of Thailand's new industrial thrust. About 75 percent of the population of 55 million are ethnic Thai, 14 percent are Chinese, and 4 percent (mostly in the south) are Malay Muslims; the remainder of the population is made up of tribal peoples and Cambodian and Vietnamese refugees.

Ninety-five percent of Thailand's people are Buddhists. Prayers to Buddha (and to the king) are offered in the public schools every day. Many children receive part of their education in Buddhist monasteries, and most males will live the life of a monk for at least a few weeks or months in their youth. Thai Buddhist monks are extremely sensitive to any comments or behavior that seems to insult or denigrate the Buddhist faith.

DEVELOPMENT

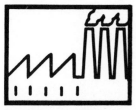

Nearly 70 percent of Thailand's workforce are small-plot or tenant farmers, but the government has energetically promoted economic diversification. Despite high taxes, Thailand has a reputation as a good place for foreign investment. Electronics and other high-tech industries from Japan, the United States, and other countries have been very successful in Thailand.

FREEDOM

Since 1932, when the absolute monarchy was abolished, Thailand has endured numerous military coups and countercoups, most recently in February 1991. Combined with the threat of communist insurgents, these have resulted in numerous declarations of martial law, press censorship, and suspensions of civil liberties.

HEALTH/WELFARE

Thailand's literacy rate is 89%, and about 2,000 young men and women out of every 100,000 inhabitants attend college (as compared to only 200 per 100,000 in Vietnam). Thailand has devoted substantial sums to the care of refugees from Cambodia and Vietnam. The rate of nonimmigrant population growth has dropped substantially since World War II.

ACHIEVEMENTS

Thailand is the only Southeast Asian nation never to have been colonized by a Western power. It was also able to remain detached from direct involvement in the Vietnam War. Unique among Asian cultures, Thailand has a large number of women in business and other professions. Thai dancing is world-famous for its intricacy.

Vietnam (Socialist Republic of Vietnam)

GEOGRAPHY

Area in Square Kilometers (Miles):
329,560 (121,278) (slightly larger than
New Mexico)
Capital (Population): Hanoi
(3,100,000)
Climate: tropical

PEOPLE
Population

Total: 66,171,000
Annual Growth Rate: 2.1%
Rural/Urban Population Ratio: 81/19
Ethnic Makeup of Population: 90%
Vietnamese; 3% Chinese; 7%
Muong, Thai, Meo, and other
mountain tribes
Languages: official: Vietnamese;
others spoken: French, Chinese,
Khmer, tribal languages

Health

Life Expectancy at Birth: 62 years
(male); 66 years (female)
Infant Mortality Rate (Ratio):
50/1,000
Average Caloric Intake: 91% of FAO
minimum
Physicians Available (Ratio): 1/3,140

Religion(s)

Buddhists, Confucians, and Taoists
most numerous, Roman Catholics,
animists, Muslims, Protestants
(percentages not available)

RELIGION IN VIETNAM

Religious belief in Vietnam is an eclectic affair. Many of the mountainous peoples, collectively called Montagnards by the French, continue to practice animism, the worship of spirits they believe reside in nature. Most Vietnamese are Buddhists or Taoists, or both. They pray to ancestors and ask for blessings at small shrines inside their homes. When the French were in power in Vietnam about 15 percent of the population were Roman Catholic—a church that was strongly opposed by the Buddhist hierarchy.

In recent years several new religions have emerged. The most prominent is called Cao Dai and claims about 2 million believers. It models itself after Roman Catholicism in terms of hierarchy and religious architecture but differs in that it accepts many gods—Jesus, Buddha, Mohammed, Lao-Tse and others—as part of its pantheon.

Education
Adult Literacy Rate: 94%

COMMUNICATION
Telephones: 106,100
Newspapers: 4 dailies

TRANSPORTATION
Highways—Kilometers (Miles):
approximately 85,000 (52,700)
Railroads—Kilometers (Miles): 3,059
(1,896)
Usable Airfields: 100

GOVERNMENT
Type: communist state
Independence Date: September 2,
1945
Head of State: Chairman of the
Council of State Vo Chi Cong;
Chairman of the Council of Ministers
(Premier) Do Mvoi
Political Parties: Vietnam Communist
Party
Suffrage: universal at 18

MILITARY
Number of Armed Forces: 1,149,000
(reductions have been announced)
*Military Expenditures (% of Central
Government Expenditures):* 19.4%
Current Hostilities: boundary disputes
with Cambodia; sporadic border
clashes with China; other boundary
disputes with China, Malaysia,
Taiwan, and the Philippines

ECONOMY
Currency ($ U.S. Equivalent): 4,515
new dong = $1
Per Capita Income/GNP: $215/$14.2
billion
Inflation Rate: 40%
Natural Resources: phosphates; coal;
manganese; bauxite; chromate;
offshore oil deposits; forests
Agriculture: rice; corn; potatoes;
rubber; soybeans; coffee; tea; animal
products; fish
Industry: food processing; textiles;
machine building; mining; cement;
chemical fertilizer; glass; tires; oil;
fishing

FOREIGN TRADE
Exports: $1.1 billion
Imports: $2.5 billion

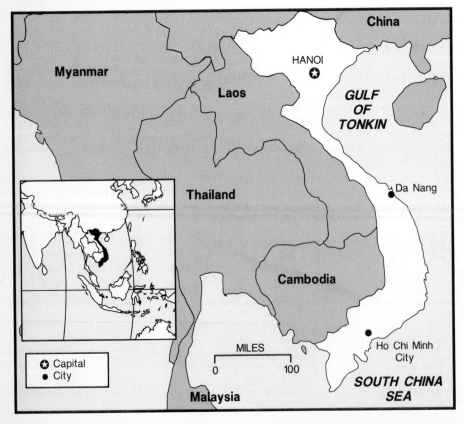

FOREIGNERS IN VIETNAM

Foreign powers have tried to control Vietnam for 2,000 years. Most of that time it has been the Chinese who have had their eye on control—specifically of the food and timber resources of the Red River Valley in northern Vietnam.

Most of the northern Vietnamese were ethnically Chinese themselves, but over the years they had forged a separate identity for themselves and had come to resent Chinese rule. Vietnam was conquered by China as early as 214 B.C. and again in 111 B.C., when the Han Chinese Emperor Wu Ti established firm control. For about 1,000 years (until A.D. 939, and sporadically thereafter by the Mongols and other Chinese) the Chinese so thoroughly dominated the region that the Vietnamese people spoke and wrote in Chinese, built their homes like those of the Chinese, and organized their society according to Confucian values. In fact, Vietnam (*viet* means "people" and *nam* is Chinese for "south") is distinct among Southeast Asian nations because it is the only one whose early culture—in the north, at least—was influenced more by China than by India.

The Chinese did not, however, directly control all of what constitutes modern Vietnam. Until the late 1400s the southern half of the country was a separate kingdom known as Champa and inhabited by people called Chams, who originally came from Indonesia. For a time Champa was annexed by the north. However, between the northern region called Tonkin and the southern Chams-dominated region was a narrow strip of land occupied by Annamese peoples (a mixture of Chinese, Indonesian, and Indian ethnic groups), who eventually overthrew the Cham rulers and came to dominate the entire southern half of the country. In the 1500s the northern Tonkin region and the southern Annamese region were ruled separately by two Vietnamese family dynasties. In the 1700s military generals took power, unifying the two regions and attempting to annex or control parts of Cambodia and Laos as well.

In 1787 Nguyen-Anh, a general with imperial ambitions, signed a military-aid treaty with France. The French had already established Roman Catholic missions in the south, were providing merce-

nary soldiers for the Vietnamese generals, and were interested in opening up trade along the Red River. Eventually the Vietnamese came to resent the increasingly active French involvement in their internal affairs and took steps to curtail French influence. The French, however, impressed by the resources of the Red River Valley in the north and the Mekong River Delta in the south, were in no mood to pull out. War broke out in 1858, and by 1863 the French had won control of many parts of the country, particularly in the south around the city of Saigon. Between 1884 and 1893 France solidified its gains in Southeast Asia by taking the city of Hanoi and the surrounding Tonkin region and by putting Cambodia, Laos, and Vietnam under one administrative unit, which it called Indochina.

Ruling Indochina was not easy for the French. For one thing, the region was comprised of hundreds of different ethnic groups, many of whom had been traditional enemies long before the French arrived. Within the borders of Vietnam proper lived Thais, Laotians, Khmers, northern and southern Vietnamese, and

President Ngo Dinh Diem, premier of the interim government of South Vietnam, proclaimed the Republic of Vietnam on October 26, 1955. Here he is seated center, attending ceremonies on November 6, 1963, marking the 8th anniversary of his takeover. One week later a military coup overthrew his regime.

China begins 1000 years of control or influence over the northern part of Vietnam 214 B.C.

Northern and southern Vietnam are ruled separately by two Vietnamese families A.D. 1500s

Military generals overthrow the ruling families and unite the country 1700s

General Nguyen-Anh signs a military-aid treaty with France 1787

After 5 years of war, France acquires its first holdings in Vietnam 1863

France establishes the colony of Indochina 1893

Anti-French sentiment begins to surface 1920s

Ho Chi Minh founds the Indochinese Communist Party 1930

The Japanese control Vietnam 1940s

mountain peoples whom the French called Montagnards. Most of the people could not read or write—and those who could wrote in Chinese, because the Vietnamese language did not have a writing system until the French created it. Most people were Buddhists and Taoists, but many also believed in animism.

In addition to the social complexity, the French had to contend with a rugged and inhospitable land filled with high mountains and plateaus as well as lowland swamps kept damp by yearly monsoon rains. The French were eager to obtain the abundant rice, rubber, tea, coffee and minerals of Vietnam, but found that transporting these commodities to the coast for shipping was extremely difficult.

VIETNAMESE RESISTANCE

France's biggest problem, however, was local resistance. Anti-French sentiment began to solidify in the 1920s; by the 1930s Vietnamese youth were beginning to engage in open resistance. Prominent among these was Nguyen ai Quoc, who founded the Indochinese Communist Party in 1930 as a way of encouraging the Vietnamese people to overthrow the French. He is better known to the world today as Ho Chi Minh, meaning "He Who Shines."

Probably none of the resisters would have succeeded in evicting the French had it not been for Adolf Hitler's overrunning of France in 1940 and Japan's subsequent military occupation of Vietnam. These events convinced many Vietnamese that French power was no longer a threat to independence; the French remained nominally in control of Vietnam, but everyone knew that the Japanese had the real power. In 1941 Ho Chi Minh, having been trained in China by Maoist leaders, organized the League for the Independence of Vietnam, or Viet Minh. Upon the defeat of Japan in 1945 the Viet Minh assumed that they would take control of the government. France, however, insisted on reestablishing a French government. Within a year the French and the Viet Minh were engaged in intense warfare, which lasted for 8 years.

The Viet Minh fought the French initially with weapons supplied by the United States when that country was helping local peoples to resist the Japanese. Communist China later became the main supplier of

assistance to the Viet Minh. This development convinced U.S. leaders that Vietnam under the Viet Minh would very likely become another communist state. To prevent this occurrence, U.S. President Harry S. Truman decided to back France's efforts to re-control Indochina (although the United States had originally opposed France's desire to regain its colonial holdings). In 1950 the United States gave $10 million in military aid to the French, an act that began a long, costly, and painful U.S. involvement in Vietnam.

In 1954 the French lost a major battle in the north of Vietnam, at Din Bien Phu, after which they agreed to a settlement with the Viet Minh. The country was to be temporarily divided at the 17th Parallel (a latitude about which the communist Viet Minh held sway and below which noncommunist Vietnamese had the upper hand), and country-wide elections were to be held in 1956. The elections were never held, however; and under Ho Chi Minh, Hanoi became the capital of North Vietnam, while Ngo Dinh Diem became president of South Vietnam, with its capital in Saigon. Ho Chi Minh viewed the United States as yet another foreign power trying to control the Vietnamese people and continued his military operations against the U.S.-backed south.

THE UNITED STATES ENTERS THE WAR

The United States, concerned about the continuing attacks on the south by northern communists and by southern communist sympathizers called Viet Cong, increased funding and sent military advisers to help prop up the increasingly fragile southern government. By 1963 President John F. Kennedy had sent 12,000 military advisers to Vietnam. In 1964 an American destroyer ship was attacked in the Gulf of Tonkin by North Vietnam. The U.S. Congress responded by giving then-President Lyndon Johnson a free hand in ordering U.S. military action against the north; before this time, U.S. troops had not been involved in direct combat.

By 1969, 542,000 American soldiers and nearly 66,000 soldiers from 40 other countries were in battle against North Vietnamese and Viet Cong troops. Despite unprecedented levels of bombing and use of sophisticated electronic weaponry, U.S. and South Vietnamese forces contin-

ued to lose ground to the communists, who used guerrilla tactics and built their successes on latent antiforeign sentiment among the masses as well as extensive Soviet military aid. At the height of the war, as many as 300 U.S. soldiers were killed in a week.

Watching the war on the evening television news, many Americans began to withdraw emotional support. Anti-Vietnam rallies became a daily occurrence on American university campuses, and many people began finding ways to protest U.S. involvement: dodging the draft by fleeing to Canada, burning down ROTC buildings, and publicly challenging the U.S. government to withdraw. President Richard Nixon had once declared that he was not going to be the first president to lose a war, but after his expansion of the bombing into Cambodia to destroy communist supply lines, and after significant battlefield losses, domestic resistance became so great that an American withdrawal seemed inevitable. The U.S. attempt to Vietnamize the war by training South Vietnamese troops and supplying them with advanced weapons did little to change South Vietnam's sense of having been sold out by the Americans.

Secretary of State Henry Kissinger negotiated a ceasefire settlement with the north in 1973, but most people believed that as soon as the Americans left, the North would resume fighting and would probably take control of the entire country. This, indeed, happened, and in April 1975, under imminent attack by victorious North Vietnamese soldiers, the last Americans lifted off in helicopters from the grounds of the U.S. Embassy in Saigon, the South Vietnamese government surrendered, and South Vietnam ceased to exist.

The war wreaked devastation on Vietnam. It has been estimated that nearly 2 million people were killed during just the American phase of the war; another 2.5 million were killed during the French era. Four-and-a-half million people were wounded, and nearly 9 million lost their homes. Among the casualties were 58,000 killed and 300,000 wounded Americans.

A CULTURE, NOT JUST A BATTLEFIELD

Because of the Vietnam War, many people think of Vietnam as if it were just a battlefield. But Vietnam is much more

France attempts to regain control Post-1945	The United States begins to aid France to contain the spread of communism 1950s	Geneva agreements end 8 years of warfare with the French; Vietnam is divided into North and South 1954	South Vietnam's corrupt regime is overthrown by a military coup 1963	The United States begins bombing North Vietnam 1965	Half a million U.S. troops are fighting in Vietnam 1969	The United States withdraws its troops and signs a ceasefire 1973	North Vietnamese troops capture Saigon and reunite the country 1975	Vietnamese troops capture Cambodia; China invades Vietnam 1979

1980s–1990s

The U.S. economic embargo of Vietnam impedes economic growth	Communist Vietnam begins liberalization of the economy	U.S. and Vietnamese officials begin meetings to resolve the Cambodian war

than that. It is a rich culture made up of peoples representing diverse aspects of Asian life. In good times, Vietnam's dinner tables are supplied with dozens of varieties of fish and the ever-present bowl of rice. Sugarcane and bananas are also favorites. Because about 80 percent of the people live in the countryside, the population as a whole possesses a living library of practical know-how about farming, livestock raising, fishing, and home manufacture. Today only about 214 out of every 100,000 Vietnamese people attend college, but most children attend elementary school and 94 percent of the population can read and write.

Literacy was not always so high; much of the credit is due the communist government, which, for political-education reasons, has promoted schooling throughout the country. Another thing that the government has done, of course, is to unify the northern and southern halves of the country. This has not been an easy task, for upon the division of the country in 1954 the North followed a socialist route of economic development, while in the South, capitalism became the norm.

THE ECONOMY

When the communists won the war in 1975 and brought the capitalist South under its jurisdiction, the United States imposed an economic embargo on Vietnam. It remains in effect today, despite repeated attempts by the Vietnamese to have it removed.

The United States and some of its allies by various means impeded efforts by the communist Vietnamese government to strengthen the economy. Thus, the first

decade after the war saw the entire nation fall into a severe economic slump. For example, whereas Vietnam had once been an exporter of rice, it now had to import rice from abroad. Inflation raged at 250 percent a year, and the government was hard-pressed to cover its debts. Many South Vietnamese were, of course, opposed to communist rule and attempted to flee on boats—but, contrary to popular opinion, most refugees left Vietnam because they could not get enough to eat, not because they were being persecuted.

Beginning in the mid-1980s the Vietnamese government began to liberalize the economy. Under a restructuring plan called *doi moi* (similar in meaning to the Soviet term *perestroika*), the government began to introduce elements of free enterprise into the economy. Japan and other countries have begun to do business with Vietnam, and the country is once again exporting large volumes of rice; indeed, it is currently the world's third-largest rice exporter.

The government has also made it clear that it would like to normalize relations with the United States. But, apparently feeling the need to punish Vietnam for winning the war (it was the first time the United States had ever lost a war), the United States resisted any attempts at bridge-building until 1990, when a desire to end the Cambodian conflict created opportunities for the two sides to talk together.

HEARTS AND MINDS

As one might expect, resistance to the current Vietnamese government comes largely from the South Vietnamese who,

under both French and American tutelage, adopted Western values of capitalism and consumerism. Many South Vietnamese had feared that after the North's victory, South Vietnamese soldiers would be mercilessly killed by the victors; some were in fact killed, but many former government leaders and military officers were instead sent to "reeducation camps," where, combined with hard labor, they were taught the values of socialist thinking. Several hundred such internees remain incarcerated a decade and a half after the end of the war. Many of the well-known leaders of the South fled the country when the communists arrived and now are making new lives for themselves in the United States, Canada, Australia, and other Western countries. Those who have remained—for example, Vietnamese members of the Roman Catholic Church—have occasionally resisted the communists openly, but their protests have been silenced. Hanoi continues to insist on policies that remove the rights to which the South Vietnamese had become accustomed. For instance, the regime has halted publication and dissemination of books that it judges to have "harmful contents." There is not much that average Vietnamese can do to change these policies except through passive obstruction, which many are doing even though it damages the efficiency of the economy.

DEVELOPMENT

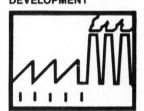

Recent liberalization in the direction of a market economy has not yet brought an end to the U.S. embargo of the Vietnamese economy. Although Vietnam is a major exporter of rice, the average Vietnamese earns less than almost any other Asian worker.

FREEDOM

Vietnam is nominally governed by an elected National Assembly. Real power, however, resides in the Communist Party and with those military leaders who helped defeat the U.S. and South Vietnamese Armies. Civil rights, such as the right of free speech, are curtailed. Private-property rights are limited.

HEALTH/WELFARE

Health care has been nationalized and the government operates a social-security system, but the chronically stagnant economy has meant that few Vietnamese receive sufficient health care or have an adequate nutritional intake. The World Health Organization has been involved in disease-abatement programs since reunification of the country in 1975.

ACHIEVEMENTS

Vietnam provides free and compulsory schooling for all children, but the curricular content has been changed in an attempt to eliminate Western influences. New Economic Zones have been created in rural areas to try to lure people away from the major cities of Hanoi, Hue, and Ho Chi Minh.

Articles from the World Press

Annotated Table of Contents for Articles

Topic Guide to Articles

TOPIC AREA	TREATED IN:	TOPIC AREA	TREATED IN:
Health and Welfare	9. The Dream Out of Reach for Japanese 16. Raising Hiroko 17. Japan: Model of Sustainable Development 25. China: The Great Leap to Disaster 32. Democratic People's Republic of Korea 35. Myanmar: Ayadaw Township 40. Thailand: People Power	**Politics**	12. New Awareness 24. China One Year Later 25. China: The Great Leap to Disaster 27. Indonesian Rebellion 29. Lurching Toward Democracy in Seoul 33. Looking for Laos 36. Recouping the Boom 37. Aquino's Fragile Government 38. Jostling for Control of the Island
History	6. The Civilization of the Forest 13. Japan's Invisible Minority 18. The Floating World 19. The Pavilion of the Second Moon 23. Rock Dreams	**Private Enterprise**	3. The Rising Power of the Pacific 4. Fair Winds in the West 22. The Pacific Rim 42. Hanoi Goes to Market
Hong Kong	26. To Leave or Not to Leave	**Religion**	6. The Civilization of the Forest 19. The Pavilion of the Second Moon 23. Rock Dreams
Human Rights	28. Uprooting People, Destroying Cultures	**Rural Life**	24. China One Year Later
Industrial Development	3. The Rising Power of the Pacific 4. Fair Winds in the West 30. South Korea	**Sex Roles**	14. Japanese Women 15. Under New Management 16. Raising Hiroko 18. The Floating World
Inflation	9. The Dream Out of Reach for Japanese 10. People Measure Affluence	**Social Reform**	18. The Floating World 24. China One Year Later 29. Lurching Toward Democracy in Seoul 33. Looking for Laos
Legal System	21. Japan's Gangsters		
Migration	28. Uprooting People, Destroying Cultures	**Social Unrest**	27. Indonesian Rebellion 28. Uprooting People, Destroying Cultures
Minorities	13. Japan's Invisible Minorities 28. Uprooting People, Destroying Cultures	**Special Administrative Region (SAR)**	26. To Leave or Not to Leave
Natives	6. The Civilization of the Forest 13. Japan's Invisible Minority 23. Rock Dreams 28. Uprooting People, Destroying Cultures		
Natural Resources	2. ASEAN Takes Off 5. Main Grain 17. Japan: Model of Sustainable Development 25. China: The Great Leap to Disaster 39. Thai Loggers Devastate Forest	**Standard of Living**	9. Japan's Role in the Post–Cold War World 10. People Measure Affluence 11. How the Japanese Are Changing 12. New Awareness
Peasants	24. China One Year Later 25. China: The Great Leap to Disaster	**Taiwan Independence**	38. Jostling for Control of the Island
Philosophy	6. The Civilization of the Forest 20. The Shape Changer Kitsune	**Tiananmen Square**	24. China One Year Later
Political Reform	24. China One Year Later 25. China: The Great Leap to Disaster 27. Indonesian Rebellion 29. Lurching Toward Democracy in Seoul	**Urban Life**	9. The Dream Out of Reach for Japanese 10. People Measure Affluence 11. How the Japanese Are Changing
		Women	14. Japanese Women 18. The Floating World

Article 1

THE WORLD & I
MARCH 1990

SPECIAL REPORT—SOUTHEAST ASIA: REGION ON THE RISE

Competition or Cooperation

The steady growth and interaction of the economies in the region suggest that substantial cooperation may finally be achieved.

by Dalton West

Dalton West, executive vice president of the Global Strategy Council, specializes in Asian affairs.

The idea of an enlarged Asia Pacific economic community is one whose time has come—and gone—several times in recent years. But now it looks like it's here to stay. For some, this marks the emergence of the Pacific Century (PC) and although Europe may continue to capture the front pages, the world's economic and political center of gravity will shift from Europe and the Atlantic to Asia and the Pacific. Others, however, see it as a sign of rising protectionism and the division of the world into competing trading blocs in Europe, Asia, and the Americas. Neither view is quite correct.

The most recent initiative, known by its acronym APEC (Asia Pacific Economic Cooperation), was set in motion by Australia's prime minister, Bob Hawke. It began with a speech by Hawke in South Korea in January 1989 and led slowly to a preliminary meeting of ministerial-level representatives from twelve countries in November.

In his speech, Hawke cited supporting multilateral trade liberalization, lifting Asia Pacific trade barriers, and encouraging regional policy coordination as major objectives. A year later, these remain the declaratory objectives of APEC.

Some give the initiative little chance of succeeding in the long term because the participating nations are separated by vast distances and widely divergent cultures. On the other hand, its mission has never been clearly defined. Given the history of diversity and rivalry in the region, success might well be defined simply, as it is in ASEAN (the Association of South East Asian Nations): namely, coming together, a paramount achievement. That yardstick, however, leaves unanswered questions about timing and its future prospects.

There is a carrot-and-stick element in the thinking of Asia Pacific leaders. The answers to the question "why now" rest in conditions both inside and outside the region. The primary answer lies in the area's economic strength (at an all-time high and set to continue) and in developments surrounding three prominent, seemingly contradictory trends in the world's trading system. These are global economic integration, growth of bilateral or regional trading arrangements, and the poor performance of multilateral trade negotiations.

On one level, the speed of worldwide economic integration, fueled by technological change, swelling capital flows, and burgeoning trade, has outgrown the international mechanisms designed to manage change. The rapid march to maturity of the Asia Pacific economies has transformed several countries into both regional and global commercial rivals, not only in such sectors as electronics and telecommunications but also in finance and services.

The speed and magnitude of change have given rise to problems of adjustment as the global system tries to accommodate the new dynamics. One factor is huge regional surpluses, such as Japan's nearly $100 billion and Taiwan's $75 billion. Other pressures include measures that in effect would erect protectionist barriers.

Examples of recent trends toward regional or bilateral cooperation include the European Common Market plans for further integration by 1992, the U.S.-Canada Free Trade Agreement, the Closer Economic Relations agreement between Australia and New Zealand, and plans for an Arab Cooperation Council. Other initiatives have all contributed to general perceptions in the Asia Pacific region about adverse trends in world trading practices.

At the same time, Asia Pacific countries share the generally pessimistic view of multilateral trade negotiations such as the GATT (General Agreement on Tariffs and Trade). In their largely bureaucratic attempt to reduce trade barriers, many feel that such attempts are too cumbersome in a rapidly changing world.

Impelling the PC are other factors of a more positive nature, including the strength of the Asia Pacific markets and their attractiveness to outside trading partners. After decades of false starts and failed initiatives, some analysts feel that the region has finally developed enough strength and cohesion to mount and sustain a meaningful trading presence on the world scene. But will it be a regional economic initiative with a difference?

The APEC challenge is to find ways to resolve difficulties without destroying the trading and financial systems that have

For more than a decade, trade across the Pacific has surpassed trade across the Atlantic.

created regional successes. According to Gareth Evans, Australia's foreign minister and chairman of the Canberra meetings, the APEC countries "vigorously and universally expressed commitment to the principles of multilateral trade liberalization."

Even a cursory glance at the raw statistics of success illustrates a solid foundation for the region's growing feeling of strength. The dozen largest economies of the Asia Pacific region account for nearly a quarter of the world's GNP, and for more than a decade trade across the Pacific has surpassed trade across the Atlantic. In 1989, Pacific Basin commerce totaled about $300 billion, about 50 percent more than Atlantic trade.

During the 1980s, Japan became the world's second-largest economy, and the four "Little Dragons"—South Korea, Singapore, Hong Kong, and Taiwan —averaged 9 percent annual growth over the decade. In the next ten years they will be joined by Thailand and Malaysia as leaders among the world's NICs or NIEs (newly industrializing countries or economies).

But the APEC initiative unfolds against a bleak historical record and in the face of some monumental political, cultural, and physical problems. Many observers feel that if APEC is to succeed it will need to address a far wider range of issues than trade.

Past attempts

Attempts to create a wider Pacific Basin economic initiative go back at least two decades when Japanese and Australian academics and politicians, led by Australian economist Peter Drysdale and Japan's Okita, inspired by the success of the European Community, began to promote Pacific cooperation. This effort led a group of businessmen in 1967 to form the PBEC (Pacific Basin Economic Council). In 1968 ASEAN was created, and its signatory nations made a major commitment to regional, economic, and cultural cooperation and development.

In the late 1970s, under Japan's Prime Minister Masayoshi Ohira and Australia's Prime Minister Malcolm Fraser, a tripartite body of academics, businessmen, and government officials was formed and named PECC (Pacific Economic Cooperation Conference). Through the 1980s this conference gradually built a consensus on Pacific cooperation in specific areas where common interests could be identified.

Neither PBEC nor PECC made much headway against fears and suspicions, mainly among the ASEAN countries, about being dominated by the larger industrial economies. The less-developed countries of ASEAN have a history of antagonistic relations. They came together in the wake of the Vietnam War and have always worried that a broader group would be run by the advanced countries, thus undermining the role of the fledgling ASEAN. Similarly, they feared that attempts to create an organization along the lines of OECD (Organization for Economic Cooperation and Development, a Paris based group of advanced nations) would lead to the creation of a permanent secretariat that might supersede ASEAN's. Nevertheless, as early as 1984, the ASEAN states had created a dialogue process with their major trading partners, and this represented an important step toward wider discussions.

In addition to PBEC and PECC, there have been numerous plans and initiatives intended to promote wider regional cooperation. These include plans put forth by American officials in the latter part of the Reagan administration, under Secretary of State George Shultz, and later, during the first months of the Bush administration, under Secretary of State James Baker. Senator Alan Cranston and others have promoted comparable congressional initiatives.

Perhaps the most important American contribution has been to ease ASEAN fears about participating in the APEC initiative last year. In the end, ASEAN went to the Canberra ministerial meetings on an "exploratory basis" and wound up hosting the second organizational meeting in Singapore, no doubt to keep a close eye on APEC's evolution. South Korea has agreed to host a third meeting, and Indonesia has expressed an interest in hosting one in the future. The stage appears to be set for annual APEC meetings, hosted alternately by ASEAN and non-ASEAN members.

The Canberra meetings intentionally avoided certain problems, in an effort to start off the initiative on a positive note. Among these was the question of membership. Invited to the gathering were representatives from Australia, Brunei, Canada, Indonesia, Japan, South Korea,

APEC is a non-formal forum for consultations among high-level representatives of significant economies in the Asia Pacific region.

Malaysia, New Zealand, the Philippines, Singapore, Thailand, and the United States. These nations represent virtually all the market economies of the region, with the notable exceptions of Taiwan and Hong Kong.

The socialist economies of the People's Republic of China, Vietnam, and the Soviet Union were excluded from these preliminary meetings on the grounds that, given the nature of the discussions, they did not fit well in the grouping. Taiwan and Hong Kong, which certainly would have blended well into the meeting, were excluded as part of the attempt to avoid the "three Chinas problem" at the first, formative meeting of APEC.

The way was left open for other regional nations to join the process with the consent of the participants. The organizing group for the Singapore meeting has already indicated that the issue of membership for the PRC, Hong Kong, and Taiwan will be on the agenda at that gathering.

It was widely recognized that the countries attending the APEC meeting had a special interest in the future of the multilateral GATT system. Almost immediately after the Canberra meeting, representatives from

Japan, the United States, Canada, and the European Community (EC) met in Japan, and these quadrilateral negotiations will be followed by informal meetings of ministers from 27 countries in the Uruguay Round of GATT negotiations.

In the view of many participants at Canberra, the principal intention and most immediate benefit of the first APEC meeting was to inject fresh life into the flagging GATT negotiations. The Uruguay Round is due to be completed in 1990, and all proposals for this year's discussions needed to be submitted by the end of 1989; hence the importance of the APEC gathering. The ministers agreed to cooperate closely and to meet at least twice before the closing sessions of the GATT negotiations in December 1990.

Overcoming obstacles

On the issue of liberalizing trade within the Asia-Pacific region and the APEC countries, it was recognized that the main trade barriers were highest for those goods in which regional rivals had a comparative advantage. For example, Japan and Korea maintain agricultural barriers against Australia, New Zealand, North America, and Thailand, whereas the latter nations protect against labor-intensive production from Asian countries. In certain areas, such as textiles, clothing, and footwear, the equation is more complicated.

It was widely recognized that the APEC's larger aim must be to go beyond trade difficulties and to reinforce the region's positive trends by promoting cooperation in areas like human-resource development, information and data, tourism, telecommunication, shipping, energy, and fisheries. In this respect, the prior work of organizations such as PECC have provided invaluable foundation studies for possible areas of cooperation.

Foreign investment and technology transfer are two particularly important areas for future cooperation. Already a second wave of foreign investment within the region appears to have started, flowing from the NICs to such ASEAN countries as Thailand, Malaysia, and Indonesia.

As the 12 nations involved in the APEC initiative prepare for their second meeting, a number of issues remain to be settled. The first is very basic and concerns the fundamental reasons for APEC's existence and—especially—ASEAN's attitudes toward it. It is difficult to comprehend the organization as a permanent, major player in world economic terms without an institutional infrastructure, however minimal. Yet institutionalizing APEC will be problematic. Many ASEAN states argue that virtually all of the APEC 12 are in dialogue already through the annual ASEAN postministerial dialogue conferences. Furthermore, these meetings include the EC and will soon include South Korea.

For the time being, rather than commit itself to creating a controversial permanent secretariat, APEC deems itself to be in a period of evolution, and arrangements for the next one or two ministerial-level meetings will be overseen by senior officials from the participating countries, joined by representation from the ASEAN secretariat.

Some proposals put forward at the first APEC meeting contain the seeds of future problems. For example, the Japanese have offered to act as a central data-processing base for APEC. If that offer is taken up, Tokyo will emerge as a logical choice for a permanent secretariat in the event that APEC decides to create one.

An exclusive club?

Membership in APEC remains a more immediate issue, for both the short and long term. Missing from the Canberra meetings were China, Taiwan, and Hong Kong. Nobody doubts their future inclusion. Present at the first APEC meeting was a representative of the South Pacific Forum, a grouping of the smaller Pacific island countries, and their membership will be reviewed at the next APEC meeting.

In the longer term, participation by Vietnam and Cambodia will become an issue. They are not well integrated into the regional economy, and such a criterion will remain a major test of eligibility for APEC membership. Soviet participation is also likely at some future point, although this relationship will involve more political than economic considerations, given the commitment to consensus decisions in APEC.

The decision to include Canada and the United States, but to exclude Mexico, the Pacific seaboard countries of Central and South America, and India, stemmed largely from attempts to define what constitutes the Asia Pacific region. This is a permanent and dynamic element in a real political equation and is subject to constant change. In the interim, according to the Canberra ministerial communiqué, APEC is evolving as a "non-formal forum for consultations among high-level representatives of significant economies in the Asia Pacific region." And, one might add, with a slowly emerging but steadily increasing, comprehensive agenda.

Article 2

THE WORLD & I
MARCH 1990

SPECIAL REPORT   SOUTHEAST ASIA: REGION ON THE RISE

ASEAN Takes Off

*If dynamic development continues, ASEAN is
scheduled to give birth to Asia's newest Tigers.*

by Frank Tatu

*Frank Tatu, a former American Foreign
Service officer who has served his entire
career in Southeast Asia, is currently
writing a book on ASEAN.*

A s the much-touted "Pacific
Century" approaches, the
miracle of economic development around the Asian
Rim continues apace with few
signs of abatement.

Prime spokes of the Pacific hub are the Association
of Southeast Asian Nations
(ASEAN) members. Brunei and
Singapore have the most robust
economies. The remaining four
members are, in order of 1987
per capita income, Malaysia,
Thailand, the Philippines, and
Indonesia, at: $1,800; $850;
$590; and $450, averaging out to
$925.

Note that Singapore is the
only ASEAN member that is an
Asian Tiger. Because of its growing economy, like Singapore,
Brunei is also, to its distress,
ineligible for American trade
preferences. Brunei's $15,390
per capita income exceeds the
$8,500 limit for GSP preferential
treatment. Brunei, however, a
tiny sultanate ruled by the
world's richest man, is absolutely sui generis and cannot be
addressed in any general discussion of either economic dynamics
or ASEAN, to which it became
the sixth and last member in

■ *The Komtar Building towers over West Malaysia. Tourism and film
shoots contribute to Malaysia's dynamic economy.*

FOO YONG KOON/THE WORLD & I

1984 [see, "Brunei's Abundant Fortunes"].

While the six ASEAN nations occupy a total land area less than a third of that of the United States, the ASEAN population of 321.2 million exceeds both that of the United States (247 million) and of the European Community with which it expects to be in direct economic competition after 1992.

ASEAN was established in August 1967 primarily as a regional instrument of economic, social, and cultural cooperation to enhance cohesion, self-reliance, and "resilience" (an ASEAN signatory term). Because of competitive aspects of the economies and the lack of complimentary goals, ASEAN was, as noted, accorded short-shrift, even by some of its members.

With some jump-starts, however, provided by significant economic spin-offs from the Vietnam War, (both Thailand and the Philippines contributed troops in support of Saigon) and foreign assistance (after World War II, U.S. bilateral economic assistance to ASEAN countries through 1987 totaled $8.6 billion), ASEAN forged ahead. It is now described by official U.S. publications as "a dynamic group of developing countries with some of the highest growth rates in the world."

Collectively, ASEAN constitutes the United States' seventh-largest trading partner. In 1987 total U.S.-ASEAN trade was about $27 billion. A generally favorable investment climate has stimulated a doubling of American direct investment in ASEAN from 1982 to the present.

America's principal exports to ASEAN are capital goods, chemicals, transportation equipment, and agricultural products. The United States imports 90 percent of ASEAN's natural rubber, and 38 percent of its tin, in addition to petroleum, sugar, palm oil, textiles, and electronic components.

An ASEAN model?

With the exception of Singapore, which won its spurs as an entrepôt par excellence, the ASEAN states have prospered by judicious exploitation of rich natural resources and all have driven their economies by export-led growth strategies and are market-oriented with a minimum of—or at least diminishing—government intervention.

The ASEAN experience, as well as the panoply of Asian development, is being studied by various groups to determine the extent to which the lessons are transferable to presently underdeveloped areas.

ASEAN also occupies a special place in U.S. regional equations. Former Secretary of State George Shultz referred to ASEAN as "the central focus of our policy in

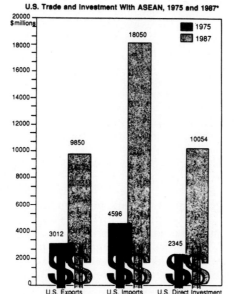

U.S. Trade and Investment With ASEAN, 1975 and 1987*

■ 1975
▨ 1987

*Direct investment is the yearend book value of US direct investors' equity in, and net outstanding loans to, their foreign affiliates. This does not include US oil company expenditures in exploration and development. It does not include investment in Brunei.

Source: US Department of Commerce

Southeast Asia." And in speaking of the region's economic growth and its global implications, Secretary of State James Baker has said that the United States is going to see in Asia "the necessity for closer coordination with ASEAN." Baker told an Asia Society audience during a speech in June that ASEAN was "one of the Pacific's most constructive regional organizations."

In answer to the question "Who will be the next Asian Tigers?" the resounding response from most sources would be: all four (that is to say, those remaining after Singapore and Brunei).

In an extensive report issued last January, the State Department wrote that "Thailand and Malaysia are fast approaching levels close to those of the newly industrialized economies, while the Philippines and Indonesia have economic reforms underway that, if sustained, will enable them to capitalize on their impressive potential."

In August 1989, the respected Washington-based Atlantic Council issued a policy paper entitled "The Role of Industrializing Economies in the World Economy" in which it also predicts that "the next generation of NIEs will be Thailand, Malaysia, the Philippines, and Indonesia."

Without addressing time factors, the State Department and Atlantic Council would seem to have put the up-and-coming ASEAN states in proper order.

A Tiger poised to leap

In response to the question "Which ASEAN state will become the next Tiger?" observers confidently answer—"Thailand."

Indeed, Thailand is already developed enough to be classified a Tiger. And Thailand has apparently benefited from the economic destabilizations of China's recent cataclysm. While tourism has always been a major factor in Thai development strategy, Bangkok hotel managers now report soaring occupancy rates, presumably as a result of tourists diverted from China. There have also been reports of foreign consumers, most notably Australians, transferring supply sources from Chinese to Thai producers.

According to another study, Thailand has in recent years enjoyed spectacular development rates. Thailand is "in a position to join the ranks of the fastest growing economies in the world" with a 1988 GDP growth rate up from 10 to 11 percent.

Thailand's status as a "near NIC" was acknowledged when it was invited to attend, as an observer, the Organization for Economic Cooperation and Development exploratory meeting with the four Tigers in mid-1989.

In August 1989, Thailand became the first Southeast Asian nation to join the Yankee bond market with an issue in New York of $200 million worth of 8.7 percent 10-year bonds. The success of the issue prompted it to file for "shelf registration" with the U.S. Securities and Exchange Commission, presumably to facilitate additional bond issues over the coming months. This is not bad for a "near NIC" which seems to be heading for the big leagues with rapid strides.

And riding the fifth Tiger's tail into Pacific Rim success will be the remaining ASEAN members—cubs six, seven, and eight.

Article 3

FORTUNE/ PACIFIC RIM 1990

THE RISING POWER OF THE PACIFIC

ASIA'S GROWING power is the corporate challenge of the 1990s. If as manager or tourist you have always found the region intriguing, the stories on the following pages will inform as well as delight you. If you think you know all about the countries of the Pacific Rim, from a couple of trips or a couple of dozen, the details we've uncovered on the pivotal trends and the fascinating people who are reshaping the East will surprise you.

Urgency is needed in learning more about Asia. The long-anticipated emergence of its countries as economic powerhouses is happening now, not tomorrow. Steel consumption is higher than in the U.S. and in Europe. Within two years Asia's demand for semiconductors will exceed that of the European Community.

By the end of the decade Pac Rim economies will be bigger in total than those of the EC, and about equal to North America's. An exciting consumer market is bubbling up, especially now that Japan and other prosperous nations are removing many barriers to foreign goods.

Western companies will have to move swiftly into the region or lose the most vibrant third of their global market. Eastern Europe, for all its potential, won't approach the dynamism of Asia for several decades—if ever. Embracing free enterprise is just the first step. The hard part will be catching up with the work habits and entrepreneurship of Asians. Says Singapore Premier Lee Kuan Yew, the most global-minded Asian leader: "As China has discovered, it is not easy to shed the effects of 40 years of Marxism-Leninism and become a spirited and gung-ho people like the Japanese and those of the newly industrializing economies."

The Pacific Rim is loaded with opportunities for American and European companies. Asia is the world's hottest market for cars, telecommunications equipment, airliner seats, paint, and a host of other products. It also is crowded with competitors, not only potent Japanese companies but aggressive, growing conglomerates from other countries in the region. Asian producers outside Japan have already gained 25% of the global market for personal computers.

Without much fanfare or a common market, Asia is becoming an economically cohesive region. A new division of labor in manufacturing is taking place. Japan and the four not-so-little dragons—Singapore, Hong Kong, Taiwan, and South Korea—provide most of the capital and expertise for Asia's developing countries, which have abundant natural resources and labor.

Toyota plans to invest $215 million in Indonesia, Thailand, Malaysia, and the Philippines to produce components for export. Sony makes videocassette recorders in Malaysia, using parts from both Singapore and Japan, and sells the finished product to customers around the world.

Japan is more open than it used to be to Western imports and investment. The country is finally settling into an economic maturity that resembles that of the U.S. and Europe. An aging population has tightened Japan's labor supply. Younger Japanese, less workaholic than their elders, are clamoring to buy more Western products.

Still, the costs and hassles of entering Japan remain formidable; the rest of Asia may offer even richer rewards.

The collective muscle of the region's new industrial economies is tremendous. The dragons together export almost as much to the U.S. as Japan does. Behind them are a group of efficient, low-cost manufacturers: Thailand, Malaysia, and Indonesia.

All these countries are more amenable than is Japan to buying Western products and forming manufacturing alliances with Western companies. Singapore in particular is promoting what it calls a growth triangle, in which multinational companies can offset the high wages of Singapore's skilled workers by also using lower-paid, less-skilled workers in nearby Indonesia and Malaysia.

The lowest-cost factory hands ($110 a month) are on the Indonesian island of Batam, just 12½ miles from Singapore. A $214 million industrial park is taking shape there for labor-intensive operations of such companies as Western Digital of the U.S. and Philips of the Netherlands. The highly technical phases of production will be done in plants in Singapore, where skilled workers earn up to $400 a month, while midlevel assembly would go to the nearby Malaysian state of Johore. Says George Yong-Boon Yeo, Singapore's Minister of State for Finance and Foreign Affairs: "Linked with Singapore, Malaysian and Indonesian labor will be very competitive in the markets of the world."

Astute U.S. and European companies are spreading operations around the region, gaining the best comparative advantages of each Asian country. Seagate, the California disk drive maker, assembles its products in Singapore, using printed circuitboards from South Korea, metal parts from Taiwan, and magnetic heads from Hong Kong that are put together in Thailand. Thomson of France makes color TV sets in Singapore, mainly for European markets, using components from five other Asian countries.

Texas Instruments has found that Acer, the fast-growing personal computer maker in Taiwan, is a valuable ally, not a threat. TI has joined with Acer to build a $250 million memory chip plant in Taiwan. Until late last year, when Acer built its own California factory, TI assembled Acer machines in Austin, Texas, for the U.S. market. Acer, whose sales could reach $1 billion this year, has been a very profitable investment for American backers, including Citicorp, Chase Manhattan, and Prudential.

AMERICAN investments in Asia generally pay off handsomely. A Commerce Department survey for 1989 shows an average annual return of 31.2% in Singapore, 28.8% in Malaysia, 17.9% in South Korea, 23.6% in Hong Kong, 22.2% in Taiwan, and 14.1% in Japan—vs. 15.2% for U.S. investments in all foreign countries.

For all its burgeoning strength, Asia faces risks. The region's long run of political stability could be shaken here and there as strong leaders hand over power. Warns one Asian business analyst: "The risk profile in Asia will change tremendously over the next several years." South Korea and Taiwan have become more democratic—and more chaotic. No one is quite sure what will follow when China's tired old leaders depart. In Indonesia, President Suharto, 69, who has ruled for 23 years, has no clear successor. Almost everywhere, including Japan, political transitions will affect business confidence.

The greatest danger in Asia for any global competitor would be failure to get there. What company can afford to pass up a market that soon will be larger in total GNP than the European Community? The risks of not tapping its potential are global. If Western companies do not establish a firm position in Asia, competitors from Japan, Taiwan, and Korea will gain more strength at home for even bigger assaults on markets in America and Europe.   **–Louis Kraar**

Article 4

SOUTH JULY 1989

FAIR WINDS IN THE WEST

Trade between the dynamic economies of the west Pacific grew faster than in any other region in 1988. Trade between the region and the US has surpassed that across the Atlantic in recent years. The latest development is an explosion of commerce between the west Pacific countries themselves, which looks set to continue for some time.

As far as the authorities in Beijing and Tapei are concerned, there is no trade between the two countries, yet the unofficial flow of goods was worth US$2.6-billion last year. In May, a Thai trade delegation went to Hanoi regardless of political tensions between the two countries. And officials from Canberra have been canvassing the idea of a Southeast Asia-Australasia trade zone, despite the fact that if it ever gets off the ground it could be the Australian industrialists who are the ones struggling to survive in a more open regional market. These three paradoxes are among the signs of the change in the old order on the Pacific's western rim.

Trade among these countries is growing as exporters reorient their markets

The golden trade triangle

Trade flows, 1988 ($bn)

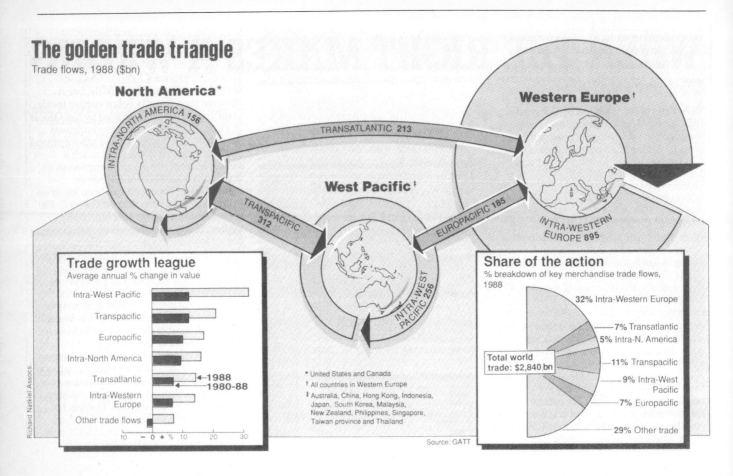

North America*

INTRA-NORTH AMERICA 156

TRANSATLANTIC 213

Western Europe †

West Pacific ‡

TRANSPACIFIC 312

EUROPACIFIC 185

INTRA-WESTERN EUROPE 895

INTRA-WEST PACIFIC 256

Trade growth league
Average annual % change in value

- Intra-West Pacific
- Transpacific
- Europacific
- Intra-North America
- Transatlantic ←1988
- ←1980-88
- Intra-Western Europe
- Other trade flows

10 − 0 + % 10 20 30

Richard Natkiel Assocs

* United States and Canada
† All countries in Western Europe
‡ Australia, China, Hong Kong, Indonesia, Japan, South Korea, Malaysia, New Zealand, Philippines, Singapore, Taiwan province and Thailand

Source: GATT

Share of the action
% breakdown of key merchandise trade flows, 1988

32% Intra-Western Europe
7% Transatlantic
5% Intra-N. America
11% Transpacific
9% Intra-West Pacific
7% Europacific
29% Other trade

Total world trade: $2,840 bn

away from the US and its protectionist policies. Within the west Pacific, trade increased by more than 30 per cent in 1985, the fastest growth in the world, according to Gatt, the international trade watchdog. In the 1980s, average annual trade flows among the 12 countries on the rim have grown by more than 10 per cent a year – roughly equal to the growth in trade across the Pacific and much faster than that among Western European countries.

Despite this rapid growth, in money terms trade among the west Pacific countries still accounts for only 9 per cent of the US$2.84-trillion world merchandise trade in 1988. This is a long way behind intra-Western European trade (31.5 per cent), and even trans-Pacific trade (11 per cent). But the shift is likely to gather pace as Asian economies diversify in what they can make and in what they want to buy.

Japan is the region's powerhouse, supplying the surrounding economies and consuming much of their output. Tokyo has been obliged to strengthen its regional links because of the yen's appreciation against other leading currencies, and because of pressure from the US and the European Community to reduce its huge trade surpluses and open up its domestic market.

Most of Japan's investment is directed at the members of the Association of South-east Asian Nations – Thailand, the Philippines, Malaysia, Indonesia, Brunei and Singapore. Investing in such low-cost neighbouring countries as Thailand, Indonesia or the Philippines has been one way that Japan has remained competitive against rivals in South Korea, Hong Kong and Taiwan province, whose currencies have risen less. In addition, a Japanese subsidiary or joint venture in Thailand can gain easier access to the US or EC markets than a home-based one because of more favourable tariff treatment and fewer quotas.

The supplies of capital equipment, spares and technology needed for these new overseas plants have boosted Japanese exports, while the flow in the other direction of raw materials, food and items such as textiles is being supplemented by finished products and components. Semiconductors are now an important Thai export to Japan, along with the established ones of rice and T-shirts.

Japan has also adjusted to the rising yen and low-cost foreign competition by shifting upmarket, and by discarding less viable operations or transferring them overseas, although this has been at the cost of jobs. Elsewhere in the west Pacific, the process of change has also been treated positively. The four tigers – Hong Kong, Taiwan province, Singapore and South Korea – have been restructuring away from exports as the chief engine of growth in favour of satisfying rising domestic demand. They have been pushed in this direction by the mounting trade restrictions in the US, their benefits under the preferential system for developing countries having been largely eliminated.

According to analysts at Morgan Guaranty, in dollar terms the share of total exports which went to the US peaked in 1986 at 37.2 per cent. (In the case of Taiwan province, this was 48 per cent.) By last year the total had fallen to 30.2 per cent. As a proportion of export growth, the importance of the US market is dwindling even faster; the US accounted for more than half the expansion in the tigers' exports in 1980-86, compared with the current 20 per cent.

Instead, there has been a growth in exports to Europe and west Pacific markets. China took only 2 per cent of the tigers' exports in 1980, but by last year this had increased to 8 per cent. And sales to Japan look set to grow at a healthy pace.

Like Japan, the tigers are no longer able to compete with the lowest-cost producers. In addition, pressure from workers for higher living standards has increased labour costs in South Korea and Taiwan province. So, like their Japanese counterparts, companies in Hong Kong, Singa-

● **A matter of custom:** *brisk trade in 19th-century Yokohama customs house*

The potential of the Chinese market has led old political foes such as Taiwan province and South Korea to overcome inhibitions, albeit the trade is indirect.

The question now remaining is how soon Indochina will open up to the thriving trading community which surrounds it. Bangkok is the natural base for business expansion into the region, as shown by the recent Thai trade mission to Hanoi. The Japanese are also familiar faces in Vietnam. However, much will depend on the availability of funds from the IMF and other financial institutions to help restructure the economy once the withdrawal of Vietnamese troops from Kampuchea clears the way for political accommodation with the West (*South May*).

On the southern fringe, Australia and New Zealand will have a difficult time competing. Natural resources, skilled workers and a highly developed services sector are their best assets, but they face deep structural problems.

Australia's Prime Minister, Bob Hawke, sent his special envoy, Richard Woolcott, shuttling around Asia promoting the idea of a Pacific economic region. This would be more trade-based than the Pacific-type organisation for economic cooperation and development proposed by the US.

More open trading zones are hardly a new idea, but the region's dynamism and competition could make such a grouping a formidable force.
Paul Melly

pore, Taiwan province and South Korea have opted for overseas assembly rather than for direct exports. This helps hold down trade surpluses with partners such as the US. Dealing with the protectionist polices of the developed countries may be the "single greatest reason for the newly industralising economies of Asia to work urgently to correct their surpluses, and for South Korea and Taiwan province to liberalise their economies fully," a Morgan Guaranty official says.

China has emerged as an attractive low-cost manufacturing base for Asian companies. In Hong Kong, for example, 80 per cent of re-exports have passed through China, in particular through the nearby special economic zones, such as Shenzhen.

Article 5

Sojourn, no. 17, Winter 1990

MAIN GRAIN

The Rites of Asian Rice

Jane Knight

As rosy-fingered dawn creeps over the vast snowy massif of Mt Rakaposhi, towering 8,000 meters over the Hunza valley in northern Pakistan, another workday begins. Swathed in coarse blankets against the chill air, two old farmers put the final touches to an intricate system of ridges and hollows between delicate apricot orchards. This ethereal place is the original Shangri-la, and both figures in the awesome landscape are more than 100 years old. They are planting rice, which along with vegetables and fruit as their staple diet, may be the secret of their longevity.

In these remote mountains, as in those of Madagascar or in the hot deserts of the Middle East, rice is grown as a dry-land crop. In southern China, Thailand and Indonesia, by contrast, it's cultivated in flooded fields, forming those mirrored patchworks, fringed by palms and wallowed in by buffalo, which constitute for many Westerners the archetypal images of Asia. Peopling such picture postcards are brightly-clad women wading knee-deep in the muddy water, painstakingly planting each seedling by hand. Not so in California, or New South Wales, however, where thousands of square miles of rice fields are sown from aircraft at the simple push of a button.

Rice is grown as far south of the equator as central Argentina, as far north as the Sino-Russian border. Unique among cereals in its adaptability to a wide diversity of environments, it can also thrive in many different kinds of soils. In southern India, farmers plant seedlings on the tops of mounds of earth that stick out of salt water. In Bangladesh, there's a rice plant that reaches a length of six meters and floats on top of flood waters.

Almost half the world's population eats rice as a staple food. Healthily, too, since brown rice — that is, rice which has been hulled but not polished — is one of the most nutritional of cereals, second only in food value to the soya bean. Though inferior in protein volume to wheat, rice beats wheat in protein quality. In addition to carbohydrates (72.5 percent) and protein (7.4 percent), the embryo and bran coat of rice contain fats, water and valuable minerals, plus vitamins B and E. Hopes are that, with appropriate aid, the planting of huge tracts of uncultivated land in Africa could one day provide enough rice to feed the world.

But if rice will grow happily from the Punjab to the Pampas, from Spain to New South Wales, 90 percent of the world's rice is grown in Asia. And here, rice is less a cereal, more a way of life — one which goes back thousands of years. Rice is mentioned in the earliest Hindu scriptures, and the great Chinese philosopher Confucius, born in 551 BC, promised prosperity if people followed the rule of a rice-growing society. Rice cultivation, with its habitual cycle — the planting of seedlings, flooding of the fields, transplanting, ripening, harvest and fallow — provided the basis of social order in many ancient civilizations. It was an existence which demanded hard work, according to a strict timetable, in addition to cooperation within family or community groups. A conservative sense of respect for the past and for the family are values that remain alive and well in every major Asian rice-growing country today.

Oryza sativa, or cultivated rice, is in fact a land, not a water plant. Early farmers probably planted it in dry hillsides, with implements as simple as sharpened sticks, much as the centenarians in Hunza do now. But some 7,000 years ago, in the river valleys of Southeast Asia, farmers noticed that their rice actually grew better when their fields were flooded in the aftermath of a storm. Thus the home of irrigated rice became part of Asia subject to the monsoon, with its guaranteed long, hot summers and equally reliable torrential rains. This system of rice growing quickly spread throughout Asia wherever the monsoon prevailed.

Nor was it confined to flat plains. The fabled rice terraces of Banaue in the Philippines, dating back at least to 1,000 BC, have been called the eighth wonder of the world. An almost incredible human achievement, these spectacular terraces cover every contour of a series of valleys in the rugged Gran Cordillera Central, soaring to between 1,800 and 3,000 meters along a 320-kilometer stretch in Northern Luzon. Researchers believe the current inhabitants — the Ifugao ("people of the sky world") — are descendants of a clan that's lived there since prehistoric times, building more and more terraces over the centuries to feed an ever-growing population. No one, however, can be quite sure who inaugurated this massive engineering feat.

The Ifugao devised an ingenious method, still employed today, of fertilizing and irrigating the land in a single operation. Water is diverted from its source and runs through manure, loam, ashes and other nutrients on its way to the rice terraces. The liquid flows by force of gravity, distributing its rich load evenly as it covers the soil.

The early Banaue rice farmers also invented a calendar of 13 seasons, dedicated to specific activities such as "weeding and planting" or "rest and feast." Each season was divided into 28 days and was represented by a length of string kept by a priest. Knots tied in the string allowed them to reckon the days, a colored bead or stick being added for special occasions. Bundles of 13 strings were kept as records of years.

Even today, the daily life of the Ifugao remains dominated by the worship of many gods and rituals performed to appease them. Foremost among these is Bulul, the fertility or rice god, in honor of whom buffalo, pigs and chickens are sacrificed amid much chanting and dancing.

For the Balinese, rice itself is sacred — so each mouthful is, in itself, an offering to the gods. In Bali, too, where every available inch of volcanic hillside is terraced, miracles of hydraulic engineering have provided irrigation by damming high mountain streams and delivering the water via hand-built conduits to the field below. Before planting, the terraces are silvery pools, covered with a glistening sheet of water. Then they turn a vivid green when the young plants begin to grow, before turning a golden yellow at harvest time. After the harvest, the straw is burned, leaving a dry stubble.

Rice is believed to be a manifestation of Dewi Sri, the Rice Mother, who is in turn a manifestation of the supreme deity, Sanghyang Widi. During Bali's harvest season, the image of Dewi Sri, called Dewa Nini, is present in the fields and adorns every rice barn. A Dewa Nini is made by tying a string round the middle of a bunch of stalks, forming an hour-glass-shaped figure called a *cili*, the symbol of the island.

The auspicious day on which to begin the rice cycle is chosen by the head of the *subak*, or cooperative, in consultation with the priest, who consults the lunar calendar and the 210-day Balinese calendar. At each stage of procedure — before the hoeing, after the plowing, at the transplanting of the seedlings when three to five are inserted poked together into the mud at one handbreadth intervals in neat rows — offerings are made at a small temple in a corner of the field. Two weeks before harvest, all irrigation is stopped and another ceremony is held.

But the most magnificent rice ceremony, Ngusaba Nini, is held as a thanksgiving after the harvest. Thousands of people in the subak make Dewa Nini and bring them to the temple, already decorated with flags and banners. There is a great feast, with music and entertainment to please Dewi Sri. At some point in the three-day festival, the Dewa Nini are paraded on the heads of their makers to the nearest holy spring, or to the sea. Afterwards, the whole cycle begins again.

That Bali now produces thousands of tons more rice annually than it consumes, despite a steady population growth (in the 1960s and 70s the island was forced to import 10,000 tons a year), is due to the miracle-working International Rice Research Institute (IRRI). Located in Los Baños, near Manila in the Philippines, this multinational organization was established in 1960 by the Ford and Rockefeller Foundations to develop new high-yield, disease- and insect-resistant strains of rice.

IRRI rice has also turned the Philippines from a rice-importing nation into an exporter, and it's thanks to IRRI that Indonesia can feed most of its 150 million people from domestic production.

"BROWN RICE IS ONE OF THE MOST NUTRITIONAL CEREALS, SECOND ONLY TO SOYA BEANS IN FOOD VALUE."

The miracle rice that saved Asia from famine threatened by a population growth of 55 percent was IR8, a plant with a short, strong stem, capable of holding the heavier grain yields achieved as a result of the introduction of fertilizers. It was developed by crossing a traditional Indonesian variety with a hybrid from Taiwan bred by Japanese and Chinese scientists after the Second World War. An even bigger step forward was taken in the 1970s, when high-yield strains were cross-pollinated with a wild rice growing in the Himalayas known to resist pests. The resultant IR36 had immunity to the brown planthopper, the most serious rice predator. Now grown on some 11 million hectares, IR36 is the single most popular food crop on earth.

Yet the race is constantly on to keep ahead of the brown planthopper, which changes to adapt to resistant varieties. To this end, 70,000 varieties of rice seed are kept by IRRI in a giant refrigerated storehouse, each computer-classified for properties such as yield, pest-resistance, response to cold, drought, saline and alkaline soils, and so on.

Although the introduction of miracle rice, as well as fertilizers and insecticides, has enabled farmers to produce three or four times as much rice per hectare as with the old *padi Bali*, there has been human resistance, largely because age-old rituals are threatened. Unlike the beautiful, tall, swaying padi Bali, cut and baled and carried home on the heads of women to be dried in the sun and stored in the rice barn, the new rice is short, ugly and must be threshed in the field because the grains fall out so easily. Some Asian farmers grow new rice but reserve a small field of old rice for family consumption, contending that it tastes better and can be stored longer.

There are other disadvantages to progress. Years ago, fish lived in the canals and flooded fields, but they have been exterminated by modern insecticides and fertilizers. Farmers also used to grow vegetables as well as rice, but with today's multiple cropping, their land is constantly wet and unsuitable for vegetable growing. Of course, income from rice has increased, but farmers now have to buy vegetables and fish in the market to ensure a diet with enough protein and vitamins. For instance, around the middle of the 19th century, there were many deaths, particularly in Malaysia, from a tropical disease called beriberi. This was just after many people switched from eating brown rice, removed from the husk by pounding, to polished white rice. It wasn't realized until well into the 20th century that beriberi was caused by a lack of thiamine, or vitamin B, in diet. White rice is especially deficient in thiamine.

"THE INTRODUCTION OF MIRACLE RICE HAS ENABLED FARMERS TO PRODUCE THREE OR FOUR TIMES AS MUCH RICE PER HECTARE."

Change has also inevitably come to Japan, that modern economic giant whose society is also based, historically, on rice growing. The earliest Japanese lived on roots and shellfish, for the long, narrow island chain, mostly volcanic, gave up little that was edible. But in the third century BC, rice cultivation was introduced from China, probably via Korea. Japan's apparently hostile terrain turned out to be ideal for rice. Over the centuries, massive human endeavor, as in Banaue, tamed the landscape. Based on rice growing, the population grew and the individual valleys formed natural political units. From 1573 to 1868, Japan was officially administered by daimyo, feudal lords,

whose lands were measured in the amount of rice they could in theory produce. They in turn paid the samurai, loyal military followers, wages calculated in koku, a sum that would keep a man in rice for one year.

Modern Japanese language is peppered with references to a life centered around rice, not least company names that we take for granted: Honda, for example, means "Main Rice Field;" Toyota translates into "Bountiful Rice Field."

If rice ripens in Japan's tropical summers, the onset of her bitter winter is ideal for sake or rice wine. Sake is best drunk young, and warm or piping hot to stave off the chill of long, dark evenings. In addition to supplying food and drink, rice also provides the glue to make shoji, the paper window screen in Japanese homes, and the straw for tatami mats Japanese sleep on, among many other uses.

Today, the Japanese are eating more bread and less rice. Many rice farmers have an office job during the week, and work the rice fields only on weekends, using up-to-date machines which eliminate the old drudgery. But every grain of rice eaten in Japan is homegrown and, quite justifiably, since the nation was formed around it, rice continues to hold a revered place in Japanese life.

But nowhere is rice more central to life than in China. For 2,000 years rice has been the staple food for most Chinese, although archaeological excavations have turned up cultivated rice grains dating back 7,000 years. Today, China produces over 140 million tons of rice a year, about one third of total world output. The Chinese word for "a meal" actually translates into "a rice." And instead of "How do you do?" the common greeting is "Have you had rice?" The milestones of life, too, have always been associated with rice. When a young girl becomes engaged, for example, her family prepares fragrant rice crackers to ensure a happy marriage. On the wedding day, they must make sweet rice dumplings in syrup using rice presented by the groom. After the ceremony, bride and groom eat a bowl of the dumplings together. She must try and pick up two together in one spoon to symbolize eternal union in a lucky marriage.

When a baby is born, on the third day the parents should send plates of mixed fried rice to close friends and relatives, who must return them covered with uncooked white rice. On top of the rice they place a strip of red paper for good luck, and also two stones, representing the hope that the baby's fontanel will harden like stone. At the end of life, bowls of rice were often placed at the feet of corpses lying in state before burial to provide nourishment in the afterlife, and further rice rites followed the burial.

In China, as in most rice-growing countries, people consider that a meal without rice is not a proper meal at all. On formal banquet occasions, rice is served at the end of a meal, or even not at all, to show that the guests have already feasted amply on the dishes served. In both China and Japan, rice is served in small bowls which are held in the left hand a few inches off the table, while the rice is being eaten with chopsticks. In parts of Southeast Asia, though, rice is eaten with a spoon and fork off a plate. In some rural areas, and throughout India, rice with curry is eaten with the fingers.

Rice is mainly boiled or steamed but is also used to make steamed breads and, by the Chinese, to make noodles. Most Asian rice belongs to one of two subspecies, *indica* and *japonica*. The rice grown in Japan, Korea and Taiwan is *japonica* and is slightly sticky, ideal for making sushi. Elsewhere the rice in everyday use is *indica*, drier and more aromatic.

For making rice sweets or wines, a special sticky or glutinous rice is used. The sweets are prepared from the rice itself or from rice flour, and usually include coconut milk, sugar, egg and seasonings. Popular rice sweets include biscuits and cakes made with nuts, dates, bananas and sesame, but especially favored by the Chinese is the famous "Eight Treasure Rice," a delicious confection of dried fruits, red-bean paste, sugar and glutinous rice.

In Hong Kong, more than 90 percent of the population eats two or three meals each day which include rice. Yet rice is no longer grown locally. Instead, local farmers now concentrate on vegetables with short growing seasons and quick,

fat returns. Nowadays, the colony's rice supply comes from mainland China, Thailand and Australia. Chinese rice has the right taste and texture for local taste and is usually blended with Thai rice for added fragrance.

The shops of Hong Kong's rice merchants, lining the waterfront in Sheung Wan — near where Captain Elliott first planted the British flag at Possession Point in 1832 — have not changed much in the last 50 years. For many traders, rice has been a life-long business. They live in a dormitory above the shop and return to their native village and family in China only at festival times. Most are from the Pearl River delta region, whose inhabitants have traditionally dominated the rice trade.

Hong Kong people also eat less rice today: consumption levels have not changed in the last 30 years, despite the population explosion. Demand averages about 10,000 sacks or 1,000 tons a day. Of the 5,000 or more rice outlets the colony once boasted, only about 2,000 remain, as supermarket chains take over, buying vast quantities at very favorable prices. The family "rice tank" — once regularly refilled with 50 to 100 *catties* by the local rice merchant — is now a thing of the past.

All rice in Hong Kong is mediated by one of the 45 licensed rice importers and life on the waterfront is calm. In contrast, trade among the mainly Chinese rice brokers in Bangkok is cutthroat indeed, each one wheeling and dealing to clinch deals involving millions of dollars and mountains of rice. Thailand is the world's fifth largest producer of rice (after mainland China, India, Indonesia and Bangladesh).

But trace the rice back up through the network, up the mighty Chao Phraya River, beyond the mills and middlemen, to the millions of Thai farmers with their palm-fringed paddies, their patient buffalo, their brightly-clad women. There you will still find a quiet, regulated existence shaped by the rice cycle, where the day begins with a greeting of "morning rice" and ends with "evening rice," where rice, in short, is life.

Article 6   Summer 1990 NPQ

The Civilization of the Forest

Takeshi Umehara

Takeshi Umehara   *Director General of the International Research Center for Japanese Studies in Kyoto, Takeshi Umehara is Japan's most prominent – and most controversial – philosopher.*

Formerly president of the Kyoto Municipal University of the Arts, Professor Umehara is author of such books as The Concept of Hell, The Exiling of the Gods *and* Japan's Deep Strata. *Also a Kabuki playwright, he is presently working on a drama based on ecological themes.*

In the following article, he addresses with a fresh perspective rooted in Asian thought the theme raised by Western thinkers from Arnold Toynbee to Lewis Mumford: the central role of the religious imagination in the rise and fall of civilizations.

The experience of losing the war in 1945 brought to Japan a sudden collapse of the value structure that had supported and guided it in the past. It was probably then, for the first time, that the Japanese were capable of understanding the nihilism of European existentialism.

In the immediate postwar period, young intellectuals like myself understood – on the basis of our personal experience – what this philosophical position meant. Having had the experience of the death of those around us and having faced almost certain death ourselves – particularly with the horrifying specter of the nuclear holocaust at Hiroshima and Nagasaki – we simply could not place any faith in a secure life. I devoured the works of Frederich Nietzsche and Martin Heidegger and spent my youth filled with doubts and anxieties. Like so many others, consciously or unconsciously, I became an existentialist who could not place my faith in any claim to objective values, including those of the traditional Japanese moral code.

Yet, as I married and became established, and as Japan itself began to get back on its feet, I started to feel that I could not continue living by staring into the void. I began to feel that I could not survive by a philosophy which emphasized the uncertainties of existence. Since the latest thinking in the West offered only this emptiness, perhaps, I began to think, there were certitudes of great import for all of humanity to be found hidden in the culture and religious history of Japan, which survived all around me.

First, I became interested in the teachings of the various sects of Japanese Buddhism – teachings that became part of our mental makeup without being part of our conscious thought.

Then I began to study Shinto, the indigenous religion of Japan. It was at this time that I came to believe there was something in the Shinto religious orientation of Japan, rooted in its ancient cultural origins, that could offer a philosophy of existence that fundamentally differed from the inevitable dead end of European thought. Further, through my research on the religions of native Japanese tribes, Ainu and Okinawan, I found common elements peculiar to both Japan and to Shinto.

For a variety of reasons, little was taught in our universities about Japan's cultural origins. Ever since the Meiji period, Japanese academic circles had regarded mastering the theories and scholarly disciplines of the advanced European countries as of the utmost importance. Additionally, during the nationalistic prewar days, fears that the sanctity of the national polity would be desecrated – a polity which consisted of chauvinistic State Shintoism linked to the notion of divine rule by the Emperor, or *tennō* – independent research into traditional Japanese topics was severely constrained.

Frankly, I had an allergic reaction to Shinto for many years, due to my bitter memories of chauvinistic State Shintoism linked to the war. And, precisely because of the close link between State Shintoism and the war, the American occupiers after the war harbored no enthusiasm for the recovery of Japan's cultural identity.

Even as Japan's economic recovery took on the sheen of world-class might, our cultural recovery lagged far behind. Although I have now been pursuing my research for years, it was not until the period of the Nakasone government in the mid-1980s that the first major institute – The International Research Center for Japanese Studies – was established in Kyoto to delve fully into the founding truths of Japanese culture.

My hope now is to discover in the cultural origins of Japan not only a new value orientation, which would benefit us as we forge the values our children can live by in the 21st century, but also to contribute to the whole of humanity a new value orientation that suits the post-Modern age with its overriding ecological imperative.

Western modernity, so fertile in its scientific discoveries and technological explosion from the 16th to the 19th century, seems to have exhausted itself in nihilism, the obsessive pursuit of pleasure through economic growth and the destruction of nature.

In order to overcome the present-day crises of human civilization, we must return to the wisdom of the starting point – the original idea of the "other world" – which regards all living beings as basically equal and regards life as a continuous eternal cycle of life and death. Since this basic thought is at the root of the development of our civilization, the earliest origins of religious belief in Japan's past have a great deal to offer the future.

∎

Japan's Pride | Some of my compatriots are proud – to the point of arrogance – of the dramatic development of Japan's economy, which has indeed turned the country into an economic superpower. There are even those who argue that Japan's prosperity is destined to last forever, since it is the product of some special quality of the Japanese national character.

But even if we grant that some psychological element or elements of the Japanese character may have led the country to its current economic heights, it strikes me as untenable to maintain that other people can't learn from the Japanese model and achieve economic success just like Japan's.

It is hard to avoid being pessimistic about the outlook for Japan's leaving a valuable legacy after its days of economic glory are over. It will be very sad if Japan in fact leaves nothing of value for posterity. Personally, I would have to agree with those who say that mere economic prosperity is evil if it fails to produce things of cultural value – and that a country that pursues this sort of culturally empty prosperity is harming rather than helping the rest of the human race. So, I am forced to conclude that we are not in a position to take pride in our economic prowess.

What else does Japan have to be proud of? Is it perhaps the long-reigning imperial family, as the Japanese thought before the war – and certain members of the right wing continue to believe to this day? It certainly cannot be denied that the dynasty has endured for a very extended period. According to *Nihon Shoki*, or Chronicle of Japan, which was compiled in the eighth century, the present line stretches back for 2,600 years. This is certainly an accomplishment. But there is nothing mystical about it, and it is certainly not something that should make the Japanese feel superior to the other peoples of the world.

It was early in the seventh century that the Japanese started calling their rulers *tennō* – the same time, incidentally, that they started calling their country by its present name, Nippon. *Tennō* is now almost always translated as "emperor," but this translation is misleading. Right from their start, these monarchs tended to hold little real power. Often they were women or small children. True power was wielded by their hereditary advisers, like the Soga and Fujiwara families. The *tennō* was basically a religious figure and a symbol of the country's unity – in Western terms, more like a pope than an emperor.

Since the *tennō* has not been directly involved in politics, the fact that the dynasty has endured through the changes on the political scene is actually not the least bit remarkable. I can hardly see why anybody in Japan would expect people in other countries to take a mystical view of this phenomenon, nor can I believe that our current democratic monarch would wish anything of the sort. There would be much less confusion about the institution of *tennō* if the word "emperor" had never been used as the English translation.

In any case, *tennō* pride is now a thing of the past.

What, then, can serve as the source of pride for today's Japanese? If Japan's civilization has any value, it rests in the fact that it retains the strong imprint of the forest civilization of its origins, the civilization of hunting and gathering. Two-thirds of Japan is covered by forests, and about 40 percent of their total area is growing in its natural state without human intervention. No other major industrial nation today can boast such a large share of forest land. This is a feature peculiar to Japan. I believe we should be more proud of our forests than of anything else, and that we must continue to treasure them.

There are two historical reasons why Japan has so much forest land left. One is that farming came to our country relatively late; only about 2,300 years ago. Japan basically became an agricultural nation during what we call the *Yayoi* period, which began about three centuries before Christ and lasted for about 600 years. Before the *Yayoi* period, the Japanese – like people in other countries in early times – were hunters and gatherers, or, it might be more accurate to say, fishers and gatherers. And it appears that the fishing and gathering culture was particularly highly developed in Japan. Evidence for this is found in the earthenware that has been excavated in Japan, some of which has been scientifically dated as twelve or thirteen thousand years old. Together with some earthenware that has recently been found in Siberia, this is the oldest anywhere in the world.

Japan's warm and humid climate produces luxuriant vegetation, which fostered the development of a fishing and gathering culture. This culture was probably at its apex about five or six thousand years ago, just when the farming culture of the Yellow River in neighboring China was rapidly developing.

This early Japanese civilization, which is represented by the earthenware found around the coun-

try, particularly in eastern Japan, is called *Jomon*. I believe that it can be considered a true forest culture, in contrast to the *Yayoi* civilization that followed it, which was a rice-growing culture. One reason for the persistence of forests in Japan is the fact that the *Jomon* civilization lasted so long and the introduction of agriculture came at a relatively late date.

Another reason for the survival of Japan's many forests is the fact that the agriculture that reached Japan's shores was from the rice-growing culture of China's Yangtze River basin. This form of agriculture made use only of the plains, leaving the mountains and hills mostly untouched. This is different from the practice of a wheat-growing culture, which also cultivates the slopes. Another point is that the form of agriculture introduced into Japan did not involve the raising of animals on pasture land, which could also have meant cutting down the trees on the hills and mountains.

In my view, Japan's culture is not unitary, as has traditionally been thought, but binary. It is analogous to Greek culture as viewed by Nietzsche, who analyzed two sorts of elements: the Apollonian and the Dionysian. In Japan's case, the two elements are the *Jomon* fishing and gathering, or forest civilization and the *Yayoi* rice-growing or paddy civilization. Recently, some physical anthropologists have been advancing the view that the races of people who were the principal carriers of these two civilizations were themselves distinct. They suggest that the forest culture was carried on by an early type of Mongoloid people living in Japan since ancient times, while the paddy culture was the product of a newer type of Mongoloid people who arrived during the *Yayoi* period. Various research supports this hypothesis, which destroys the traditional assumption that the Japanese come from a homogeneous race of farmers.

Shinto: Religion of the Forest | This background has also had a major impact on the shaping of religious thought in Japan. Japan's major religions are Buddhism and Shinto. Buddhism is known to have come originally from India, passing through China on its way to Japan, but Shinto is generally thought of as an indigenous religion.

Shinto has come to the fore as Japan's national religion twice during the course of the nation's history. The second time this happened was in the latter part of the 19th century and the earlier part of the 20th century, when it was used as an ideological expression of Japan's nationalistic philosophy – influenced at that time by European thinking, particularly by the model of Prussia and by Bonapartism.

The previous period of State Shinto, so to speak, was in the seventh and eighth centuries, when Japan first took shape as a nation-state. As I mentioned earlier, this was the period when the name Nippon was adopted for the country and the title *tennō* was first applied to its monarchs. Shinto was the established religion of this new state. Two of its key rituals were *harai* and *misogi*. *Harai*, which may be translated as "purification," or "exorcism," represented the driving out of elements or persons harmful to the state. *Misogi*, or ritual cleansing, was the forced correction or reform of such harmful persons.

I believe, however, that Shinto originated as a form of nature worship, rooted in the civilization of the forest, and had nothing to do with this sort of nationalism. It is hard to determine exactly what sort of world view was present in the original Shinto, but based on various forms of conjecture, I would suggest that it may have been something like this:

When people die, their souls depart from their body and go to the world of the dead. The old Japanese word for conducting a funeral is *hofuru*, which means to discard, or throw away. And the word for corpse is *nakigara*, which might be translated as "empty remains." It is like the word *nukegara* that is used for the cast-off skin of a snake or shell of an insect. In other words, it is something that no longer has any use or meaning. And the ancient practice was simply to leave the remains exposed in the woods or fields, like any other item to be discarded.

The world of the dead in this original Shinto view is located somewhere in the sky. The spirits that go there live in families, just as on earth. Life in that world is similar to life in this world, with the exception that everything there is backwards. Here we walk with our feet down, but there they walk with their feet up. Here we dress with the right side of the kimono underneath and the left side on top; there the left side is underneath and the right side on top. When it is morning here, it is evening there; when it is summer here, it is winter there, and so forth.

What is particularly noteworthy about Shinto is that this view of the afterworld contains no vision of heaven or hell. Neither is there any figure who passes judgment on people after they die. In the Shinto view, almost everybody gets to go to the afterworld. In some cases, the soul may refuse to go because it remains too attached to the world of the living, and of course, if a person has been too evil while alive, the ancestral spirits may refuse to welcome that person's soul. In cases like these, the priest conducting the funeral must make doubly strong invocations to be sure that the soul actually makes it to the other world.

All the souls that reach the afterworld become *kami*. The word *kami* in this context is generally translated as "god" with a small g, but actually it refers to any being that is more powerful than normal humans. For example, snakes, wolves, foxes, and other animals that often harm people are also considered to be *kami*.

Thus, in the Shinto view, the souls of the dead go to the afterworld, where they live with their families more or less as they lived on earth. Furthermore, the two worlds – the world of the living and the world of the dead – are not cut off from each other. There are four Buddhist memorial days during which the spirits of the departed return to the world of the living: at New Year's, at midsummer, and at the equinoxes in spring and fall. They spend about three days with the families of their descendants, who wait on them and then send them off on their return journey to the afterworld. By waiting on the spirits of their ancestors during these four annual visits, the people of this world ensure that these spirits will look after them for the rest of the year.

After living in the other world for a time, the spirits of the dead are reborn in this world. When a child is conceived, the representatives of the ancestors on both sides of the family get together and decide whose turn it is to go back. The spirit of the person so selected then returns to the world of the living and slips into the womb of the mother, where it enters the unborn child.

Shinto Influence on Buddhism | What I have been describing are the beliefs of the Japanese before the arrival of Buddhism, but these beliefs continue to live among the Japanese of today. Most people in Japan are both Shintoists and Buddhists. To the Japanese mind, there is nothing contradictory about this.

In general terms, rites relating to the dead are the province of Buddhism, while the rites of the living are the domain of Shinto. More specifically, Buddhist rituals are used for funerals, anniversary memorial services, and the services for the dead that are conducted at New Year's, mid-summer, and the equinoxes. Shinto rituals are used for weddings, birth celebrations, and *shichigosan*, the special celebrations for boys at ages three and five and for girls at ages three and seven.

Originally, of course, all these rites must have been Shinto, but when Buddhism appeared on the scene, it took over the central rites, namely, those relating to the passage from this world to the next, such as funerals.

It is hard to trace the way Buddhism changed after being introduced to Japan, but it seems fair to state that the Buddhism that developed in Japan and won the belief of the Japanese people is a religion quite different from that originally created in India by Syakamuni Buddha and his followers.

In the Buddhism of Gautama, the world is seen as a place of suffering. Human beings, and in fact all living creatures, are reborn each time they die, and thus they must face a perpetual cycle of pain. According to the teachings of this creed, the reason humans are trapped in this unending cycle is because of their passions. Accordingly, the only way to break out of the cycle is to conquer these passions. This requires a life of following the commandments, meditating, and learning. Through such a life, a person can hope to attain a state of quiet enlightenment, or *nirvana*, that will make it possible to leave the world of suffering forever. Buddhahood, in other words, means breaking free of the cycle of reincarnation.

In this form of Buddhism, only human beings are candidates for Buddhahood. And even for humans, the only way to become a Buddha is through religious training, including mortification of the senses, and study. But after being introduced into Japan, this religion changed dramatically. In contrast to the original teaching, which held that only a minority of people were eligible to become Buddhas, the religion as it developed in Japan gradually widened the scope of potential Buddhahood to encompass all human beings, and ultimately even non-humans. Around the 10th century, an influential school of thought arose that proclaimed that "mountains and rivers, grasses and trees, all can become Buddhas."

This school of thought has formed the basis for the various forms of Buddhism that have evolved in Japan since then, though the methods that are prescribed for attaining Buddhahood – such as chanting and meditation – differ from one sect to another.

Another feature of Buddhism in Japan is the common practice of giving posthumous religious names to dead people. This, in effect, certifies that the deceased person has become a Buddha. Even in today's Japan, people often refer to the dead as *hotoke-sama*, or Buddhas. In other words, the Buddhism that has taken root in Japan seems to have been influenced by the traditional Shinto belief that all people become *kami*, or gods, when they die.

Another interesting parallel between Buddhism in Japan and the original Shinto beliefs is to be found in *Jodo Shinshu*, or the True Sect of the Pure Land, which was founded by Shinran in the 13th century and continues to be one of the main sects. Shinran preached the value of two types of *eko*, or transferences of one's virtue to others for the attainment of Buddhahood. One, called *oso-eko*, means that a Buddhist devotee calling Amitabha's name at the death bed could attain Buddhahood by being reborn in the Pure Land, or Amitabha's paradise after his or her death. This was preached by Honen, Shinran's teacher, in the 12th century. In addition to this, Shinran stressed the other type of *eko* called *genso-eko*, which refers to the return of a dead person to this world from the Pure Land in order to save others.

According to Shinran, this is the sort of act performed by a *Bodhisattva*, who is a person who seeks to relieve the sufferings of others and to save their souls. In other words, through the practice of *nembutsu*, or chanting the praises of Amitabha Buddha, a person can go to paradise; being a

Bodhisattva, however, such a person will not be content to remain there forever but will return to this world to relieve the living of their pain.

Shinran maintained that the true practitioners of *nembutsu* were those who would keep returning to the world of the living time after time for the salvation of other humans. This seems quite similar indeed to the Shinto belief in reincarnation. Over the centuries of its evolution in Japan, culminating with the teaching of Shinran, Buddhism developed thinking that was amazingly similar to that of the indigenous religion.

The Eternal Cycle | To sum up, it seems clear that the belief in an eternal cycle of life and death is a basic element not only of Shinto but also of Japanese Buddhism. This is a belief that is surely not just Japanese; it was probably held in common by all human beings during the Stone Age. People who lived in the forest probably developed similar philosophies. The difference in Japan's case is that this primitive thinking has shown a stronger ability to survive here than elsewhere.

It may be a primitive philosophy, but I believe that the time has come to reexamine its merits. Modern science has demonstrated that all life is basically one, and it has shown that living things and their physical surroundings are all part of a single ecosystem. Further, we have learned that even though the individual dies, his or her genes are carried on by future generations in a lasting cycle of rebirth. Even more important, the human race has finally realized that it can survive only in "peaceful coexistence" with the other life forms of the animal and plant worlds.

Ever since human beings learned how to raise crops and livestock, they have been attempting to control, or conquer, nature. And in the process of this conquest, they have come to see themselves as somehow superior to other living things. We must now reconsider this feeling of human superiority. In order to do so, we need to refer back to the wisdom of the people of the hunting and gathering age that preceded the age of farming and livestock raising.

The Rhythms of History | Arnold Toynbee understood world history as the rise and fall of various civilizations. He placed religion at the center of civilization, because he believed that it is religion that supports civilization. From this standpoint, it seemed to Toynbee that modern Western civiliza-

---

Ego As The Result, Not The Cause

The Japanese do not treat ego as grave as the Westerner, nor consider it the indispensable origin of philosophical speculations. This is why some say René Descartes' famous "Je pense, donc je suis" can't exactly be translated into Japanese.

But I do not believe that the Japanese ignore ego totally.

Ego for the Japanese is not the cause but the result. As in Japanese syntax, in which sentences are made up of layers of general and special qualifiers, its ideology places ego at the end. The phenomenon is the result coming out of complex structures formed by social and professional groups. Thus ego matures as the last place where one belongs.

The Japanese construction of ego from outer elements, shows in the language. Japanese try to avoid personal pronouns.

This also is reflected in various forms. Since implements invented in China, such as planes and chisels,

were brought to Japan 600 or 700 years ago, the ways to use them have been changed.

Instead of pushing them forward, the Japanese redesigned them to use for pulling toward oneself. Even when they work on things, they are at the arrival point, not the starting point.

This represents a similarity to the Japanese psychology that tries to construct the ego from outside in accordance with their positions in the families, occupations and the environment, as well as in their society and country.

According to traditional Western ideology, all the natural phenomena are carved with the seal of rationality and move in one direction with logical inevitability. In order to liberate us from the Western notion, there is nothing more effective than adapting the Japanese conception.

– Claude Lévi-Strauss

tion, which had arisen from Christian civilization but had now weakened, was in grave danger.

I hold a pluralistic view of history, according to which any individual civilization or nation inevitably and repeatedly both rises and falls.

Any individual civilization necessarily has certain central ideas. When these ideas are valid and effective at a certain stage of history, then that civilization and the nation founded upon its principles are strong and prosperous. When, at another stage, the principles of that civilization go against the movement of history, then that civilization faces a decline. The principles of a single civilization can never be equally valid in all historical situations.

No doubt the nations of Europe, led by the principles of their civilization, have indeed played an overwhelmingly important role in history between the 16th century and the present. However, the times have now clearly changed. Nations based consciously or unconsciously on principles other than those of European culture have arisen and are now proclaiming principles that are unique to themselves. Moreover, the times are now such that the US and the countries of Western Europe are having difficulty forcing the principles of their own civilization upon other nations. What the people of the world need to do under these circumstances is to form a clear idea of what the principles of European civilization really are: to determine what it is about those principles which no longer work in the present and, if civilizations other than that of Europe do indeed have some significance, to judge coolly just which aspects of those non-European civilizations may serve as a medicine to remedy the defects in the civilization of Europe.

I would like to turn my attention here to three principles that are inherent in European civilization:

- **Individualism** | In European terms, the individual is always the point of departure for any consideration of humanity at large. In the early 17th century, René Descartes expressed this principle as "I think, therefore I am." In other words, the most solid and stable of all entities is the "thinking self." This "self" was the point of departure not only for almost all pre-19th century Euro-

pean philosophers, but also for the world view of the people actually living within European civilization. In the society of the time, the highest value was placed upon the rights of the individual. Even when duty to society and respect toward the state were stressed, this was done, as in the case of Jean Jacques Rousseau and Thomas Hobbes, from a conception of some sort of contract founded upon a community of individual wills.

- **The Conquest of Nature** | In the philosophy of Descartes, matter is opposed to this rational "self." The better this rational "self" knows the laws of nature, which stands in opposition to it, the better it can subdue nature. Modern European civilization employs the natural sciences as a technology to further man's conquest of nature. Thanks to this technology, based on the natural sciences, man's conquest of nature is now complete and mankind is able to use nature as its slave.

- **Denial of Life After Death** | Modern Western civilization arose from Christian civilization. In Catholic Christianity, human beings go after death to purgatory where they await the Second Coming of Christ. At the end of time, Christ presides over the Last Judgement and decides the fate of each person: either to fall into everlasting hell or to receive eternal bliss in heaven. In other words, the soul of a person lives on even after death until the Last Judgement, when it is consigned either to heaven or to hell.

Modern European civilization rejected this concept of life after death as an unscientific delusion. Thus, people ceased to believe in the afterlife, and took it that victory is possible in this present life only. It is thanks to so powerfully realistic an outlook that Westerners have conquered the world in modern times.

As far as the human conquest of nature is concerned, in primitive societies there is no clear distinction between humans and animals. Further, while humans in the dominant religion of East Asia have been accorded a position higher than that of animals, they have been conceived as being in a harmonious relationship with the world. In this East Asian religion, the concept of man subduing nature hardly exists. Perhaps this concept is in fact unusual in human society.

Regarding my point that Western civilization no longer believes in life after death, most civilizations in the past, as Toynbee has pointed out, considered themselves to be founded upon religion. Each religion had its own conception of the "other world," and this "other world" already existed in the primitive religions created by mankind tens of thousands of years ago.

Modern Western civilization destroyed this "other world," which mankind had preserved for thousands of years. No doubt this destruction had something to do with the development of the scientific world view.

It is certainly true, however, that modern European civilization gave rise to truly brilliant arts and learning. Such an achievement can hardly be praised too highly. Thanks to the absolute value accorded the individual, mankind has been able to realize a hitherto unimagined potential. This in turn has made possible not just world preeminence for the European nations, but complete human domination of the earth and a revolution in the destiny of mankind itself. We who live in non-Western societies can only be amazed.

Nonetheless, an idea which, under one set of historical circumstances plays a positive role in the development of a civilization may at another stage of the same development turn out to be a liability. For myself, I cannot see that the three principles I outlined above are wholly assets at the present stage of the development of civilization. On the contrary, I believe that they have begun to play a negative role.

In an East Asian society, it is one's public duty that comes first. As a Japanese proverb has it, "You can't be there when your parent dies." This means that someone who has an important public duty to perform cannot stay on and on by his parent's bedside even when that parent is dying. The same thing is even more true in the case of a sick wife or child. For the Japanese, a child's illness is a private matter, and cannot possibly stand as a reason for neglecting one's public duty. A business executive or an actor could never get away with neglecting his company or his theater because a child of his was ill. However, since according to Western principles the value of the individual is absolute, it is no doubt perfectly natural for a Westerner to absent himself from his work when faced with a problem so important to himself, an individual, as the illness of his child.

In Western society, the rights of the individual are the alpha and omega of all values. This fact is unquestionably linked with the constant strikes and excessively numerous lawsuits which are taken for granted in Western societies.

I obviously do not mean to suggest, of course, that a society which denies human rights is good. I only wish to point out that as far as economic productivity and social harmony are concerned, an absolute valuation of individual rights cannot be a good influence.

I believe the situation is clearer still with respect to the conquest of nature. The ambition to conquer nature certainly called forth human courage and resolve in the past, when mankind seriously believed that the earth was boundless and that by conquering nature mankind would create unlimited power.

As a result of such thinking, however, the earth has become all too finite, nature has been almost wholly subjugated by man, and the resulting devastation is easier and easier to see every day. The transformation of the earth into a desert and a toxic dump is a fearful phenomenon which daily poses a growing threat to future generations. One can only conclude that mankind has no choice but to embrace ideals not of the conquest of nature, but of harmony with nature.

Above all, it is the denial of life after death – the loss of faith in the "other world" – which is the issue that will exercise a decisive influence on the fate of mankind in the future.

Nietzsche and Dostoyevsky very seriously considered the Europe of their time to be in the "age of the death of God," and lamented that Europe was surely courting grave danger. I believe that their concern is now realized. No matter how tenaciously humans cling as individual's to the "self," in the end this "self" is limited and destined to die. And if there is nothing beyond death, then what is wrong with giving oneself wholly to pleasure in the short time one has left to live? The loss of faith in the "other world" has saddled modern Western society with a fatal moral problem.

The time has come when mankind must consider these three issues seriously. If the thought and religion of East Asia have any significance for the present world, it is as a remedy for the principles inherent in Western civilization.

Confucius and Productivity | All the countries now making rapid economic progress, such as Korea, Taiwan, Singapore and Japan, are countries which have been profoundly influenced by Confucian ideas.

There is no doubt that the Confucian thought that exists, consciously or unconsciously, in the countries of East Asia, has had a helpful influence on their economic development. Confucian thought, unlike the philosophy of the modern West, treats man in society. Man is born into a certain society and reaches maturity within it. Confucianism discusses the ethics of that society, and its fundamental tenet is, "Be filial to your parents and loyal to your master." The weight of value is thus on the side of society, and a person's existence has meaning by virtue of his fulfilling the role which has been given him within that society. It is "public duty" which has priority, not "private concerns." This priority given to "public duty" is a special feature of Confucianism.

Those Asian countries which have succeeded in developing economically are probably reworking their Confucian principles, although quite unconsciously. Their principles are perhaps Confucian, but they are not Confucianism itself.

Animism and Ecology | Problems directly related to production are important, but more important still are the problems which involve the very survival of mankind. These have to do with preventing the spread of deserts across the entire globe and preventing the devastation of nature. In this connection, I believe it is necessary to radically reconsider the principle of modern European society which upholds as an ideal the conquest of nature. What is needed is an attitude that considers man and nature to be fundamentally one, and which aims at harmony between the two. This attitude flourishes in Taoism and in Mahayana Buddhism, and particularly in the Kegon Buddhism which is so strong in Korea and Japan. For that matter, the animistic and shamanistic ideas which underlie East Asian culture deserve re-evaluation. Animism holds that human beings share life equally with plants and animals, and that their coexistence is necessary for human survival. The worship of trees is particularly significant in this regard. The worship of *soto* in Korea and the worship of pillars in Japan are both manifestations of this worship of trees. At bottom, it assumes that the root of human beings is the same as that of plants, animals and other natural phenomena.

Heraclitus and The Eternal Return | Concerning religion, I believe that we must re-examine the notion of the "other world," especially this notion as it is found in primitive religion. For example, in the animistic world view of the "other world" that is widespread in East Asia, the souls not only of humans but all living things repeat an endless cycle of migration to and fro, between "this world" and the "other world."

This world view, which is to be found in animistic cultures, somewhat resembles the concept of "eternal return" associated with Heraclitus of ancient Greece as well as Nietzsche. I believe that despite its unscientific appearance, this concept tells a great scientific truth: that of the death and rebirth of life.

How very shortsighted is the view that denies this vast continuity of life and which elevates the "individual" into an absolute! Animistic thought requires re-evaluation on this score as well.

Mankind now stands at an important crossroads. Since it is not at all obvious that humanity will survive in the 21st century, we must re-examine human civilization and return to its point of origin. There is no doubt that toward this end, the thought of East Asia offers rich possibilities for finding a solution. Surely all people regardless of nationality, especially the people of East Asia, must make this task their own.

Article 7

WORLD PRESS REVIEW ● MARCH 1990

The Search for A New World Role

Tokyo prepares for an era of economic interdependence

The collapse of the East-West divide has left governments from Tokyo to Tunis in a state of disequilibrium. While few are mourning the end of the bipolar standoff, it at least offered a measure of stability. Its absence will inevitably lead to calls for another framework to insure global security. To many observers in Japan, that security can increasingly be defined in terms of commercial ties rather than military alliances. Put another way, international economic interdependence is becoming the strongest guarantor of peace.

Japan—overflowing with capital, technology, and manufacturing expertise—is perhaps in a better position than any other country to contribute to that new order. But the nation also faces the daunting task of reconciling such expectations with its international image as a mercantilist nation interested mainly in promoting its own aims. The nation's prosperity will depend on how thoroughly it transforms itself from a potentially disturbing factor into a stabilizing force.

Looking around, you might not think that the world is heading for economic interdependence. Trading blocs in Western Europe and North America might well turn into members-only clubs that restrict the activity of Japan and other outsiders. The threat of protectionism looms in the U.S., and Japan itself is still coming under fire for not importing enough from its Asian neighbors. Furthermore, economic interdependence will have to include the Soviet Union, China, and Eastern Europe, whose feeble economies will render them unable to compete seriously on the world market for years to come.

Yet there are reasons for optimism. The rapid globalization of many corporations has already made interdependence a fact in numerous vital industries. And the breakup of the socialist bloc offers unparalleled opportunities for Japan and other developed nations to insinuate themselves into the economies of those nations.

If tension between Washington and Moscow in the Far East decreases, however, Japan's importance as the key Pacific ally of the U.S. is likely to diminish. If the U.S. chooses to disengage militarily from the Asia-Pacific region, there will be pressure in Japan to assert its independence from Washington. But most opinion leaders in Japan want the country to maintain the Japan-U.S. Security Treaty and, if anything, to strengthen its ties with Washington as long as tension remains in the Korean peninsula, China, and other parts of Asia. "After the cold-war security system is finished," says Hisashi Owada, deputy minister for foreign affairs, "the security treaty will become even more beneficial for Japan than for the U.S." If the U.S. succeeds in reducing its $170-billion military budget for Europe, "it may no longer have to depend on Japan to heavily purchase government bonds to finance the budget deficit," says Takehiko Kamo, professor of international politics at the University of Tokyo.

Critics contend that Japan and the U.S. are headed for more trying times in the 1990s. Makoto Kuroda, former vice minister in the Ministry of International Trade and Industry, sees it differently. Such conflict, he says, "can also be explained as a reflection of the increased economic interdependence between the two countries. When you begin sleeping in a double bed, you tend to complain about one another's snoring and tossing." As long as Japan strives to respond to "proposals by its close friend," there will not be serious problems in relations with the U.S.

The end of the East-West confrontation has also given Japan a chance to reassess its relations with socialist countries, especially the Soviet Union. To stabilize these ties, many business executives say, Japan should take a major role in assisting Soviet economic reform. Keiji Hirano, director and general manager of Toyo Engineering Corp., says, "Interdependence with the Soviets will be the largest contributor to Japan's security. The Soviet Union needs Japan's economic cooperation." Susumu Yoshida, a managing director of Nissho Iwai Corp., adds, "If Japan can seek an alternative market in the Soviet Union, it will help rectify the trade imbalance with the U.S."

The biggest obstacle in relations with Moscow is the issue of the Northern Territories, the islands whose occupation by Soviet troops since the end of World War II has kept bilateral trade semi-frozen for years. Soviet President Mikhail Gorbachev is expected to visit Tokyo in 1991. Yoshida and other business leaders believe that his visit may lead to a resolution of the issue in the 1990s.

From the financial "Japan Economic Journal" of Tokyo.

Japan is also expected to step up its economic and technological assistance to developing countries, mainly in Asia. Tokyo's official development-assistance budget in 1989 exceeded $10 billion, making Japan a major power in overseas aid. But Hirohiko Okumura, director and chief economist at Nomura Research Institute, complains that the country lacks a clear principle in its economic assistance and is not using it to make the country a stabilizing force in the world economy. Although Tokyo will provide $150 million to Poland and Hungary, "it should offer such assistance of its own accord, not under prodding by Washington," Okumura says.

Because of the 1989 U.S.-Canadian free-trade pact and the European Community's decision to integrate its markets by the end of 1992, the Asia-Pacific region is expected to grow in importance for Japan. "Japan should organize a similar economic sphere in the Asia-Pacific region by using its economic clout—basically its buying power," says Kamo. Although Japan seems reluctant to take such overt initiatives as a result of lingering memories of World War II, it has a responsibility to buy more from Asian countries, says James C. Abegglen, president of Asia Advisory Service, a consulting firm in Tokyo. Many Japanese agree that such regional integration will continue in

The Quality of Life

By Kimindo Kusaka, senior managing director of the Softnomics Center, Tokyo; from the leftist "Libération" of Paris:

These days, Japan has more money than it knows what to do with. The man on the street says, "Rich? Us? Are you kidding?" Despite the world's second-highest gross national product and a per-capita GNP that surpassed that of the U.S. in 1987, Japan suffers a high cost of living, poor housing, and the world's longest working hours.

True prosperity, however, does not consist of having a big house or a shorter work week; it is also made up of a life style defined by cultural values. After the war, we Japanese envied the American Dream. Today we need a Japanese vision of the good life.

Some of Japan's obstacles may turn out to be assets. Take prices: According to a recent government report, Tokyo residents pay $2.50 for a cup of coffee that would cost them only 70 cents in New York.

However, Tokyo coffee shops create a private space where customers can relax. Also, a Tokyo coffee shop is worth at least $60,000 per square foot. Personnel costs are high. Taking everything into consideration, $2.50 is a bargain.

In housing, too, the invisible "added value" must be taken into account. Some Americans transferred to Tokyo are shocked to learn that their companies pay $7,000 per month for their cramped apartments. But after a year, most of these people understand the advantages. Because there is less space, homes are easier to clean and maintain. Having no yard means having no grass to cut or leaves to rake. Most neighborhoods in Tokyo are free of violence and have shopping districts and restaurants. In the 21st century, most of the world's people will live in large cities. They will have to accept small homes. Japan can demonstrate that "small is beautiful."

Critics say that exces-sively long work hours are also keeping the Japanese from attaining a better life. We do have very long work hours. But not all of the time in the office is spent working. A strong feeling of group loyalty makes it difficult for an employee to leave the office before his colleagues do. Employees dawdle until the work day is declared over by common accord.

Nonetheless, the old work ethic is changing. Faced since 1985 with the rapid rise of the yen against the dollar, many companies have reduced their work forces, closed, or set up shop overseas. Many middle-aged executives, after years of loyalty to the company, have been forced to accept early re-tirement, transfers, or secondary positions. Many employees have lost confidence in management as a result. In addition, Japanese young people, products of a new education, are now distinguishing between company time and private time. They tend to leave the office at

5 o'clock sharp and will change jobs rather than accept onerous working conditions.

Some economists maintain that Japan has just brought down the final curtain on the industrial revolution. By the year 2000, it will have to muster the forces necessary to launch a radically new revolution, which will marry high technology and a creative ethos based on service.

"Personalization," an integral part of the Japanese way of life, will be a crucial factor in this revolution. Some companies are already experimenting with flexible manufacturing systems capable of using mass production methods to design products adapted to specialized demands.

This coming industrial leap will reduce consumers' alienation from production by allowing them to participate in the manufacturing process. The variety of goods and the role of the service sector will expand, leading to a higher standard of living.

the 1990s. Says Owada: "An increasing number of global issues such as environmental hazards, overpopulation, and disease will prevent protectionism in the 1990s because no single country can solve these problems by itself."

Although some government officials complain that the U.S. has been too aggressive in trade negotiations, "clearly Japan has to change some of its business practices," says Kyoto University economics professor Takamitsu Sawa. Measures are being taken by Tokyo to change the nation's industrial structure, but Sawa attributes their slowness to the infancy of Japanese democracy and the weakness of individualism. The Japanese are so bound to their families, companies, and communities that they cannot easily change their habits, says Kinji Yajima, director of the Institute for International Affairs.

Economists, however, predict that such patterns will be remolded in the 1990s by the decreasing number of extended families, increasing career mobility, and an influx of foreign workers. Nobuyoshi Namiki, a professor of economics at Nagoya City University, believes that young people, especially, will start behaving in a more individualistic manner. The increased number of foreign workers in Japanese companies will cut the traditional closed linkages of employees. Namiki and other economists predict that when such individualism arrives in Japan in the 1990s, the ruling Liberal Democratic Party will face difficulty in representing such diverse interests, and Japan's de facto single-party system will end.

—WAICHI SEKIGUCHI

Prosperity, lapping at the shores of Asia-Pacific nations, promises to keep the region economically afloat throughout the 1990s. But Japan, saddled with its dual role of economic superpower and former military aggressor, is still groping cautiously to find its place.

The Japanese government, which has repeatedly expressed its intention to contribute significant resources to regional economic development, will apparently be held to that promise by its neighbors, who are anxious to see Japan open its markets, although they also hope that the country's contributions do not make it dominant over the region. Japan's leaders, highly sensitive about being accused of wanting another Greater East Asia Co-Prosperity Sphere, are pondering how high a profile Japan should take among its neighbors.

Most export-oriented Asian countries depend on far-off markets to maintain their fast economic growth, because regional spheres of trade are not big enough. Kazuo Nukazawa, managing director at the Japan Federation of Economic Organizations, says that Japanese firms are under pressure to accept more products from such countries and to help them become competitive on the world market. In 1988, Japan's imports from other Asian nations increased 25.3 percent from the previous year, to $57.6 billion, accounting for 30.7 percent of the nation's total imports. With exports of $76.5 billion to Asia, however, Japan's trade surplus in the region stood at $18.8 billion.

Neighboring countries are also urging Tokyo to permit the entry of unskilled laborers, plentiful in their nations but painfully scarce in Japan. In December, Japan amended its laws to allow in more skilled foreign workers and to penalize recruiters of unskilled foreign workers and the firms employing them. It is estimated that 100,000 foreigners are already working illegally in Japan.

"Japan talks of internationalization but opposes the opening of its labor market," says Yang Woo-jin, managing director of the Korea Foreign Trade Association. But despite such criticism, the Japanese government is taking things slowly. A recent special cabinet meeting on foreign workers apparently resulted in little more than a statement by Prime Minister Toshiki Kaifu that Japan "will have to continue studying the issue carefully."

Japan's direct official development assistance to East Asian nations—Indonesia, Thailand, the Philippines, Malaysia, Burma, South Korea, and China—reached $2.9 billion in 1988. But the quality of such assistance is now under question. In 1989, loans made up 59.4 percent of Japanese official development assistance to East Asian nations, up from 57 percent the year before. At the same time, grants dropped from 28.8 percent to 21.1 percent.

"We need to raise the ratio of grants, as well as insure that the assistance is being put to the best use," says Hisashi Owada, a deputy minister at the Foreign Ministry. He says that Japan's stance will continue to be based on the doctrine outlined by former Prime Minister Takeo Fukuda in 1977: Japan will never again become a big military power, and it will strive to establish mutual trust with other Asian nations, contributing to peace and prosperity in the region.

—KONOSUKE KUWABARA

Japan, which has long had its defense policy shaped by the Pentagon, will be defining more of its own strategic interests. That, at least, is the view of some analysts in Japan, who see changes ahead in the bilateral relationship, including a re-evaluation of the Japan-U.S. Security Treaty as East-West tensions relax and a budget-strapped Washington leans toward cutting defense spending. Many politicians and scholars even envision the establishment of a security system in Asia involving the U.S., the Soviet Union, China, and other Asian nations, to supplement a weakened bilateral security pact.

To be certain, many others believe that future arms-control agreements will have little impact on the Asia-Pacific region. Gorbachev's doctrine of "reasonable sufficiency" in the Far East is belied by a quiet Soviet campaign to improve and modernize its armaments in the region, says Hachiyo Nakagawa, a professor at Tsukuba University. According to Nakagawa, the Soviets built an annual 50,000 tons of destroyers during 1985-88—up more than 40 percent from the yearly average of 35,000 tons during 1973-84. Construction of attack submarines increased 16 percent during the same period.

Makoto Momoi, a defense analyst, says that the U.S. and the Soviet Union have merely shifted the emphasis of their strategic deployment to underwater systems. "I wouldn't be surprised if the two superpowers agree on the withdrawal of ground forces, sooner or later, from South Korea and Japan," says Momoi. "Japan's defense posture will suffer greatly if the U.S. withdraws its troops."

But events have become so unpredictable that few can discount the possibility that the Far East will eventually be caught up in the whirlpool of change that has engulfed Europe. Already the Soviets have pledged to reduce their Far East forces by 120,000.

For other Asian nations, the Japan-U.S. Security Treaty has been a reassuring check on Japanese rearmament. Under the pact, signed in 1952 and revised in 1960, the U.S. has taken the leadership role in defending Japan, and Tokyo has virtually accepted a junior role in the alliance. Détente will certainly lead the U.S. to rethink its strategic designs on the region, some analysts say. And this could lead Japan to exert more strategic influence in Asia than it has since World War II.

The *Washington Post* recently reported that a military source in the capital said the U.S. Defense Department is studying the possibility of sharply reducing American forces in Japan, South Korea, and the Philippines. In that case, the security treaty would no longer function as an exclusively military alliance; more emphasis would be placed on economic cooperation, says Momoi. And ultimately, Japan must have greater say in the alliance, says Takeshi Sasaki, a professor at the University of Tokyo.

Motofumi Asai, another University of Tokyo professor and a former diplomat, says that Japan should terminate the security pact altogether and shift its diplomatic atten-

tion from the U.S. to Asia. "Now that the potential Soviet military threat has diminished," he says, "any sharp increase in Japan's defense spending within the framework of the Japan-U.S. security pact would be the most destabilizing factor for détente in Asia."

Some members of the Japan Socialist Party, the country's leading opposition group, also say that the security pact will lose its raison d'être. Though the party has retreated from its outright opposition to the pact, it will oppose the more than 6-percent increase in defense spending planned for next year, to about $29 billion, although that figure will fall below 1 percent of the gross national product for the first time in years. Japan's defense budget is now the third largest in the world, though that figure is deceptive, since it is computed in dollar terms at a time when the yen is so strong.

Analysts claim that Japan's defense ability is still weak, stating that some 41 percent of the budget goes to salaries, while only 28 percent is allocated for equipment purchases and the rest to the upkeep of U.S. bases and other support services. At present, 50,600 U.S. soldiers are stationed in Japan. The analysts also say that Japan's Self-Defense Forces are too strategically integrated with U.S. troops, lacking the ability to defend Japan on their own. Yet many signs point to an even greater integration of the two countries' military forces, indicating that close Japan-U.S. defense ties will continue into the 1990s, whatever the fate of the security pact. "The relationship," says Momoi, "is like a thick leather family Bible for those who stop going to church on Sundays."

—Yuko Inoue

Article 8

CURRENT HISTORY, APRIL, 1991

Our issue on Japan examines the effects of the "new world order" on Japan's foreign policy. In our introductory article, Hideo Sato discusses how Japan should adapt to the changes in the global power balance: "To the extent that the United States is no longer willing and able to bear alone the cost of maintaining a stable international economic and political order, the nations of the world may have to depend on a system of plural leadership by major economic powers. . . . Japan would be a core member of such a system."

Japan's Role in the Post-Cold War World

By Hideo Sato

Professor of Political Science, Tsukuba University

Hideo Sato's books include *The Textile Wrangle: Conflict in Japanese-American Relations 1969–1971* (Ithaca: Cornell University Press, 1979) and *Taigai Seisaku* [Foreign Policy] (Tokyo: Tokyo University Press, 1989).

THE world today is markedly different from the world of the 1950's and the 1960's. The cold war, which defined international relations during the postwar period, has come to an end. During the cold war, the United States had an obvious reason to maintain a substantial military presence in Europe, Asia and other parts of the world. Moreover, in shoring up the Western coalition against the Soviet bloc, it had a strong foreign policy incentive to guarantee "free trade for the free world." With Soviet President Mikhail Gorbachev's perestroika and the changes in East Europe, however, the United States may be less willing to maintain its military commitment overseas and may be less generous and patient with Japan and other allies over bilateral economic issues.

Another important change concerns the relative decline of American economic hegemony, as reflected in declining United States industrial competitiveness. In the immediate postwar years, the United States enjoyed international competitiveness in practically all domestic industries. But over the years it has lost its advantage in an increasing number of them, like textiles in the 1950's, steel in the 1960's, household electronics in the mid-1970's, automobiles in the late 1970's, and even high-technology industries, such as semiconductors, in the 1990's. In 1955 the share of the United States gross national product (GNP) in world GNP was about 40 percent, but it has been reduced to about 23 percent today. Until recently the United States was the world's largest creditor nation; it now labors under huge public and private debts. Under these circumstances, one cannot help assuming that the United States may not only be less willing but also less able financially to bear the cost of maintaining peace and the liberal economic order that has brought enormous prosperity to Japan and other trading partners.

The United States response to Iraq's invasion of Kuwait in August, 1990, shows that the United States is still willing to exercise leadership for the stated purpose of restoring peace and justice outside its borders. Indeed, without timely and effective leadership by the United States, it might have been impossible to enforce economic sanctions against Iraq or to mobilize the multinational force in the Gulf. However, this time the United States had to ask Saudi Arabia, Japan and other wealthy countries to share the expenses of maintaining the multinational force.

TOWARD A JOINT LEADERSHIP SYSTEM

To the extent that the United States is no longer willing and able to bear alone the cost of maintaining a stable international economic and political order, the nations of the world may have to depend on a system of plural leadership by major economic powers. Japan would be a core member of any such system.

Similar ideas have been expressed by others. C. Fred Bergsten has called for a "Big-Three Steering Committee" for the world economy, involving the United States, Japan and Europe.[1] Stanley Hoffmann advocates "a deal to redistribute power — now still largely in the hands of the United States — among the main actors in the international financial and economic organizations — the United States, Japan, and the European Community."[2] Robert Kuttner has suggested that

> in some respects, a U.S.-dominated grand alliance was simpler and stabler than a plural system. But, for better or worse, a plural system is where we are headed. America cannot afford to "bear any burden, pay any price" to defend liberty and safeguard its interests — at least not single-handedly. Rather than going broke resisting that reality, the United States should seize the moment and work to build a stable, plural world order.[3]

Once important policymakers in key countries have embraced this scenario and have developed a common vision of the world they hope to build together, they will be in a good position to manage specific economic issues cooperatively. But the shift to a joint leadership system will not be easy. The United States would have to reject hegemony and refrain from projecting its own foreign policy onto the rest of the world. It would also have to consult and coordinate closely with key countries when making decisions that concern others. Of course, the other members of the joint leadership system would have to be more willing to share burdens and responsibilities, making necessary policy changes despite domestic opposition. Japan would be no exception.

JAPAN'S IMAGE PROBLEM

According to David Rapkin, Japan suffers from a "legitimacy deficit" overseas that may impair Japanese efforts to exercise international leadership. Sources of this problem include "the legacy of militarism and colonialism, a mercantilistic reputation, and disbelief that Japan can articulate universalizable norms, values, and principles."[4] Japan's lack of universalizable values and principles may not necessarily handicap it in exercising leadership as one of the primary countries in a joint leadership system. Besides, Japan already shares with the United States, West Europe and other countries such fundamental values as freedom, democracy and human rights.

Japan's militaristic history certainly constrains its

relations with neighboring Asian countries, and any regional initiative coming from Japan tends to look suspicious to these countries. They are naturally wary of increasing Japanese economic influence, and some even wonder if Japan is again attempting to build the "Greater East Asia Co-Prosperity Sphere," its master plan to control the region during its 15 years of war with Asia and with the West. Although Japan allocates only about 1 percent of GNP to defense, its economy is so productive that its allocations for the armed forces rank third in the world, behind the United States and the Soviet Union. This factor, combined with memories of Japan's military aggression, seems to contribute to the Asian perception of Japan as a potential security threat.[5]

Many Japanese have a strong aversion to militarism—a reaction to the tight thought control exercised by the prewar military regime as well as to the scourge of war itself. In fact, the Japanese government found it difficult to send even unarmed Japanese military personnel to the multinational force in the Persian Gulf, fearing it would create a precedent for bypassing the postwar Japanese policy of not sending military units abroad. Japan must face the dark side of its modern history and sincerely demonstrate a repentant attitude in public education and in speeches by its politicians and officials in order to win the trust of its neighbors.

Japan's contributions to a joint leadership system would have to be basically nonmilitary. But this would be perfectly in tune with the demands of the post-cold war world. As Assistant Secretary of State for East Asian and Pacific Affairs Richard H. Solomon put it in a recent address,

> We now face a future in which technological and commercial capabilities more than military strength are the significant determinants of state power and influence. National security is ever more reckoned in terms of economic and environmental concerns.[6]

In short, what Richard Rosecrance calls "the military-political world" is giving way to "the trading world," and Japan, as a "trading state," could provide a potentially useful model.[7]

However, Japan's mercantilistic reputation will be a serious drawback if it attempts to take on the role of trading state. Efforts must be made to erase Japan's protectionist image and convince other countries that Japan is a reliable leader committed to reciprocal and multilateral free trade. First and foremost, Japan must reduce its enormous global trade surplus, which was approximately $64 billion in 1989. The surplus has been decreasing gradually

from a peak of about $83 billion in 1986, but more deliberate efforts are needed.

Over the years Japan has liberalized and expanded its market, and has increased manufacturing imports. Obviously, these kinds of changes can be accelerated. Japan must also play a more active role in preserving the multilateral free trade system from which it has greatly benefited.

SPECIFIC TASKS FOR JAPAN

Japan can overcome its "legitimacy deficit." Apart from practicing and promoting free trade generally, it should also carry out the following steps to pave the way for a viable joint leadership system.

One of Japan's first tasks is to accept greater responsibility in international financial markets. Japan became the world's largest creditor in 1985 and will remain so for the foreseeable future, despite the recent fluctuations in international stock and bond markets. Ironically, the yen is not regularly used in international transactions. If the yen can achieve a higher profile, Japanese policymakers will have to take international repercussions more into account. How can Japan increase the yen's role in international transactions? It cannot force foreign governments and companies to make greater use of the yen, but it can render the Japanese currency more attractive by further opening up Japanese capital markets.

Promoting economic growth and regional cooperation in Asia and the Pacific is a second task for Japan. As suggested earlier, national security is increasingly reckoned in economic terms. Sustained economic growth and prosperity can be a credible deterrent to aggression and instability. In Asia, dynamic economic growth is no longer a purely Japanese phenomenon. The "four tigers" of Asia—South Korea, Taiwan, Singapore and Hong Kong—have as a group one of the world's highest annual growth rates and have become major players in international trade. Their growth has been largely dependent on trade and investment with the United States and Japan, with United States imports far larger than Japanese imports. But the United States is less and less able to pay the cost of sustaining the region's economic growth. Moreover, it presumably has less of an incentive to do so with the decline in the perceived threat from the Soviet Union. Japan could step in and share burdens as an "import absorber."

There have been increasing calls for some form of enhanced regional cooperation, including a proposal to form an Asian and Pacific free trade zone to counter the economic integration of the European Community in 1992 and the Canadian–United States free trade agreement. The diversity of the region in terms of country size, level of development, economic objectives, culture and political tradition make it impracticable to constitute formal policymaking bodies along European lines. The Asia–Pacific Economic Cooperation Conference, which held its first meeting in Canberra, Australia, in December, 1989, and its second in Singapore in July, 1990, appears to be a better alternative, because it is mainly a forum for discussion on economic issues and policies.

This does not mean that Japan does not have a security role in the region. Japan must share defense burdens with the United States, according to their mutual security treaty. Its most important security task is to help the United States remain a Pacific power by increasing support for stationing United States troops in Japan (though the number of troops could be gradually reduced in the future). Japan's own defense expenditures could be frozen or gradually decreased, depending on security concerns in the region. At some point Japan would have to define "minimum deterrence" for itself, while helping the United States to function as a balancer. As for its extraregional security role, Japan should provide personnel for United Nations peacekeeping operations and monetary contributions commensurate with its economic power.

Allocating its foreign aid effectively is a third task for Japan. Japan's official development assistance budget in 1990 was about $10 billion, helping to make the country the largest donor of foreign aid among the 18 members of the development assistance committee of the Organization for European Cooperation and Development (OECD). But Japan's disbursements constitute only 0.32 percent of GNP, below the OECD average of 0.35 percent.[8]

Japan has generally refrained from attaching political conditions to its aid. This traditionally apolitical stance may need to be reevaluated as the cold war ends and the effect of Japan's aid program on world politics grows. Japan may want to adopt an aid policy more directly linked to democratic values, with special consideration given to countries that are seriously working toward greater democracy.

The condition that it be used for peaceful purposes may also be attached to aid money; Japan could deny assistance to developing countries that spend an inordinate amount of money on military resources. Basically, Japan must articulate its aid

objectives and prove that it, too, is interested in promoting universalizable values and principles.

A fourth task for Japan is to take the initiative in combating environmental problems. The world has become keenly aware of threats like acid rain, global warming, erosion of the ozone layer, the spread of deserts and the destruction of rain forests. Global warming, which is believed to be caused mainly by carbon dioxide emissions, is perhaps the most threatening problem. It could result in serious flooding as sea levels rise, in falling crop production and in the extinction of thousands of species.

On October 23, 1990, the Japanese government adopted a program to stabilize at 1990 levels by the year 2000 emissions of carbon dioxide and other gases, like methane and nitrous oxide, that contribute to global warming. At the Geneva environmental conference that immediately followed, Japan and 18 West European nations announced plans to freeze or cut emissions of harmful gases by the year 2000. The United States has refused to develop a policy addressing gas emissions; apparently, it is more concerned with the economic costs of such a policy than with protecting the global environment.

Japan is often seen as a major environmental villain, perhaps because it is a chief exporter of industrial finished goods, including automobiles, and because it imports large amounts of timber. But the United States and West European countries buy most of the timber exported from Latin America and Africa, where 81 percent of the world's tropical forests were destroyed between 1978 and 1981. In 1986, the Japanese share of timber imports from Africa was only 2 percent, and from Latin America, 0.7 percent.[9]

Japan could take the initiative on global warming and other environmental problems, since its leadership would not be perceived as a threat by other countries. Japan's pollution control measures are more advanced than those elsewhere. Japan has also developed effective energy conservation technology and is one of the few countries to resolve successfully the dilemma of economic growth and energy conservation. Consequently, it could be a model for other countries.

Creating a global partnership with the United States is the fifth task Japan must undertake. If the world's two largest economies fail to manage their relations with each other, an international joint leadership system is nothing more than a pipe dream. Unfortunately, a recent speech by United States Under Secretary of State for Economic Affairs Richard McCormack does not lead one to be optimistic:

> Japan has become a domestic issue in the United States. We see polls which label Japan as a greater threat to this country than the Soviet Union. Part of the reason for this is the correct perception that the Soviet military threat has decreased. But it also reflects a twofold concern about our economic position: apprehension that the U.S. is in decline, and that the Japanese have gained economic strength against us. . . . Our deficit with Japan is coming down, but a [$40-billion] trade deficit with Japan is still politically unsustainable.[10]

Reduction of the bilateral trade imbalance is the main issue dividing the two countries. Japan has made a series of market-opening concessions, and the value of the yen in relation to the dollar has appreciated substantially since the United States, Japan, Great Britain, France and West Germany agreed in September, 1985, to intervene in the currency market to drive down the dollar's value. Yet the United States trade deficit has not come down as much as was hoped. The problem is that both the United States and Japan need to make changes in order to reduce the trade imbalance. United States officials have often admitted that a large part of the imbalance stems from the United States federal budget deficit, declining industrial competitiveness and lack of aggressive marketing efforts. In addition to further liberalization and expansion of its own market, Japan could step up direct investment by building manufacturing plants in the United States. The automobile industry and other industries in Japan have been moving in this direction. In the long run this would moderate growth in Japanese exports, provided that most of the necessary parts are procured in the United States.

Both countries could also identify and remove barriers to market-determined trade and investment flows. The so-called Structural Impediments Initiative (SII) is an example of this approach. In June, 1990, the United States and Japan concluded a year of intensive talks by issuing a joint report that committed them to comprehensive measures to reduce structural impediments to the flow of trade and investment. The United States asked Japan for changes in six areas: savings and consumption, investment balance, the distribution system, land-use policies, exclusionary business practices, and pricing. For its part, Japan asked the United States to address its budget deficit, its low savings rate and educational and worker-training difficulties. In short, each side "interfered" in the internal affairs of the other country.

The SII talks represented one of the few times that postwar Japan and the United States made demands on each other. Japan should be more assertive in dealing with the United States since Americans are used to resolving conflict through argument and debate. Avoiding issues for fear of confrontation can only add to confusion and misunderstanding. Effective leadership requires the ability to articulate and initiate moves. Robert Samuelson wrote in the *Washington Post* a few years ago that "great nations do not negotiate so much as they initiate. Japan is a great nation. It should begin acting like one."[11] Indeed, providing the initiative is a precondition for Japan to establish a working partnership with the United States in the framework of an international joint leadership system.

[1]Quoted in David Gergen, "For the Tripolar World, a Big-Three Steering Committee," *International Herald Tribune,* May 7, 1990.

[2]Stanley Hoffmann, "A New World and Its Troubles," *Foreign Affairs* (Fall, 1990), vol. 69, no. 4, p. 120.

[3]Robert Kuttner, "The Former Free Riders Will Require a Say," *International Herald Tribune,* September 19, 1990.

[4]David P. Rapkin, "Japan and World Leadership?" in D.P. Rapkin, ed., *World Leadership and Hegemony,* International Political Economy Yearbook, vol. 5 (Boulder, Col. and London: Lynne Rienner Publishers, 1990), pp. 196–199.

[5]Steven Erlanger, "As Economic Competitors, Asians Rearm," *International Herald Tribune,* May 7, 1990.

[6]Assistant Secretary of State for East Asian and Pacific Affairs Richard H. Solomon, "Asian Security in the 1990s: Integration in Economics; Diversity in Defense" (Address to the University of California at San Diego Graduate School of International Relations and Pacific Studies, October 30, 1990; official text from the American embassy, Tokyo, November 1, 1990), p. 2.

[7]Richard Rosecrance, *The Rise of the Trading State* (New York: Basic Books, 1986).

[8]*JEI Report* (Washington, D.C.: Japan Economic Institute), October 19, 1990, p. 8.

[9]Kyohiko Arafune, "Kankyo Hakaisha-Nihon no Hihna ni taishite" [In Response to Criticisms of Japan as Environmental Destroyer], *Gaiko Forum,* no. 16 (January, 1990), pp. 80–84.

[10]Under Secretary of State for Economic Affairs Richard McCormack, "Japan Must Revaluate Its World Role" (Address to the North Carolina–Japan Forum, November 1, 1990; official text from the American embassy, Tokyo, November 9, 1990), pp. 4–5.

[11]Robert Samuelson, *Washington Post,* March 6, 1985.

The Dream Out of Reach for Japanese

SUMMARY: The Japanese take a great deal of pride in their nation's economic achievement. For many, however, pride is no longer enough. They are asking why the nation's fabulous riches have not been translated into more dramatic improvements in the quality of everyday life. The cost of living in Tokyo is spectacularly high. Tiny apartments sell for hundreds of thousands of dollars. Government ministries are now pledging to make consumer issues a higher priority.

M*asuo-san gensho,* the Japanese call it, in their penchant for catchphrases. Translated, it means "the phenomenon of Mr. Masuo." Mr. Masuo is a cartoon character in one of Japan's most popular and (after 20 years) longest-running prime-time TV programs, an animated version of Ozzie and Harriet. Recently, however, he has come to symbolize the increasing number of Japanese shut out of the real estate market. Poor Mr. Masuo has never been able to afford a house of his own and suffers the indignity of living with his mother-in-law. The six-room Tokyo dwelling the family of newspaper comic strip characters began in back in 1946 would cost about 1 billion yen in today's market. At 150 yen to the dollar, that is nearly $6.7 million. A lot of money for a cartoon character.

But no laughing matter. The Japanese have created an economic juggernaut. The nation has become a world leader in technology. Its investments span the globe. Its huge reserves of capital prime the international financial markets and, some say, keep the United States from sinking in its own deficits. But just as Japan's tireless efforts have come to fruition, the Japanese find themselves stalled at home, confronted by diminishing personal expectations. Though they have attained the highest per capita income in the world, they are less able than at any time in the postwar era to buy a home of their own, and owning a home is the dream of every Japanese.

The hyperinflation of the real estate market has had both direct and indirect effects on the quality of life in Japan. In numerous polls, more than half of the highest-paid people in the world say they do not feel affluent, a sense shared even by Japan's truly wealthy. Those with incomes double the national average complain that they are frustrated with their standard of living — the tiny, ravenously expensive apartments; the long, crushing commutes to work; the tedious days at the gray office. A refrain from a Japanese folk tune repeats: "Getsu, Getsu, Ka, Sui, Moku, Kin, Kin." It is a recitation of the workweek: "Monday, Monday, Tuesday, Wednesday, Thursday, Friday, Friday."

MITI, the Ministry of International Trade and Industry, the bureaucratic engine propelling Japan's economic miracle, calls it the "paradox of prosperity": rich Japan, poor Japanese. The government worries that without the incentive of home ownership, Japanese workers will lose their will to do the hard work that keeps the economy booming. And so for the past year, Prime Minister Toshiki Kaifu has been holding regular meetings on "The Society We Should Aim for in the 21st Century."

Such talk has been heard in Tokyo before, however. Shuichi Kato, a noted commentator on Japanese society, doubts that change will come easily or soon. "The extraordinary growth of Japan over the last decades and the lagging quality of life are two sides of the same coin. To a large extent, we grow at the expense of our living standards." Tinkering with such trade-offs, he fears, "might result in economic catastrophe." But he also acknowledges that there may be little choice. "In the years immediately after World War II, it was all right to live in this state of emergency. But after 40 years? And with all this prosperity? These conditions are not acceptable."

Just how bad are things? Tokyo is to Japan what Manhattan, Washington, Chicago and Los Angeles together are to the United States. The city serves as a compass of national priorities, the heart of cultural, financial, industrial and political life. This metropolitan center, with nearly 12 million residents, has taken the brunt of Japan's headlong rush from a war-ravaged economy into the 21st century. And the people of Tokyo say the pressures are becoming intolerable.

Yumiko Miyakawa lives with her husband, an art teacher at a design school, in a middle-class section of western Tokyo called Shibasaki. She looks much younger than her 38 years. She works at home three days a week doing word processing for a company that promotes sales of Philip Morris Inc. cigarettes in Japan. Together, the Miyakawas, both of whom have college degrees, earn approximately 4 million yen a year, about $27,000, close to the national average. "Japan became rich," she says, "but most of the people are not rich."

Her apartment, which is favorably situated just a short walk from the local train station, is about a 75-minute commute to central Tokyo. The apartment building the Miyakawas live in is about 15 years old and, from the outside, resembles the sort of small complex that might be found on the outskirts of many American cities.

The obvious difference between this apartment and its U.S. counterpart is size. The Miyakawas' place consists of a dinette kitchen, a bedroom, study and bath. The bedroom and study are both about 8 feet wide, just a little wider than the outstretched arms of a man. It is about twice as long. The kitchenette serves as an entryway to the apartment and is cramped by a small dining table. Altogether, the space measures about 450 square feet, half the size of a typical Manhattan apartment. *Usagi goya*, the Japanese mockingly call their places: rabbit hutches.

For this, the Miyakawas pay 90,000 yen a month in rent, $600. They pay an additional $100 a month to park their six-year-old car in front of their building. (Filling its tank costs $33.) And they pay all utilities — water, gas, electric — which tacks on an average $113 per month. To secure the place, the Miyakawas paid four months' rent in advance, of which they will get back only two when they move out, a common scenario in the Tokyo real estate market.

Usually, apartments like this offer no Western-style amenities. They do not offer such fundamental appliances as a water heater, customary even in the poorest U.S. dwellings but rare in Japan. The Miyakawas had to buy their own. What is more, the apartment came without washer or dryer. No dishwasher. No refrigerator. No stove. No microwave. Few Japanese homes have ovens. The Miyakawas cook on a double hot plate, which they had to buy for themselves. There was no air-conditioning. No central heat. Again, a standard arrangement. Kerosene is delivered to their door in winter and they warm themselves with space heaters. Without a trace of irony, such apartments are offered by real estate agents under the designation "mansion." This is a standard mansion.

Yumiko says hers is a little better than average. She is accepting of her situation. The phrase she uses is echoed through Japan's big cities, *Shonagai*: It cannot be helped. This apartment is not a halfway house to a brighter future, either. She does not expect to be able to buy a home. "Not in Tokyo," she says. "Too expensive." And like many Japanese, she must live in Tokyo, because it is bad form for Japanese to change jobs in search of greater opportunity. It brands them as unreliable. Most Japanese spend their lives with one firm.

The western suburbs of the city where Shibasaki is located are generally considered well-to-do. Like the rest of Tokyo, it is a warren of winding streets little more than one car wide. There are no sidewalks, except in the center of town, and only a broad white road stripe marks the way for pedestrians between the two-way traffic cramming past.

Many of the homes here are detached single-family dwellings. This is where Kayo Yoshikawa and her husband, Giichi, live, with their two sons, age 23 and 19. Giichi heads a branch office of the globe-trotting Mitsubishi Trust & Banking Corp. He earns a yearly income of more than 10 million yen, or $67,000, double the national average.

His wife, who has completed two years of college, works part-time, 20 days a month, as a hotel domestic. She considers herself "middle-middle class." Her pleasant two-story home has five rooms and one bath. Out front is a small, immaculate garden, a reminder that nature has not entirely been lost to the city's concrete. Downstairs, in what would correspond with the dining room in the United States, is a traditional tatami room, named for the floor mats of woven rice straw. Only stockinged feet are permitted on tatami. It is a ceremonial room, a formal receiving and dining room that often doubles, as it does for the Yoshikawas, as a bedroom. They sleep on traditional futons, large folding cushions, hidden during the day behind wooden panels at one end of the room. Upstairs the two bedrooms are reserved for the sons.

The Yoshikawas bought their home 20

> ## The average price for a home in Tokyo is $432,000. Its size is 675 square feet. Nationwide, in 1986, it was $192,700.

years ago and now place its value between $600,000 and $1 million, possibly more. The rule of thumb for home ownership is that the cost of a property should not exceed five times the family's gross annual income. Today, despite the Yoshikawas' substantial earnings, they could not afford to buy the home they live in — which is why Kayo Yoshikawa can say in all candor, "We don't feel that we are rich."

Home ownership is down from 62 percent of all households in 1983 to 61.1 percent in 1988. Although the percentage of ownership is high, the trend is troubling. As a November 1989 "White Paper on the Life of the Nation" produced by the Economic Planning Agency said, "The main reason for the decrease is the rising cost of housing in recent years. . . . For those who rent their dwellings, the situation is bleak."

The deliriously high cost of Tokyo housing becomes plain from a quick perusal of listings at the city's real estate offices. Cubbyholed in racks outside the entryways of each office are sheets of red, green and yellow floor plans describing each apartment's offerings and monthly charges. The average price for a home in Tokyo is $432,000. Its size is 675 square feet. Nationwide, in 1986 (the last year for which figures are available), it was $192,700 for 788 square feet. But land prices skyrocketed after 1986, and that figure is now grossly low. By comparison, last year the average price in the United States for a new home was $148,000, with about

132

2,000 square feet of floor space, according to the Department of Housing and Urban Development.

In Tokyo's Ikebukuro section, a lower-middle-class residential area close to the center of town, there are offerings for a 512-square-foot apartment at $552,000 and a 133-square-foot apartment at $185,300. In the more tony Shinjuku section, which will soon be home to the city's towering new government buildings, a 420-square-foot apartment is offered at $1,033,000. In the less desirable east end of Tokyo, in the old Edogawa section, a newly built 660-square-foot condominium is on the market for $466,000, plus $100 per month for maintenance.

Last year, 60 of Japan's top 100 taxpayers made their money in real estate. Since 1955, the price of land in Japan has risen an average of 54 times. Prices in Tokyo and five other major cities have ballooned 128 times, according to a May report by Japan's National Land Agency. Perhaps the most dramatic example of the high cost of land in Japan was produced by Masaru Yoshitomi, the director general of the Economic Research Institute of the Economic Planning Agency, a government think tank. In a 1988 speech, he noted that the land under Tokyo's Imperial Palace was more valuable than all the land in Canada. Today, he would add the state of California into the bargain.

Yoshitomi's office is located in Tokyo's Kasumigaseki, the nation's seat of bureaucratic power, inside the same four-block power quadrangle that holds the mighty Ministry of International Trade and Industry and its economic counterpart, the Ministry of Finance. Two "mansions" could easily be fit in the area occupied by Yoshitomi's large desk and the conference table opposite. A noted economist, he was one of the first Japanese to hold a directorship in the 24-nation Organization of Economic Cooperation and Development, the powerful international market council.

Yoshitomi begins explaining the stifling price of housing by talking about Japan's limited land resources. What he says is heard everywhere in Japan, at many levels of government, and has grown into something of a catechism. Although the figures sometimes vary, the essential proposition is the same: Japan is about the size of California. Seventy percent of the land is mountainous. Only about 17 percent of the available land is suitable for housing and farming. Nearly 124 million people call this home. Hence, the high price of land.

But the explanation is not entirely sufficient, as Yoshitomi explains. "Land value comes from economic activity," he says. The measure of economic activity he employs is gross national product per acre, the amount of money earned on an acre of land. For example, the gross national product per acre in Germany is seven times that in the United States, and land values are about seven times U.S. land values. In Japan, however, the gross national product per acre is 40 times that in the United States, but land is 90 times more valuable.

The huge gap between actual land prices and GNP per acre is partly explained by the combination of low interest rates and high expected growth rate, Yoshitomi says. The economic rule of thumb is that when interest rates are low, asset prices are high. Interest rates in Japan are considerably lower than anywhere in the West. And economic forecasts call for continued high growth rates for the Japanese economy, as much as 5 percent a year, promising ever higher value added per acre. Put another way, there is good reason for speculators to bid up the value of land.

"So if you have low interest rates and high growth rates, you might explain this gap," he says. "But to what extent is very difficult to say. The remaining difference could be a bubble, speculation. But bubbles burst, and the Japanese bubble hasn't, so perhaps it is not a bubble."

One result of these prices is that people are moving farther and farther from the center of Tokyo. This makes commuting, which has always been a problem, an issue of public policy, and it raises questions more easily dodged than dealt with. "Commuting time in Tokyo is not so far from New York," Yoshitomi says. "There, it is one hour, 10 minutes. Here, it is one hour, 20 minutes" each way. There are important differences, however. Nearly everyone in Tokyo uses mass transportation to commute to work. But more to the point: The rigors of commuting make it life's single worst indignity.

Fifty-five percent of Tokyo's workers travel more than two hours to and from work; of those, one worker in five travels more than four hours each day. And commuter trains, though running at three-minute intervals with added cars during rush hours, fill to 250 percent of the capacity for which they were designed. At times, riders have the sense that their feet do not touch the ground or that the forces of acceleration or deceleration on the packed car will crush them. Subway attendants help jam people into trains so the doors can shut. Riders complain that they are physically and psychologically molested by the daily experience, and they arrive at work exhausted.

Between commutes, they endure one of the longest workdays in the developed world. Usually, Japanese office workers —

known in Japan as "salary men," who are roughly the U.S. equivalents of white-collar workers but who harbor an ethic of total company commitment—arrive at 8:30 in the morning and stay long past their 5:30 quitting time. Almost always, they are at their desks until 8 in the evening, with many working even later. Schmoozing after-hours is a virtual institution for salary men, in many cases a requirement. (In Japan, corporate expenditures for entertainment are greater than the government's expenditures for defense, according to the Economic Planning Agency.) With the long commute, it is not uncommon for them to arrive back home at midnight.

A health elixir popular among Tokyo's working stiffs is called Regain. TV ads for the energy drink pose a high-powered salary man asking, "Can you fight 24 hours a day?" Regain, of course, will make this possible. Its ingredients include caffeine, nicotine and vitamin C.

Drinks like Regain are popular in Japan because work hours have actually increased as the country has grown in prosperity, up from 2,064 in 1975 to 2,111 in 1988. Last year, a national record for overtime hours was set in Japan, with 190. U.S. workers average about 1,900 hours per year on the job, German workers, 1,600. The six-day week is still commonplace in Japan. Overall, only 30 percent of Japanese workers had two days off a week. However, in those companies employing fewer than 100 persons—the vast majority of firms—only 5 percent offer a five-day week. Most often, companies work one weekend out of two or three.

Japan's giant Nippon Telegraph & Telephone Corp., for example (a company larger than American Telephone & Telegraph Co. and International Business Machines Corp. combined), still keeps office hours every other Saturday. This, four years after the government promised a campaign to reduce hours below 2,000 a year by 1990 and 1,800 a year by 1992.

The possibility of working even longer hours than at present is taken so seriously that there has been resistance to moving the nation onto daylight saving time, or "summer time," as the Japanese call it. Starting in May in the Land of the Rising Sun, the sun will rise at 4 a.m. The economics of switching are obvious to this energy-starved nation, which is fueled almost entirely by oil imports. But the Japanese fear that whatever gain summer time may bring in terms of conservation, it will ultimately lead to more hours at the office.

Makoto Takei, who works for the giant telephone company, says he is resigned to his arduous schedule. Until he was promoted to special assistant to the senior vice president for international affairs, he rarely left the office before 10, often not until midnight. Now things are better. He says he is usually home by 9 p.m. and has time for himself and his family after dinner, usually about 10 p.m. "The situation is not so bad," he says, although he spends little time relaxing. "I seldom watch TV." He is back at his desk the next day at 7:30 to catch up on reading or to prepare for assignments.

In return for his conscientiousness, Takei earns a good bit more than 10 million yen a year and can look forward to Japan's system of lifetime employment, at least until age 55. Then, in the typical pattern, he will retire to a less prestigious position, with considerably lower pay, in a subsidiary of his firm. Contrary to conventional wisdom, only one worker in five enjoys such guaranteed lifetime employment in Japan.

Technically, Takei gets 22 paid vacation days each year. But he rarely takes more than a week or two off. Few Japanese make full use of their vacations. In fact, the free time taken has decreased 10 percent since 1980. Nowhere do employees allow themselves more than 50 percent of the time they are due, according to the November 1989 Economic Planning Agency white paper.

Largely, this is a result of peer pressure. No one likes to be seen as shirking work, and only hard workers who put in long hours are rewarded with promotions. But there are also pressing financial considerations driving the Japanese. The 1989 report found that 55 percent of employees age 30 to 39 keep their brutal schedules because they need the extra wages, which they earn in addition to their vacation pay.

When Takei does take time to himself, he rarely travels. "Everywhere you go is crowded," he explains. Because Japanese usually take their vacations at the same time of year, resort areas are frequently overcrowded. So are the already jammed roads. A weekend jaunt from Tokyo to the seashore some 60 miles away can take up to six hours. And highway tolls are exorbitant, gouging riders for $41 between Tokyo and Nagoya, a distance equal to a trip from New York to Washington. From Tokyo to Osaka, a distance equal to a trip from Chicago to Cleveland, costs a staggering $67 one way. Just to ride the narrow two-lane expressway cutting over Tokyo's maze of winding streets costs $4.

Unlike most Japanese, Takei says the

majority of his income goes to pay for his home loan, instead of into savings. He lives in a modern, well-appointed house, located in the wealthy suburb of Kamikitazawa in western Tokyo. His home resembles a small two-floor subdivision town house in the United States. It is built on land owned by his father. "Otherwise, I could not afford it," says Takei, whose income is nearly three times the national average. "I would still be living in company housing."

Company and public housing are Tokyo's answer to the high price of real estate. A 1987 survey of 742 Japanese firms found that 96.2 percent of them offered some form of housing. In the past, such places, with their low, low rents, were a way for people to salt away cash for home purchases. Such places are often undersized, even by Tokyo standards, but they are usually well-located, just a short commute from the office. Such subsidized housing bears no social stigma. Even small and medium manufacturing firms, which form the backbone of Japanese industry, offer their workers housing.

Near the Edo River, which forms the city's eastern boundary, is an industrial-residential area crammed with such small factories. These firms do not have names, only owners, like Shinsaku Seto. His business, which chrome-plates metal tool parts — rollers for extruding plastics, for example — was founded 35 years ago by his father-in-law. The company remains closely held and last year had revenues of about 400 million yen, $2.7 million, about average. He has 40 employees.

The front office of the factory could pass for any small manufacturing company anywhere in the world. The industrial-grade decor — gray furniture, metal cabinets — gives the place a gritty air. There is no computer, only a copy machine and a facsimile machine. An abacus sits at the ready on one desktop. Only Seto's office, which is up a flight of steel spiral stairs, is air-conditioned against the humidity of the summer rainy season. It is a small, immaculate room.

"Once we employed 100, but automation has replaced workers," he says. Just as well, perhaps, as labor shortages are now a serious issue in Japan. Compounding the problem is a shrinking birthrate, which reached an all-time low for the postwar period last year. Young people claim that cramped housing makes it impossible for them to have more than one child and still live close enough to their offices to maintain some semblance of family life.

"When this business began, money was a problem," Seto says. "Now the problem is finding young workers." The young shy away from what they call 3-D jobs (or 3-K

in Japanese): those that are dirty, dangerous, difficult. Like many employers, Seto turned to foreign workers, but he found them unreliable, leaving work to take language classes in midday, he says.

Seto's workers earn 1,000 yen an hour, about $6.60. Overtime in Japan earns time and a quarter. The first Saturday of each month is an unpaid holiday at Seto's. Wages average about $20,000 a year. There is an employee restaurant on the floor above the plant, where the men take half an hour for lunch. Today the menu calls for salad, rice, hamburgers, eggs and pickles. Food odors waft through the room. An upright cabinet stands against one wall. It holds the workers' drinking cups and chopsticks. The various designs on the utensils suggest the personalities of their owners.

Four of the workers in the factory make use of company housing. There is a row of individual rooms down the hall from the lunchroom. Each is the size of a storage locker, about 8 feet by 12 feet, and costs 10,000 yen a month, $67. The walls are paneled in wood veneer. They buckle in places and show their age. The carpeted floors are stained. There is no air-conditioning, just one sliding window glazed with corrugated translucent plastic.

Across the hall is a game room where the workers have pushed the few pieces of furniture to one side. Here, they relax on the floor after work, playing cards or mahjongg. A red ashtray the size of a hubcap spills over with cigarette butts.

But for the incandescent light, this could be a sweatshop scene from the 19th century. The floor where the men sit and smoke is located above the factory's plating vats, where rainbows of chemicals are puddled on the factory floor. The atmosphere is part Dickens and part gold rush. The $800 a year Seto's workers pay in rent, the free board, leaves much of their yearly $20,000 in earnings for savings.

If the living conditions Seto reveals are questionable, they are nonetheless typical. Some of the men have lived here for years and may never move. Though they have money to spend, there is little room for storage of furniture — some stereo equipment, televisions, an auto. "They do this to buy a house," Seto says, "but that is getting difficult." In a survey done by the Bank of Japan, 32 percent of Japanese in 1978 said they were saving to buy a home. In 1988 that figure had plummeted to 19 percent, a symptom of the despair Japanese feel over real estate values.

Savings rates are also down from 1979 levels of 18.5 percent to 15.1 percent in 1988, although the overall value of savings has grown. Last year, the average Japanese family had a 13.1 million-yen nest egg,

$87,300, according to a March survey by the government's Management and Coordination Agency. Significantly, however, over the same period, debt for the average worker showed the greatest increase in 10 years, up 20.9 percent in 1988, to $25,000.

Indications are the Japanese are on something of a spending bender. Says social critic Shuichi Kato, "People cannot afford to buy homes, so they buy other things." Prestigious cars are becoming a substitute for home ownership. "More and more, you see Benzes parked in front of

former battlefield that has metamorphosed into a tropical island resort.

Nakajima works for Japan Air Lines Co. Ltd. and is a graduate of Tokyo's prestigious Sophia University. She exemplifies the young women captured by the phrase *Hanako gensho*. Hanako is the name of Tokyo's most popular magazine for young women. It is a life-style magazine, but the weekly is more than a Japanese version of Mademoiselle, Glamour or even Elle. Hanako is to shopping what travel guides are to touring.

Such an attempt at accommodation is one way the Japanese are dealing with their diminishing expectations. Still, the lack of public outcry about the real estate crisis is surprising to many observers. The past two parliamentary campaigns bubbled with talk of consumer unrest, but such sentiments never boiled over into vote-casting issues.

Masao Kunihiro, an opposition member of the Diet, Japan's parliament, blames this seeming indifference among voters on national character. "The Japanese are like sheep," he says. "They call themselves *shachachiko*" — a portmanteau expression, he explains, that means corporate livestock. "The word is pronounced very wryly, very sardonically," says the former television personality, whose flare for the dramatic has become a political asset. He thinks the Japanese have armored themselves against adversity with large doses of cynicism.

The ability to endure harsh circumstances is basic to the social compact and has its roots in the culture. There is even a word for it: *gaman*, a mix of fighting spirit and true grit. It explains as much about the quiet resignation of the Japanese in the face of this paradox of prosperity as does *shachachiko*.

"People cannot afford to buy homes, so they buy other things. More and more, you see Benzes parked in front of shabby houses in Tokyo."

shabby houses in Tokyo." The Japanese do not say Mercedes-Benz, Kato points out. "They say 'Benz,' as if the word had power."

Here, too, the paradox of Japan's prosperity emerges. "The cars are largely a psychological satisfaction," Kato observes, "because there are no roads." In all of Japan, there are only 7,100 miles of expressway, a number the government has promised to triple this decade.

Although there are 46 million passenger cars in Japan, few are used for commuting. In Tokyo, traffic is nearly impacted, and parking is virtually impossible. Those who do commute by car leave their homes at 5 a.m. and can be seen parked on the street, snoozing or eating a brown bag breakfast before restaurants and offices open.

The freewheeling spending evident in luxury car sales is visible elsewhere, in other ways, particularly among young working people. Japanese marry late, so their early 20s are years blessed by disposable income. Tokyo's shopping districts — such as the Ginza, Shinjuku and most especially Rippongi — are promenades, teeming with handsome, well-dressed young people. This is Japan's answer to the trendy fashion parade along Paris's Boulevard St. Germain.

ost of these young bons vivants, like Yuki Nakajima, 22, live with their parents. "Women like me lead a good life if we are not married," she says. She has recently returned from a weekend in Okinawa, a

With an average take-home pay of 100,000 yen a month, nearly $700, and no rent to pay, young women like Nakajima are wellsprings of disposable income. A recent magazine survey found that young women dished out an average of $554 a month on clothing, food and drink. Nearly 10 percent of the record 9 million Japanese who traveled abroad last year were women age 20 to 24.

Seated in the cushy environs of the Rainbow Lounge in Tokyo's pricey Imperial Hotel, Nakajima is in her milieu. She glances through her crowded appointment book to recall what she did on her last night out. Her date book is organized with colored stick-on symbols. It is almost a childlike touch. There are green circles to indicate holidays and gold stars to mark office events, such as meetings and conferences. The red heart posted over Saturday night needs no explanation. Last Wednesday, she notes, pointing to a gold star on the calendar, she attended a casual after-hour party thrown by her company.

High-priced real estate is something Nakajima says that she worries about. A friend recently related a story to her regarding a young woman in her early 30s who was unmarried. Although she was conducting a far-reaching search for the right man, she was fussy. She wanted to find a fellow who was born and raised in Tokyo. The reason for this particular qualification was immediately apparent to Nakajima. The woman wanted a Tokyo native because it was more likely that his parents would own a home in town. *Masuo-san gensho*. Inheriting a place is the only hope most young people harbor for owning a home of their own in the city.

Not to be overlooked, however, is the more practical circumstance. For despite the hardships, Japan has made huge strides in living standards since the war. Stores overflow with food. Everyone has shelter, excellent medical care. The Japanese electronics and auto industries are the envy of the world. The country has become a direct challenger to U.S. technological leadership and ranges ahead in many areas. The nation has real economic muscle. Japanese businesses own Rockefeller Center, Tiffany's, 50 percent of the prime real estate in Los Angeles, 30 percent of Houston, Washington. The people count such accomplishments as their own. Their sacrifices are realized — and assuaged — by the nation's achievements.

And they may be proud that their nation works. The trains run on time, as do the ultrasafe subways; the mail gets delivered; streets are clean; crime is virtually nonexistent; drugs are no problem. One may more safely drink the tap water in Tokyo than in Paris.

Philosopher Kato points to still another factor in the lack of reaction by the Japanese electorate: "The relationship between the government and the people is different in Japan from the West." He cites taxes as an example. "People hate taxes but they never question them. [The exception was a fire storm last year over a 3 percent consumption tax.] We just had a royal wedding in Tokyo. No one talked about the budget."

Grass roots movements in Japan are practically unheard-of, particularly in recent years. For the most part, people are too consumed by their long hours to become involved. Instead, when change is in the winds, it flows down from the lofty and powerful ministries. That is why a recent "vision paper" issued by the Ministry of International Trade and Industry drew so much comment. While the paper ranged over such issues as Eastern Europe and Japan as an emerging global power, it took the unusual step of calling attention to consumer issues.

Such "visions" have been issued each decade since the 1960s. They have set the agenda for Japan's ascendancy in computer hardware, autos and consumer electronics. MITI's reputation for realizing its visions remains virtually unchallenged.

And now, says the ministry, the target is consumers. "To date, in Japan, we have adopted policies in response to the times," says Kunio Morikiyo, director of the policy planning office at MITI, who introduced this latest vision. "In the 1990s, that calls for programs that benefit the people. We call our industrial policies of the 1990s 'human-oriented.' "

The summary report delivered by Morikiyo, which was uncharacteristically issued in English as well as in Japanese, came right to the point: "If we simply look at numbers, there is no question Japan has left a trail of superior economic performances. However, there is increasing doubt among the Japanese people that their standard of living has risen accordingly. The problem is too serious to simply say that it is a 'matter of personal viewpoints' or 'an extravagance of a newly wealthy Japan.' "

MITI says it is concerned about public reaction. The fear, however, is not that the paradox of prosperity will result in civil unrest, or even that it might send Japan's ruling Liberal-Democratic Party to its first outright defeat since 1955. Instead, the ministry worries that the mixing of Japan's deep cultural strength, *gaman*, with its dark opposite, cynicism, will result in nihilism. "If changes are not made to realize this goal, and there are increasing gaps in wealth and among regions, a feeling of frustration may permeate society. This in turn could undermine motivation and creativity in individuals," the paper warned.

ITI delivered its vision for the 1990s just as the year-long Strategic Impediments Initiative talks ended across the street at the Ministry of Foreign Affairs. Its timing raised brows among the skeptics. Much of

the trade talks focused on Japanese promises to pump up its skinny infrastructure and to make progress on land prices. Such impediments have so much impact on the Japanese economy that the United States believes remedying them will improve the one-sided trade imbalance between the nations. (The prohibitive cost of real estate, for example, excludes midsize U.S. companies from opening their doors in the Japanese market.)

Unofficially within MITI, it was acknowledged that the vision was issued for external consumption, to form a coda to the Strategic Impediments talks. Doubts about the true significance of the vision even percolated up from those who contributed to the document: 200 independent consultants from giant corporations such as Mitsubishi Heavy Industries Ltd., Nomura Securities Co. Ltd., Dentsu Advertising; foreign firms like Citibank NA; powerful associations like the Keidanren (the Japan Federation of Economic Organizations) and Nikkeiren, its nominal counterpart in labor.

Hidehiko Sekizawa, a consultant on the vision and executive director of Hakuhodo Institute of Life & Living Inc., a subsidiary of Japan's No. 2 advertising firm, remains cautious. "We must keep our eyes fixed on what MITI will do, not what they say."

To gain perspective on Japan's living standards for the vision, Sekizawa says he interviewed 30 Westerners who had been working in Japan for more than three years. He wanted to know how the quality of life in their home countries differed from Japan's. The study found that the Japanese lack three things. As Sekizawa summarizes, "We lack space, because we live in rabbit hutches. We lack time, because of long hours, long commutes and no leisure. And we lack private lives, because most of our time is spent with colleagues or clients."

In search of a catchphrase to vivify the findings, Sekizawa arrived at the Japanese word *manuke*. "The meaning of *manuke* is that 'we lack three things,' " he says: "time, space and family interaction." The purpose of the catchphrase was to attract press attention. The hope was to galvanize public opinion, because the Japanese instantly recognize that the catchphrase is a stinger. It has a double meaning. "*Manuke* is also the Japanese word for 'stupid,' " he says. "We are stupid to live without these three things."

But Sekizawa is not entirely discouraged by the situation. He takes MITI's invitation to him and to other top marketing people as a signal that the ministry is aware of the issues. "I have little knowledge of industry," he points out. "I study consumers." Asking him to join the study "may show that MITI is serious about under-

standing consumer needs." Still, he adds, the question remains: "Can MITI change anything?"

One potential target of reform for the ministry is Tokyo's urban farmer. In people-packed Tokyo, farmers control 15 percent of the land. Only 1 percent of the city's people live on these preserves. The National Land Agency survey found that within one hour's commuting time from central Tokyo, 17,400 hectares of land, nearly 43,000 acres, were suitable for housing. If only 15 percent of that land were developed, there would be enough room to build 500,000 detached homes. At 3.19 persons per household, Tokyo's average, that is enough housing for almost 1.6 million residents, 13 percent of the capital's population.

The farmers who own these lands are at great advantage, borrowing against their huge land assets to make lucrative investments or subdividing the land and selling it for substantial profits. Then there are the tax breaks. Because land prices are so high, the effective tax rate has shrunk to almost nothing, about 0.1 percent, compared with 1.5 percent in the United States. "Farmers pay about one-fiftieth the rate paid in the rest of Japan," says the Economic Planning Agency's Yoshitomi. That means that a farm plot worth $10 million would pay yearly taxes equal to a dinner for four in Tokyo's Ginza, about $200.

The largest, most luxurious homes in most of Tokyo's neighborhoods are those owned by local farmers. In the little town of Takaido, for example, in the wealthy western suburbs, a family of farmers who have lived in the area for years keep large parcels of land nominally under the till. A wag in the Ministry of Construction has said that if this one particular owner's land were sold in a single year, its buyer would become the largest taxpayer in Japan.

On one section of the land is a chestnut grove the size of two football fields. It is worth millions. In season, the chestnuts from the grove are sold by the side of the road in paper bags for 500 yen, 35 cents a bag. There is an honor cup to collect the 500-yen coppers. The small transaction that takes place atop that chair seat satisfies the definition of farming in the tax code. Nearby stands a sign that says, "This agricultural land is maintained as greenery for the benefit of Tokyo's children." The sign sits behind a 4-foot concrete wall, too tall for young children to get the message.

Says the Economic Planning Agency's Yoshitomi, "There are two separate questions: Do we deal with the price of land or the more effective use of land?" The government prefers the former, he says. But he thinks higher land prices are inevitable. "The purpose of our policy should be aimed at increasing the utility of the land for the people." In other words, more space, lower unit prices. "That obviously will end up raising land prices on the underlying property."

Tokyo is a low, flat city. Across its endless urban sprawl, few buildings rise up above the treetops, about 2½ stories. The city's seismic instability partly explains this low-slung phenomenon. But Yoshitomi says that buildings can be built to withstand earthquakes. "We are technology optimists," he says. "The problem we are trying to overcome now is glass." During an earthquake, glass shattering from skyscrapers could have terrible effects on those below. "So we are developing special windows." The future of Tokyo, he believes, will be upward.

"We are not talking about turning Tokyo into Manhattan," he says. Instead, he sees a city of 20- to 50-story buildings in Tokyo's 10-kilometer radius inner core. "In the next 10 kilometers there would be seven- or eight-story Paris-style apartments, with their own parking garages. Beyond 20 kilometers would be American-style suburbs."

What he describes is known as the Tokyo Doughnut. It is an idea so well institutionalized that it is taught in elementary schools. Most consider such plans for the city to be dreams, virtually impossible to implement. MITI's paper suggested a sec-

> ## "Encouraging young people to buy land is mistaken. They should have more space in a less costly apartment. This would make them happy."

ond solution, reducing the pressure on Tokyo by directing national resources to other cities. That scenario also seems unlikely.

A more realistic near-term solution, which is already being acted upon, is leveraging out living space through the tax code. The government's Tax Commission began hearings on the subject in May. A full report on real estate, farm and inheritance taxes is expected in October.

Yoshitomi says the effective tax rate for real estate will certainly be increased. Higher real estate taxes would be balanced by lower local taxes. The effect would be to maintain purchasing power but to reduce the incentive to hold on to housing. "We have to squeeze the people to make them sell their land." Already, he says, a consensus is forming in the government to support the change. "It will take five to 10 years to accomplish."

While these are not draconian measures, the message they contain is not a pleasant one. The dream of owning land, at least in Tokyo and possibly in the other

large cities, is coming to an end. "Encouraging young people to buy land is mistaken," Yoshitomi says. To avoid the downward spiral that comes with diminished expectations, the loss of incentive, he suggests an alternative. "They should have more space in a less costly apartment. This would make them happy."

By trading expectations, land for living room, the government hopes to make a dent in the paradox of prosperity. It entails sacrifice. But this is the only possible future, Yoshitomi says. This generation of Japanese now in their early 30s will be the generation of *Masuo-san gensho*.

"Young people, sorry to say, must give up the idea of owning their own land in Tokyo," says Yoshitomi. "It is not economical. We will build more comfortable apartments with more reasonable rents. They won't have to pay the high price of land to own their own homes. We must put an end to that illusion."

— Jeff Shear in Tokyo

Article 10

The Japan Times Weekly International Edition
April 23–29, 1990

Our Own Vision Needed:
People measure affluence with the wrong yardstick

Kimindo Kusaka

Kimindo Kusaka is senior managing director of the Softnomics Center. This article originally appeared in the Voice magazine (July 1989). This translation was prepared by the Asia Foundation's Translation Service Center.

A quiz in a popular American magazine asked readers three questions.

(1) Which country exports massively to the United States but imports almost no American goods? Hint: An island nation heavily bombed during World War II.

(2) Which country invests most heavily in the United States? Hint: A small nation whose inhabitants have a reputation for hard work and frugality.

(3) Which country owns the most U.S. real estate? Hint: Its trade imbalance with the United States is a long-standing bilateral issue.

If you answered "Japan" to all three questions, you swallowed the bait. The correct responses are Britain, the Netherlands and Canada.

Few people on either side of the Pacific know the correct answers. After all, Japanese purchases of prime property in Honolulu and Los Angeles grab the headlines. Americans perceive Japan as a threat because it is the newcomer.

Of course, if our trade surplus continues to swell, and Uncle Sam fails to trim his budget deficit and improve competitiveness, Japan will probably take the lead in every category. But that day is not yet here.

Japan is awash with money these days, but you would never guess it from talking to the man in the street. "We're rich? You've got to be kidding!" is a common refrain. Despite the world's second largest gross national product (GNP), Japan has some of the highest prices, worst housing conditions and longest working hours.

Many Japanese wonder whether we will surpass the U.S. economically in the 1990s. Will we improve the quality of life? Many doubt that we will ever catch up with the Americans in terms of housing, working conditions and urban amenities.

But people measure affluence with the wrong yardstick. Real wealth is not a big house or shorter workweek. It's our lifestyle and many of the cultural intangibles we take for granted. Today, we need a Japanese vision of the good life.

But that is easier said than done. Can we build a prosperous postindustrial society without creating the cleavages between haves and have-nots that plague America?

Japan is already overdeveloped. Automobile exhaust and industrial pollutants contribute to the greenhouse effect. We manufacture about 10 percent of the world's chlorofluoro-carbons, a major cause of ozone depletion. Japan is a heavy user of pesticides and other farm chemicals. Will the public accept a lower standard of living in order to protect the environment and produce safe food?

In 1986, an ad hoc commission headed by Haruo Maekawa, former Bank of Japan governor, warned that we would have to shift from an export-based economy to one driven by internal demand. To boost domestic consumption of goods and services, the report said, Japanese would have to overcome three major obstacles to a standard of life comparable with the West: high prices, inadequate housing and long working hours.

But the Maekawa report didn't define that standard. In 1987, our per capita GNP surpassed that of the United States. But people who can't afford to take a vacation, life in "rabbit hutches" and put in 10-hour workdays don't feel affluent.

In the past two years, government and media surveys comparing Japan's living standards with those of other countries have reinforced the perception that we are poor, not rich. But these studies, too, fail to define the quality of life.

Will lower prices, larger houses and a 40-hour week make us happy? What is happiness, anyway? No one seems to know.

If Japan were really as poor as many commentators say, who would buy, for example, the $5,400 electronic bicycle made by Matsushita Electric? Yet the custom-built bike is selling well.

The experts consider only one dimension of the problem. There is another side to the high cost of living, substandard dwellings and worker-bee mentality. Many so-called obstacles to a better life are actually assets. These disguised benefits constitute a distinctive Japanese lifestyle.

Take prices, for example. According to a recent government report, Tokyoites pay $2.50 for a cup of coffee that costs only 70 cents in New York and 60 cents in Paris. But the Japanese consumer gets more than just a hot beverage.

Coffee shops here strive to create a special ambience, a private space where patrons can relax and savor their favorite blend. Well-groomed, courteous waitresses enhance the mood.

Moreover, there is a coffee shop for every preference. Some feature the classics, others jazz or popular music. Many people transact business in these congenial surroundings. Even executives like to hold low-level meetings there.

The floor space of a Tokyo coffee-house is worth upward of $60,000 per square foot. Personnel and maintenance costs are also expensive.

Considering the atmosphere, service and overhead, the $2.50 price of admission is cheap.

It is difficult to put a value on first-rate service. Yet you can't compare prices in New York or Paris without taking these hidden costs into account.

The people who complain the loudest about Japan's unreasonable prices are the political and business elite. Few Maekawa commission members, for example, spend much time in coffee shops. They should take a good look at how the rest of us live.

Housing is another area where invisible "quality-added" factors must be considered. American families transferred to Tokyo are astonished to learn they must pay $7,000 per month for an apartment that seems impossibly cramped.

But after a year, most appreciate the advantages of smaller quarters. Japanese rentals come with all the modern conveniences, including electronic kitchens, central heating and air conditioners. Because there is less space, they are easy to clean and maintain. No yard means no lawn to cut or leaves to rake. Most neighborhoods are crime-free by U.S. standards and include a shopping district with supermarkets and restaurants.

Japanese rarely entertain in their own residences because of the lack of space. Businessmen wine and dine clients at night-spots or restaurants, and at company expense. After-hours relaxation with colleagues is done in bars. Americans living here are spared the expense and bother of U.S.-style socializing at home.

In the United States, an executive's career prospects depend on impressing the boss and important business associates. Guests are frequently invited to dinner, and wives are expected not only to be good hostesses but interior decorators as well. Stylish drapes, furniture and table settings are de rigueur in the competitive world of U.S. business.

For Americans, a spacious, well-appointed house is a career asset and therefore a business investment. Yet no one includes this additional cost when comparing the prices of Japanese and U.S. housing.

In the 21st century, the bulk of humanity will live in large cities. Most people will have to accept small dwellings and congested living conditions. Japan can show the world that small is beautiful. In fact, we have already begin to do so.

Ten years ago, the New York branch of a large Japanese bank held a Christmas party on Dec. 23. American employees were surprised that the Japanese brought their wives and children and then took them to dinner later. New Yorkers assumed the families attended because, having made few friends in New York, they had not been invited to a yule party.

Today, however, the Americans have caught on. Like their Japanese colleagues, many now take their families to the bank's office party. They do their pre-Christmas socializing there and then go to a restaurant, dispensing with the burden of entertaining at home.

Critics say Japan's long working hours are an impediment to a better life. Some U.S. legislators even cite them as a nontariff trade barrier.

Japanese and Western attitudes toward work, however, are fundamentally different. The Bible, for example, says that God condemned Adam to live by the sweat of his brow as punishment for yielding to Eve's temptation. Japanese work hard largely because they enjoy collective effort.

Granted, we put in long hours. But not all of that time is spent on the job. The strong sense of group loyalty makes it difficult for a person to leave the office before his colleagues. Employees tarry until everyone is ready to call it a day.

But the old work ethic is changing. Following the rise of the yen vis-a-vis the dollar from 1985, many companies trimmed their work force or closed down and moved offshore. After years of loyalty to the firm, large numbers of middle-aged, white-collar employees were forced to retire early or accept permanent transfers to lower-paying subsidiaries. More workers now distrust management and look out for number one.

Young Japanese, dubbed the "new breed," make a clear distinction between company time and private time. They tend to leave the office at 5 p.m. sharp and will switch jobs rather than accept onerous working conditions.

The top jobs in government and industry now go to people with diplomas from the University of Tokyo and other prestigious schools. Most companies organize study groups; participation is mandatory for those who want to get ahead. Once on the job, young would-be managers must cram to pass qualifying exams required for promotion.

On their way up the ladder, junior executives often neglect their families, leading to marital discord. They may also alienate friends and colleagues.

But increasingly, a degree from a leading university and a good job do not guarantee happiness.

Women, for instance, are no longer content with an elite-track spouse. Many now want a companion, not a dull breadwinner interested only in his job. The ideal mate is one who likes to do things together, helps around the house and is paying off the mortgage.

Our children will inherit a very different world. In the 1990s, a new age in international relations will dawn. Detente and perestroika have already made conventional political and economic theories obsolete. To cope with the future, the men and women of tomorrow will need an entirely new set of concepts.

Article 11

FORTUNE/ Pacific Rim 1990

HOW THE JAPANESE ARE CHANGING

Japan is finally trying to live like the wealthy country it is. And that means new opportunity for the West. Selling to Japan, while never easy, is no longer impossible. ■ by Carla Rapoport

CONJURE UP AN IMAGE of Tokyo Bay. Are you thinking only of rows of factories and warehouses? Try again. Today sailboards, cruise ships, fancy hotels, and trendy new skyscrapers dot Tokyo's shoreline, along with dozens of noisy construction sites where

REPORTER ASSOCIATES *Sara Hammes and Cindy Mikami*

a variety of new projects are under way.

These changes are just the most visible signs of Japan's new effort to live like the wealthy country it is. The world's champion workaholics are starting to loosen up and play more. Japan's consumers are enjoying more choices than ever before, from imported cars to U.S.-made cockroach killers. Top Japanese business and government leaders

have begun calling for less economic aggressiveness overseas. Even the once unthinkable notion of importing rice is beginning to seem possible.

Look behind these developments and you'll find *gaiatsu*, or external pressure. Japan is finally starting to respond to U.S. prodding that it buy as well as sell. But there are significant internal forces for change too. Many young Japanese are starting to realize that some aspects of Western lifestyle are preferable to their own. As a result of both outside diplomacy and a growing national sense of confidence, today's Japan also is more willing to cooperate with other industrialized countries rather than go its own way.

OF COURSE, all this is just a beginning. The qualities that brought Japan out of the desolation of World War II—hard work, dedication, and respect for the established order—remain dominant. But the changes are real enough to present the West with new opportunities.

Selling to Japan, while never easy, is no longer impossible. Japan is now the world's fastest-growing market for imported cars. As more luxury houses, sports clubs, and leisure facilities go up around the country, the Japanese will want more foreign expertise and services as well as consumer goods and hardware. This won't make the U.S. trade deficit go away, but it will push it in the right direction. Most analysts think that the deficit will drop from $49 billion last year to between $40 billion and $44 billion this year.

As competitors, the Japanese remain harder working and richer than almost everyone else. But they have altered or stopped outright many of the practices that once annoyed, even outraged, their rivals. In response to strong complaints, they have virtually stopped dumping goods abroad below cost. Exports of cars, steel, and semiconductors—all the target of past U.S. trade restrictions—are now falling. Even banks, known for lending around the world at low interest rates, are raising them in line with those of other international banks.

Inside Japan, certain segments of society are changing faster than anyone outside the country would have imagined. A prime example is the rapid development of a leisure industry. In Tama New Town, about 50 minutes by train from Tokyo, a huge indoor amusement park decked with candy stripes and curlicues is taking shape. This $400 million pink colossus, opening in December, marks the first attempt by a Japanese company to tap into the market with a distinctly local product. Dreamed up by Sanrio, Japan's leading toy company, it will feature robotronics and a crop of new Japanese cartoon characters—but no Disney-type thrill rides.

Sanrio is gambling that the Japanese are finally getting serious about leisure. In other industrialized countries, rising wealth has brought a reduction in working hours. In Japan, largely because of the country's weak labor unions, workers have not been so lucky. Some 60% still spend Saturdays on the job.

But rising corporate profits have led to higher wages. Workers' disposable income grew nearly 8% last year. Leisure-time spending as a percent of total consumer spending reached 29% last year, vs. 27% in the U.S. The figure for Japan is up from 25% in 1984. Japan's leisure industry is betting that good-time spending is just beginning. According to industry analysts, Japanese companies will invest nearly $40 billion in resorts alone over the next ten years.

Behind this urge to spend are some deeper currents that may make $40 billion seem puny. The primary one is the changing attitude of Japanese young people toward fun. While just as hardworking as their parents, they think that a vacation is supposed to be more than a week off to pray at their ancestors' graves. Says Toshio Kagami, managing director of Oriental Land, which owns Tokyo Disneyland: "Young people want longer vacations, closer to the American style. Their parents are happy with two or three nights away. Not the children. As the young people grow and take more responsibility,

The younger generation thinks that a vacation is supposed to be more than a week off to pray at their ancestors' graves.

the entire society will change the way it thinks of leisure."

Japanese companies are beginning to give in to demands for shorter hours and longer vacations, but not out of altruism or because they want to help spin the turnstiles at Disneyland. Japan's booming economy and rapidly aging work force have led to the worst labor shortage in 15 years, and employers are scrambling for young workers. A government survey shows that 80% of today's college graduates list a five-day workweek as a prime requirement when choosing a job. Sony, often the industry maverick, has taken the unusual step of allowing employees to take vacations anytime they want. Canon recently boosted vacation time for first-year employees from ten days to 20.

Backing all this up are a number of government initiatives aimed at creating more ski areas, marinas, resorts, and sports facilities of all kinds. Almost every government ministry and municipality is offering developers tax breaks and other incentives. The Japanese have a long way to go. Last year ten million Japanese chose to vacation outside the country, spending so much money that they helped drive the country's current account surplus down by about $12 billion. More would go abroad if Japan's inadequate airports weren't already full to bursting.

This almost grim determination to enjoy life more translates into opportunity for foreign builders and consultants. Sanrio, for example, hired Landmark Entertainment of Los Angeles to advise it on almost every aspect of its new amusement park. Oriental Land is expecting to build another theme park in 1992, and Disney plans to bid. In Osaka, government authorities commissioned Cambridge Seven Associates of Boston to design a $107 million aquarium on the waterfront. The attraction, which opened last July, is expected to attract two million visitors a year. Marketing opportunities beckon. Most of the new cruise ships afloat around Japan are losing money because they haven't been able to lure enough customers.

Along with the need to play more, the Japanese have a new itch for foreign goods. Five years ago a Japanese consumer could buy domestic goods at reasonable prices or imports at punitive prices. Today, for the most part, imports are available at affordable prices. Consumers can now find cut-rate prices on Japanese goods at the mushrooming number of discount stores.

To speed up this process, Prime Minister Toshiki Kaifu, responding in part to U.S. demands, last June announced huge increases in public spending over the next decade to improve Japan's miserable roads, housing, and sewers. At the same time, the government vowed to declaw the patchwork of regulations, including restrictions on size and hours among other things, that make it hard for big retailers to compete against mom and pop stores. Kaifu also proposed a variety of other measures aimed at increasing imports and pushing up spending.

Already trade numbers are starting to reflect the change. Total imports climbed from $130 billion in 1985 to $210 billion last year, with U.S. sales to Japan jumping from $23 billion to $45 billion. This year imports are likely to climb another 6% to 8% overall, with 10% from the U.S. More than a dozen U.S. companies have sales around $1 billion or more in Japan. No one accuses Japan of maintaining a closed economy anymore, but no one says it's easy to break into. Still, imported cars now account for 5% of the total sales, and BMW alone claims 6.3% of the Japanese luxury car market.

Behind these public manifestations of change is a growing undercurrent of reform within the political leadership. This summer the Ministry of International Trade and Industry (MITI) issued its industrial policy paper for the 1990s with a positively mellow subtitle: "Creating Human Values in the Global Age." Dispensing with its time-honored tradition of business first, MITI argued for longer vacations, more consumer protection, higher imports, and better child care facilities before mentioning industrial goals. Japan's bureaucracy is also working on schemes to assist both the elderly and the young. One result: a nursery school combined with a home for the aged. The seniors help watch the youngsters and get companionship in return.

LEADERS of the ruling Liberal Democratic Party are now traveling overseas in unprecedented numbers and are starting to transform Japan into a more open member of the world community. In recent months, Prime Minister Kaifu has been boosting Japan's profile abroad by taking stands on such issues as resuming loans to China and the embargo of Iraqi oil. The new emperor gave an outright apology to South Koreans for Japan's prewar colonization of that country.

The hysteria over Japan's relentless pursuit of world markets also is no longer confined to Lee Iacocca and U.S. trade officials. Some of the most acerbic criticisms are now coming from Japanese businessmen. Says Masaji Shinagawa, the dapper chairman of Nippon Fire & Marine: "Our process of economic development has been multiplying without any brakes. This has to stop, or we risk total isolation from the world." As head of corporate reform for the Japan Association of Corporate Executives, Shinagawa recently issued a blueprint for change that calls on Japan's bureaucracy to stop coddling industry, on companies to cut back on exports and boost imports, and on business in general to put the needs of the community and consumers first.

More startling to veteran Japan watchers has been this summer's debate over rice imports. Since the 1960s Japanese leaders have always insisted that Japan's security would be compromised if foreign rice were allowed in. This silly argument has merely been a cover-up for the real reason—the tremendous political power of farmers. But suddenly, it seems, that balance of power is shifting. In three recent surveys by leading national newspapers, 60% to 65% of those queried said they favored some liberalization of the Japanese rice market.

In July, Toshio Yamaguchi, a senior LDP leader, shocked his colleagues by announcing that Japan's rice market should be opened to allow imports of about 5% of domestic demand. Prime Minister Kaifu followed a week later by admitting that a total ban on rice imports was not necessarily a good course for Japan. Both men were playing to Washington, of course, where the ire over Japan's large trade surplus remains high. But both are savvy politicians who recognize that the influence of farmers is on the wane. This is primarily because the rural population is shrinking and because electoral reform within the next two years should give more power to urban voters.

While unlocking 5% of the Japanese rice market might not seem like much to Americans, it would have a very large effect on the Japanese economy. First, it would force rice prices down from their ridiculously high protected rate, freeing billions of yen in disposable income for other purchases. It would also force farmers to vacate nonproductive plots, liberating much-needed land for housing and recreational purposes.

Indeed, land reform remains the one area most crucial to change in Japan and the one most difficult to solve. The biggest stumbling block is Japan's tax system, which penalizes those who sell land. Even so, hardy developers, both public and private, are creating some striking alternatives to Japan's cramped living quarters.

Increased public spending is expected to boost substantially the number of government housing projects around the country over the next few years. Dozens of public and private projects are taking shape. The new skyscrapers of Makuhari New Town on Tokyo Bay, which is also home to the newly opened Convention Center, is drawing businesses out of central Tokyo. Already 160 companies have made the move.

After 30 years of debate, the multibillion-dollar Tokyo Bay Bridge project is finally under way, with completion scheduled in 1996. The Yokohama section of the bridge is completed, easing traffic congestion in that area. When finished, the Bay Bridge will open access to cheaper land and better recreational sites for crowded Tokyo.

FOR THE VERY RICH who want a second home, the choice until recently was a condo in Hawaii or Queensland, Australia. Late this summer a new option appeared in Chiba, a Tokyo suburb. Tokyu Land is putting the finishing touches on a lush development it calls One Hundred Hills. The project sports such curiosities for Japan as rolling green lawns, private tennis courts, swimming pools, palm trees, and sidewalks. Designed by the Los Angeles architectural firm of Richardson Nagy Martin, all 33 of the $3 million to $6 million houses put on the market so far were sold months before completion.

All these changes are occurring slowly, with most Japanese admitting that it will be ten years at least before Japan will really enjoy the lifestyle it can afford. In the meantime, even with both the yen and the stock market below their previous highs, few complain. Those who won't inherit a house and have no chance of buying one are not particularly alienated. As Naoyuki Hasegawa, 25, a researcher at the Japan External Trade Organization, puts it: "If we get our parents' house, we can spend all our money without worrying. If we don't inherit one, we know we can't buy one, so we can enjoy all our money anyway. Either way we have a lot of disposable income." That disposable income will become one of the most powerful forces in the world's economy in the decade to come. And those who heed the winds of change in Japan should be best able to harness it.

Carla Rapoport

Article 12

The Wall Street Journal, June 20, 1989

New Awareness

Disparities in Wealth Affront Japan's Vision Of Itself as Classless

'Recruit' Scandal, Fortunes In Speculation Give Rise To Resentment of Rich
A Chateau and $6.50 Cigars

Urban C. Lehner

Staff Reporter of The Wall Street Journal

TOKYO—Before Japan's Recruit scandal, Kayoko Ishizuka might never have given a second thought to Takao Fujinami's house. Now it's outrageous, the moral equivalent of Imelda Marcos's 2,000 pairs of shoes.

Mrs. Ishizuka lives with her husband and three children in a cramped three-room apartment in a Tokyo public-housing project. Although the rent is subsidized and both the Ishizukas work, they have no hope of affording a bigger apartment, much less a house.

Mr. Fujinami, a powerful politician, lives a few miles away in a two-story house of 1,800 square feet, twice the size of the average Japanese home. To help build the $900,000 place, he allegedly used gains on the sale of 10,000 shares of Recruit Cosmos Co., the Japanese firm whose issuance of cheap stock to politicians precipitated the biggest political scandal in years.

"I was so angry, I couldn't even look at my place," says Mrs. Ishizuka. "My whole apartment would fit into the entranceway of Fujinami's house—maybe into the bathroom."

The Rich-Poor Gap

Never mind that Mr. Fujinami has pleaded innocent to a bribery indictment. For many Japanese he will remain the man who built a house they could never afford, with easy money they will never have. The Recruit symbol has come to symbolize not merely political corruption but also entrenched privilege in Japan's social and economic system.

In Japan, as elsewhere, some people labor long hours, commuting great distances between their tiny homes and the workplace, while others ride in limousines and deal in vast sums of money. But Japan has long prided itself as a classless society. The disparities showing the contrary usually have been ignored. "The Recruit affair," says Sumiko Iwamoto, Mrs. Ishizuka's neighbor in the public-housing complex, "has made us conscious of this gap."

Class-consciousness is rising. More than 90% of Japanese who responded in an opinion poll last year still considered themselves middle class. But 29.2%, the highest percentage in 20 years, called themselves lower middle class. "A wealth gap has been opening," says Hiroyuki Hisamizu, a private economist: "Consciousness of it is just beginning, but in five to 10 years, this could be a big social issue."

Speculative Wealth

Underlying the widening economic gap and its embodiment in the Recruit scandal is the explosive rise in Tokyo land prices. Salaried income remains remarkably evenly distributed here, reinforcing the illusion of classlessness. But inflation in land has made the rich a lot richer and the poor more perceptive. Government statistics show that in 1987, the landholdings of the richest fifth of the Japanese population were worth 10 times as much as those of the middle fifth. As recently as 1985 the gap was only 5.5 times.

Japan's haves borrowed against their land to buy stocks that also have soared. The have-nots, unable to borrow on their meager landholdings, have missed an easy ride in the stock market, too. "Mr. Fujinami bought an expensive house out of the money he made from selling Recruit Cosmos shares, which went up because the company speculated on Tokyo real estate, bidding up land prices," says Akio Mikuni, president of Mikuni & Co., a bond-rating outfit.

Some critics say that the Japanese work ethic and tight social fabric may wear thin. Some other critics have a different concern. They say that obsession over the gulf between rich and poor could retard Japan's natural evolution into a society more preoccupied with consumption than production. "Now is the time when we ought to be working less hard and spending more," says Kenichi Takemura, an author and television commentator. "This Recruit scandal reduces Japan's chances of becoming a more spendthrift society."

The Artist as Consumer

Japanese *nouveaux riches* are spending freely. The studio-office of Noriyoshi

Ishigooka, artist and real-estate speculator, is decorated with expensive art, including some of Mr. Ishigooka's own $80,000-and-up abstract paintings. Glass shelves hold his collection of fine European porcelain; some cups are worth $20,000 each. Drawers are crammed with boxes and boxes of fat Cerdan cigars, bought in France for about $6.50 a cigar.

The artist himself is dressed in a lemon-sherbet-colored kimono. He wears a gold watch, three gold bracelets and a gold-set ruby ring the size of a bird's egg. He puffs on a Cerdan and offers a late-morning visitor a glass of 50-year-old Calvados. He looks a decade younger than his 60 years as he tells how he made his millions.

"The answer is very simple," he says. "It's just because land in Japan has risen rapidly. The rest is all borrowing. Now I'm borrowing again to buy more land."

Mr. Ishigooka owns a $3 million house in Bronxville, N.Y., which he bought from the king of Morocco. He owns two office buildings in midtown Manhattan. He owns a chateau in France on 740 acres; the place cost $1.3 million. He is converting the chateau into a museum for his own paintings. He is shopping for land in the U.S. to build another museum.

"I lead a luxurious life," Mr. Ishigooka says unapologetically. "If an artist is poor, even his heart becomes hungry."

While none of this would cause much comment in America or Western Europe, it strikes traditional Japanese as unseemly.

Their society historically has considered conspicuous consumption distasteful. The Buddhist and Confucian ethic encouraged even the old samurai nobility to live poorly and purely. Merchants, at the bottom of the social ladder in feudal Japan, were expected to hide their wealth. (Some wore kimonos with cotton outers and silk linings.) In the economic rebuilding after World War II, an industrialist's fondness for sardines and rice, a poor man's diet, won his widespread respect.

The rich today flaunt it. A television network recently filmed university students as they crowded into French restaurants to order $100 courses and vintage wines. Worse, many people today got rich not through hard work or merit—or so the popular perception has it—but by inheriting land, a business or professional practice or even a political career from their parents. "This feeling is exploding," says Kazuhiro Ono, author of a book on Japan's new rich.

Few Japanese begrudge wealth earned by effort or talent. Many profess respect for Hiromasa Ezoe, Recruit's chairman and founder, who built his big company from scratch. "They are in awe of his ability," Mr. Ono says. "His problem was, he tried to enter the old system later and make all these connections. People think that was wrong. But they think that even worse than him were the people who took the money from him, the politicians."

Mr. Ono says most Japanese envy the new rich not so much for their BMWs as for their free time. Mitsui Research Group surveyed Japanese in their 20s and 30s earlier this year and found that only 19% defined new richness as "having an abundance of material things"; 51% saw it as "having a life style of your own." But however they define rich, most Japanese agree that they're not. Some 69% of Mitsui's respondents said they would need to double or even triple their income to have a new-rich life style.

"We all think we're the same middle class, but there's a gap," says Ken Kono, a free-lance photographer and an Amway distributor.

The new rich themselves don't see it quite that way. Mr. Ishigooka, the artist, says those who missed the land boom can still get rich in Japan by finding something else to speculate on. "If you don't own land, you can own jewelry," he says.

Takashi Nagaoka, a 35-year-old middle manager at Mitsubishi Bank, considers himself upper-middle class. He says that those who are merely middle-class remain so because of their own way of thinking, not because society is unfair. Mr. Nagaoka, who says his salary is in the range of $66,000 to $87,000 a year, is an aggressive investor. In recent years, he has accumulated more than $100,000 in stocks and other liquid assets, built a $200,000 house on his father's land in Yokohama, purchased land on a resort island that is now worth $170,000, and bought a $50,000 membership in a golf club.

"If I hadn't made all these investments, maybe I would have remained just middle class," he says. "Class depends on your way of thinking about life. If there's something you want, whether you buy it really depends on what you think is enough for you. I feel I ought to demand a lot, even if I have to borrow money."

Mr. Takemura, the television commentator, says many ordinary Japanese do have money and leisure time but just won't use it. "We must first get rid of this Japanese guilty conscience toward spending money and taking time off," he says. On a recent midweek airplane trip to a ski resort, he says, "I was appalled to find I was the only middle-aged man on the plane. All the other skiers were students."

Mr. Takemura believes the "difference between the richest and the poorest" in Japan is still "so small that everyone can dream of being a rich man, and that's why they become jealous." He decries as petty the bad outcry over Mr. Fujinami's house. It is, he says, "a small house for a political leader who might have become the prime minister of the world's richest nation. I'm sad that the Japanese are so narrow-minded and jealous of others."

It's not so simple as that, others say. They mourn the narrowing of their country's avenues of social mobility. In the postwar meritocracy, talented youths, however poor, could go to the best schools and get the best jobs. Now both increasingly are filled by sons and daughters of the privileged. Some 25% of the seats in the Diet, or parliament, are held by politicians whose fathers had held the same seats.

Educational competition is fierce. But the "cram schools" that prepare students for entrance examinations are too expensive for low-income students.

Takako Inoue grew up in a large house with a swimming pool, a rarity in the early postwar years. She went to a private school where she rubbed shoulders with members of the emperor's family. She married an heir to a small but successful manufacturing business, and she manages—along with several partners—a successful chain of 16 shops that rents fancy dresses. She lives in an expensive apartment in a fashionable neighborhood with her husband and two children and her Pomeranian, Shachan. Her family has land in resort areas and takes lengthy vacations.

Even so, Mrs. Inoue professes astonishment at the wealth required to send a child to the right school. To qualify for medical school, one friend's son joined a tutorial group that required him to live for three months in Tokyo's posh Hotel Okura, where rooms go for hundreds of dollars a night.

For poorer Japanese, such spending is out of the question. Mrs. Ishizuka complains: "Unless you graduate [from college] you can't go anywhere, and you can't enter if you don't have money."

Article 13 THE CHRISTIAN SCIENCE MONITOR January 9, 1991

After centuries of discrimination, Japanese with burakumin backgrounds fight bias by publicly denouncing their detractors

Japan's Invisible Minority Rejects Life on the Margins

By Clayton Jones

Staff writer of The Christian Science Monitor

SEKIYADO, JAPAN

LEAGUE SYMBOL:
*Buraku Liberation
League fights bias.*

A YEAR ago, just after a Japanese school board decided to relocate an elementary school here, a man named Daikichi Sekiguchi received an unsigned letter.

"It will be sad if our children go to this school – they will be considered burakumin," it said, using the euphemistic term for a Japanese minority whose ancestors worked in occupations once regarded as "unclean."

Burakumin literally means "village people," but it describes an "invisible" group of Japanese who lead humbled lives on society's margins, victims of an ancient bigotry. Although physically and ethnically Japanese, *burakumin* are often set apart. Their plight is rarely acknowledged, their stories rarely revealed.

The letter to Mr. Sekiguchi continued: "We are happy just to live in a separate community and to have different bloodlines." After that, a petition against moving the school was presented by some resident associations. The school board shelved the move.

"Now we know other people still really despise us," said Sekiguchi, the local leader of Sekiyado's *burakumin*.

He has seen many types of bigotry over his seven decades in this town, home to some 50 *burakumin* families. They have lived for centuries near the fork of a river in Chiba prefecture near Tokyo. Most eke out a living by recycling other people's refuse.

"In my youth, discrimination was so common we didn't think it was discrimination," Sekiguchi explains. Kids would openly taunt him with derogatory names. During festivals, religious icons would not be brought into *burakumin* areas for fear they would be "polluted."

Even in the allegedly egalitarian Japan of today, *burakumin* carry a cruel social stigma and are often victims of subtle discrimination. Sekiguchi's son, for instance, lost a chance for a job at a Tokyo company after revealing that his father was a *burakumin* leader.

The stigma is a remnant from the days of the last shogunate. Under a rigid hierarchy set up by the Tokugawa clan, which ruled Japan with sword-wielding repression from 1603 to 1867, an untouchable group was created below and outside the official classes of warrior, farmer, craftsman, and merchant.

These outcasts lived by slaughtering animals, working with leather, or doing other jobs deemed religiously impure under old Shinto and Buddhist beliefs.

They were openly mistreated and tagged as either *eta* (much filth) or *hinin* (nonhuman), terms now eschewed. They lived in separate hamlets, often by rivers, and developed a type of theater which some scholars say is the origin of kabuki.

In 1871, soon after the shogunate was overthrown, a reformist government legally emancipated this caste, giving it a less demeaning label of *burakumin*. But over a century later, few *burakumin* will reveal

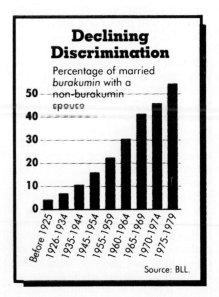

Declining Discrimination

Percentage of married *burakumin* with a non-burakumin spouse

Source: BLL.

their ancestry, fearful of social ostracism.

The acute sensitivity about *burakumin* prevents an accurate tally of their numbers. The government estimates there are 1.16 million, but *burakumin* leaders claim over 3 million.

Either way, this hidden minority makes up 1 to 2.5 percent of the population.

While the original excuses for discrimination have long since passed, *burakumin* remain social pariahs due to a common Japanese belief that one's status flows along bloodlines.

Detective agencies have compiled lists of *burakumin* names and sell them to hundreds of companies that try to avoid hiring *burakumin*, and who sometimes share them with others on computer networks.

Another reason for lingering discrimination, say observers, is that prestige-conscious Japan operates on a hierarchical structure that puts an emperor on top and minorities such as *burakumin* at the bottom.

"The tragic fate of the outsider confirms to the Japanese just how lucky they all are to lead such a restricted, respectable and in most cases, perfectly harmless lives," writes Ian Buruma in a 1984 book, "Behind the Mask."

"Many *burakumin* wish they could leave their districts and start a new life elsewhere," says Toshikazu Kondo, a *burakumin* activist.

"But their past will follow them. We never tell outsiders where we live, or what our fathers do," says Mr. Kondo.

An antidiscrimination group of *burakumin* activists was first formed in 1922, and later named the Buraku Liberation League.

The BLL uses a tactic known as a *kyudan* – denunciation campaign – to confront those who act or speak against *burakumin*, demand a confession, and try to "reeducate" the offender.

Fear of *kyudan* among many Japanese has helped to end the most open and vicious name-calling and prejudice.

Though the government estimates that there are 1.16 million *burakumin*, their leaders claim over 3 million. Even in the Japan of today, *burakumin* remain social pariahs due to a common Japanese belief that one's status flows along bloodlines.

In 1969, spurred in part by the civil rights movement in the United States, the government began to upgrade living standards and education for *burakumin*.

Known as *dowa* (assimilation), these projects were partly an attempt by Japanese leaders to control the left-leaning BLL, says Sueo Murakoshi, a Osaka City University sociologist and chairman of the Buraku Liberation Research Institute.

But, says BLL official Tamio Yamanaka, "*Dowa* has drastically improved housing for *burakumin*. Slums have been eliminated and roads widened." Nonetheless, much more needs to be done, he says. *Burakumin* suffer from higher rates of illiteracy, unemployment, poor health, and poverty than other Japanese, surveys reveal.

The government, however, plans to end *dowa* in March, 1992. Officials say *burakumin* need no extra support after 23 years of assistance that has cost over $26 billion.

The BLL not only demands more *dowa*, but wants parliament to pass a law to make discrimination an official crime and to teach it in classrooms.

What the government really wants, says Mr. Yamanaka, "is for the problem to just go away."

Indeed, many *burakumin* themselves ar-

gue that *dowa* and the BLL just perpetuate discrimination by spotlighting the group's existence. They prefer not "to wake up a sleeping baby," a Japanese idiom, hoping *burakumin* can slowly blend into society. Others, however, say prejudice runs too deep to be ignored and might increase during an economic recession when *burakumin* would become scapegoats.

"It's difficult to know if discrimination decreases in a community that does not declare itself *burakumin*," says Dr. Murakoshi. The BLL claims there are close to 6,000 *burakumin* communities, but only 4,603 have declared their existence to obtain *dowa* projects.

In recent years, high land prices have driven many non-*burakumin* to seek housing in *burakumin* communities.

The integration has created new social frictions.

By 1992, the government, under foreign pressure, plans to allow massive imports of shoes, many one-third the price of those made by the protected leather industry.

Burakumin shoemakers say they are being sacrificed to a trade-off with the European Community. To gain access for Japanese autos and electronics in the post-1992 EC market, Japan has to open its market to European exports such as Italian shoes.

Already, some leather imports have put a few *burakumin*-run firms out of business. In the meat industry, too, the first full-scale imports of foreign meat starting in April are threatening *burakumin* butchers.

"All we ask is for government to give us time and financial support to modernize," says Yamanaka, the BLL official. "So far they are not very serious."

He adds that more than Japan's internal harmony may be at stake. "Japanese look for differences between people – that's why they discriminate against *buraku*, or other Asian people. They will not be truly internationalized until they learn how to coexist inside Japan."

Article 14   THE WALL STREET JOURNAL   JULY 27, 1990

Japanese Women Are Truly Putting Aside a Tradition

'Oyaji Girls' Bring Femininity To Nation's Golf Courses; They Also Play Pachinko

Yumiko Ono

Staff Reporter of The Wall Street Journal

CHINO, Japan—Megumi Negishi wouldn't have been caught dead playing golf a few years ago. She is a woman—and the links were the domain of middle-aged businessmen known as *oyaji,* or "old boys," for their coarse ways. The beer-swilling oyaji, dressed in gaudy striped shirts and tight-fitting polyester trousers, gave Japanese golf a locker-room tone.

Things are changing, though. The 24-year-old Ms. Negishi, wearing bright pink designer golf clothes, now is happy to shell out 58,000 yen, about $385, for a two-day golf tour. "I used to think I'd never do things that oyaji did," she says. "But when I tried it myself, it was fun."

Many of the newcomers are certainly not obsessive about their scores. They are more interested in the latest in golf fashion—this year, tropical prints with labels such as "Cute Story." Many of the women, in fact, never make it to a golf course. They settle for urban driving ranges.

Duffers' Outing

On a stormy day at the fancy Mitsui no Mori Tateshina Golf Club, 120 miles from Tokyo, Mrs. Negishi is playing her first round on a real course with a group of women touring with the Loft Sports Golf School. She began weekly lessons six months ago. The women are scurrying after their designer golf-balls. Some of the balls have plopped into ponds, and others have bounced onto the green—the previous hole's green.

The women play at less than the speed of divine lightning. One vows to break 200 in her next round—nearly three times par. Ms. Negishi, shielding her outfit under a raincoat and hat, slices her ball off a tree trunk. A group of men impatiently pace the fairway behind her, and a caddy pleads with her to hurry.

Oyaji say they really welcome women to golf but bemoan their giggly manner and slow pace. "I wouldn't mind them if they practice and become good," says Hiroyoshi Sugano, a 38-year-old electric appliance company worker. Still, he says, if women take up too many pastimes of the old men, they are going to become old themselves.

Those pastimes are just what the women are pursuing, however. Bored with discos and chic bars, young women have used their rising purchasing power to assert themselves in the male domain of "out-of-the-ordinary experiences, just like eating ethnic food, or going to Bali and Tahiti," says Hikaru Hayashi. She is senior research director at the Hakuhodo Institute of Life & Living Inc. and a specialist in youth culture. Young women are joining the oyaji at pachinko parlors, *karaoke* sing-along bars, and even seedy horse-racing tracks. The women, mostly single clerks and secretaries in their 20s, call themselves "oyaji girls."

Costly Game

Golf appeals to them most. The number of women golfers in Japan has doubled in the past five years to three million, or 20% of all the golfers in a country that spends $13.3 billion a year on the game.

"I'm sick of going to discos," says 23-year-old Mika Takaara after finishing her round with Ms. Negishi. Ms. Takaara, who works for a securities company, says, "If there's something fun to do, we should all do it." In addition to golf and pinball, her oyaji pastimes include betting at the track and downing vitamin drinks marketed as energy fixes for the overworked.

Clothes-consciousness weighs heavily on the women. Young skiers here often buy two skiing outfits a season so they won't always be wearing the same clothing in photographs. Golf is even more demanding, fashion-wise. "I feel I have to change my outfit every time I play," says Kumiko Koga, a 23-year-old Tokyo secretary who took up the game a year ago.

She plays with her company's clients and occasionally even with her 56-year-old boss, who, she says, encourages her fashion spending. She has spent as much as $465 on clothes for a single round of golf. She likes this year's hot colors, gold and silver, and especially sequins. She saves money by borrowing her mother's golf clubs, but she recently invested $865 in a blue golf bag with embroidered figures of Mickey and Minnie Mouse swinging their clubs.

All over Japan, golf shops with shelves of pastel balls and racks of clothing with such labels as "Papas" and "Popo Club" are opening. Designers offer the oyaji girls slim leather bags, holding only a few clubs, especially made for the driving range. New magazines for neophyte women golfers advise on proper makeup, and advertise gloves that emit a fragrance when a wearer grips a club. The Kapalua Golf Course in Hawaii sells its own brand of designer clothes exclusively in the Japanese market.

High greens fees, often well above $180 on weekends, give the sport prestige for those oyaji girls who can afford them. Other young women swing their clubs only at golf schools on the rooftops of Tokyo department stores. Still others, like 18-year-old Megumi Sakaguchi, are satisfied with urban driving ranges. Unlike America's

driving ranges, with their broad swaths of green that stretch for 150 yards or more, Japan's cramped ranges look like batting cages. Some, draped with nets as high as 80 feet, are no longer than two tennis courts.

The country's 4,500 ranges attracted more than 120 million customer visits in 1989, compared with 90 million by those who teed off on courses. Driving at the trendy Meiji Jingu Gaien Golf Practice Range in Tokyo, where a flashing electronic board warns of a one-hour, 50-minute wait, Ms. Sakaguchi admits she has never played on a real course. She has been practicing for three years.

Yutsuko Chusonji claims to be the first oyaji girl. She says she coined the term two years ago when, in the comic books she writes, she started portraying young women golfers pretending to be men. The 27-year-old Ms. Chusonji, herself an avid golfer, says golf is an important status symbol for young women.

Not all, however, like being called oyaji girls. Ms. Koga says she gets upset when middle-aged men on the golf course ask if she's one. "If you call me an oyaji girl," she warns a reporter, "I'll cry."

Article 15

The Unesco Courier, July 1989

Under new management

BY KURIMOTO KAZUO

KURIMOTO KAZUO, of Japan, is a Unesco staff member specializing in educational administration and management.

Bound by economic ties as well as kinship, the traditional Japanese family has undergone sweeping changes in modern times. Its members have achieved greater independence...but at what cost?

THE traditional form of the Japanese family is designated by the word *ie*, which denotes an original concept embracing not only the structure of the family but the bonds uniting its members, the family assets, and the activities connected with it.

In most cases, this basic family unit consists of a son—usually the eldest son living with his parents after marriage—his children, and his unmarried brothers and sisters. But *ie* also includes deceased forebears and unborn descendants. The continuity of the family depends largely upon the maintenance of the material basis which guarantees its social status and way of life. Since its survival is closely connected with the maintenance of its activities, the Japanese family is often defined as a family business. The heritage is just as important as the continuation of the family line, and more so than the prosperity or even the life and death of individual members of the household.

The *ie* is primarily based upon family ties, the most important of which are those with parents and ancestors. The eldest son is responsible—in most cases alone—for perpetuating the *ie*. When they get married, the younger sons will in turn be called upon to found other *ie*. In theory the younger branches continue to owe allegiance to the senior branch, but in practice they soon achieve autonomy and their founders become ancestors of new *ie*. The only ones which remain linked are those families which are bound to each other by strong financial interests, or which live in the same neighbourhood. Few Japanese are well acquainted with their collateral family, and it is not uncommon for a Japanese to be incapable of quoting the exact names of his eight great-grandparents.

The wife as servant of the ie

In this typical organization, the wife's role is essentially to provide heirs for her husband's family. If the marriage proves to be sterile, the wife is sent back to her parents, and the adoption of a male child must then be considered. A wife's entire education prepares her to become the servant of her husband's lineage. In the early eighteenth century, the principles which should govern a wife's behaviour were defined by the moralist Kaibara Ekiken. They can be summarized as follows:

• When a wife enters her husband's house she must follow the instructions of his parents, wait upon them and be agreeable to them at all times. They should avoid excessive affection which would make her capricious, and they should not allow her to have a will of her own.

• A wife must respect her husband's brothers and sisters.

• She should be prudent and strict in her personal behaviour, rise early, retire late, and her attention should be concentrated upon the house throughout the day.

• She should rarely appear in public before the age of forty.

• Her behaviour should be dignified and reasonable, because her misconduct would ruin the house.

• Even a wife who is surrounded by servants should take an interest in everything, because "that is the wife's law".

And so the heavy task of maintaining the peace and ensuring the proper functioning of the house falls upon the wife. Her personality should be relegated to the background.

By contrast with the subordinate status of the wife, the powers enjoyed by the head of the family are very extensive. He can remove from the family register *(koseki)* any member who might harm the *ie*. Since the end of the nineteenth century, he has been the sole owner of the family assets. No other member of the family, even an adult, may enter into a contract without his permission. His powers, which may seem exorbitant, are based upon a profound consensus within the family.

The head of the family

On the other hand, the head of the family has certain responsibilities, and he may be stripped of his authority if he proves incapable of managing the family fortune. The "instructions for the head of a family" of a retail kimono merchant in Kyoto laid down that "even the head of the family may not neglect his work by lying in bed late or going out frequently in the evenings and indulging in gambling. If this happens, the older members of the shop's staff, who are responsible, should report the matter to his parents. When the family's capital and goods have been valued, compensation shall be paid to the head of the family and he shall be obliged to retire from management of the family business". The head of another Kyoto family stipulated that "if any of my potential successors begins to spend irresponsibly, and there is reason to think that he is not a trustworthy heir to the family business, the family, after consulting the parents, shall give him 5 per cent of the family assets and create a branch for him. When this separation has been completed, a reliable person shall be chosen to succeed him".

Although succession is hereditary, the head of the family or any other undesirable relative can be excluded. Such is the overriding importance of the *ie*'s continuity, that it is not uncommon for a new member to be adopted.

The basis of the nation

The traditional *ie* is more in the nature of a socio-economic institution than a community linked by blood-relationships. The head of the family strongly resembles the head of a business. When the question of his succession arises, this business does not necessarily give priority to his "blood child". The paramount consideration is that the enterprise be headed by a competent manager.

The *ie* system is of very ancient origin. It goes back to the eleventh century, but it was during the second half of the Tokugawa shogunate that it became consolidated and officially established, partly under the influence of Confucian doctrines. The *ie* type of organization soon ceased to be confined to the samurai caste and the rich merchant and farmer class, and became a model for all Japanese families. It became the very basis of the nation and one of the main components of Japanese identity.

Although it was criticized after the Second World War on the grounds that it had justified militarism and was an obstacle to democratization, the *ie* concept has survived in big firms, although divested of its former political and ideological connotations.

Absentee fathers

The Japanese family has evolved considerably since the 1946 Constitution came into force. Although the traditional *ie* still survives, new legal structures favour the development of nuclear families (63.4 per cent in 1970) by granting equal rights to men and women and imposing a distribution of the estate among the children. This trend has been strengthened by post-war industrial and urban changes. Nowadays, families are much smaller, usually consisting of only one or two children. The generations live apart from each other and the children, even the unmarried ones, soon acquire their autonomy.

This trend accelerated from the 1960s onwards, with the growth in the number of jobs and the resulting mobility. Initially it was mainly young workers who left rural areas for the urban industrial centres. Then, many heads of rural families took seasonal employment in expanding urban areas, leaving the cultivation of the land to their wives, children, or other members of their families. These seasonal jobs soon became permanent and so it became common for heads of families to be absent most of the year. This trend is not confined to manual workers. Transfers of managerial and executive staff to new project sites are becoming increasingly necessary because of economic expansion.

It is difficult for a family to follow the father if he is moved around too often. Finding family accommodation is quite a problem, and too many moves are bad for children and their studies.

The phenomenon known as *tanshin hunin* (unaccompanied transfer of a member of the family) is common in Japan today, but it is giving rise to problems. The family head may find a substitute for *ie* in his links with his firm—employment for life, membership of a community, concern for its prosperity and its perpetuity—but he suffers from the loosening of family ties. Many men only see their families at weekends. This may be one of the causes of the depressions, stress and alcoholism which afflict so many men.

The solitary wife

The wife suffers no less than her husband. She is increasingly isolated. Even when he lives at home during the week, her husband goes to work early in the morning and comes back late in the evening. Children are at school all day or go off in the afternoon to *juku* (extra private lessons). Many married women react to this solitude by looking for a job or taking part in the activities of cultural groups.

Relations between mothers and their children are also changing. The bonds between them are close and exclusive. Because of the decline in the birth rate, children find fewer playmates in their neighbourhood and almost none at home. Deprived of contacts with children of their own age, they cling to their mothers' apron strings. In the extended families of the past, the psychological link with the mother was only one family relationship among others. Since children formed their own society within the group, they had less difficulty leaving home. Now separation from the mother is becoming much more painful for both mother and child. For the mother, the chief concern is her child's success at school. Forty years ago a child who was accompanied to secondary school by his mother would have been the laughing-stock of his schoolmates. Nowadays, many mothers accompany their children, not only to secondary school, but even to the university. Newspapers wax ironical about mothers who accompany their sons as far as the door of the firm on their first day at work.

The ageing of the population is having other consequences. For a long time life expectancy in Japan was 50 years, but by 1982 it had risen to 75 for men and 80.4 for women. In 1930 most fathers died before their youngest child had completed university studies, and the mother rarely outlived the head of the family. Now, when the youngest child has finished his or her studies, it is common for the father to have a life expectancy of a further twenty years and the mother thirty. In many cases the parents are neither financially nor psychologically prepared for the departure of their children. This is an unprecedented situation, and no cultural model exists to help them to cope with it. A new life-style will have to be created which will enable older people to take an active part in the life of the community, assume their social responsibilities and define their new identity. In fact, there is no ready-made answer to this problem.

Many elderly persons live with their children, whereas in the past it was the children who lived under their parents' roof. Under the present law, each descendant receives an equal share of the family estate, and the question arises which of the children shall take in the elders. The average household rarely possesses the necessary resources and space. The nuclear family is often faced with a crisis when it has to assume responsibility for the health care of its elders.

The broken bond

This crisis is reflected in customs relating to the organization of meals. Formerly, meals were ritu-als which strengthened the cohesion of the family group. Now this essential function is on the wane and in many families most meals are no longer taken in common. About 60 per cent of fathers do not take part in the family breakfast, and 30 per cent of them are absent at dinner time. Most mothers have lunch alone at home. The decline in the frequency of meals eaten in common is weakening the psychological bonds between members of the same family.

Developments in the mass media also run counter to the family spirit. The family is ceasing to be a place for the exchange of news. With the growth in the number of channels, cable television and the diversification of programmes, watching television is becoming an individual activity. Increasingly, each member of the family has his or her own sources of information and tends to share them less and less with the rest of the family.

However, this may be just a passing phase, and new modes of behaviour may emerge. For instance, there is an increase in the number of "houses for two generations", in which elderly parents and their children can live together while preserving their independence. It is also probable that the revival of traditional feasts, bringing together members of different generations, and in which everyone has a role to play, points to a tightening of family links. Perhaps a new cultural model is about to emerge?

Article 16

The American Enterprise, March/April 1990

RAISING HIROKO

The Child-Centered Culture of Japan

KARL ZINSMEISTER

Karl Zinsmeister is an adjunct scholar at the American Enterprise Institute. He writes frequently about demographic and family issues.

WE READ A GREAT DEAL about Japanese economic success these days, success usually credited to factors such as powerful social discipline, attention to quality, cooperation between their government and their industries, low tax rates, and the rigor of their education system. All of these are indeed important factors. But there is an even more vital one that rarely gets mentioned: their powerfully nurturant families.

Japan possesses few natural resources, and after World War II, it had meager financial resources. Its single great strength has been in what economists sometimes call human capital—the attitudes, health, and intelligence of its people. And there is a reason the Japanese population is so healthy and talented: stable, supportive homes get youngsters off to a very good start in life.

There is a mountain of scientific evidence showing that when families disintegrate, children often end up with intellectual, physical, and emotional scars that persist for life. This is widely acknowledged to be one of the great problems facing America today. We talk about the drug crisis, the education crisis, and the problems of teen pregnancy and juvenile crime. But all these ills trace back predominantly to one source: broken families.

Today, 27 percent of American children live with just one parent or neither, and 60 percent of all children will spend at least some time in a single-parent family before they reach adulthood. That means growing up with financial strains, with less parental direction, with less time in a secure and loving environment. Of course, illegitimacy, divorce, and weaker family ties are on the rise in most modern nations. Not in Japan, however, where family integrity remains the rule.

Amazingly, 95 percent of Japanese children live in married, two-parent households (and in nearly a third of these, there is the additional presence of a grandparent). Only 1 percent of Japanese births are illegitimate versus nearly 24 percent in the United States, and Japanese divorce rates are only about one-fourth of those in the United States (see figures 1 and 2). These powerfully stable families—where children can develop into good students and good workers with fewer strains—are the deepest source of "the Japanese miracle."

A Closer Look

Marriage in Japan is explicitly viewed as a rite of passage into full adulthood and social responsibility. There are advertisements for "wedding-ceremony palaces" that urge, "Get married! The final act of filial piety." Once a young Japanese reaches the traditional marriage age (25 for women, a little older for men), pressure to marry—to please one's parents

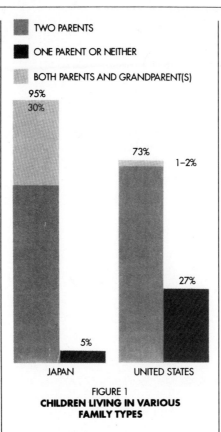

FIGURE 1
CHILDREN LIVING IN VARIOUS FAMILY TYPES

SOURCE: JAPANESE STATISTICAL BUREAU; UNITED STATES BUREAU OF THE CENSUS.

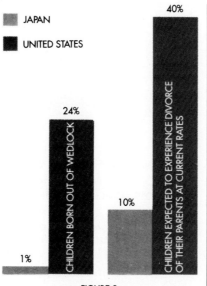

FIGURE 2
CHILDREN'S EXPERIENCE

SOURCE: EDITOR'S CALCULATION FROM JAPANESE STATISTICAL BUREAU DATA AND U.S. NATIONAL CENTER FOR HEALTH STATISTICS; KONO AND PRESTON, "TRENDS IN WELL-BEING AMONG CHILDREN AND THE ELDERLY IN JAPAN."

and peers, to fulfill one's social obligations—mounts rapidly. Even now, between one-quarter and one-half of Japanese marriages are "arranged."

The ideal of romantic love is gaining popular acceptance, but it runs up against certain cultural constraints. Japanese sociologists point out that the basic social unit in Japan is the coalition of mother and child, rather than the husband-wife orientation common in the West. More than 90 percent of adults opposing divorce cite "the influence of divorce on the children" as their principal reason.

Japan's extraordinary child-centeredness leads to some remarkable behavior. For one thing, the child is rarely left alone under traditional Japanese child-rearing—sleeping with the mother, being tightly bound to her back whenever she goes out, and breast-feeding in some cases until the age of six. Some observers have identified powerful maternal indulgence as both the source of the "womb-like group life the majority of Japanese feel most comfortable leading" and the key to understanding the individual Japanese personality. (Unlike mothers, Japanese fathers sometimes see their children only when they are asleep.)

Amaeru, "playing the baby" through a show of passive dependency, is a common way of gaining favor in Japan, according to psychiatrist Doi Takeo. Author Ian Buruma points out, "Juniors do it to seniors in companies . . . women do it to men, men do it to their mothers and sometimes their wives, the Japanese government does it to stronger powers such as the United States." Of course, "playing the tyrant" is another trait sometimes seen in indulged personalities in Japan and elsewhere. "Obsequious conformity and callous egotism can alternate in many a Japanese personality with disturbing and unpredictable ease," writes Buruma.

The healthy aspects of this focus on the child's welfare and interests, however, can hardly be overstated. With almost all Japanese children growing up in intact homes, childhood poverty is extremely low. Less than 1 percent of Japanese live in households that are receiving public assistance, and only a small minority of welfare households contain children (see table 1). Behavioral problems like juvenile delinquency are also comparatively rare in Japan. Juvenile arrest rates for murder are only 7 percent of those in the United States; levels for rape and assault and battery are about one-fourth of ours.

Crime in general is minimal in Japan. In a nation of 120 million, there were fewer than 2,000 instances each of homicide, robbery, and rape. (The

Table 1

JAPANESE RECEIVING PUBLIC ASSISTANCE

	1965	1986
Persons in welfare households as a percentage of total population	< 2%	< 1%
Welfare households by type:		
Single parent and child/children	14	14
Aged	23	32
Disabled	29	44
Other	34	10

Source: Japanese Ministry of Health and Welfare.

United States, approximately twice as populous, totaled 20,000, 518,000, and 91,000, respectively.) And Japanese crime rates have been falling dramatically over the last three decades (see figure 3). The crime rate is but one of several major social indicators that has improved in Japan while deteriorating in other parts of the industrial world. The rate of welfare dependency in Japan has fallen by 30 percent since 1950.

Smaller Families Ahead

The population of Japan is aging faster than any on earth. In one lifetime, from 1947 to 2025, Japan will go from being one of the globe's youngest nations (with less than 5 percent of its population 65 years old or more) to quite likely the oldest (with nearly one-fourth of all citizens elderly). Japan is currently at its productive peak in demographic terms, with nearly 70 percent of its population being of working age, 15–64 years old. The ranks of retirees will soon grow rapidly, however. Viewed in terms of the change in median age, Japan is now aging twice as fast as the United States (see figure 4).

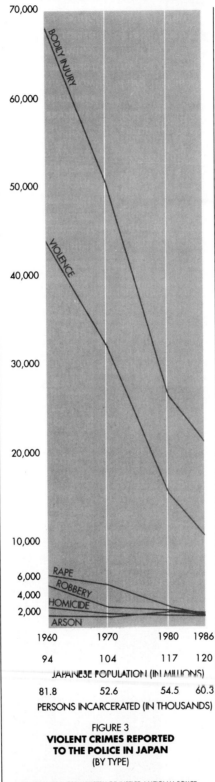

FIGURE 3
VIOLENT CRIMES REPORTED TO THE POLICE IN JAPAN
(BY TYPE)

SOURCE: JAPANESE MINISTRY OF JUSTICE; NATIONAL POLICE AGENCY.

The explanation for this lies in Japan's unusual birth patterns. There was a small upward blip in the Japanese birth

rate immediately after World War II. Then from 1947 to 1957, the total fertility rate plummeted from 4.5 lifetime births per woman to 2.0. While this rapid child-bearing tumble was taking place in Japan, the other industrial countries were experiencing varying degrees of baby boom. Since 1957, Japanese fertility rates have stayed constant at about 1.8 births per woman, somewhat below the population replacement figure. Because of this early and steep decline in fertility, the Japanese population pyramid has taken on a "pot-bellied" shape, lacking the traditional base of ever-fuller younger generations.

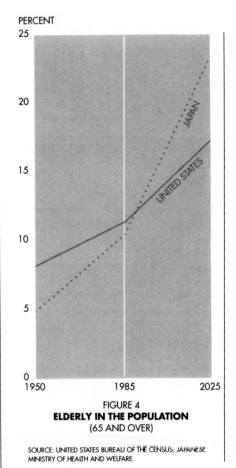

FIGURE 4
ELDERLY IN THE POPULATION
(65 AND OVER)

SOURCE: UNITED STATES BUREAU OF THE CENSUS; JAPANESE MINISTRY OF HEALTH AND WELFARE.

Longevity

Another factor increasing the age of Japanese society is the rapid rise in life expectancy—from 52 years in 1947 to 68 years in 1960 and 78 years today. Along with Icelanders, Japanese now live longer than any other people in the world. Health-care expenditures per capita are less than half U.S. levels, so spending patterns do not account for the longevity. (Most experts think the explanation lies in the Japanese diet, high in fish and rice.)

Whatever their secret, most Japanese are survivors, and they tend to spend their later years close to their children (see figure 5). Two-thirds of the elderly live with one of their offspring (of whom roughly two-thirds are married); usually it is their eldest son. (This is more often a case of the child residing in the parents' home than the reverse.) Forty-one percent of eldest sons who married in 1980–1982 lived with their parents afterwards.

The Family and the Community

The limits of personal loyalty for Japanese are often defined by the family and the work place. Despite their much-vaunted social cooperation, relations with relatives and co-workers to a large extent substitute for broader community ties. For instance, while almost 40 percent of American elderly report daily conversations with neighbors, less than 20 percent of Japanese do. Close to one-third of elderly Japanese report hardly any neighborhood contact, compared to only 7 percent of Americans. The Japanese are much less likely to accept nonrelated caregivers than Americans. Compared to older Japanese, older Americans are much more likely to participate in community activities.

This is part of the larger distinction Japanese draw between life within and outside of identifiable groups. While strict codes of etiquette and respect for hierarchies govern behavior within established groups, among strangers Japanese can be very uncooperative and impolite. In the words of one guide to Japanese culture, "In the outside world, anarchy sometimes reigns. Pushing and shoving in crowds . . . and reluctance to form orderly queues are commonplace." Unity and estrangement exist side by side.

This same paradox increasingly applies to Japanese attitudes toward the elderly. While respect for age remains an essential rule within families and defined groups, the society-wide posi-

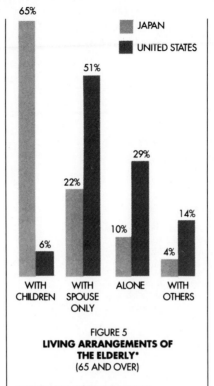

FIGURE 5
LIVING ARRANGEMENTS OF THE ELDERLY*
(65 AND OVER)

NOTE:* U.S. DATA ARE 1980, JAPANESE 1985.
SOURCE: JAPANESE STATISTICAL BUREAU; UNITED STATES BUREAU OF THE CENSUS.

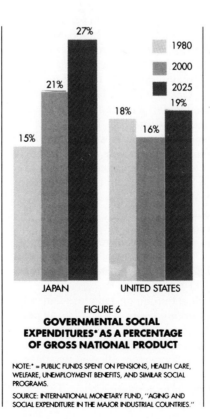

FIGURE 6
GOVERNMENTAL SOCIAL EXPENDITURES* AS A PERCENTAGE OF GROSS NATIONAL PRODUCT

NOTE:* = PUBLIC FUNDS SPENT ON PENSIONS, HEALTH CARE, WELFARE, UNEMPLOYMENT BENEFITS, AND SIMILAR SOCIAL PROGRAMS.
SOURCE: INTERNATIONAL MONETARY FUND, "AGING AND SOCIAL EXPENDITURE IN THE MAJOR INDUSTRIAL COUNTRIES."

tion of elders is not so clearly positive. There are temples where the elderly can go to pray for a quick death, and suicide rates for older Japanese are relatively high. "The modern Japanese seem increasingly to place youth before age," reports *The Economist*. "It is not unusual for a frail old lady to be deprived of a seat by a healthy young child."

No Generational Politics

The orientation toward youth and the conformity of Japanese to the interests of their family unit can confer benefits beyond the obvious ones. One of Japan's longstanding economic advantages *vis-à-vis* competitors has been the modest load imposed on its economy by state spending (long the lowest among the industrial democracies as a fraction of national income). A bulge of retired and sick elderly, however, could change this by necessitating sharp increases in public expenditure. Government social payments (most of which are for pensions and health care) amounted to 5 percent of Japanese gross national product in 1950 and less than 7 percent as late as 1970. Today, social spending is 16 percent of GNP, still comparatively moderate but rising rapidly. A 1986 report of the International Monetary Fund estimated the ratio would nearly double from 1980 to 2025, due largely to population aging (see figure 6).

The Japanese public's attitude toward aging and families, however, seems to have allowed them to dodge the first of what may be several dangerous punches in this area. Alarmed by projections that pension costs would eat up from 38–50 percent of workers' earnings by the early part of next century, the Japanese government mounted a major reform in 1986. Over a 20-year period, pension benefits per unit of contribution will be reduced considerably, to a level that should keep their cost down to 29 percent of workers' earnings. Health benefits were also trimmed. Americans familiar with the eruptions that issue forth from the old-age lobby any time far gentler tinkerings with our own Social Security program are proposed will appreciate the enormity of this accomplishment. And it was achieved with almost no protest. "The close identification of

Japanese with their family unit," sociologists Sam Preston and Shigemi Kono point out, "seems . . . to have impeded the development of strong age-based constituencies."

Pressures on Family Life

There is a relatively high level of stress in Japanese life. The pressures of the education system on immature children are well known and sometimes result in self-esteem problems and even suicide. Under the system known as *gakureki shakai* (loosely, "the credential society"), individual social mobility is sharply limited by the particulars of one's formal education. Parents as well as students come under strain. "In homes where there are teenagers striving to enter ranking universities, there are no Saturdays, Sundays, and holidays for them or their parents," write Preston and Kono. "While their sons and daughters are preparing for examination upstairs, parents walk on tiptoe downstairs. 'Examination war' or 'examination hell' in Japan is a kind of social trauma."

In management ranks, too, life can be stressful. Japan has kept statistics on suicides by business executives since 1979—there were 475 in the most recent year. A more common way to vent frustration and pressure is through heavy drinking. Ritual imbibing after work is an important part of business life, and the Japanese are tolerant of even extreme drunkenness. A recent survey showed that two-thirds of Japanese men get drunk at least once a week, and one in eight does so daily.

A few years ago, an Indiana University survey of more than 7,000 factory workers in Japan and the United States found that American workers were much more satisfied with various aspects of their work (tasks, co-workers, bosses, and so forth), were four times as likely to recommend a job like theirs to a friend (62 percent versus 15 percent in Japan), and were more satisfied with life in general (84 percent to 45 percent). Each year, one office worker in three in Tokyo needs treatment for mental disorder, stress, or alcohol-related disease.

The choked physical conditions in Japanese cities add to the generalized strain. One-fourth of all Japanese—30

Table 2

HOUSING IN JAPAN AND THE UNITED STATES

	United States	Japan
Average floor area per dwelling, square feet	1,700	925
Average number of persons in household	2.6	3.2
Percentage of dwellings with:		
Piped water	100%	94%
Flush toilet	99	58
Bathing facilities	99	88
Average number of baths purchased annually in public bathhouses, per household	0	15
Percentage of population living in houses with shower connections	76%	36%

Note: U.S. data are 1985, Japanese 1983.
Source: Japanese Statistical Bureau; United States Bureau of the Census.

million people—live within a 30-mile radius of the emperor's palace in central Tokyo. New Yorkers have ten times as much public green space as Tokyo residents. Land prices, having risen 24 percent in 1986, another 76 percent in 1987, and then 44 percent in 1988, are astronomical—the 16.7 acres under the American embassy buildings are worth $5.1 billion dollars at current prices.

One unhappy effect of this on Japanese families has been to make housing almost unaffordable. The average daily commute for Tokyo workers is three hours round trip (the average U.S. two-way total is 39 minutes), and even far out in the suburbs, a typical house costs about 20 times the median annual white-collar salary, up to $1 million frequently. And for that price, they get a structure with minimal comforts (see table 2).

A Staggering Workload

A final burden on Japanese family life is working hours. As of 1986, 49 percent of all businesses with 30 or more employees were still requiring a six-day work week. Six percent allowed two days off every week, and the rest provided two days off on a rotating basis. The largest firms are moving faster toward a five-day

work week, so 28 percent of all workers are now on that pattern. But total hours put in by employees did not change significantly in the 1980s. On average, Japanese workers rack up 2,110 hours per year, about 500 more than West Germans and 200 more than Americans.

Workers get an average of only 3.3 days of annual leave. Adding in national holidays, the average employee gets a total of 17 days off a year. Traditionally, it has been frowned upon to use all allowed leave. But a 1987 revision in labor laws made it illegal to punish workers who take their full entitlement of vacation days, and 80 percent of firms now require employees to take their summer holidays. Even so, many executives take only 60 percent of their allowed time off, and few take more than ten days.

This does not translate into increased production in any simple way. To quote *The Economist*'s reference book on Japanese business: compared to their Western counterparts, Japanese workers' "commitment to the company is greater. In the corporate sector, particularly, the job comes first, ahead of family, holidays, and other commitments. On the other hand, they generally work less hard during the course of the day—notably in offices—and their productivity, by Western standards, is lower." It is a largely unappreciated fact that outside of a few manufacturing sectors Japanese output per hour continues to fall well below American levels, sharply lower in certain important industries.

In sheer time on the job, however, the Japanese are unsurpassed in the industrial world. This is particularly so if one takes into account the elaborate after-hours social requirements of white-collar jobs. Few business "salarymen" dash home after work. Instead, groups of colleagues reconvene in bars, where extended drinking and informal business transactions take place every evening (on fat, tax-free corporate allowances). A second rush hour commences at 11:30 p.m. as businessmen stagger for last trains and storm available taxis.

No ambitious salaryman can afford to opt out of this more casual extension of the business day. In Japan, Ian Buruma writes, "The pressure to conform outwardly to fixed rules of conduct is far more relentless than it is in Western countries. Most Japanese are mortally afraid of seeming odd or strange, or in any way different from their neighbor. 'Ordinary' (*heibon*) is cited by the majority of Japanese as the most desirable thing to be." Buruma recounts the story of a wife who pushes her husband to stop coming home promptly after work, to go out drinking with the boys (and the bar hostesses and geishas) instead. This she does despite the loneliness and occasional drunken late-night abuse it brings her, out of fear that excessive time spent with family might lead neighbors and, worse, bosses to conclude that a failing career and a disloyal attitude were at work.

In the case of the Japanese family, the relationship between prosperity and inner health is quite mixed.

Article 17

New Perspectives Quarterly, Summer 1990

Japan: Model of Sustainable Development

Saburo Okita   *The foreign minister of Japan from 1979 to 1980, Saburo Okita was also a member of the UN's Brundtland Commission on the Environment and Development. He presently heads the Japan Worldwide Fund for Nature.*

Japan's environmental situation has improved dramatically since the early 1970s. One indicator, the yearly average emission of atmospheric sulfur dioxide in Japan's 15 major regions, has been reduced to about one-sixth over the 20-year period from 1967 to 1987. This improvement was achieved on the back of technological advances and massive investment in state-of-the-art desulfurization equipment at electrical power plants, steel production factories, chemical manufacturing plants, and other smokestack facilities.

The composition of the energy supply is a major determinant of air pollution levels. Japan was able to reduce its dependence on oil to 55.6 percent – down from 77.6 percent. The country also managed to raise its use of natural gas to 9.8 percent from 1.6 percent and of nuclear power to 10.9 percent, up from 0.6 percent, during the period 1973-88. This shift away from petroleum has done much to help cut down on the amount of carbon dioxide spewed into the atmosphere.

According to the 1985 Energy Statistics Yearbook, put out by the United Nations, the US was responsible for 25.8 percent of the carbon dioxide emissions coming from the major industrial countries in 1985; the Soviet Union 17.5 percent; China 9.6 percent; and Japan 5.3 percent. Thus even though Japan's GNP, at $1.2 trillion, was fully one-third of the United States' GNP in 1985, Japan's carbon dioxide emissions were only one-fifth of the United States'.

Regarding automobile emissions, Japan enacted strict standards based on a bill introduced by Senator Edmund Muskie in the US – but not enacted there because the proposed regulations were considered too strict – that forced major emission reductions. In fact, Japan now has the most stringent automobile emission standards in the world.

Japan gets virtually none of its petroleum and natural gas from domestic sources and is self-sufficient for only one-fifth of its coal. With hydroelectric power supplying five percent or less of its energy, Japan must depend primarily on imported energy. Japan recognized the need for nuclear power early on and is expanding capacity while promoting stronger safety measures. As of 1987, nuclear power supplied 31 percent of all generated electricity and 11 percent of Japan's primary energy.

Japan's oil imports peaked at 289 million kiloliters in 1973, a figure that has declined to 198 million kiloliters – a 30 percent reduction – by 1988. During this same period, GNP grew by 80 percent in real terms. The fact that economic

> Japan now has the most stringent automobile emission standards in the world.

growth was not accompanied by oil consumption growth can be attributed to the determined energy-conservation measures that were taken, as well as to the restructuring of industry away from energy-intensive heavy industries to energy-frugal electronics and other high-tech sectors.

As a result of these and other anti-air-pollution efforts in a variety of industrial sectors, Japan has become a world leader in the area of pollution-prevention.

When the "Global 2000 Report to the President" was published in 1980 by the US government, Japan's then-Prime Minister Zenko Suzuki took note of it and decided to set up the Ad Hoc Group on Global Environmental Problems, under the auspices of Japan's Environment Agency. I was asked to chair the Group and, in 1981, we published an interim report that included a recommendation that a group of experts be formed under UN auspices to study this issue. This idea was then proposed by the Japanese delegation to the United Nations Environmental Program special session in Nairobi in 1982 and was approved by the UN General Assembly in 1983.

As a result, the World Commission on Environment and Development was born, with Mrs. Gro Harlem Brundtland of Norway appointed chairperson. I participated in the Commission as a member. Its report, "Our Common Future" was published in April 1987 and has been widely read worldwide. Among other things, this report clearly indicates the importance of attaining "sustainable development," pointing out the interrelationship between the global environment and development in a very comprehensive manner.

The Ad Hoc Group then followed up on the Commission report by presenting its own report to the Environment Minister of Japan in June 1988. Entitled "Japan's Activities to Cope with Global Environmental Problems – Japan's Contribution Toward a Better Global Environment," it outlines Japan's role in global environmental protection. The report emphasizes strengthening and enhancing scientific knowledge, developing and spreading technology for global environmental protection, participating positively in international efforts, enhancing environmental assistance, assisting environmentally-sound development and reforestation, and preventing environmental destruction by Japanese companies in the developing countries.

Additionally, the Japanese government invited the International Tropical Timber Organization (ITTO) to locate its headquarter in Japan. Established in 1986 in Yokohama, ITTO is specifically entrusted with overseeing the development and implementation of crucial issues regarding forestry resource utilization and conservation. In this same vein, Japan plans to further increase its financial contribution in support of UNEP activities.

At the 1989 summit of industrial powers held in Paris, Japan announced its plan to implement the following three items concerning environmental problems. ❶ An additional $2.2 billion over a three-year period to enhance bilateral and multilateral environmental assistance. *[And Japan allocated $850 million in loans to Mexico in June, 1990 to help battle air pollution there. – ed.]* ❷ Enhanced assistance to the ITTO and the CGIAR (Consultative Group for International Agricultural Research. ❸ Cooperation in the establishment of a Joint network for earth-watch satellite monitoring.

Japan plans to further increase its financial contribution in support of UNEP activities.

Article 18   # The Floating World   BOSTONIA · SEPTEMBER/OCTOBER 1990

Attitudes of Japanese Intellectuals toward Foreign Cultures

BY YOSHIYUKI FUJIKAWA

OR A LONG TIME, JAPANESE INTELLEC-tuals' interest in foreign cultures was aroused by works published in translation. This was particularly true before World War II when only the elite were able to travel to foreign countries. Translated literature provided the only means for these intellectuals to come into contact with mysterious Western cultures, their only mental passport.

Many scholars, writers, and poets engaged in translation, struggling to absorb foreign cultures directly through such pursuits. For them, translating Western literature was a kind of personal initiation into foreign cultures.

Through their efforts, which were frequently of the highest art, many intellectuals gained at least a vague understanding of foreign culture. At the same time, they became more aware of the gap between Japanese and other cultures. For them, the problem of harmonizing the yearning for foreign culture and their own traditions became a lifelong task. It is a dilemma that recalls Henry James, who took as his literary mission the reconciliation of "Americanness" with Americans' envy and longing for European culture. Unlike Henry James, however, most Japanese intellectuals were not proficient at foreign languages and had little opportunity to become acquainted at first hand with foreign cultures, customs, and people. Thus, this awareness of a cultural gap gave rise to psychological complications. At least occasionally, these scholars adopted ambivalent attitudes toward foreign cultures, both idolizing and belittling what they only dimly understood.

This kind of ambivalence among intellectuals is common even as Japan increasingly emulates Western ways. This is clearly evident in the work of the two writers most representative of modern Japanese literature, Ogai Mori and Soseki Natsume. The more Mori and Natsume understood the West, the less they could disguise their displeasure towards those imprudent Japanese who worshiped the West. At the same time, they were irritated with those who turned their backs on foreign countries, convinced it was impossible to understand the West. In this sense, Mori and Natsume were typical modern Japanese writers who tilled in the no-man's-land between Japan and the West. Ogai Mori especially is known for excellent translations of H.C. Andersen's *Improvisatoren* and Goethe's *Faust*, and as a novelist had a great deal of influence in the development of modern Japanese literature, and on such writers as Junchiro Tanizaki and Yukio Mishima.

The attraction/repulsion toward foreign culture was more or less shared by many Japanese intellectuals born prior to World War II. For those born after the war, however, the situation appears quite different. For the present-day Japanese who secured the nation's meteoric economic growth, and whose culture has been Americanized in almost every respect, the important question still remains: To what extent should one adopt Western culture? The way in which Japanese writers now acknowledge foreign cultures, however, is quite different from writers of the era of Mori and Natsume.

Let us take as an example Haruki Murakami's *A Wild Sheep Chase*, recently translated into English, and popular in England and America. Of this novel Robert Carver wrote, "The unnamed hero is a young existentialist, adrift in the Shinjuku coffee bars, who reads Ginsberg, listens to rock, and philosophises about sex, whales and consciousness. The death of an ex-girlfriend sets him off on what begins as a Chandleresque private, quasi-Zen exploration of the Japanese soul through elaborate metaphor." (*The Sunday Times*, June 10, 1990.)

This "quasi-Zen exploration of the Japanese soul" in Murakami's novel went unrecognized by most Japanese critics. Yet it is reasonable to suspect that Murakami, an admirer of J.D. Salinger, was more directly influenced by the novels of the Zen-influenced Salinger than by Zen itself. It is characteristic of young writers such as Murakami to re-import from the United States even such significant Japanese cultural elements as Zen, a tendency beyond the imagination of the older generation of writers. Murakami presents Zen philosophy as a kind of modern trend. While Soseki Natsume entered a Zen temple to save his soul, Murakami sees even that which originally belonged to Japanese culture as blended into American culture.

Haruki Murakami is not only a best-selling novelist (more than 1,000,000 copies sold), but also a prominent translator of Raymond Chandler, Paul Theroux, and most recently, the late Raymond Carver. He is now presiding over the publication of an eight-volume translation of Carver's works.

Murakami is passionate about the modern American novels he adores, and seems to have taken translation as a kind of mission. In that sense, he reminds us of Ogai Mori, who in the late nineteenth and early twentieth centuries energetically translated Austrian and German modern literature while simultaneously engaged in creating his own work. Murakami's position is shared by some older Japanese contemporary writers, including Shinichiro Nakamura, Kenichi Yoshida, Saiichi Maruya, Kunio Tsuji and Tatsuhiko Shibusawa, while the phenomenon of writer as novelist and translator would probably be quite rare in the United States today: imagine Salinger translating books of Buddhist philosophy, or Carver translating the works of Chekhov.

Yet, unlike Mori, who struggled with the conflict of cultural values, for Murakami the Americanization of Japanese culture was a self-evident premise. Born in 1949, he must have acquired from his childhood the skills needed to deftly swim through the swells of Americanization which inundated Japan. In addition, this young writer, unlike most intellectuals from his father's, grandfather's, and great-grandfather's generations, doesn't exhibit an intensely self-conscious ambivalence towards the Americanization of Japanese civilization. He recognizes American culture — jazz, rock, pop art, the Beat Generation, and Salinger — as being deeply rooted in his inner self.

This self-confirmation is a characteristic of Murakami's novel, *The Wild Sheep Chase.* In the long history of modern as well as contemporary Japanese literature, Murakami is the first writer who almost never evinces any discomfort toward the Western shadow within him. This is the reason why he is enthusiastically hailed as a new champion of Japanese literature by readers of his own, as well as of the younger generation. His novels reflect the present Americanized customs and living conditions which have swept over Japan. His understanding of America through Chandler, Carver, jazz, and rock may well seem superficial and mistaken from an American point of view. However, the Westernized modern Japan he depicts is clearly a reality with which many youths empathize. It is practically impossible to talk about the current condition of Japanese culture without touching on this fact.

Yoshiyuki Fujikawa is a professor of English at the University of Tokyo, the author of Poetics of Landscape, *and the translator of 15 books including Nabokov's* Pale Fire.

On Japanese Mountains

BY NOBUYUKI KONDŌ

FIRST DISCOVERED THE JOY OF MOUNtain-climbing in the summer of 1946, when I was 16 years old. Setting out for Mount Fuji from the Tokyo area from the hills of Kantō I entered the central mountain range. On that first trip, I remember being moved by the beauties of nature that still remained in the war-battered land of Japan.

It is well-known that Japan is a country of islands with ocean on all sides. It is also a country of mountains. Since three quarters of its area is occupied by mountains, which are visible from any place in Japan, their images always remain in our subconscious mind, whether we like them or not. From Hokkaidō in the North to Kyūshū and the southwestern islands in the South, the Japanese Islands stretch into an archipelago of mountains: ruggedly steep peaks, graceful volcanoes, and gently rolling hills; they lack only glaciers. In its geography, climate, in the distribution of fauna and flora, Japan is extremely colorful. This spectacle of nature, changing so markedly from season to season, has had a tremendous influence on Japanese sensibilities.

The Japanese people's relationship with mountains is not only ancient, but profound. For example, the *Hitachi Province Topography* of 712 describes in abundant detail Tsukuba mountain (876 meters), its beautiful shape rising out of the middle of the Kantō Plain. Compared to the "continually snow-covered, and thus impossible to climb" Fuji (3,776 meters), Tsukuba has "climbing groups singing, dancing, drinking and eating, that

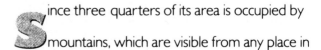

since three quarters of its area is occupied by mountains, which are visible from any place in Japan, their images always remain in our subconscious mind, whether we like them or not.

to this day have not ceased (coming to the mountain)"; the men and women of the Kantō provinces, looking for the cherry blossoms of spring or the crimson maple leaves of autumn, would climb carrying *sake* and snacks, and hold a party. As for the "unclimbable" Fuji, in the second half of the eighth century there appear people who actually reached the summit. In the record written by Miyako-no Yoshika (834–79) is an accurate and precise scenic description of Fuji: the topography of the summit, the crater-lake, the smoke, the rocks, the snow, the plants, and so forth. Without actually standing on the summit of Fuji, no one could have written such a description. Thus we know that more than 1000 years ago there were mountainclimbers who ascended this realm of mystery. As a record of reaching the summit of a high mountain, Yoshika's account may be the oldest such account in the world. From these early documents we know that in Japan, mountains provided sites for enjoying life, as well as sites for adventuring into the unknown.

After the introduction of Buddhism into Japan in the middle of the sixth century, indigenous ideas of mountain worship, blending together with an esoteric Buddhist faith, gave birth to the distinctively Japanese religious form known as Shugendō. Sacred sites were founded on mountains of each district, most notably Tateyama (3,015 meters), Hakusan (2,702 meters), Kiso Ontake (3,063 meters), Ishizuchiyama (1,981 meters), Hikosan (1,200 meters), and the three peaks of Dewa, highest peak, Gassan (1,979 meters). Shugendō represents a group of complex beliefs, religious practices, and wizardry; centering on the mountain bonzes or monks called *yamabushi* (literally "hidden in the mountains"), Shugendō formed the basis of mountain worship in Japanese folk religion.

While the *yamabushi* were relegated to the Shingon and Tendai sects of Buddhism (or perhaps they simply returned to the soil) in the latter half of the nineteenth century, they accomplished much over a span of more than a millennium: they built a mountain religion and culture, and were the first to reach the summits of many high mountains. There are still *yamabushi* who are guides for people wishing to study the mountains, and there are still people who, like the traditional *yamabushi*, spend their lives going up and down the mountains.

When climbing, one frequently chances upon traces of these ancient religious mountain-climbers. In fact, there are nearly no mountains without such signs. At the entrance of a trail there is a shrine, along the route are stone tablets, and at the summit is a small shrine that offers tribute to some deity. Then there are the mountains that have been made into sacred precincts, with a long history literally chiseled into them.

Mountain worship, the carrying out of religious rituals to achieve greater emotional harmony, is a tradition that continues down to the present. On the other hand, secular mountain-climbing groups have flourished from the sixteenth and seventeenth centuries. The first groups were the Fuji, Tateyama, and Ontake Pilgrimage Societies; later there were groups for each region. Wrapping themselves in white robes, chanting incantations of purification and strength, climbers ascend, following their religious and mountain-climbing guide. With the gradual increase of organized groups came the consolidation of trails, the establishment of places and rooms of worship, and the plentiful religious buildings and stone tablets donated by pilgrimage societies. Those who could not actually climb a mountain could approximate their wish by climbing one of the many hill-size facsimiles of Fuji that were built throughout Edo (Tokyo).

A new trend came with the "Civilization and Enlightenment" of the Meiji Restoration (1868). Modernization, which opened the country to Western science, rapidly illuminated hitherto unknown areas of mountain regions. First came foreign geographers, climatic, mineral, and botanical researchers, mountain-loving diplomats, and religionists; they were joined by Japan's scientists. The development of transportation brought the mountains closer to people, and the growth of surveying enterprises further spurred on the spread of mountain-climbing.

The Japan Alpine Club was founded in 1905 under interesting circumstances. An English missionary, Walter Weston (1861–1940), published a book in London, *Mountaineering and Exploration in the Japanese Alps* (1896), based on travels in the mountains during his first stay in Japan. Seven years after its publication, two young men in Yokohama happened to come across this book. Coincidentally, Weston, who had made his second trip to Japan, was living in Yokohama and happened to make the acquaintance of these two young mountaineering enthusiasts. From this chance encounter was born the Japan Alpine Club. At Kamikōchi, a famous resort at the foot of the Japanese Alps, is still held the annual service to honor Walter Weston, during the opening ceremony of the season in June.

Since then, Japanese mountain literature has become extremely vast and rich, quite different from the mountain-travel genre that preceded it. The book I first read that left the deepest impression was a posthumous manuscript by Ōshima Ryōkichi (1899–1928), who fell to his death from the cliff of Hotaka Dake. It was titled *Mountains—Research and Occasional Thoughts*, and contains the fruits of scientific research, personal travel accounts, and reflections on the theme, "A Feeling of Intimacy Rather than a Battle Against Mountains." The author was well-read in the works of such Western climbers as Albert Frederick Mummery (1855–95), Coolidge, Arnold Runn (1888–1974), and perhaps Hans Morganthaler (dates unknown). Ōshima was someone who demanded harmony in all aspects of mountain-climbing. Thus he sought not only to practice modern mountain-climbing, but to taste fully the beauty and peacefulness of Japanese mountains. His book represents the most important

characteristics of the Japanese "mountain literature," as well as the attitudes of the Japanese toward mountains in general.

Nobuyuki Kondō is a journalist and councilor of the Japanese Alpine Club. He won the Osaragi Prize in 1978 for the biography of a mountaineer.

Yamakawa Kikue and Women of the Mito Domain:

A Modern Feminist and the Mirror of the Past

BY KATE NAKAI

IN 1943, IN THE MIDST OF THE PACIFIC War, Yamakawa Kikue (1890–1980), one of Japan's earliest socialist feminists, published a slim book entitled *Women of the Mito Domain*. Mito (today an hour's ride by express train northeast of Tokyo) was the birthplace of Kikue's mother, who had been born there in 1857 to a family of well-known Confucian scholars. On one level *Women of the Mito Domain* is a family history built around anecdotes that Kikue had heard from her mother and other relatives. The focus of this history is not the major events in the lives of Kikue's forebears, however, but the texture of daily life as experienced by the samurai class, particularly samurai women, on the eve of the Meiji Restoration of 1868. As such, it has been described by one contemporary scholar as a native forerunner of the currently popular approach to history associated with the French *Annales* school.

Interwoven with Kikue's Annales-life history of diet and dress, housing, grooming, games, and schooling in mid-nineteenth-century Mito is another element. Mito was the home of the fervently nationalistic ideology expressed as "revere the emperor and expel the barbarian." This ideology, proclaimed by the activists who overthrew the Tokugawa shogunate and rallied around the Imperial cause in 1868, was reacclaimed by the military governments of the 1930s and 1940s. Not unrelated to the intensity of its ideological atmosphere, Mito also had been driven in the 1960s by sharp factional divisions and fratricidal infighting as each faction that gained power "sought to revenge blood with blood."

For Kikue these circumstances found an obvious resonance in the twentieth-century political environment, as she had experienced it. Considered from one angle, the factional fighting that had destroyed Mito from within mirrored the equally damaging divisions that had split and weakened the socialist movement in the 1920s. Viewed from another, the ideological orientation of the Mito imperial loyalists of 1868 paralleled that of the military government of the '30s and '40s. In the 1940s it was no longer possible for Kikue to criticize openly the current course of events: since the 1920s she and her husband, Yamakawa Hitoshi, a leading theoretician of the pre-World War II socialist movement, had been under constant police surveillance as "dangerous elements." With the outbreak of the China War in 1937, the government had banned Hitoshi from publishing anything whatsoever and at the end of that year had arrested him as part of a large-scale roundup of leftist intellectuals. Kikue, too, met with increasing difficulty in publishing even innocuous social commentary. Given this situation, *Women of the Mito Domain* was more than simply a portrayal of late Tokugawa samurai life and an account of how Kikue's forebears had lived through the "terror" of Mito in the 1860s. It also contained an implicit critique of Kikue's own times.

The opening and closing passages of the chapter entitled "Clothing" provide a good example. The chapter begins with an almost lyrical description of the growing of cotton in Mito: "In late Tokugawa Mito people wore cotton clothes virtually

> **"E**ven those rattling their swords and demanding 'the expulsion of the barbarians' wanted nothing so much as Western guns and imported felt for military field jackets." —*Women of the Mito Domain*

exclusively and, in principle, the raw material for those clothes, like other agricultural products, was obtained from within the domain. Of course, there were limits to self-sufficiency. Samurai households did not grow the cotton they consumed; they bought it from peasants who cultivated it in areas like the broad flat plain along the Naka River. When summer came the fields through which the river meandered were white with the blossoms of cotton plants, the snowy white expanse accentuated here and there by variegated touches of green—the dark green of a stand of trees, the brighter hues of the grassy embankment and adjoining rice fields."

Underlying this idyllic setting, however, was an inescapable reality: "However striking the scene, an autarchic economy centered around the single Mito domain . . . could hardly yield an ample supply of goods":

> Once the country was forced open (in the 1850s), new things appeared on the scene with an increasing rush, just as water having breached a dike floods in with ever greater force. Imported cotton yarn, referred to as "Chinese" yarn, first made an appearance about this time. Thanks to it, within a few years the constant sound of the spinning wheel in Mito households and the cotton fields along the banks of the Naka River had both disappeared. . . . Another new imported item was merino wool, known at the time as "Chinese crepe". . . . That smooth, soft fabric so different from either silk or cotton! Once one had worn it nothing else would do. People began to use "Chinese crepe" for

sashes, for the cords for fastening the kimono around the waist, for the sleeves of underrobes.

> Even those rattling their swords and demanding "the expulsion of the barbarians" wanted nothing so much as Western guns and imported felt for military field jackets. Since they were willing to pay out huge sums of money to acquire these things, however much they might call for "expulsion of the barbarians" or "rescinding the opening of the country," the unrealistic nature of that goal was a foregone conclusion. Whatever the situation before the opening of the country, after it there was not anyone in Mito who truly believed in the feasibility of expelling the barbarians or who really in his heart thought that a policy of isolation was better.

In pointing out this contradiction Kikue was not talking solely about Mito in the late Tokugawa period. The contemporary parallel was obvious, as was the lesson to be drawn: the costly military adventure mounted by "those people wearing imported felt and carrying imported guns," who had deluded themselves and others with their promise to "drive the Westerners out and restore the world to its proper state," had ended in failure and brought only tragedy to the lives of the people of the domain.

Along with criticism of the government leadership and its policies, one can see in Kikue's *Women of the Mito Domain* a reflection of her own views as a social activist. Distrustful of "romantic" and "heroic" approaches to social and political reform, Kikue consistently advocated adherence to a principled path of action founded on the realities of ordinary existence. In 1922, in the heyday of the socialist movement, Yamakawa Hitoshi had issued a manifesto calling for the movement to cease being the purist enterprise of a few. While avoiding the trap of seeking merely palliative measures, the socialists, he asserted, should take up the task of positively representing the demand of the masses for improvements in working and living conditions. In the same period Kikue developed a similar argument concerning the situation of women. The socialist movement, she held, should take account of the special needs of women in its platform. Specifically, it should advocate equalization of the status of men and women within the family, equal educational opportunities, and equal wages. When fellow leftists said that these aims were *petit-bourgeois* in nature she responded that as a practical measure the socialist movement had to adopt such a platform in order to draw women into it. Given the fact that female workers constituted a major component of the factory labor force, she contended that the socialist movement would have to win women supporters in order to bring about a proletarian revolution.

In the late 1920s and early 1930s, however, it became increasingly difficult to maintain such a "realistic" position. Rejected on the one hand by extremists within the leftist movement who advocated more "heroic" efforts, Kikue and Hitoshi's stance was circumscribed on the other by unrelenting government repression of all shades of socialist activism. In *Women of the Mito Domain* these experiences are reflected in Kikue's evocation of the pathos of those people who, in times past, opposing both the hotheaded extremists and opportunistic collusion with an unprincipled government, "were swept, regardless of their wish, into the vortex of the fighting which racked the domain." It was the same in Kikue's day.

While describing the tragedy of those people "of common

decency" who, despite an abhorrence of terror, became trapped in a situation dominated by it, in *Women of the Mito Domain* Kikue also described one means of coping with such a situation. This was an approach, largely unconscious, adopted by women associated with both factions who, struggling to keep their households going in the face of politically motivated confiscations of hereditary stipends, held as best they could to the routine of daily life.

Such concentration on the details of ordinary life was an important aspect of Kikue's own strategy for dealing with the darkening political environment of the 1930s. In 1932 she and Hitoshi, confronting the growing difficulty of supporting themselves through writing and translating work, had moved to a village on the outskirts of Kamakura. There they raised weasels for their fur and then, when that enterprise proved unsuccessful, took up the commercial raising of quail.

To be sure, Kikue recognized that concentration on the routine of daily life would not in itself ensure the preservation of political independence. The situation of women in Mito showed that such a stance could lead to ignorance of the larger world impinging on them and to passivity in responding to that larger world. That Kikue's fundamental concern remained the reform of that situation is shown by the fact that after the war, in changed political circumstances, she resumed a more active approach. Among other things, as the first head of the newly created Women's and Minors' Bureau within the Ministry of Labor, she worked directly to improve the status of women as she had called for in the 1920s. Nevertheless, in 1943, *Women of the Mito Domain* testifies, holding to the routine of daily life in the face of adverse circumstances was for Kikue the only possible, the only feasible course.

Kate Nakai's *translation of Yamakawa Kikue's* Women of the Mito Domain *will appear next year, published by the University of Tokyo Press.*

Article 19   *The Unesco Courier,* December 1989

The Pavilion of the Second Moon

BY LAURENCE CAILLET

The Japanese greet the New Year with a time-honoured religious ritual inspired by the myth of the water of youth

FOR many years the West pictured Japan as a land of geishas and cherry blossom. Today this once-familiar image has been displaced by that of a country of contrasts between old and new, a land of samurai and motorcycles.

It would be wrong, however, to see tradition and modernity as opposing forces in Japan, a country which ever since the seventh century has been a centralized state and where time-honoured community traditions have actually served to encourage, not hinder, modernization. The picturesque and joyful festivals which periodically strengthened community ties have survived industrial development and still attract pilgrims and tourists. And although their purely religious function has atrophied, they still transmit the centuries-old syncretic beliefs of Great Vehicle Buddhism and of Japan's indigenous religion, *Shinto,* the Way of the Gods.

Japan's main festive period was and is the New Year, which under the ancient lunar-solar calendar was celebrated shortly before spring ploughing. This was the time of the festival of the water of youth, a rite which is generally known as *Omizutori* (the drawing of water) and whose observance is traditionally believed necessary to bring about the return of spring. The best description of the meaning of *Omizutori* is found in a *haiku* by the poet Riôta (1718-1787):

Drawing of water!
The water of whirlpools warms
From this day also.

Every year since the eighth century the festival has been celebrated at the Buddhist monastery of Tôdaiji, at Nara, an ancient capital of Japan. Today it takes place in the first and second weeks of March, at a time corresponding to the second moon of the old calendar.

In the Pavilion of the Second Moon, a vast wooden building on the top of a hill to the east of the monastery, twelve monks meet to honour Kannon, the bodhisattva of infinite compassion and mercy. Guided by giant torches whose embers are collected by the faithful as talismans, they return to the pavilion fifteen nights in succession. They walk around the altar, tirelessly intoning hymns of praise and penitence. From the prayer room, which is separated from the holy of holies by a long veil of transparent linen, the pilgrims can see the outsize shadows of the monks praying for the peace and prosperity of the world.

On each of the fifteen days of ritual, six services are celebrated at specific moments of the day and night. Through ten or more hours of incantation to Kannon, of chanting and ritual kneeling, the participants seek to expiate sins committed the previous year and to accumulate merit.

The thousand circumambulations

Almost every night, special ceremonies are held as part of the penitential rites. According to the "Illustrated History of the Origins of the Pavilion of the Second Moon", the oldest manuscript of which dates from the sixteenth century, a Tôdaiji monk named Jitchû celebrated the feast of the drawing of water for the first time in 752. When he reached the paradise of the bodhisattvas, Jitchû contemplated their ceremonies and asked how they could be imitated and performed by men. The bodhisattvas replied as follows: "A day and a night here correspond to 400 human years. And so it is all the more difficult, in the short human time-span, to perform the rites according to the rules and to carry out the thousand circumambulations solemnly, without overlooking any detail. Furthermore, how could men reproduce these rites without a Kannon with a living body?" Jitchû then said: "The ceremony must be speeded up and the thousand circumambulations per-

formed at a run.... If I call on him with a sincere heart, why should a Kannon with a living body not come?" And he returned to transmit these rites to men.

Because of the difference between human time and godly time, the monks run a strange race around the altar dedicated to Kannon on the last three days of each of the two weeks of ritual. At first the monks walk very slowly, rolling up the sleeves of their robes and their stoles; then they fasten the lower parts of their garments to their legs. Meanwhile, the curtain concealing the holy of holies is lifted so that the crowd of pilgrims suddenly sees the splendour of the rites and experiences a joy equal to that felt by Jitchû when he reached paradise. Bells are loudly rung during this part of the ceremony.

Suddenly all noise ceases, and in the astonishing silence that follows, all the monks begin to run barefoot around the altar. One of them abruptly leaves the group and rushes into the antechamber of the prayer room where a wooden board known as the plank of prostration is fixed parallel to the floor by a kind of spring. He leaps onto the plank, striking it energetically with his knee, and then returns to his place. Each time the monks go around the altar, one of them runs and strikes the plank with his knee, the part of the body which symbolizes the forehead, elbow and knees, with which the worshippers must touch the ground as a sign of penitence. Eventually the pace slackens, the curtain falls, the intonation starts again, and the silhouettes of the monks are only visible as grey shadows.

On other evenings, the gods themselves come and dance, disguised as eight monks whose faces are masked by their hair. The first to arrive is the water divinity, who skips and runs with tiny steps and sprinkles the prayer room with lustral water. Next come the god of fire, who scatters embers, and the god Keshi, who sprinkles grains of rice cracked in the fire. Everyone dances and leaps to the noisy rhythm made by three other gods with a rattle, a conch shell and a bell. Two more brandish a sabre and a willow rod to drive away evil spirits.

The well of the god Onyû

During these nights of dancing the water of youth is drawn and distributed to the pilgrims. What is the origin of this ritual? The "Illustrated History of the Origins of the Pavilion of the Second Moon" records how "In the province of Wakasa, Onyû, a god who possessed the river Onyû, lingered while out fishing and arrived late at the rites of the twice seven days and seven nights. Profoundly regretful, the god said to Jitchû the monk that as a sign of contrition he would make the lustral water spring near to the place of the feast, and at that very moment two cormorants, one black and the other white, suddenly rose from the rock and perched on a nearby tree. From the traces of these birds sprang water of incomparable sweetness. Stones were laid there and it became the spring of lustral water, aka-i..."

And so, on the second day of March, the priests of the sanctuary of Onyû pour into the river a phial of lustral water which is supposed to flow through an underground channel and reach the spring of the Pavilion of the Second Moon during the night of the twelfth to the thirteenth.

On that night, at two o'clock in the morning, the "master of esoteric rites", wearing a brocade hat, leaves the pavilion and turns towards the hill where the miraculous spring is located. With him is a faithful layman wearing a hermit's white robe. He is followed by monks bearing magic rods to which conch shells and bells are fastened. The conch shells are sounded and then, guided by a lay torch-bearer, everyone goes down the steps leading to the spring. At that moment, an orchestra begins to play ancient Chinese music and the monks pray for the water to gush out.

Today the spring is concealed beneath a flimsy building with a grey-tiled roof, the four corners of which are adorned with birds. Some think the birds are pigeons, others that they are messenger cormorants of Onyû, the god of fishing and sovereign of the waters which according to Japanese beliefs form a reservoir of longevity, if not of eternity. He is also associated with cinnabar, the essential component of the elixir of immortality which the Taoists of China and Japan tried to concoct in ancient times.

Only the hermit and the master of the esoteric rites enter the building which covers the spring. The water, carried three times in buckets to the Pavilion of the Second Moon, is poured into a wide tub of light-coloured wood which is immediately covered with a white cloth and offered to Kannon. From that day on it is distributed to the thousands of pilgrims who flock to receive in the palms of their hands a few drops of this extraordinary liquid which encourages longevity and is a panacea for all ills.

In spite of its extreme solemnity, this rite is not very different from that with which peasant families welcome the spring. On the eve of the first day of spring, the master of the house, his eldest son or a specially chosen servant rises while it is still dark. He dons a traditional kimono and bows before the altar of the household gods after sprinkling himself with a few drops of purifying water. Then he puts on new straw sandals and goes to the nearest spring. Beside the spring or on the lip of the well, he offers the water-god rice cakes and, while reciting a magic formula, draws with a new ladle and bucket the first water of the year.

Without speaking to the people he meets on his way, he returns home and places the freshly drawn water on the household altars. Then he awakens the members of the family and each one drinks tea brewed with this water of youth which as far as possible compensates for the aging caused by the New Year. According to tradition, people become a year older at New Year, not on their birthday.

The origin of this marvellous water is described in the following story from the southern island of Miyako: "Once, long ago, when men settled on the beautiful island of Miyako, the Sun and Moon wished to give them an elixir of immortality and sent them Akariyazagama, a young servant with red hair and a red face. On the night that marked the changing of the season, Akariyazagama came down to Earth with two buckets, one of which contained the water of immortality and the other the water of mortality. The Moon and the Sun had ordered him to bathe men with the water of immortality and to bathe the snake with the water of death. As Akariyazagama, tired after his long journey, put down the buckets beside the road and urinated, a great snake appeared and bathed in the water of immortality. Weeping, Akariyazagama had men take a bath of death and then returned to heaven. When he described how he had carried out his mission, the Sun was furious and said to him: 'Your offence against men is irreparable...'

"Since then, the snake is reborn when it sheds its skin, whereas men die. However, the gods took pity on men and wished to enable them, if not to live for ever, at least to grow somewhat younger. And so each year, on the night before the day of the feast of the new season, they send from heaven the water of youth. That is why even now, at dawn on the day of the feast of the first season, water of youth is drawn from the well and all the family bathes in it."

The water of youth which rises at the foot of the Pavilion of the Second Moon, like that which bubbles up in family wells, thus comes from the other world. It is carried by waves from the distant land of the gods, the land of Tokoyo, a world both sombre and luminous, a land of abundance and immortality, but also the resting place of the dead on the other side of the sea.

Penitence and the absorption of holy water are two facets of a single hopeless desire to obliterate the wear and tear of time and establish in the world of men something of the eternity which is the prerogative of the gods.

Article 20

THE WORLD & I
APRIL 1990

≡

The Shape Changer Kitsune

The Many Faces of the Japanese Fox

Thomas Wayne Johnson

Other than the four-footed animal that one sometimes sees in rural areas, the fox is at least three separate characters in Japanese folklore, one of which is its major trickster figure. The living creature and these three (or more) different personae are frequently interwoven in interesting and confusing ways.

The first fox that the foreign tourist is likely to find in Japan is the messenger of the Shinto deity Inari-sama. Inari is responsible for many important aspects of Japanese life. He began as the god of the rice harvest, but over time he has been vested with powers over many other related areas and he is today most frequently seen as devoted to prosperity and fertility in general. By extension, he has also become a patron deity of prostitutes as well as modern business.

Even the casual tourist in Japan will come across roadside shrines with a pair of foxes at the gate. These may be elaborate stone carvings several times larger than life-size, or they may be miniature white porcelain statues decorated with gold and red. There are tens of thousands of shrines to Inari throughout the country. In rural Japan nearly every household has a small shrine dedicated to him in the yard, or at least an amulet and a pair of miniature statues on the family shrine indoors. The largest of the shrines in Inari, Fushimi Inari Taisha in Kyoto, covers much of a mountain and contains thousands of statues and red *torii* (shrine gates) dedicated to the deity. Shrine gates painted red invariably signify a place sacred to Inari.

A second fox, and one that the tourist is much less likely to find, takes possession of the spirit of an individual and must be driven out by various means. Fox possession is sometimes diagnosed when a person becomes irrational and begins behaving strangely. One of the many modern religions of Japan, Sukyo Mahikari, frequently cures alcoholism by exorcising thirsty fox spirits. (The fox is generally seen as fond of *saké*, fried tofu and fried rats, and these are often used to trap him as we will see below.)

A frequent means used to drive out a fox spirit is through pain. In the first half of this century there were several cases reported in the newspapers of people who died during the process of having a fox spirit driven from them. One case tells of a mad woman who died during treatment by being denied all food, having red pepper applied to her nose, eyes, and mouth, and having her body rubbed with red-hot fire tongs. Another police case reported in the newspaper tells of a woman who had been insane for several years. Eventually, after all other attempts at a cure had failed, her kinsmen became convinced that she was possessed by a fox spirit. She died during the "usual" curing process of having her eyes and nostrils filled with sulfur while onlookers chanted Buddhist sutras. Even today, small children who are cranky and cry too frequently may be perceived as possessed by foxes. The exorcism is far more gentle today, however.

The Fox as trickster and shape changer

The third fox, and the one that concerns us most, is the fox as trickster and shape changer. When a fox attains a great age (the exact age depends on the text and varies from fifty to a thousand years) it gains the power to change its shape. Usually it assumes human shape, frequently that of a beautiful woman, but it may also take the form of other animals or inanimate objects. Sometimes this is with evil intent, but more often it seems to be as trickster. Many legends and/or jokes are told of foxes in disguise, how to recognize them, and how they are exposed.

Folk belief tells of several ways that we might recognize a fox in disguise. A fox always emits a slight glow and even on the darkest night she will be visible. A fox in human form will have a long face with eyebrows that grow together in the middle—a trait that may cause this American anthropologist to have to convince some elderly residents in rural areas that he *is* what he appears to be, not a fox posing as a foreigner. Dogs are not fooled by the disguised fox and will bark incessantly at one—just as they will at a strange foreigner.

Foxes also have difficulty in pronouncing certain words. *Moshi* is one of the words that foxes are supposed to have great difficulty with, and a folk explanation for the continual use of *moshi-moshi* in telephone conversations is the need to convince the other party that he is not talking to a fox. If in doubt, the quickest way to expose a fox is to place a fried rat on the road where it will pass. The fox is so fond of fried rats that he will abandon his disguise to eat it.

Shape-changing foxes have been around for a long time in Japan. They have been written about since the eighth century and have been spotted or spoken about as recently as the moment you are reading about them here. They do seem to be more frequent during times of intense social change, however, and there was a tremendous increase in their number as Japan entered the modern age.

In 1889, a tale was widely circulated and believed of a fox having taken the shape of a railway train on the Tokyo-Yokohama line (whch opened in 1872). The phantom train seemed to be running straight toward a real train, but never got any nearer to it. The engineer of the real train, seeing that all his signals were useless, put on a tremendous burst of speed. He eventually caught up with the phantom, which suddenly disap-

A folk explanation for the continual use of moshi-moshi in telephone conversations is the need to convince the other party that he is not talking to a fox.

*M*any folktales tell of men who have married beautiful women only to learn later that their brides were foxes in disguise.

peared. When he stopped his train, a crushed fox was found beneath the engine wheels. Similar phantom trains have been reported as being seen in some parts of Japan as late as the 1950s and the foxes may still be running on some rural rail lines yet.

D.C. Buchanan, an early observer of Japanese folk belief, reported that the priest of the Inari Shrine at Wakayama told him the following story as true:

> Late one evening, a man was walking along the narrow and steep road known as *Kurumazaka* ("Cart Hill"), which leads down from the Inari Shrine when

■ Inari shrines are a commonplace sight in Japan and account for the most common use of the fox image. These scenes are from the Toyokawa-Inari shrine in the Akasaka district of Tokyo. *Left:* Statue of vixen and cub. *Below:* A worshiper prays at the shrine.

a large automobile, blazing with lights, rushed up and came within a hair's breadth of hitting the pedestrian, who stepped to one side in the nick of time. Several days later, in the wee small hours of the night, this same man was in his own motor-car carefully making his way down *Kurumazaka* when again up the hill came a larger car going at tremendous speed. There was no room to pass and no time to stop. The driver in the first car put on his brakes and braced himself for the collision. There was a dull thud, and the huge car disappeared. Getting out, the driver saw beneath the wheels of his car an old, dead fox!

Another legend found in rural Japan tells of a farmer who smoked a fox from its den by burning pine needles. He then killed the fox and sold its fur. Several days later he was awakened by six men, armed with shotguns, who demanded money. After giving them all the money that he had in the house he managed to escape from them and ran into the village. When he returned with the policeman, several fireman, and others, he found his money untouched on the floor, but his rice cooker was empty, his food supply had been ransacked, and there were fox paw prints all over his floor.

The Fox as woman

The most common stories about foxes, however, portray the fox as changing into a woman. A large number of folktales tell of men who have married beautiful women only to learn much later that their brides were foxes in disguise. One of the oldest (attributed to the reign of the Emperor Kim Mei in the sixth century, but first written down in the eighth century) tells of a farmer who had waited until late in life to marry, as he was searching for the perfect wife. One day, while walking home from his fields, he met a strikingly beautiful woman on the path. After talking with her for a while he ascertained that she was not yet married. When he asked her to be his bride, she agreed. Eventually, a son was born to the cou-

ple. On the same day, a pup was born to the man's dog. As the puppy grew up it became very hostile to the mistress of the house—snarling at her and frightening her. The man refused to kill the dog, however, and one day it attacked the woman so fiercely that, in despair, she returned to fox form and fled. The man was crushed, as he loved his wife in spite of her being a fox, and he cried out to her, *"ki tsu ne"* (come and sleep). This folktale is often given as a folk etymology for the word *kitsune* (fox).

Another story, still widely told in Japan, has a physician summoned to aid with a difficult childbirth in a remote area. He is led to a magnificent house where he is received with great courtesy. After the beautiful young mother has safely delivered a fine, healthy baby boy, the physician is treated to an excellent dinner, entertained elegantly, and given a much more than ample payment before being sent home. The next day he returns to thank his hosts and to check on the mother and the new baby. Search as he might, he can find no house in the area, only empty woods. Upon arriving home he reexamines the payment that he had received. All is good except for one bill that has changed into a leaf. Other versions of this legend have the physician spend the night with the family only to awaken in the morning on a grassy knoll far from any house. The remains of the banquet are seen in scattered leaves and horse droppings.

The fondness of foxes for red beans and fried bean curd is their undoing in a number of stories. One tells of how three foxes thought that they had found a good way to indulge in their favorite foods when one of them saw three warts on the bottom of an old woman when she stooped to relieve herself in her garden. They came disguised as three police officers the next day and announced that a government official had heard of the woman's three warts and wanted to see them for himself. The three officers had been sent to get the warts. The old woman was frightened, but to delay matters, she offered the policemen lunch. When she asked what they would like to eat, they replied that their favorite was *sekihan* (a

Shape-changing foxes are more frequently reported during times of intense social change, as when Japan entered the modern age.

festival dish made of rice and steamed with red beans) and fried bean curd.

After they had eaten their fill, they told the old woman that, as it was getting late, they would excuse her for the day, but would return to fetch her warts on the following day. They repeated the trick for several days. Finally a neighbor happened to pass the neighborhood shrine at night and heard loud goings-on. He saw three foxes dancing and singing about their sport with the old woman. He reported this and loaned his dog to the woman. The next day, when the three "policemen" came for the warts—and their lunch of red beans and fried bean curd—the dog attacked and killed the three foxes that they were.

The fox is not the only animal that can change its shape, however. Many Japanese legends and folktales concern a shape-changing badger. The favorite of these tales concerns a badger who changes himself into a teakettle to fool a monk, but he is forced to change back to badger form and run for his life when he is put over the fire to boil water for tea. One tale even has the fox and badger engaging in a contest to see which could appear in the best disguise. The fox returned to the contest site first in the guise of a youthful bride. As she walked down the path toward the place they were to meet, she spied a piece of fried bean curd that someone had apparently dropped while on the way out to the rice paddies. She reached down and picked it up, but as she started to take a bite, it shouted "You lose, fox!"—and changed back into the badger.

While belief in the power of the fox to change shapes and to delude the observer has declined greatly in modern Japan, it has not yet fully disappeared and likely will never disappear from popular folktales. The strength of this Japanese folk belief is most strongly expressed, however, in the best first-person account of the great eruption of Bandai-San in 1888. In the eruption the entire mountain was blown to pieces, devastating an area of many square miles. Forests were leveled, rivers were turned from their courses, and several villages were buried with all of their inhabitants. Casually observing this from another mountain peak several miles away was an old farmer who later described the black cloud of steam and ashes rising to a height of twenty thousand feet and spreading out in the form of a giant umbrella. He described the strange black rain that fell over him, hotter than the hottest bath. He felt the mountain shake beneath him and heard sounds louder than the loudest thunders. He remained quiet, watching it all, however, as he had decided that it was a fox attempting to frighten and delude him.

If you are ever traveling in Japan, remember the many tales of the fox whenever you pass a shrine to Inari with its red torii (gates) and its statues of the fox messengers. Think of foxes when you eat that favorite Japanese picnic food of *Inari-zushi* (a piece of fried bean curd stuffed with rice, occasionally containing red beans). Remember that the wild drunk whom you meet on the train may simply be possessed by a fox spirit and need exorcism. Especially remember that the beautiful woman in the striking kimono might be a fox in disguise. If you are unable to check to see if she glows in the dark, you can always look for a fried rat.

Additional Reading

D.C. Buchanan, "Inari: Its origin, development, and nature," *Transactions of the Asiatic Society of Japan*, Series II, 12 (1935).

Richard M. Dorson, *Folk Legends of Japan*, Charles E. Tuttle: Rutland, Vt., 1962.

Thomas W. Johnson, "Far Eastern fox lore," *Asian Folklore Studies*, 33 (1974).

Kiyoshi Nozaki, *Kitsune: Japan's fox of mystery, romance, and humor*, The Hokuseido Press: Tokyo, 1961.

Thomas Wayne Johnson is professor of liberal studies at California State University in Chico.

Article 21

THE ECONOMIST JANUARY 27 1990

JAPAN'S GANGSTERS

Honourable mob

Even in organised crime Japan is ahead of other countries. Its criminals carry business cards, not submachineguns

"BLACK RAIN", Ridley Scott's gripping film about Japanese gangsters, sacrifices reality for drama in only one respect. Its villains are always to be found in steel mills, deserted farmhouses or underground carparks.

In fact, when the *yakuza*, as Japan calls its mob, have important business, they do it in their own offices, clearly marked and open 24 hours a day. Like other Japanese, they greet strangers with a business card showing their organisation and rank. The biggest crime syndicate, the Yamaguchi-gumi, prints an 18-page internal telephone directory, complete with a bland code of practice on the inside front cover.

For proof of this well justified confidence, look at a videotape showing the installation ceremony last year of the syndicate's fifth *kumicho*, supreme chief. As well as the Shinto ceremony and the new don's sword of office, the film also shows the gangster guests, scores of them, dressed in formal kimono and recorded carefully, one by one, as they entered the ceremony, with their name and rank subtitled on the screen. A startling piece of undercover police work, you might think. Not at all. The video was made for the syndicate, which circulated copies in elegant white-and-gold presentation boxes bearing on the front the name of the group, its logo (below) and the characters for "happy occasion".

When a Tokyo television station, TBS, got hold of one of the tapes and broadcast a short section of it, the syndicate's second-in-command, Mr Masaru Takumi, promptly—did what? Declared this was just the annual outing of the Ginza canary-fanciers club? Threatened the station? Fitted up the newscaster with a concrete waistcoat? No, he sued for breach of copyright, claiming ¥10m ($70,000) in damages.

War, victory and turning-point

The ceremony shown in the videotape was perhaps the most momentous event in the history of the Yamaguchigumi since its foundation in 1915. It had a membership of only 25 after the second world war. But under the American occupation, the gang's third boss, Kazuo Taoka, began to build it up by hostile takeovers. By the end of the 1960s he had become the chief of 10,000 gangsters and the most powerful mobster in Japan.

He died in 1981, and the gang was thrown into turmoil. After three years two candidates for his mantle submitted themselves to a vote. The loser refused to concede, set up a syndicate of his own called the Ichiwa-kai, and declared war. In January 1985 the official winner was murdered outside his mistress's apartment, along with his two top sidekicks.

That bloodshed did not end the war, however. It merely embittered the survivors inside the Yamaguchigumi against their breakaway rivals. For four more years, the two gangs battled it out for supremacy.

The old syndicate had fewer members than the new. But it had two useful things on its side. First, the logo, which has acquired tremendous brand recognition over the years. Many non-criminal Japanese know the sign, and react with fear and awe when they see it. Gangsters who wear it in their lapels do better business than those who do not. Second, the Yamaguchi-gumi had allies. It struck deals with smaller gangster groups from Kyushu to Hokkaido, and made them promise to have nothing to do with the upstart Ichiwa-kai.

It worked. When a truce was eventually called last March, the renegade was forced to dissolve the Ichiwa-kai and retire. After a

brief skirmish with their murdered chief's younger brother (who had kept the ceremonial sword, and had ideas of his own), the leaders of the Yamaguchi-gumi last July chose Mr Yoshinori Watanabe as its boss.

His installation ceremony was therefore a turning-point in the gang's history. It has stemmed the sporadic inter-gang warfare that had become common. By re-establishing solidarity, it has reduced the vulnerability of organised crime to police crackdowns. And it has boosted its membership to 21,000. "The Yamaguchi-gumi is now stronger than it has ever been in its history," says Reikichi Sumiya, editor of *Asahi Geino*, a Tokyo magazine that devotes much of its coverage to the doings of gangsters.

Rooted in society

A golden age for gangsters? In Japan? The country where women walk through the streets of the capital late at night without fear, where children hardly big enough to climb on to the seats travel the subway alone, where a dropped wallet will as likely as not be sent back to the owner within a day or two by post?

Yes. Japan's National Police Agency estimates that Japan has 80,000 gangsters. True, 25 years ago it had 180,000, outnumbering the army; but 80,000 is still more than 20 times the membership of America's mafia. Almost a third of all the prisoners in Japanese jails are said to be *yakuza*; 80% of the criminal-defence work paid for by the defendants themselves (rather than through public legal-aid funds) is *yakuza* business.

One explanation is that Japanese crime, like so many other things in Japan, is done in orderly, organised groups. Gangs have their patches, and their own lines of business. Woe betide the intruder who tries to collect protection money from an already protected street market; still more woe betide the pickpocket whose activities drive away that market's customers. In their internal structure, the gangs are highly central-ised and becoming more so.

Gangster groups also have shadowy links with politics. A couple of years ago, a Liberal Democrat member of parliament was videotaped singing songs at a gangster party. He was alleged to have visited gangsters in jail, and to have accepted *yakuza* support in his successful bid for re-election.

Some say the *yakuza* have their own members in parliament. Certainly some gangster bosses keep offices next door to those of members of parliament. And the industries in which organised crime is most active—such as construction, which must rely on casual labour, and *pachinko*, the pinball gambling game that is one of the country's biggest businesses—make hefty political contributions.

The gangsters' relationship with the police is unclear. Almost any suburban street in Japan has its *pachinko* parlour, protected if not owned by organised crime and offering theoretically illegal money prizes, under the eyes of the police. Tokyo's leading red-light district, thronged with *yakuza*, carries

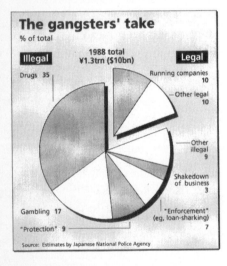

The gangsters' take
% of total

1988 total
¥1.3trn ($10bn)

| Illegal | Legal |

Drugs 35

Running companies 10

Other legal 10

Other illegal 9

Shakedown of business 3

Gambling 17

"Enforcement" (eg, loan-sharking) 7

"Protection" 9

Source: Estimates by Japanese National Police Agency

on its business—also illegal, since the late 1950s—within a stone's throw of the local police-box.

The Japanese magazine writers who know the gangsters best say actual bribes to the police are few, but both parties know how far they can go and take care not to overstep the mark. To help the police save face after an underworld assassination, the gang that carried it out may offer up a junior gangster who will confess and go to prison on behalf of his boss. The Yamaguchi-gumi has even organised leaflet campaigns and street marches against drug-taking.

The police certainly get to know their adversaries well. When the *Far Eastern Eco-*

nomic Review sent a reporter to talk to a gangster in 1984, the reporter found him "having tea and a friendly chat with a highly placed official of the Osaka police".

Popular heroes

These ambiguities reflect the ambivalent attitude of Japanese society to organised crime. "The gangster's lusts are for money, power, politics," says Mr Yukio Yamanouchi, a lawyer who often acts for the Yamaguchi-gumi and who has written two books about gangsters. "These are all human values."

They certainly strike a chord with the public. Tales of the gangsters, with their shoulder-to-knee tattoos, flashy suits, diamond-studded watches and stretched Mercedes limousines, bring a touch of the exotic to the life of the humblest salaryman. Mr Yamanouchi's first book, "The Lonely Hit Man", sold 180,000 copies and was made into a film. Mass-market magazines do a roaring business in sensational gangster articles. The public also laps up *yakuza* films, in which the gangster is glorified as the modern equivalent of the samurai.

The *yakuza* themselves are outstanding at public relations. Their claim to be the champions of the outcast and the downtrodden holds more than a grain of truth: the underworld is one of the few areas of Japanese society where being of Korean ancestry or a *burakumin* (a member of Japan's old untouchable caste) does not matter. The gangsters have a moral code of their own which is nearer the samurai tradition than modern urban life is.

The relation between an *oyabun*, a boss (literally, father), with his *kobun*, his sidekick (child), is a sacred one; gangsters are extraordinarily conscious of seniority and loyalty. Their picturesque way of atoning for mistakes or of expressing solidarity is to lop off the second joint of their own little fingers and to send the grisly morsel in a bottle as a peace-offering. Syndicates even provide social services for their members.

When *The Economist*'s reporter went to interview Mr Masao Katsuragi, one of the Yamaguchi-gumi's top ten, he was treated to an extraordinary display of politeness. Mr Katsuragi, who has the twinkling eyes of a favourite uncle, has served 12 years in jail for murder. He had been the chief of the syndicate's hit squad, he said; some of his victims were killed with pistols, others with Japanese swords. Now his official occupation is antique-dealing; but at a lavish dinner in an Osaka restaurant—one of those offers that even an upright paper like this one cannot refuse—he was quite willing to talk about real business.

Did he not regret his criminal life? "Absolutely not," replied Mr Katsuragi, launch-

ing into a monologue about the chivalry of the *yakuza* lifestyle, and the danger and fear it imposes on the gangster's family.

As if confirming the suspicion that he was the model for "The Lonely Hit Man", he called for a record of a popular song he had written about the sadness of a gangster's wife. Asked why his standing at the restaurant seemed so high, he answered simply: "We tip well. And we're the best-behaved, most polite customers there are."

Speed, sex and new religion

The size and sources of the gangsters' money are a matter of guesswork. Our chart shows a police estimate; some estimates are several times higher. But at least the figures give an idea of the breadth of *yakuza* activities. The list is familiar: drugs, gambling, blackmail, loan-sharking, protection. Organised crime has grown fat on Japan's growing wealth.

The drugs figure looks surprising, given the Yamaguchi-gumi's supposed hostility to drug-dealing. Yet it shows merely the difference between appearances and reality. Almost half the 20,400 people arrested in Japan in 1988 for trading in or owning illegal stimulants such as "speed" were members of crime syndicates. The gangsters also deal in heroin and cocaine when they can get them. So far, these drugs are not widespread in Japan; arrests in the narcotic and opium categories ran to a total of only 300 last year. No thanks are due to the syndicates for this.

Some *yakuza* activities are more peculiarly Japanese. The system of *dango*—the rigging of bids in the construction industry, which has drawn fierce criticism from America—is said to be enforced by the gangsters. Another traditional activity is to blackmail companies by threatening to ask embarrassing questions at shareholders' meetings; once paid off, the gangsters instead shout down legitimate questioners.

Other kinds of business are newer. As Tokyo's property boom took off in the mid-1980s, more and more little old ladies found themselves sitting tenants in a small house, the last obstacle to the construction of a million-dollar office block. Gangsters have made a thriving business of *jiageya*, terrorising them into leaving, and then profiting hugely from the resulting rise in site value.

As their activities grow, the syndicates are beginning to see the virtues of integration. They do not merely run brothels but also launder the towels and sheets. They make gambling machines, and have moved into sports shops. Some say *yakuza* have taken advantage of the recent shortage of doctors and nurses to buy into private hospitals, and have profited from the boom in new religions by setting up priests in new temples whose plastic Buddhas are supplied by gangster companies.

And now the world

The next step seems inevitable. If Japanese cars, banks and consumer electronics can conquer the world, why not Japanese gangsters, too?

Police have observed *yakuza* representatives in the Philippines, hiring girls to come and work in Japan as "hostesses". They know about the amphetamine supply routes from Taiwan to Tokyo, and from the South Korean port of Pusan to the Japanese port of Shimonoseki. They know that the *yakuza* organise sex tours abroad and arrange gambling for Japanese citizens on holiday in California. Thanks to some smart investigative reporting by the *Honolulu Advertiser*, they even have details of Japanese gangsters' penchant for buying into Hawaiian golf courses.

So far the *yakuza* have gone abroad mostly for three things: to fleece Japanese tourists there, to invest or spend their ill-gotten gains legitimately, and to buy drugs for their domestic market. Two senior Yamaguchi-gumi gangsters whom the FBI caught in Hawaii offering to sell heroin had sought to be paid with firearms, which are strictly controlled in Japan and cost about ten times as much as in the free-killing United States. So even that intended transaction was mainly directed to the home market. (The two men got off, by the way: the FBI's undercover agents, in trying to entrap them, went rather far in offering them deals. The gangsters' reply, according to their defence, was "Hai! Hai!"—"yes, yes", which in Japanese is likelier to mean "Yes, we understand" than "Yes, we agree".)

In fact the *yakuza* have two good reasons not to make a bid for market share in Europe or America. First, they do not have the necessary foothold: they neither control the supply of a popular drug, as the Colombian rings do, nor can they work from the base of a poor immigrant community, source of much of America's organised crime. Second, their home business continues to grow at a healthy pace. There is also the small matter of language: few gangsters know English.

The good days are passing

Yet life at home cannot for ever stay as comfortable for the *yakuza* as in the past. The threat comes from the possible breakdown of public tolerance. A few citizens, refusing to be cowed by the might of the Yamaguchi-gumi and other organisations, have even gone to court to have gangsters evicted from the apartment next door.

More significantly, the Japanese police are studying ways in which the law might be changed. Under present rules, they cannot follow the practice, routine in America and Europe, of buying drugs on the street so as to have an accurate idea of the state of supply. Nor do they carry out "controlled delivery", which means persuading a drug courier whom they have caught to carry on with delivery of his package to the next person in the chain. Instead, they are required to put him behind bars immediately. "They are trying to cut down a tree by pulling off the leaves," says a frustrated American law-enforcement officer.

Perhaps most importantly, Japanese law does not have any statute specifically directed against illegal organisations, like America's catch-all RICO laws. This would make it possible to declare a syndicate such as the Yamaguchi-gumi illegal, and then take action against its declared members.

Under present rules, the police are sometimes put in a ludicrous position. They knew every one of the gangsters who came to pay their respects to the new, fifth boss of the Yamaguchi-gumi. But the only man they could do anything about was one who had been silly enough to come to the party with a gun. The rest made their way in and out watched but not troubled; and their tributes to the new leader, delivered in cash, were handed over in envelopes with their seals still unbroken.

Article 22

Presidential Studies Quarterly, Summer 1990

The Pacific Rim: The View From Down Under*

JOHN R. KELSO
Australian Consul-General, Los Angeles

There is an obsession, not least here in the West, with the perceived challenges presented by the economic success of Japan and several smaller Western Pacific countries.

All too seldom is it mentioned that these sustained successes have made an enormous contribution to prosperity, investment and economic development world-wide for at least a quarter of a century.

Moreover, peoples from the Western Pacific are making outstanding contributions to the societies of Australia, Canada, and the U.S.A. This is very evident here in Los Angeles, as well as in Sydney, Vancouver and elsewhere.

There is far too much negative comment, accompanied by calls for retaliatory action and the like. This should not be permitted to creep into the policies of government nor cause us to overlook important realities. For example, the Association of Southeast Asian Nations (ASEAN) and the South Pacific Forum currently receive very little media attention and are not widely known, studied or discussed.

Rational comment, study and policy must strive to overcome such distortions.

Asia-Pacific Dynamism

The Asian-Pacific region has become the most economically dynamic in the world. Moreover, its vitality is outward-looking. The proportion of GNP dependent on trade is high and is, by and large, open and dispersed, not dependent on groupings or blocs.

The centre of gravity of world production has already shifted from the Atlantic to the Pacific. The Asia-Pacific region as a whole, including North America, generates the largest of the world's bilateral trade flows, and is likely in the next decade to create more than half the world's economic output. Per capita incomes are growing quickly. Singapore and Hong Kong already rival the lower-income European countries. More than half of Australia's exports and nearly half our imports are directed to or sourced from our Western Pacific neighbors.

The region is politically, culturally and militarily diverse. If one considers the distinctive character of the larger Asian powers alone—Japan, China and Indonesia, plus India—and the economic achievements of several more—South Korea, Taiwan, Thailand and Singapore—it is obvious that if this is a distinct region, it is one of vast diversity in cultures and living standards.

The elements of dynamism and diversity, together with the element of openness, lend a strongly pragmatic flavour to many countries in the region. But there are also regional conflicts, territorial disputes and political disagreements. It is far from being a stable region of settled and shared values. The constant challenge for policy is to harness the dynamism and the pragmatism to the resolution of problems and difficulties.

Both superpowers are Pacific powers. But economically and culturally, the U.S. presence is much more substantial. Moreover, as in other parts of the world, the communist states have singularly failed to deliver economic prosperity and to match the economic pace of their neighbours.

Regrettably, the recent improvements in the U.S.-Soviet relationship have not been reflected in the Asia-Pacific region to the same extent as in Europe. In large part this reflects the multipolar nature of the region. U.S.-Soviet competition has been an important axis around which Asia-Pacific security issues have been defined since World War II. But, unlike Europe, it has not been the only axis.

Gorbachev's Asia-Pacific agenda is still largely unclear, though the Soviet withdrawal from Afghanistan, the Soviet-Chinese Summit before Tiananmen and signs of a more forthcoming Soviet position on Cambodia were warmly welcomed. But Gorbachev's 1986 Vladivostok speech, and subsequent variations on its theme, have not struck a responsive chord in the region. This is probably because serious fault lines in regional circumstances have still to be repaired. Moreover, there are some disconcerting actions by the U.S.S.R., mostly in the northern sector, such as supplying sophisticated weaponry to North Korea, maintaining a disproportionately large and aggressively deployed military presence, and being unyielding with Japan in discussion on various matters, including the northern territories.

Setting Australian Priorities

What do all these changes in the international and regional scene augur for Australia? In foreign policy, as in domestic policy, coping with *rapid change requires skilful political management.*

One: Maintaining a Positive Security and Strategic Environment in Our Own Region

We identify first a 'zone of direct military interest' (embracing our own territories, New Zealand and the nearby island countries of the South-West Pacific, Papua New Guinea and Indonesia), and second, an 'area of primary strategic interest' (embracing the eastern Indian Ocean, and the rest of South-East Asia and the South-West Pacific).

With our partners in the South Pacific Forum, 15 members including the Federated States of Micronesia and the Marshall Islands, we have sought to develop a relationship of 'constructive commitment'.

This policy recognises that, notwithstanding our very much greater size and economic capacity, we should approach the South Pacific within a framework of regional partnership, not dominance. We do not regard the South Pacific as our sphere of influence, either in our own right or as a guardian of larger western alliance interests. Such influence as we do exercise we want to be in the context of a network of close, confident and broadly-based bilateral relationships, in which we promote regional stability through economic development and the encouragement of shared perceptions of common strategic and security interests. Indeed, traditional 'sphere of influence' approaches are quite misplaced in a region of fragile micro-states where politics and institutions are highly personalised and less susceptible as such to the brutal logic of relative size and power. The Island states are preoccupied above all else with questions of economic and environmental security and these are the matters which we emphasize. The initiative to launch the project for a South Pacific nuclear free zone was devised to meet and to manage specific regional concerns with French nuclear testing and protection of the Pacific environment against the dumping of nuclear waste.

We give particular priority to relations with *Papua New Guinea*. The conclusion of a joint declaration of principles in 1987 and the inauguration late in 1988 of the PNG-Australia Ministerial Forum have provided valuable new structures through which to manage the political, strategic and economic interests which Australia and PNG share. We remain extremely careful not to intrude into issues of PNG-Indonesia border relations, which must remain a matter for bilateral resolution between the two countries. We have also made a serious effort — and one which I think is understood and appreciated by both sides — to play a constructive role in encouraging communication and generally helping to reduce tensions.

With *Indonesia*, we have actively sought — with the cooperation of the Indonesian government, and with good results — to re-invigorate relations. Our approach to this diverse and complex country is focused not on constantly taking the temperature of 'the relationship', but rather on getting on with the task of building the relationship, layer by layer. We have paid particular attention to identifying mutual interests and areas of practical mutual benefit. We have given the relationship a new institutional structure which can, among other things, systematically address potential problems in their early stages and help to stabilise what has in the past been a rather volatile association. The establishment of the Australia-Indonesia ministerial meetings, the resumption of senior officials talks, the decision to establish an Australia Indonesia institute, and the conclusion of a full-scale working agreement on the joint development of petroleum resources in the Timor Gap: all of the foregoing add real weight to a relationship which necessarily remains among our most important — and which covers a vast area.

Defence Policy

The corner stone of Australia's defence policy is self-reliance. The main elements are defence in depth, and strategies of early detection, long-range sea and air-strike capability, highly mobile ground forces and the joint operation of communications and intelligence facilities with the United States.

Much of the focus is obviously on regional capability and regional defence cooperation. It is very far removed from the so-called 'forward defence' posture of earlier decades. Today our defence posture emphasises self-reliant forces able to meet unaided, credible threats in our own region, should such threats ever emerge. But our other policies, and our defence policy itself, are designed to manage relationships so that the threats do not arise.

Alliance with the United States remains fundamental in our defence and foreign policies. While our defence policy is one of self-reliance, it is self-reliance within an alliance framework. We have placed a high priority on explaining that we accept the risks of hosting communications and intelligence installations as potential nuclear targets and that the existence of the Australia, New Zealand, United States (ANZUS) Alliance relationship does not absolve us of our responsibility to think and act for ourselves, and to pull our full weight in our own protection.

Australia and others have an interest in, and actively encourage, continued U.S. security, political and economic engagement in the wider Western Pacific area. While the future of the U.S. bases at Subic Bay and Clark is very much a matter for the U.S. and Philippines to resolve bilaterally, we do take the view that their presence has had a stabilising effect in the region, and that their presence or absence will be an important element in encouraging multi-polar equilibrium. We also encourage the view that continuation of a healthy, multi-dimensional, U.S.-Japan relationship is manifestly vital to the stability and progress of the whole Asia-Pacific. At the same time, in the North Pacific—where the U.S. and Soviet Union continue to deploy considerable forces, and where there has been little arms control momentum developed to date—we will continue to quietly encourage the consideration of both sides of measures that could improve the East-West dialogue in the region: such confidence-building measures have worked with good effect in Europe, and we believe they could help to reduce potential tensions, and the risk of miscalculation, in the North Pacific Theatre.

Australia's position in the Asia region is quite distinct. The cultures, traditions and languages of our nearest neighbours are very different from ours. Through the restructuring of our domestic economy and a non-discriminatory immigration policy, we seek to be open to international change. But we have few natural allies and, because of our limited economic and political power, are particularly dependent on the multilateral system. We are a multiracial community but, although in Asia, we are manifestly not an Asian people. We cannot continue to claim respect and acceptance from Asian countries without continuing to demonstrate our right to it—one of the major demonstrations has to be a commitment to racial tolerance.

Two: Pursuing Trade, Investment and Economic Co-operation

The Hawke government, more than any previous Australian government, has brought trade concerns into the mainstream of foreign policy and has abandoned an artificial distinction between trade policy and foreign policy. Our activities in this respect have spread across the full range of bilateral, regional and multilateral relationships.

We have invested enormous effort in the multilateral trade field because we have made the unequivocal judgement that a strengthened multilateral trading regime is far and away the best system for Australia. *We have as one of our very highest foreign policy objectives a successful outcome to the current Uruguay MTN Round—in all fields, including new ones like services and intellectual property, and especially in agriculture.* Through our chairmanship of the cairns group of agricultural traders and through our active involvement in the whole range of GATT negotiations we have sought to increase our influence in the MTN Round. We do not want the field left to the EC and to the USA with whom we strive to identify common interests based on free trade principles. We aim to strengthen the ranks of those who see a liberal multilateral trading system as serving the interests of all nations. For Australia the stakes could not be higher.

Regionally, we believe that greater economic co-operation is an idea whose time has come. A full scale ministerial meeting on APEC is being held in Canberra on November 6 and 7. Ten regional countries plus Canada and the USA will send high level representatives. Those coming are from the 6 ASEAN countries, Japan and the ROK.

The countries of the region are increasingly interdependent, and our economic futures inevitably intertwined. The potential benefits of wider co-operation are essentially threefold: improving the chances of success of the Uruguay Round; further dismantling of trade barriers within the region on a non-discriminatory basis; and capitalising in new and more effective ways—especially in the areas such as infrastructure development—on the complementarities of regional economies.

We stress that we are not interested in any new restrictive trading bloc, nor would any be credible in the diverse context of the Western Pacific.

So far as bilateral relations are concerned, Japan, because it is overwhelmingly our most important trading partner, remains at the top of our priorities. Our exports to Japan are more than two-and-a-half times our exports to our next largest single-country market (USA) and five times our exports to our third largest market (New Zealand).

We do not see relations with Japan in bilateral trade terms only. Both sides are working at developing what we have recently agreed to describe as a 'constructive partnership', extending to co-operation in regional and multilateral economic affairs and on non-trade issues such as the protection of the global environment. This will ensure that as our region and world changes, and particularly as Japan increasingly seeks for itself a more multifaceted international role going beyond its traditional narrowly commercial one, the Australia-Japan relationship continues to adapt and develop.

In our commercial relations with Japan, as with our trading relations elsewhere in the region, we seek to ensure that the structure of our bilateral trade reflects our broader strategy of becoming more fruitfully integrated into the dynamic Asia-Pacific regional economy.

This objective—which is closely linked to economic restructuring at home—is aimed at expanding and diversifying Australia's export base to increase exports of processed minerals, manufactures and services and make us less vulnerable to fluctuations in world commodity prices.

This is a strategy which infuses our commercial dealings with established regional partners like New Zealand, China, Taiwan and the ROK, as well as with what we hope will become important new markets in Thailand and the other ASEAN states, India and, further down the track, we would hope with the states of Indo-China.

Our bilateral trade initiatives have a strong focus on the Asia-Pacific region, reflecting the opportunities there. At the same time the government recognises that North America and Europe are, and will continue to be, very important trading partners for Australia. Our increased efforts in our region should not be seen as a down-grading of our commercial links with Europe and North America. Indeed the opposite is true and we are working actively to expand even further these crucial markets, not least through removal from them of some of the barriers that have limited the access to which our efficiency would otherwise have entitled us.

What Europe 1992 will bring remains to be seen, but currently both the US and European markets remain, for good reason, very attractive to Australian business firms. Far from there being any conflict between our focus on the Asia-Pacific region and our relations with the European Community, much of the future economic interest of European countries in Australia will in fact depend on our economic success— and perceived success—in the Asia-Pacific region. This is simply because success in the region will encourage European firms to see Australia, as we are constantly urging them to, as a congenial springboard for their participation in the Asia-Pacific region.

Three: Contributing to Global Security

Australia makes a very distinctive contribution to global stability through our hosting of the Australia-US joint facilities. These facilities, through their early warning functions and their role in the verification, play a crucially important part in maintaining a system of stable nuclear deterrence.

We have been placing in recent times particular emphasis on the early conclusion of a comprehensive convention to ban all chemical weapons. There is regional as well as global sense in this focus. The competitive introduction of CW/BW would be highly destabilising for the region. Our leading international role on chemical weapons issues is reflected in three major ways: chairmanship of the Paris-based Australia group on export controls; the hosting of the successful international conference in September 1989 which brought together government officials and chemical industry representatives from all over the world to discuss how best to avoid the inadvertent diversion of industry products to the manufacture of chemical weapons; and an initiative in the South East Asian/South Pacific region to increase awareness of the complex issues involved in the negotiation and verification of a chemical weapons convention.

The government has been a staunch advocate of nuclear non-proliferation and of the NPT, which is the single most important—and to date most successful—arms control agreement in existence. We have used our position as a major supplier of uranium to strengthen that non-proliferation regime. Australia took a leading role in the conclusion of the South Pacific Nuclear Free Zone Treaty and we have sought to encourage support for non-proliferation in South Asia and other regions. We have also given a high priority to the early conclusion of a comprehensive test ban treaty which would ban all nuclear tests in all environments for all time: although that endeavour has not yet met with conspicuous success.

Global International Issues

The reality of international interdependence requires global solutions for global problems. There has not been time to look into the implications of these in this short intervention, but the region is deeply affected by threats to the global environment and protection of the ocean environment of special concern to the vulnerable island states of the Pacific, international health problems like AIDS, the international narcotics trade, refugee care and resettlement, the many human rights issues, population growth, the range of debt problems, etc. The region is touched by all of these and more. We should be conscious of their relevance and the scope for trying to manage them.

* This essay is based upon an address by Ambassador Kelso October 27, 1989 in Los Angeles at the 20th Annual Leadership Conference of the Center for the Study of the Presidency.

Article 23

MOTHER JONES   OCTOBER 1989

Rock Dreams

Between Australia's Caucasian and Aboriginal cultures is Ayers Rock, one of the country's most spectacular sites and symbol of its emerging identity struggle.

Robyn Davidson

IN THE BEGINNING, before the world took on its present form, carpet-snake people journeyed from the east and settled at a sand hill containing what they came to call the Uluru water hole. Soon after, a party of venomous snake men came from the west to attack their peaceful settlement. At the close of the battle, Uluru rose up—a monolith bearing all the physical and metaphysical signs of epic destruction. A water hole that now sits at the foot of the Rock came from the blood of a dying carpet-snake man; a fragment of stone is the severed nose of a venomous snake warrior; a large cave was formed from the mouth of a woman weeping with grief for the loss of her son and spitting *arukwita,* the spirit of disease and death, over her enemies.

Thus was created Ayers Rock, one of the most spectacular sites in Australia. For the Pitjantjatjara aborigines, descendants of the ancient carpet-snake people, the Rock, located at the center of a vast tract of desert spreading over three Australian states, forms an axis around which the universe turns. Ethnocentricity perhaps, but when you gaze for the first time at Ayers Rock, floating like Leviathan in a sea of orange sand, it's easy to agree

with them. Uluru, as they call it, is like nothing else on earth.

It rises, isolated and improbable, over a thousand feet above the dunes. From a distance its size is difficult to appreciate, but as you travel closer, its grandeur begins to penetrate your consciousness until, walking around the six-mile base, you are receiving a powerful dose of what Jorge Luis Borges called "the wonder distilled from elementary things." Europeans, who have been on this continent for only two hundred years, also have a special feeling about the place, clinging as they do to anything that enhances a sense of national identity.

Aboriginal people not only come from the land, they are the land. Concepts of ancestor, descendant, country, story line, and ritual art form an eternal continuum. Or, as a Pitjantjatjara elder put it, "This is not a rock, it is my grandfather. This is a place where the dreaming comes up, right up from inside the ground."

I FIRST VISITED ULURU PARK over a decade ago. It was under the control of the Northern Territory government, which promoted state rights and economic development at any cost. The government

was pro-mining, anti-land rights, and decidedly antagonistic toward "southern do-gooders," of which I was one.

During the protest years of the seventies, land rights for aborigines became an article of faith across the spectrum of left and moderate politics. Liberal whites—lawyers, anthropologists, advisers of all sorts—arrived in Alice Springs, about two hundred miles northeast of Uluru, to work for newly formed black organizations. I had gone there to prepare for a journey across Australia by camel, and soon became involved emotionally and professionally in the aboriginal battle for land. But in 1977 it was time to leave politics, along with everything else, behind me. I set out with my camels on a journey that would take me right through Pitjantjatjara country, and that would, years later, provide the materials for my book *Tracks.*

When I first came upon Uluru, I had been walking for two weeks without seeing a soul. Up one sand hill, down another, and on either side of me an infinity of dunes stretching away into blue. I was not looking forward to seeing the Rock, having overdosed on its shape on billboards advertising life insurance and on

T-shirts sold in kitsch shops in Alice Springs. But when I saw that great blue mass shimmering on the horizon, I was spellbound. Uluru was too ancient to be corruptible.

I spent a week there, exploring every cave, fold, and gully of it. There were three small motels at its base, a little shop, and some houses for the rangers. Aborigines lived in humpies just outside the settlement; tourists wandered into those camps taking photographs. I spent another week there before continuing west into blissful emptiness.

In 1983, after eight years of lobbying, the Pitjantjatjara were granted freehold title to the park, which they then leased back to the government. They received a share of the financial benefits of tourism and, more importantly, acquired a majority on the board of management. Since the arrival of Europeans in the area during the early part of the century, the Pitjantjatjara had been forced off their country by ranchers and miners, been employed as virtual slave labor on the great cattle estates, and had their half-caste children taken from them by welfare agencies. They had watched their young men force-marched three hundred miles to prison in neck chains for the spearing of a sheep and seen relatives blinded or killed by the British nuclear bomb tests at Maralinga. In returning the Rock to its original owners, white Australia made a gesture toward acknowledging those injustices. The hand-over ceremony was, by most accounts, very moving despite the outrage expressed in the local press. As one headline put it, "Ayers Rock is white man's dreaming too."

A DECADE IS A LONG TIME TO LIVE WITHOUT experiencing the sand-hill country of central Australia. When a friend came out for a holiday last autumn, I decided to return to Uluru. After getting off the plane, I gave in to nostalgia and pantheism and walked the five miles to Yulara—a village built twelve miles north of the Rock to house tourists, taking the ecological pressure off the Rock and the social pressure off the aborigines who still live at its base. My friend, reluctant to walk such a distance, climbed into a bus along with all the American, Japanese, and German tourists.

The dunes were the color of conch shells, of rosebuds. Thanks to the rain, there were explosions of color everywhere—purple parakeelya, bright yellow grevillea, blue shrubs sprouting scarlet flowers, silky orange trunks of desert poplars, and, furring the ridges of the dunes, pincushions of pale green spinifex. I struggled to the top of a sand hill, and there it was: the Rock, bruise-colored, striped by waterfalls, and capped with gray mist. The rain came down in buckets, but what did it matter? I was in the heart of the world and I was happy.

Until I turned a corner and saw Yulara. This was no village; this was a blueprint town complete with a Sheraton hotel, a mock Greek amphitheater, and tourist-trap boutiques. We rented a car and drove straight to the Rock.

As it swelled before us, the "skin" of the Rock was changing from steel gray to purple to shiny red. We parked the car and stepped out into the freezing wind. The path took us around the western face, past the white line painted up the side of the Rock. By the time I had walked a mile, I was so numb with cold that it seemed perfectly sensible to take off my drenched clothes and plunge into one of the new water holes beneath a cascade thundering down at us from the gods. The water was pure as crystal, and so deep in places that it was bluish black.

After my impromptu swim, we continued walking around the Rock, struggling through the needles of rain until we came to a sign notifying the public that this small fenced-off area was a sacred site closed to visitors. A group of tourists was reading it; one of them crossed the fence and headed off for the cave. I called him back and explained in my most polite voice that the Rock belonged, morally and legally, to the aboriginal people, and that he was their guest and about to break their law. Since he could explore every part of the Rock except two or three tiny sections, I added, why did he feel the need to trespass? He walked on.

I recalled the words of a frail, elderly aboriginal woman who once told me, "When ignorant men go into a women's place, they rape all women—not just us [aboriginal women], but all women everywhere. They ruin everyone with their ignorance."

TOURISM IS NOT A BENIGN INDUSTRY. Unless it is rigorously controlled, it can fundamentally alter the natural environment and adversely affect the host culture that tourists wish to experience. The custodians of Ayers Rock are lucky in many respects: they have the power to veto the use of Uluru. (Recently they turned away a musician who offered enormous amounts of money to make a video on top of it—a new definition of "rock clip.") Even so, many of them are abandoning it for more private settlements out in the desert—away from public display. They worry about and feel responsible for the climbers who fall to their deaths, and they are powerless against the trespassers who blunder about in fertility caves, ignorant of the deep distress this causes.

Eventually, the very element that now attracts so many visitors to Uluru Park— aboriginal culture—could be subsumed by a kind of tourist imperialism; or the Rock itself, the return of which was such an important aboriginal victory, could be taken over by commercial interests after all. As one disgruntled Pitjantjatjara elder put it, "You are money people, with money to burn. You work like hell for money. We work for the land, to look after the land."

All this isn't to say that we shouldn't join the hordes visiting this wonder of the world —only that tourism is full of uncomfortable ironies. Even with the best of intentions, cross-cultural travelers can never be a neutral presence.

Robyn Davidson is an Australian writer living in London. Her latest book is Ancestors, *published this month by Simon & Schuster.*

Article 24   WORLD MONITOR   JUNE 1990

CHINA
ONE YEAR LATER

■

Emperors come and go—even Red emperors.
  But China remains.
  Emperors' calls-to-arms also come and go.
  They leave memorable slogans (Expel the Barbarians; Let One Hundred Flowers Bloom; Combat Spiritual Pollution). But those too pass.
  And TV cameras—the supreme rulers of popular conception—come and go, as they did last June in Tiananmen Square. But daily life goes on.
  In the absence of intense world scrutiny—after camera crews fly off to Eastern Europe, Central America, South Africa—what is happening in China? Who is on stage? Who waits in the wings? What is the mood of 1.1 billion ordinary Chinese?
  The three articles that follow are unusual. The first reveals what big-city Chinese—the talent on which future governments must rely—are thinking and doing. The second is a remembrance from a student now in the US. The third, by China scholar and author Ross Terrill, explains the thinking of China's vast peasantry, the backbone of the nation. These dispatches won't tell you what has happened to gross national product or food markets in the year since the massacre in Tiananmen Square. (That is relatively easy: GNP growth is down sharply from the roaring 10% of recent years, but food supplies are fine.) What the writers do reveal is subtler, deeper. Don't be deceived by their typically Chinese flavor—images of "cutting mountains" and "sea of bamboo." Stick with them and you will understand what moves this greatest single bloc of humanity and why.

BEIJING'S SECRET LIFE

*A Tiananmen survivor looks at a strong
new current behind the façade*

If you looked around Beijing, you would think people were doing nothing but perusing government propaganda statements. Yet if you were observant, you would see rising a huge wave. It is called "cutting the mountains wave" or "wave of cutting the mountains."

The phrase "cutting the mountains" can mean "chatting." Yet in 1990 the word "cut" carries a more trenchant idea of slicing a mountain—a topic of discussion—into two parts with the mouth. The word "mountain" suggests that the scope of our talking is immense.

We cut mountains usually in a group of close friends. We gather in a room with tea, better still if we can manage food. The topic can rise to astronomy and descend to geography. We get so fascinated with our cutting that we forget to sleep, to go to work. At times we even forget who we are. Yet when we disperse we find we are still ourselves, and the real world is still real.

Today's "cutting the mountains wave" is quite different from all previous phases of social behavior since the founding of New China in 1949.

First there was an "INDUSTRIAL WORKER WAVE." The government told us to "learn from the workers" as a frenetic drive began to industrialize. Farmers flocked to the cities to become factory workers. The idea was that we were to sprint toward communism.

The author, who requests anonymity, works in a Beijing government ministry. He was a graduate student when he joined in last year's democracy demonstrations.

All this, alas, ended up in the Great Leap Forward of the late 1950s, which exhausted the people and drained the government coffers.

A "FARMER WAVE" came next. With gongs and drums, intellectuals and young people were sent from the cities to "receive re-education" at the hands of the simple farmers. But hot passion gave way to cold truth: No one wanted to live the life of the farmer, with one's face to the yellow soil and back to the blue sky.

A "SOLDIER WAVE" was born. For village people especially, to go into the army was to kill several birds with one stone. It was a good route to becoming part of a cadre and a member of the Communist Party. Everything was provided free in the People's Liberation Army (PLA), so money could be saved for one's mother and father. After coming out of the army, one generally could exchange rural life for city life.

After the death of Mao and the fall of the "gang of four" in 1976, being a soldier went quite out of fashion. The intellectuals turned from a "stinking"

A Voice from Tiananmen Square

Jinqing Cai's brother, a student in the United States, was watching a television report from Tiananmen Square last spring when he thought he heard his sister's voice addressing the crowd over a loudspeaker. He telephoned their parents in China, found that he was right, and was able to help Jinqing move quickly to escape the Beijing crackdown and join him in the US. She has now completed her first year of study—and star basketball playing—at Wellesley College in Massachusetts. Here she recalls the proudest moment of her life.

Exactly a year ago I was among thousands of students camping in Tiananmen Square, demanding political changes. Buoyed by the extraordinary response of the Chinese people, our emotion was soaring. We thought we had waked up the nation's consciousness and changed the course of China. It was the proudest moment of our lives.

On the night of June 4, 1989, however, tanks and armored vehicles of the People's Liberation Army moved into Tiananmen Square. The "Goddess of Democracy" statue, the symbol of our movement, was smashed amid bloody bodies of demonstrators. So—for the moment—was our dream of pushing China into a democracy.

After the massacre I left Beijing to study in the United States. I consider myself extremely lucky. My fellow students still in China have had to endure the blast of big lies and bear the endless indoctrination by the government. Their future is in serious jeopardy. Most of the students graduating this summer will be sent to outlying factories to "learn from the real experiences," as their predecessors were during the notorious Cultural Revolution of the 1960s.

The fundamental cause of the democratic movement last year was the profound conflict between the government and the people. The one-party monopoly had resulted in astounding abuses of power. Chinese people, usually reserved, had never shown their emotion in such an open way as they did during the democratic movement. Whenever I recall those moments I still cannot hold back my tears.

Though the buds of democracy were crushed before they blossomed, the people's display of courage, confidence, and determination was powerful evidence that the will of the people cannot forever be denied.

As I greet a new spring in a new country, the last spring will be always with me. I remember each day:

• April 22 was the day of despair. We were totally humiliated by the government's refusal of our letter of petition for democratic reforms.

• April 27 was the day of fear mixed with hope. We defied the government's intimidation and walked away from our campuses to demonstrate. We broke countless police blockades and reached Tiananmen Square. For the first time, the government was forced to agree to talk to us.

• May 13, when the students' hunger strike started, was the day beginning the most unbelievable and unforgettable days and nights of my life. My fellow students and I experienced perhaps every possible emotion. We were relieved and gratified over the outpouring of support from the people; desperate over the collapse of hunger strikers one after another; absolutely indignant over the declaration of the martial law.

• June 4 was the night of horror and disbelief. Tanks, helicopters, and machine guns were only for movies. We never imagined we would have to face them in Beijing.

Yet, even with the power of the army, this government is a "paper tiger," since it does not have the trust and support of the people, the ultimate power. As recently as the beginning of this April, the government sent a huge army to close off Tiananmen Square when a letter written by a group of students called for a silent walk in the square during Qing Ming, the Spring Festival, to commemorate the dead.

In the year past, I have grown up. I feel so fortunate to be a part of a new generation that will eventually push China into being a country of democracy and freedom. Chairman Mao once said: "The world is yours, also ours. But it will eventually be yours. You are young, just like the rising sun in the morning. The future is yours."

—Jinqing Cai

element to a "fragrant" element. In the drive for modernization led by Deng Xiaoping, it was said that knowledge was a key ingredient.

So we experienced a "DIPLOMA WAVE." There was a saying, "Master math, physics, and chemistry, and there is nothing under heaven you will not reach."

But the diploma was soon devalued. A lot of incompetents ended up with diplomas. The saying of that time was, "Better to sell tea eggs than to be a professor." And there was another one: "The barber's knife is sharper than the doctor's scalpel."

Deng Xiaoping's policies of reform and the open door brought a deep material and spiritual influence from the West. It made Chinese people realize how poor they were. Poverty gives rise to a burning desire for change. The "diploma wave" gave way to a "BUSINESS WAVE."

If knowledge promised little, going into business seemed to promise much. Like all the other waves, the "business wave" stemmed from a call by the government. Deng said: "It's fine for part of the people to get rich first." Yet, looking back, it's a pity Deng did not say *how* we were to get rich, and *which part* of the populace should be the first to get rich.

In the end, the "business wave" sadly added to the inequity of distribution. Since the Tiananmen massacre, the "business wave" is a thing of the past. For this there are two reasons. People really felt the "business wave" was not the right path. And Premier Li Peng's new austerity policy just makes the business life hopeless.

Today's great "CUTTING THE MOUNTAINS WAVE" serves many purposes. It satisfies our thirst for news. The government blocks the news, which gives us an extra craving to know what is going on. The news each night from VOA (Voice of America) and BBC (British Broadcasting Corporation) is known next morning in the bus, at the workshop, in the office.

News about China is an export that turns into an import—all Chinese people know this. We exchange news about everything, from an inside story about a High Person to information from beyond the Iron Curtain (that is, from outside China), to ideas about making money, to techniques of lovemaking. In our sessions of "cutting the mountains" there is nothing we may not eventually learn.

While we are "cutting" we depart from reality and for a sweet while become men. As we sit there talking, society seems to change in the direction of our dreams.

I believe "cutting the mountains" will eventually promote a change in our sick society. Our activity is creating a new public opinion. There is an ancient saying: "Facing a thousand pointing fingers, he died without any disease." Public opinion can not only put a big shot to "death" but also wreck an organization or stymie a policy.

It was the student democracy movement that made "cutting the mountains" a widespread activity. First people discussed the student democracy movement. Then they supported it. Later came criticism. In the end came terror.

After the Tiananmen massacre, "cutting the mountains" was mainly for grumbling and blaming. But as the wind of change swept Eastern Europe, and especially after the fall of the Romanian boss Ceausescu the grumbling and blaming gave way to analyzing our current situation. We are developing the momentum to "cut" away at our terrible feudal system and our discredited one-party rule. We want to fashion a future for which we take a deliberate responsibility.

Years ago Deng Xiaoping criticized the people for "eating meat from the bowl then attacking the mother that provided it." Later this same mother opened fire on her own sons and daughters. Now, as we respond quietly with "cutting mountains," the government is worried. The propaganda machines are running full tilt to "guide" and "lead" us.

Yet a crucial feature of "cutting the mountains" is that it's safe. The government cannot get a handle on us.

We are realistic enough to know that nowhere in the world is freedom absolute. Yet we also know that we are not fundamentally different from people around the globe. We have a brain to think, a mouth to speak. We have ears, we have eyes.

This sixth wave is totally different from all the others. It was not called forth by the government, and not given any approval by the government. This time you do not see the blind obedience of a people but a quiet revolt.

The "industrial worker wave" led to the Great Leap Forward and much starvation. The "farmer wave" scattered families. The "soldier wave" was no more than a way to escape the hard life. The "diploma wave" went too far and became formalistic. The "business wave" confused people and led to the worship of money. What will the "cutting the mountains wave" bring to the Chinese people?

Mao Zedong said New China had overturned "three big mountains"—imperialism, feudalism, and colonialism. Why are Chinese people still trying to tackle mountains? Perhaps it is because a huge mountain still stands in our path—autocracy!

Our "cutting the mountains" shows that we have not given up the hope to become our own masters. We are trying to actively and subtly and correctly use our brains, mouths, ears, and eyes toward this goal. If we can reach a common understanding, may we not turn our thought into action, leading at last to freedom and democracy?

Indeed the "wave of cutting mountains" is a sign of the consciousness of people of Chinese race. That consciousness is like the rumble that comes before the eruption of a volcano.

A REPORT FROM THE GREAT MAJORITY

In a village nation any 'current emperor' has to worry how he plays in Jiang An

By Ross Terrill

Ross Terrill is a writer and scholar in the field of international affairs. A regular visitor to China, he was there during the student uprising of 1989 and is there now. An earlier trip this year took him deep into the countryside. His books on China include "Mao: A Biography," "Flowers on an Iron Tree: Five Cities in China," and "Madame Mao: The White-Boned Demon."

In the sea of bamboo within Jiang An county in Sichuan Province, on a cliff of orange sandstone, I came upon a grotto of Buddhist statues. Above this natural cathedral of religious art stretched groves of smooth-trunked bamboo, curving together at the top like oversized feather dusters. Below lay a jigsaw puzzle of terraced wet-rice fields, so far away that I felt I was in an airplane.

In conciliatory Chinese fashion there were Taoist figures among the Buddhist, all bearing interesting inscriptions. One sign beside a fearsome Taoist imaginary creature with huge feet and a snarling face read: "With a sharp eye you can look right inside an evil spirit."

The most arresting piece of philosophy on the figurines accompanied a tablet of the nine dragons—a standard Buddhist image: Nine dragons came from the sky to bathe Sakyamuni Buddha after his birth from his mother's right armpit. Dating from the Ming Dynasty (1368-1643), the inscription of dedication read: "To the Emperor of Current Times, Ten Thousand Years, Many Tens of Thousands of Years!" I was intrigued by the blend of religious feeling and shrewd accommodation to political winds. The "emperor of current times" indeed!

That evening in Jiang An county town, the chief magistrate gave a hearty dinner party for me and two companions from Chengdu, the Sichuan capital. I mentioned to the magistrate the tablet of the nine dragons and quoted the 500-year-old inscription. He smiled broadly on learning I had noticed this piece of farmers' wisdom.

"And who is the 'emperor of current times' as of today?" I asked. The chief magistrate of Jiang An tossed back his head and laughed. Recovering his composure, he replied:

"Well, you know, we don't have emperors anymore in China." The whole banquet table quietly chuckled.

What touched everyone, I think, was the aptness and tenacity of the Chinese peasant tradition of doing just enough to satisfy the desire of the supreme leader of the moment in Beijing for loyalty. And the slightly nervous chuckles stemmed from a realization that the tradition goes right on into the 1990s. The inscription on the tablet of the nine dragons served the needs of the times under a dozen

incumbent emperors. It continued to do so in the era of Mao Zedong (1893-1976)—and still does under Deng Xiaoping, today's sagging "emperor."

DIALOGUE WITH NATURE

The power of nature is great in China, and the thinking of rural people encapsulates it. This power derives from the crucial role of harvests; the capacity of rivers' tantrums to adjudicate life and death; the sheer size of China (the Sea of Bamboo is 1,500 miles from Tiananmen Square); and the long corridor of time down which peasant wisdom has evolved in dialogue with the natural order.

Beijing itself is a city designed to relate to the cosmos. It was built to partner the planets and stars. The Temple of the Sun was erected in the east. The Temple of the Moon faced it from the west. To the Temple of Heaven, in the south, emperors went to pray for a good harvest. Still today, the taxi drivers speak more of "east" and "west," than of "left" and "right."

The greatest of Chinese festivals, Qing Ming or the Spring Festival, is a time when the dead are honored. Families clean the graves of their ancestors and put offerings of food on them. At Qing Ming the living and the dead are joined, each needing the other, the one returned to nature, the other reminded of its destiny to return to nature. It was at Qing Ming in 1976 that the honoring of Zhou Enlai, who had died three months earlier, produced the demonstration that turned into a riot and led Mao to dismiss Deng Xiaoping from the government.

In the Sea of Bamboo, Beijing seems far away, though not entirely to be disregarded, while the rivers and mountains and storms are immediate, if not always benevolent. It is rural China in particular that lives with nature's power. Peasant China has twisted many an ideology into a cozier shape. Otherworldly Buddhism from India was brought down to earth by an infusion of Confucian filial piety and Taoist sense of nature. Marxism from Europe was shorn of its linear view of history and given a modest place in the Chinese cyclical view of history.

In the countryside, from the 1930s to the 1950s, Marxism was a useful weapon to undermine landlord power. Thereafter the farmers of China often turned their backs on its pretensions but still bowed a knee on necessary occasions to the Red Emperor of the moment.

MAO, MARX, AND FERTILIZER

Mao himself, raised in a farming family, used nature's imagery in his speeches and writings. "Don't peasants weed several times a year?" he remarked. "The weeds removed can be used as fertilizer."

It was a chilling metaphor for the "weeding out" of unacceptable intellectuals he desired in the Hundred Flowers period—and again in the Cultural Revolution.

The same Mao was alone among world Communist leaders in seeming at times to transcend Marxism. "In a thousand years," he said to Edgar Snow, "won't Marx and Engels and Lenin seem rather ridiculous?" (It would seem a prescient remark to East Europeans today.)

A major significance of the Deng Xiaoping era in Chinese history has been that this flinty anti-Mao appeased rural China. By the end of the 1970s, farmers' faith in the Communist Party was low, and Deng put political necessity ahead of ideology and boldly began to decollectivize the countryside. Even since the Tiananmen massacre a year ago, the Chinese countryside remains a tolerably steady base for Deng. Farmers grumble about prices and slow payment from the government for their grain, but few of them hate Deng as Beijing intellectuals hate him.

Historically, nature was put into the center of Chinese thought not only by Buddhism, Taoism, and (to a degree) Confucianism, but also by the monarchical political theory of successive dynasties. The emperor was called "Son of Heaven." The realm he governed was known as "All Under Heaven."

WEATHER A STATE SECRET

Because the polity was a cosmology, dissent from political orthodoxy was a deviation from nature. Weather reports were state secrets. The emperor's power stemmed from the same source as the power of wind and sun—heaven—and so ruler and weather were presumed to have a special bond.

Rural China is a place where the overriding imperative has generally been to survive, and that explains the naturalistic world view of the individual farmer—and the inscription on the tablet of the nine dragons. Nature's power makes for fatalism, and it makes for what to city people seems like apoliticism.

Mao attached high importance to overturning nature's power. He covered the face of the countryside with red and white political slogans. He set targets for economic growth that blithely disregarded the limits of nature's capacity. He ordered rice planted in the north and wheat in the south, in disregard of rainfall levels and soil quality. He sent city graduates to remote barren areas and told them to create prosperity from nothing, by sheer willpower.

In traditional Chinese painting the landscape dominated and human beings were tiny. By contrast, Mao's Communists sponsored a painting style in which nature receded and burly proletarian heroes loomed from the canvas.

One day years ago I was visiting Yanan, Mao's base prior to his capture of full power. A Communist official, in the course of relating Yanan's rich revolutionary history, said: "Even the mountains were pleased to receive Chairman Mao's telegrams" to various localities during the war against Japan.

COUNTRYSIDE CREDIBILITY

Yet in China today the Communists have partially retreated from the countryside. Replacing Mao's collectivism with family farming more than trebled farmers' income in one decade. The farmers in the Sea of Bamboo live as always between nature and Beijing. But during the Deng era, Beijing's grip loosened, and the natural order and the philosophies flavored by it reasserted themselves. Ironically, Deng's popularity in the villages has nothing to do with the Marxism he staunchly upholds in post-Tiananmen-massacre Beijing.

One dimension of the fate of Marxism in China is that, since the 1970s, it has been ground down, diluted, and outlasted by nature. The farmer sees himself in a functional relation with nature. He has found it harder, much of the time, to see any positive function for the Communist Party in rural China. Communism lost its credibility in the villages long before it lost it in Tiananmen Square.

Amid the bamboo groves of Jiang An county, I lunched with a wealthy farmer named Chen and some county economic officials for whom he is a star of the reform era. After an interview with Chen, who in 1988 made a profit of 20,000 yuan at his bamboo products factory (half went in tax and fees to the government), I was ready to leave when a guide rushed up and said, "Party secretary Li wants to say a word of farewell to you." I had quite overlooked Li, though he had been introduced to me before the copious lunch. Photos in various groupings somehow had not included him.

Secretary Li shook my hand lengthily. He didn't seem to have anything particular to say to me. The guide hissed in English: "He wants a Polaroid picture of himself with you!" Farmer Chen and county economic officials smiled benignly as a photo was taken with my Polaroid camera. At a gala county function the county's party secretary had been an afterthought.

POLITICS IN RETREAT

In rural China, politics has for some years been in retreat. The muscle-power of society and the economy have grown at the expense of the muscle-power of party and state. The party reminds people of failure and yesterday; the new economic forces suggest success and tomorrow.

With Deng Xiaoping at age 85, the politics of succession becomes an inescapable issue. The end of an emperor's reign used to bring uncertainty, often crisis, and in a Communist system the tension is accentuated. No representative elective mechanism exists for a succession to Deng. In China (unlike in India) the farmers do not vote for the top leadership of the country. Mao could not pin down a succession (he chose three successors, and all quickly fell). Can Deng arrange what Mao failed to arrange? Already he has chosen two successors and discarded both.

In the Sea of Bamboo I reflected that for most Chinese, the farmers, it matters who is the supreme leader in Beijing, yet not all that much. Rural society has its own sedate dynamic, evolved over millennia, and Beijing politics seldom cuts its flow.

A portent from heaven is just as likely as an editorial from Beijing to convince farmers of a political point or shift. So it was that the falling to earth of a huge meteorite in northeast China not long after Zhou Enlai's death convinced hundreds of millions of village folk that Zhou was marked as a man whose legend would endure. When a terrible earthquake killed a hundred thousand people at Tangshan a few months later, the disaster was widely seen by rural folk as a portent that Mao soon would die—he died three months later.

"To the Emperor of Current Times, Ten Thousand Years, Many Tens of Thousands of Years!" Guests at the chief magistrate's banquet in Jiang An county smiled at the way tradition encounters the politics of the day, because that protective tradition continues to wear pretty well. China still is a peasant nation, with 80% of its people living in villages, and for as long as it remains so, nature's power will be great over body and mind alike.

Article 25

Focus   Fall 1990

China: The Great Leap to Disaster

or

China: The Great Famine

or

China: The Harvest of Death

or

A. John Jowett

The recent murderous brutality in Beijing was portrayed as China's worst disaster of the past 40 years. The first time the People's Liberation Army had been turned on the people. China's official explanation - "a shocking counter-revolutionary rebellion" - is rated as the biggest lie since the communists came to power in 1949. Yet the massacre of the demonstration for democracy was none of these things. Not the worst nor the first but just the most recent of the disasters which the party has inflicted on the people over the past 40 years.

The People's Liberation Army savagely suppress the call for freedom in Tibet. Sino-Soviet relations rise to the top of the geopolitical agenda. Death and devastation are inflicted on the people of China and the state-controlled media spins its web of misinformation. How history repeats itself. For I speak of 1959 not 1989, when the devastation was nationwide rather than localized, when the disaster lasted for years not days and when the dead were counted not in hundreds or thousands but in tens of millions.

Thirty years ago China was heading for a major disaster. Yet the political rhetoric was pointing everywhere except in the direction of disaster. Mao Zedong was encouraging the peasants to eat as much as they wished. Five meals a day was his offer to the peasants of Hebei. Deng Xiaoping was feeding expectations with his proclamation that per capita grain distribution would be 625 kg in 1958, 1050 kg in 1959 and 2500 kg in 1962. *The People's Daily* noted that a life of abundance in food and clothing, which the Chinese peasants had aspired to for thousands of years, was now within their grasp.

Feast turned to famine

Yet somehow the leadership turned this projected feast into the world's worst famine. By 1960 the nutritional deprivation in China was such that people were eating chaff, grass, tree leaves, bark and roots, wild plants and anything that might keep them alive. Nutritional diseases and disorders, famine oedema, beri beri, night blindness, rickets, and diarrhoeal diseases were widespread. Incidents of cannibalism added to the shame, the guilt, the devastation. In many provinces entire villages were 'deserted and dead' and the countryside was in 'total desolation'. Corpses lay by the roadside, the living were too weak to bury their dead.

ADMINISTRATIVE SUB-DIVISION OF CHINA

Province	GUANGDONG
Autonomous Region	*GUANGXI*
Centrally Administered Municipalities	1 BEIJING 2 TIANJIN 3 SHANGHAI

0   1000km

Yvonne Wilson

Nowadays the combination of advanced technology and China's open door policy have allowed the outside world an armchair view of the butchery in Beijing. Thirty years ago it was very different. No newspaper headlines, no photographs of death and despair, just a veil of conspiratorial silence drawn across this colossal, human-made famine. Indeed for almost a quarter of a century there would be few in the outside world who were aware of the existence, let alone the dimensions of the disaster.

The contemporary view of the London *Times* was that it was a case of malnutrition that nowhere amounted to famine. Others claimed that the well organized administrative structures of the communist regime, in particular an effective food rationing and distribution system plus a greatly improved transport network, meant that few if any starved outright, and the regime averted a major disaster. This optimistic stance was maintained throughout the 1970s and into the 1980s.

Twenty-five years would pass before we got access to the relevant demographic data and were able to assess the magnitude of the disaster. The horror is now apparent. The event which contemporary observers reported as mild malnutrition now ranks as probably the worst famine-related, demographic disaster the world has ever seen. Grain production declined by over 50 million tons which meant that food supplies which in normal times would have fed about 150 million people were missing

in 1960 and the situation improved only marginally in 1961.

The impact of the famine was such, that by 1960 the soaring death rate surpassed the plummeting birth rate and China's population went into decline. Over the four years 1958-61, China suffered some 25-30 million more deaths and experienced some 30-35 million fewer births than might have been expected under normal conditions. Imagine half the population of the United Kingdom dying of starvation and you have a measure of China's misery and misfortune. Such was the severity of the famine that in China as a whole the annual number of deaths rose from 11.5 million in 1957 to a peak of 29.0 million in 1960. Even in the relatively more prosperous coastal province of Liaoning the death rate doubled, in Henan, it trebled, Guizhou registered a fourfold increase, Sichuan suffered a fivefold increase and devastated Anhui was racked by a sixfold increase in mortality.

Under famine conditions the demographic sub-groups exposed to the highest risk of mortality are normally assumed to be infants, children and the elderly. Infant mortality rises as malnutrition increases, as disease becomes more widespread, and as birth weights decline. Current estimates suggest that by 1960 infant mortality may have doubled, rising to almost 300 deaths per 1000 live births, while life expectancy at birth was probably

China, Guizhou Province - rural housing, poverty.

halved, falling to less than 25 years in 1960. The rise in mortality among the young was such that half of China's deaths in 1960 related to children under 10 years old.

The substantial decline in the number of births, down from over 27 million in 1957 to around 14.5 million in 1961, emphasizes the important point that famine is just as severe on fertility as it is on mortality. It is obvious to everyone that famine increases mortality; less obvious, but equally important, is the realization that famine decreases fertility. A variety of physiological, stress and behavioral mechanisms link nutritional deprivation with temporary infertility. In China's case famine-induced infertility meant that the birth rate was halved.

Birth rates dropped: The reasons why
At least four factors contribute to the decline in fertility.

• Severe malnutrition causes a decrease in fecundity (the latent ability to reproduce) because when food consumption falls below a critical minimum level women stop ovulating and therefore cannot conceive.

• Patterns of sexual behavior are substantially changed with a lower frequency of intercourse and an increased level of birth control, the latter achieved through increased contraception, abstinence and abortion.

• Famines are generally associated with large scale migrations as people go off in search of food. Husband and wife are often separated in this process and therefore fertility is lowered.

• Famine conditions are normally associated with the postponement of marriage and that was certainly the case in China. Fewer marriages mean fewer births.

Fluctuation in birth rates and death rates are immediately transmitted to the age structure of a population, as can be seen on the accompanying population pyramid. The rapidly fluctuating number of annual births, trimmed by variable rates of survival, appear as a series of peaks and troughs on the age structure of a population. The severity of the disaster in China's most populous province of Sichuan is reflected in the depth to which the

Jowett

Peoples Republic of China, Guangdong Province - farmer posing for the camera.

demographic scar is incised into the provincial population. At the time of the 1982 census Sichuan had 2.7 million 18 year olds (born in 1964) but only 0.6 million 21 year olds (born in 1961).

The dearth of population in the 20-23 age group, survivors from the reduced number of births in 1959-62, is a clear indication of the extent to which the famine impinged on Chinese levels of fertility and mortality. This missing cohort is generating important social and economic repercussions as it passes through the various stages of life. School rolls, for example, have varied dramatically as these large and small cohorts have moved through the education system. In China as a whole, the 1982 census recorded 19.5 million 24 years olds, 27.4 million 19 year olds but only 10.7 million 21 year olds.

The Great Leap Forward: Mismanaged

The major responsibility for the disaster rests with the monumental mismanagement of Mao's Great Leap Forward (GLF) which was launched in 1958. On the agricultural front the GLF was associated with the arrival of the communes. Instead of rapid advancement, the country suffered a great leap backwards.

The years 1958-60 were characterized by the most exaggerated claims for agricultural output. Foodgrain production was targeted to increase to 525 million tons (Mt) in 1959. We now know that output was only 170 Mt in 1959 and slumped to 143.5 Mt in 1960. Yet the leadership had become mesmerized by their politically inspired production figures.

For almost a quarter of a century there would be few in the outside world who were aware of the existence, let alone the dimensions of the disaster.

Because the claims for foodgrain production in 1958 were so large and the predictions for 1959 were even larger, it was decided to reduce the grain acreage in order to prevent over-production! Between 1956 and 1959 the land sown with foodgrains declined by over 20 million hectares or 50 million acres.

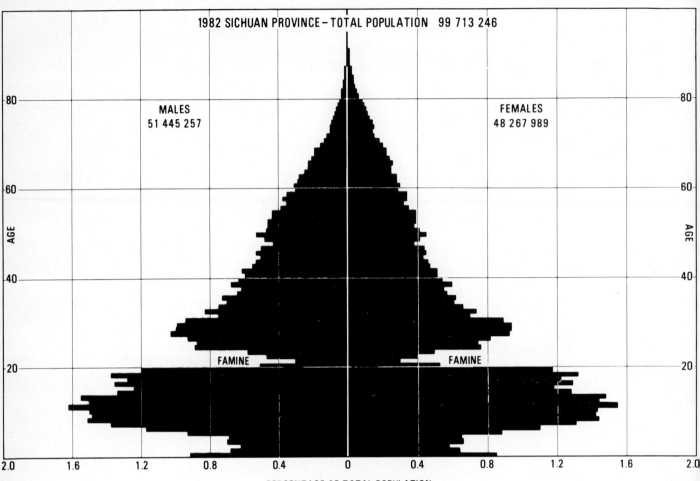

1982 SICHUAN PROVINCE – TOTAL POPULATION 99 713 246

MALES
51 445 257

FEMALES
48 267 989

In addition to the dramatic impact of the famine on China's population, the rapidly tapering base of the pyramid (ages 2-12 at the time of the 1982 census) bears testimony to the dramatic decline of fertility that occured in Sichuan and elsewhere in China, in the 1970s.

The pursuit of massive and rapid industrialization during the GLF, led to the large-scale transfer of labor from agriculture to industry. Government sanctioned a 20% reduction in the agricultural labor force. The notoriously inefficient backyard iron and steel furnaces swallowed up people and materials.

The agricultural sector was drained of both human and animal power. At the time of collectivization many peasants slaughtered their livestock and enjoyed the meat before entering the collectives. The number of draught animals in China declined by almost 20 million. A 50% decline in the pig population dramatically lowered the supply of pork and severely curtailed the supply of organic fertilizer.

China has a labor-intensive, low-technology agriculture. Substantially reduce the inputs of land, people-power and animal power and you inevitably lower the output. And so it was. Between 1958 and 1960 total foodgrain production declined by 56.5 million tons, per capita grain consumption was down by 30 percent and meat almost disappeared from the menu. Famine stalked

the land. Calorie intake declined to the levels currently experienced in the famine-devastated areas of Africa.

Such was the climate of the Cold War that international food aid was neither requested nor delivered. However, food parcels sent through the mail from relatives and friends in Hong Kong soared from 870,000 in 1959 to 13 million in 1961. In the reverse direction a sizeable wave of illegal immigrants flowed from the mainland into Hong Kong. Come 1997 will the United Kingdom allow these people the freedom to once again vote with their feet?

The official Chinese explanation for the disaster is that it arose from the unprecedented bad weather over the period 1959-61. It was one of nature's whims, what the Chinese call *tianzai* or heavenly calamities, which precipitated the 'three years of difficulty'. Yet the weather was by no means as severe as the Chinese claim. The leadership saw the opportunity of diverting the blame for the disaster from human-made to natural causes. If scapegoats were edible what a feast they would make.

East Asia were not devastated by agricultural and demographic disasters. It is difficult to accept that weather problems were precisely confined within China's national boundaries.

Internal opposition to the policies of the GLF was voiced by the minister of defence, Peng Dehuai. A widespread purge was launched against Peng and anyone who shared his views. To survive in opposition in China you need courage, support and luck. Deng Xiaoping, at various times, has had all of these. Peng Dehuai did not. He lost his job, was vilified and never returned. President Liu Shaoqi opposed Mao in the Cultural Revolution. He was tortured to death in 1969. What future will there be for the man currently in opposition, secretary-general, Zhao Ziyang?

Whether one's point of reference is 1959, 1969 or 1989; whether Han Chinese or Ethnic Minorities, one is forced into the uncomfortable conclusion that China's leaders have scant regard for the consequences of their policies and no compunction regarding the use of force to maintain their power and authority. In Deng's own words "bloodshed is a necessary tool in controlling opposition".

Yet amidst the harvest of death are there no straws of hope we might cling to? In 1959, as in 1989, a decade of reforms and development seemed in danger of being cast aside. Yet after three years of turmoil Mao was effectively deposed by an obsessive bridge player and his 'new rightists'. Liberal measures and substantial reforms were introduced. A new economic order got underway. "Whatever style the masses want, adopt that style. What may be illegal, make it legal. By whatever means, produce more food". Is it too much to hope that similar reformers might emerge in the early 1990s to nurture those seeds of freedom and democracy, sown in the spring of 1989?

Unfortunately the obsessive bridge player, who spearheaded the economic reforms in the early-1960s and offered the masses a new world of their own choosing was, believe it or not, Deng Xiaoping. Ah well, the biological time-clock ticks away. The old guard cannot live forever.

Photo of Mao Zedong, overlooking Tian'an Men Square, Beijing.

While it appears that some of the provinces, such as Anhui, Sichuan and Qinghai, suffered far more than the border provinces of Heilongjiang, Inner Mongolia, Xinjiang, and Tibet, the entire country fell victim to the famine.

Given that the disaster was nationwide rather than localized, one tends to conclude that policy failures, rather than weather problems, were the primary cause of the catastrophe. Weather-induced harvest failures within China normally have a localized impact, with some areas devastated while others are virtually unaffected. But if national policies fail then the whole country suffers. It should also be noted that the surrounding countries, Hong Kong, Taiwan, South Korea, USSR, South and South-

(John Jowett, senior lecturer at the University of Glasgow, Scotland, specializes in the geography of China. He is director of the University's Applied Population Research Unit. A visitor to China since 1975, he recently spent six months undertaking population research in the People's Republic. His current research and publications on China are concerned with the demographic impact of famine and with the one-child policy).

Article 26

NEWSWEEK : SEPTEMBER 24, 1990

To Leave or Not to Leave

Where's the 'next Hong Kong'? Business is placing most of its bets on Singapore.

Now faster than ever Hong Kong is swept toward its next incarnation. We are too soon for epilogue ... but I have to say it is not at all unlike contemplating the mysteries of death ...

—JAN MORRIS, "Hong Kong"

On July 1, 1997, the British government will return the world's foremost enclave of unfettered capitalism to the control of one of the world's last remaining communist regimes, the People's Republic of China. The transition is already wrenching. Consider Richard Yung, scion of a wealthy Chinese family and founder of a successful Hong Kong-based electronics firm. He recently contemplated the mysteries of doing business in Hong Kong after 1997. His conclusion? Last week he announced he was moving his company's headquarters to Singapore. Yung is hardly alone. He is, in fact, just the latest in a stream of executives—Chinese and Westerners alike—hedging their bets on Hong Kong's future as the 1997 return to Chinese sovereignty draws closer.

To leave or not to leave is the question asked daily, not only by the hundreds of Hong Kong citizens who line up at embassies seeking visas, but by scores of business executives in the crowned colony of capitalism. Already suffering from the colony's intensifying brain drain and haunted by the uncertainties 1997 poses, more than 70 companies have moved their headquarters out of Hong Kong since 1985. They include the regional headquarters of multinational corporations like Union Carbide and giant financial institutions like Chemical Bank. "Everyone talks about whether to leave or not," says one high-ranking American banker in Hong Kong, "and prudence

dictates that you at least consider it. But the question is, where do you go?"

The answer, more and more frequently, is Singapore, 1,600 miles southwest across the South China Sea. According to many analysts in Southeast Asia, its quiet but persistent efforts to step into the commercial void left by a Beijing-controlled Hong Kong has already made Singapore the principal commercial hub of the world's most dynamic economic region. Its success, moreover, has spawned similar efforts by Southeast Asia's other fledgling commercial centers, most prominently Bangkok and Taipei, the capitals of Thailand and Taiwan, respectively. Though their officials would never say it so bluntly, both cities believe that they, too, can reap opportunity from Hong Kong's anguish, siphoning off business if things go seriously sour come 1997.

HONG KONG The question is, when the British flag comes down, what businesses will be left?

For now and the foreseeable future, Singapore remains the prime choice for companies bailing out of Hong Kong. On the surface that seems an incongruous choice. The two cities could hardly be more different. Prime Minister Lee Kuan Yew's Singapore is as tightly ordered as Hong Kong is frenetically chaotic. Wide, palm-tree-lined highways and avenues move traffic along smoothly. Pedestrians wait patiently for

traffic lights to change before crossing the streets, lest they get nailed with an $11 jaywalking fine. The streets themselves look clean enough to eat off, thanks to the prospect of a $50 fine for littering. Undercover police patrol the subway, fining commuters for eating. Another law requires that public toilets are flushed.

Real problem: Of more concern to executives, though, is what critics see as the government's inclination to tinker with the free flow of information, the engine that drives open markets. Most significantly, Singapore closely restricts the circulation of The Asian Wall Street Journal, the result of a bitter legal battle in the Singapore courts between the prime minister and Dow Jones & Co., the Journal's majority owner. A banker whose firm has considered but rejected moving operations to Singapore says the government's restrictions on the Journal amount to a "competitive disadvantage. The flow of information there is a real problem." Singaporean officials contemptuously dismiss those complaints. "We're not that concerned that some bankers can't check on what their own stock portfolios did first thing in the morning," says Yeo Seng Teck, chief executive officer at the Singapore Trade Development Board. "There are no restrictions on the flow of information here."

Indeed, in the minds of many Singaporean government officials and businessmen, the question of the "next Hong Kong" has already been decided. If the title means the trade and finance capital of Southeast

SINGAPORE The country is tightly controlled but already is a leader in trade and finance.

TAIPEI
Taiwan's capital is a commercial center in a fast-growing economy. Basic services? Forget it.

Asia, Singapore, as far as they're concerned, is already it. They have some impressive evidence to back up the claim. In currency trading, for example, Singapore has already outstripped Hong Kong and trails only Tokyo in all of Asia. In trade, Singapore this year also surpassed Hong Kong as the leading container port in Southeast Asia, thanks in part to a government effort that has fully automated all customs procedures. That typically forward-thinking step means paperwork that takes shipping companies hours in Hong Kong now takes only minutes in Singapore.

Since 1986, the Trade Development Board has lured more than 30 multinational companies (not all from Hong Kong) by offering a generous array of incentives. Not surprisingly, there is a full-time Singapore Trade Development Board office in Hong Kong, devoted mainly to greasing the way for edgy corporations to move. Says the TDB's Teck: "Why do companies come to Singapore? The reason is there is a total symbiosis between government and business. There is no divergence at all. For us it is very simple, very clear. All we want to be is very competitive and very successful."

Some Hong Kong administrators don't believe Singapore's constant assurances that it is refraining from specifically targeting business in Hong Kong. Nonetheless, the belief that it's doing exactly that is clearly beginning to grate. "Singapore is playing with our future," charges Paul Cheng, a Hong Kong businessman. According to one bank study, only 35 Hong Kong Chinese citizens have so far opted to move to Singapore. Jack So, head of Hong Kong's Trade Development Council, delivers what may be the ultimate insult, by Hong Kong standards: "You can't make big money there."

Less formidable but no less ambitious at the moment are government planners in Bangkok and Taipei. Their cities are the commercial centers of rapidly growing economies, and both "now speak dreamily of one day taking over Hong Kong's role as the gateway to China and regional financial center," says Robert Broadfoot, a political-risk analyst in Hong Kong.

Phone calls: Is that rhetoric realistic? For now, no. Both cities have become victims of their own success. Basic mundane services—getting from one place to another in

BANGKOK
It's a nice place to visit, but many businesses may not want to go there.

a reasonable amount of time, having phone calls go through, transmitting computer data over phone lines—remain naggingly real aggravations. In both places, growth quite plainly has outstripped both governments' abilities to manage it effectively.

Not even Bangkok's exotic reputation as a place that offers a shot at big money during the day and an anything-goes atmosphere at night helps much anymore. To any number of managers who have evaluated it recently, Bangkok is a nice place to visit, but you wouldn't want to locate there. "If your idea of doing business is sitting in a monumental traffic jam inhaling exhaust and missing your appointments all day, then by all means, come on down," says one British banker. As for Taipei, says one currency trader in Hong Kong—cruelly—"it's not even a nice place to visit."

For Hong Kong executives voting on the colony's future with their feet, then, Singapore's efficiency and political stability dwarf its reputation for Big Brother-style regulations and boredom. That by itself should send a message about Hong Kong's plight to Beijing, but it probably won't register as loudly as Richard Yung's decision to bail out last week did. Yung's uncle is the chairman of an agency called the China International Trust and Investment Corp. (CITIC). His cousin Larry Yung is CITIC's highest-ranking representative in Hong Kong. And CITIC, based in Beijing, is the overseas investment arm of the government of the People's Republic of China.

BILL POWELL *and* PETER McKILLOP

Article 27　　　THE CHRISTIAN SCIENCE MONITOR　　August 14, 1990

Indonesian Rebellion Defies Jakarta's Rule

Long-standing bitterness toward the central government and growing Muslim militancy fuel revolt by fiercely independent Acehnese

By Sheila Tefft
Staff writer of The Christian Science Monitor

ALULHOK, INDONESIA

STUNNED and angry, the Acehnese villagers milled near shuttered shops beside the deserted main road.

Just a half hour before, a farmer was shot and wounded while fleeing from patrolling Army troops. Villagers said that the military crackdown in Aceh (pronounced "Achay") was deepening their long-standing bitterness toward the central government in Jakarta.

JOAN RAPAPORT – STAFF

"The Acehnese will not obey the republic. We must free Aceh from the republic," said a local resident, who claimed the wounded man was involved in antigovernment politics.

"They have promised many things, but the people do not get them. We don't want to live under colonialism."

A shadowy rebellion is gripping Aceh, for years a center of defiance in the tumultuous Indonesian archipelago. Aceh is also a mainstay of Indonesia's economy. In recent months, about 80 people have been killed, most of them soldiers and Javanese settlers, who symbolize central rule to the fiercely independent Acehnese.

Motives for the ongoing uprising are murky. The government links the violence to common criminals involved in the area's thriving marijuana production.

Also suspect are about 40 disgruntled soldiers discharged last year for indiscipline in a military crackdown on the drug trade.

But Indonesian and foreign observers say the violence draws on Aceh's long-standing restiveness and opposition to Jakarta and Javanese dominance of the central government.

Aceh has a long history of rebellion. The Dutch, who colonized Indonesia for its spice trade, battled the Acehnese for four decades before conquering them earlier this century.

Since Indonesia won independence in 1949, resource-rich Aceh has been both a thorn in the side of Jakarta and a key contributor of export earnings from oil and gas.

Positioned at the head of the strategic Strait of Malacca, Aceh was the first foothold for Islam in predominantly Muslim Indonesia. Today, its residents practice a form of Islam more orthodox and intense than that of the rest of the country.

"The Acehnese resent any outsider," says a Sumatran businessman who worked in Aceh for years. Aceh's religious fervor and

and palm oil from the province, but gives little in return. The best jobs and land go to outsiders, particularly the Javanese, they say.

In the 1970s, an independence movement led by a group called Aceh Merdeka or Freedom for Aceh spread but was crushed after the death of its top leaders. People in Aceh revere the militants as martyrs.

Today's trouble is reviving that movement, some observers say. Recently, an extremist group called the National Liberation Front Aceh Sumatra has claimed responsibility for the deaths of 30 soldiers. Buses and settlements of

Aceh's religious fervor and the potential militancy of Islamic leaders have long worried Jakarta, which fears the emergence of a more fundamentalist and politicized Muslim population.

the potential militancy of Islamic leaders have long worried Jakarta, which fears the emergence of a more fundamentalist and politicized Muslim population.

The Indonesian government, which relies on Aceh's oil and gas operations for badly needed export dollars, has crushed periodic separatist outbreaks.

Acehnese contend the government takes oil, gas, wood, rubber,

Javanese immigrants have been attacked, sending thousands fleeing. "It's not all independence. It's also religion and economics," says a Western diplomat, who sees the violence as a cyclical outbreak rather than a serious threat.

In recent months, however, the Army has rushed 5,000 crack troops to the area. Acehnese say there have been house-to-house searches and many arrests. Curfew has been imposed in Banda Aceh, the main town, and authorities, who for weeks refused to publicly acknowledge the trouble, talk openly of Acehnese guerrillas.

The daring daytime attacks and sophisticated automatic weapons of the extremists have fueled rumors of outside help from Libya or other Islamic countries.

"In the past, this problem resulted in only isolated cases of violence because there was no support from the local population. This time it's much better organ-

ized," says a foreign diplomat familiar with the insurgency.

"The problem is more complex than the government is saying," he continued. "The government and military seem to be getting control." But heavy-handed measures by the military are fueling resistance, Acehnese say. Military officials in Medan and Jakarta were not available for comment.

Recently, a group of oil exploration workers hurried for cover when two truckloads of soldiers pulled up beside their cluster of

ramshackle tents. At gunpoint, a soldier confiscated film of a foreign photographer. "We are afraid they will arrest us or shoot us," says one of the workers. "We feel fearful of the Army and the Acehnese."

The trouble is starting to slow the local economy. There have been explosions near the natural gas facilities at Lhokseumawe. Prices have been rising, fishing is being disrupted, and Javanese settlers working on palm-oil plantations are leaving their jobs and deserting their settlements.

Article 28

MULTINATIONAL MONITOR

OCTOBER 1990

UPROOTING PEOPLE, DESTROYING CULTURES
Indonesia's transmigration program

By Carolyn Marr

Carolyn Marr works in London on a project, managed by Survival International, which monitors environmental and development issues in Indonesia.

DESPITE OBJECTIONS by human rights and environmental organizations, the Indonesian government and the international lending community defend and continue the controversial transmigration program which moves poor farming families from the crowded islands of Java, Bali and Madura to less densely populated islands of the archipelago. Human rights organizations charge that the program destroys indigenous communities, and environmentalists focus on its ecological devastation, including deforestation. The Indonesian government dismisses these concerns, arguing that transmigration is necessary to reduce overpopulation and develop undeveloped territories, and asserting that everyone benefits from the program.

The government claims that families participating in the transmigration program do so voluntarily. Indeed, as its supporters describe it, the government's offer is very attractive. In theory, participants receive two hectares of

land, a house and the basic necessities which enable them to build new, more prosperous lives in settlements with schools, health facilities and access to markets. The conditions in which transmigrants actually live, however, are less appealing. They are sent to Sumatra, Kalimantan (Indonesian Borneo), Sulawesi, the Moluccas and most controversially, the disputed territories of West Papua (referred to as "Irian Jaya" by the Indonesian government) and East Timor where the land is infertile and there are few or no facilities. Most find their living conditions worse than on their native islands.

There is little public criticism of transmigration within Indonesia, where the government ruthlessly suppresses democratic organizations and press freedoms and imposes harsh prison sentences on those who dare question Indonesia's presence in those disputed territories. President Suharto's 25-year-old military regime tolerates no dissent.

Millions of people have already been resettled under transmigration, the world's largest resettlement program. And the program is growing rapidly. According to official data, between 1950 and 1986, 698,200 families (about 3.5 million people) were moved, most of them to Sumatra. In 1985, Indonesia intensifed the program and announced a five-year transmigration target of 750,000

Savunese people

families (3.75 million people). When critics voiced objections, the transmigration department backtracked, saying, "We are realizing that it may now be impossible to achieve this ambitious target, because of unpredictable budgetary constraints and related problems." Nevertheless, the lack of funds was overcome by encouraging the participation of self-financing transmigrants. The target for the current five-year plan (1989-1994) is 550,000 families (2.5 million people), requiring an estimated 4.5 million hectares of land.

Population transfer or territorial management?

In 1987, Indonesia's Ministry of Transmigration claimed, "Transmigration is the name of the Republic's bold program to help spur the development of the sprawling island nation and give its poorest families the chance to own their land and significantly improve their living standards." It went on to list the aims of the resettlement program: to encourage development; raise living standards; generate new jobs; increase food and tree crop production; relieve population pressure; control environmental degradation; and foster greater national interdependence.

In fact, internal documents of the government's transmigration department acknowledge that transmigration does not achieve its publicly stated goals: it makes virtually no dent in the population pressure on Java and it exacerbates the country's environmental degradation instead of reducing it, as forests are destroyed to make way for the new sites.

The Transmigration Ministry does not mention, however, one of transmigration's most important goals: national defense and security. The World Bank makes the same omission in its justifications for continued funding. But at home, Indonesian officials have been very clear about it. In 1989, for example, Defense Minister General Murdani said that transmigration is not only concerned with population redistribution but is "related to the importance of territorial development," which means "spreading out human resources as a defense and security potential." Transmigration Minister Lieutenant General Soegiarto also included strengthening defense and security when he described the program's purpose. In practice, this means resettling ethnic Javanese in sensitive border areas. The government also plans to populate border sites with retired army personnel. One such settlement was established in 1986 on the island of Natuna, located in the China Sea between Borneo and Vietnam. And according to the head of the provincial transmigration office, 500 retired army families will soon be sent to the Malaysian border in West Kalimantan.

Voluntary?

Transmigration promoters say the program is voluntary. But an official in the province of Aceh described transmigrants as "poor people who were thrown out of

194

Java like rubbish." Indeed, some of those who end up at transmigrant sites, including beggars and vagrants, have been rounded up in some of the larger cities and bundled off to transmigration sites. One site established especially for this category is on the island of Buru, where thousands of political prisoners were sent in the wake of President Suharto's 1965 anti-communist reign of terror.

As part of a campaign to "modernize" Jakarta, government officials confiscated the vehicles of the becak (trishaw) drivers who throng the streets of many Javanese cities, and sent the drivers to start new lives as farmers on other islands. Some families join the ranks of transmigrants after natural disasters such as floods and volcanic eruptions destroy their land, while others — such as the familes displaced by the World Bank-funded Kedung Ombo Dam in Central Java — are coerced into joining to make way for large-scale development projects. In Gresik, a major industrial zone of Java, people living on land earmarked to accommodate the expansion of a chemical plant have been offered transmigration as an escape from the increased pollution.

But the bulk of transmigrants are drawn from landless and poor farmers. On Java, where 60 percent of Indonesia's population lives on only 7 percent of the total land area, the population density is one of the highest in the world. Still, industrial and tourist projects gobble up more and more land, exacerbating the land squeeze and accelerating the marginalization of poor farmers. Transmigrants are lectured about the scarcity of land in Java and Bali as a justification for transmigration, while big business interests with ties to the Suharto family announce plans for luxury tourist resorts, golf courses, industrial estates and chemical complexes. Transmigration is primarily a "safety valve," designed to defuse pressure for the redistribution of land and for political change.

A catalogue of failures

A recent survey by a French consultant found that 80 percent of sites fail to improve the living standards of transmigrants. Even Indonesia's Transmigration Minister, Lieutenant General Soegiarto, admits that conditions in 903 sites throughout Indonesia concern the government. Similarly, the World Bank acknowledged this year that the expectation that transmigrants would raise their household incomes through the introduction of cash crops has not been met. The Bank reports that agricultural support services and supply of inputs are "inadequate;" access roads are "of poor quality and inadequately managed;" and the general management and coordination of the program is "weak."

The Indonesian daily, *Kompas*, recently outlined the problems faced by transmigrants on one of the earliest sites. Settlement began in Kurik, in the southern part of West Papua, even before the territory had been officially incorporated into Indonesia. Here, where the soil is rockhard in the dry season and waterlogged in the wet seaseon, the meager crops that can be grown are likely to be devoured by pests.

Women usually fare worse than men when families transmigrate; they have no part in the decision to transmigrate, and they receive no training or preparation for the move. Typically, the men are forced to leave the site, often for months at a time, to find work after the government support has run out. The women must stay behind to tend the plot and look after the children. Kurik, however, was an exception. There the women left the site — with the blessings of their husbands—to become prostitutes in the town.

Many transmigration sites have been abandoned altogether. One woman, living in makeshift accommodations in the provincial capital after leaving a settlement, says "the land was too acidic to grow crops and there were so many mice." She and other "failed" transmigrants eke out a living as rubbish recyclers. Others live on the rubbish dump itself. These people are not calculated in the rate of return to Java, which signifies the failure of the program and which is officially at least 15 percent.

Government spending on transmigration was cut during the mid-eighties slump in the price of oil, Indonesia's major foreign exchange earner. Falling revenues from the oil sector and the spiraling foreign debt left fewer funds for the program. A plan to save money by encouraging transmigrants to pay their way to the site (370,000 of the current 550,000 families target is for these so-called "spontaneous" transmigrants) was introduced and the program was directed away from the original food crop model to state-run or private plantations and processing projects for export.

Transmigrants working on these projects, which were first introduced in the mid-eighties, are given a house and 0.25 hectares for growing subsistence foods and are required to work on a plantation as wage laborers. After a number of years, the transmigrants are supposed to gain ownership of plantation plots and from then on sell their produce to a processing plant. In reality, projects rarely reach this stage; instead transmigrants are exploited as cheap labor.

The government responds to the failure of many sites by blaming the transmigrants themselves. Last year, Vice President Sudharmono told transmigrants in South Kalimantan who appealed to him for funds to improve their site that they should use their own skills and resources. "Don't rely only on the government and don't wait for divine intervention to overcome your problems," he said. Sudharmono surely would not approve, however, of the increasingly popular survival tactic which the transmigrants have developed on their own: familes register as transmigrants, receive free government supplies for the six-month period, and then sell their land, return to Java and re-register as transmigrants to begin the whole cycle again.

Transmigrants as colonists

The families which are thrown out of Java and Bali are not the only ones to suffer. The indigenous communities and the environment at the transmigration sites are also victims of the program.

The government claims that the islands are appropriate sites for the new settlements because they are "virtually empty" or "underpopulated." But it is no accident that the population density is lower than in Java; the rainforests there cover thin soils which cannot sustain intensive agriculture without the massive and unsustain-

Indonesian President Suharto.

The notion that indigenous people are "backward" and "primitive" informs the policy of the Social Affairs Ministry, the government ministry reponsible for their interests. If not relocated directly on transmigration sites, many communities are resettled in transmigration-style accommodations locally, under the development program for "isolated tribes."

As "local transmigrants," they are expected to learn what are considered advanced agricultural techniques from the Javanese newcomers, whose intensive farming methods are generally not suited to the vastly different soils and climatic conditions of the islands.

The prejudice against traditional forms of agriculture runs deep; the government blames shifting cultivators for forest destruction despite the fact that they have used the land in a sustainable manner for generations. The same prejudice is found in the international community; before leaving to take up his post as U.S. ambassador to Indonesia, John Monjo told the Committee on Foreign Relations that some of the residents of West Papua, "are virtually stone-age people ... [who] might do better" if they were able to live with Javanese and Balinese transmigrants who are "fairly advanced in their farming techniques."

Indigenous communities regard transmigration as a major threat. In the submission to the UN Working Group on Indigenous Peoples, the Netherlands-based West Papua *Volksfront* said, "it is because of the transmigration projects and activities of transnational corporations that Papuans are forced to leave their ancestral homeland. ... Jakarta's homogenizing approach to development, i.e. the creation of a centralized state, poses a threat to the lifestyle and culture of the Papuans and therefore creates antagonism and social unrest."

The World Bank — propping up transmigration

Despite the plethora of criticisms and problems, the World Bank has invested a total of US$500 million in the transmigration program since 1976. Campaigners have long sought to pressure the World Bank and other donors to withdraw their support, but the money keeps rolling in. In response to criticism, the Bank has limited its funding to the improvement of existing sites. But this simply enables the Indonesian government to spend more of its transmigration funds on establishing new resettlement sites.

Indonesia also collects large amounts of bilateral support for the program. Canadian funds are directed to transmigration in Sulawesi. German money funded a transmigration site improvement scheme in East Kalimantan, and Japan donated tractors and pesticide sprayers for sites in Sumatra. The UK government Overseas Development Administration has carried out a land satellite mapping project to identify suitable sites for transmigration.

Cheap labor

With the support of the World Bank, the Indonesian government is relying more heavily on transmigration as a component of its efforts to develop the non-petroleum sectors of the economy. Transmigrants are increasingly used as cheap labor, just as Javanese were exploited by the Dutch colonial administration under *kolonisasi*, the fore-

able use of fertilizers. The indigenous peoples of these islands have evolved strategies to live in and from the forests without destroying them, but they are being displaced by transmigration settlements. They are losing their land because the Indonesian government refuses to recognize their traditional land rights. And their indigenous cultural heritage is threatened with extinction by the large influx of outsiders.

Some indigenous groups have responded militantly to the invasion of their territory. A government official in Aceh expressed particular pity for transmigrants who he said had been "thrown out of Java," and were now being chased out of Aceh too — in fear for their lives. A recent upsurge of separatist violence in the province, where, alongside the military and police, transmigrants have come to symbolize Javanese domination of this fiercely Islamic region, has prompted thousands of settlers to abandon their sites. The violence is partly inspired by Acehnese opposition to the large mining, gas, oil and pulp and paper projects which are exploiting Aceh's resources but which are controlled by Jakarta. Many Javanese transmigrants in Aceh have returned to Java with all their portable possessions to escape attacks by the Free Aceh Movement.

Attacks on transmigrants have also been reported at the Arso transmigration site close to the Papua New Guinea border in West Papua, where the transmigration program is widely seen as a direct attempt to outnumber the indigenous inhabitants. The indigenous people's resentment is justified; outsiders identify their traditional land as suitable for transmigration, clear their forests, destroy their sacred sites and deny them their basic needs. Then the government gives them the "choice" of joining a transmigration site where they will live as a minority group.

runner of the transmigration program which procured labor to work on plantations in Sumatra. Two hundred thousand families are destined for plantations under the current five-year plan. The transmigration department also plans to send 40,000 transmigrant families to work on new-style timber estate projects, 90,000 to fisheries and 40,000 to tertiary industries.

How successful these plans will be is uncertain. In March, transmigrants working on an oil-palm estate in Central Sulawesi protested about wages too low to buy basic necessities, and in East Kalimantan hundreds of transmigrants abandoned their sites to seek work elsewhere, as they could no longer survive on the wages paid by the company.

More certain are the effects of plantations, timber estates and other massive development projects on indigenous communities, since they deprive indigenous people of their subsistence resources. Recently, yet another product was made available for commercial exploitation. Sagindo Sari Lestari, a company owned by Indonesia's most powerful timber tycoon, Bob Hasan, has been licensed to process sago — a staple food of many indigenous peoples — for export from a 45,000 hectare concession in Bintuni Bay, West Papua. The government will bring 200 transmigrant families to the site to work for the company.

International parallels

Indonesia garners support for the resettlement program from many countries which have implemented similar plans. In a recent meeting with Transmigration Minister Soegiarto, Japan's ambassador to Indonesia praised the transmigration program and likened it to Japan's own scheme to resettle its northernmost island, Hokkaido, in the last century. Indonesia has also drawn parallels between transmigration and the homesteading program of the western United States a hundred years ago. Officials say the United States was "knitting together a continent and developing underutilized land into one of the most productive areas of the world." But these complimentary comparisons fail to point out that in each case, resettlement was achieved at the expense of indigenous people — the traditional owners of the land. Like the indigenous Ainu of Hokkaido and the Native American communities in the United States before them, the indigenous people of the Indonesian islands are in danger of annihilation. ∎

Article 29

WORLD PRESS REVIEW
● FEBRUARY 1990

Lurching Toward Democracy in Seoul

Still a lack of respect for opponents' opinions

Le Monde

By PHILIPPE PONS

The Berlin Wall has become porous, but the 38th parallel cutting Korea in two—the last vestige of the cold war—remains impermeable. While the North treads water in the name of the ideology of self-sufficiency, the South is crowning its economic success with political liberalization. But that liberalization remains vulnerable: Shifting from a military regime to a democracy is no simple matter.

The No. 2 industrial power in the Far East, after Japan, South Korea has been going through a difficult transition to democracy during the past three years. It is realizing that it is perhaps easier to crash the gates of prosperity than to move from authoritarianism to a more open system.

Too lenient for some and too repressive for others, South Korea's President Roh Tae Woo is entering the second half of his term in office with one thing to his credit: a remarkable revolution of the country's political system. Parliament has been given powers that it can actually use, and a working multi-party system has been set up. Moreover, the idea of an independent press is now accepted, and freedom of expression is generally respected. Finally, the government has to some extent stopped abusive practices in law enforcement, although the opposition claims that there are still more "prisoners of conscience" than there were during the days of the former president, Gen.

From the liberal "Le Monde" of Paris.

Chun Doo Hwan. But Roh has a long way to go before he fulfills all of the promises he made upon election in 1987.

Concerned with disorder, the government has resumed a strong-arm approach to containing dissent and social ferment, which disrupt production and endanger the competitiveness of industrial exports. Specifically, Roh's government has been reining in the dissent that followed his announcement in July, 1989, that South Korea would open up to the socialist countries, including North Korea. This policy was made to insure that the government controls dialogue with the North—a blow to the militant minority in South Korea that feels strongly about reunification.

The dividing line between legitimate governmental authority and authoritarianism seems easily blurred in this country, which, since its liberation from Japan after World War II, has known only strong-man regimes. Because of its history and culture, and thanks to the very high level of education it has achieved, South Korea stands apart from the Third World. But what it lacks at the moment—and this holds true especially for its politicians, majority and opposition—is one of the working principles of democracy: respect for the opinions of one's opponent.

The blossoming of a panoply of publications should contribute to accustoming South Koreans to debating ideas. But a history marked by sharp divisions, the civil war, the partition of North and South, and the current effervescence following years of repression is not conducive to such change. It is more conducive to radicalism. This applies, for example, to labor-management disputes. Workers feel, not unreasonably, that they have borne the brunt of growth for too long and now want to be compensated for it with better working conditions, working hours, and salaries. Their aggressive impatience is not allayed by the attitude of management, which strives to maintain authority.

South Korea is also in the throes of deep social change. Two-thirds of the population has grown up in a country whose economic growth was driven by a generation that had lived through war and poverty. The generation born after the Korean war makes up the urban middle class. These young people are avid consumers, and they demonstrated with the students in 1987 against Gen. Chun's authoritarianism and forced the government to set a course for reform.

The urban middle class was comfortable with Roh's apparent enlightened conservatism, and benefited from reform—from freedom of expression and improved purchasing power. Today, the middle class is probably torn between the fear of social instability, which could endanger its prosperity, and the disappointment of seeing a return to authoritarian ways.

Roh's government is steering a narrow course, seeking to muzzle the opposition and, in some measure, to lessen social inequalities. (A system of social security has been in force since last July.) But the government seems to have backtracked from the policy of tolerance that it pursued until mid-1988. Under pressure from an increasingly influential right wing, is the government inching toward a form of neo-authoritarianism? That is a delicate political option faced by President Roh in the second half of his term. ∎

Article 30

THE ECONOMIST
AUGUST 18 1990

SOUTH KOREA
Good to be big, better to be good

COMPARE Korean business with that of Hongkong, Singapore and Taiwan, and one difference glares out: economic concentration. Whereas the other newly industrialising countries (NICs) have grown mostly as a result of the efforts of small or middle-sized companies, South Korea has not. Its economic power is concentrated in fewer hands, and its present success is the triumph not of thousands of entrepreneurial minnows but of a handful of big-business fish. Ten of the country's firms are responsible for more than half its exports.

This is no accident. Korea's last military dictator but one, Park Chung Hee, made up his mind in the early 1960s that the way to make his country rich was to favour a few companies with carefully channelled credit and subsidies. In return for those favours, he asked a lot: those few firms had to meet the government's expectations. Sometimes they were given export targets; sometimes they were even told which new businesses to go into.

Civil servants under President Park followed these policies until his assassination in 1979; under President Chun Doo Hwan, they continued them until 1988. Economists still argue about whether Korea's spectacular economic success in the past three decades was a result of those industrial policies, or whether it was achieved despite them. Two things, though, are inescapable.

One is that Korea now has a number of business groups, or *chaebol*, so big that they are comparable in size to their strongest competitors in Japan, America and Europe. The four best known are

Hyundai, Lucky-Goldstar, Samsung and Daewoo; but six others had sales last year of over $3.5 billion.

The other is that as the *chaebol*'s profile has risen abroad, their popularity has fallen at home. The big firms and their founders are respected, it is true. Who could fail to admire Mr Chung Joo Yung, honorary chairman of the Hyundai group, who worked himself up from manual labourer to the owner of the world's biggest shipyard? Or Mr Kim Woo Choong, a turn-around merchant who built

The top ten		
Sales, 1989	won bn	$bn
Samsung	21,894	32.6
Hyundai	17,284	25.7
Lucky-Goldstar	13,304	19.8
Daewoo	9,523	14.2
Sunkyung	6,048	9.0
Ssangyong	4,164	6.2
Kia	3,039	4.5
Lotte	2,829	4.2
Hanjin	2,772	4.1
Hyosung	2,343	3.5
Source: James Capel		

the Daewoo group from a series of apparently hopeless acquisitions, and whose recent book, "It's a Big World, and There's Lots to be Done", has sold more than 1m copies in Korea?

Yet many Koreans feel that the government's life-and-death power over big business has been an invitation to corruption. In one famous case in 1985, the Kukje group, then Korea's seventh-largest company with almost 40,000 workers and sales of $1.5 billion, went bust for reasons more to do with politics than with business. In countless other cases, radical Koreans say, the relationship between government and big business has been far too cosy: in return for their favours, businessmen have been able to get away with paying their workers badly and suppressing free trade unions.

Under the new political system, in which President Roh faced an opposition-dominated parliament from April 1988 to May 1990, these complaints have come out into the open. The government, embarrassed, has found it hard to respond. Indeed, it has joined in the outcry, blaming the big business groups for driving up house prices by speculating in land, and for promoting "excessive consumption" by importing expensive things Koreans want to buy. And it has announced (several times) measures to promote small and medium-sized businesses.

For all the rhetoric though, Korea is still firmly committed to big business. Many of the industries in which Korea is most competitive—textiles, shipbuilding, steel—are ones in which being big is a great help. Even more so the industries into which the government wants Korean firms to expand in the future, like semiconductors, aerospace and telecommunications. In those industries, size is such an advantage that many firms in Europe, America and Japan are forging "strategic alliances" with foreign

competitors. Korean companies need to be mammoth just to survive.

Leviathans on the run

Big though they are, Korean firms have been battered by a series of shocks in the past two years. Wage bills have doubled since 1987, as workers demanded higher pay to compensate for the huge improvements they have made in productivity since 1980. The value of the won is 11% higher against the dollar than in 1987, even after devaluations in the past 12 months. Protectionism in Europe and America is more of a threat, with the "super-301" provisions of America's 1988 trade act and the wide powers of the European Commission to make foreign firms pay "anti-dumping" duties on exports to the EC. Foreign partners previously willing to give Korean firms technology almost for free have become more wary.

Individually, any one of these changes might have been manageable. Together, they amount to a crunch. In the past, Korean firms could take advantage of their size and low labour costs to sell mediocre products at low prices, and still make fat profits. No longer. To continue to grow, they must be well managed—not just big, but good.

What kind of companies are they now? Unlike Japanese companies, Korean firms are relatively unknown to outsiders and business writers. The few books about them are sketchy and uninformative. Like Japanese companies, they have become strongly hierarchical, full of *kajang* (section chiefs) and *bujang* (general managers), each demanding to be called by his title and bowed to at the right angle. Also like Japanese companies, they have a strong streak of the "collective" spirit; workers often wear company uniforms, sing the company song, live in company dormitories.

There the similarities end. Unlike their Japanese counterparts, Korean companies are still young enough to be led firmly from the top. The Japanese system of *nemawashi*—coming to decisions by a sort of collective consent—is unknown. Rather, the boss tends to make the big decisions. Perhaps as a result, workers are much freer to leave one company and join another than workers in Japan.

Given the differences between firms (of which more later), it is hard to generalise. But a balance-sheet of their general strengths and weaknesses would look like this:

Weaknesses:
• **Bureaucracy.** In contrast to their factories, Korean companies' offices are often inefficient and overmanned. Workers put in long hours, but great swathes of time are often wasted in pointless meetings or waiting for small decisions to be approved from on high.
• **Lack of focus.** Partly to insure against the risk that the government may restrict entry to a new industry, partly to satisfy the founder's vanity, many of the *chaebol* have dived into scores of disparate businesses without asking themselves why. One of them actually trumpets this fault with a series of corporate advertisements asking

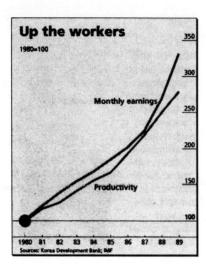

Up the workers

1980=100

Monthly earnings

Productivity

1980 81 82 83 84 85 86 87 88 89

Sources: Korea Development Bank; IMF

"Who is in everything from A to Z? Daewoo, that's who."

● **Lack of creativity**. Rarely have Korean firms come up with truly innovative products; many times they have pinched a good idea—whether a logo, a semiconductor design or a manufacturing process—from foreigners. Late starters often have to, but many Korean firms still spend too little on R&D. Their corporate culture sometimes discourages the creativity their workers possess.

Strengths:

● **People**. Despite their recent strikes and pay rises, Korean workers are still good value. They are highly literate, well-trained and hardworking.

● **Persistence**. Like their workers, Korean managers do not give up easily.

● **Agility**. Although they are slow in small things, the *chaebol* move fast in big ones. They do not fear risk. Samsung's decision to enter the semiconductor market with its own chip just before the industry's worst-ever recession in 1984 stunned its competitors. But the company threw $150m at its new venture in 18 months, and emerged a winner.

● **Financial strength**. With cross-holdings between group firms and obscure balance sheets, the *chaebol* can use the strong cash flow of a core business to finance another division's losses. Although they are still highly geared by world standards, the *chaebol* also have deep pockets.

Samsung to the rescue

One company—the Samsung group—seems to have a head start on the rest. Its labour relations are better, partly because it pays the highest salaries. Its balance sheet is stronger, because electronics, in which it specialises, has done better in the late 1980s than the heavy industries on which Hyundai and Daewoo depend more. It has a team of talented managers, the result of a system of hiring by open examination since 1957, while some other groups are encumbered with gormless members of the founder's family.

Two years ago, just after its 50th anniversary, the founder of the Samsung group died, and his son, Mr Lee Kun Hee, took the reins. Mr Lee understood clearly the problems his firm would face in the future. He told his employees to ignore the high profits they were making that year, and think instead as if they had a crisis on their hands. His managers took him at his word. They have virtually turned the firm upside down since then.

First, they have cut costs. Production lines are shorter; their running speeds are higher. Taking advantage of the fact that most of its light-manufacturing workers are women, who stay for only a few years, the company has reduced its docile workforce where necessary, by natural wastage. It has saved money by reducing inventories—at one plant from six weeks' stocks to an hour's stocks for most parts in the space of half a year. It has also introduced just-in-time management systems throughout the factory in order to cut the amount of time each worker spends idle. One Samsung factory plans to cut costs by 10% and raise productivity by 30% this year.

What matters even more is that Samsung is trying to move away from its niche as a low-cost, medium-quality producer. It aims to build strong brands in up-market products, backed up with high quality and a reputation for innovation like Sony's.

This is no small ambition. The first step has been to tackle the quality challenge head-on. In every Samsung plant visited for this survey, the production line's quality statistics were prominently displayed. By drumming the idea into workers that quality counts, the managers of the firm's microwave-oven plant at Suwon, which supplies almost a fifth of world demand, have cut its defect ratio from 6% to 2% in the first six months of 1990.

Product lines are being changed, too. In June Samsung Aerospace started to sell a new ultra-small autofocus camera called the AF Slim, which sells in the home market for $375, and is the world's most advanced model—bar one made by Konica of Japan. To make way for production of 30,000 cameras a month, the company is dropping two cheaper models. The same is happening at Samsung's colour-picture-tube plant at Kachun, which is the world's biggest maker of the tube that is a television's key component: the plant is being closed for two months this summer to be retooled so it can turn out 29-inch screens, which have far fatter margins than the humbler 20-inch screens that were its stock-in-trade before.

To make the fatter margins, the firm must sell more of its goods under Samsung brand names, rather than as a contractor for more famous firms like Sony. It recognises the need to become better known. This year the consumer-electronics division plans to raise its advertising spending from $46m to $70m. In that budget is one special project: to put the Samsung name on every baggage cart in every airport in the world. As a result of these efforts, says Mr Chung Dam, who is in charge of international consumer-electronics marketing, more than half Samsung's electronics sales this year will be under its own name.

Management methods have had to change, too.

The presidents of each company in the group have been given more responsibility. "The chairman's power today," says Mr Lim Dong Sung, president of the company's research institute, "is probably only 10% of what his father's was a decade ago." Line employees are being told more. Samsung companies seem perpetually to be in the middle of campaigns to improve something or other: posters announce this year's "MVP" (microwave victory plan), or JUMP 90. Change is reaching even the company's white-collar workers. One campaign exhorts them not to waste time in meetings. Before any Samsung meeting begins, the man in charge is supposed to tell the participants what it is for, how long it will take—and, as an added incentive to brevity, how much an hour it will cost to hold it.

Much remains the same, however. Little has been done to introduce flexible production, in which lots of different-seeming products can be made on the same production line. Japanese companies, by contrast, are steaming ahead, knowing that flexible production will radically lower their break-even points and allow them to respond faster to what the customer wants.

Like the rest of Korean society, Samsung remains extremely hierarchical. Talented middle managers complain that their best ideas are stymied by their dull-witted bosses. In style, relations between juniors and seniors are an eye-opener to foreigners. During one interview, a Samsung boss waved an empty cigarette-packet; his colleague (a deputy general manager, so quite high in the firm in his own right) dutifully rushed out of the room and came back with a new one. During another, a Samsung manager was interrupted by a shoe-shine man. The manager continued to talk as the shoe-shine man took off his shoes for him and replaced them with a clean pair.

More seriously, Samsung remains a group of 27 companies with little in common except ownership. "Our sugar and textile companies rank first in productivity, first in R&D, first in sales," says Mr Lim. "This year they made big profits. Why should we sell them?" Far from it: the firm is still looking for new lines of business. It hopes to get into the car industry, despite the fact that Korea already has three big struggling carmakers. It also has a finger in aerospace, with sales last year of $100m derived mostly from engine assembly, spare-part manufacture, and maintenance. It hopes to use the Korea Fighter Plane project to boost this still further.

Yet the company has changed irrevocably. It has become more internationally minded, recognising not Lucky-Goldstar but firms in America and Japan as its competitors. And if its factories look like their Japanese equivalents, that is because it shares with them a relentless policy of making small marginal improvements all the time. "Last year we were ready to raise productivity in order to stay afloat if the won rose to 600 [to the dollar]," says Mr Won In Ki, director of the picture-tube plant. "Since then, it has depreciated. So we're working on quality instead."

That, in sum, is what has made Samsung Korea's most promising company: the pressure to raise standards now comes from within. Samsung clamours for a weaker won with the best of them. But it does not make the mistake of taking its own rhetoric seriously. It knows the won and wages must continue to rise; whatever needs to be done to remain competitive, it will do.

Not all firms are the same. Most need a push from the government if they are to raise quality, invest more, use more technology or improve their management. Three years ago there was no doubt that the government was able to deliver that push. Now, businessmen say, they are not so sure.

Anything for a quiet life

IN DECEMBER 1988 President Roh made an interesting choice for the job of deputy prime minister and head of the Economic Planning Board. He appointed Mr Cho Soon, a distinguished professor of economics who had taught at Seoul National University, the country's most prestigious, for 20 years. Half of the country's top politicians and bureaucrats learnt their economics from him. Mr Cho occupied the job, which is Korea's top economics post and senior to both the finance minister and trade minister, during a fascinating period of his country's history.

After little more than a year of putting his theories to the test, however, Mr Cho was unceremoniously sacked—along with the rest of his economic team. He is now a private consultant. Mr Cho is too high-minded to spill the beans about his time in office. But in conversation, he gives a lucid account of how the job of making economic policy has changed.

Before 1987 the government of Korea was run by an authoritarian system in which the president had almost absolute power. Because the president supported the economic planning board and the deputy prime minister who heads it, the deputy prime minister had great visible influence and was firmly in charge of his subordinate ministers. That was the structure.

The objectives were more or less simple: during the 1960s, to maximise economic growth and export volume; and during the 1970s, to stabilise prices. All measures were directed towards fulfilling these aims, which were visible and understandable.

The means were more or less simple, too: direct controls. Although these direct-control measures—such as the power to set interest rates or the wage rate—caused lots of distortions, the tools at the government's disposal were very powerful... In many respects, Korea was like a command economy—particularly in monetary policy.

Since the authoritarian regime went in 1987, all that has changed.

What Mr Cho found was that the job had become a job for a politician, not an economist. First, the deputy prime minister could no longer count on his boss's support. He also had to deal with an opposition-dominated parliament that could summon him or his officials to justify their policies. Clarity of purpose had gone, too: success meant not just high growth or exports, but juggling them against a host of other things, such as satisfying the demands of labour and farmers, improving welfare, thinking about the environment. And even as the job had got more taxing, the tools had become less effective. No longer could the deputy prime minister manage micro-policy with a few well-placed telephone calls to the heads of the *chaebol*. He had to rely on the slower responding, less reliable macro-measures familiar to finance ministers in the industrial world.

Because Mr Cho has no plans to write his memoirs, the details of his travails in office are unlikely to be known. But one thing is clear: the transformation from the "command economy" Mr Cho talks of to an economy where the government allows the market to take more decisions is proving politically difficult.

This is because the public is confused about what government can or cannot do. Newspapers splashed their front pages last year with headlines like PRESIDENT ORDERS MINISTERS TO HALT RISE IN HOUSE PRICES—an order about as sensible as telling them to stop the waves lapping against the shore. Mr Cho himself was a victim of these misconceptions: his departure was forced by a downturn in exports and a deterioration in the balance of payments, which his fellow ministers and the ruling party thought he could have done more to prevent.

In general, Mr Cho's policy line was clear: he pressed for a gentle appreciation of the won, and a gradual opening of Korea's markets to imports, heralding a trend towards higher domestic consumption, less reliance on growth through exports, and more welfare spending. It was a modest downturn in the economy—exports down 7% in volume terms in 1989, a sticky period of strikes, a falling stock-market and signs of rising inflation—coupled with a damaging rise in land prices that precipitated his departure.

In March a new team was installed, committed to a return to export-led growth and to domestic austerity. Its leading light is Mr Park Pil Soo, the new trade and industry minister, who used to be a career civil servant responsible for export promotion. "My policy direction", says Mr Park, "is to increase exports which were discouraged by my predecessor. That's the difference."

The new team has moved fast. Its first act was to cancel a proposed reform of the financial system which would have forbidden investors to use pseudonyms, as they can at present. Next it began to depreciate the won, claiming that the fall of the yen

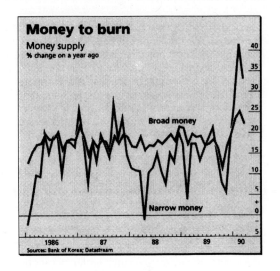

Money to burn

Money supply
% change on a year ago

Broad money

Narrow money

1986   87   88   89   90

Sources: Bank of Korea; Datastream

against the dollar this year has made Korea uncompetitive against Japan. "According to my information," says Mr Park, "720 [won to the dollar] is the rate at which Korean companies can be competitive."

The government has cracked down on labour disputes more strictly this year than last. It has also made it more expensive for Koreans to buy foreign cars, by using an existing rule that says they must make a compensating "investment" in government subway bonds. The required investment is higher for foreign than domestic cars, and also higher than before. The government has also encouraged its taxmen to investigate people who buy expensive imports. "Most of the haves," says Mr Park, "have acquired their money from irregular transactions such as land and building speculation. The tax office is therefore very eager to find out who spends his money on big cars but has a limited income."

There have also been allegations that the government has put direct pressure on importers to stop them bringing "luxury" goods into the Korean market. The countries of the European Community took the claims seriously enough to send their ambassadors *en masse* to Mr Park's office in June to bang the table. He denied everything, saying that it was citizens' groups, not the government, that had applied the pressure. It is still too early to say, but many outsiders fear that the government is trying to return to its old meddling ways. Mr Koo Bon Young, one of the president's economic secretaries, denies this: the differences between the old and the new teams have been overstated, he says.

The surplus fetish

At the root of today's problems is a policy failure dating back four years. Because Korean workers' productivity rose much faster than their wages in the first half of the 1980s, it became clear around

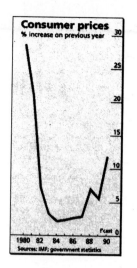

Consumer prices
% increase on previous year

30
25
20
15
10
5
0
f'cast

1980 82 84 86 88 90
Sources: IMF; government statistics

1986 that the won was undervalued. Yet the government, understandably keen to shake off its history of chronic trade deficits, refused to let the currency appreciate. Instead, it kept the won low, and clocked up huge current-account surpluses in the next four years.

At first, all seemed well. The economy boomed along, growing by 12.5% a year between 1986 and 1988. Hyundai made a splash with its cars in America in 1987—partly because of the low won, partly because the Japanese cars with which it was competing were subject to quantitative restrictions. Other firms had similar Indian summers, making big profits and paying them out to their employees in wage increases in 1988 and 1989.

Eventually, however, the extra money in the system began to push up domestic prices. Despite the government's efforts to keep down prices and to sterilise the surpluses by forcing big companies to buy government bonds, the price of one of the few goods the government could not control, land, began to rise dizzyingly.

The result is that although Korea's economy is likely to grow by an impressive 9% this year, it has two pressing problems: inflation, which official figures say is running at 8.9% but is probably more than double that, and the prospect of a modest trade deficit for 1990. These are the problems that the government is trying to solve by quick-fix direct intervention. Yet the trouble is that the government's meddling in the economy has itself become part of the problem.

Take the housing market. Thanks to migration into the capital and the green belt around it, the long-term trend of house prices in Seoul has necessarily been upwards. Successive governments' meddling, though, has made the housing market less efficient.

First, the government's promotion of corporate investment has restricted the supply of credit for house-buying. Mortgages are scarce and almost im-

possible to get for more than 20% of the value of a house or apartment. A lunatic system has thus grown up which forces a tenant, who needs a house at short notice, instead of paying rent to stump up a lump sum, called *chonsei* and running to up to two-thirds of the value of the property, which the landlord has free use of until the tenant leaves and then gets his *chonsei* back.

Second, in an attempt to provide low-cost housing to the poor, the government has built houses and sold them off outright at a hefty discount. The result has been predictable: the poorest people cannot put together the capital to join in, and so never get helped. Middle-class people, on the other hand, buy government houses and later sell them on at a market price. There is even a secondary market in the certificates that guarantee a place in the queue.

Third, the government tried until last November to control house prices directly, by setting maximum retail prices per square metre for new houses. In order to protect their profits, builders have therefore avoided areas with high land prices, such as the centre of Seoul, and built only in places where land can be picked up more cheaply. They have also concentrated on big houses, which are cheaper to build per square metre. The result has been an artificial shortage of normal-sized dwellings where people want to live—and a spiral in the price of houses already built (which are not liable to these restrictions). Since the end of last year the government has allowed minimum prices to rise a little. But the guts of the system remain the same.

Like many such distortions, the policy has created a political lobby of people who benefit from it. When the construction minister suggested last year that the controls should be eased, the howl of protest from owners forced the president to sack him.

Mr Yoo Jae Hyun, president of the Hanssem Housing Research Institute, an independent research body, thinks still more radical reform is necessary. He wants the government to:
- Scrap the price controls, after waiting for the present boom to subside.
- Make mortgages more freely available, and formalise the grey market for housing credit.
- Improve the density of use of the 78% of land which is devoted to one-family occupancy.
- Acquire a small slice of the green belt, perhaps 10%, for building new houses.

The trouble with these reforms—and others like them in other parts of the economy—is that they go against the grain of the extensive intervention which has been part of Korean economic policy for a generation. The bureaucrats are understandably reluctant to change a recipe which has served their country so well in the past. Yet there is hope for change all the same. "The hardest thing for economic policy-makers," says Mr Lawrence Krause, a professor at the University of California in San Diego, who specialises in Korea, "is to unlearn the lessons of the past." Outsiders, such as the World Bank, are becoming less shy of advising the Korean government to reduce its microeconomic intervention.

Before the present economic team can do that, however, they must have some clear macro-policies to follow. At a time when inflation is accelerating and domestic demand is overheated, the government has been hinting to business that it will let the currency slide. Suppose it did the opposite, however. A steady rise in the value of the won over the next year or two would cut the cost of imports; and it would squeeze corporate profits. Companies would be inclined to pay their workers less, so domestic demand would ease.

Revaluing the won has just one drawback. After four years of surplus, Korea's balance of payments is likely to go back into the red this year. A stronger won will make the deficit bigger—something which the present economic team wants to avoid at all costs. Is it right to be so cautious?

Article 31

THE ECONOMIST
JULY 14 1990

TAIWAN AND KOREA

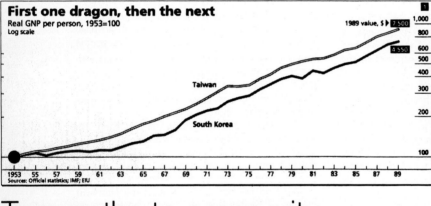

First one dragon, then the next
Real GNP per person, 1953=100
Log scale

1989 value, $ ▶ 7,500

Taiwan

South Korea

1,000
800
600
500
400
300

200

100

1953 55 57 59 61 63 65 67 69 71 73 75 77 79 81 83 85 87 89
Sources: Official statistics; IMF; EIU

Two paths to prosperity

Taiwan and South Korea have both grown out of poverty, and have both avoided gross disparities of income while doing it. They took radically different paths. Which is better placed to move on now to real wealth?

THIS is a happy story, even though it is about economics.

In 1950, the year after Chiang Kai-shek's Nationalists fled China's victorious Communists for "temporary" exile on the island of Taiwan, the incomes of Taiwanese and of mainland Chinese were much the same. For the next four decades, Taiwan's real GNP grew at an average of 8.7% a year: enough to raise the island's GNP per person by 1989 to $7,500. Count in the large black economy and that could mean around $10,000, about as much as in Ireland or New Zealand. That same year each of mainland China's 1.1 billion people could claim a share of GNP equal to maybe $350.

South Korea's rise too has been spectacular, but it started only in 1961, the year a general called Park Chung Hee staged a coup, promising to "end starvation" there. He did better than that. In 1960 South Korea's GNP per person was about $675 in today's money, probably not much more than that of the communist North. Since then the South's real GNP has grown by 8.4% a year, giving each citizen a share of official GNP last year equal to $4,550. Each North Korean had maybe a quarter as much.

Behind these curt figures stands an immense increase in human well-being. A Taiwanese child born in 1988 could expect to live 74 years, only a year less than an American or a West German, and 15 years longer than a Taiwanese born in 1952; a South Korean born in 1988 could expect 70 years on earth, up from 58 in 1965. In 1988 the Taiwanese took in 50% more calories each day than they had done 35 years earlier. They had 100 times as many televisions, telephones and cars per household; in Korea the rise in the possession of these goods was even sharper. Virtually all Taiwanese and Koreans go through elementary school, and 45% of Taiwanese and 37% of Koreans get at least some higher education (like 60% of Americans, but only 22% of Britons).

Best of all, Taiwan and Korea grew in ways that spread the benefits to practically everybody. Rural incomes rose to urban levels and stayed there, and unemployment in both countries has been low. Taiwan's unemployment rate was 1% in 1988; the last time it exceeded 2% was 1964. Korea's rate has hovered between 2% and 4% for all but one of the past 20 years.

Unlike most developing countries, Taiwan and Korea grew fast and sharply reduced income inequalities at the same time. In 1970, when Korea's GNP per head was still only about $1,300 in today's money, by one measure it had a more equal income distribution than Japan or the United States. In 1952 the income of the best-off 20% of Taiwanese households was 15 times the income of the lowest 20%; by 1980 the multiple was only 4.2. The equivalent in America that year was 7.5, in Sweden a year later 5.6, in Japan a year earlier 4.4. For much of the past two decades Taiwan has been the world's

Living longer, living better					
	Daily calories per person	Life expectancy, years	Telephones	Televisions	Passenger cars
			per 1,000 population		
Taiwan	2950	74	360	275	53
South Korea	2900	70	200	200	29

Latest available figures. Sources: EIU; World Bank; Telecommunications Research Centre.

most egalitarian society, as well as one of the half-dozen fastest-growing ones.

Growth through exports

Taiwan and Korea have few resources, little arable land and the highest population densities of any country save Bangladesh and the city-states of Hongkong and Singapore. How did they succeed so well? Essentially, by trying to keep prices at the level that a free market would find. To do this, though, the two used quite different methods. At least until the 1980s the differences made Taiwan a better performer than Korea.

One policy that both have pursued—and it is a crucial one—is to be export-oriented. This simply means, contrary to the suspicions of American congressmen, that they did not handicap their exports in world markets. Almost all developing countries do this, by bans, quotas or tariffs on imported goods. This both makes the home market more attractive to a might-be exporter and raises the cost of his inputs, so hampering him if he does try to sell abroad.

Shrewd governments try to make up for this by giving exporters tax rebates and the like. In the 1950s Korea's government was not shrewd. It pursued an import-substitution policy. Growth was slow. But from 1961 it combined a lot of protection with a lot of correction to keep domestic and international prices roughly in line, and growth

took off. Taiwan had less protection, but was zealous in correcting for it. See chart 2 overleaf for the spectacular results.

Korea and Taiwan also tried to keep relative domestic prices in line, and both more or less succeeded; but the way each succeeded explains how different they are. A World Bank study in 1983 showed that Korea had one of the least price-distorting regimes in the world. It offsets penalties in one place (enforced low selling prices, for instance) with rewards in another (subsidised credit). Taiwan generally got the same result by letting the market have its way.

The contrast was most marked in the case of credit and interest-rate policy, which more than anything else determined the present shape of the two economies. From the 1950s Taiwan pursued a policy, almost unique in those days, of letting interest rates rise to—high—market levels. This brought it the world's highest rates of savings and investment, an atomised industrial structure and equal incomes.

It happened that way for a simple reason. When a government keeps interest rates below the market-clearing rate, it usually does so in the vague belief that this will help the little guy. It does the opposite. Cheap money helps borrowers, mostly big firms. It also encourages more capital-intensive methods of production—reducing employment growth—and larger firms.

From 1961 to 1979 South Korea's credit policy was just the opposite of Taiwan's. The planners kept interest rates low, using their control over bank credit to direct cheap money to those borrowers whom they thought should be favoured. These were export-oriented groups, which quickly grew into giant conglomerates known as *chaebol*.

Those basic choices about credit were at the root of the two countries' contrasting models of development. Taiwan's companies were small and equity-based. Along with tight money, it also had a tight fiscal policy, with a budget surplus every year but one from 1964 to 1988. Korea's companies were big and debt-based. Its macroeconomic policies were both looser and more erratic.

What resulted was higher savings and more tightly costed, therefore more efficient, investment in Taiwan (chart 2); more foreign borrowing and far higher inflation (chart 3) in Korea; and a pair of industrial structures that could almost have originated on different planets.

Taiwan is dominated by small, lightly indebted firms: by one reckoning, more than four-fifths of its firms in 1981 had fewer than 20 employees. Brooding over Korea's economy are the huge, heavily indebted *chaebol*. In 1984 the sales of the top ten *chaebol* equalled two-thirds of South Korea's GNP, and by one estimate the sales of the top four alone equalled half of GNP in 1989. A Korean government survey of 2,500 goods found that in 1988 21% of the country's markets for them were monopolistic and 56% oligopolistic.

Korea catches up

Korea, which started the 1980s by letting interest rates move towards market levels, outperformed Taiwan until the very end of the

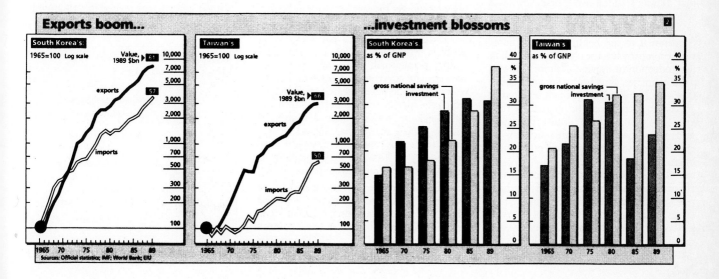

Exports boom... South Korea's 1965=100 Log scale. Taiwan's 1965=100 Log scale. **...investment blossoms** South Korea's as % of GNP. Taiwan's as % of GNP.

Sources: Official statistics; IMF; World Bank; EIU

There's inflation and inflation
Consumer prices, 1952=100
Log scale

South Korea

Taiwan

1952 54 56 58 60 62 64 66 68 70 72 74 76 78 80 82 84 86 88 90 estimate
Source: Official statistics; IMF; EIU

30,000
10,000
5,000
3,000
1,000
500
300
100

decade. Faster GNP growth for Korea seems natural: it is poorer. But Korea's savings rate has risen to Taiwanese levels and its investment rate has held up well, while Taiwan's crashed in the mid-1980s.

Land and stockmarket booms have widened income disparities in both countries, but probably faster in Taiwan: that 4.2 multiple of top-fifth to bottom-fifth incomes had grown to 4.7 by 1987. And though both countries' stockmarkets lost touch with reality late in the decade, Taiwan's flew into space. The Seoul market index rose eightfold from its trough in 1985 to its peak in 1989; the Taipei index went up 20-fold before it started falling this February.

Many observers shrug off these disquieting signs about Taiwan. In its 1990 annual report on world competitiveness, the Swiss-based International Institute for Management Development rated Taiwan ahead of South Korea on nine of the ten factors it uses to rank countries. Among ten developing countries, it ranked Taiwan second (after Singapore), Korea only fourth (after Hongkong) and well behind Taiwan in its overall score.

Nonsense, says Mr Robert Wade, a New Zealand economist at Princeton. He argues that Taiwan's falling investment, low R&D spending (around 1% of GNP, as against Korea's 2%) and puny marketing punch will condemn it to fall behind. As wage rates rise, a company has the choice of upgrading its production or moving offshore to lower-wage countries. Small firms in small countries, says Mr Wade, are strongly tempted to go abroad rather than to upgrade. If they keep doing so, and he thinks Taiwanese firms will, growth in Taiwan's productivity will slow and so, eventually, will other kinds of growth.

Many Taiwanese share this worry. Makers of shoes and textiles, they say, are happier sending their factories to China and Indonesia than upgrading them at home. And in 1986-89 Taiwan had a net loss of 300,000 manufacturing jobs. Yet the quality of the labour force suggests there is nothing to

stop it moving rapidly upmarket. In 1988-89 nearly a third of its students in higher education were studying engineering; 165,000 of them, a remarkable figure, in relation to population, by world standards. They come cheap too: Mr Stan Shih, who heads Acer Computer, Taiwan's most successful high-tech company, says he has to pay his engineers at only 35-40% of world levels.

The success of Acer in particular, with its $700m in sales last year, and of the computer-hardware industry in general (Taiwan is the world's sixth-biggest producer), argue against the idea that upmarket industries are not going to thrive on the island. Mr Shih says the small size of Taiwan's firms does not disadvantage them in the competition against American, Japanese and Korean giants. Taiwanese computer firms benefit from good infrastructure, low overheads and a good network of local suppliers.

Being small hurts in consumer electronics, Mr Shih says, but, for any product with a longer life, technology (meaning engineering talent and R&D) and marketing are what count, and being a big firm is not essential for either. Acer has marketing and production links with American companies, and Mr Shih is confident that in the next ten years he can get his company's brand-name recognised worldwide.

Overall, however, Taiwan does have a problem with R&D, which is fragmented among many small firms, and poorly financed. The government's answer has been to set up co-operative research institutes, of which the biggest is the Industrial Technology Research Institute, with a budget of $150m-180m a year. It has a good record, but hardly seems capable of raising the level and quality of Taiwan's R&D spending to match those of competing countries.

A more convincing explanation than smallness for Taiwan's relative weakness these past few years is finance. Like Japan and South Korea, Taiwan ran vast current-account surpluses in the mid-1980s, and the cash flooded through the economy: the

money supply went up 1½ times in 1985-88, five times faster than the economy grew.

Property prices shot up. Spurred on by deregulation of stockbroking—the number of brokers rose from 28 in 1986 to 320 by the beginning of 1990—the stockmarket became more frenzied than any casino ever was. No productive investment could compete. Nor, in many cases, could productive labour: one economist guesses that as many as 100,000 people (1.2% of the workforce) quit their jobs to play the market full-time. But money supply is now being squeezed, and the central bank intends to keep squeezing it. Its governor, Mr Samuel Shieh, says stock prices, land prices and the "grey" financial system are all going down, "and it's a good thing".

Blame the government
Koreans have a saying which suggests what mainly ails their economy: "When crops are good, thank God. When they are bad, blame the king."

This habit of mind is hard to correct in a country still going through the turbulence generated by a sudden switch in 1987 from military dictatorship to democracy. (Taiwan has made a much smoother and slower transition to near-democracy.) The first economic consequence of the switch was a wage explosion. Over 1987-89 wages rose by 45% or so; manufacturers' unit labour costs rose 43% from mid-1988 to mid-1989 alone. Growth in real GNP slowed from 12.2% in 1988 to 6.5% in 1989, and in the dollar value of exports from 28% to 3%.

With inflation also on the rise, Koreans early this year were talking of a "crisis". It is no such thing. The unions are getting used to democracy, and have already seen that wage increases cannot outstrip productivity growth for long. Wage settlements this spring were reportedly down to 10%. In June the government revised its GNP growth

Only one step down
GNP per person, 1989, $'000

0   4   8   12   16   20   24

Japan

Taiwan

South Korea

Malaysia

Philippines

China

Source: Official statistics; IMF; EIU

projection for 1990 up from 6.5% to 9%.

The government's behaviour during this unjustified gloom showed how prone it is to leap in and try to correct every market distortion it finds—and indeed some market non-distortions which just happen to be unpopular. When the public outcry over land prices became deafening this spring, the government brought in a detailed programme of regulation, limiting the size of plots and ordering *chaebol* to sell off property. When the stockmarket began its well-deserved tumble and small investors rioted in brokers' offices, the government began to slow moves toward financial deregulation.

Mr Suh Sang Mok, a member of the National Assembly and the ruling party's chief economic-policy man, says the government wants to start using indirect instruments of control like interest rates and tax policy. But that is hard to do in an economy as heavily regulated as Korea's (the taxman even tells liquor producers what shape their bottles have to be), and one in which "everybody is used to taking and resenting orders". So, in true Korean fashion, the government is aiming to correct distortions with interventions—the difference this time, says Mr Suh, being that the aim of the intervention is to enable the market in 5-10 years' time to do the regulating instead of the government.

Easier said than done. The main target of regulation, the *chaebol*, used to bask in government favour. Now, says Mr Suh, official intervention, instead of favouring them, does the opposite. The banks, for instance, have been told to make 35% of their loans to small and middle-sized businesses. But neither government nor *chaebol* will find it easy to kick old habits. With the generals no longer in power, the *chaebol* are inclined to turn a deaf ear to officialdom and go their own sweet way. On the other side, public resentment against them and the rich families that control them makes it politically expedient to push them around.

Yet for all their collective power, the *chaebol* are absurdly diversified—one runs from shipbuilding to textiles to microchips to aerospace to sugar-processing—and compete with each other in almost everything. Provided it can expose them to foreign imports, the government may find the market quite able to keep the *chaebol* in line.

Their more thoughtful executives are, in fact, concerned about the position the *chaebol* have got themselves into. They have financial power and good international marketing resources. A lot of non-Koreans have heard of Hyundai, Samsung, even Goldstar; what non-Taiwanese has yet heard of Acer? Yet the *chaebol* will find it increasingly hard to keep all their businesses going. Can they, asks a top financial man at one of the big groups, really afford the investments needed to drive petrochemicals and semiconductors at the same time? Yet the internal pressures not to sell off any of their businesses—from family owners and workforces alike—are intense.

A greater problem is that not much of an undergrowth of smaller firms seems to be developing in the shade of the giant *chaebol*. Managers of the conglomerates say that their small suppliers on long-term contracts do all right, but do not seem to learn and grow; the 35% of bank loans going their way are not doing what they are intended to.

The verdict

So what is the verdict between Taiwan and Korea? Taiwan has the edge. Its economy is more flexible; it looks likelier to produce flourishing large companies than does Korea to produce small ones. And Taiwan's government ought to find it simpler to do some more of the things it needs to, like providing infrastructure for the choked and dirty capital, Taipei, than will Korea's government to do fewer of the things it should not have been doing in the first place.

But keep some perspective. Different though they are, both these economies have been among the best in the world for the past 30 years, and should continue to be so for the next 20. As Tolstoy didn't write, all unhappy countries resemble each other, but each happy one is happy in its own way.

Article 32

WORLD HEALTH, September-October 1990

DEMOCRATIC PEOPLE'S REPUBLIC OF KOREA

Healthy aging

by Dr Choe Chun Hyon

Head of WHO Collaborating Centre in Gerontology and Geriatrics, Pyongyang

"Nothing is more precious than man in the world ... Man is the master of everything and decides everything." With its emphasis on humanity – and here "man" means "woman" too – this is the philosophical base for the health policy of the Democratic People's Republic of Korea (DPRK). This principle applies equally to the elderly, since protection of the elderly is an important part of the state's policy.

Populations are aging rapidly not only in the developed world but also in developing countries. There are an estimated 416 million older people (aged 60 years and over) in the world. By the year 2025, they will number 806 million, accounting for 11.9 per cent of the world's total population.

In the DPRK, life expectancy in 1986 was 74.3 years. The Socialist Labour Law stipulates that the state takes charge of and provides for the life of every citizen, and pledges as a matter of supreme principle to continuously increase the material and cultural life of all citizens. It also lays down that men are entitled to a state pension when they reach the age of 60 and women at the age of 55, and that every citizen has a right to work and eventually to have access to nursing homes and homes for the elderly without any charge.

The elderly are entitled to primary health care, and there is much emphasis on the pre-disease status of older people.

In March 1974, the Supreme People's Assembly published a law entirely eliminating the taxation system, thus making it a tax-free country.

Free medical care

The Public Health Law stipulates that every citizen shall enjoy the benefit of completely free medical care from the state and has a right to be treated without charge. The document "Theses on Socialist Education" ensures universal and continuous education for all people throughout their lives, from childhood to old age, and including pre-school, school and adult education.

The latter is considered of great importance in consolidating and developing people's world outlook and in increasing general knowledge, as well as improving their technical and cultural levels. The education provided is not only universal and compulsory but also free of charge.

The social relationship of people is based on the collective principle of "One for all, all for one;" everybody helps each other. The state is responsible for providing the elderly (and indeed everyone) with food, clothing and housing almost without any charge. As for family relationships with elderly people, the young traditionally respect the old and share their homes with them.

The Public Health Law lays down the state's policy and the principal ways to consolidate and develop the Section Doctor System. This is a system of health care with doctors in charge of certain sections, performing prophylactic and therapeutic activities, taking good care of the citizens' health. Accordingly, every elderly person is registered and cared for by the section doctor, without charge.

The elderly are entitled to primary health care, general examination and guidance on activities from the doctors in charge. There is much emphasis on the pre-disease status of the elderly. Important areas receiving attention are hygiene propaganda, physical and mental training, observance of personal hygiene, diet and nutrition, guidance for a regimen for healthy living, the supply of gerotonics, facilities for rest and recreation, and anti-epidemic measures including vaccination.

In 1986 there were 135.9 hospital beds per 10,000 population. Beds for the elderly far exceed this number. In the capital, Pyongyang, there is a centre for medical services and research for the elderly, which has 1,700 beds and a specialised experimental unit. The other big hospitals and provincial hospitals also have departments and beds for specialised medical services for the elderly.

Modern medicine is combined with traditional medicine on a scientific basis. Special attention and efforts are

WHO/DPRK Mission, Geneva

directed at preventing and controlling geriatric diseases, from their early diagnosis to the prevention of relapse. Most of these diseases are chronic and incurable, calling for long-term treatment. So it is rational to prevent and treat diseases on the basis of normalising the structure and function of the organs and systems in elderly people. This requirement is met by traditional medicine.

We differentiate the gerontologica clinic from the geriatric clinic. For continuous maintenance of the health status of the elderly, relatively healthy elderly people are admitted as patients to gerontological clinics for investigation and assessment. These patients are given special medicaments and offered training and rehabilitation.

Medicaments based on traditional medicine and manufactured on a scientific basis are used to prevent and treat ischaemic heart disease, Parkinsonism and senile mental disturbances, or to raise the immune resistance in the aging.

There are five or six kinds of activities that the elderly can pursue. They can continue to do their work or act as an adviser or honorary official. They can participate in associations of retired persons, which are voluntary organizations for retired persons. Or they can undertake light activities in workshops or in neighbourhood work teams for the elderly. They can live in

---

National policy in the DPRK aims to ensure that all the elderly live long and happy lives, under the most favourable conditions.

---

nursing homes or homes for the elderly, while those with chronic diseases receive treatment in special hospitals.

Facilities where the elderly can lead an active life are run by the state. These have well-equipped clinics designed for a full cultural, recreational and emotional life. The residents are given nutritious meals and an opportunity to enjoy films, opera and drama, to visit historical places and recreation grounds, or to organize their own artistic performances.

The elderly receive education from skilled health and social workers in such matters as social hygiene, public health and disease prevention. Short scientific films and television offer excellent means of conveying this kind of education.

Meanwhile studies are being carried out on various aspects of the elderly. These include epidemiology – aimed at identifying the determinants of aging as well as the risk factors and favourable factors. Social studies try to identify ways to remove risk factors and use favourable factors, and to develop facilities for "healthy aging" which will ensure an active mind, health lifestyles, relaxation, organized work, education, and cultural and emotional interests.

Other studies seek to clarify the mechanism of aging, to find ways to delay its onset, and to identify rehabilitation measures that will maintain structure and function in the elderly through physical and mental training and the use of traditional medicines. Also under investigation are the prevention, early diagnosis, treatment and prevention of relapse of diseases in the aging, especially by applying traditional medicine.

The health of the elderly in the DPRK is an integral part of the state's policy, which aims to ensure that all the elderly live long and happy lives, on a sound structural, functional and social basis, and under favourable conditions of universal and completely cost-free state support.

Article 33

DISCOVERY MAY 1990 137

LOOKING FOR

LAOS

This tiny Southeast Asian country is now slowly awakening to the realities of life beyond its borders and possibilities beyond socialism

Essay by Grant Evans

Several years ago, I happened to be in Vientiane, the capital of Laos, to film a documentary with the BBC. The producer and I sat at an outdoor bar drinking a beer and discussing the script. We became so engrossed in the subject that when we left the producer forgot to pick up his jacket. In it, he had left US$1,000. A few hours later, we noticed that it was missing and rushed back to the bar.

"Have you seen a white jacket?" I asked with an edge of panic.

"You mean the one with a thousand dollars in it?" came the disarming reply. We fell over with relief. The money was meticulously counted out as it was handed back, and the manager of the bar pointedly remarked: "If this was Bangkok you might never have seen your money again."

Whether that's true or not, the Lao enjoy scoring points against the Thais. They have a few points to tally. The potholed, dusty streets of Vientiane are free of traffic congestion and high-rise buildings, though since 1988, noisy, Thai *tuk-tuk* taxis have made an appearance in the tiny capital. For the most part, however, the city still has the agreeable atmosphere of a provincial town rather than a political and commercial nerve centre. There is an appealing, small-town innocence about the place that has long been lost in Bangkok.

In Laos, mornings in the cities and the rural villages begin with young saffron-robed Buddhist monks making their rounds of the urban "villages" surrounding each wat (temple). The faithful who wait outside their houses offer the monks food as a way of gaining religious merit. Buddhists believe in a cycle of death and rebirth, and by accumulating merit they hope to be reborn at a higher level in their next life. Few expect to break this cycle of rebirth and achieve nirvana. Watching this daily ritual unfold gives the outsider a glimpse of the importance the Lao people place on Theravada Buddhism.

While Laos is, nominally at least, a communist country, there is no apparent antagonism between Buddhism and the state. Most Lao communists I have met also claim to be Buddhists and see no inconsistency in this. One of the major Buddhist shrines in Vientiane is the imposing That Luang where, every November, a major Buddhist/nationalist celebration takes place. It is always attended by at least one senior figure from the communist party leadership.

The Lao will tell you that this is part of the "Lao way to socialism," a more relaxed and more tolerant variety than one is likely to find elsewhere. This wasn't always true. From December 1975 until the early 1980s, more orthodox communist policies were enforced. Among other things, it was extremely hard for foreigners to travel in Laos. Only in the past two years have tourists been allowed to visit in significant numbers. Even today, however, tours outside Vientiane are generally restricted to government-arranged groups.

Nearly anyone who has had anything to do with Laos will tell you that the people are charming and friendly. Even in the late 1970s, when the government was at its most puritanical, it could not suppress the spontaneous Lao love of a good party, or a *boun*, with drinking and traditional *lam vong* dancing late into the night. Nowadays, younger people flock to Vientiane discos such as the Vienlaty Mai; there, I begin to feel as if I am back in Bangkok.

Road travel in Laos is another story. Few of the roads outside the main towns can take all-weather traffic; breakdowns are frequent and repair workshops are few and far between. In the mountains, roads are replaced by pony tracks up the hillsides. Some adventurous travellers have gone all the way up to Luang Prabang, the former royal and religious capital, from Vientiane by road. But most of them are forced to turn back when they reach the Vang Vieng valley with its marvellous forest of vertical granite hills. Thankfully, there are plans to upgrade this route to the magical old royal capital in the near future.

To get to the northern or southern provinces from Vientiane, air-travel is essential. There is a regular and reliable plane service from Vientiane to Luang Prabang, and to the major southern cities of Savannakhet and Pakse. But only a helicopter will get you to the remote northern provinces of Phong Saly, Xieng Khouang or Houa Phan, and unfortunately they run irregularly.

A few years ago I travelled into these provinces in rickety old Russian biplanes, AN-2s. Although I now

About five years ago, this H'mong tribe family settled in Nasom village, about seven kilometres west of Vang Vieng. There are about 70 ethnic tribes in Laos.

travel into the mountains by helicopter, I feel only marginally safer. One of the sidelines of helicopter pilots is to fly fresh buffalo meat — or live lizards — back to the capital for sale. Sitting in the belly of a helicopter resting your feet on an animal slaughtered only an hour before hardly inspires confidence in the service.

Laos is one of the poorest countries in Southeast Asia. The majority of people are rice-growing peasants in the countryside; there is little industry and cash incomes are meagre. One of the country's most serious problems is health care, and there is a high infant mortality rate.

In an attempt to stimulate the country's economic development, the government has recently moved away from orthodox communist policies. And foreign investors from the West have begun to trickle in. Small-scale private commerce has been encouraged, and all varieties of state and private-sector joint ventures are emerging, particularly in Vientiane. The capital's Morning Market, Talat Sao, is a must for any visitor to Vientiane. Among other goods, its long lanes of stalls are draped with some of the most exquisite embroidery and patterned silk weaving found in Asia — an art that has faded in most other countries.

One of the most imposing monuments in Vientiane is the baroque Anousawali, or Arc de Triomphe monument, at the top of the Avenue Lane Xang. A bizarre imitation of the Arc in Paris, it is decorated with angels from the Buddhist pantheon. The story behind its construction is a very Lao one. Under the old government, which was backed by the United States, Uncle Sam supplied Vientiane with concrete to build a runway. Instead the Lao built the Arc as a monument to their war dead. Today,

it is affectionately known as "the vertical runway."

Ratsannajak Lane Xang, or Land of a Million Elephants, was the old name for Laos. If there were ever a million elephants, they have almost all disappeared. In more sentimental moments, I fear that many of the most

endearing things about Laos will also soon disappear.

Gerhard Jörén *is a freelance photographer based in Hong Kong.*
Grant Evans *is a senior lecturer in anthropology at the University of Hong Kong and has written widely on Laos and Indochina.*

Article 34

THE NEW YORK TIMES **INTERNATIONAL** *NOVEMBER 27, 1990*

Temple Rises Grandly; Will the Strongman Fall?

Sheryl WuDunn

Special to The New York Times

Yangon, Myanmar—The nation is watching as construction workers put the finishing touches on this city's newest temple, with its golden stupa that swells into the sky, for in whispers and prayers people are saying that it could spell the end for the most controversial man in this country: their leader.

He holds no official posts these days, but General Ne Win has wielded ultimate power in this nation ever since he staged a military coup in 1962. Thus, when he began building the Maha Wizaya, a Buddhist temple, people started recalling the legend of Narathihapati.

Narathihapati was a 13th-century ruler, the last King of Pagan, an ancient capital of Myanmar, as Burma is now officially known. The story goes that when the King began to build a giant pagoda in honor of himself, he was told by an astrologer that as soon as it was finished he would die. He stopped construction until a monk counseled him that building the pagoda would be a great service to his people. The king completed the pagoda, but then the Mongols invaded Pagan and the King was killed.

It may be more hope than belief that has popularized this legend throughout the country, but it nonetheless points to the anger its people feel for the 79-year-old General Ne Win. Every person interviewed in a 12-day visit to Myanmar had

bitter words about him—if they dared say anything at all.

"He is worse than Satan," a young Burmese man whispered in a restaurant. "People hate him."

Consulted on Decisions

General Ne Win believes in astrology and numerology, and his fortune-tellers appear to have significant influence on national policy. One day in 1987, he told his people that most of their money was invalid. Then he issued new money in denominations of 90 and 45, his lucky numbers, and this money is still used today.

In the summer of 1988, General Ne Win resigned as chairman of the ruling

> **'He is worse than Satan. People hate him.'**

party amid dramatic demonstrations for political change, and some Burmese say that he has slightly reduced his control of the country. While he probably is not involved in day-to-day operations, Burmese say he is consulted on all major decisions by his fiercely loyal military subordinates who now hold the official positions. For instance, he is

likely to have played a role in a recent wave of arrests of monks and opposition members.

These days, General Ne Win rarely emerges from his large residence by a lake in the northern part of Yangon, also called Rangoon. When he appeared in public in March 1989, Burmese say he looked healthy and even spry. Some Burmese say that while they do not like General Ne Win, his power must derive from heaven, because he has held it for so long.

"Even when protesters were calling for the overthrow of the Government, they never dared to march to Ne Win's house and demand to see him," a Burmese teacher said.

Some Burmese and diplomats based in Yangon say that as long as General Ne Win is alive, there is only a remote possibility that an issue could split the military and therefore lead to a change in the Government.

"If Ne Win dies, some say it is possible this would cause the military to split," said a diplomat in Yangon. "But they have tried to reduce the influence of Ne Win. At least they want to show the people that they are preparing for post-Ne Win's death; and that if Ne Win dies, there will be no split."

Because of General Ne Win, the army has become the only efficient, unified and organized institution in the country. While schools and hospitals all have old equipment, the military is modernizing, diplomats in Yangon say. It recently bought patrol boats from Yugoslavia and artillery and other equipment from China, and it has also discussed the purchase of F-7 fighters from China.

The army has also expanded since 1988, and diplomats say it has nearly 250,000 men, many of whom are recruited from poor, uneducated families in rural areas. Under General Ne Win, the army has become an enclosed society, and the officers and troops are often isolated in military camps across the country. Even in Yangon, military families have better living arrangements and special treatment.

"They have no idea that the people don't like them," said a Burmese woman, a writer. "They are stunned when they find out."

A Million Dollars or More

Although many Burmese intellectuals dislike the Government, the military is still considered an elite institution, and even in educated families some boys still speak of joining.

"The sons of some of my friends want to join the military," said a Burmese intellectual. "It often shocks their parents."

In Yangon, the distaste for General Ne Win seems to have been sharpened by the construction of his pagoda. The project, which is expected to be completed soon, was built with public funds and contributions—possibly forced—totaling the equivalent of $1 million at the unofficial exchange rate. But other estimates say the investment was much higher.

Though it is not yet finished, people have already started to visit it. Inside the hall sits a Buddha beneath a dome with elaborate carvings of mango and bayan trees, an elephant, an alligator, a rooster and other animals along the walls and on the sky-blue ceiling. The designer was reportedly sent to Hollywood as preparation for the project.

"We don't like this stupa," said a Burmese man who visited recently. "It has taken too long to build and it costs so much money."

Article 35

WORLD HEALTH, September-October 1990

MYANMAR

Ayadaw Township

by Dr Tin Tun Oo
Health Education Officer, Department of Health, Yangon

Ayadaw Township lies between the River Chindwin and the River Mu, north-west of Mandalay in central Myanmar (formerly Burma). It used to be a water-scarce area in the dryest zone of the country. Life was by no means easy there, and local people would say: "We need water, not gold and money."

Then in 1975 the township conceived a plan for providing clean, safe water. The plan worked, and the townsfolk moved on to improving public health and environmental sanitation. To ensure that the measures being taken under the People's Health Plan were both quantitatively and qualitatively effective, health workers received training, while the people held regular discussion sessions, evaluated the progress of what was being done, and studied new methods.

The People's Health Plan which the government began in early 1979 attracted the enthusiastic involvement of the administrative authorities and the local populace, and the results were encouraging. So was the significant success achieved on a national scale. Improvements in health were followed by progress in the social and economic spheres. And among all the townships, Ayadaw ranked top.

At a time when only 52 per cent of the villages throughout the nation had at least one midwife or an auxiliary midwife, this was already true of 100 per cent of the villages which constitute Ayadaw Township. In addition,

WHO/SEARO

A community health worker admires the handsome Sasakawa Health Prize awarded to Ayadaw Township, Myanmar, in 1986.

Mothers have to be made aware that only if they get their children immunized will they be free from the dangers of many killer diseases.

97.2 per cent of the population had clean and safe water, and 90 per cent used sanitary fly-proof latrines. This latter figure was well above the national average of 30 per cent.

Every baby born in the township made its appearance with the help of either a trained traditional birth attendant (TBA), an auxiliary midwife or the midwife herself. The coverage of infants with immunization against the main killer diseases of childhood rose steadily from 60 to 90 per cent.

Consequently Ayadaw Township became the model for others in the country, as regards the supply of clean and safe water, environmental sanitation and the building of fly-proof latrines. It managed to eliminate such communicable diseases as cholera and plague, and even the incidence of diarrhoeal diseases is on the decrease.

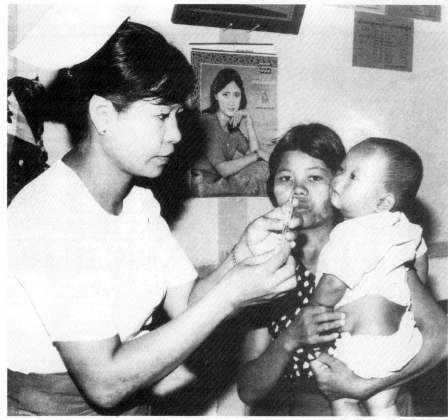
WHO/SEARO

Sasakawa Health Prize

In May 1986, at a ceremony during the 39th World Health Assembly in Geneva, Switzerland, Ayadaw Township proudly received the annual Sasakawa Health Prize in recognition of its contribution towards the fulfilment of Myanmar's People's Health Plan.

Besides the active participation and cooperation of the people, the township's accomplishment was due to the higher skills and conscientious performance of duties by the basic health staffs, community health workers, auxiliary midwives and trained TBAs. And while serious attention was being paid to people's health activities, there was much emphasis on developing the social and economic spheres.

So what were the other main factors which contributed towards the success of winning the Sasakawa Health Prize? They included:
– accepting the leadership, guidance and necessary assistance from the

government in Yangon (formerly Rangoon);
– receiving the wholehearted help of various professional and mass organizations;
– holding training courses to ensure that health staff are better qualified;
– outstanding performances on the part of health staff;
– full intersectoral cooperation;
– active participation by such social activists as voluntary health workers and midwives;
– motivating the local populace and arousing their enthusiasm;
– the active participation of the local people, their financial assistance and their adherence to health guidelines;
– all-round development in the health, educational, social and economic fields;
– proper keeping of accurate health data and records of activities;
– continuous monitoring and evaluation of the progress of work.

Other townships in the central

province of Myanmar Naing-Ngan which did not win the Health Prize had also actively participated in the health plans, and had their own successes to show.

The over-riding factor in all these achievements was the active participation of the local community in health matters. Everyone worked with the conviction that "if we really strive, we will surely achieve success."

Carrying out primary health care measures through the strength of the people is a fundamental part of the People's Health Plan laid down by the state. Voluntary health workers such as community health workers and auxiliary midwives are playing a leading role in effectively bringing primary health care to every village. No less important is the role of Red Cross youths and other local youth groups.

Comprehensive state-run health programmes will be of little use unless people adhere to health guidelines. For instance, if villagers – especially mothers – refuse to get their babies aged under one year immunized when the Universal Childhood Immunization teams come to the villages, they will not reap the benefits. In fact, only if the mothers get their children immunized will the children be free from the dangers of many killer diseases.

It is essential for parents to have an ardent desire to protect their children in this way.

The townships of Myanmar Naing-Ngan today enjoy high standards of health – clear proof that community participation is the main factor contributing to success in carrying out health plans. It follows that the active participation of the whole community is crucial when health activities are being put into effect, anywhere in the world, with a view to promoting good health.

Article 36   *Seattle Times,* February 25, 1990

RECOUPING THE BOOM

A coup attempt hurts the Philippines' economic surge and world image—but the nation is bouncing back

Byron Achohido

Times staff reporter

Manila, Philippines—For 11 months last year, the Philippines basked in an unprecedented economic boom.

Month after month, the Manila and Makati stock markets set new records for volume and prices. High-rise condominiums and hotels and sprawling shopping malls began sprouting all over Manila. Real estate prices soared.

On the islands of Cebu and Mindanao, squalid *barangays* (neighborhoods) bustled with villagers who were too busy fashioning jewelry and tourist trinkets from wood, stone and carabao horn and exotic furniture from rattan to listen to communist recruiters.

Acute problems still beset this country of 60 million, to be sure. Abject poverty is pervasive, archaic transportation and utilities systems are crumbling, the environment is being destroyed and a communist insurgency supported by thousands of starving peasants poses a threat to the immature democratic government.

Yet, in deposing Ferdinand Marcos during the miraculous People's Power revolution of February 1986, Filipinos seemed to be a shining light for democracy in Asia.

Out went a plundering dictator whose spendthrift economic policies, monopolistic cronyism and brutal strong-arm tactics had drained the nation's life blood over the course of two decades.

Enter the saintly, if politically naive, Corazon Aquino, the widow of Benigno Aquino, slain opponent of Marcos, the one person who could unify a fractious opposition movement, oust the evil Marcos and put the country on the road to prosperity.

For most of last year, Aquino's third as president, the housewife-turned-president seemed to be handling Act III of that script with aplomb. Financiers with deep pockets from Taiwan, Singapore, Japan and Hong Kong underscored with hard investment cash the hope of many Filipinos that the country was finally and emphatically jumping on board the bandwagon of progress. In a November trip to the West, Aquino personally took that message to investors in the United States and Canada, prodding them to follow suit.

But a subplot was brewing.

Each year between June and November, an average of 22 typhoons rip through the Philippine archipelago, killing hundreds and destroying millions of dollars worth of property.

Just after dawn on Dec. 1, an off shore typhoon darkened the skies of Manila. Rebel soldiers commandeered a squadron of 1950s-era T-28 dive bombers, nicknamed Tora Toras, and attacked the presidential palace and two suburban military compounds.

In a fierce suburban firefight, a large contingent of rebel soldiers very nearly captured the Philippine armed forces command staff. Upon being beaten back, the rebels retreated downtown into the upper floors of several high-rise towers, turning the Makati financial district and the posh residential communities surrounding it into a perilous freefire zone and trapping tourists in their hotel rooms.

By the time the attempted coup was squelched a week later, 113 people had been killed and more than 600 maimed or injured.

And the Philippine boom went bust.

Aquino may have survived the sixth and most stringent attempt to topple her government, but the sales pitch about internal stability that she had brought with her to the West just a few weeks earlier suddenly had a very hollow ring.

Filipinos still have the December coup attempt very much on their minds. Virtually everyone lost something, from beggars, who don't have as many tourists to beseech, to high-powered businessmen and politicians, who now must scramble to keep their pet projects on track.

They seem to fall roughly into two camps, being either staunchly optimistic about the future, despite widespread speculation that the year won't end without another bloody grab for power, or resigned to a never-ending cycle of political intrigue and economic stagnation.

An hour's drive south of Manila, perched on a ridge above a spectacular crater lake, sits the bustling town of Tagaytay. Downtown Tagaytay has everything you'd expect of a rural Filipino hamlet—ramshackle sari sari (variety) stores, street vendors galore, pedicabs blaring U.S. pop tunes from giant speakers, garish jeepneys weaving expertly in and out of traffic, children playing with simple toys ingeniously concocted from the materials at hand.

But the homes on the outskirts of town set Tagaytay apart: opulent, sprawling villas that rich Manilans maintain as weekend retreats or, in times of civil unrest in the capital city, as safe shelter.

Defense secretary Fidel Ramos owns a cliffside home here with a panoramic view of Lake Taal and the still active Taal volcano rising from the center of the lake. Town lore has it that a major amusement park on the scale of Disneyland was once envisioned for Tagaytay, but then the volcano erupted in the mid-1960s, killing 2,000. The park developers haven't been heard from since.

No one doubts the volcano will erupt again someday, perhaps soon, wreaking havoc. These days, the residents of Tagaytay feel the same way about the threat of another attempt to overthrow the democratic government.

Yet that hasn't stopped Dante Carandang, a prominent Makati attorney, from securing the developments rights to tiny Napayan Island, lolling peacefully alongside the potentially explosive Taal volcano.

Angels to the rescue

On Friday morning, Dec. 1, Manilans woke to the scream of Tora Tora bombers swooping down on Malacanang Palace. Most of the bombs fell harmlessly in the Pasig River and on the palace gardens, apparently because the goal of rebels was to force Aquino to resign, not to kill her.

On ensuing runs over Camp Crame and Camp Aguinaldo,

the bombers very efficiently obliterated the personal residence of armed forces chief of staff Gen. Renato de Villa (his wife, children and maids had left a scant 10 minutes earlier) and other key military targets.

By Friday afternoon, when all commerce in Manila had ground to a halt and the air strikes were continuing, thousands of Filipinos flocked to their parish halls to attend Mass in response to a nationwide call to prayer by Cardinal Jaime Sin.

Jose Cervantes and his wife dutifully participated in the exposition of the Blessed Sacrament at the Shrine of the Holy Rosary church in suburban Paranque.

Afterwards, Cervantes stepped outside into the church parking area and immediately noticed that the buzz of the rebel dive bombers had been replaced by the deep growl of U.S. F-4 Phantom jets.

With her government teetering on the brink, Aquino had requested and received military support from the United States. The U.S. jets forced the rebel prop planes down by flying in low, wide circles over Manila.

"Those black Phantom jets were like dark angels swooping down from heaven," recalled Cervantes, manager of the Manila stock exchange. "It was as if our prayers had been answered."

Back to square one

Eruption or no eruption, coup or no coup, Dante Carandang has big plans for Napayan Island.

He intends to anchor floating pavilions on one side of the island and carve a gun-shooting range into the adjacent hillside, creating the exclusive Lake Taal Shooting Club. Members will come from the Manila upper class, perhaps a few of the Tagaytay villa crowd, and from foreign tourists; Carandang has targeted the Japanese because they are avid patrons of gun clubs in Manila, where one can blast live chickens with assault rifles, and in Hong Kong, which feature the very latest in large-caliber, high-tech weaponry.

A small irony is that Japanese members would be blasting happily away in the shadow of Mount Makulot, looming majestically on the opposite shore. Makulot is a cave-ridden sanctuary where diehard Japanese soldiers held out for years after World War II.

Eventually, Carandang wants to erect a 24-unit waterfront "boatel" on the island where gun club members could arrive via speedboats for a few days of relaxing target practice. He has staked out other sites for a 36-unit resort hotel, a helicopter landing pad and a personal residence.

Caranbdang was about to begin construction of the gun club when the coup erupted, setting his plans back by two months. He said he is determined to open the club by this summer.

"Even if the coup had been successful, it would have meant only a changing of the guard. Everything else would be the same," he said. "The coup attempt definitely delayed the advancement of the economy. We were in square four and now we have to go to square one. But this lake will always be there. The Philippines will always be here."

Saving penthouses

The appearance of the U.S. fighter jets the afternoon of the coup began was a major setback for the rebels, but they had more aces to play. By Saturday afternoon rebel troops had moved into position for a pivotal showdown at Camp Aguinaldo, the Philippine military headquarters in the White Plains suburb half an hour's drive from downtown Manila.

Meanwhile, rebel soldiers disguised as loyal troops had started moving weapons and supplies into the lobbies of high-rise condominiums and hotels in the Makati financial district.

Occupying the most expensive buildings in the city proved to be a shrewd fall-back strategy. After rebel soldiers failed to take Camp Aguinaldo Saturday night, they regrouped in buildings owned by the corporate elite, those known to have significant influence with the president.

If firepower couldn't bring Aquino down, internal political pressure, applied by the country's richest citizens, interested in preserving their opulent penthouse condos, might do it.

Aquino's hard-line public statements seem to suggest she was ready to go with recommendations by her military advisers to blast the rebels out of their luxurious stronghold.

While the building owners did not call publicly for Aquino's resignation, their intense lobbying did help persuade the president to back down from her "surrender or die" ultimatum and negotiate with the rebels, a source close to the owners said.

"They (the building owners) marched into Malacanang and implored the president not to let her troops fire their howitzers and recoiless rifles on what amounted to the most expensive apartments and hotel rooms in the Philippines," the source said. "They said they would give her the money to negotiate the rebels out, anything she needed. Had those buildings been destroyed they would have never been replaced."

An armed society

If the Philippines is to swiftly industrialize on a wave of foreign investment, following the pattern of neighbors such as Taiwan and South Korea, Filipinos must lead the way, injecting capital into the home economy and, thus, giving foreigners reason to follow suit.

This is something Aquino is trying to encourage, and it is something visionary Filipinos such as Dante Carandang fervently believe. Too often in the recent past, affluent Filipinos have opted for real estate in Los Angeles or certificates of deposits in Swiss banks, Carandang said.

But a shooting club? To give a visitor a sense of the demand for such a thing in the Philippines, Carandang, a 9mm pistol tucked in a velcro-strapped holster belted to his Bermuda shorts, led the way on a short hike beyond a picturesque stone grotto to the roughed-in site of his proposed shooting range.

There a handful of his guests were joyfully swigging Johnny Walker Black Label scotch whiskey and firing haphazardly at makeshift targets on the hillside. They were using handguns and armalite assault rifles. These weren't rich Manilans, but officials from the villages surrounding the lake and their heavily armed bodyguards, blowing off steam.

One of the officials, Rommel Arguellos, explained how guns are an integral part of the Filipino male persona. "If you are a man of means, one of the first things you will acquire is a good gun," he said, reloading his nickel-plated .45 caliber magnum handgun.

He attributed this mainly to a strong sense among Filipinos that a government, military and police force historically rife with corruption and duplicity could not be depended on to mete out justice. The armored car holdups frequently pulled by maverick soldiers and police using the very latest in assault weapons, not to mention frequent coup attempts by a military seemingly always ripe for mutiny, only reinforce this perception.

In the Philippines, Arguellos said, it is expected that a strong male will look after his own, and this translates into an infatuation with firearms. A Western visitor will notice this soon enough. In Manila, private security guards clad in navy blue uniforms and armed with sawed-off shotguns and metal detectors routinely search patrons of virtually every major retail store, bank and hotel.

Blasting the rich

Randy and Cecil Limjoco were in their master bedroom listening to the ominous bark of an M60 machine gun coming from down the street when a grenade blasted the outside of their $2 million Makati mansion.

The Limjoco residence is in Urdaneta Village, an enclave of palatial homes bordering a row of five-star hotels and exclusive condominium towers in Makati. In this neighborhood, two Mercedes vehicles per household is the norm, as is maintaining a live-in staff of domestic help that includes— at the minimum—a security guard, a driver, a gardener, several maids and a cook.

When they built the house in 1979, the Limjocos had the exterior walls made of concrete, three feet thick, to withstand typhoons and termites.

As a result, the wall that absorbed the explosion of the rifle-launched, 40mm grenade was merely charred, a nearby rain gutter mangled and a flower bed wrecked.

Still, Limjoco had made his fortune as a weapons broker for the Philippine armed forces. So he well knew what a 60mm mortar shell or stray howitzer round would do if it struck the tile roof.

"It would have ignited the superstructure, the house would have been gutted by fire and, for all intents and purposes, destroyed," he said.

The war had moved from strategic military targets onto the front lawns, literally, of Manila's rich and famous.

The rebel leader

Whether they agree with his politics, most Filipinos would probably concede that Gregorio "Gringo" Honasan, clad in combat fatigues, his hair grown over his ears, a neatly trimmed mustache offset by dazzling brown eyes, cuts a dashing figure.

In another era, Honasan might have been a Filipino movie star. As it stands, he is the most wanted man in the Philippines, a cashiered lieutenant colonel in his 40s, with a price on his head of $1.5 million pesos ($75,000) for allegedly orchestrating the December coup attempt.

Honasan's problems seem to stem from the fact that his loyalties shift with the wind, as long as the wind is blowing more power his way. It was Honasan who, following his boss' lead, organized the Reform the Armed Forces of the Philippines Movement, or RAM, four years ago as the Marcos regime seemed ready to crumble.

Honasan's boss at the time was Marcos' defense minister, Juan Ponce Enrile, who was about to switch allegiance to Corazon Aquino and help turn the tide against Marcos.

It was RAM that attempted a coup against Marcos, after the dictator brazenly stole a snap presidential election clearly won by Aquino. Marcos, who had called the election to certify his power base, instead ignited an unprecedented peaceful protest by the masses, the now famous People Power movement.

Marcos dispatched his imposing tank corps to quash Honasan's ill-equipped RAM forces, but there was no fight because 2 million unarmed citizens waving yellow ribbons blocked the tanks. The military capitulated, and Marcos fled to Hawaii.

Defending mansions

Late Sunday afternoon, the third day after the Tora Toras buzzed overhead, Randy Limjoco drove his wife to her father's home in a safe suburb 30 minutes away, then made his way home through several military checkpoints. Before long he found himself taking charge of the defense of Urdaneta Village.

The posh community was caught smack in the middle of the crossfire of government troops deployed along Gil Puyat Avenue on one side, and rebel troops ensconced in Makati's pricey high-rise towers on the other side.

In Manila's fanciest five-star hotels—the Peninsula, the Intercontinental, the Manila Gardens, the Mandarin—hotel guests settled in their rooms (away from the windows) to wait out the full-scale guerrilla war unfolding just outside.

Limjoco was among only five out of 385 Urdaneta home-owners who refused to evacuate the area. Those who fled left behind befuddled security guards and frightened maids and gardeners to protect homes brimming with ostentatious possessions.

Limjoco disarmed the guards, to signify their neutrality, and organized regular patrols of the village. At a critical juncture, he persuaded the commander of the government troops, who happened to be a business acquaintance, not to occupy the village and thus turn it into an open battlefield.

"My main goal was to prevent the occupation of Urdaneta Village by either the rebels or the military," Limjoco said. "The damage from stray bullets and grenades was minimal compared to the destruction that would have resulted had either of the forces occupied us."

By the time the rebel troops surrendered and agreed to "march back to barracks," only three Urdaneta homes had been burglarized and only one heavily looted.

Among the casualties was a cigarette vendor who ignored warnings to stay out of Makati streets. The vendor had come to cater to "usieros," bold spectators who took to the streets, ignoring military barriers, to cheer on the action and loot fallen soldiers.

"It was a terrifying experience," Limjoco said. "Bullets flying overhead, the constant threat of soldiers bursting into our homes and threatening bodily harm. The house help spent much of the time on their knees saying the rosary. They were convinced we were all going to die."

Spoiled by perks

In August 1987, a little more than a year after playing a bit role in bringing Corazon Aquino to power, Lt. Col. Gringo Honasan, apparently dissatisfied with his place in the new democracy, turned RAM loose in an unsuccessful coup against the fledgling president.

The skirmish lasted three days. Honasan was captured, stripped of his officer's commission and imprisoned. But he soon escaped by persuading his guards to join RAM.

Now Honasan is taking credit for the latest overthrow attempt, with his affluent patron Enrile, now an opposition senator, charged by the government with conspiring with his protege in the grab for power.

For all his bravado, Honasan is viewed with disdain by his peers—high-level professional soldiers loyal to Aquino—and not just because he is the enemy. Opposing soldiers often respect each other's military record. But Honasan's résumé, according to Brig. Gen. Lissandro Abadia, armed forces chief of operations, is woefully thin.

"He stayed in combat (fighting communists in the provinces) less than a year before he was taken under the wing of Sen. Enrile and given a cushy office job," Abadia said. "He's a handsome, charismatic guy who can parachute from an airplane with a python wrapped around his body, but he has never commanded a battalion."

Honasan's leadership ability, or lack of it, may be more of a factor than is widely acknowledged. He can succeed in toppling the government only by winning over a majority of loyal senior military officers through bribes or promises of powerful positions in the new regime. But, Abadia says: "I know a lot of senior officers who cannot and will never take orders from him. He hasn't paid his dues."

Abadia points out that Honasan and other key coup leaders all graduated from the Philippine Military Academy in the early 1970s, and so cut their teeth as young officers during the height of marital law.

"They came to believe in political patronage. They got spoiled by the perks of high office," Abadia said. "They don't understand the role of the professional soldier in a democratic system with checks and balances."

On the Manila coffee shop circuit, where food and drink comes second to lively discussions of political intrigue, Honasan is said to have a powerful guardian angel whose wings are painted red, white and blue. Speculation is spreading here that Honasan enjoys the covert backing of the United States.

Military sources say the coup attempt got as far as it did because Honasan was able to spend freely from a war chest of about $2.5 million.

As the coffee shop wisdom goes, Honasan's war chest had to have come from the U.S. government acting in concert with rich Filipinos still loyal to Marcos, who died in exile in Honolulu last September.

RAM was thought to be unfocused and in disarray, but Honasan was able to revitalize the movement by luring several of Aquino's key generals, and the men under their command, to his cause. His selling point: not impassioned ideology, but hard, cold cash paid in U.S. dollars.

Generals were paid as much as $250,000 for joining the coup attempt. Junior officers received $1,250, while enlisted men were persuaded to throw their lot in with Honasan's so-called Ramboys by means of a one-time payment of $500, for them the equivalent of 10 months' pay.

Many Filipinos now read into the uprising a no-risk, hedged bet on the part of a United States keenly interested in gaining favorable renewal of its Philippine military bases lease agreement, which expires next year.

Since just after World War II, the Philippines has been the home of the largest foreign U.S. naval base, Subic Bay, and the largest U.S. Air Force installation in Asia, Clark Field. The bases represent the only substantial U.S. military pres-

ence between Japan and the Indian Ocean.

They also provide about 70,000 jobs for Filipinos and annually pump an estimated $1 billion a year into the economy, although a good chunk of that comes from the hundreds of discos, topless bars and massage parlors just outside the bases.

If the Americans were to pull out, studies by both the Philippines and the United States suggest, part or all of the bases could be put to civilian uses that would boost the Philippine economy. Ideas include a resort or retirement community, an industrial estate and a hub airport for Asia.

Relocating the bases to Guam or Tinian Island in the Marianas or to Singapore or Australia is possible, but, for the United States, it would be bothersome and very expensive. Coincidentally, or perhaps not, negotiations for a new lease, scheduled to begin the week the coup began, were postponed until next month.

Serving U.S. interests

"If you ask me, it is clear that Uncle Sam was behind this last coup attempt," said Jesus "Sunny" Garcia, a civic leader and newspaper publisher in Cebu City. "It was a 'heads I win, tails you lose' situation for the United States."

Had the coup succeeded, Garcia explained, the United States would have benefited from a cozy inside relationship with a new government it surreptitiously helped install.

Never mind that any ruling junta that grabbed control of the country through military action would seem predestined to plunge the nation back into the dark days of Marcos-style "authoritarian democracy."

After all, U.S. interests were well served by Marcos for two decades even as poverty advanced and human rights violations flourished under the wily, self-aggrandizing potentate.

As it turned out, the coup failed, and yet the United States still came out smelling like a rose. At a crucial moment, with antiquated rebel dive bombers pinning her down in Malacanang Palace and threatening to wipe out her staff of loyal generals at nearby Camp Aguinaldo, Aquino had no choice but to summon the angelic U.S. Phantom jets.

That move, many Filipinos believe, may have irrevocably weakened Aquinos' bargaining position with the United States. How can she demand substantially higher lease payments from the United States, much less succumb to a swelling nationalist sentiment that the U.S. bases should be removed altogether, when the Phantom jets proved so pivotal in preserving the young Philippine democracy?

As if he were pouncing on the United States' post-coup advantage, Adm. Huntington Hardisty, commander of the U.S. Pacific Command, this month made what even most pro-base Filipinos consider an insulting proposal—that the bases stay, rent-free.

Foreign policymakers point out that a stable, democratic

Philippines government with close ties to the United States is crucial to stability in Southeast Asia and to the United States' interests both inside and outside the region.

Yet today, Honasan and a dozen or so top-echelon rebel leaders remain at large, posing the very real threat of triggering another coup and perhaps this time overthrowing Aquinos' democratic administration. In its place would rise a junta manned by the unsavory combination of opportunistic military officers and scheming Marcos loyalists.

As the fractured and unpredictable Philippine military jockeys for power, egged on by behind-the-scenes financiers, the communist insurgents it should be fighting continue to recruit supporters and plot revolution.

Yet if the coup attempt of August 1987 is any indication, the Philippine economy, however shaky the leadership from Malacanang Palace, may already have enough momentum to get quickly back on the upswing.

After a slight dip in late 1987, the country's gross national product roared to more than 5 percent in 1988 and 1989, heady stuff for a nation whose economy actually shrank in the final Marcos years.

Aurelio Periquet Jr., for one, predicts a similar comeback this year. A dapper insurance executive and president of the Philippines Chamber of Commerce and Industry, Periquet acknowledges that stock markets and tourist traffic dropped precipitously in December and January.

But he points out that there have been no cancellations of any major development projects that were in the works before the coup attempt.

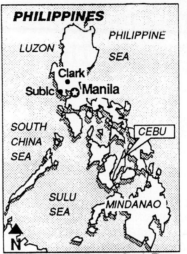

James McFarlane / Seattle Times

He reads into this the reasoned business judgment of savvy investors who have made huge profits weathering similar periods of strife in other developing nations and who see too much promise in the Philippines to be scared off now.

"A slowdown during the first few months of 1990 is to be expected, but the economy should register a substantial bottom line by the end of the year," Periquet predicted. "Time and time again, the Filipino has shown himself to be resilient. I'm certain that will be the case once again."

Article 37

THE CHRISTIAN SCIENCE MONITOR   August 16, 1990

As negotiations over two strategic US bases loom,
the embattled Philippine president seeks to revive
the 'people power' movement that won her office

Aquino's Fragile Government Faces Tests Over Bases, Elections

By Sheila Tefft
Staff writer of The Christian Science Monitor   **MANILA**

PHILIPPINES President Corazon Aquino was again toying with trouble.

Last week, tensions between the armed forces and the government were high after a controversial July drug bust. Three military men suspected of drug dealing had been killed by drug enforcement officials.

This Philippine City Wants Bases, Despite Their Seamy Side Effects

OLONGAPO CITY, PHILLIPINES

MANY Filipinos wonder if keeping US military bases is worth it.

Not in Olongapo City. A rowdy bazaar of bars, massage parlors, and prostitutes, this honky-tonk town of 250,000 people depends on nearby Subic Bay Naval Station for its economic life.

Olongapo City has paid a high price for its years as a recreation stop for American servicemen. Pornography, child abuse, venereal disease, and drug addiction are widespread, critics of the US facilities say.

Still, the continued presence of the US bases is almost gospel here. "My position isn't to keep the bases forever," says Mayor Richard Gordon. "But withdrawing them now will simply make for more suffering."

Owners of the city's many nightclubs, which are interspersed with VD clinics and slums where many of the bar girls live, say that business has nose-dived after a spate of attacks on Americans by communist rebels.

The attacks soured relations between the two countries. Fearing further communist-instigated strife, the US government this summer withdrew its Peace Corps volunteers from the Philippines.

US and Philippine officials agree that relations improved a bit after the massive United States relief effort for earthquake victims and the return of a kidnapped Peace Corps worker two weeks ago.

But through the ups and downs, Olongapo City has stood by the bases.

Carolina, who says she is about 21, waits on the street outside the New Pussycat Disco. The mother of a two-year-old, she says she hopes the base will remain so she can find a husband.

"I hope my daughter and I can go to the United States," she says.

– S. T.

The United States, which had three agents working with Philippine officers in the sting, watched anxiously. Coup rumors flew. The military went on alert. Manila waited.

Crisis has become almost routine for the embattled four-year-old Aquino government. However, in this Philippine capital made blasé by six unsuccessful coup attempts, analysts and politicians say the president's most crucial months are immediately ahead.

The Philippine leader confronts her most important foreign policy decision over the future of US military bases here. The issue could reshape Philippine politics, and also hurt the economy, already buffeted by the devastating July 16 earthquake, rising energy prices, and the forced return of Filipino workers from the Persian Gulf.

Manila, the country's sprawling, decaying capital, has become a metaphor for the administration's failure to deal with problems. Garbage piles up, power is often out, traffic chokes movement, searing poverty abounds, and government seems at a standstill.

The threat of another coup attempt looms large after Mrs. Aquino's close call in an uprising by military dissidents last December. The government was saved after the US intervened and sent Air Force jets to ground rebel pilots controlling airfields.

Imelda Marcos, wife of the late dictator Ferdinand Marcos, who was overthrown by the military in a popular revolt in 1986, has new political life here after her triumphant acquittal by a federal court in New York on racketeering charges.

Aquino blames the Marcoses for the 1983 murder of her husband, Benigno, the chief opposition leader.

Eyeing the 1991 presidential election, Aquino has launched a grass-roots organization aimed at regaining the "people power" momentum that brought her to power in 1986.

The group, known as Kabisig ("arm in arm"), will promote an alternative to cronyism and traditional feudal politics, Aquino's aides say. Or it could promote her, if she changes her mind and decides to run again, as some analysts believe she will.

"This is the most crucial six months of this administration," says an Asian diplomat here.

Given Aquino's shaky track record, many question if she can rise to the challenge. Corruption thrives and feeds instability in the country's fledgling democracy.

Critics, and even some supporters, say Aquino should honor her pledge not to seek a second six-year term. Several public opinion polls show that since last summer, her approval rating has fallen by more than 10 points to below 50 percent.

"Cory has ruined herself. Because of the stagna-

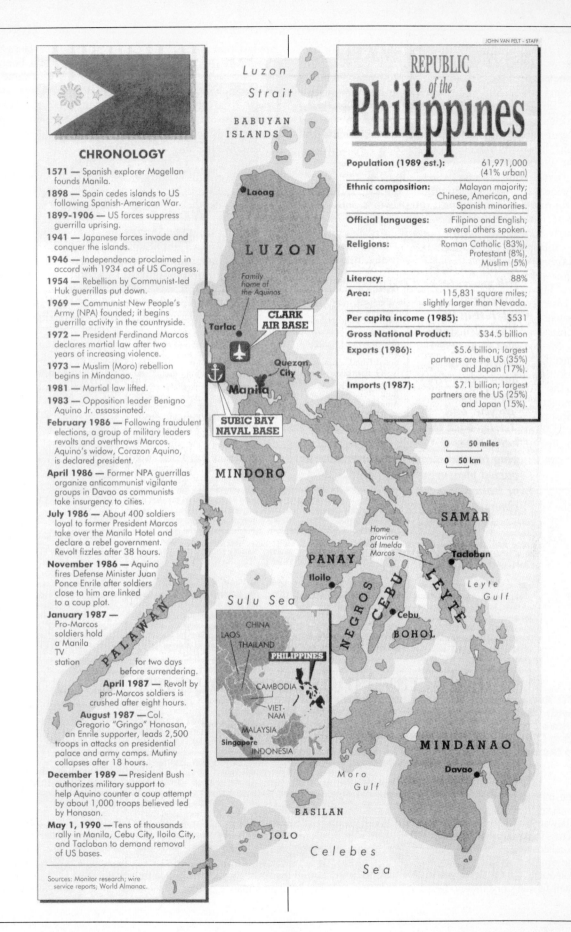

JOHN VAN PELT – STAFF

REPUBLIC *of the* Philippines

Population (1989 est.):	61,971,000 (41% urban)
Ethnic composition:	Malayan majority; Chinese, American, and Spanish minorities.
Official languages:	Filipino and English; several others spoken.
Religions:	Roman Catholic (83%), Protestant (8%), Muslim (5%)
Literacy:	88%
Area:	115,831 square miles; slightly larger than Nevada.
Per capita income (1985):	$531
Gross National Product:	$34.5 billion
Exports (1986):	$5.6 billion; largest partners are the US (35%) and Japan (17%).
Imports (1987):	$7.1 billion; largest partners are the US (25%) and Japan (15%).

CHRONOLOGY

1571 — Spanish explorer Magellan founds Manila.

1898 — Spain cedes islands to US following Spanish-American War.

1899-1906 — US forces suppress guerrilla uprising.

1941 — Japanese forces invade and conquer the islands.

1946 — Independence proclaimed in accord with 1934 act of US Congress.

1954 — Rebellion by Communist-led Huk guerrillas put down.

1969 — Communist New People's Army (NPA) founded; it begins guerrilla activity in the countryside.

1972 — President Ferdinand Marcos declares martial law after two years of increasing violence.

1973 — Muslim (Moro) rebellion begins in Mindanao.

1981 — Martial law lifted.

1983 — Opposition leader Benigno Aquino Jr. assassinated.

February 1986 — Following fraudulent elections, a group of military leaders revolts and overthrows Marcos. Aquino's widow, Corazon Aquino, is declared president.

April 1986 — Former NPA guerrillas organize anticommunist vigilante groups in Davao as communists take insurgency to cities.

July 1986 — About 400 soldiers loyal to former President Marcos take over the Manila Hotel and declare a rebel government. Revolt fizzles after 38 hours.

November 1986 — Aquino fires Defense Minister Juan Ponce Enrile after soldiers close to him are linked to a coup plot.

January 1987 — Pro-Marcos soldiers hold a Manila TV station for two days before surrendering.

April 1987 — Revolt by pro-Marcos soldiers is crushed after eight hours.

August 1987 —Col. Gregorio "Gringo" Honasan, an Enrile supporter, leads 2,500 troops in attacks on presidential palace and army camps. Mutiny collapses after 18 hours.

December 1989 — President Bush authorizes military support to help Aquino counter a coup attempt by about 1,000 troops believed led by Honasan.

May 1, 1990 — Tens of thousands rally in Manila, Cebu City, Iloilo City, and Tacloban to demand removal of US bases.

Sources: Monitor research; wire service reports; World Almanac.

tion, people now say that any change is for the better," says Max Soliven, a Manila newspaper publisher and political commentator. "This government is very shaky. She won't survive her term."

"She probably was the right kind of leader to bring us together in the beginning," says Rene Saguisay, a senator sympathetic to Aquino. He admits, however, that "most of us are terribly scared of the alternatives."

Even Aquino's supporters admit that her indecisiveness has created a political vaccuum. Given her own privileged upbringing and previous political inexperience, she has been hesitant to plunge into the hurly-burly of Philippine politics, observers say.

Still, aides defend her and, with the launch of Kabisig, have been circulating the idea that a new, more political Aquino is emerging.

"The president ran reluctantly without promising a rose garden," says an Aquino loyalist. "The corruption is not worse than during the Marcos era. We are saints compared to those thieves."

Mrs. Marcos, fresh from her court victory, but still mired in legal problems in the US, remains a major question mark. Marcos is still banned from returning to the Philippines on security grounds. But she is still expected to help choose and bankroll the opposition. Most prominently mentioned is Eduardo Cojuangco Jr., Aquino's cousin, a businessman and Marcos loyalist who fled to Hawaii with the late dictator.

Mr. Cojuangco, who entered the country secretly late last year after a four-year exile in the US, faces a myriad of corruption accusations but has not been formally charged. Widely known by his nickname, Danding, Cojuangco represents the tradition of political patronage in the Philippines. He remains close to the Marcos family which, along with business associates, is accused by the Philippine government of illegally amassing up to $10 billion.

Cojuangco's growing clout on the political scene could force Aquino to run, observers say. "The enmity runs so deep that she would respond to Danding's candidacy the way she would respond to an Imelda candidacy," says Francisco Tatad, a former official in the Marcos government.

Perhaps more imminently, the Philippine president confronts simmering discontent among the young, educated military elite who have spearheaded recent coup attempts. They make up the Reform of the Armed Forces Movement, which planned the 1986 military uprising against Marcos that led to Aquino's rise to power.

But Felipe Miranda, a political scientist and military expert at the University of the Philippines, says that Aquino is trying to counter this dissent by strengthening her ties with young loyalist officers. American support during the last coup shored up her position with these officers, he says.

While the president's public support has deteriorated, he says, Aquino could rebound with a show of political will and leadership.

Article 38

INSIGHT / NOVEMBER 26, 1990

Jostling for Control of the Island

SUMMARY: Taiwan's reformist President Lee Teng-hui has to contend not only with China but with his newly popular premier, Hau Pei-tsun. Lee may have seen Hau as a compromise to appease mainlanders bent on reuniting China. But observers say the hard-liners may be grooming Hau to be the next leader, one poised to wrest control from Lee.

When military head Hau Pei-tsun was appointed prime minister of Taiwan last May, pandemonium broke out across the country. In the streets, protesters torched buses and lobbed firebombs at government buildings, warning that the appointment of the four-star general would threaten Taiwan's first moves toward democracy. Fistfights erupted in the Parliament, in a physical filibuster to prevent Hau from making his first address.

Yet almost six months later, he is toasted as the most popular premier in the republic's history. Some say Hau, 71, is being groomed to take over the presidency; others see him as a forceful representative of the mainland-born faction of the Nationalist Party, intent on preventing Taiwanese independence.

The official press paints a flattering picture of Hau. On Oct. 17, when Taiwan's Legislative Yuan (notorious for gridlock, it passed only three bills in the last session) rejected a controversial spending proposal in its first-ever veto, government media painted the vote as a historic event and a vote of confidence in Hau. "Hau has filled the old bottles with new wine," crowed a typically laudatory editorial in the government-owned Free China Journal.

Nevertheless, some Taiwanese say the

media blitz is but the latest attempt to sculpt a popular leader out of a ham-fisted strongman, in order to challenge Taiwan's reformist President Lee Teng-hui.

"The media in Taiwan is not independent at all," says Dr. Wen-yen Chen, echoing the complaints of the opposition Democratic Progressive Party. Chen, a Taiwan watcher and associate dean at the University of the District of Columbia, says, "If you look at the boards of directors [of the newspapers], many are military men." Members of the party complain that they are not allowed to express their viewpoints either on television or in the newspapers. "They are engaging in image-making, to show Hau as the man who can lead Taiwan," says Chen.

Critics of the nationalist Kuomintang government say the media campaign reflects an underlying plan by hard-liners to reclaim ground lost to reformers. "General Hau is preparing to take back authority that President Lee had wrangled for himself," says a Taiwanese academic, who requested anonymity. "The Kuomintang is polishing his image so that the mainlanders can take back the presidency, although that is now completely inappropriate." Hau is one of a vanishing breed of Taiwan politicians born on the mainland, while President Lee is a native Taiwanese. Although their relations are cordial, they represent conflicting camps.

The Kuomintang, which was defeated by communist insurgents in mainland China and set up a government-in-exile on Taiwan in 1949, sees itself as the only legitimate government of all China and looks toward an eventual reunion. Kuomintang leaders stress their successful economy as an example for the mainland and proof of the market economy's superior performance (per capita gross national product in Taiwan is 13 times that of the People's Republic), and say that rapprochement is unthinkable until Beijing renounces both communism and the specter of unification by force.

Beijing, on the other hand, views Taiwan as a renegade province that must eventually return to the fold under a "one country, two systems" framework. Previous re-unification bids from China would have guaranteed Taiwan an autonomous government and army, as well as 100 years of noninterference from the mainland.

But mainland leaders insist that they would invade Taiwan before they would allow it to realize independence. When Hau was defense minister, he assured the communist Chinese that he would not defend Taiwan if independence were declared and it was attacked by the mainland. This conflict grows sharper as fewer Taiwanese

are able to remember the battle for the mainland, let alone identify with their elders' sense of historical mission.

Within this context, the choice of Hau for prime minister illustrates the balancing act that is Taiwanese politics. "Hau was a compromise choice for President Lee Teng-hui," says the Taiwanese academic. The mainland faction threatened to oppose Lee's election as president. "Selecting Hau as PM kept him from joining the anti-Lee contingent," says the academic.

Others say Hau was, in effect, kicked upstairs. "The reason Hau is premier is so he won't be head of the army," says a Western analyst. "Democratization policies in Taiwan have undermined the power base of some parts of the bureaucracy and taken away certain privileges; for instance, the defense budget must now be reviewed and approved by the legislative Yuan. Hau has opposed some of these things — and lost." Hau's move from the military has opened senior slots there for younger Taiwanese. This may lead to greater rapport between the new generation of Kuomintang military and civilian leaders.

Whatever the reasoning behind Hau's selection, the choice of an aggressively pro-unification prime minister set both Taiwanese hard-liners and Chinese communists at ease. But among moderates and pro-independence Taiwanese, the choice of a strong leader who says he would not resist a Chinese invasion is cause for worry at a time when unification stories abound.

Taiwan fears that mainland China has read the news. The enviable power of a unified Germany and the apparent ease with which Iraq's President Saddam Hussein invaded smaller, richer Kuwait might encourage China to step up plans to consolidate its empire. "In Taiwan, the people know they are not sitting on oil," says Mark Chen, former president of the Formosan Association for Public Affairs. "There are no illusions" regarding superpower intervention in the scenario of Chinese invasion, he says.

This troubles many Taiwanese, who have neither might nor its best substitute, mighty friends, on their side. Central Intelligence Agency statistics peg Taiwan's military manpower of 5.6 million as outweighed almost 57-to-1 by China's. China-bashing over the June 1989 Tiananmen Square massacre has subsided, as evidenced by the United States' renewal of most-favored-nation status in May. The Bush administration's threat to veto legislation tying renewal to an improved human rights record shows that all is forgiven as far as the president is concerned.

Former Secretary of Defense Caspar

Weinberger made a mid-October visit to Shanghai, where he told a conference on foreign investment that he could not see how "simply taking sanctions or taking away most-favored-nation status is going to be in any way effective" in promoting political and economic freedoms in China. He urged instead "quiet diplomacy." Other friendly nations, such as Saudi Arabia, now find themselves in greater need of Chinese-made arms than of Taiwan-made foreign aid.

"Saudi Arabia has just suspended diplomatic relations with Taiwan," says an official of the Taiwanese trade office in Washington. "However, we hope to maintain trade relations."

Hau is a trade booster and favors increased investment in and trade with China. This has been a source of his popular support, as Taiwanese swallow shrinking growth forecasts — plummeting from 7 percent to less than 4.5 percent this year, in a country that has averaged 9 percent growth for the last 30 years. In the past, 2.5 percent of growth came from Taiwan's stock market. This year's crash of the Taipei Stock Exchange pushed its index down 70 percent.

The government hopes to rechannel its citizens' speculative drive into a new will to work and reinvest. "The prime minister's first priority is to correct the economy and keep Taiwan in a good climate for investment," says an official of Taiwan's Coordination Council for North American Affairs. "Toward that end our government is planning a major [national infrastructure] project worth more than $100 million." Improved relations with China could provide the labor force needed for infrastructure development and growth in manufacturing exports.

Taipei has established a handful of official committees and associations to coordinate the expanding contacts between the two nations. The most significant of these is the National Unification Council, inaugurated Oct. 7, with President Lee leading the special task force to speed unification of all China and the premier serving as vice chairman.

The council is "a positive step in learning to deal with each other at arm's length," says Ralph Clough, a professorial lecturer at the Johns Hopkins School of Advanced International Studies in Washington. Taiwanese political skeptics say it is a tool for Lee to appease those suspicious of the Taiwan-born leader's commitment to a unified China and a means for the high echelons of the Kuomintang to reserve their seats, come the revolution.

Analysts say a revolution may be in the offing, should Hau challenge Lee in the near future. "Hau is a powerful guy to begin with," says Dr. Chen. "After two or three years of image polishing, President Lee could be overshadowed. No one will be able to defeat Hau."

The prime minister's law-and-order stance has won converts, and although the media praise may be a bit lavish, his leadership experience is substantial. "He fought the Japanese and the communists," says a Taiwanese academic. "He has serious credentials as a nationalist fighter. And he didn't get to the top because he's an amateur."

— Deanna Hodgin

Article 39   THE CHRISTIAN SCIENCE MONITOR   December 26, 1990

Thai Loggers Devastate Forest

Timber companies cross international borders
in race to get concessions for dwindling trees

By Sheila Tefft

Staff writer of The Christian Science Monitor

BANGKOK

FOR Sueb Nakasathien, the future of Thailand's forests and wildlife was dark.

"The government says it has banned logging in Thailand, but it still continues," the outspoken conservationist said in a Monitor interview earlier this fall. "The time is coming when we will have nothing left. It's hard to see how we can turn it back."

Two weeks later, Mr. Sueb, a government official who headed the country's most pristine rain forest and wildlife reserve, killed himself. He died, friends said, in personal turmoil and professional anguish over Southeast Asia's mounting environmental crisis.

Thailand, long admired as one of Asia's most gentle and gracious cultures, is becoming a byword for environmental rapacity.

Thai logging lords continue to slash the country's slim forest cover, despite a two-year-old ban, Thai and Western environmentalists say. And the country's influential logging companies are even impinging on the forests of Cambodia, Laos, Burma, and Malaysia. Since 1980, Thailand,

once famed as a teak exporter, has had to import large amounts of timber to fill demand for furniture exports and meet construction needs during a period of unparalleled growth.

The race for logging concessions crosses international borders and has become a major force in shaping Southeast Asian politics, analysts say.

"Thailand has become an agency for destroying the forests of this region," says a Thai environmental activist who asked not to be named. "The logging companies don't care about politics or the environment. They will go wherever they can make business."

Thailand's growing confrontation over logging mirrors spreading alarm about runaway deforestation in Southeast Asia. Although its crisis has yet to attain the profile of that in Latin America, the region is consuming its forests at double the rate of a decade ago.

More than 42 million acres of tropical rain forest are destroyed worldwide each year, 11.75 million of that in Asia, according to the United Nations Food and Agricultural Organization.

In Southeast Asia, the logging lords have economic and political clout. The region accounts for al-

most 90 percent of the $7 billion annual trade in tropical timber products.

Yet, in some countries, the impact of deforestation is stirring outcry, forcing governments to prohibit logging. In early 1989, after scores of Thais died in flooding and landslides in southern Thailand, Prime Minister Chatchai Choonhavan imposed a logging ban. The disasters were widely blamed on illegal logging.

As a result, the government claims forest plunder has dropped and a turnaround has begun. With only 28 percent of the country still forested, officials have set a goal of rebuilding wooded cover to 40 percent.

The ban, however, is having an unsavory side effect. Because of the desperate need for new sources of commercial hardwood, a valuable trade in teak has sprouted between Thailand and its heavily forested neighbors.

To placate Thai businessmen, bureaucrats, and Army officers who held timber concessions, the government and top military leaders have cut controversial deals to keep the logs rolling.

Despite a cutoff of aid to Burma, Thailand conducts a lucrative timber border trade with Rangoon which earns dearly needed foreign exchange. Thai logging companies also have been granted concessions by Karen insurgents to fund their uprising against the Burmese regime.

In Cambodia, the Khmer Rouge guerrillas, whose rule in the 1970s is blamed for the deaths of 1 million Cambodians, sells wood to Thailand to help fund its battle against the regime in Phnom Penh. In turn, the trade pays off for the Thai military, which controls the border.

Logging also underpins Thailand's growing commercial relations with the communist-led government in Laos. Last year, the Viangchan regime took control of logging concessions from provincial administrators in a move to control Thai loggers. But the forests continue to dwindle.

"Laos is at the mercy of Thailand, which is stripping the forests and taking the profits home. No replanting is being done," says a Western aid worker with extensive experience in Laos. "Logging is being done by Laotian companies which are fronts for Thai financing."

As Thailand exports its devastation, the ravaging at home continues despite the ban, environmentalists say. Indeed, Western and Thai environmental experts say official figures for forest cover underestimate the problem.

"We can't expect to increase forests in Thailand back to 40 percent," says Witoon Permpongsacharoen, director of the project for Ecological Recovery, a private environmental lobby in Bangkok which estimates forest cover at 18 percent, down from 53 percent in 1960. "Now our concern must be to protect the forests we have."

As Sueb discovered, however, that is hard to do. The logging industry operates within a web of

JOAN RAPAPORT – STAFF

politics and corruption that includes prominent officials and senior military officers, Thai and international environmentalists say.

Logging circles are so high-powered that the chorus of critics is afraid to speak openly of the environmental exploitation. Thai foresters in the field, like Sueb, are high-risk policemen who frequently find themselves in gun battles with poachers and illegal loggers.

Not long after Sueb became chief of Huay Kha Khaeng wildlife sanctuary in 1989, the conservationist had a price on his head, friends say. Located 100 miles north of Bangkok, Thailand's last major rain forest became a frontline against poachers and illegal loggers.

Hundreds of poor villagers

trying to scrounge a living had encroached on the sanctuary and were cutting trees and hunting and trapping the reserve's unique wildlife. Encouraging the pillaging were powerful logging companies, wildlife traders, and corrupt military and government officials, according to Sueb and Western environmental officials.

Although the forces arrayed against Sueb appeared to overwhelm him, his Sept. 1 suicide became a symbol of Thailand's troubling environmental future.

Bangkok's press likened him to the late Brazilian environmental crusader Chico Mendes, and, in a unique honor, Thailand's King Bhumibol Adulyadej lent his name to Sueb's funeral rites and backed a foundation to fund conservation projects and welfare benefits for forest rangers. The Army also threw its support behind policing Huay Kha Khaeng as a showcase sanctuary.

Environmental experts say Thailand's problems run far deeper, however. The Thailand Development Research Institute recently estimated that about 10 million poor farmers and landless laborers have encroached on the forests in the struggle to survive.

Calling for widespread land reform, the institute contends that the poor "provide the smoke screen for forest encroachment by others such as illegal loggers and land speculators.

"There can be simply no successful forest policy unless the issue of land ownership over encroached forest lands is clarified and settled," the report says.

Sueb agreed. "Without poor people having their own piece of land, the forest cannot be saved," the forestry official said. "The people have to rise up. It can't be left to the government alone."

Article 40

WORLD HEALTH, September-October 1990

THAILAND

People power

by Dr Prapont Piyaratn

Adviser to the ASEAN Institute of Health Development, Mahidol University, Thailand

The locale is rural, the setting spartan, the principal character is a lithe and diminutive lady with smiling eyes and a definite nasal twang. The audience is of men, women and children of all ages, some wide-eyed, others open-mouthed in an apparent effort to take in the message from this lady.

At the rear of the room, several *farangs* (the Thai word for fair-skinned foreigners) listen in silence to the translation by a Ministry of Public Health staff member who seems oblivious to the searing heat and high humidity. The shrill voice of the lady rises to a crescendo as she reaches the climax of her discourse.

What is this all about? Why the crowd? Why the devout attention? Why the presence of farangs who have braved Thailand's atrociously famed summer temperatures?

The setting is the province of Nakorn Rachasima, known by its residents as Korat, lying some 256 km (160 miles) north-east of the capital city of Bangkok. Korat has a population of nearly two and a half million people in an area of 21,000 square km, and a population density of 115 per square km. It has an annual population growth rate of 1.3 per cent and a birth rate of 1.6 per cent. The infant mortality rate is 10.42 per 1,000 live births and the maternal mortality rate is 0.13 per 1,000 live births.

The hall is passably clean and well ventilated, with rows of chairs laid out in anticipation of large audiences. Posters paper the walls, colourful enough to distract any peevish child. The messages on the posters are carefully written in Thai script. This is one of Korat's health centres.

The leading character in the drama they are all watching is the village head woman – though she looks more like an archangel of health. Beneath her unpretentious exterior, however, lies a backbone of steel and an iron will. She has never been known to cede to a challenge – provided the challenge relates to her constituency and its Basic Minimum Needs (BMN). She is a living testimony to the high respect that the Thais have for their womenfolk.

Adopt and adapt

The audience is a merry mixture of indigenous villagers and visitors from neighbouring and distant villages. They have come to listen, to adopt and adapt what they have heard. The lecture approach rapidly gives way to include audience participation. The villagers ask questions, seek clarification, volunteer their own experiences, share their constraints and suggest feasible alternatives. This is the "people power" approach that gave birth to TCDV (Technical Cooperation among Developing Villages) – an innovative offspring of WHO's TCDC (Technical Cooperation among Developing Countries).

Human resources

The group of foreigners attending the meeting are but a few of the many international guests who are fascinated by Thailand's BMN approach. They come from different disciplines; some are social scientists, others policymakers, many are themselves health personnel. Their reactions vary from scepticism at one end to complete acceptance of the BMN approach at the other. Certainly all of them leave the country fully convinced that, notwithstanding the poverty, human resources represent a country's best asset.

At the time of the 1978 Declaration of Alma-Ata, Thailand was among the WHO member countries which subscribed to WHO's goal of Health for all by the year 2000, to be attained through primary health care. BMN is an acronym that in Thailand is almost synonymous with Health for all. A brain-child of the former Permanent Secretary of Public Health, Dr Amorn Nondasuta, the BMN approach is in turn an innovation of the primary health care approach. When primary health care itself fell short of its projected expectations, brainstorming among officials of the Ministry of Public Health and of the inter-ministerial agency gave birth to Basic Minimum Needs.

Nationwide needs

Trial and error led to the formulation of eight such "needs" which apply nationwide. Among them are that every family should have adequate meals of nutritional and hygienic quality, appropriate shelter within a proper environment, and the right to receive basic social services.

It is widely accepted that health is bound to be an elusive commodity in the absence of development. Recognising this fact, the authorities saw that a mechanism for an integrated approach was immediately called for. They designed, experimented with, adapted and applied different models of community health programmes with the people's participation. They developed, trained and re-trained various groups of health cadres, and introduced several financing schemes to fund village-based, self-managed activities.

All these strategies took years of unrelenting effort. Yet the achievements have been, to say the least, rewarding. At the close of the Fifth Five Year Development Plan (1982 to 1986), health coverage had reached 87 per cent of all Thai villages – that is to say, it embraced roughly 73.6 per cent of the country's total population of 53,605,000.

Article 41

INSIGHT / DECEMBER 3, 1990

A Battlefield Again – for Business

SUMMARY: Diplomatic relations between the United States and Vietnam have thawed recently, but U.S. businesses still feel left out in the cold. The extension of a trade embargo has set off a wave of protests, but the issues of peace in Cambodia and missing American servicemen could be stumbling blocks for years.

The two U.S.-built A-37 Dragonfly fighter jets were abandoned near Saigon in 1973, when U.S. fighting forces pulled out of Vietnam. The jets, rusting reminders of a brutal conflict, weathered years of neglect and monsoons until Cenon Rey Avelino purchased them last year, shipped them to Canada, then tried to sell them to a Florida aircraft restorer for $306,000. Avelino was arrested and went on trial Nov. 12 in U.S. District Court in Buffalo, N.Y., on charges of violating the Trade with the Enemy Act, a felony that could carry a penalty of four years in prison.

If a vocal group of U.S. businessmen has its way, trading with Vietnam will soon be a much less risky business. A growing number of businessmen and politicians argue that economic sanctions are a hobbling war relic that is freezing the United States out of potentially lucrative opportunities. Corporate appetites were whetted in early November when Vietnamese Communist Party General Secretary Nguyen Van Linh offered to let U.S. and Japanese investors develop Cam Ranh Bay — where U.S.

forces built a naval base during the war, one that until now has been occupied by the Soviets — if they would lift the embargo. (Japan has generally followed the U.S. lead.) "If you want to use [the facility] you can make technical improvements," Linh told a Japanese television crew. Vietnam must develop port facilities if it is to reorient its economy to exporting to the West.

President Bush extended the 15-year-old U.S. trade embargo against Vietnam Sept. 6. In response, Senate Foreign Relations Committee Chairman Claiborne Pell of Rhode Island, Indiana's Richard Lugar, the ranking Republican on the committee, and seven other senators wrote to the president Oct. 29 protesting the resistance to trade normalization with Vietnam and pointing up lost business opportunities.

"The main opposition to trade normalization are members of the National Security Council and in the administration who think we should not remove the embargo until Vietnam delivers a comprehensive peace settlement in Cambodia," says Gerald Warburg, vice president for international affairs at the lobbying and government public relations firm Cassidy and Associates and representative of the Multinational Business Development Coalition, which is lobbying for the resumption of Vietnamese trade.

Despite a thaw in U.S.-Vietnamese relations — Secretary of State James A. Baker III met with Hanoi's Foreign Minister Nguyen Co Thach in September, the highest-level contact between the two countries in 15 years — government officials have let it be known that relaxation of the

embargo is at least two years away and is tied to two conditions.

"Baker has been very firm in saying the administration will not consider changing its policy until there is a fair settlement in Cambodia," says Stephen Graw, coordinator of the U.S.-Vietnam Friendship and Aid Association. A coalition of three militant groups, headed and largely controlled by the Khmer Rouge, has fought the Hanoi-backed government of Cambodia since 1977. The United States only recently withdrew its support of one of the smaller factions of the coalition. The administration also demands "an accounting for the more than 1,600 American soldiers listed as missing in action or prisoners of war," Graw says.

Warburg maintains that meeting the conditions is easier said than done. "We're asking the Vietnamese to deliver their sworn enemies: the Khmer Rouge, the Chinese, things that aren't in their power to deliver." Preliminary negotiations, held in early November in Djakarta, bode well for U.N.-administered elections in Cambodia. Warburg and other advocates of normalization complain, however, that the U.S. demand of a "fair settlement" is vague and may not be satisfied until the conclusion of elections in Cambodia, by which time the majority of construction contracts and development projects could be committed.

Resolution of MIA and POW cases is also problematic. "The U.S. claims the Vietnamese have been intransigent on this issue, but they don't understand what an explosive domestic issue that is in Vietnam," says Graw. "The Vietnamese are still

227

trying to resolve the 600,000 to 700,000 cases of their own MIAs." Even those who press for investigation of POW and MIA cases say they do not expect complete resolution.

"We want the return of all remains," says Jack Clark, a director of the Vietnam Veterans of America and chairman of the group's POW-MIA committee. "But we have to acknowledge that not all of those missing can ever be recovered. War destroys. It does not permit 100 percent recovery of every person lost." Clark favors establishing a U.S. interest section in Hanoi "as a first step. That would put someone on the ground in Hanoi to be a contact between the two governments, but short of diplomatic recognition. After that, normalization of relations is not a matter of if but a matter of when."

At stake is a foot in the door of a country hungry for investment and development. Trade advocates speak of the potential for billions of dollars in business, but so far these are blue-sky estimates. Cuts in Soviet economic aid and a switch from traditional barter deals with the Soviets and former East Bloc countries to trade on a hard currency basis have sent the Vietnamese in search of venture capital. But the collapse of unregulated credit cooperatives last summer, and resultant runs on banks, have decreased trust in Vietnam's centrally managed financial sector and led to the failure of an estimated 2,000 small businesses when loans were called early. The value of the Vietnamese dong has fallen against the U.S. dollar, from 4,200 at the beginning of the year to 6,450 at present, and inflation is at a crushing 60 percent.

Still, "prospects for the Vietnam market are more promising than China," says Warburg. "In Vietnam, you have a highly educated population, with exposure to European and American culture, with a legacy of a free market economy." Transportation, retail, telecommunications and various service industries are eager to enter the market. The value of the market, aside from its raw materials and a limited consumer market, is in inexpensive labor. But more than

anything else, Vietnam's oil resources have piqued the interest of U.S. companies.

Although Vietnam's oil resources have been in development for only five years, 40 wells are operating and are projected to produce 25 million tons of crude oil in the next four years. "That isn't much, compared to your wells in the Middle East," says a U.S. oil executive. "But it's a nice, producing well."

"We've had a man there talking to their people, and so has everyone else," says another representative of the same company. "We'd be happy to drill in Vietnam. With oil, you've got to go where God put the stuff." Oil companies from France, Belgium, the United Kingdom, Canada, Italy and Spain have signed contracts with the Vietnamese government in the past year. "You don't see this sort of a barrier confronting businesses from Europe and Japan," says William Archey, vice president for the U.S. Chamber of Commerce's international division.

Business boosters advance various arguments for normalizing trade with Vietnam. "Everyone else is out there making money," says Warburg. "A continued economic blockade only penalizes American business."

Trade advocates also dispute the value of unilateral sanctions. "A lot of the moral argument — about inseparability of our principles and our foreign policy — presupposes that we have the power to cause change with unilateral sanctions," says Archey. "We've got to realize that the days the U.S. could dictate policy or 'punish' nonconforming nations are past, or else be isolated."

Another popular defense of renewed trade falls under the rubric of "boring out communism from within." "The more contact we have, the more Vietnam's opened up, the better for all," says Warburg. "How did Eastern Europe fall? It was the presence of Western business, Western ideas, Western products, exposure to Western ways of doing business. That's how you collapse communism: You show them what a free

market economy can do." The theory is that economic liberalization would lead to political liberalization.

While corporate America lobbies for economic liberalization, others say it has the equation backward: Social progress must begin with political freedom. "Everyone who is responsible about opening relations with Vietnam wants certain conditions; it's just a question of how much is enough," says Kenneth Conboy, acting director of Asian studies at the Heritage Foundation. "The business people don't care much about political relations, they just want trade. A lot of people on Capitol Hill want the conditions to be more economic freedom. And Vietnamese immigrants say since we aren't going to make much money there, let's use our power to improve political conditions for our relatives." Economic conditions could include the Vietnam government's living up to the open-trade provisions in its 1987 Foreign Investment Code. Politically, a lift of the ban on opposition parties would encourage the Bush administration to look more charitably upon trade with Vietnam.

The political winds within Vietnam, however, are blowing away from such reform, with new crackdowns on religion and the press. Vietnamese dailies announced in early November the reorganization of the publishing industry "to correct historical lies" in translations of foreign books. A recent Vatican delegation visit to Vietnam's Religious Affairs Committee ended Nov. 9, without a decision on filling five vacant bishoprics. Religious practice has opened in the past few years, but government leaders are suspicious of the Roman Catholic community and speak critically of the church's role in East European democracy movements.

"They have to do more to convince us that we need a relationship with them," says Conboy. "The Soviets are leaving Cam Ranh Bay, Vietnamese troops are mostly out of Cambodia, so we don't need [relations with Vietnam] that much."

— *Deanna Hodgin*

Article 42

SOUTH MARCH 1990

HANOI GOES TO MARKET

Ever since the era of *doi moi*, or renovation, ushered in at the end of 1986, Vietnam has been introducing market reforms in an attempt to end its economic woes. Socialist economic theory has taken a back seat with the lifting of many price controls, cuts in public spending, and the abolition of state monopolies. But some party leaders fear economic liberalisation has veered out of control. Unemployment has emerged as a serious problem and there is a growing disparity of wealth as businesses seize opportunities to make money. ■

The First Weaving factory, on the outskirts of Ho Chi Minh City, has not only survived but thrived in Vietnam's increasingly vibrant economy, now undergoing what the IMF describes as "a remarkable reorientation".

First Weaving met all its sales targets for 1989 well before the end of the year, and its high-quality material is in great demand. But it has been a hard slog for the factory's Czech-trained manager, Huynh Thanh Ut. When he took over the 1,000-strong firm in 1987, his job was to prepare it for the era of *doi moi*, or renovation, ushered in by the landmark sixth Communist Party congress in December 1986.

Since then, the party has been steadily scrapping socialist economic dogma in favour of market reforms to pull the country out of its economic morass.

Huynh undertook an extensive restructuring of First Weaving. He trimmed the workforce by 300, upgraded the equipment and rationalised production. But the company's most novel departure was its marketing campaign – Huynh and his colleagues travelled around the south to push the company's products. The results have been gratifying. The company has managed to hold its own – unlike many other Vietnamese textile companies – in the face of fierce foreign competition, especially from Thailand.

First Weaving provides, in microcosm, an example of the far-reaching economic changes now taking place in Vietnam. These transformations have deeply impressed the growing number of visiting World Bank and IMF economists.

The speed of change has been dramatic. Vietnam has carried economic liberalisation further in the last two years than China has in 10, according to a World Bank regional specialist.

Implementing an IMF stabilisation programme in all but name, Vietnam has restructured and sharply reduced current budget spending; kept monetary growth within a targeted range to curb inflation; linked interest rates to inflation; and depreciated its currency, the dong, to eliminate the difference between the official and the parallel market exchange rates.

In addition, price controls on most staples and services have been lifted, domestic monopolies and subsidies for companies have been abolished, and bosses have been given the right to fire workers.

One result has been to halt runaway inflation, which was close to 500 per cent in the mid-1980s according to the IMF. By late 1989, it was heading towards zero. The current account deficit has also been reduced, and the black market largely eliminated. Output in 1988 is estimated to have risen by almost 6 per cent, against 2.5 per cent in 1987.

A confidential IMF report says the new policy initiatives "have begun to show favourable results", and cites a near record rice crop and greater availability of a wide range of goods. "These are signal developments," the report says, "harbouring great potential for a reversal of the prolonged economic deterioration in Vietnam."

IMF amd World Bank staffers agree Vietnam has done enough to warrant an IMF loan. But the US continues to oppose funds to Vietnam, even though it has carried out what amounts to a Fund reform programme and has frequent contact with IMF staff to deal with its US$100-million arrears to the institution.

It is political spite on the part of the US, says one Fund economist. He says some people in Washington have still not come to terms with losing the Vietnam war.

The lack of finance to boost the reform programme is creating problems for Vietnam. It will take time for the reforms to pay off and produce extra tax and hard currency revenue. In the meantime, the country needs foreign exchange to pay for vital imports, particularly raw materials and capital items that will ultimately boost exports. The result is that the budget deficit will increase this year. This increase will probably be financed by expanding the money supply, with a danger of rekindling inflation.

Although the changes introduced appear to have more to do with free-market than socialist economic theory, Vietnamese economists are unabashed. "I defy anyone to define what socialism is," says Le Ngoc Hien, an economic adviser in Ho Chi Minh City. "Our immediate objective is to see that everyone has a good standard of living." The more liberal-minded members of the government believe they can emulate South Korea.

Evidence of the success of the reforms abounds in Ho Chi Minh City. Fruit and vegetables are plentiful, and visitors no longer need to patronise the hard currency Intershop store as most of the goods there are available in the markets.

Success, however, has brought new challenges. Unemployment has emerged as a serious problem as firms rationalise operations. The demobilisation of thousands of troops returning from Cambodia has compounded the problem. Official sources estimate about 20 per cent of the labour force is unemployed or without regular employment. Underemployment is also common. Altogether perhaps as much as 40 per cent of the country's workforce is unemployed or underutilised. With salaries averaging only US$20 a month, almost everyone in Ho Chi Minh City has to moonlight to make ends meet.

While there is evidence that business activity is beginning to stir in the north of the country, it is in the south, traditionally the economic powerhouse, that improvements are most apparent. The persistent flow of boat people from the north is sad testimony to the grinding poverty there. Even so, there is an increasing variety of goods for sale on the streets of Hanoi.

Without the internal resources to soak up the existing pool of labour, Vietnam's leaders are counting on foreign investment and the fledgling export sector to provide jobs. Growing numbers of foreign businessmen fly into Ho Chi Minh City and Hanoi

Vietnam's key economic indicators

seeking investment opportunities. But Vietnam's legendary red tape and woeful infrastructure, as a result of the war, are serious •disincentives. Vietnam has 100,000km of roads, but only 10 to 13 per cent is tarmac, and a shortage of bridges is a severe impediment to transport. The rail system is extremely inefficient; trains are slow and have small load capacity.

The government says that since the December 1987 launch of a liberal foreign investment policy – allowing 100 per cent

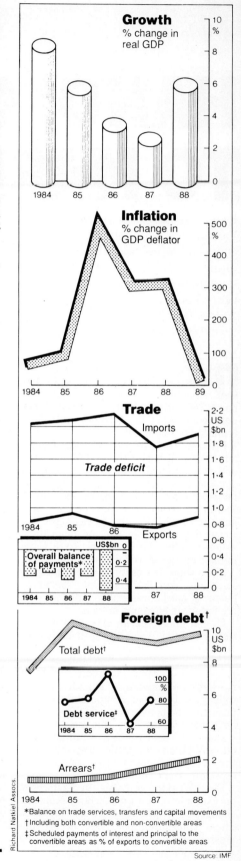

A pioneer of profit

Tran Duc Nam likes to think of himself as the pioneer of a private sector renaissance in Ho Chi Minh City. Starting with an investment of US$27,000 in 1988, he has rapidly built up his Saigon Private Garment Export Enterprise by exporting to Eastern Europe. The company is beginning to make inroads into the West.

Tran is notable not only for being the first serious private entrepreneur, but also for being a former captain in the South Vietnamese army. His new-found respectability in today's Vietnam can be measured by his recent election to a district people's committee in Ho Chi Minh City and the patronage of Vo Van Kiet, the leading Communist Party reformer. Although his company is not the biggest of the 15 private garment exporters in the city, he continues to hog the limelight. Since overseas interest grew after the launch of *doi moi*, the reform programme, Tran has received more than 100 foreign delegations.

In its first year, Tran's garment export company had a total turnover of about US$110,000, a figure which rose threefold to more than US$330,000 in 1989. Tran predicts a further doubling to more than US$660,000 this year, on the basis of contracts already signed. All the company's products, mainly men's shirts, are exported. Turnover could be a lot higher if contracts are signed with Southeast Asian companies still negotiating

production or joint venture agreements.

Although the company has already grown rapidly, the deputy director, Vu Thi Kim Loan, says it has yet to achieve important economies of scale. It has about 300 production workers, but they are in five different workshops. The company wants to move into a new purpose-built six-storey building which will cost about US$500,000 to build.

With revenues averaging only US$2.80 per shirt exported to West Germany, it has been a long, hard road to develop the company. After overheads and taxes, Tran says the average net profit per garment is about US35¢ to US40¢. All foreign currency earnings must be deposited with Vietcombank (the foreign trade bank), and 45 per cent must be converted into dong immediately. This restriction does not apply to state-owned trading companies which can, with permission, retain all their foreign currency earnings. Private sector products are also restricted by having to export via a state-owned company, which charges about 2 per cent commission.

Tran says he has already applied for permission to export directly. Vo has promised to study the case. Tran is also organising a non-state garments association, a loose confederation of the 15 private garment exporters. It has applied to set up offices in Ho Chi Minh City.

For the time being, however, the garment export company's ambitious expansion plans are being financed at staggering Vietnamese interest rates of 7.5 per cent per month. The company is lucky to have access to funds over one year from Vietcombank. But the monthly interest bill on its US$110,000 loan is more than US$8,000. ∎

Neil Wilson

The rice bowl overflows

Vietnam suddenly became the third largest rice exporter in 1989, exporting more than 1.4-million tonnes. Although some observers think this performance will be difficult to sustain, Vietnamese officials have few doubts. They see the sudden leap as a direct result of highly successful agricultural reforms.

"The rice export figures were wonderful," says Nguyen Xuan Oanh, managing director of the Investment & Management Consulting Corporation of Ho Chi Minh City. "This is the result of allowing the market to operate," he argues. "Far-mers could get a better price, so they produced more. It's as simple as that."

It was indeed a remarkable performance, and one that raised eyebrows – not least in the US. But how much did Vietnam earn from it, especially given that Vietnamese rice is not regarded as being of very high quality and that most of it was sold in Third World markets in Africa, India and East Asia? And is such a high level of export really sustainable?

Observers suggest that Vietnam did not make as much as some officials claim. Nguyen, for instance, says the rice was sold at an average of US$230 to US$250 per tonne; US$200 might be a more conservative estimate, these observers suggest. But they admit that continuing high levels of exports should prove sustainable, at least for this year. "Last year's exports were achieved despite the country suffering 10 typhoons," a foreign banker in Ho Chi Minh City points out. "This year may not prove quite so good because there were also some reductions in stockpiles by peasant farmers, particularly in the south. But barring catastrophic weather conditions they should still be significant net exporters." ■
N W

foreign ownership of local enterprises and minimal controls on profit remittance – 105 licences have been granted to potential investors, worth a notional US$800-million. This is more in two years than either South Korea or Thailand received over a similar period following their investment liberalisation, according to the government.

However, some businesses already in Ho Chi Minh City are sceptical about the entrepreneurs making a beeline for Vietnam. "A lot of these guys are fly-by-nighters intent on ripping off the Vietnamese," says an Australian business-person in Vietnam's seafood industry.

Some party leaders fear that economic liberalisation has veered out of control. "In certain areas, the spirit of anarchy reigns," says minister without portfolio Tran Bach Dang. "Videos from Thailand are flooding into the country (decimating the Vietnamese film industry) and the government can barely collect taxes in some provinces."

Adding to the debate is the demand by respected southern revolutionaries, such as retired General Tran Van Tra and former Ho Chi Minh City people's committee chairman Nguyen Ho, for increased investment in the south. Reflecting a resurgence in southern nationalism, they argue the south should become the economic locomotive that will drag the country out of poverty. Most foreign investment is already concentrated in the south.

Apart from domestic constraints on foreign investment, Vietnam still faces a US economic embargo, imposed after the National Liberation Front's victory in 1975 and tightened after the 1978 invasion of Cambodia. Vietnam's leaders complain bitterly about the embargo being maintained despite Hanoi's withdrawal from Cambodia last year. The Bush administration now says it will remain until there is a peace agreement on Cambodia.

Vietnam is also burdened with a US$10-billion foreign debt, and is in arrears on about US$2-billion. Repayments and interest on the debt absorbs about 80 per cent of export earnings; much of this debt will have to be rescheduled if Vietnam is to continue building its export capacity. But this means overcoming US opposition to re-entry into the international economy. Japan has also tended to back the US line, although it has growing investments in Vietnam.

Despite the contradictions emerging from economic liberalisation, the leadership is determined to press ahead with *doi moi*. But at the same time, Hanoi's old men are retrenching politically in response to the democratic revolution in Eastern Europe. The political atmosphere was worsening after August's party plenum, and the mood of defiant conservatism was most recently underlined in January with the introduction of a restrictive press law.

The economic repercussions of the upheaval in Eastern Europe will also be serious. Vietnam has been relying on foreign aid from Comecon in the form of loan disbursements of about US$1-billion annually. The new regimes in Eastern Europe are unlikely to uphold the spirit of solidarity shown in the past. ■
Mark Tran in Ho Chi Minh City

Credits

Glossary of Terms and Abbreviations

Animism The belief that all objects, including plants, animals, rocks, and other matter, contain spirits. This belief figures prominently in early Japanese religious thought and in the various indigenous religions of the South Pacific.

Anti-Fascist People's Freedom League (AFPFL) An anti-Japanese resistance movement organized by Burmese students and intellectuals in the 1940s.

ANZUS The name of a joint military-security agreement among Australia, New Zealand, and the United States. New Zealand is no longer a member.

Asian Development Bank (ADB) With contributions from industrialized nations, the ADB provides loans to Pacific Rim countries in order to foster economic development.

Association of Southeast Asian Nations (ASEAN) Established in 1967 to promote economic cooperation between the countries of Indonesia, Malaysia, the Philippines, Singapore, Thailand, and Brunei.

British Commonwealth of Nations A voluntary association of nations formerly included in the British Empire. Officials meet regularly in member countries to discuss issues of common economic, military, and political concern.

Buddhism A religious and ethical philosophy of life that originated in India in the fifth and sixth centuries B.C., partly in reaction to the caste system. Buddhism holds that people's souls are endlessly reborn and that one's standing with each rebirth depends on one's behavior in the previous life.

Burma Socialist Program Party (BSPP) The only political party allowed to exist in Burma (now called Myanmar) between 1974 and 1989. It was renamed the National Unity Party in 1989.

Capitalism An economic system in which productive property is owned by individuals or corporations, rather than by the government, and the proceeds of which belong to the owner rather than to the workers or the state.

Chinese Communist Party (CCP) Founded in 1921 by Mao Zedong and others, the CCP became the ruling party of the People's Republic of China in 1949 upon the defeat of the Nationalist Party and the army of Chiang Kai-shek.

Cold War The intense rivalry, short of direct "hot-war" military conflict, between the Soviet Union and the United States which continued from the end of World War II until approximately 1990.

Communism An economic system in which land and businesses are owned collectively by everyone in the society rather than by individuals. Modern communism is founded on the teachings of the German intellectuals Marx and Engels.

Confucianism A system of ethical guidelines for managing one's personal relationships with others and with the state. Confucianism stresses filial piety and obligation to one's superiors. It is based on the teachings of the Chinese intellectuals Confucius and Mencius.

Cultural Revolution A period between 1966 and 1976 in China when, urged on by Mao, students attempted to revive a revolutionary spirit in China. Intellectuals and even Chinese Communist Party leaders who were not zealously communist were violently attacked or purged from office.

Demilitarized Zone (DMZ) A heavily guarded border separating North and South Korea.

European Economic Community (EC, or the Common Market) The organization of Western European nations that have, since 1952, worked toward the establishment of a single economic and political European entity.

Extraterritoriality The practice whereby the home country exercises jurisdiction over its diplomats and other citizens living in a foreign country, effectively freeing them from the authority of the host government.

Feudalism A social and economic system of pre-modern Europe, Japan, China, and other countries, characterized by a strict division of the populace into social classes, an agricultural economy, and governance by lords controlling vast parcels of land and the people thereon.

Greater East Asia Co-Prosperity Sphere The Japanese description of the empire they created in the 1940s by military conquest.

Gross Domestic Product (GDP) A statistic describing the entire output of goods and services produced by a country in a year, less income earned on foreign investments.

Hinduism A 5,000-year-old religion of India that advocates a social-caste system but anticipates the eventual merging of all individuals into one universal world soul.

Indochina The name of the colony in Southeast Asia controlled by France and consisting of the countries of Laos, Cambodia, and Vietnam. The colony ceased to exist after 1954, but the term still is often applied to the region.

Islam The religion founded by Mohammed and codified in the *Koran*. Believers (called Muslims) submit to Allah (Arabic for God) and venerate his name in daily prayer.

Khmer Rouge The communist guerrilla army, led by Pol Pot, that controlled Cambodia in the 1970s and is currently attempting to overthrow the Vietnamese-installed government.

Kuomintang The National People's Party (Nationalists), which, under Chiang Kai-shek, governed China until Mao Zedong's revolution in 1949; it continues to dominate politics in Taiwan.

Liberal Democratic Party (LDP) The conservative party that has ruled Japan almost continuously since 1955 and has overseen Japan's rapid economic development.

Martial Law The law applied to a territory by military authorities in a time of emergency when regular civilian authorities are unable to maintain order. Under martial law, residents are usually restricted in their movement and in their exercise of such rights as freedom of speech and of the press.

Meiji Restoration The restoration of the Japanese emperor to his throne in 1868. The period is important as the beginning of the modern era in Japan and the opening of Japan to the West after centuries of isolation.

Monsoons Winds that bring exceptionally heavy rainfall to parts of Southeast Asia and elsewhere. Monsoon rains are essential to the production of rice.

National League for Democracy An opposition party in Myanmar that was elected to head the government in 1990 but that has since been forbidden by the current military leaders to take office.

New Economic Policy (NEP) An economic plan advanced in the 1970s to restructure the Malaysian economy and foster industrialization and ethnic equality.

Newly Industrializing Country (NIC) A designation for those countries of the Third World, particularly Taiwan, South Korea, and other Asian nations, whose economies have undergone rapid growth; sometimes also referred to as newly industrialized countries.

Non-Aligned Movement A loose association of mostly non-Western developing nations, many of which had been colonies of Western powers but during the Cold War chose to remain detached from either the U.S. or Soviet bloc. Initially Indonesia and India, among others, were enthusiastic promoters of the movement.

Opium Wars Conflicts between Britain and China in 1839–1842 and 1856–1866 in which England used China's destruction of opium shipments and other issues as a pretext to attack China and force the government to sign trade agreements.

Pacific War The name frequently used by the Japanese to refer to that portion of World War II in which they were involved and which took place in Asia and the Pacific.

Shintoism An ancient indigenous religion of Japan that stressed the role of *kami,* or supernatural gods, in the lives of people. For a time during the 1930s Shinto was the state religion of Japan, and the emperor was honored as its high priest.

Siddhartha Gautama The name of the man who came to be called the Buddha.

Smokestack Industries Heavy industries such as steel mills that are basic to an economy but produce objectionable levels of air, water, or land pollution.

Socialism An economic system in which productive property is owned by the government as are the proceeds from the productive labor. Most socialist systems today are actually mixed economies in which individuals as well as the government own property.

South Pacific Forum An organization established by Australia and other South Pacific nations to provide a forum for discussion of common problems and opportunities in the region.

Southeast Asia Treaty Organization (SEATO) A collective-defense treaty signed by the United States and several European and Southeast Asian nations. It was dissolved in 1977.

Subsistence Farming Farming that meets the immediate needs of the farming family but that does not yield a surplus sufficient for export.

Tiananmen Square Massacre The violent suppression by the Chinese Army of a prodemocracy movement that had been organized in Beijing by thousands of Chinese students in 1989 and that had become an international embarrassment to the Chinese regime.

Taoism An ancient religion of China inspired by Lao-tze that stresses the need for mystical contemplation to free one from the desires and sensations of the materialistic and physical world.

United Nations (UN) An international organization established immediately after World War II to replace the League of Nations. The organization includes most of the countries of the world and works for international understanding and world peace.

World Health Organization (WHO) Established in 1948 as an advisory and technical-assistance organization to improve the health of peoples around the world.

Bibliography

GENERAL WORKS

Wm. Theodore de Bary, *East Asian Civilizations: A Dialogue in Five Stages* (Cambridge: Harvard University Press, 1988).

> The development of philosophical and religious thought in China, Korea, Japan, and other regions of East Asia.

Robert L. Downen and Bruce J. Dickson, eds., *The Emerging Pacific Community* (Boulder: Westview Press, 1984).

> Proceedings of 1983 conference on the Pacific Rim.

John E. Endicott and William P. Heaton, *The Politics of East Asia: China, Japan, Korea* (Boulder: Westview Press, 1978).

> Treatment of the political ideology undergirding the modern states of China, Japan, and Korea.

Hans Hoefer and Geoffrey Eu, eds., *East Asia* (New York: Prentice-Hall, 1988).

> A travel guide that contains useful historical sketches as well as anecdotes about contemporary life in Hong Kong, Indonesia, Japan, South Korea, Malaysia, Myanmar, the Philippines, Singapore, Taiwan, and Thailand.

Charles E. Morrison, *Japan, the United States and a Changing Southeast Asia* (New York: University Press of America, 1985).

> A review of the work of the Asia Society regarding the new roles of Japan and the United States in Southeast Asia.

Michael P. Smith, ed., *Pacific Rim Cities in the World Economy* (New Brunswick: Transaction Books, 1989).

> The growing role of selected Pacific Rim cities in the world economy.

Colin E. Tweddell and Linda Amy Kimball, *Introduction to the Peoples and Cultures of Asia* (Englewood Cliffs: Prentice-Hall, 1985).

> A useful introduction to the many ethnic groups and socioreligious ideologies that make up the fabric of modern Asia.

Donald E. Weatherbee, ed., *Southeast Asia Divided* (Boulder: Westview Press, 1985).

> Reprints of papers delivered at the 1984 International Studies Association meeting as well as copies of documents of note for the Southeast Asian region.

NATIONAL HISTORIES AND ANALYSES

Australia

Roderick Cameron, *Australia: History and Horizons* (New York: Columbia University Press, 1971).

> A review of Australian history during the 1800s. Intended for the general reader, it is liberally illustrated.

W. J. Hudson, ed., *Australia in World Affairs* (Sydney: George Allen & Unwin, 1980).

> Australia's foreign relations since 1945.

David Alistair Kemp, *Society and Electoral Behaviour in Australia: A Study of Three Decades* (St. Lucia: University of Queensland Press, 1978).

> Elections, political parties, and social problems in Australia since 1945.

John Gladstone Steele, *Aboriginal Pathways in Southeast Queensland and the Richmond River* (St. Lucia: University of Queensland Press, 1984).

> A description of Aboriginal culture in Australia.

Andrew C. Theophanous, *Australia Democracy in Crisis: A Radical Approach to Australian Politics* (Melbourne: Oxford University Press, 1980).

> The role of capitalism and the maintenance of democracy in Australia.

Brunei

Nicholas Tarling, *Britain, the Brookes, and Brunei* (Kuala Lumpur: Oxford University Press, 1971).

> A history of the Sultanate of Brunei and its neighbors.

Cambodia

David P. Chandler, *A History of Cambodia* (Boulder: Westview Press, 1983).

> A short history of Cambodia.

Craig Etcheson, *The Rise and Demise of Democratic Kampuchea* (Boulder: Westview Press, 1984).

> A history of the rise of communist government in Cambodia.

William Shawcross, *The Quality of Mercy: Cambodia, Holocaust, and Modern Conscience; with a report from Ethiopia* (New York: Simon & Schuster, 1985).

> A report on political atrocities, relief programs, and refugees in Cambodia and Ethiopia.

China

Frederick H. Chaffee, *et al.*, eds., *Area Handbook for Republic of China* (Washington, DC: United States Government, 1982).

A careful treatment of all spheres of modern Chinese life, from population, to education, to governance.

David S. G. Goodman, ed., *Groups and Politics in the People's Republic of China* (Armonk: M. E. Sharpe, 1984).

Special-interest groups and the Chinese government, 1949–1976, are explored.

A. James Gregor, *The China Connection: U.S. Policy and the People's Republic of China* (Stanford: Hoover Institution Press, 1986).

Foreign relations of China and the United States.

Alfred Kuo-liang Ho, *Developing the Economy of the People's Republic of China* (New York: Praeger, 1982).

A discussion of the economic conditions and policies in China beginning in 1949.

D. Gale Johnson, *Progress of Economic Reform in the People's Republic of China* (Washington, DC: American Enterprise Institute, 1982).

Economic policy in China since 1949.

Hong Kong

Ambrose Y. C. King and Rance P. L. Lee, eds., *Social Life and Development in Hong Kong* (Hong Kong: Chinese University Press, 1981).

Essays on the nature of modern Hong Kong society.

Lennox A. Mills, *British Rule in Eastern Asia: A Study of Contemporary Government and Economic Development in British Malaya and Hong Kong* (New York: Russell & Russell, 1970).

A description of Britain's administrative practices in Hong Kong and the former British Malaya.

A. J. Youngson, ed., *China and Hong Kong: The Economic Nexus* (Hong Kong: Oxford University Press, 1983).

A description of the close economic relationship between China and Hong Kong.

Indonesia

Frederica M. Bunge, *Indonesia: A Country Study* (Washington, DC: United States Government, 1983).

An excellent review of the outlines of Indonesian history and culture, including politics and national security.

Audrey R. Kahin, ed., *Regional Dynamics of the Indonesian Revolution: Unity from Diversity* (Honolulu: University of Hawaii Press, 1985).

A history of Indonesia since the end of World War II, with separate chapters on selected islands.

Hamish McConald, *Suharto's Indonesia* (Australia: The Dominion Press, 1980).

The story of the rise of Suharto and the manner in which he controlled the political and military life of the country beginning in 1965.

M. C. Richlefs, *A History of Modern Indonesia c. 1300 to the Present* (Bloomington: Indiana University Press, 1981).

A detailed review of Indonesian history, especially the early colonization era and the creation of a united Indonesian state.

Japan

Marjorie Wall Bingham and Susan Hill Gross, *Women in Japan* (Minnesota: Glenhurst Publications, Inc., 1987).

A historical review of Japanese women's roles in Japan.

Ray F. Downs, ed., *Japan Yesterday and Today* (Toronto: Bantam, 1970).

A good source for abstracts of important documents, speeches, and commentary related to Japanese history.

Benjamin Duke, *The Japanese School: Lessons for Industrial America* (New York: Praeger, 1986).

A description of the nature of modern Japanese schooling.

Tadashi Fukutake, *Japanese Rural Society* (Ithaca: Cornell University Press, 1967).

A sociological study of the Japanese countryside.

Tetsuya Kataoka and Ramon H. Myers, *Defending an Economic Superpower: Reassessing the U.S.–Japan Security Alliance* (Boulder: Westview Press, 1989).

The security alliance is evaluated in light of Japan's economic strength and changes in the international alignment of military, political, and economic power.

Solomon B. Levine and Koji Taira, eds., "Japan's External Economic Relations: Japanese Perspectives," special issue of *The Annals of the American Academy of Political and Social Science,* January 1991.

An excellent overview of the origin and future of Japan's economic relations with the rest of the world, especially Asia.

Chie Nakane, *Japanese Society* (Berkeley: University of California Press, 1970).

A classic study of modern Japanese society by a Japanese sociologist.

Nippon Steel Corporation, *Nippon: The Land and Its People* (Japan: Gakuseisha Publishing Co., 1984).

An overview of modern Japan in both English and Japanese.

J. A. A. Stockwin, *Japan: Divided Politics in a Growth Economy* (New York: W. W. Norton & Co., 1975).

An Australian political scientist's description of the workings of Japanese politics.

Ezra F. Vogel, *Japan as Number One: Lessons for America* (Tokyo: Charles E. Tuttle Co., 1979).

A challenge to the United States to catch up to Japanese education and commerce.

_____, *Japan's New Middle Class* (Berkeley: University of California Press, 1963).

One of the best studies of the nature of life among the middle classes in Japan.

An excellent overview of the history, politics, and culture of contemporary Philippines. It includes an extensive annotated bibliography.

Singapore

Robert E. Gamer, *The Politics of Urban Development in Singapore* (Ithaca: Cornell University Press, 1972).

A discussion of Singapore's efforts at urban renewal and city planning.

Hafiz Mirza, *Multinationals and the Growth of the Singapore Economy* (New York: St. Martin's Press, 1986).

Foreign companies and their impact on modern Singapore.

Garry Rodan, *The Political Economy of Singapore's Industrialization: National State and International Capital* (New York: St. Martin's Press, 1989).

An analysis of the sources of Singapore's amazing rise in economic productivity.

South Pacific

Ernest S. Dodge, *Islands and Empires: Western Impact on the Pacific and East Asia* (Minneapolis: University of Minnesota Press, 1976).

Early European explorers' impact on the social values and economic fortunes of the peoples of the South Pacific.

William S. Livingston and Wm. Roger Louis, eds., *Australia, New Zealand, and the Pacific Islands Since the First World War* (Austin: University of Texas Press, 1979).

An assessment of significant historical and political developments in Australia, New Zealand, and the Pacific Islands since 1917.

Taiwan

Philip S. Cox, ed., *United States–Taiwan Relations and Western Pacific Security: A Study in Pacific Security Problems* (Washington, DC: American Foreign Policy Institute, 1984).

Issues affecting the security of the Pacific region around Taiwan.

Yu-ming Shaw, *Beyond the Economic Miracle: Reflections on the Republic of China on Taiwan, Mainland China and Sino-American Relations* (Taipei: Kwang Hwa Publishing Co., 1989).

Economic conditions and government economic policy in Taiwan and the People's Republic of China, from the early 1970s to the present.

Mary Sheridan and Janet W. Salaff, eds., *Lives: Chinese Working Women* (Bloomington: Indiana University Press, 1984).

Case studies of working-class women in Hong Kong, Taiwan, and China.

Richard W. Wilson, Amy Auerbacher Wilson, Sidney L. Greenblatt, eds., *Value Change in Chinese Society* (New York: Praeger, 1979).

Changes in popular culture in Taiwan and China.

Thailand

Ganganath Jha, *Foreign Policy of Thailand* (New Delhi: Radiant Publishers, 1979).

Thailand's political relations with its immediate neighbors and the world.

Ross Prizzia, *Thailand in Transition: The Role of Oppositional Forces* (Honolulu: University of Hawaii Press, 1985).

Government management of political opposition in Thailand.

B. J. Terwiel, *A History of Modern Thailand, 1767–1942* (St. Lucia: University of Queensland Press, 1983).

The history of Thailand during the crucial years of European colonization in Southeast Asia.

David K. Wyatt, *Thailand: A Short History* (New Haven: Yale University Press, 1984).

A history of Thailand from its beginnings to the present.

Vietnam

Ronald J. Cima, ed., *Vietnam: A Country Study* (Washington, DC: United States Government, 1989).

An overview of modern Vietnam, with emphasis on the origins, values, and life-styles of the Vietnamese people.

John Pimlott, ed., *Vietnam: The History and the Tactics* (New York: Crescent Books, 1982).

A pictorial history of the Vietnam War, including a review of the events leading up to it.

Andrew J. Rotter, *The Path to Vietnam: Origins of the American Commitment to Southeast Asia* (Ithaca: Cornell University Press, 1987).

A discussion of the events and the thinking of key political leaders that catapulted the United States into the Vietnam War.

PERIODICALS AND CURRENT EVENTS

The Annals of the American Academy of Political and Social Science
  c/o Sage Publications, Inc.
  2455 Teller Rd.
  Newbury Park, CA 91320
  Selected issues focus on the Pacific Rim; there is an extensive book review section.

The Asian Wall Street Journal, Dow Jones & Company, Inc.
  A daily business newspaper focusing on Asian markets.

Current History: A World Affairs Journal
  Focuses on one country or region in each issue; the emphasis is on international and domestic politics.

The Economist
  25 St. James's St.
  London, England
  A newsmagazine with insightful commentary on international issues affecting the Pacific Rim.

The Japan Foundation Newsletter
  The Japan Foundation

North and South Korea

Korean Overseas Information Service, *A Handbook of Korea* (Seoul: Seoul International Publishing House, 1987).
  A description of modern South Korea, including social welfare, foreign relations, and culture. The early history of the entire Korean Peninsula is also discussed.

————, *Korean Arts and Culture* (Seoul: Seoul International Publishing House, 1986).
  A beautifully illustrated introduction to the rich cultural life of modern South Korea.

————, *Korean History* (Seoul: Seoul International Publishing House, 1986).
  A brief, beautifully illustrated review of Korean culture and history.

Callus A. MacDonald, *Korea: The War Before Vietnam* (New York: The Free Press, 1986).
  A detailed account of the military events in Korea between 1950 and 1953, including a careful analysis of the United States' decision to send troops to the peninsula.

Laos

Arthur J. Dommen, *Laos: Keystone of Indochina* (Boulder: Westview Press, 1985).
  A short history and review of current events in Laos.

Martin Stuart-Fox, ed., *Contemporary Laos: Studies in the Politics and Society of the Lao People's Democratic Repub-* *lic* (St. Lucia: University of Queensland Press, 1982).
  Events in Laos since 1975.

Macau

Charles Ralph Boxer, *The Portuguese Seaborne Empire, 1415–1825* (New York: A. A. Knopf, 1969).
  A history of Portugal's colonies, including Macau.

W. G. Clarence-Smith, *The Third Portuguese Empire, 1825–1975* (Manchester: Manchester University Press, 1985).
  A history of Portugal's colonies, including Macau.

Malaysia

Richard Clutterbuck, *Conflict and Violence in Singapore and Malaysia, 1945–1983* (Boulder: Westview Press, 1985).
  The communist challenge to the stability of Singapore and Malaysia in the early years of their independence from Great Britain.

Harry Miller, *A Short History of Malaysia* (New York: Frederick A. Praeger, 1965).
  A history of Malaysia, from its earliest beginnings until the creation of the modern state in 1963.

R. S. Milne, *Malaysia: Tradition, Modernity, and Islam* (Boulder: Westview Press, 1986).
  A general overview of the nature of modern Malaysian society.

Myanmar (Burma)

Michael Aung-Thwin, *Pagan: The Origins of Modern Burma* (Honolulu: University of Hawaii Press, 1985).
  A treatment of the religious and political ideology of the Burmese people and the effect of ideology on the economy and politics of the modern state.

David I. Steinberg, *Burma, a Socialist Nation of Southeast Asia* (Boulder: Westview Press, 1982).
  A description of how socialism has been meshed with traditional Burmese life.

New Zealand

Roderic Alley, ed., *New Zealand and the Pacific* (Boulder: Westview Press, 1984).
  Focus on New Zealand's economic and foreign policy as well as excellent treatment of issues affecting the islands of the South Pacific.

Joan Metge, *The Maoris of New Zealand Rautahi* (London: Routledge & Kegan Paul Ltd., 1976).
  An introduction to Maori life before and after European contact.

W. H. Oliver with B. R. Williams, eds., *The Oxford History of New Zealand* (Wellington: Oxford University Press, 1981).

The story of the early settlement of New Zealand by Polynesians and its subsequent colonization by Europeans; detailed coverage of events until the end of World War II, with less in-depth treatment thereafter.

Papua New Guinea

Timothy P. Bayliss-Smith and Richard G. Feachem, eds., *Subsistence and Survival: Rural Ecology in the Pacific* (London: Academic Press, 1977).

Environmental conditions in Papua New Guinea and Melanesia.

Robert J. Gordon and Mervyn J. Meggitt, *Law and Order in the New Guinea Highlands: Encounters with Enga* (Hanover: University Press of New England, 1985).

Tribal law and warfare in Papua New Guinea.

Kenneth E. Read, *Return to the High Valley: Coming Full Circle* (Berkeley: University of California Press, 1986).

An anthropological study of life in Papua New Guinea.

The Philippines

Frederica M. Bunge, ed., *Philippines: A Country Study* (Washington, DC: United States Government, 1984).

Description and analysis of the economic, security, political, and social systems of the Philippines, including maps, statistical charts, and reproduction of important documents. An extensive bibliography is included.

David Joel Steinberg, *The Philippines: A Singular and A Plural Place* (Boulder: Westview Press, 1982).

Park Building
3-6 Kioi-cho
Chiyoda-ku
Tokyo 102, Japan
A quarterly with research reports, book reviews, and announcements of interest to Japan specialists.

Japan Quarterly
Asahi Shimbun
5-3-2 Tsukiji
Chuo-ku
Tokyo 104, Japan
A quarterly journal, in English, covering political, cultural, and sociological aspects of modern Japanese life.

The Japan Times
The Japan Times Ltd.
C.P.O. Box 144
Tokyo 100-91, Japan
Excellent coverage, in English, of news reported in the Japanese press.

The Journal of Asian Studies
Association for Asian Studies
1 Lane Hall
University of Michigan
Ann Arbor, MI 48109
Formerly *The Far Eastern Quarterly;* scholarly articles on Asia, South Asia, and Southeast Asia.

Journal of Southeast Asian Studies
Singapore University Press
Singapore
Formerly the *Journal of Southeast Asian History;* scholarly articles on all aspects of modern Southeast Asia.

Korea Economic Report
Yoido
P.O. Box 963
Seoul 150-609
South Korea
An economic magazine for people doing business in Korea.

The Korea Herald
2-12, 3-ga Hoehyon-dong
Chung-gu
Seoul, South Korea
World news coverage, in English, with focus on events affecting the Korean Peninsula.

The Korea Times
The Korea Times Hankook Ilbo
Seoul, South Korea
Coverage of world news, with emphasis on events affecting Asia and the Korean Peninsula.

News from Japan
Embassy of Japan
Japan–U.S. News and Communication
Suite 520
900 17th St., NW
Washington, DC 20006
A twice-monthly newsletter with news briefs from the Embassy of Japan on issues affecting Japan–U.S. relations.

Newsweek
444 Madison Ave.
New York, NY 10022
A weekly magazine with news and commentary on national and world events.

The New York Times
229 West 43rd St.
New York, NY 10036
A daily newspaper with excellent coverage of world events.

Pacific Affairs
   The University of British Columbia
   Vancouver, BC
   Canada, V6T 1W5
   An international journal on Asia and the Pacific including reviews of recent books about the region.

South China Morning Post
   Tong Chong Street
   Hong Kong
   Daily coverage of world news, with emphasis on Hong Kong, China, Taiwan, and other Asian countries.

Time
   Time-Life Building
   Rockefeller Center

New York, NY 10020
A weekly newsmagazine with news and commentary on national and world events.

U.S. News & World Report
2400 N St. NW
Washington, DC 20037
A weekly newsmagazine with news and commentary on national and world events.

The World & I: A Chronicle of our Changing Era
2800 New York Ave., NE
Washington, DC 20002
A monthly review of current events plus excellent articles on various regions of the world.

Sources for Statistical Reports

U.S. State Department, *Background Notes* (1990).

C.I.A. *World Factbook* (1990).

World Bank, *World Development Report* (1990).

UN *Population and Vital Statistics Report* (January 1991).

World Statistics in Brief (1990).

Statistical Yearbook (1990–91).

The Statesman's Yearbook (1990).

Population Reference Bureau, *World Population Data Sheet* (1990).

World Almanac (1991).

Demographic Yearbook (1990).

Index